The Italian legal system

Butterworths' Legal Systems of the World

EDITOR: PROFESSOR W. E. BUTLER

Other books in the series:
Soviet law by Professor W. E. Butler

The Italian legal system

G. Leroy Certoma, Dottore in Giurisprudenza (Florence), BA, LLM (Sydney)

Senior Lecturer in Law, Faculty of Law,
University of Sydney,
Solicitor of the Supreme Court of New South Wales

London
Butterworths
1985

England	Butterworth & Co (Publishers) Ltd, 88 Kingsway **London** WC2B 6AB
Australia	Butterworths Pty Ltd, **Sydney, Melbourne, Brisbane, Adelaide, Perth, Canberra** and **Hobart**
Canada	Butterworth & Co (Canada) Ltd, **Toronto** and **Vancouver**
New Zealand	Butterworths of New Zealand Ltd, **Wellington** and **Auckland**
Singapore	Butterworth & Co (Asia) Pte Ltd, **Singapore**
South Africa	Butterworth Publishers (Pty) Ltd, **Durban** and **Pretoria**
USA	Butterworth Legal Publishers, **St Paul**. Minnesota, **Seattle**, Washington, **Boston**, Massachusetts, **Austin**, Texas and D & S Publishers, **Clearwater**, Florida

© Butterworth & Co (Publishers) Ltd 1985

British Library Cataloguing in Publication Data

Certoma, G. Leroy
   The Italian legal system.——(Butterworths' legal systems of the world, ISSN 0264-8636)
   1. Law——Italy
   I. Title
   344.507   [LAW]

   ISBN 0 406 3999 3
   ISSN 0264-8636

Typeset by Phoenix Photosetting, Chatham
Printed and bound in Great Britain by
Biddles Ltd, Guildford and King's Lynn

Series preface

This is the second study in Butterworths' *Legal Systems of the World*, a series devoted to single-country or, where appropriate, multi-country studies of the principal contemporary legal systems of the world, reflecting a high level of scholarship but suitable for a broad audience. Each study treats briefly the historical development of the respective legal system and its place in the larger family of legal systems or legal traditions in which it originates or by which it has been significantly influenced, the structure and organisation of legal education and the legal profession, the principal institutions involved in the administration of justice and dispute settlement, the sources of law, the constitutional or state system, the basic elements of the principal branches of law, including attention to conflicts of law and foreign relations law, and an analytical bibliography of the principal official gazettes, court reports, and other relevant materials. The studies are designed to serve as a basic reference tool for the particular legal system and to be suitable as preliminary or supplementary reading for courses in international or comparative law, a resource for practitioners, executives, and government legal advisers engaged in legal transactions with the country concerned, and background for area students and specialists who require an introduction to the legal orders of their area of concern.

In the case of Italian law, the introduction by Mauro Cappelletti, John H. Merryman, and Joseph M. Perillo, *The Italian Legal System* (1967) is nearly two decades old. That accomplishment, the translation of *The Italian Civil Code* (1969) by M. Beltrano, G. E. Longo, and Merryman, with Supplement (1978), Cappelletti and Perillo's fine study *Civil Procedure in Italy* (1965), E. M. Wise's translation with introduction of *The Italian Penal Code* (1978), specialist studies such as that by M. Guttieres and U. Ruffolo, *The Law and Practice Relating to Pollution Control in Italy* (1982), and the expanding links between Italy and other nations both within and without the European communities have laid the base for a comprehensive survey of Italian law, including areas never treated in the general comparative literature: labour law, environmental law; foreign relations law; and commercial law. Dr Leroy Certoma brings to his study a thorough command of the Italian legal system based on research in leading Italian centres and a background in Anglo-American law enabling him to relate salient features of the Italian Romano-Germanic tradition to English experience.

The present volume presupposes no knowledge of the Italian language. Because most Italian legislation is not available in English translation, the author has been unusually attentive to detail, but in the interests of narrative textual references have been kept to a minimum. The principal doctrinal orientations are set out, with ample reference to the most important writings cited in ch 12.

London   W. E. Butler
September 1984

Preface to the Italian legal system

The principal object of this work, which forms part of Butterworths' *Legal Systems of the World*, is to present the first comprehensive study of the Italian legal system. Since the majority of subjects covered have not hitherto been dealt with in the English language, a comparatively greater emphasis has been placed upon these rather than those subjects whose treatment is readily to be found in other works.

It is hoped that the work will inspire a better understanding and further studies of the Italian legal system, which is not only a modern example of the Romano-Germanic system of laws but whose very history, until relatively recently, has coincided with the origins and development of the Romano-Germanic tradition. Because the contemporary Italian legal system has had, before many others, to face numerous and diverse challenges necessitating an active, even if not always successful, search for new solutions, its experiences provide a timely and valuable insight into the general types of problems that may well concern our own societies in the future.

The writer is indebted to numerous persons and institutions but desires particularly to express his gratitude and appreciation to the following for their assistance in the various tasks connected with the preparation of the manuscript: Josephine Di Fava, Graeme Coss and Ethel Bohnhoff. The writer especially thanks his wife Maria who bore the unexpected task of typing much of the manuscript. He is also grateful to Dott.sa Iolanda Calamandrei and numerous other members of the Faculty of Law of the University of Florence who were always ready to lend their assistance, as well as to various government officials including Dott. Mario Venditti, whose practical expertise in regional affairs was particularly valuable.

September 1984   G. L. Certoma

Contents

Table of principal Italian legislative Acts

Abbreviations

A	Article
Artt	Articles
C	The Republican Constitution (1947)
Cass	Court of Cassation
Cass Sez Un	The Full Court of Cassation
cc	Civil Code (1942)
CCA	Company Labour Agreements
CCNL	National Collective Labour Contracts
Citations to Case Law	For example, 120/1967 signifies case no 120 of 1967 of the particular court under consideration.
C*l*	Constitutional legislation
cn	Navigation Code (1942)
Corte Cost	Constitutional Court
cp	Criminal Code (1930)
cpc	Code of Civil Procedure (1940)
CPL	The Communal and Provincial Law (1915)
cpp	Code of Criminal Procedure (1930)
DL	Legislative decree
DM	Ministerial decree
dp	The Preliminary Provisions of the Civil Code
dPR/DPR	Presidential Decree
DPR ra	The Presidential Decree on Administrative Review (1971)
HL	The Health Law (1934)
l	law
*l*f	Bankruptcy Law (1942)
l for	The Law on Legal Practice (1933)
ll	Labour Law (1970)
LM	'Legge Merli' on Soil and Water Pollution (1976)
*l*n	The Notarial Law (1913)
l TAR	The Law on the Regional Administrative Tribunals (1971)
rd/RD	Royal Decree
RDL	Royal legislative decree

Sez Un	Full court
snc	The ordinary partnership
SpA	Public company
SRL	Private company
TAR	Regional Administrative Tribunal
TUCP	The Consolidated Law on the Communes and Provinces (1934)
TUPS	The Consolidated Law on Public Safety (1931)

Part I

General aspects of the Italian legal system

Chapter 1

The historical development of the Italian legal system

A HISTORY OF ITALIAN LEGAL THOUGHT

Introduction

The Italian legal system combines the legal tradition of the *jus commune*, the ideology of the French Revolution and German legal scholarship of around the nineteenth century. It is this combination of influences that makes the contemporary Italian legal system a prototype of the so-called Romano-Germanic family of legal systems. A history of the Italian legal system is, for the most part, a history of the Romano-Germanic family. In common with all of the members of this family of legal systems, the Italian legal system has a legal culture whose origins are to be found in the law of Rome. As with other members of the family, Italian law has gradually departed from its Roman origins; today it incorporates the influences of the universities, Canon law, mercantile law, together with the impact of the French Revolution and German legal scholarship. In other words, the chronological development of the Italian legal system, and indeed of the Romano-Germanic family of legal systems as a whole, originated in Italy and then, from the sixteenth century onwards, developed in France and later still in Germany.

The Roman law of Justinian

The basis of the contemporary Italian legal system is the Roman law of Justinian, although the modern law is less indebted to Roman law solutions than to its vocabulary and classifications. By Justinian's time the law had become so complex, principally because of the large number of commentaries and treatises written by the jurisconsults, that Justinian (Emperor from 527-565 AD) set about to codify and systematise the Roman law in the form of the so-called *Corpus iuris civilis*. Synthesising the heritage of Roman legal thought, it comprised the *Codex*, which was a codification of Imperial legislation, the *Digesta seu Pandectae*, which was a codification of the work of the jurisconsults, and the *Institutiones*, which was an elementary treatise of the law for

3

scholastic use. With the compilation of the *Corpus iuris civilis* the evolution of Roman law can be regarded as concluded. Post-Justinian law cannot be regarded as Roman Law in the strict sense because in the Eastern Empire it underwent Greek and Byzantine influence, whilst in the Western Empire it suffered the consequences of the German invasions.

The Dark Ages and the renaissance of the law of Justinian

At the fall of the Western Empire, and until the close of the Dark Ages, the Roman law entered a period of deterioration. The destiny of the Roman law in this period, however, is relatively unimportant to the development of modern Italian law, for it was the Roman law of Justinian's times that was to be re-discovered and to form the direct source of the Italian legal system and, indeed, of the Romano-Germanic family of legal systems.

The renaissance of law in Italy coincided with the re-birth of the idea of law in the twelfth and thirteenth centuries. The *Corpus iuris civilis* occupied a central role in this renaissance which essentially occurred in the universities. Several factors explain the selection of Justinian's law as the object of study. First, it had no territorial limits. It enjoyed a wider application than the local laws which had established themselves after the fall of the Western Empire. Second, its intellectual quality set it apart from the outdated and inadequate local laws. Third, it was readily accessible in the compilations of Justinian. And finally, the Roman law was no longer considered anti-Christian. St Thomas Aquinas was instrumental in removing this latter criticism of the Roman law by showing that pre-Christian philosophy based on reason was largely in conformity with divine law. The Roman law had not only influenced the development of Canon law, but also been influenced in turn by the latter. In the post-classical period of the absolute monarchy, that is, from the time of Diocletian (284 AD) to Justinian (527 AD), Christianity progressively replaced paganism. The new religion triumphed with Justinian, and this led to the radical modification of many legal institutions, e g the abolition of slavery, limitations upon divorce, and a different conception of private property. For all of these reasons the basis of teaching in all European universities was Roman law. The universities, by adopting a body of law, a legal language, and a method of teaching and scholarship common to all Europe, created in this way a common law, the so-called *jus commune* of Europe.

Canon law

During the renaissance of law, Canon law likewise became the object of study. It comprised that body of law developed by the Church to regulate its own government and the rights and duties of its members. It was collected, reconciled, and systematised by the Bolognese monk, Gratian, in his *Decretum* of around the middle of the twelfth century. This compilation drew on a method similar to that followed in Justinian's *Institutes* and, like the latter, subsequently received its own gloss. Canon law, unlike Roman law, was the product of those forces operating in medieval times but, like Roman law, was to influence the development of the *jus commune*, particularly in the fields of marriage, succession, criminal law, and procedure. During early medieval times the Church acquired either an exclusive or concurrent jurisdiction in many subjects, as well as over certain categories of persons, and many of the principles developed by the Ecclesiastical courts in these areas were to survive the later divestiture of the courts' civil jurisdiction. In the end, both Roman and Canon law were studied in Italian universities and both influenced the development of the *jus commune*.

Local law

Alongside Roman and Canon law, both of which had a potentially universal character, there were local custom and legislation. Although local law little concerned the universities, it did influence those fields in which the Roman law was underdeveloped or non-existent. One area in which local custom and statutory law became significant was commercial law. The medieval Italian cities were transformed into commercial centres and developed the first major system of commercial law. The Italian merchants, as early as the twelfth century, formed themselves into corporations known as guilds and established rules for the conduct of commerce. These rules were interpreted and applied by specialised commercial courts composed of merchants. Thus, unlike Roman and Canon law, commercial law met the practical needs and interests of the men of commerce and gradually became a common commercial law which even penetrated into England, where the Roman law had failed to displace the common law.

The evolution of Roman common law

The teaching of the *Corpus iuris civilis* in the universities, the first of which is reputed to be the University of Bologna in Italy, underwent an evolution marked by a succession of 'schools', each having its own method of study. This was the beginning of the modern law of Italy and the legal systems of the Romano-Germanic family of legal systems.

The first school, the Glossators, developed at Bologna and coincided in time with the intellectual revival that began at about the end of the twelfth century. Bologna became the centre of legal studies and attracted students from all over Europe. The University of Bologna, and other schools modelled on it, gave rise to a class of jurist with a common background in the study of law. These jurists, in their practical work, regarded local law as an exception to the *jus commune*. They interpreted the local law restrictively and adapted it to the concepts and terminology of the Roman law. In this manner the *jus commune* became the law of the greater part of the continent.

The aim of the Glossators was to rediscover and clarify the original meaning of the Roman law. Their method was that of the gloss, a literary explication of the text. This literal exegesis of the text began as a simple explanatory interpretation and later evolved into more elaborate systematically connected interpretations. The work of the Glossators, however, was restricted to the Roman law and neglected both the evolving Canon law and the local statute law. The work of this school reached its apogee in the middle of the thirteenth century with the work of Accursius, which contained some 96,000 glosses. The law by now was no longer studied directly, but only through the glosses.

The study of the literal text of the *Corpus iuris civilis* was then superseded by the emergence of the school of the *Post-Glossators*. Their method was that of the 'comment', which constituted the search, through a process of synthesis and abstraction, for the general principles and rationale of the law. The emphasis changed to one of creating an analytical structure of the law, what modern Italian legal theory calls 'dogmatic construction'. Jurists no longer sought to discover Roman solutions but rather used the Roman texts to justify rules adopted in contemporary society. In the fourteenth and fifteenth centuries an evolved form of Roman law influenced by Canon law concepts such as the principle of *pacta sunt servanda* was taught in the universities.

By the end of the fifteenth century legal scholarship had become rigid and pedantic. Nonetheless, the style of the comment continued to be used in Italy throughout the sixteenth and seventeenth centuries, during which Italian legal science lost its pre-eminence. The scholars and the courts had relied increasingly upon the *communis opinio doctorum*, that is, the opinions of the principal jurists. It was the reaction against this excessive attachment of the Post-Glossators to the doctrine and the mechanical procedure requiring adhesion to the *communis opinio doctorum* that gave rise, in the fifteenth and sixteenth centuries, to a legal humanism that affirmed the liberty of interpretation. However, the humanist school was centred elsewhere in Europe, mostly in French universities, as a result of which there arose a clear contrast between the Italian and French manner of legal teaching. The former, in the tradition of the Glossators and Commentators, looked to Roman law for practical ends. The latter sought to obtain a historical and scientific knowledge of Roman law without practical pre-occupations; it was interested in Roman law as a historical phenomenon and not as an existing body of law. The French school accordingly sought to reconstruct the original Roman law texts by freeing them of the interpretations of Justinian's codifiers and the Glossators.

The growth of nationalism from the fifteenth century onwards also contributed to the weakening of the *jus commune*: where the Roman law was received, it was received by the will of the Prince, and its continued force depended, in theory, on his will. But where, as in most of Europe including Italy, there was no formal reception of the Roman law, the nationalisation of law took place under conditions which foreshadowed legal positivism. There was the emergence of the state as the only source of legislation which the lawyer merely accepted and studied, as he was preconditioned to do so by centuries of acceptance and study of the *Corpus iuris civilis*.

Natural law and the reception of its results in Italy

A. THE DEVELOPMENT OF THE NATURAL LAW SCHOOL OUTSIDE ITALY

Whilst Roman and Canon law continued to develop in Italy, the natural law school, which was to flourish between the sixteenth and eighteenth centuries, began to develop, for the most part, in France. Unlike Thomistic ideas of natural law, however, the natural law of this era was secular and had little effect in Italy, which was going through the counter-reformation. The method of the Post-Glossators continued to thrive in the Italian universities throughout this period with the consequence that, until the French Revolution, the medieval legal system remained the basis of law in Italy, although it was supplemented by numerous fragmentary and unsystematic legislative changes. During the Enlightenment, Italy was influenced by various European cultural movements, all of which had considerable effects on legislation, but however important this development was, it did not abrogate the Roman common law.

Natural law was a major component of the Enlightenment. It regarded objective reality as the prime and exclusive purpose of philosophical enquiry, and consistent with this approach it adopted as its fundamental method the empirical one of the natural sciences. The natural law school affirmed the validity of a universally rational and absolute law, that is to say, a perfect legal model with which it was necessary to conform. This would enable the transformation of the then confused and uncertain law into certain and rational positive legal norms conforming with the universal and patent dictates of reason.

The demand of the intellectual revolution to define and stablise the law was met, between the end of the eighteenth and the beginning of the nineteenth centuries, by codification. The codification movement was a direct consequence of the obscure, uncertain, contradictory, and arbitrary state of the law, a state of affairs which arose out of both the inability of the *jus commune* to adapt to new conditions and the continuing existence of feudal law, individual sovereign states, local customs and legislation, and a series of privileges and autonomies. The codification movement was also encouraged by the doctrinal works of scholars who transformed Roman law into natural law by giving it that logic and reason which characterised the latter. In other words, there occurred a 'nationalisation' of the then existing positive law which was Roman common law or the *jus commune*. The codification movement was also aided by the political interests of the absolute state.

Codification did not produce any revolutionary reform, at least in the private law where the codes were primarily consolidations of existing Roman and customary law, which had been nationalised in the light of the natural law, thereby satisfying the practical demands for stability and certainty in the law. The case of public law was otherwise. The public law of contemporary Romano-Germanic legal systems is still largely the product of this period, that is, of the intellectual revolution beginning at the end of the eighteenth century. The Roman law could not serve as a model, for it did not know constitutional or administrative law, and the public law of Justinian's times was inappropriate to modern society.

In essence the intellectual revolution combined ideas of natural human rights, which ought to be recognised and secured by the government, and the separation of powers which, inter alia, was aimed at isolating the judiciary, who in the past had frustrated progressive legislative reforms through its failure to distinguish between applying and making law. It was the age of rationalism, anti-feudalism, secularisation, and nationalism. There was an exaggerated emphasis on private property and the freedom of contract, the loss of what temporal jurisdiction the Ecclesiastical courts still had, and the combination of separate legal traditions into a single national legal system which expressed national ideals and unified the national culture. The authority, although not the content, of the *jus commune* was rejected.

B. THE SPREAD OF FRENCH IDEAS TO ITALY

The influence of the French Revolution spread both because of the prestige of the ideas of 1789 and because of the Napoleonic expansion.

The ideals of the Revolution produced a peculiar theory as to what law is, as well as determining the form and style of the basic codes. The legislative results of the revolution within France were the Code Napoléon of 1804, the Code of Civil Procedure of 1807, the Commercial Code and the Code of Criminal Procedure, both of 1808, and the Criminal Code of 1810. As it happened, Italy received both the ideology of the revolution and the French Codes. The French occupation from 1796, and its foundation of several Italian Republics and vassal kingdoms, brought the French legislation, which was readily received, both because it satisfied new socio-economic needs, and because of the common legal tradition which, for the most part, had been absorbed into the Napoleonic Codes. The codes represented a new law which would supplant the old. Although many rules and institutions were those of the *jus commune*, they were theoretically effective only because of their re-enactment as part of a new and complete legislation. There was a formal rupture with the *jus commune*, which could no longer be considered a general residual law. Notwithstanding the break with the past, however, the Codes were necessarily the product of the existing legal culture and were made up of familiar concepts, institutions, and attitudes about law.

The Restoration

At the beginning of the Restoration when the Napoleonic regime collapsed, in 1814, most Italian Princes ordered an immediate re-enactment of pre-revolutionary legislation. Soon afterwards they authorised the drafting of new codes. But the local codifications in the Restoration period came at a time when Italian legal scholarship lacked both vitality and originality, with the natural consequence that there was a general reliance upon French legal science and the French Codes which embodied many of the reforms of the changed ideological and political times. Therefore, notwithstanding the conservative and reactionary policies of the State and Church, a factor which had also inhibited doctrinal activity, there was no return to the pre-Napoleonic situation. Many of the reforms suited the monarchs because they suppressed various privileges that had limited central power. In the end, the Napoleonic experience left its mark on the Italian law of the Restoration.

From natural law to the new legal positivism

Natural law, within the context of the broader cultural movement of the Enlightenment, placed objective reality as the foremost and exclusive object of philosophical enquiry. This kind of thinking lasted only until the first decade of the nineteenth century. One may have thought that with such a successful cultural and legal revolution legal positivism would have disappeared. The Enlightenment proved to be merely a short interlude between one kind of positivism based on the dogma of the State within the person of the monarch, and another form of positivism based on the dogma of the separation of powers.

The Enlightenment, which contributed so much to the codification process, did not give rise to a renewal in accordance with natural law principles of the substantive law contained within the Code Napoléon, except to a minor extent. The principal natural law tenet that did penetrate the Code in a substantive sense was the individualistic ideal, that is, the protection of those innate rights of man identified by the natural law, particularly ownership and liberty. These manifested themselves in the right to enjoy and dispose of things in an absolute manner, the introduction of divorce, and the freedom of contract between employee and employer in recognition of the right to work. However, the other basic principle of the Enlightenment, viz, that of the limitation of judicial powers, a principle which, inter alia, later gave rise to the thesis that the legal system is complete, had an important theoretical and practical effect even though it only affected the formal structure and not the normative substance of the Code.

Although the principal reason for the limitation of judicial powers was a preoccupation with the certainty of law, there were other reasons, including an interest in maintaining an absolute distinction between judicial and legislative powers even though the theoretical justification given for prohibiting the judges from resorting to any source of law other than legislation was that the latter incorporated natural law or, in other words, the dictates of reason. To safeguard the separation of powers and the law-making monopoly of the State, the Code prohibited the judges from resorting to equity or usages in cases of legislative silence, obscurity, or insufficiency. This prohibition was regarded as a command to find an exclusively legislative solution in every case, an approach translated by the French exegesis school of thought into the principle that the positive legal order is complete and contains no lacunae.

It was through this process that the demands born out of the Enlightenment and, in particular, out of its legal component, natural law, namely, the demands for a clear and certain legislation incorporating rational national law, led, instead, to legal positivism. While the aim was that only legislation could produce valid law, the basis of this process was to be that the legislator would translate reason into law, and law therefore could not be other than natural law. Instead, however, the source of law was taken to be the will of the legislator; natural law, although for some time thought to be the essence of the Code, was quickly forgotten. As between reason and legislative discretion, the latter came out victorious.

The principle that the positive legal order is complete, and that therefore all law takes the form of legislation which represents the will of the state, was theorised by the *école de l'exégèse*, the French exegesis school of the nineteenth century. This school of thought considered the study of law to be a commentary on the Code in the same order as that defined by the legislator. It considered that the literary interpretation of the Code would furnish the answer to any problem. It accepted the already rational structure of the legislative order so that any further elaboration or systematisation of concepts would be superfluous. This was reinforced by the belief that the Code ensured both the certainty of law and the division of powers. It excluded any reference to other than the law imposed by the State, and the only canon of interpretation was the search for the intent or will or the legislature. This was a static concept of law tied to the authority of law understood as an objective datum: strict submission to certainty meant that it sacrificed the social evolution of law, thereby reviving the very approach which had instigated the natural law movement of the eighteenth century.

In this way codification became an involuntary bridge between natural law and legal positivism. The result favoured positivism: all law was transformed into State legislation; a positive legal order, moreover, was regarded as complete. But these consequences were attributable to political and technical, not philosophical, reasons because the philosophy of codification always remained that of natural law. Notwithstanding the strong sentiments at the beginning of the Restoration in favour of unification and of freedom from foreign domination, the Italian doctrine followed the French influence. The dogma of the strict separation of powers, combined with legislative unity and codification, and their corollary that the Code was self-sufficient, dominated Italian legal life until the advent of Pandectist thought.

The influence of the German Pandectist school

The next change in Italian legal culture dates from the middle of the nineteenth century under the influence of the Roman law scholars educated in the German Pandectist school of the middle and late nineteenth century. The Pandectists transformed the study of Roman law and achieved the highest systematic conceptual legal structure ever attained. Their aim was to extract from the mass of Roman law, and in particular from Justinian's Pandects, pure concepts and principles pitched at an appropriate conceptual level and to combine them into a systematic legal structure or system that could then be utilised in resolving every conceivable problem arising in a modern society. The

Pandectists, in creating their systematic conceptual legal structure, were concerned with the private law only, mainly because this was the scope of Justinian's Pandects. The culmination of this process is represented by Windscheid in his work *Lehrbuch des Pandektenrechts*. The ultimate triumph of the Pandectists was the German National Civil Code which entered into force in 1900. The structure of the Code bears testimony to the influence of the Pandectists. It begins with a General Part whose principles are pitched at a high level of abstraction sufficient to encompass every aspect and institution of the private law. The Code then proceeds through descending levels of abstraction, always from the general to the more particular. Thus it moves from obligations to contractual obligations, particular contracts, non-contractual obligations and so on. All of these provisions logically interlock, so that the more particular fits within and is comprised by the more general and so on, and must therefore be constantly kept in mind.

Positivism

The natural law approach had lasted in Italy until roughly the first decade of the nineteenth century when positivism began to penetrate. The positivist mentality spread rapidly in European culture, but only as a set of mind or general approach rather than as a precise doctrine. Every theory which was not, or did not intend to be, metaphysical adopted the term 'positivism'. The expression 'legal positivism' enjoyed extraordinary success; it linked to philosophical positivism a theoretical legal approach which is at the opposite pole of sociology and the positivistic vision of law.

Positivists like Maine and Post extracted abstract general concepts from historical and ethnological data and thus remained within the ambit of sociology and the true and proper positivism. Others applied a similar method to data furnished by 'positive' legal systems understood in a formal sense, that is, as systems of formally valid norms. These are two clearly different procedures, even if both are qualified as 'positive': one is the positivism constituted by an effective and concrete human behaviour, and the other is the positivism constituted by the formal existence of a norm. It is true that neither has anything to do with values or ethics, and are thus distinct from natural law, but notwithstanding this similarity the two methods remain very different from each other.

The belief by a majority of jurists in the second half of the nineteenth century that they were positivists was not only due to the ambiguity of the phrase 'positive law'. Apart from the fact that it meant the negation of natural law, the metaphysical, and indeed of philosophy itself, positivism seemed to make possible the construction of a science of law, the dream of jurists. A formal theory of norms and legal institutions could give rise to a rational system analagous to those of the natural sciences, something which the sociology of law, as an approximate science, could not give. To limit this system to positive law, as well as taking advantage of the name, simplified the problem.

In reality that which is called 'legal positivism' is formalism. However, formalism had other than positivistic origins, and the aspirations of jurists in the second half of the nineteenth century of creating a science of law—an aim which they had hoped to achieve through the formalistic method—also went far back in time. The first to conceive that which the supporters of legal positivism were to later call 'the general theory of law' were two Wolfian natural lawyers, Nettelbladt (1719–1791) and Pütter (1725–1807), who had abandoned the style of the comment in the study of the Roman law and urged the introduction into the study of positive law of a 'general part' which would place the general concepts and propositions into a logical order. They elaborated concepts such as 'legal subjects', 'subjective rights' and the like through a rationalistic, deductive process long before John Austin, who was unknown on the continent until the end of the nineteenth century, did the same thing on an empirical basis. Their work was continued by jurists of a Kantian philosophy, again with the aim of systematising the positive law into a logical order. They were then followed by the Pandectists Savigny and, above all, by Puchta, but as already noted, the most perfect logical-systematic construction of positive law—which was always, in Germany, the *jus commune*—was by the Pandectist Bernard Windscheid (1817–1892) in *Lehrbuch des Pandektenrechts* (1862–1870).

It is also possible, of course, to construct empirically a formal theory of law through abstractions from comparative and related data, as in fact did John Austin. But this 'scientific' method was also regarded as being positivistic, because it utilised the comparative-inductive method of the positivists and because of the general enthusiasm for positivism and the related aversion to philosophy which was identified with metaphysics. In any event, it was formalistic and therefore naturally fell into the same general mould.

This gave rise to what jurists call 'dogmatism', that is, the elaboration of general legal concepts upon the basis of existent legal norms or 'dogma'. Its opponents call it 'conceptual law'. It has dominated the legal science of Germany and other countries, particularly that of Italy, and it directly influenced the German Civil Code promulgated in 1900. The method, restricted at first to private law, was later extended to public law. It led to a refinement of the instruments of legal science through the elaboration of concepts, the most celebrated of which is that of the 'legal transaction'. These concepts have remained fundamental to both the study of law and the identification of its 'differentiating characteristics'.

The conceptualism and formalism of dogmatism find their ultimate expression in doctrine, or the general theory of law, which is the identification and systematisation of the 'fundamental legal concepts' extracted from an analysis of the general principles of the various branches of the positive legal system. It is this contraction through observing the various branches of the legal system that distinguishes the general theory of German jurists from the analytical jurisprudence of John Austin who, instead, arrived at general concepts through the observation and comparison of the norms and institutions common to several legal systems. Otherwise they are both positive systems of general and formal concepts. In effect, German legal theory which was an ulterior development and perfection of dogmatism, and as such of the science of law and not philosophy, posed itself as the philosophy of law.

Italian legal science had adopted purism as the ideal and rejected all but legal data in order to interpret and arrange that data into a system. This was the direct influence of German legal science, of the formalism inherent in the Pandectist school. Although there was some interest in law and sociology in the second half of the nineteenth century, as in the case of the criminal law whose major representatives were Cesare Lombroso (1835–1909) and Enrico Ferri (1856–1929), Italian legal sociology went into decline. The odd philosopher of Italian law who still professed to be faithful to philosophical positivism at the end of the nineteenth century tended to avoid its naturalistic-sociological determinism and instead assigned to the philosophy of law functions other than sociological research. This was the case, for instance, of Icilio Vanni (1855–1903).

There was in the early twentieth century a rebirth of idealism which, particularly in the person of Giorgio Del Vecchio (1878–1970), threw Italian legal positivist philosophy into a definite crisis. The appearance of Del Vecchio's work not only introduced turmoil into Italian legal-philosophical studies by giving them a lever with which to develop their dormant anti-positivist elements, but it also shook many positivists out of their dogmatic incantation. There was a change of perspective in relation to the philosophical problem of law that was to be later radically developed by the neo-Hegelian idealists. Del Vecchio reabsorbed the fundamental legal concepts of the general theory of law into philosophy, combining it with the phenomenological and deontological aspects of law.

Although the twentieth century anti-formalistic doctrines of a sociological nature did not destroy formal legal positivism, they weakened it. The anti-formalistic doctrines emphasised that formal legal positivism needed to create a new basis for itself. Formalism, born from the work of the Pandectists, comprised an elaboration of concepts abstracted from historical data. However, to create a true formal science of law it was necessary to find a criterion for indentifying the juridical character of a norm. Conceptual jurisprudence, whether it admitted this or not, found this criterion in the statutory nature of the norm. For this reason formalism became synonymous with legal positivism. That, this criterion was unsatisfactory became apparent as a result of the sociological doctrines and through the difficulties experienced by the neo-Kantians in building a formal theory of law. One could have resorted to *norms* in order to identify law and to then extract legal concepts, but the work of the neo-Kantians demonstrated that one cannot accept an empirical datum as a criterion to identify law. All of this became apparent in Kelsen's pure theory of law.

Kelsen's normative doctrine was a vigorous attempt to give legal formalism both a logical basis and a systematic structure. There appeared at the same time the most important and consequential of the anti-normative theories of law, namely, that of Santi Romano based on the concept of an 'institution'. This concept, or at least the term 'institution' is to be found in the doctrine of Hauriou and perhaps Romano adapted it from him but, unlike Hauriou the 'institution' of Romano is not so much based on sociology as upon the observation of concrete legal experiences without any systematising ambition. Equally, Romano remains outside philosophy as his theory is based solely upon the empirical observation of law.

Romano's approach was the exact opposite to that of Kelsen. Whilst Kelsen begins from the norm and only subsequently arrives at the legal system, Romano begins with the legal system and within its ambit also explains law as a norm. In other words, Romano explains that although social order is imposed through the existence of norms, the latter are merely utilised and comprised within the orbit of social order. Thus law, before becoming a norm, is an organisation or structure, that is, a position taken by the society within which the norm will operate. This approach does not deny the validity of a norm but, rather, places it within that complex reality which is society. Therefore, for Romano, law is first linked to the concept of society and only subsequently does it embody the idea of social order. Thus the importance of the concept, 'institution', which is both necessary and sufficient to explain law as it gives law the significance of a legal order considered as an entirety or unit. For Romano every legal system is an institution, and every institution is a legal system. However, Romano does not give an exhaustive definition of the concept of 'institution'. He says that it is 'every social entity or corpus' but then renders the concept vague by saying that in some cases you cannot speak of an institution, e g a queue in an office, so that not every human society gives rise to legal phenomenon. He, in essence, concludes by saying that only those social groupings which are effective, concrete and objective in the legal world are institutions. Therefore, he falls into that vicious circle of saying that a legal institution is legal when in effect it is legal.

Institutionalism has had certain important effects. In the first place, it disturbed the dogma of the statutory character of law that was at the basis of nineteenth century positivism. It challenged Kelsen's identity between the legal system and norms because it pointed out that law, before becoming a norm, is an organisation and exists before the organs of the institution start to legislate. In other words, organisation or law is prius and not posterius to society. A consequence of the institutionalistic approach is that, because law is considered as a social phenomenon independent of the State, there can be numerous legal systems, as many as there are 'institutions' or 'associations' which must necessarily have three characteristics: an association of persons, a common object, and a normative order to discipline the functioning of the organisation. They range from simple forms (such as the family) to more articulate and permanent forms (such as the State).

The two very different ways of understanding the legal system, namely, as either a system of norms (as Kelsen) or as an institution (as Santi Romano), remain important in Italian doctrine. Most private lawyers are inclined to the normative approach because the private law manifests itself in the form of positive norms. On the other hand, public lawyers generally adopt the institutional approach which is of greater relevance in the study of the life and regulation of the State.

The present state of Italian legal thought

Although the reaction to positivism led to a rebirth of Hegelian idealism, which attained an influence in the early twentieth century of an extent no less than that attained by positivism in the second half of the nineteenth century, there came about a division between the philosophy of law and legal science that was even deeper than when jurists believed that the philosophy of law was dominated by natural law. Idealism has had little influence on Italian legal science. Jurists continued to cling to the natural science of nineteenth century positivism and to put forward models based on that science; some continued to build systems based on concepts, like Francesco Carnelutti, whose *General Theory of Law* appeared in 1940. Thus the philosophy of law, dominated by idealism, and legal science each proceeded on their own paths in an atmosphere of reciprocal indifference. Nonetheless, some degree of reconciliation between the two arose through the work of the philosopher Giuseppe Capograssi, who shook the Italian legal world from its unquestioned faith in formal legal positivism and opened it up to a more concrete approach to law. It was in this atmosphere that analytical legal philosophy appeared in Italy. The supporters of legal positivism, or formalism, sought a new philosophical basis for legal science which was the general theory of law into which, through the logic of legal positivism, the philosophy of law had been transformed. They sought a basis which would be sounder than the rather naive naturalistic one upon which Italian jurists had hitherto continued to operate. Outside Italy, jurists had already undergone the influence of analytical philosophy, such as Kelsen, Ross and above all, Hart. This philosophy, also called neopositivism, was born as a theory of science and is based on a rigorous scientific methodology. For the neopositivist the essential characteristic of science is not its absolute veracity but its validity. Neopositivism is based upon defined principles which, although not absolutely certain, are taken as fixed because they are necessary to the purpose at hand, and from which there is extracted all of those consequences that follow according to a strict and coherent logic. Thus a given form of knowledge acquires a scientific character, not because of the truth of its content, but because of the rigour in its methodology. Norberto Bobbio, by taking such an approach, sought to resolve the old problem of a science of law. He affirmed that the work of the jurist has a scientific character insofar as it makes the language of the legislature exact by clarifying the initial propositions (or norms), defining and integrating the rules for their transformation, and organising them into a coherent system. The type of legal science which takes the form indicated by Bobbio is, essentially, the general theory of normative and formal law, in effect Kelsenism. However, Bobbio does not draw from his new theory the conclusion of the old legal positivism, namely, the futility of the philosophy of law and therefore the need to force it into the general theory of law. Rather, he assigns to the philosophy of law the functions of a theory of justice (the traditional 'deontological' function) which is concerned with the ideals and values of law, to legal science the study of the validity, rather than the value, of law, and to legal sociology the study of the effectiveness of law. He then deals with law, because of the analytical approach itself, under the sole aspect of its formal validity, at the expense of its other two aspects. This unitary vision of law is the defect in his school of thought; it has been responsible for leading all of his followers along the path of a reductionist formal analysis because of their excitement with the novelty of the analytical approach. It therefore runs the risk of overshadowing that complete and concrete vision of law that Bobbio himself had advocated. This explains the diffidence towards analytical philosophy by certain other streams of Italian legal culture notwith-standing that they also adhere to a scientific approach and a rigorous methodology.

To conclude, it may be said that the dogma of legislative positivism, which arose as a consequence of codification, has become weaker. This is evident from the more open recognition of the role of the doctrine and case law in the formation and evolution of law, as well as the tendency of legal scholarship in extending its scope into other aspects of society. However, the accomplishments of traditional legal science, especially the systematisation and the construction of an orderly structure in the law, still survive. Although many jurists are critical of the traditional doctrine, most still cling to it and it dominates the literature used in teaching and practice. The typical private law manual begins with a general part, similar in nature and style to the general part of the German Civil Code. Traditional legal science, which takes the form of the 'General Theory of Law', remains a significant element of contemporary Italian legal scholarship.

THE GENERAL THEORY OF LAW

Introduction

The function of the science of law is to describe systematically and explain the legal system understood as an organism or unitary structure. This function necessarily presupposes the utilisation of general concepts and categories applicable to every branch of the law. It is these concepts and categories which form the object of the general theory of law. This method contributes to an orderly, systematic, and logical organisation of the legal system and provides the framework within which the more detailed study of law is undertaken. Although the general theory of law was developed in the private law, it was later extended to encompass public law.

The general theory of law has its origins in the German Pandectist school which, through the general theory, arrived at the most elaborate and abstract systematisation of fundamental legal concepts ever achieved. The results of the German school have been embodied in the so-called General Part of the German Civil Code which, in its subsequent Parts, proceeds, through descending levels of abstraction, to deal more specifically with particular legal institutions. The German school greatly influenced Italian legal scholarship which continued to develop and refine the general theory of law. However, unlike the German Code, the Italian Civil Code of 1942 does not contain a general part because the Italian legislature, in accordance with Latin tradition, preferred not to incorporate abstract principles into the Code. In Italy both the creation and the study of the general theory has been the province of the doctrine. Nonetheless, the general theory is of fundamental importance since the Code is interpreted and applied by lawyers who are trained and educated in the doctrinal methods of the German school.

The most enlightened of the Italian doctrine acknowledges the existence of other schools of thought as well as the limitations of traditional legal science. However, the Italian doctrine continues to adhere to the general theory which best responds to the traditional reasoning and methodology of civil lawyers. The education of Italian lawyers always begins with the systematic general theory of law, the traditional legal science. The doctrine continues to consider its task as being the scientific treatment of the law with the object of extracting general principles and creating a system. It considers every legal norm as falling within that rational system. Italian legal studies always commence with the general part, and only after the exploration of the general concepts and their characteristics does a more specific study, which comprises legislation, case law, and doctrine, take place. The process is from the more general and abstract to the less general and specific institutions which are always, however, studied within the conceptual structure established by the general part. This process is patently manifest in the organisation of university law curricula in which the abstract concepts and categories of the general theory are studied in the introductory institutional private and public law courses, whilst the detailed principles of both private and public law are studied in later and more specialised courses of the law degree. Moreover, every private and public law manual commences with a general part which systematically discusses the principal concepts and structure of the legal system. In this way the general theory becomes a permanent framework or reference for academics, judges, and practitioners. In adherence to the traditional approach it is now appropriate to examine the general concepts and structure of traditional Italian legal science, or the general theory, which is still at the basis of Italian professional legal life.

The legal relationship (rapporto giuridico)

The first fundamental notion of the general theory is the legal relationship. It may be defined as that relationship, regulated by law, which exists between two or more subjects giving rise to a right in one subject with a corresponding subjection of one or more other subjects. To extend this notion to all legal relationships, including those which do not involve a right-duty relation, it can be said that the legal relationship is every interpersonal relationship regulated by law. In its simplest form, the legal relationship is the relation between the holder of a legally-protected interest (the so-called active subject of the relationship) and a subject who is bound to perform or respect that interest (the so-called passive subject of the relationship) e g the relationship between creditor and debtor of a sum of money.

The legal relationship arises when a subject acquires a right. The right may be acquired as either an original right which arises without its transmission from another subject, e g the right of a fisherman in the fish which he catches, or a derivative right which arises by its transmission from another subject. Succession by derivative right may, furthermore, be either a universal succession in which case all of the relationships of another person are acquired, e g succession mortis causa, or a particular succession in which case only determinate relationships are acquired, e g a purchase. It follows, therefore, that a legal relationship may be either modified or extinguished. It is modified where there is the transmission of a derivative right, there being both an alienation and an acquisition of the right at the same time, and it is extinguished where the right is lost without its corresponding acquisition by another subject, e g the revocation of a right.

Legal subjective situations (situazioni giuridiche soggettive)

The expression *legal subjective situations* describes the totality of rights, powers, obligations, and the like which appertain to a legal subject. There are two broad categories of subjective situations: first, active situations, or positions of advantage, which involve freedom or discretion of action, and second, passive situations or positions of disadvantage, which involve positions of subjection, limiting the freedom of the individual.

The active subjective positions (or situations of advantage) are the subjective right (*diritto soggettivo*), the legitimate interest (*l'interesse legittimo*), the simple interest (*l'interesse semplice*), the authority (*potestà*), expectations (*aspettative*) and powers (*diritti potestativi*). The passive subjective positions are the obligation (*l'obbligo*), the general duty of abstention or observance (*il dovere generico di astensione o soggezione*), and the burden (*l'onere*).

The subjective right is traditionally defined as the power to act for the satisfaction of an interest which is recognised and protected by the legal system. It is the power to act within the limits indicated by the relevant norm or, in other words, the legal possibility of taking a stance in relation to a given legal situation. It is the maximum protection that the legal system gives to individual interests. It consists of two elements: first a voluntary power which, according to Savigny and Windscheid, manifests itself in either a dominion over an external object or a pretence that someone (the passive subject of the legal relationship) conduct himself in a given way; and second, according to Jhering, an interest which is granted by the legal system to the subject so that he can avail himself of it for the fulfilment of a legally recognised interest. The content of the subjective right consists of all of those faculties inherent in the right, e g ownership of land implies rights of enjoyment, disposition, modification, definition of boundries, and the like. It follows, therefore, that the faculties cannot exist without the right.

In public law, and especially in the case of administrative law, the notion of a subjective right is of practical importance because the division of jurisdiction between the ordinary and administrative courts, in relation to disputes concerning the public administration, depends upon the type of subjective position which is being enforced: if the plaintiff claims a subjective right, then he must proceed in the ordinary courts to protect his right; if, instead, he has only a legitimate interest, then he must proceed in the administrative courts to protect his interest.

The traditional doctrine divides subjective rights into private subjective rights and public subjective rights. Private subjective rights concern those rights which are independent of the individual's relationship with the State, e g personal, family and real rights, and obligations, all of which form the object of private law. On the other hand, public subjective rights, although variously defined by the doctrine, are those rights which have public law relationships at their base. They concern those rights inherent in the relationship between citizen and State, and may be divided into four categories: civic rights, political rights, rights of freedom, and 'social' rights. Civic rights entitles citizens to particular State services, unrelated to the exercise of State functions, upon payment of the relevant fee, e g the right to attend school, the right to use postal and telegraphic services and the right to obtain certificates of civil status. Political rights entitle citizens to participate in State activities including the formation of State and public bodies, e g access to public office and the right to vote. Rights of freedom comprise the traditional fundamental rights, e g freedom of the press. Finally, the so-called 'social rights' entitle citizens to social welfare assistance if they are impaired from, or unable to, work. The most recent doctrine, however, disputes the necessity for the distinction between 'public' and 'private' rights because subjective rights comprise a unitary category, a criticism which even the traditional doctrine acknowledges is not without foundation.

There are also various other classifications of subjective rights, the most important of which are as follows: First, absolute and relative rights. The former are rights which are generally enforceable against *all* other subjects who have corresponding negative obligations not to disturb the rights in question. Examples of absolute rights include real rights (such as ownership) and rights over incorporeal property. Relative rights, on the other hand, are those rights which can only be enforced against one or more determinate persons who have the obligation to do or not to do something, e g obligations. Second, patrimonial and non-patrimonial rights. The former are economic rights which can be quantified in money terms, whilst the latter are primarily rights of a moral nature, e g those appertaining to family relationships. Third, transmissible and non-transmissible rights. The former are rights which may be alienated, whilst the latter cannot be transferred to another subject. Examples of non-transmissible rights include strictly personal rights such as the right to life, certain patrimonial rights (such as usufruct), rights which regulate relationships that satisfy superior interests (such as family rights), and the public subjective rights. Fourth, real rights and obligations. The former are, in fact, the most important category of absolute rights and give to their holder either a total or partial dominion over property. Real rights are always immediate, absolute, and nominate. Obligations, also known as rights of credit or personal rights, are relative rights which can only be enforced against one or more determinate persons who, as passive subjects, owe a certain conduct or prestation.

Finally, perfect and conditional subjective rights. This is a distinction which is generally made in administrative law. Perfect subjective rights are rights which are directly protected by a legal norm and give rise to correlative obligations in the public administration and private individuals to abstain from their violation. The protection of perfect subjective rights generally falls within the jurisdiction of the ordinary courts. Conditional subjective rights, on the other hand, are those rights whose acquisition or continuation are conditional upon an administrative decision. They are rights which may prejudice the public interest and are therefore subject to the power of the public administration to limit or extinguish them, e g the resumption of land for the construction of a highway. There are two types of conditional rights. First, conditional prospective rights or rights in expectation of expansion, which are rights subject to a legal obstacle whose removal depends upon an administrative measure. If the obstacle is removed, the right expands and attains its potential fullness, e g the grant of a building permit. Second, rights subject to a resolutive condition, or the 'weakening of rights'. These are rights which may be limited, in the public interest, by an administrative measure and therefore weaken into legitimate interests, e g the right of ownership weakens into a legitimate interest when the public administration legally exercises its power to resume land. It is controversial in the doctrine as to whether rights which weaken into legitimate interests can constitute an autonomous subjective position. Part of the doctrine denies such an assertion, maintaining that they are simply subjective rights which later become legitimate interests.

The second most important type of active subjective situation is the legitimate interest (*l'interesse legittimo*). There is a lack of consensus in the doctrine as to the exact meaning of this concept. One theory regards it as an interest which is only incidentally or indirectly protected because the interest is so intricately connected with the general interest that it only receives protection because it happens to coincide with the direct protection of the latter. It is, therefore, only protected when the public or general interest is protected. Another theory regards it as an interest which finds protection through the ability of the subject to seek the annulment of a measure which injures it. However, the modern doctrinal approach is to define a legitimate interest as the pretence that the administration validly exercise its power to sacrifice or expand a right, that is, the pretence that the administration exercise its power in accordance with the norms which regulate the exercise of that power. This pretence is not a general one, but only belongs to those subjects who are in a particular position vis-à-vis the administrative measure or the exercise of the power by the administration. This so-called legitimating position (*posizione legittimante*) has its basis in a pre-existing public or private law relationship between the actor and the administration.

A legitimate interest may, therefore, be said to differ from a subjective right in three ways. First, a legitimate interest presupposes subjection to a public power. Second, the remedy for an injured legitimate interest is limited to the annulment of the offending administrative measure, that is, the injured legitimate interest can only be re-integrated by the elimination of the unlawful administrative act. Finally, a legitimate interest presupposes the existence of a prior private or public law relationship.

Legitimate interests may be divided into three types. First, legitimate interests connected with the weakening of rights. The substance of these interests is the pretence that the administration comply with the law in exercising its powers to affect rights, e g requisitions and resumptions. Second, legitimate interests connected with rights awaiting expansion. The substance of these interests is the pretence that the administration remove the restrictions upon the exercise of a particular subjective right, e g authorisations and the issue of passports. Third, legitimate interests unrelated to rights. These include interests connected with status (e g the concession of citizenship), situations of advantage (e g admission to a competition or selection, or the issue of a licence), and subordinate positions (e g promotions).

The third type of active subjective situation is the simple interest (*l'interesse semplice*). It is an interest which is only protected administratively and therefore receives a protection which is inferior to that of the legitimate interest. Whilst the legitimate interest is the pretence that the administration exercise its non-discretionary powers in accordance with the law, the simple interest is the pretence that the administration exercise its discretionary powers in accordance with the criteria of expediency and opportuneness which relate to the merits of the administrative measure. The simple interest, unlike the subjective right and the legitimate interest, never receives judicial protection but is only reviewable within the administrative structure itself by recourse to a hierarchically superior organ.

The three remaining types of active subjective situations may be described as follows. The authority (*potestà*) is a right granted to a subject for the fulfilment of interests which are not directly his. The holder of such authority is not as free as the holder of a subjective interest but is nonetheless bound to protect those interests in respect of which he is given the authority, e g parental authority which is conceded in the interests of the children (A.316 cc) [Abbreviations are listed in the preliminary pages at the beginning of this book]. Expectations (*aspettative*) arise where the acquisition of a right is dependent upon the happening of several conditions, some of which have already occurred and the others remain to be satisfied in the future. In some cases the law protects such interests, e g an inheritance conditional upon acquiring a diploma in which case the subject possessing the conditional interest may take conservative and protective actions in respect of his future interest. It is a preliminary interest which is provisionally protected by the legal system so as to make the acquisition of the true and proper right a possibility. Powers (*diritti potestativi*) are subjective rights which do not involve a dominion over a thing nor a pretence vis-à-vis other subjects. Instead, a power is a right in respect to which the opposite party is not required to perform any particular act but is in a position of mere subjection, e g the right to request the dissolution of a communion of property or the right to seek a divorce, both of which are situations in which there are no true and proper passive subjects.

The passive subjective situations may be briefly described as follows. The obligation is the sacrifice of an interest belonging to one subject in the interests of another, e g the obligation to pay a sum of money to a creditor. An obligation is usually complementary to the subjective right of another subject within the context of a legal relationship. The general duty of abstention (or observance) is the legal situation of a subject who must respect the superior right of another. It is the mere passive duty of observance, and only gives rise to concrete legal relationships where there is an opposition to the exercise of a superior right. For example, the position of the subject who must respect another's right of ownership. Finally, the burden is the sacrifice imposed upon a subject as a condition for obtaining or maintaining a legal advantage. The interest of the subject is therefore made conditional upon a certain conduct which, however, is not an obligation. For example, registration requirements for the protection of interests against third parties.

Legal subjects (I soggetti giuridici)

Legal subjects comprise natural persons (*persone fisiche*), legal persons (*persone giuridiche*), and defined de facto entities (*enti di fatto*). The qualification as a legal subject indicates that the legal system regards the subject as existent and capable of possessing rights and obligations. However, the subject only acquires this qualification if and when the legal system concedes it legal personality (*personalità giuridica*).

The term 'legal personality' is generally restricted to legal persons who acquire their legal existence, or legal personality, at the point of their recognition by the State, that is, after satisfying certain defined pre-requisites. Legal capacity (*capacità giuridica*), on the other hand, is the equivalent expression for natural persons and denotes their eligibility as holders of rights and obligations. As there cannot exist natural persons without legal capacity, which is automatically acquired at birth (A.1 cc), every natural person also acquires 'legal personality' at birth.

The capacity to act (*capacità di agire*) is the ability of the subject *independently* to acquire and deal with subjective rights and to assume obligations. The capacity to act is acquired by natural persons on attaining the age of 18 provided that they are not declared to lack legal capacity to act.

Legal persons

The doctrine classifies legal persons in various ways. The first and most important of such classifications is that between corporations (*corporazioni*) and institutions (*istituzioni*). This distinction is based upon the fact that legal persons consist of an organisation of persons or property. The corporation is an entity in which the personal element predominates. They are, in turn, either associations in a strict sense (*associazioni*) whose principal objects are not of a purely economic nature, e g cultural, sporting and political organisations, or companies (*società*) which have lucrative or mutualist objects. Institutions, on the other hand, are organisations in which the property element predominates and include foundations (*fondazioni*) and committees (*comitati*). There are several distinguishing features between corporations and institutions. First, whereas property is a constituent element of the foundation, it is only a *means* of achieving an object in the case of an association. Second, the objects of a foundation are external, in the sense that they confer advantages on non-members, whilst they are internal, or confer advantages on members, in the case of associations. Third, the government of the organisation is external in the case of foundations because it originates from the founders, whilst it is internal in the case of associations because it is manifested by the members through the apposite organs. It follows from this last characteristic that although the management organs of a foundation remain subject to the will of the founder, they predominate in the case of an association.

A second classification of legal persons is that between public and private. Public legal persons, or public entities, pursue the general interests of the State and often occupy a position of supremacy vis-à-vis the subjects with which they come into contact. Private legal persons, on the other hand, do not pursue the interests of the State and are therefore in an equivalent position to that of the private subjects with whom they enter into legal relations. This criterion for the distinction, however, is controversial but notwithstanding the large number of theories which have been advanced no one theory has succeeded in formulating a universally valid criterion, although the 1975 legislation concerning the reorganisation of public entities and public employment has made the individuation of public entities less difficult than in the past.

In the Italian legal system there are a number of subjects which exercise administrative functions and duties and which can therefore be regarded as public entities. The public legal person par excellence is the State, which is therefore itself subject to the requirements of public or private law depending upon the legal situation in question. An important distinction here is between autocratic public entities (*enti pubblici autarchici*) which operate in the sphere of administrative law, through administrative measures, and exercise the public power, and economic public entities (*enti pubblici economici*) which operate in the private law sphere but are, formally, public legal persons. Because the latter operate in the private law sphere, through the legal transaction and in competition with private associations, they are subject to the private law. Another distinction between public entities is that between territorial and non-territorial public entities. The territorial entities are those in relation to which their territorial jurisdiction is an essential element and comprise the communes, provinces, and Regions. The non-territorial entities are all other public entities in relation to which the territorial element is not a constituent element, although their activity may in fact be limited to a particular territory.

A third classification of legal persons is that between civil and ecclesiastical legal persons, but this distinction is only operative within the category of private legal persons. The ecclesiastical legal person is that which pursues religious objects and, as such, is regulated not only by the civil law but also by canon law. All other private legal persons are civil. A further and final classification is that between national and foreign legal persons. This distinction is based upon the recognition of legal persons by the State. Thus all legal persons which are recognised by the Italian State are national, whilst all of those which are not recognised by the State are foreign. However, commercial companies are an exception to this principle because their recognition is based upon mere registration and their nationality is governed by Artt. 2505 ff cc. The latter provisions have, moreover, been affected by A.58 of the EEC Treaty according to which all companies, whether national or foreign, having their seat and activity within the Community are recognised by the Italian legal system.

De facto entities

The third type of legal person is the de facto entity or unrecognised association, which is commonplace and enjoys a particular legal position. It comprises the same elements as a legal person but lacks formal State recognition. Nonetheless, although the legal system concedes neither the importance nor the capacity typical of a recognised association, it does not impede its operation as a collective unit. The lack of recognition means that the members, even if acting on behalf of the entity, remain personally liable. However, the property of the association and all contributions constitute a common fund and the members or their creditors cannot, unlike the ordinary case of co-ownership, request its division for so long as the association continues to exist. Article 36 cc, moreover, expressly enables the president or directors of the association to bring or defend actions on behalf of the association.

The committee is a particular type of unrecognised association. It consists of a group of persons who, through the accumulation of material means, seek to fulfil an object which is generally one in the public interest and for this purpose seek contributions through public subscription or invitations to donate. Article 39 cc enumerates in an exemplary fashion the more frequent types of committee, e g charities. Part of the doctrine assimilates committees with the foundation because of the prevalence of the property element. The members of the committee are personally liable to the donors for the conservation of the fund and its expenditure on the stated objects, and to third party creditors in respect of the obligations assumed by the committee.

The dynamics of subjective situations: legal facts and acts (i fatti e gli atti giuridici)

A subjective situation is established, modified, or extinguished by so-called legal facts (*fatti giuridici*) which are natural or social facts, the occurrence of which produce a legal consequence. A norm, which is an abstract command, does not directly give rise to a subjective situation but rather provides and regulates the causes for the establishment, modification, or extinguishment of rights. It is these causes which are the so-called legal facts. All those facts of life which give rise to legal consequences in human relationships are considered legal facts, e g birth, an agreement for sale, or an assault. The legal system, through its norms, regulates all of those facts which affect social relations.

The doctrine classifies legal facts in accordance with the incidence of human intervention. Therefore, the doctrine distinguishes between:

(a) Legal events in which human activity is irrelevant. These may, in turn, be divided into two categories. First, natural facts (*fatti naturali*) such as lightning, floods, the mere passage of time, and the like. These are facts which are free from human intervention and are the sole consequence of the natural order of things. Second, the pure and simple legal act (*atto giuridico puro e semplice*) in which the human contribution is irrelevant, e g planting and construction.

(b) Legal events in which human activity is relevant, that is human acts (*atti umani*), also known as 'legal acts'. These are acts knowingly and voluntarily determined by a capable subject who has the power to modify an existing situation. Legal acts may be classified in two ways. First, according to whether or not the acts conform with the legal system, so that they may be either lawful acts (*atti leciti*), if they conform with the legal system, or unlawful acts (*atti illeciti*), if they are in conflict with the legal system, in which case they are said to be illegal (*antigiuridici*). An illegal fact may give rise to either a criminal or civil illegality. The former, after the conclusion of the criminal process, results in the imposition of a criminal penalty and forms the subject matter of criminal law and criminal procedure. The latter, on the other hand, gives rise to compensation for damages in accordance with A.2043 cc, that is, tort liability. If, instead, the illegality is a consequence of a natural fact, or a pure and simple legal act in which the human contribution is irrelevant, there is generally an objective responsibility in the subject connected with the happening of the event. Second, legal acts may be classified according to the degree of autonomy enjoyed by the parties, so that they may be either legal acts in the strict sense (*atti giuridici in senso stretto*) which are those acts where the human agent determines the act and the legal system exclusively and directly determines the legal consequences, e g torts, or legal transactions (*negozi giuridici*) which are those acts where the human agent enjoys the autonomy of determining both the act and its effects, e g contracts and wills.

The 'legal acts' of the public administration

A legal act of the public administration may appertain to either public or private law. It is a public law act if it originates in accordance with the principles and forms of public law, e g all of the so-called administrative acts (*atti amministrativi*) issued by the public administration. On the other hand, the public administration may create a private law transaction in which case the public administration is on a level of parity with other private subjects and the legal act in question is entirely regulated by the private law.

The 'legal acts' of public law are not divided like those of the private law between legal acts in the strict sense and legal transactions, the latter being largely irrelevant to public law, but between normative acts (*atti normativi*) and measures (*provvedimenti*). Normative acts are those which stipulate rules of general application, and are therefore characterised by their general and abstract nature, e g legislation, delegated legislation, and regulations. Measures, on the other hand, are those acts of the public administration that are directed to one or more specific situations or subjects. They are individual measures in that they do not contain general and abstract provisions but rather modify a specific and defined situation, even if at the same time the measure is applicable to more than one subject. Measures, may be divided into three broad categories. First, authorisations (*autorizzazioni*) which enable a defined subject to exercise an existing power which could not, however, be exercised in the absence of consensus by the public administration. Second, concessions (*concessioni*) which are measures that confer on a grantee new legal rights which, prior to the measure, fell outside his legal sphere. And finally, measures creating legal situations of disadvantage (*atti creativi di situazioni giuridiche di svantaggio*) for the subject to which they are directed. These may either impose positive or negative obligations.

Legal acts are voluntary facts and therefore, although of particular significance in the case of legal transactions and the private law, they are, as already stated, only of a limited relevance in public law. However, some writers introduce a voluntary element to distinguish between (i) administrative transactions which *cannot* be freely negotiated (the voluntary element here is limited to whether or not they are to be put into existence as their effects are already predetermined by law), and (ii) administrative transactions which *can* be freely negotiated (these are voluntary as to both their creation *and* effects). However, the doctrine generally denies that such a distinction may be drawn in public law because the freedom of negotiation inherent in the concept of the 'legal transaction' is absent in the administrative act which is always conditioned by institutional objectives. This fact also explains why the legal system, inter alia, does not provide for the invalidity of the administrative act by reason of a defect in the intent or capacity of its agent.

La fattispecie

The concept of *fattispecie* (or typical fact situation) describes the relationships between legal facts and their normative regulation, on the one hand, and between the same legal facts and their legal consequences, on the other hand. The doctrine distinguishes between abstract and actual *fattispecie*. The abstract *fatttispecie* (*fattispecie astratta*) is that combination of elements which the legal system requires in abstract to produce the modification of a legal relationship. It is the typical abstract situation regulated in a norm which links to it certain legal effects. The abstract *fattispecie*, therefore, is necessary both for the application of the norm and the production of certain legal effects. The abstract *fattispecie* may comprise one legal fact only (e g death which gives rise to the opening of a succession) or several legal facts (e g the consensus of the parties and the declaration of the marriage celebrant both of which are necessary for the celebration of a marriage). The actual or concrete *fattispecie* (*fattispecie concreta*) is the factual situation which actually verifies itself and is taken into account in determining whether it coincides with, and is therefore regulated by, the abstract *fattispecie*. It is clear, therefore, that legal facts are the dynamic element of social life. They are the vital factors which give the legal world its dynamism. They produce given legal effects (*effetti giuridici*) because the legal system gives to each legal fact a certain relevance and effect.

The legal transaction (il negozio giuridico)

The concept of the legal transaction, a particular product of the German Pandectist school of the last century, is the fundamental manifestation of private autonomy. It confers a power upon individuals to constitute freely, in the desired form, certain legal acts and to stipulate norms which bind the parties to the transaction with the force of law. However, because the Italian legal system, like most western legal systems, is seeking to achieve a balance between laissez faire and state intervention, an increasing number of limitations have been placed upon private autonomy in defence of group interests, e g the predominance of collective contracts in labour law. Moreover, private autonomy has been limited by certain legislative provisions. First, those norms which prescribe the requisites for the legal transaction, that is, the requirements as to form, cause, and intent. Second, the restrictions on creating atypical legal transactions in certain subjects, e g family relations, real rights, dispositions *mortis causa*, and commercial companies. Third, the prohibition against eliminating certain effects of defined (typical) transactions. And finally, the limits arising out of the overriding principles of legality, public order, and good custom.

In essence, the legal transaction is an abstract notion created by the doctrine to unite different types of acts which share certain common characteristics. It is generally defined as a lawful legal act whose effects are not predetermined by law but freely stipulated by the parties; such effects being in accordance with both an express manifest intent and a cause which the act is objectively capable of achieving. From all of the usual doctrinal definitions it can be said that the 'legal transaction' has four basic characteristics. First, it is a 'legal act', which means that it is a conscious and voluntary human act whose effects are not pre-determined by law but freely stipulated by the parties. Second, it is lawful in that it must conform with the general rules of the legal system. Third, it consists of a manifest declaration of intent. And finally, it is directed to defined legal effects which are both recognised and protected by the legal system, that is, it has a valid cause.

The legal transaction has a complex structure. In the first place, the parties to the transaction must satisfy certain requisites in order that that transaction may come into existence, namely, the parties must have legal capacity (*capacità giuridica*), the capacity to act (*capacità d'agire*), and the necessary locus standi (*legittimazione*) to be party to the type of transaction in question. Second, the transaction itself comprises various elements: first, the essential elements, without which no transaction can validly come into existence. They are intent, form and cause. In certain categories of transaction there may be additional necessary elements, e g the requirement of revocability in the case of wills. Second, natural elements or effects, which are the consequences that flow from the particular nature of the transaction in question, although these may be excluded by the parties. Finally, the incidental elements, which although not part of the abstract structure of the transaction may be incorporated as a result of the freedom to transact. The incidental elements which may be incorporated into every transaction are conditions, terms, and burdens. In addition, certain types of incidental elements may be incorporated into defined transactions, e g contracts may contain penalty clauses and deposits.

The doctrine has devised various classifications of the legal transaction employing various criteria of which the most important are as follows: first, in relation to the number of parties to a transaction, which may therefore be unilateral (e g a will), bilateral (e g a sale), or plurilateral (e g a company constitution). This distinction is of practical relevance in relation both to the date of the formation of the necessary intent and the interpretation of transactions. Second, in relation to the nature of the object of the transaction which may therefore be strictly personal (e g transactions concerning ones own person), domestic (e g marriage), or patrimonial. Third, in relation to the nature of the counterprestation, which is a criterion applicable to patrimonial transactions only, as a result of which transactions may be either onerous or gratuitous. Moreover, onerous transactions may be further divided into commutative, where the counterprestations are certain, and aleatory where they are uncertain (e g contract of insurance). The distinction between onerous and gratuitous transactions has broad practical relevance, e g in relation to the capacity to act, defects in intent, and form. Finally, in relation to death according to which transactions may be either *mortis causa* or inter vivos. The Italian legal system permits only one type of *mortis causa* transaction, the will. Every other type of transaction to take effect on death and *donationes mortis causa* is prohibited.

The essential elements of a 'legal transaction'

A. THE INTENTION TO CREATE LEGAL RELATIONS

The intent to enter into a legal transaction must be externalised in order to become relevant. Therefore, if in a normal transaction the external and internal intents of the subject must coincide, it follows that there may be a divergence between the two. Such divergence may be of three basic types. First, where there is a declaration but without an effective internal intent, so that the transaction is totally without intent and therefore null ab initio. This may arise in the case of a declaration made during a performance; a declaration in the course of instruction; or a declaration as a result of physical force. Second, where the internal intent does not correspond with the declared intent. This may arise because of so-called hindering-error (*errore ostativo*) which is a fundamental mistake in the declaration caused by distraction or ignorance, or a mistake in the transmission; dissonance (*dissenso*) which arises when the recipient of a declaration agrees because of a misunderstanding as to the substance of the negotiations; or simulation which is when the external declarations deliberately fail to reflect the real intent of the parties, as a result of which there is both a simulated (or fictional) transaction and a latent transaction. Third, where, although the internal and external intent correspond, the former has been abnormally formed. This may be because of general error, which is a misrepresentation to induce the opposite party to enter into the transaction; moral violence which is the inducement of an agreement through an unlawful and effective threat; or fraud which is any device or trick utilised in deceiving another person so as to induce him to enter into the transaction. All of these defects in the intent to enter into legal relations have varying consequences on the transaction in question: in some cases the transaction is invalid in which event it may be either null and void or merely voidable; in other cases the transaction may remain valid but give rise to damages.

The validity of transactions defective for intent basically depend upon the good faith of the recipient of the declaration. Thus, in general, if the recipient did not, or could not, know of the divergence between the effective and declared intent and therefore relied on the faith of the declaration, the transaction is valid; otherwise it is invalid. However, this general approach has been tempered in certain circumstances so that the following broad propositions may be stated. First, the validity of inter vivos property transactions for value depend, in accordance with the general rule, upon the good faith of the recipient so that the risk falls upon the declarant. Second, the validity of domestic transactions, dispositions *mortis causa*, and gratuitous property transactions depend upon the strict internal intent of the declarant so that any divergence between the effective and declared intents will necessarily lead to the invalidity of the transaction, so that the risk, in these cases, rests with the recipient. Finally, in the case of the erroneous payment of a debt, the good faith of the declarant (the payer) is decisive. Thus if the divergence between internal and external intents is due to the non-excusable error of the payer, then the latter must bear the risk so that the transaction remains valid and he cannot obtain restitution of the sum paid.

B. FORM

As a consequence of the principle of contractual autonomy, the law does not generally require any particular form and therefore most transactions may even be created orally. Only exceptionally does the law specify formal requisites essential to the validity of the transaction in question.

C. CAUSE (CAUSA)

(*i*) *Definition*. The dominant and accepted view is that cause is the socio-economic function that a transaction is objectively capable of achieving, e g in a sale it is the exchange between object and price. However, this approach has been criticised as being a futile repetition of the definition or concept of the particular transaction without taking into account its *purpose*, which is the very element inherent in the term 'cause'. Cause, according to this latter approach, is the purpose or objective result which the subject proposes to achieve by placing the transaction into existence. Cause, therefore, is the typical, constant, objective and impersonal purpose of every legal transaction. This definition, moreover, highlights the difference between the cause and the motives of a legal transaction. Whilst the motives for which a subject enters into a transaction may be many and varied, its cause is the constant and typical purpose of the transaction.

Legal transactions may be divided into three types according to their cause. First, typical (or nominate) transactions which are those transactions expressly contemplated and defined by law, e g the sale. They are also known as transactions with a typical cause. Second, atypical (or innominate) transactions (A.1322(2) cc) which do not correspond to any transaction expressly regulated by law. However, atypical transactions are subject to two limits: they must conform with the general principles of the legal system (A.1323 cc) regarding their requisites and effects, and must have a purpose worthy of protection (A.1322(2) cc). Third, mixed transactions which are atypical transactions formed by the fusion of two or more typical transactions, e g a parking contract which combines the causes of both the lease and a deposit.

Legal transactions may also be divided into causal and formal transactions. The former are those in which their cause is an essential and constituent element, whilst the latter, because they are expressly contemplated by law, produce their effects apart from their cause.

(ii) Absence of cause. A transaction may lack cause either ab initio or from a point of time subsequent to its formation. Cause will be totally lacking ab initio, in a typical transaction, when it does not fulfil the typical purpose of the transaction as, e g in the acquisition of a thing which already belongs to the purchaser, and, in an atypical transaction, when the cause is not worthy of protection by the legal system because it is either futile or unlawful. The total absence of cause ab initio results in the nullity of the transaction. However, when cause is only partially absent ab initio, viz. when there is a mere inequitable disproportion between the counterprestations in a bilateral contract, the injured party may seek termination only. Cause may, moreover, fail subsequent to the formation of a transaction because of supervening impossibility, an excessive burden, or non-performance by one of the parties, in which cases rescission is available to the party for whom the cause failed.

(iii) Unlawful cause. Cause is unlawful when it is contrary to an imperative norm (which expressly or implicitly prescribes nullity as its sanction, e g A.458 cc which prohibits any agreement which is to take effect *mortis causa*), public order or good custom. The two latter concepts are roughly equivalent to the 'public policy' of common law countries. The principles of public order are not necessarily contained in express statutory provisions but may be deduced from the general legislative system as affected by contemporary social needs and development. Good custom, on the other hand, is not restricted to matters of sexual morality but comprises all of those elastic principles relating to the current and general social morality. Unlawful cause is only relevant in the case of atypical transactions as the defined cause of a typical transaction must necessarily be lawful. An unlawful cause results in the nullity of the transaction (A.1418 cc) and in addition, a

right of restitution which, exceptionally, is not available in the case of an immoral cause.

The pathology of the legal transaction

If one of the elements or requisites of a legal transaction is missing or defective, the transaction remains, or becomes, ineffective. A transaction, however, may be ineffective in either a wide or narrow sense. The former is a serious defect of a permanent and pathological nature which affects the structure or substance of the transaction, whilst the latter is only a temporary inability of the transaction to produce its effects, e g pending the happening of a condition precedent.

Ineffective transactions, in a wide sense, may be divided into three types. First, non-existent transactions. Whilst part of the doctrine disputes this category which, in practice, produces the same effects as a null transaction, another part of the doctrine observes that this category concerns a situation beyond mere 'vitiation', that is, where there is the absence of even that bare 'minimum' for a transaction to be conceived, categorised or identified as a legal transaction.

Second, invalid transactions which may be either null and void or voidable depending upon the seriousness of the defect. According to A.1418 cc, a transaction is null and void if it lacks an essential element, is contrary to public order or good custom, or contains an unlawful condition. When a transaction is void there is nonetheless a right of restitution in favour of the party who performed (A.2033 cc) unless it is an immoral transaction (A.2035 cc). However, the general principle that a purchaser takes no better title than his transferor has been modified to protect a purchaser acting in good faith. In particular, a judgment declaring nullity does not prejudice the rights of bona fide purchasers if the commencement of the nullity proceedings was registered more than five years, in the case of immovables, or more than three years, in the case of registrable movables, after the registration of the transaction whose nullity is requested provided that the third-party purchaser has registered his purchase prior to the registration of the commencement of the nullity proceedings.

On the other hand, an invalid transaction may be merely voidable and will be so regarded when nullity is too serious a penalty. The transaction, therefore, produces its effects until it is annulled. A transaction will be voidable when one of its elements is defective, when an essential element is missing but this is not sufficiently serious to give rise to nullity, and in all other cases provided for by legislation. An action for the annulment of a voidable transaction must be brought within a prescriptive period of five years (A.1442 cc). A judgment which declares the nullity of a voidable transaction is retrospective and thereby eliminates all of the effects of the voidable transaction as well as giving rise to restitution. However, except in the case where the voidability of the transaction is due to the incapacity of a person who was previously declared to be an interdict, the retrospective effect of the judgment does not prejudice the rights of a bona fide third person for value. A voidable transaction, unlike a void transaction, may nonetheless be made effective by its express or implied ratification by the party entitled to seek its annulment (A.1444 cc). Moreover, there is a general principle that transactions made pursuant to the freedom to contract must be saved from nullity whenever possible and, similarly, another principle according to which a null transaction may be considered valid if it contains all of the necessary elements of a different type of transaction provided that it can be presumed that the parties would have desired its conversion had they been aware of the nullity.

Finally, a transaction may be impugnable where, unlike void or voidable transactions, its validity is not affected by any defect in a constituent element or other requisite of the transaction but some extrinsic circumstances upon which the validity of the transaction is also dependent. Impugnment does not necessarily destroy all of the effects of a transaction. Moreover, the effect of the judgment which impugns the transaction is generally limited to the parties to the transaction, subject to any registration requirements. There are four types of impugnment. First, rescission of contracts for either non-performance or excessive burden. Second, termination of contracts concluded in a state of necessity (A.1447 cc) or by taking advantage of the contractual weakness of the opposite party as a result of the latter's state of need (A.1448 cc). Third, reduction of gifts inter vivos and testamentary dispositions so as to enable a favoured beneficiary to receive the share due to him under the rules of forced inheritance. Finally, revocation of transactions disposing of property, at the instance of a creditor who is prejudiced by the transaction. This action, also known as the Paulian action, subject to any registration requirements, does not affect a bona fide purchaser for value.

Transactions may be ineffective in a narrow sense in two broad situations. First, where the transaction is valid but ineffective, e g where it is subject to a suspensive or resolutive condition. Second, where the transaction is said to be irregular. This arises where the transaction violates a legislative provision which does not affect the validity of the transaction but merely imposes a penalty on its author.

The elements and pathology of the 'legal act' in public law

As already stated, the legal transaction, which is a particular form of legal act, is only of a limited significance in public law because in this area the autonomy of the actor is limited to the creation of the 'legal act' and not also its effects which are, instead, predetermined by law. It follows therefore that the elements of a legal act have a different importance in public law.

First, as to the subjective elements of the legal act, namely, the capacity to act and the locus standi of the actor to act in a given situation, the latter element is much more complex in public than in private law because here it not only involves a consideration of the relevant legal norms or their relationship to the actor, but also the validity of the relationship between the actor and the organ of the public administration which he represents. The latter relationship comprises the valid investiture of the public function in the actor, the regular formation of the relevant public organ and the functional competence of the organ which issues the act.

Of the essential elements of the legal act itself, the element of intent is of a more limited significance in public law. In public acts, what is relevant is not the intent of the person who is physically acting but the intent of the entity or organ for which he acts. Thus the private law notions which concern a defect in intent are not applicable to public law in which, instead, the element of 'intent' relates solely to the formal legal rules which prescribe the procedure with which an organ or entity must make a decision or issue a measure. In relation to the element of cause, the public law doctrine is equivocal. Some writers consider that it is irrelevant because all public acts are 'typical' whilst other writers maintain that cause may be understood as the function attributed by the legal system to a given act so that the emanation of an act for a purpose or function different to that prescribed by law will give rise to the defect known as 'excess of power'. Finally, the requirement of form is more important in public than in private law as in the majority of cases public acts must comply with a prescribed form, in the absence of which the act will be invalid or even non existent.

In respect to the ineffectiveness of public acts, the main differences with the private law are as follows. First, the common grounds for nullity in public law are the failure to comply with the form prescribed by law, the lack of jurisdiction to issue the administrative act in question, uncertainty as to the content of the administrative measure, and conflict with the general principles of the legal system. Second, as in the case of the private law, defects in an administrative act of a less serious nature than those for nullity will merely render the act voidable which means that the act will remain effective until it is declared null. However, unlike the private law, the typical defects which give rise to a voidable act in administrative law are incompetence, excess of power, and violation of law. Third, ineffectiveness in a narrow sense may arise in administrative law for two basic reasons. In the first place, for the failure to submit the act to the relevant controlling organ, e g the failure to 'register' an act with the Court of Accounts where this is required. In the second place, for the failure to communicate the act to the subjects required to observe it. Such communication may consist of either service upon the interested parties, or publication where the act is one of general application.

ITALIAN LEGISLATIVE HISTORY FROM THE RESTORATION TO THE PRESENT

The constitutional history of Italy

Italy, prior to unification, comprised a number of independent states. Modern Italy grew from the State of Sardegna by a process of annexation of various states culminating with the Proclamation of the Kingdom of Italy in 1861. The *Statuto albertino*, as the Constitution of the State of Sardegna was known, through the same process of annexation became the Constitution of Italy and remained so, at least formally, until 1 January 1948, although in 1944 it was almost entirely superseded by the 'Provisional Constitution'. However, the *Statuto albertino* was, for several reasons, a weak constitution. It was conceded by an absolute sovereign, Charles Albert, in 1848; it was flexible and therefore of a status equal to ordinary legislation only; its provisions were general and subject to differing interpretations; it had an unsatisfactory institutional framework, placing the sovereign in a pre-eminent and powerful position vis-à-vis the legislative, executive, and judicial branches of government; and not least it was so brief in the area of civil and individual liberties that, even before fascism, it was unable to guarantee satisfactorily the rights of the citizen. This last factor abundantly demonstrated the profound weakness of the Constitution, a weakness which was to remain even after the evolution of the constitutional system into a parliamentary form, as was evident from the passage of the police laws in the second half of the nineteenth century. But the ultimate evidence of the weakness of the constitutional system emerged in October 1922 with the march on Rome by the fascists. Instead of signing the decrees proclaiming a state of emergency, as proposed by the government of the day, to contain the fascist advance, the King, through an unconventional practice, designated Benito Mussolini as prime minister. The Crown was apparently motivated in its action by a belief that the fascists would assist the Crown's conservative politics. Mussolini, after having obtained the confidence of the Parliament through intimidation, initiated a series of institutional changes which converted the parliamentary system into a dictatorship.

After the fall of fascism in June 1944, the National Liberation Committee, temporarily given the functions of government, became the provisional organ which substituted for Parliament and represented Italian public opinion. By legislative decree dated 25 June 1944, the government also provisionally assumed the legislative power. The decree provided that the institutional choice between monarchy and republic be put to the Italian people through the election of a constituent assembly. Simultaneously there was an 'institutional truce' to the effect that until the constituent assembly came into being neither party would do anything to prejudice the institutional choice.

In March 1946 it was provided by legislative decree that the institutional question be, instead, put to a popular referendum, and that the ordinary legislative power of the government continue during the period of the constituent assembly. On 9 May 1946, King Victor Emmanuel III, who in accordance with the 'institutional truce' had retired into private life without abdicating, in violation of the truce, reappeared to abdicate in favour of his son Umberto, the Lieutenant-General of the Realm. Notwithstanding this violation of the constitutional truce the government recognised Umberto as King in order not to delay the referendum. However, the referendum decided in favour of a republic, as a result of which Umberto was King for only a few days until his expulsion from the national territory.

The Constituent Assembly, which convened on 22 June 1946 and continued to operate until 31 January 1948, immediately asserted its total sovereignty and, in conflict with the 1946 legislative decrees which had reserved the legislative power to the government, it instead delegated such power to the government on the clear understanding that the assembly had the power at any time to assume the legislative function for itself. The assembly created from its number the *Commission of 75* which divided itself into three sub-committees and after six months presented a draft constitution. The draft was dealt with in 173 sittings and finally approved on 22 December 1947. It was proclaimed five days later and became effective on 1 January 1948.

The origins of the present Italian Codes

Although most Italian City States partially returned to pre-Napoleonic legislation at the collapse of the Napoleonic regime in 1814, they soon after introduced Codes which, as already noted, were heavily affected by French legal science and the French Codes. In Piedmont, for instance, the restored King Emmanuel I of Savoy re-enacted the pre-Napoleonic compilations. Charles Albert, his successor, provided for an almost complete re-codification, comprising the Civil, Criminal, Military, Commercial, and Criminal Procedure Codes. The next monarch, Victor Emmanuel II, the last King of Piedmont, also officially known as King of Sardegna, who was to be the first King of unified Italy, completed this process with the promulgation of the Code of Civil Procedure in 1854. In 1859 he introduced a new Criminal Code which was later to become applicable to all of Italy (except Tuscany) and remain in force until 1890.

The proclamation of the new Kingdom of Italy in 1861, the beginning of Italian unification through a process of annexation of territories to the old Kingdom of Sardegna, also brought with it a corresponding unification of law by the annexation of the Codes and laws of Piedmont. This was followed by the promulgation, in 1865 and later, of new Codes for the united Kingdom of Italy: the Civil, Commercial, Civil Procedure, Navigation, and Criminal Procedure Codes. These early unification Codes were modelled on the French Napoleonic ones; for some time to come Italian legal scholarship was to be influenced by the French exegesis school (see pp 7 ff, above).

The Civil Code of 1865 was modelled on the Napoleonic Code, although it was innovative in some places and adhered to Italian legal traditions in others. The Code was to be criticised for its poor analytic structure, especially after the reception of the Pandectist school of thought. The Code did not have a general part, and did not deal with abstract concepts such as the 'legal transaction' which is a fundamental concept in Italian legal analysis. It was the school of civil lawyers influenced by Pandectist scholarship that led the movemement for the reform of the 1865 Civil Code; a movement which culminated in the introduction of the present Civil Code of 1942.

The first Italian Commercial Code, which was introduced in 1865, also largely incorporated the principles of the corresponding French Code. However, Venice, which was not annexed until 1866, retained the Austrian mercantile legislation. Therefore, the first uniform commercial law came about as late as 1882 with the promulgation of the new Commercial Code. This Code, modelled on the French Code de Commerce of 1807, took into account the commercial and economic developments of the nineteenth century. The separation of commercial and civil law meant that certain transactions, such as the sale, were sometimes regulated by the civil law, and at other times by the commercial law, depending upon the presence of certain requisites. However, because of the always more widespread relevance of commercial principles, it was decided to unite, and 'commercialise', the whole of the private law into a single Code. Thus the present Civil Code, which became effective on 21 April 1942, replaced the Civil Code of 1865 and the Commercial Code of 1882, thereby ending the separate regulation of civil and commercial relationships. It united the law of obligations, utilising the unitary concept of the 'commercial entrepreneur' to distinguish every form of economic activity.

The 1865 Code of Civil Procedure was the direct descendant of the corresponding Sardinian Codes of 1854 and 1860 and therefore incorporated the influences upon the latter, namely, the formalism of the old Austrian model as well as the nineteenth-century individualism and liberalism of the French 1806 Code of Civil Procedure. The Italian legislature, following the old Austrian model, did not introduce the principle of orality from the French Code, and as a result Italian civil procedure basically remained a written process under the 1865 Code. Even the summary process, which was an oral and concentrated process based on the French Code, was in practice transformed into a formal procedure. However, the 1865 Code was to remain in force until the introduction of the present Code of Civil Procedure, which became effective on 21 April 1942. The 1942 Code manifests the partial success of the demands for reform by Pandectist scholars, led by Giuseppe Chiovenda, who had been influenced by the modern German and Austrian Codes, which had employed concepts and institutions of Roman and Italian origin in order to change the formalistic procedure inherited from the Canon law and the *jus commune*. The recent renewal in the level of Italian legal studies had stimulated Italian procedural scholars to seek out the historical origins of procedural institutions and to rediscover the Roman, Germanic and Italian traditions behind existing rules. The 1942 Code, therefore, partially implemented the demands of the scholars for a procedure characterised by flexibility, orality, and a more active participation of the court in evidentiary matters.

In respect of criminal law, unification did not come about until 1889. On political unification, the Piedmont Criminal Code of 1859 became effective throughout Italy, except in Tuscany whose Criminal Code of 1853 was far superior. The latter, a product of the Enlightenment, is considered the masterpiece of the 'classical school' of criminal law. The classical school, moreover, inspired the uniform Criminal Code of 1889 which was characterised by the abolition of the death penalty, milder punishments, and an overall liberal spirit. This Code remained in force until the introduction of the present Criminal Code of 1930 which became effective on 1 July 1931. The present Code takes an approach which is midway between the classical and positive schools of criminal law. It combines the teachings of the classical school, by requiring conduct which is both blameworthy and imputable to the actor before a criminal penalty can be imposed, and the influence of the positive school, in providing for the imposition of indeterminate precautionary measures in the cases of conduct which, although not criminal, nonetheless indicates that the actor is a danger to society. The essential difference between the classical and positive schools of thought is that the latter is based upon strict causation and therefore disregards the element of imputability, or free will, which the classical school considers indispensable. Therefore, according to the classical approach, a criminal sanction cannot be imposed where the actor lacks a free will, even if he is socially dangerous. Thus the new Code introduced a new type of sanction which does not have the object of punishment but prevention or social defence, namely, the so-called precautionary measures which must always be proportional to the dangerousness of the actor and not, as in the case of a penalty, to the seriousness of the fact.

Soon after unification, in 1865, there was also the enactment of a new Code of Criminal Procedure but this Code was to be replaced by the Code of Criminal Procedure of 1913 which was motivated by liberal anti-authoritarian ideals. It was partially because of this characteristic that it was later repealed and replaced by the so-called 'Rocco Code' of 1930 which became operative on 1 July 1931.

In conclusion, it may be noted that fascist ideology had, generally speaking, little influence on the Codes. Although the fascists, for propaganda reasons, claimed that both the Civil Code and the Code of Civil Procedure were products of the regime, neither in fact had much to do with fascism. Rather, they represented the results of legal scholarship and doctrinal pressures for reform ante-dating the regime. The only Codes into which the authoritarian ideology of fascism penetrated to any extent were the Criminal Code and, to a greater extent, the Code of Criminal Procedure. However, both, but particularly the Code of Criminal Procedure, have undergone extensive amendment, although this is not to say that they are not in need of fundamental reform to bring about a coherent ideological outlook.

Chapter 2

The Italian legal profession

The general categories of the Italian legal profession and the university law degree

The Italian legal profession can be divided into three broad categories: academics, practitioners, and the magistracy. The latter comprises the judiciary in a strict sense and the *pubblico ministero* who, inter alia, performs the function of public prosecutor. The fundamental academic requirement for entry into any of the above branches of the legal profession is a degree in law (*laurea in giurisprudenza*) awarded by an Italian university. The requisites for the award of the degree comprise examination in 26 subjects and a thesis which is generally prepared at the conclusion of the course requirements. The minimum duration of the degree course is four years, although few students manage to complete all of the degree requirements within that time. The courses, which are the same in every university, cover the following subjects: private law, Roman law, the history of Roman law, political economy, constitutional law, the philosophy of law, Italian legal history, administrative law, public finance and taxation, criminal law, civil law, commercial law, labour law, international law, ecclesiastical law, criminal procedure, civil procedure, and optional courses selected amongst subjects such as agrarian law, comparative law, regional law, taxation, legal medicine, and Canon law. Under the legislative reforms of 1970 students may, with the approval of the faculty and within defined limits, vary the courses and the order in which they are taken. Nonetheless the selection of subjects is generally influenced by the requirements for admission to the various branches of the legal profession. Attendance at lectures is not obligatory and examinations are generally oral.

The practising profession

Lawyers may be either procurators or attorneys, or both. Registration on the relevant rolls, which are kept at every *Tribunale* (see p 62, below), is a necessary condition for the practice of law (A.1 of *l* 27 November 1933 n.1578, the so-called *legge forense* (cited in this book as *l.* for.)). Persons who are not on the rolls and hold themselves out as entitled to practise are punishable under Artt. 348 and 489 cp. In particular, there are three basic categories of practitioner: procurators, attorneys, and attorneys entitled to practise before the superior courts. There is, in addition, a special category comprising procurators and attorneys who are in the employ of public bodies.

The requisites for registration as a procurator are Italian citizenship, the enjoyment of all civil rights, unblemished conduct, the possession of a law degree conferred or recognised by an Italian university, the completion of one year of legal practice (or other defined periods in certain equivalent activities) subsequent to the award of a law degree, residence in the district of registration, and finally, the successful completion of bar examinations which are primarily of a practical nature and comprise two written and two oral examinations. The written examinations generally cover civil and administrative law and civil and criminal procedure. The oral examinations comprise, in addition to the subjects covered by the written examinations, commercial and tax law. Registered attorneys, persons who have exercised certain public functions for a defined period, and permanent law teachers in universities or other tertiary institutions may be automatically registered as procurators.

In addition to the first four requirements for registration as a procurator there are two further requisites for registration as an attorney. First, commendable practice as a procurator for at least six years or the completion of certain oral and written examinations which may be taken after two years of practice as a procurator. The examinations, which enable a speedier progress to the status of attorney, comprise four written and four oral examinations covering civil, criminal, administrative and commercial law as well as civil and criminal procedure. Second, residence in the district of the Tribunale on whose roll registration is sought. Registration as of right applies to public functionaries and university law teachers of a certain seniority.

The requirement for membership of the roll enabling practice before the superior courts (Cassation, the Council of State, the Court of Accounts on questions of jurisdiction, the Supreme Military Tribunal, The Superior Tribunal for Public Waters and the Central Commission for Direct Taxes) is either practice as an attorney for at least eight years or the completion of three written examinations after one year's practice as an attorney. The examinations cover civil, criminal, and administrative recourses to Cassation and administrative recourses to the Council of State and the Court of Accounts. Moreover, membership of this roll is available as of right to permanent university law teachers who are already on the roll of attorneys, senior magistrates, and State attorneys.

It follows that there are, in increasing order of seniority, four categories of legal practitioner. First, probationary procurators who are graduates in law and have entered their name on the roll of probationary practitioners; they may only practice before the *Pretura* of the district of their residence. At the conclusion of the probationary period, which is of four years' duration unless the probationary period is served in the office of a registered procurator in which case it is reduced to one year, the bar examinations for admission as a procurator may be taken. Second, procurators who have a territorial competence limited to the Court of Appeal district which contains the *Tribunale* at which they are registered. Exceptionally, however, they may practice before any *Pretura*, wherever located. Within the limits of their territorial competence, procurators may practice, in civil matters, before all courts up to and including the Court of Appeal and, in criminal matters, up to and including the *Tribunali*. The Court of Cassation has recently been inclined to holding as absolutely invalid any procedural act which has been carried out by a territorially incompetent procurator. Third, attorneys who are entitled to practise before all of the Courts of Appeal, *Tribunali* and *Preture* throughout the national territory. And, finally, senior attorneys who may, in addition, practice before all of the superior courts.

A characteristic common to every category of legal practitioner is that the practice of law is generally incompatible with a vast range of other occupations, e g those of notary, minister of religion, professional journalist, employee of a public body (except as a university or high school teacher) and merchant.

The two branches of the Italian legal profession, namely attorneys and procurators, have independent roles, although in certain circumstances the two roles may be exercised together. In practice the distinction between the two branches of the profession hardly exists as almost all attorneys are also registered as procurators and perform a dual function in the same action. The practitioner who is solely a procurator is, in practice, the young practitioner who is not yet entitled to the status of attorney. The functions of the procurator are to represent the party in the *development* of the proceedings and to perform all of those acts necessary to its progress. The attorney, on the other hand, has the more elevated function of the *defence* of the party, that is, of making oral or written legal arguments in favour of his client. In short, the functions of the procurator are of a non-discretionary and procedural nature whilst those of the attorney are primarily connected with the exercise of his expert discretion. This distinction between the two branches of the Italian legal profession is clearer than the English distinction. Comparatively speaking, solicitors are closest to the Italian procurators, except that solicitors, unlike procurators, exercise non-litigious functions and defence activities. The more elevated defence function of Italian attorneys, on the other hand, is exercised by barristers in English jurisdictions, but barristers, unlike Italian attorneys, never have a mere representation function nor do they have direct rapports with their clients who have contact with solicitors only.

The two branches of the profession are jointly organised in the same guild (*ordine*), which has a two-tier structure. The several decentralised or local bar councils have a territorial jurisdiction which coincides with the territorial jurisdiction of the various *Tribunali* and are composed of between five and 15 attorneys and procurators depending upon the number of local members. The principal functions of the local bodies are to maintain the rolls and to exercise disciplinary powers. They also have various secondary functions, such as giving opinions on the assessment of fees, the conciliation of disputes between members or between members and their clients, and a number of administrative functions such as issuing certificates and compiling the annual accounts. For the sole purpose of covering their recurrent expenses, the local bodies may impose certain defined types of fees, including an annual charge on members.

The central or national bar council is organised within the Ministry of Grace and Justice. Its members are elected from attorneys admitted to practice before the superior courts and represent the various Court of Appeal districts. It has three principal functions. First, the decision of appeals from the local bar councils. These decisions are, however, subject to further appeal to the Court of Cassation at the instance of an interested party or the *pubblico ministero* (see p 68, below) upon the grounds of incompetence, excess of power, or violation of law. Second, the exercise of disciplinary powers over the members of the council. Finally, the decision of jurisdictional conflicts between the local councils and the refusal of the latter to issue certificates.

Another central professional body is the Special Committee, which is composed of three members of the central council nominated by the president of the latter. This Committee is responsible for keeping the roll of attorneys admitted to practice before the superior courts. The decisions of the Special Committee, like the decisions of the local councils, are subject to appeal to the national council and from the latter to the Court of Cassation.

Since the practice of law is accessory to the administration of justice, it is regulated both by professional bodies and by the State, at least in relation to those aspects of practice that concern public order. Article 15 *l.* for. provides that the supreme supervision of the profession belongs to the Minister of Grace and Justice who exercises this function either directly or indirectly through various judicial officers. Apart from its supervisory role, the State also has a number of other direct and indirect controls over the legal profession, including: first, the extensive powers of the Minister of Grace and Justice over the conduct of bar examinations; second, the obligation of the guilds to inform the *pubblico ministero* within a defined time of all decisions and measures taken in relation to either the admission or discipline of members so that the former may exercise its right of appeal to the National Council and, if necessary, to the Court of Cassation; third, the obligatory initiation of disciplinary proceedings at the request of the *pubblico ministero*, who is then free to take part in the proceedings; and finally, the approval of all professional fees, which are initially fixed by the National Council, by the Minister of Grace and Justice who also has, in certain cases and circumstances, the power to seek their review.

Attorneys and procurators are required to observe a complex set of norms concerning professional conduct which must be consistent with the decorum and professional dignity of the individual member and of the profession as a whole. These norms arise partly from legislation and partly from the traditional ethics of the legal profession. Some of the duties arising out of the positive law are professional secrecy (A.622 cp), the faithful rendering of services (A.380 cp), the prohibition on representing or advising opposite parties (A.382 cp), the duty to act with 'probity and fairness' in all proceedings (A.88 cpc), the prohibition of discourteous and offensive expressions in legal proceedings (A.98 cpc), and the general duty of acting with the dignity and decorum inherent in those functions which are connected with the administration of justice. Although not beyond dispute, this range of general duties is not usually regarded as imposing upon the lawyer a duty of collaboration in the administration of justice. The procurator and attorney are generally considered as owing a duty to the client rather than to the collectivity. The non-legislative duties owed by lawyers, on the other hand, include what the French call the duties of devotion to the client and of fraternity to colleagues, as well as duties of collaboration and professional propriety.

The disciplinary powers over members of the profession, as already mentioned, are complementary to the punitive powers of the State. Therefore, in cases of inaction by the relevant guild, the Ministry of Grace and Justice or the ordinary judicial authorities have the power to provoke disciplinary proceedings and, in certain cases, even to directly initiate them and inflict disciplinary sanctions. In order to co-ordinate the disciplinary functions of the various bodies, the law regulating legal practitioners imposes duties as to the exchange of information.

The disciplinary sanctions which may be imposed upon members are warnings, censures, suspensions (ranging from two months to one year), cancellation (applied when a requisite for membership of the profession ceases to exist), and disbarment (relevant in the case of conduct which either compromises the reputation of the member and the dignity of the profession or is contrary to the national interest). Moreover, legal practitioners, like other professionals, will be criminally responsible in cases of fraud and certain other crimes concerning the monopoly over legal services, e g the illegal practice of law (A.348 cp). There are also various crimes of specific application to the legal profession, such as fees obtained on the pretence of influencing the course of justice (A.382 cp), unfaithful representation (A.380 cp), and collusion (A.381 cp). The civil responsibility of legal practitioners for professional error is, in essence, limited to cases of serious fault, inexcusable gross ignorance, or blameworthy negligence in the performance of services.

The breach of the obligation on the parties and their legal representatives to conduct themselves with probity and fairness (A.88 cpc) may result not only in disciplinary sanctions against the legal representative but also an order against the relevant party, even if successful in the proceedings, to reimburse the costs caused to the opposite party through a breach of the obligation. In addition discourteous and offensive expressions (A.89 cpc) may be struck from the records and damages awarded to the party offended when the expressions were irrelevant to the subject of the proceedings. Finally, where a party brings or defends actions in bad faith or with gross negligence, the court may, in addition to costs, order the losing party to pay damages (A.96 cpc).

In Italian law legal practitioners must receive their instructions in a particular form which varies depending upon the type of matter and whether the legal services in question are judicial or extra-judicial. Where judicial services are involved, a special or general power of attorney, according to which the lawyer will represent his client, is generally required, whilst in the case of extra-judicial services instructions may even be oral. In criminal proceedings instructions may, in addition, be received either orally during the interrogatory of the defendant at which time they are incorporated into the written depositions or from the court which has the power to appoint a legal representative for the defendant. The powers of the legal representative in judicial proceedings are to perform and accept all procedural acts necessary in the interests of his client unless the law expressly requires the litigant to perform personally or acquiesce in some particular act.

Any agreement to accept fees contingent upon the outcome of the proceedings is illegal. Moreover, any agreement with the legal representative to share a verdict or to surrender any rights arising out of the proceedings are prohibited on pain of both nullity of the agreement and damages. Where several lawyers are retained, each is entitled to a separate fee based on the full normal rates for the services rendered, but the losing party is only liable to the opposite party for the fees of a single legal representative. Where there are no fixed legal fees, A.2233 (2) cc provides that the measure of compensation must be in accordance with the importance of the work and professional decorum.

Legal representation

The requirement that a litigant must generally be represented is regarded as having its basis in the general principle now embodied in A.24 (2)C, which provides that the 'right of defence is inviolable at every stage and grade of proceedings'. The raison d'être of legal representation is said to be an effective procedural contest which, in turn, also implies a procedural parity between the parties. A party who is unrepresented does not have the necessary expertise to argue his case effectively and, moreover, is at a disadvantage if the opposite party is either a state prosecutor or a private party who is legally represented.

Only in exceptional cases of generally minor importance may a litigant appear unrepresented. In civil matters these include all causes before the *Conciliatori*, those causes before the *Pretori* in which the court, having regard to the nature and importance of the matter, exempts the party from the need for legal representation, all labour matters in which the value of the cause does not exceed Lit 250,000 and all causes in which the party is qualified to practice before the court in question. In all other civil matters a litigant must be represented by a procurator or, in the case of Cassation, by an attorney on the roll of practitioners entitled to practice before the superior courts. In criminal matters the defendant may only appear unrepresented in trials for contraventions punishable by either or both an amend not exceeding Lit 3,000 or arrest not exceeding one month. Similarly, pursuant to various pieces of special legislation, legal representation is not necessary in defined cases, e g disputes concerning legal costs, electoral causes, tenancy causes at first instance within certain values, oppositions to orders for the payment of administrative pecuniary penalties imposed for decriminalised contraventions, and causes before the taxation commissions.

In the case of civil and administrative causes, the failure to comply with the mandatory requirement of legal representation will result, in the case of the plaintiff, in the invalidity of the originating process and, in the case of any other party, in the invalidity of the document with which the latter constitutes himself a party to the proceedings. If the non-representation intervenes after the valid constitution of the proceedings for other than the volition of the party in question, the proceedings will be temporarily interrupted but will be eventually extinguished unless resumed in accordance with the prescribed formalities (Artt.301 ff cpc). In criminal trials, on the other hand, if the accused is unrepresented the court is obliged to appoint ex officio a legal representative who is entitled to be remunerated for his services by the accused, unless the latter is granted legal aid. However, the court nominee does not generally request a fee where the accused does not confirm his appointment in which case the legal representative will restrict himself to performing the essential formalities necessary for the validity of the proceedings.

Legal aid

Article 24(3) C provides that appropriate institutions are to be established to furnish impecunious litigants with the means of bringing and defending actions before any jurisdiction. Except for labour disputes, this constitutional provision has remained a dead letter; legal aid is still regulated by the outdated and inadequate legislation of 1923 which established a system of gratuitous legal aid by assigning the defence of the impecunious to 'attorneys and procurators' as an obligatory and honourable incident of their profession. A lawyer who has been assigned the duty of defending a party that has been admitted to legal aid must perform his services gratuitously subject only to the right of recouping his fees from the adversary in the event of successful proceedings.

In civil and administrative causes both the grant of legal aid and the appointment of a legal representative are made by legal aid committees which exist at every *Tribunale* and are composed of magistrates and attorneys. Notice of an application for legal aid is given to the applicant's adversary who, within the prescribed time, may dispute the applicant's entitlement either on the grounds of the latter's means or on the merits of the proposed proceedings. If the adversary appears before the committee, it may attempt a conciliation between the parties. An applicant may appeal against the decision of a committee to a committee of appeal established at each Court of Appeal. In cases of urgency legal aid may be granted by the president of a committee. In criminal proceedings, on the other hand, legal aid is granted by the chief judicial administrative officer of the court before which the proceedings are pending, and the legal representative is appointed by either the examining judge (or *pubblico ministero*) conducting the instruction proceedings (see ch 6, below) or the trial court. Although in civil and administrative matters the applicant must show both a 'state of poverty' and the 'probability of a favourable result' in order to obtain legal aid, in criminal matters the latter requisite is irrelevant.

Although the present system of legal aid is of doubtful constitutional validity, the Constitutional Court, in the expectation of an imminent reform, has avoided declaring the system unconstitutional. Reform has thus far been limited to labour disputes and causes concerning the rights of employees to social welfare and security entitlements. The 1973 legislation which introduced these reforms established the system whereby public and private employees may be admitted to legal aid at the cost of the State provided that they are 'not wealthy' and that the grounds of the proposed proceedings are 'not manifestly unfounded'. An applicant is not to be considered wealthy if he is in receipt of an annual income of less than Lit 2,000,000 net of taxes, social security contributions, life insurance premiums, and certain other payments. A copy of the applicant's declaration as to his means is eventually sent to the Superintendent of Finances, who is entitled to request the court to revoke the grant of legal aid on the basis of the applicant's means, apart from any criminal sanctions for false declaration. In the case of a married couple, their joint income is considered in determining the application although this would appear to be of doubtful constitutional validity. The application for legal aid, supported by the applicant's declaration as to his means, is lodged with the originating process or, in the case of a defendant, with his appearance, and the court determines with a reasoned decision whether the applicant is to be admitted to legal aid. If the application is granted the court nominates the legal representative selected by the applicant or, in default, by the bar council. If the party admitted to legal aid succeeds in the proceedings, the grant of legal aid will continue for all eventual appeals. On the other hand, if the applicant totally fails at first instance a fresh application must be made to the judge of appeal. Under this system of legal aid the State bears all of the costs of the proceedings subject to its right of recovering them from the opposite party where the applicant succeeds in the proceedings and is given an order for costs against an adversary who was not also granted legal aid.

The State Attorney (l'avvocatura dello Stato)

The State Attorney is that group of legal practitioners who necessarily and exclusively represent and defend the State and the public administration whenever these are party to civil, criminal or administrative proceedings. The State Attorney also has an extensive advisory function as the legal consultative service to the administration and, moreover, it has the duty of giving opinions in relation to proposed legislation, regulations, and state contracts. It should be noted that the public administration may, except in certain special cases, be represented by its own functionaries in proceedings before the *Preture* and *Conciliatori*.

The State Attorney also necessarily and exclusively represents the autonomous public authorities coming within the sphere of the State (viz. national) government unless these authorities come into conflict with a State body, in which case they may be represented by private attorneys. The State Attorney, furthermore, may be empowered by legislation or regulation to represent non-State public bodies and subsidised bodies which are subject to State supervision. Amongst the non-State public bodies which may be represented by the State Attorney are the Special and Ordinary Regions (see ch 5, below) and the other inferior territorial bodies. The representation of the Special Regions by the State Attorney is generally mandatory unless they come into conflict with the State. The Ordinary Regions, on the other hand, have been given the right, after resolution of the relevant Regional Parliament, of availing themselves of the services of the State Attorney. The State Attorney may also represent the provinces, municipalities, and other inferior territorial authorities, upon request, in respect to functions delegated to them by the Regions. These provisions, of course, do not apply in cases of dispute, or conflict of interest, with the State. The Regions always retain the right to resort to private attorneys upon a reasoned decision and 'subject to any usual administrative controls'. The State also, for 'absolutely exceptional reasons', may resort to private attorneys.

The State Attorney may represent and defend an employee or agent of the State administration or of certain of the other bodies referred to above provided that it is at the request of the administration and that the proceedings concern matters connected with official duties. In such cases, although the State Attorney directly and immediately defends the employee, it is in effect defending the interests of the administration. However, the interests of the latter are lacking when there is a conflict between the employee and the administration in which case the State Attorney, with whom the ultimate decision rests, will not generally act. Moreover, the State Attorney may represent and defend foreign administrations and representatives of foreign governments that are party to proceedings in Italy. However, this function of the State Attorney must be specifically authorised by legislation, regulation, or presidential decree, and has, for example, been conceded in relation to NATO commands in Italy.

The originating process in all proceedings against the State or its administration brought before the *Preture, Conciliatori*, the administrative and special courts, or arbitrators must be served directly upon the administrator or organ having the external representation of the relevant administration. In every other case, proceedings against the administration are commenced by citing the responsible minister and serving the originating process upon the territorially competent State Attorney. The latter form of service was introduced by the law of 25 March 1958 n.260 and had the object of overcoming the perennial difficulty of identifying the administrative officer or organ upon which the originating process had to be served. In such cases if the administration fails to raise any objection at the first audience as to the erroneous indication of the competent minister, the matter can no longer be raised. However, it is apparent that the 1958 legislation is only applicable to proceedings in which the administration is *bound* to utilise the State Attorney as its legal representative. Where the administration remains free to utilise a legal representative other than the State Attorney, as in the case of proceedings before the administrative courts and the other bodies cited above, the originating process must still be addressed to, and served directly upon, the relevant administrative authority in the person of the administrator or organ which externally represents the administration.

The State Attorney's office has both a hierarchial and territorial structure. Territorially it consists of the Attorney General, located in Rome, and decentralised district attorneys, generally located in each regional capital or in any other centre at which there is a Court of Appeal. The Rome office deals with all matters coming within the jurisdiction of the superior ordinary and administrative courts, and international and Community courts, as well as all matters which come within its jurisdiction as the district attorney for the Rome Court of Appeal district. The decentralised district attorneys, on the other hand, deal with all matters that come within the competence of the courts comprised within their respective districts.

Hierarchically, the office comes under the direct dependency of the prime minister. The office itself consists of an Attorney General, State procurators, and State attorneys. The Attorney General, nominated by the Council of Ministers, is assisted by nine deputy Attorney Generals. There is also a Secretary General and, of course, the several district attorneys. State attorneys and procurators are appointed through a competitive selection process in which State functionaries with certain career and seniority qualifications may also participate. Applicants for the position of State attorneys must generally be either State procurators with at least two years' service or attorneys of at least one year standing.

In 1979 a system of career advancement analagous to that applicable to the ordinary magistracy (see p 72, below) was introduced. Consequently, career advancement within the two fundamental classifications of State procurator and State attorney is basically one of economic progression on the mere basis of seniority which per se is taken to imply the acquisition of experience and professional ability. Although, from an external point of view, there are no differences in duties amongst those belonging to the different categories or salary divisions, the internal structure of the office is hierarchical.

However, in order to ensure a democratic organisation and decision-making structure there are various internal bodies whose opinions, even if not binding, must be heard and to which the individual attorneys or procurators may have recourse. The first of these bodies is the Council of State Attorneys and Procurators which consists of the Attorney General, the two most senior deputy Attorney Generals, the two most senior district attorneys, and four attorneys or procurators (which must include at least one procurator) elected by all of the attorneys and procurators. Its functions include expressing opinions on the allocation of various offices, formulating opinions on career advancement, deciding appeals against the substitution of an attorney in any given matter, exercising disciplinary powers, and nominating the State attorneys who are to be part of the Consultative Committee. The Consultative Committee is composed of the Attorney General and six attorneys nominated by the Council. These attorneys must be of a certain seniority and must not be members of the Council. This Committee must be heard by the Attorney General on all matters of general policy or of particular importance, and in relation to internal directives of a general nature. It is also called upon to settle differences of opinion amongst attorneys in the treatment of contentious or consultative matters, and to fix the general criteria for the distribution of business amongst members of the office. The third body is the Permanent Personnel Commission composed of the Secretary General, two State attorneys, a representative of the auxiliary personnel and a State procurator. The functions of this Commission are the administration and discipline of auxiliary personnel. The final body is the Council for Administration of the State Attorney's Office, which is comprised of the first and third of the above bodies. It expresses opinions and suggestions on the organisation and management of services, allocates funds amongst the various offices, and performs various other administrative functions.

State attorneys and procurators exercise their functions in the same independent and professional spirit as private lawyers. This is so notwithstanding that their hierarchical organisation may suggest otherwise. In the event of a difference of opinion with the Attorney General, a deputy Attorney General, or a district attorney in the treatment of a matter, the attorney in question may request in writing that the Consultative Committee decide the issue and that should the Committee decide against the attorney that he be relieved from dealing with the matter. Apart from this situation, an attorney or procurator may only be removed from a matter for absence, impediment, or other just reason, but in any event the action must be supported by a reasoned decision of the Attorney General or district attorney and that decision is subject to appeal to the Council of State Attorneys and Procurators.

Notaries

The activities of notaries are regulated by the law of 16 February 1913 n.89 and the regulations of 10 September 1914 n.1326, both of which have been extensively amended. Notaries combine a dual function;

they are both public officials and professionals. This dual function corresponds to the dual set of interests that are protected by notarial activities, namely, the public interest in the regularity of notarial acts, and the private interests of the parties to a particular notarial transaction. The same dual function is also manifest in the dichotomy between the obligatory and optional functions that a notary is called upon to perform, namely and respectively, the institutional function which he performs in his capacity as a public official, and that of private consultant which he exercises in his capacity as an independent professional.

The institutional or public function of notaries fundamentally comprises the preparation of inter vivos and testamentary instruments, the conferral of public credit upon such documents as well as their custody and the issue of copies, certificates and extracts (A.1(1) *l*n). In short, it is a function which confers legal certainty (certification) upon legal facts and, in a special sense, upon legal transactions, as well as preconstituting the means of their legal proof (documentation). The institutional function, however, is not exclusive to the notary; in certain subjects and situtations the law provides either an additional or exclusive recourse to other public officials. Article 1(1) *l*n is complemented by Artt.2699 and 2700 cc. Article 2699 cc provides that a 'public act is a document drawn up with the requisite formalities by a notary or other public official authorised to give it public faith in the place where the act is formed', and A.2700 cc which provides that a public act constitutes full proof, until *querela di falso* (see ch 6, below), of the public official who prepared it and of the declarations of the parties and other facts that the public official attests to have either occurred in his presence or were performed by him.

The institutional functions of the notary in A.1(1) *l*n have been integrated by A.1(2) of the same law but because the latter provision commences with the words 'Notaries are also conceded the faculty of . . .', it has been argued that the word 'faculty' implies that the notary is at liberty to refuse the services listed in that subsection. However, as the only intent of the amendments were to broaden the functions of the notary, it can be said that the latter cannot refuse to perform these additional functions which are: (a) the preparation and lodgement of applications in non-contentious or voluntary proceedings (*giurisdizione volontaria*); (b) the taking of sworn statements in civil and commercial matters; (c) the taking of declarations accepting an inheritance with the benefit of inventory; (d) the affixure or removal of official seals and the drawing of inventories in those cases contemplated by the civil and commercial law, as well as the arrangement of auctions, partitions and related activities upon delegation by the judicial authorities; (e) the issue of certificates verifying the continued existence of persons receiving state benefits; (f) the reception for safe-keeping of originals or copies of public and private writings and other papers or documents even if prepared abroad although the latter must generally be legalised and, if written in a foreign language, accompanied by a translation prepared either by the notary himself or an expert selected by the parties; (g) the reception of declarations which renounce an inheritance; (h) the subscription and authentication of commercial records for the purposes specified in the civil code; (i) the taking of sworn declarations as to the findings of extrajudicial experts and of translations of foreign writings; and (j) the release of copies and extracts of original documents sighted by the notary and of commecial books or registers. In addition to the above, notaries have other and innumerable functions and obligations conferred by various pieces of legislation.

The private function of the notary is that of private consultant, which gives rise to a notary-client relationship, that is, a private contractual relationship with mere private interests at its base. This relationship is primarily regulated by Artt.2230ff cc, which regulates all of the intellectual professions. Although part of the doctrine places a greater emphasis on the public aspect of the notary's functions, another part places the accent on his independent professional quality. However, according to a controversial but now authoritative doctrine it is considered impossible and futile to attempt a separation of the two functions which are inseparably intertwined in the figure of the notary.

An old problem related to the dual nature of the notary is the question of his civil responsibility. The solution to the problem varies depending upon the importance which is attached to either of his two basic functions, viz. public official and independent professional. The doctrine is basically divided between those who maintain that there exists only a responsibility to the client, with whom there is a contractual relationship, and those that maintain that the notary is also liable to third parties. The case law is generally in favour of the latter and more extensive view of the notary's liability. It may well be that the civil responsibility of the notary has a dual basis, namely, a contractual basis arising from the mandate from his client and an extra-contractual basis arising from his status as a public official. In other words, whilst contractual liability arises from the relationship between the parties and the notary, an extra-contractual liability arises from the relationship between the notary, third parties, and the State.

A consequence of the public nature of the office is that the notary is *obliged* to render his services upon any legitimate request (A.27(1) *ln*). This obligation, in a few exceptional situations, even arises in the absence of any specific instructions. However, there are two general exceptions to the obligation of the notary to make his services available. First, according to Artt.28 and 78 *ln*, a notary *may* refuse his services if the parties fail to deposit a sum sufficient to cover any duties, fees, and expenses, unless it is a matter in which either legal aid has been granted or a will is involved. Second, there are certain provisions which in fact oblige the notary not to render his services. Of these the basic provision is A.28 *ln* which provides that a notary cannot perform a service (a) if it is expressly prohibited by law or is manifestly contrary to good custom or public order, (b) if a party to the transaction is the wife, a lineal relative (whether by blood or affinity) or certain proximate collateral relatives of the notary, even if such person merely intervenes as a guardian, tutor, or adminstrator, and (c) if the notary, any of the persons mentioned in the preceding case, or a person for whom the notary is the guardian is interested in the transaction, unless the subject provision is contained in a secret will which was not drawn up by the notary or any of the persons mentioned above and was received by the notary in a sealed cover. The provisions in (b) and (c) do not apply to sales by public auction.

The essential requisites for appointment as a notary are Italian citizenship, age of no less than 21 and under 50, impeccable conduct, eligibility for jury service, possession of a law degree conferred or recognised by an Italian university, post-graduate registration with a Notarial Council and the service of articles of clerkship with a notary, and finally, the successful completion of the competitive admission examinations which may only be taken at the conclusion of the relevant period of clerkship. The admission examinations are held annually by the Ministry of Grace and Justice in order to fill the available number of positions. The examinations which have both a theoretical and practical orientation, include three written papers which concern an inter vivos transaction, a will and a non-contentious process respectively, and three oral examinations which cover civil and commercial law, notarial records and organisation, and taxation on notarial transactions. All candidates who pass the examinations are placed in order of merit and accordingly allocated to the available positions. Successful candidates who do not receive an allocation must retake the examinations if they wish to compete in future intakes but their total marks are increased by two for every prior intake at which they successfully passed the examinations. Candidates who are allocated a position must, within 90 days of the official publication of the results, inter alia, post a bond against malpractice, pay certain fees and taxes to various public bodies, take the oath of office, receive an official seal from the Notarial Council, deposit their specimen signature with the Council and open their office in the assigned locality. In order to ensure independence and a proper performance of duties, the law prohibits a notary, on penalty of removal from office, from accepting any form of employment, office or position incompatible with his functions.

The national territory is divided into notarial districts which coincide with the territorial divisions of the *Tribunali*. Each district comprises a defined number of notaries. This number, which is periodically reviewed, depends upon population, quantum of business, territorial expanse, and means of communication. The notaries in each district together form a college which at its ordinary annual general meeting elects one-third of the local Notarial Council so that each councillor has a term of three years. The functions of the Council include: first, the supervision of notaries both as to their conduct and adherence to professional duties; second, the supervision of the conduct and performance of apprentice notaries and the release of certificates in their regard; third, the expression of opinions on notarial matters upon request of the relevant authorities; fourth, the preparation of an annual report on admitted and apprenticed notaries; fifth, the conciliation, upon request, of disputes between notaries or between notaries and third parties on any matter concerning the exercise of notarial functions; and finally, the adoption of the annual accounts and estimates of the treasurer, subject to their approval by the college. The Council is also required to keep a register of all correspondence, a register of the minutes of all meetings of the college and Council, a duplicate register of apprentice notaries, a register of the specimen signatures of notaries, the roll of practicing notaries, and books of account. The Council may be dissolved for persistent violation of its duties or for any other serious reason by the Ministry of Grace and Justice after hearing the opinion of the Court of Appeal in camera, in which case the President of the Civil section of the *Tribunale* or a judge nominated by him administers the affairs of the Council until its renewal. The secretary of the Council must give an annual report which must be posted for public exhibition at the Court of Appeal and *Tribunale* located within the relevant notarial district, and a copy delivered to the Ministry of Grace and Justice.

The Ministry of Grace and Justice exercises the supreme supervision over all notaries, Councils and notarial archives and may order such inspections and visits as it deems necessary. The same kind of supervisory powers belong to the Procurator General located at each Court of Appeal and the Procurator of the Republic located at each *Tribunale*. In addition, notaries, who have the custody and security of documents drawn or received by them, must compile certain inventories and indices of all such documents and the documents, inventories and indices must, on penalty of disciplinary action for the failure to so do, be periodically presented for various inspections and controls.

The disciplinary penalties which may be imposed upon notaries include warnings, censures, pecuniary penalties, suspensions and disbarment. Apart from many specific provisions imposing various obligations on notaries, the violation of which will result in the application of defined disciplinary sanctions, the general disciplinary provision is A.147 *ln* which provides that a notary who in any manner whatsoever compromises his conduct, whether in his private or public life, dignity or reputation, and the decorum and prestige of the profession, or unlawfully competes with his colleagues through the reduction of fees and other accessory entitlements, soliciting clients, advertising or in any other manner inconsistent with the decorum and prestige of the profession, is punishable by censure, suspension up to one year and, in serious cases, disbarment. Disbarment, moreover, automatically applies if a notary has been twice suspended for contravening the present provision. A notary who has been disbarred may, in certain cases, be re-admitted upon decision of the Notarial Council. The disciplinary penalties of warning and censure are applied by the relevant Notarial Council, whilst pecuniary penalties, which are applicable for defined infractions, suspensions and disbarment are applied by the Civil *Tribunale* of the district in which the relevant Notarial Council is located.

There has also been established, by amendment of the original legislation, a National Notarial Council which is located in Rome. The Council is elected every three years and consists of 15 members representing defined territorial divisions. The National Council has the following functions: first, it furnishes opinions at the request of the Ministry of Grace and Justice on proposed legislation affecting notaries or any other matter of interest to the profession; second, it may make submissions to the Ministry of Grace and Justice or other relevant authorities on matters concening notaries; third, it collects and co-ordinates proposals formulated by the local Notarial Councils and individual notaries for the purpose of its power to make submissions; fourth, it may undertake or promote research; fifth, it acts to protect the interests of the profession; and finally, it elects from its number the members of the Administrative Commission of the National Notarial Fund. The National Notarial Fund provides, from contributions paid by notaries, allowances to practicing notaries, superannuation benefits to retiring notaries and their families, scholarships to members' children, and various other benefits, as well as ex gratia welfare payments to retired notaries and their families in deserving cases. There is, finally, an annual national congress in which all practicing or retired notaries may participate. The congress deals with all matters of interest to the profession and consists of an organising committee, an executive committee, the assembly and various sub-committees which make submissions to the assembly.

The paralegals (dottori commercialisti)

In Italy certain functions which are commonly dealt with by lawyers in English speaking countries are dealt with by non-legal professions, the most important of which are the *dottori commercialisti*. This profession is regulated by the dPR 27 October 1953 n.1067. The *dottori commercialisti* are competent in economic, commercial, financial, taxation, and accounting matters. Moreover, in accordance with the RDL 7 August 1936 n.1639 they may also advise and represent parties in taxation proceedings. In certain matters, such as bankruptcies and arrangements with creditors, they do not have an exclusive competence because the same functions may also be performed by attorneys, procurators, and accountants.

To practice as a *dottore commercialista* it is necessary to be on the roll of *commercialisti*. The *commercialisti*, as with other intellectual professions, are organised into a guild under the supervision of the Ministry of Grace and Justice. At the local level there are district councils elected by the assembly of registered members. The councils have a life of three years and their size is commensurate to the local membership. The councils elect from their number a president, secretary, treasurer, and if they consist of more than seven members, a vice-president. The principal functions of the local councils are to maintain the roll of practitioners and to exercise disciplinary powers over them. They, moreover, supervise the observance of the relevant professional legislation, give opinions in disputes relating to fees, and release certificates to members. In serious cases, the Minister of Grace and Justice may dissolve a council and nominate an extraordinary Commissioner. At the apex there is a National Council which exists within the Minstry of Grace and Justice and is composed of 11 members elected by the local councils. The National Council has a term of three years and its most important functions are the supervision of the local councils and the decision of appeals against the latter on matters of registration, discipline, and electoral disputes.

The essential requisites for registration as a *commercialista* are Italian citizenship or the citizenship of a country granting reciprocal rights, full enjoyment of all civil rights, irreproachable conduct, possession of a degree in economics and commerce or certain other qualifications, satisfactory completion of the entrance examinations, and residence within the district of the relevant council. Registration on any one roll enables practice throughout the national territory.

The practice of the profession is incompatible with state employment, the conduct of an enterprise either independently or on behalf of another, and with certain defined professions and occupations such as notary, minister of religion, and journalist. A person who cannot enrol by reason of incompatibility only may nonetheless register on the roll of non-practicing *commercialisti*; once the incompatibility ceases they are automatically transferred to the roll of practicing members.

The *commercialista* must at all times act in accordance with the dignity and decorum of the profession. Disciplinary proceedings against members may be initiated by any interested person, the council ex officio or at the request of the *pubblico ministero*. The rights of the latter emphasises the State's control over the profession. Depending upon the gravity of the infringement, the council may censure, suspend (for not more than two years), or disbar a member. An administrative appeal lies to the National Council from which a further appeal lies to the ordinary courts, namely, the *Tribunale* in the district of the local council from which the appeal originally arose. The decision of the *Tribunale* may, furthermore, be attacked before the Court of Appeal. A member who has been disbarred may, if of irreproachable conduct for a given period, be re-admitted.

Broadly speaking, another type of paralegal is the foreign lawyer. There is no provision in Italian law prohibiting foreign lawyers acting as consultants provided, of course, that they do not hold themselves out as local lawyers.

The magistracy

The ordinary magistracy (which is attached to the ordinary courts) and, in certain cases, the special magistracy (which is attached to the special courts) may be broadly divided between judicial and invocatory organs depending upon whether their fundamental function is respectively adjudication or the formulation of requests and opinions which are to be considered by a separate decision-making organ. From a functional point of view, only the former are true judicial organs. The latter, on the other hand, perform a similar procedural role and have analagous powers to an ordinary party although, unlike an ordinary party, they are always 'public' or 'impartial' bodies. In Italy, the invocatory function is generally exercised by a distinct organ known as the *pubblico ministero*. In addition to their normal functions, invocatory organs exceptionally enjoy judicial functions as well, e g the conduct of summary instructions by the *pubblico ministero* in criminal proceedings. From an organisational point of view, on the other hand, invocatory organs have certain characteristics in common with judicial organs, such as recruitment and status, as a result of which both are administered by the Superior Magisterial Council (see p 64, below). Their common administration has meant that invocatory organs have generally reaped the same guarantees as judicial organs. However, unlike judicial organs, which have a complex structure, the *pubblico ministero* has a strict hierarchical structure. Notwithstanding the precise distinction between judical and invocatory organs, it should be noted that the term 'judicial' is often used in a wide sense to include both types of organ. When this happens it is generally apparent from the context, but the reader ought to remain alert both to the strict and wide sense of the term.

The judicial organs in a strict sense

Judicial organs may be said to have two broad functions: first, an administrative function which concerns matters such as the preparation of hearing lists, the distribution of business, and the formation of adjudicatory panels or colleges where the court has a collegiate structure; and second, the judicial function in a strict sense. These functions are distributed according to complicated criteria for the division of labour as a result of which, in practice, there is hardly ever a perfect division between administrative judicial organs and judicial organs in the strict sense because the latter generally exercise both functions. Nonetheless the distinction between administrative and strict judicial functions is important, especially in a career judiciary, as a strict hierarchical structure exists in the case of administrative functions only. On the other hand, the distinction is inapplicable to invocatory organs because the hierarchical structure in the *pubblico ministero* relates not only to its administrative functions but also, although within certain limits, to the exercise of its strict invocatory functions.

The Italian judicial organs, which may be either monocratic or collegiate bodies, are, in descending order of importance: *Cassazione*, the *corti di appello*, the *tribunali*, the *preture* and the *offices of conciliazione*, as well as the *corti di assise* and *assise di appello*, the *minors tribunals*, and other specialised sections of the various courts. Except for Cassation, which is situated in Rome and is competent over the whole of the national territory, every other court has a territorial competence limited to its respective district which, with the descending hierarchical order of the courts, becomes progressively smaller and forms part of the district of the immediately superior court. Thus there are some 27 Courts of Appeal, each having a territorial competence limited to its respective '*distretto*'. Then each *distretto* is progressively subdivided into smaller territorial divisions, so that the *tribunali*, *corti d'assise*, *preture* and *conciliatori* have a territorial competance limited to their respective '*circondario*', '*circolo*', '*mandamento*', and '*comune*'.

The administrative organs of the judiciary, on the other hand, apart from the Superior Magisterial Council and its internal sections (except for the disciplinary section which is an organ of special jurisdiction) and the Judicial Councils, include the personnel within the various courts that exercise management functions, that is, the presidents of the various courts and *Tribunali*, the chief *Pretori* and *Conciliatori*, as well as the sectional heads of the various divisions of these courts. Although the judicial function is exercised by all of the magistrates in a given office on a roster system, the administrative or management function, on the other hand, is exercised exclusively by office superiors or their temporary substitutes.

The distinction between judicial and administrative functions is important because special rules are applicable in the formation of an organ which is to exercise judicial functions, e g the principle that magistrates are to be distinguished in accordance with their functions only, and not according to their rank, class, or seniority (A.107(3) C), and the principle of the 'preconstitution of the judge', viz. that judicial organs must be constituted prior to the occurrence of the events which must be adjudicated by them (A.25(1) C). In the case of administrative functions, on the other hand, the same general rules as any other administrative organisation are applicable. The end result is that there is no hierarchy amongst judicial organs other than that constituted by the normal appeal process, the rules on competency (which divide the jurisdiction of the ordinary courts amongst its component parts) and the rules on jurisdiction (which effect the division of jurisdiction between the ordinary and special courts). On the other hand, the administrative function involves a hierarchy which combines the rules inherited from the previous system, as well as those that have come about from the elimination of administrative dependence upon the Ministry of Grace and Justice, which has been replaced by the Superior Magisterial Council. The risks to the internal independence of judges inherent in such a hierarchical administrative system is obviated by the establishment of a democratic administrative structure. However, although such a structure has been effectively introduced in relation to the Superior Magisterial Council, it has not as yet affected either the office superiors or the Judicial Councils. As a result, the present judicial structure is in an incoherent transitional state.

There appear to be, at present, two general trends in the evolution of the judicial structure. First, that towards an always more independent judicial organ through the application of the principle of the 'preconstitution of the judge', which, however, has so far been regarded as applicable to each judicial seat as a whole and not also to the composition of the particular judical organs within each office. Second, an always more democratic administration through the concentration of administrative functions in both the Superior Magisterial Council and analagous decentralised bodies, together with the corresponding reduction in power of office superiors.

The administrative organs of the judiciary

The independence of the judiciary comprises two elements, especially in the Italian system which has a career judiciary. First and foremost, an 'external' independence from all other powers of State (A.104(1) C), especially from the Executive, and second, an 'internal' independence of individual magistrates from other organs within the judiciary itself.

The latter aspect has become more evident in recent times through both the various attempts by senior magistrates to occupy leading positions and the threats to judicial freedom by office superiors.

A. THE SUPERIOR MAGISTERIAL COUNCIL

The most important innovation of the Republican Constitution of 1948 on the subject of the independence of the judiciary was the establishment of a Superior Magisterial Council which was given all of the most important functions relevant to the judicial power. The predominance of magistrates on this Council assures the judiciary an automony vis-à-vis the other powers of State, both in relation to its administration and discipline. At the same time, the presence on the Council of the Head of State and a number of members elected by the parliament makes the Council the link between the magistracy and the other powers of State. These two characteristics of the Superior Magisterial Council have given the magistracy the status of a true 'power of State' as well as having severed its dependence upon the Executive, a feature which had previously given the Minister of Grace and Justice significant powers over the administration of judicial personnel. Nevertheless, the Council was not set up until some ten years after the introduction of the Constitution and the legislation which established it retained to some measure a dependence upon the Minister of Grace and Justice characteristic of the previous system, e g the continuing necessity of obtaining the 'consensus' of the Minister in certain situations.

According to A.104 C, the Superior Magisterial Council is composed of the President of the Republic, the President and Procurator General of the Court of Cassation, and a further 30 members, of whom two-thirds are elected by the ordinary magistracy from its own ranks and one-third by Parliament in joint sitting from amongst university law professors and lawyers of at least 15 years' standing. The Council, elected every four years, may be sooner dissolved by decree of the Head of State after hearing the opinions of the President of each House of Parliament and of the Presidential Committee of the Council itself.

The Superior Magisterial Council consists of a President, who is always the Head of State; a Vice-President elected from its members and who is the effective president of the Council in its ordinary activities; a Presidential Committee comprising the Vice-President of the Council and the President and Procurator General of the Court of Cassation; and a secretariat headed by the Presidential Committee. It also has various other permanent or special internal committees including the disciplinary section.

The principal functions of the Superior Magisterial Council are administrative in nature, but it also has normative and judicial functions. The judicial function of the Council concerns its disciplinary powers, exercised by the disciplinary section; its normative functions include the inherent power to regulate its own procedures, the regulation of the apprenticeship of probationary magistrates and, although of doubtful basis, the regulation of its own activities and those of judicial organs in a strict sense. Moreover, the Council may, if requested, express opinions on proposed legislation relating to the subject of justice generally.

The administrative functions of the Council may be divided into three broad groups: the organisation of the Council itself, the status of magistrates, and the relationship between the judicial and other powers of State. The first concerns the eligibility and election of its own members and officers, as well as the organisation of its internal organs. The second relates to the functions defined in A.105 C, which concerns the recruitment, placement, transfer, promotion, and discipline of magistrates; A.107(1) C, which relates to exemption or suspension from service and the variation of location and function of magistrates; and A.106(3) C, which governs the nomination of university law professors and attorneys as judges of Cassation. The Council has, moreover, been empowered to decide upon the appointment and removal of honorary deputy *Pretori*, *Conciliatori*, *vice-Conciliatori*, and the expert members of the various specialised sections of the courts, and has the right to delegate certain of these powers to the Presidents of the Courts of Appeal. The Council, furthermore, first, approves the annual rosters which both allocate magistrates to various functions within their respective seats and distribute the business of the court and, second, decides all questions put to it by the various offices as well as all complaints made by individual magistrates against the decisions of section heads. The jurisdiction of the Council in relation to career magistrates, in short, extends to every aspect of their employment. The third administrative function of the Council is its representation of the judicial power and comprises the right to formulate and place proposals before the Minister of Grace and Justice on any matter relevant to the organisation and operation of the system of justice, the expression of opinions on proposed legislation relating to the judicial system, and the presentation of reports, through the Minister of Grace and Justice, to Parliament. Moreover, the Council may pronounce itself by motion or in any other manifestation of opinion on any matter of interest to the operation of justice.

Decisions of the Council are in the form of decrees made by the Head of State or the Minister of Grace and Justice and are therefore subject to appeal like any other administrative measure. Decisions of the disciplinary section are judicial in nature and may therefore be attacked before Cassation.

B. THE JUDICIAL COUNCILS

These exist at every Court of Appeal and comprise the President and the Procurator General of the relevant Court and eight members elected bi-annually from the magistrates occupying judicial offices within the Court's territorial jurisdiction. The functions of the local Councils comprise principally the provision of promotion reports and the supervision of probationary magistrates.

C. THE OFFICE SUPERIORS

All office superiors (that is, the first President of the Court of Cassation, the President of each Court of Appeal, Tribunal and Minor's Tribunal, the Director of each *Pretura*, the Procurator General of the Court of Cassation and of each Court of Appeal and the Procurator of the Republic at each Tribunal) are appointed by the Superior Magisterial Council. Their appointment is not merely one to a particular rank, but to a particular location and specific 'management position'. Semi-management positions are also made by the Council. All of these positions are permanent and therefore continue until the occupant is transferred (which is usually either on request or promotion) or retires. The office superiors (which also include the *Conciliatori*), apart from judicial functions proper, also exercise administrative functions the most important of which are the formulation of rosters allocating the various general duties or positions amongst the members of the court or office, the preparation of the hearing lists including the composition of the adjudicating panels, and the distribution of business to the various magistrates or sections. These functions, once exercised under the supervision of the Minister of Grace and Justice, are now exercised under the control of the Council which, however, generally intervenes in cases of complaint only. As far as the judicial function proper is concerned, the office superior may allocate any matter to himself, and he may preside any adjudicating panel within his jurisdiction.

D. THE MINISTER OF GRACE AND JUSTICE

Under the previous constitutional system, the Minister of Grace and Justice, and the organisational structure of the Ministry, provided an intrinsic connexion between the Executive and Judicial powers of State, with a distinct advantage in favour of the former. Notwithstanding the clear intent of the Republican Constitution to create an independent judiciary, it provided that the Minister of Grace and Justice could initiate disciplinary proceedings against magistrates (A.107(2) C) and was to ensure 'the organisation and operation of services concerning justice' (A.110 C). This gave rise to constitutional problems as to the identification of those functions which could still be performed by the

Minister. The major problems were dealt with at the establishment of the Superior Magisterial Council, which ought to have taken over all of the administrative powers of the Minister concerning justice. However, the law of 24 March 1958 n.195, which established the Council, reserved to the Minister a general initiatory power which was binding upon the Council. This power has since been removed by the Constitutional Court so that today the only residual power of the Minister is that of granting or withholding his 'concurrence' to the allocation of management positions. The Ministry, however, still deals with 'judicial organisation and general matters' which concern, inter alia, its relationship with both the Superior Magisterial Council and the various judicial offices, the organisation of entrance examinations for probationary magistrates, the administration of auxiliary personnel, and other general matters concerning the judicial or legal system.

The organisation of individual courts

Each court is generally divided into sections, each section having the same structure as a unitary court. Thus every unitary court or section of a court has internal divisions with specific functions, for example, the Instruction Division of the *Tribunale* (corresponding to the Instruction Section of the Court of Appeal) which is distinct because of function and structure from the other divisions of the court or section of which it forms part.

Apart from workload considerations, the division of a court into sections also meets the needs of specialisation. To some extent this is manifest in the distinction between civil and criminal sections, but the objective is more specifically pursued in the creation of 'specialised sections for determinate subjects' of which those sections utilising 'suitable citizens from outside the magistracy', as provided for by A.102(2) C, are of particular importance. Typical examples of specialised sections are those that deal with agrarian and labour disputes. It must be noted, however, that the Minor's Tribunal and the Court of Assizes are not specialised sections but autonomous courts with their own registries.

Each court has a number of magistrates and lay judges in excess of the number necessary to constitute a single bench so as to enable both the simultaneous conduct of several hearings and the rotation of staff amongst the various functions to be performed by the court. It follows that the composition of the bench is not synonomous with the composition of the court. The latter depends upon appointments, transfers, promotions, and similar measures concerning staff movements taken by the Superior Magisterial Council. The former is the result of decisions taken by the office superior in relation to both the preparation of rosters allocating office members to the various collegiate and monocratic judicial functions to be performed by the court, and the temporary substitution of staff occasioned by any permanent or temporary impairment making it impossible for the regular occupant of a position to carry out his duties.

The powers of the office superior reach their limit once the rosters assigning individual magistrates to the various sections and duties have been fixed because these rosters are only prepared annually and receive the approval of the Superior Council. However, the composition of the colleges within each section remains in the discretion of the office superior or section head, as does the distribution of business amongst the various sections and between the colleges or judges within each section. This continuous discretion is to some extent mitigated by the specific duties of specialised sections and the conventional criteria for the automatic distribution of business, although the failure to observe the latter cannot give rise to complaint.

The present procedures regarding the formation of the adjudicatory colleges and the distribution of business raises problems of compliance with the principle sanctioned by A.25(1) C, namely, that 'no person can be denied his natural judge as predetermined by law'. This principle incorporates, and extends beyond, the more specific principle in A.102(2) C which prohibits the institution of 'extraordinary or special courts'. Article 25(1) C combines two requirements. First, that the competent court be defined by legislation and not, therefore, by secondary sources of law except, of course, within the normal limits of interpretation. Second, that the competent court be defined prior to the occurrence of the event to be adjudicated, so that its individuation can never be ad hoc. One problem, however, is whether A.25(1) C refers to the composition of the court as a whole or the actual natural components of each adjudicatory organ. Many commentators, and not without foundation, maintain that A.25(1) C requires not only the distribution of business to the competent court but, more particularly, to specific natural persons. However, there has been a resistance to this approach in the case law, which has been preoccupied with the practical difficulties in specifically pre-determining the particular judge or components of the adjudicatory panels. This necessitates the adoption of very rigid rules in relation to both the formation of the panels and the distribution of business, thereby eliminating every form of discretion and modifying current practices.

The invocatory judicial organs: the pubblico ministero

The *pubblico ministero* is, in essence, a public office which has the duty of giving effect to the collective interest either by initiating judicial proceedings or by intervening in proceedings commenced by private parties. The *pubblico ministero* fulfils its functions before the ordinary courts through a network of offices called '*procure (or procure generali) della Repubblica*'.

The principal function of the *pubblico ministero* is the initiation of criminal proceedings irrespective of whether they are proceedings which may be initiated ex officio or only after complaint, application, or request. A basic feature of Italian criminal procedure is that the initiation of criminal proceedings is obligatory (A.112 C) and irretractable (A.75 cpp), so that once the *pubblico ministero* is in possession of a *notitia criminis* he has the power and the obligation to initiate criminal proceedings even if only for the purpose of requesting the examining judge to discontinue the matter for the non-existence of the factual and legal requisites for the action. This function of the *pubblico ministero* gives rise to a complex set of supplementary powers, some of which are similar to those of judges, e g the conduct of 'summary instructions' and the issuance of measures which restrict personal liberty, such as warrants for arrest and summonses (see ch 6, below). The *pubblico ministero* also has certain accessory functions, for example, the execution of penalties and the supervision of penitentiaries.

The *pubblico ministero* has various functions in civil proceedings. The doctrine generally distinguishes between those in which he acts as agent and those in which he merely acts as an intervener. The former category comprises all those defined situations in which he may initiate civil proceedings. These may be divided into two groups: first, where the object of the action is to seek a measure favourable to a defined person, e g the nomination of a curator when a person is presumed dead, and the application for orders relating to parental authority, interdiction, and capacity; and second, where the object of the action concerns public order and seeks to limit the freedom of contract, e g oppositions to marriage (A.102 cc), actions for the nullity of marriage (Artt. 84, 86, 87, 88 cc), and proceedings for the annulment of decisions made contrary to law. The powers of the *pubblico ministero* to intervene in civil proceedings, on the other hand, may be either obligatory or discretionary. The obligation to intervene in proceedings arises, for instance, in the case of proceedings which could have been initiated by the *pubblico ministero* ex officio, matrimonial causes, proceedings concerning the capacity of persons, and in all matters before the Court of Cassation in which the *pubblico ministero* must give his conclusions. In those cases in which the *pubblico ministero* could have initiated the proceedings ex officio he has the same powers as if he were a party; in all other cases he has more limited powers. The discretion to intervene in proceedings, on the other hand, arises in every case in which the *pubblico ministero* considers the public interest to be involved.

Although the functions of the *pubblico ministero* are clear, there is a continuing controversy as to his status; the controversy is related to the uncertain nature of his functions. Some writers categorise the *pubblico ministero* as a judicial organ, others as an administrative organ, and yet others take intermediate positions which emphasise various distinctive characteristics of the office that differentiate it from the traditional powers of State. It is important to emphasise, finally, that the functions of the *pubblico ministero* are to be distinguished from those of the State Attorney: whilst the former is concerned with the collective interest, the latter is concerned with the private interests of the State.

The organisation of the pubblico ministero

The functions of the *pubblico ministero* are carried out by apposite offices annexed to every court and composed of magistrates which have a status equal to that of magistrates performing strict judicial functions. At the Court of Cassation and the Courts of Appeal, the offices are known as '*procure generali della Repubblica*', and at the Tribunals they are known as the '*procure della Repubblica*'. In the *Preture*, the functions of the *pubblico ministero* are exercised by the *Pretore* himself, except at the actual trial when they may be carried out by a probationary judge, an honorary vice-*Pretore*, a police officer, the mayor, municipal secretary or vice-secretary or, as is the general practice, by an attorney, procurator, or notary resident in the relevant court district.

At one time the organisation of the *pubblico ministero* was characterised by both a hierarchical structure amongst its various offices and by its general subordination to the Minister of Grace and Justice. As far as the latter aspect was concerned, A.69 of rd 30 January 1941 n.12 provided that the *pubblico ministero* exercised its functions under the 'direction' of the Minister of Grace and Justice. However, this was modified by RDL of 31 May 1946, n.511 which provides that the *pubblico ministero* exercises its functions under 'the vigilance' of the Minister. This has been taken to mean that the *pubblico ministero* is now no longer dependent upon the Minister. As far as the relationship between the various offices in the hierarchy is concerned, it appears that the present position is as follows. First, the 1946 legislation has transferred the supervision of the *Preture* from the procurators of the Republic to the President of the relevant *Tribunale*, thereby eliminating the hierarchical relationship which previously existed between the offices of the *procure della Repubblica* and the *Pretori* in their capacity as *pubblico ministero*. Second, it is doubtful whether the hierarchical relationship between the *procure generali* at the Courts of Appeal and the *procure della Repubblica* at the *Tribunali* is still operative. The previous system, unclear in any event, has not been explicitly modified by the present legislation. However, the recent tendency of Cassation has been to exclude any such hierarchical dependency, and this has met the approval of the doctrine. Finally, the *Procuratore Generale* at the Court of Cassation does not have, nor has it ever had, any hierarchical link with any of the other offices of the *pubblico ministero*. If it is correct to assume that the hierarchical relationship between the *procure generali* at the Courts of Appeal and the *procure della Repubblica* at the *Tribunali* has been eliminated, then it can be said that the functions of the *pubblico ministero* are today exercised by a plurality of offices independent both amongst themselves and vis-à-vis any other authority. However, the presence of certain other factors in the present constitutional system make this conclusion tenuous.

The internal organisation of the individual offices of the *pubblico ministero* is of the traditional hierarchical structure with the result that all functions are theoretically vested in the office superior, who may either exercise them personally or delegate them to his dependants.

Another important feature of the organisational structure of the *pubblico ministero*, and essential to the fulfilment of its duties, is its management of the judicial police, a specialised police corps dependent upon the magistracy. However, this is not to say that the judicial police is not also part of, and dependent upon, the Executive. Although this dual dependency has proved to be a serious defect, the aspirations for a judicial police which is effectively dependent upon the magistracy always meets with less favour, so much so that recent legislation has taken the opposite approach and sought merely to realise a more effective co-ordination between the different branches of the police.

Recruitment, promotion, and tenure of ordinary magistrates

Both branches of the Italian magistracy are generally a professional career service. The only non-professional magistrates in the Italian system are the *conciliatori*, the honorary vice-*pretori*, and the lay judges of the *corti di assise* and the *corti di assise di appello*, the latter two courts having a criminal jurisdiction.

A. RECRUITMENT

Appointment as a probationary magistrate (*uditore giudiziaro*) is based on the results gained in national entrance examinations. The examinations are usually held annually by the Ministery of Grace and Justice pursuant to a resolution of the Superior Magisterial Council to fill a given number of vacancies. The only possible exception to this form of recruitment is the direct appointment of full university law professors or attorneys as judges of Cassation pursuant to A.106(3) C, although this provision has never been, nor is it likely to ever be, implemented. The examinations for *uditore giudiziaro* comprise written examinations in civil, Roman, criminal, and administrative law, and oral examinations in Roman, civil, criminal, administrative, constitutional, ecclesiastical, international, and labour law, social welfare legislation, civil and criminal procedure, and elements of statistics. The examinations for the magistracy are reputed to be the most difficult of the professional entrance examinations. In the last few years, certain law faculties, in co-operation with the Superior Magisterial Council and the Regions, have conducted courses to prepare candidates for the examinations. Only persons who hold a law degree, are aged between 21 and 30, and satisfy certain physical and moral requirements are eligible to take the entrance examinations. The required number of persons are then selected from the successful candidates in order of merit and, subject to approval by the Superior Magisterial Council, assigned as *uditori giudiziari* to a Court of Appeal where they serve an apprenticeship which consists of assisting other magistrates and attending certain courses. The apprenticeship generally lasts six months.

B. PROMOTION

At one time promotion was based upon examination and merit. However, such a system was regarded as being in conflict with A.107(3) C, which provides that magistrates are to be distinguished on the basis of their functions only. Therefore, through a complex series of reforms over some 30 years, career progression has become dependent upon a purely negative criterion. Under the present system, all promotions are granted upon request at the attainment of the requisite seniority provided that the magistrate in question has exercised judicial functions for a given minimum period and is regarded suitable by the Superior Magisterial Council which, in the case of promotions up to the rank of magistrate of appeal, makes its decision on the basis of the opinion expressed by the relevant local Judicial Council. If the decision is negative, the magistrate in question is subject to a new evaluation after the expiry of a certain period ranging between two and three years.

In practice, this system has generally made it possible for every magistrate to proceed through the various promotions up to and including that of president of a section of Cassation without ever having exercised the functions corresponding to the various promotions. The requisite periods of seniority for promotion are two years from appointment as an *uditore* for promotion to a magistrate of *Tribunale*, 11 years from appointment as the latter for promotion to a magistrate of *Appello*, a further seven years for appointment as a magistrate of Cassation, and another eight years for the declaration of eligibility for superior management functions. Consequently a person appointed as an *uditore* at the age of 25 may, as a rule, attain the highest career position by the age of 53.

The reforms mean that it is possible for every *uditore* to achieve the highest remuneration level without ever having to submit to any form of positive selection. However, the equality of all magistrates in terms of economic advancement has not been accompanied by the reform of the recruitment process nor of the present hierarchical structure, thereby giving rise to various inconsistencies and disadvantages. The system has, in the first place, shifted from one which encouraged a career mentality incompatible with judicial office to one which places an excessive emphasis on seniority, thereby discouraging further professional preparation. In other words, the successful completion of entrance examinations at the start of a judicial career cannot be regarded as a sufficient indication of professional adequacy for the exercise of judicial functions at any level. Moreover, notwithstanding a philosophy of equality, the Superior Magisterial Council continues, at least theoretically, to exercise very broad powers in allocating the generally important management positions.

C. THE ALLOCATION OF VACANT POSITIONS

It follows that the introduction of promotions to open lists has led to a severance of the relationship between rank and the assignment of corresponding duties. Rather, promotion has now become both a pre-requisite for the exercise of given duties and the vehicle for transfers which have been rationalised through a complex set of rules devised by the Superior Magisterial Council. All vacant positions are filled either by transfer or the appointment of a probationary magistrate. Transfers are made competitively according to such criteria as seniority, family or health reasons, and attitudes. Senior positions, of course, are only open to magistrates who have already been promoted to the relevant rank. In the case of positions open to probationary magistrates the grades achieved in the entrance examinations are also utilised in filling positions.

A procedure similar to that in determining transfers is adopted in allocating management and semi-management positions. In the case of management positions the Superior Magisterial Council, with the consensus of the Minister of Grace and Justice, merely decides under a special procedure upon the recommendations formulated by a committee consisting of six members, four of whom are elected by the magistrates and the other two by parliament. If the committee's recommendations are rejected by the Superior Magisterial Council, the procedure is repeated until agreement is reached. All appointments to management and semi-management positions are permanent.

All non-managerial positions within a given court are allocated amongst the court personnel by annual rosters prepared by the office superior after consultation with the subject magistrates. These rosters which allocate personnel to the various civil, criminal or mixed sections of the court and other specific duties are subject to approval by the Superior Magisterial Council. The positions allocated by roster are neither appointments to specific offices nor permanent. However, the failure to make a reappointment is tantamount to a censure on the manner in which the relevant duties have been carried out. Moreover, because such action is tantamount to an attack on the independence of the incumbent the issue has often led to controversy.

D. TENURE

Although all magistrates hold office until the age of 70, their term of office may come to an end sooner for any of the following reasons: first, resignation; second, incompatibility through the assumption of another public office; third, 'permanent infirmity' or 'supervening ineptitude' rendering a magistrate incapable of 'profitably and efficiently performing the duties of office', a situation which is determined by the Superior Magisterial Council at the conclusion of defined proceedings; fourth, as a result of disciplinary proceedings; and finally, where a probationary magistrate has been twice rejected for promotion to a magistrate of *Tribunale*. It is to be noted that the powers of removal from office have been very rarely utilised nor have they assumed the role of a negative selection process as they could well have done after the reform of the promotion system.

The irremovability of magistrates is guaranteed by A.107(1) C. The guarantee has two aspects. First, it prevents transfers at the whim of the authorities. Generally speaking, removal by transfer may only arise upon application of the interested party or by promotion which may, of course, be rejected by the incumbent of an office. Second, the guarantee also extends to the functions performed by a magistrate within the particular office to which he is attached. The modification of rostered functions must always be justified on the basis of the objective needs of the particular office to which the magistrate in question belongs and must not have the object of removing him from the exercise of his functions. A magistrate may only have his functions suspended in cases of mental sickness or infirmity, or consequent upon the commencement of disciplinary or criminal proceedings against him.

E. DISCIPLINE AND RESPONSIBILITY

Disciplinary sanctions against magistrates may only be imposed by the disciplinary section of the Superior Magisterial Council subsequent to proceedings brought either by the Minister of Grace and Justice or the

Procurator General of Cassation. The decision of the disciplinary section is subject to appeal before the full court of Cassation. The disciplinary penalties are admonition, censure, loss of seniority, dismissal or forfeiture of promotion and may be applied against a 'magistrate who fails in his duties, or maintains official or private conduct which either renders him undeserving of the trust and reputation required of his office or compromises the prestige of the judiciary'. However, the very generic nature of this provision has given rise to doubts as to its constitutional validity.

The criminal liability of magistrates relates to crimes such as collusion, corruption, and the performance of official acts for a private motive. Their civil liability, on the other hand, is limited to fraud, extortion, and the denial of justice. The tendency of the doctrine and the recent case law of the Constitutional Court is to hold the State vicariously liable for every unlawful act committed by magistrates notwithstanding the present restrictions upon their personal liability.

Chapter 3

The divisions, sources and sphere of application of Italian law

The divisions of Italian law

Although traditional doctrine divides law into various categories, the fundamental division is between public and private law. However, this division raises two basic issues: first, the classical problem of the distinction between the two branches of law, and second, the continuing relevance of the division.

Prominent amongst the proposed criteria for distinguishing between private and public law is the interest theory: according to the Roman jurist Ulpiano, public law is that complex of norms which concern the public interest, whilst private law is that complex of norms which concern the private interest. This Roman formula is no longer acceptable because the same subject often forms the object of both public and private law, e g ownership which serves both individual and collective functions. Nonetheless, the same criterion in a modified version which emphasises the nature of the social interests protected by any given norm is still followed today. Thus for part of the doctrine, public law comprises those norms which regulate the general, immediate, and collective interests of society considered as a whole whilst private law comprises those norms which satisfy the particular interests of individuals.

The common failing of the various theories advanced to distinguish between public and private law has been that they all purport to formulate a universal and perpetual criterion. Since there can be nothing constant or typical about a legal system, a valid criterion to distinguish between public and private law can only be formulated in relation to any given point in the development of any legal system. It follows that the boundary between public and private law cannot be fixed in a rigorous and definitive manner and that, moreover, the division of subjects between the two spheres is relative, as it depends on historical events which cause a continuous movement of given relations from one sphere to the other.

This dynamic nature of the legal system is evident in the recent transformation undergone by private law. In the nineteenth century, private law was characterised by the freedom and autonomy of the individual in regulating his own legal relationships. As a result of changing economic and social conditions, there has been increased State intervention in the relationships which had hitherto been autonomously regulated by private individuals. It is therefore said that public law has been expanding at the expense of private law. It is, indeed, difficult nowadays to consider institutions such as ownership, contract, partnership, and employment, the very subjects which once formed the core of the private law, as purely individualistic institutions.

The reaction of the doctrine to this transformation of private law has varied. Part of the doctrine, without ignoring the changing situation, has sought to rationalise and incorporate the new datum into the system inherited from the traditional doctrine. At the opposite extreme, others have drastically proposed the abandonment of the distinction between public and private law, as now representing a superseded ideology, and the unification of the two spheres into a 'common law' with the exception of constitutional law and, perhaps, a few other sectors.

The rupture between traditional and modern private law is undeniable. This has been caused by such factors as the increasing volume of special legislation, the modification of the traditional private law institutions, the adaptation of private law to constitutional guarantees, and the increasing regulatory intervention of the State. Nonetheless, these factors have not deprived private law of its role and significance. Although it has been said that State intervention for the protection of the public interest has limited the field of individual freedom and autonomy to certain micro-relations, such as those arising out of small enterprise and the family, on the other hand, it is wrong to infer that the changes in private law have led to the absorption of the latter by public law; this inference almost suggests that the nineteenth century model was the only legitimate model of the private law.

Changing socio-economic conditions necessarily affected traditional private law institutions, which thenceforth faced the necessity of performing a plurality of functions: apart from those relations which remained individualistic in character, private law had now to deal with 'mass' relations, which required a different balance of the interests at play. Whilst these new functions could have been dealt with through either the appropriate application of elastic formulae, such as 'fault', or the differential application of general principles, such as 'good faith', the collective interest made State intervention inevitable, e g in urban planning, price fixing, and the imposition of an obligation to contract in certain cases. This does not mean that there has been a conversion of private law into public law, however, but only that there was a need for the introduction of a 'corrective' in the case of certain institutions.

Although the greater part of private law has undergone the influence of public law, another and indeed essential part of the law has undergone a progressive shift from a public law to a private law nature, e g family law and the collective bargains made by the trade unions. Yet another part, such as succession law, has been unaffected by either of these influences. This transformation is a continuing process, and although the advent of the social welfare state has led to the imposition of various limits upon individual autonomy so as to protect the public interest, the private and public law dichotomy has not entirely lost its significance.

The sub-divisions of public and private law

Public law is divided into public international and public domestic law. The former comprises both international relations, or the law of nations, and Community law which regulates the relationships between the member states of the three European Communities, viz, CEE, CECA, and EURATOM (see ch 4, below). Public domestic law comprises a wide and complex group of subjects. These include: first, constitutional law; second, administrative law; third, criminal law; fourth, procedure (civil, criminal and administrative) which regulates the administration of justice; fifth, ecclesiastical law which disciplines the activities of the religious community in its relations with the State and which must be kept distinct from Canon law which is the internal law of the Church; sixth, finance law, inclusive of tax law which concerns the imposition and collection of taxes and public finance which concerns the management of the State patrimony; and, finally, navigation law, agrarian law, and public economics. Private law is basically divided into civil and commercial law.

There are certain subjects which cannot be easily classified within the traditional public-private law dichotomy either because of the dynamic nature of their legal relationships or because they are recent subjects which have not developed out of this traditional dichotomy of legal science. A subject of the former type deserving special mention is labour law. Notwithstanding its social importance, its classification is still a matter of controversy. This, no doubt, is due to the fact that the subject has been influenced by various branches of law outside the private law sphere: constitutional, criminal, administrative, and international law. Consequently part of the doctrine acknowledges that the labour phenomenon can no longer be circumscribed to its traditional private law sphere. An influential theory here is that whilst the regulation of the collective and individual autonomy of the labour relationship (that is, unionism and the contract of employment, respectively) still belongs to the private law sphere, the regulation of worker security and assistance (social welfare legislation) belongs to the public law sphere. An example of a new subject which presents difficulties of classification is environment law whose object, the protection of the environment, is fulfilled through recourse to the most disparate sectors of the law, including criminal, civil, and labour law. Therefore, subjects such as labour and environment law may be said to form part of a hybrid group which defy the traditional dichotomy because they contain public and private law elements.

The sources of law

A. INTRODUCTION

The formal doctrinal statement as to the sources of law is restricted to a consideration of the Constitution and the sources listed in the so-called 'preliminary provisions to the Civil Code'. Article 1 of the 'preliminary provisions', which pre-date the Republican Constitution of 1948, defines the sources of law as legislation (*legge*), regulations (*regolamenti*), corporative norms (*norme corporative*, which, however, have had no practical significance since the fall of the fascist regime which utilised them to raise government approved regulations and agreements stipulated by certain corporative bodies to the status of sources of law), and usages (*usi*). The appearance of the Constitution necessarily altered the position because the Constitution, rather than legislation, became the prime formal source of law: not only does parliament derive its legislative power from the Constitution, but it must in its law-making function conform in every respect to the provisions of the Constitution upon penalty of having its legislation struck from the statute books by the Constitutional Court. However, this formal or doctrinal elaboration of the sources of law is an oversimplification of the actual position. It fails to take account of certain sources of law which although of no formal value are nonetheless influential; the most important of these are case law and legal scholarship (or doctrine). The basis of the formal doctrinal approach, with its emphasis on legislation, lies in the principle of the separation of powers; in other words, that the law-making function belongs exclusively to the legislature. However, the practical resolution of legal problems necessitates a close understanding of the complex relationships which exist amongst the various formal and informal sources of law, so much so that the strict doctrinal approach contained in the traditional manuals will give an unrealistic, or at least distorted, impression of the true situation. The Italian lawyer, in advising his client, and the Italian judge, in deciding a case, apart from considering the basic legislative provisions and, perhaps, the doctrine, will place heavy emphasis upon the existing state of the case law, which is conveniently collected in various law reports and *massimari* (collections of abstract rules which have formed the basis of previous judicial decisions).

B. THE FORMAL OR DOCTRINAL SOURCES OF LAW

The doctrine classifies the formal sources of law, in decreasing order of importance, as follows:

(*i*) *The Constitution and constitutional legislation.* The Republican Constitution of 1948, which is the fundamental law of the State, contains the general provisions concerning State organisation and functions and the fundamental rights and guarantees. The first 54 articles are devoted to the constitutional guarantees with respect to which the Constitutional Court has been instrumental as to both their interpretation and application. However, the constitutional provisions have, according to criteria which are not altogether clear, been divided by the doctrine and case law between self-executing provisions, which became immediately effective upon the introduction of the Constitution, and policy provisions, which merely contemplate future legislative programmes without producing any immediate effects.

Constitutional legislation comprises, on the one hand, legislation modifying the Constitution and, on the other hand, legislation which either has been expressly contemplated by the Constitution or concerns matters which are regarded by the parliament as integrating the Constitution. In every case the special legislative process prescribed by A.138 C must be followed (see ch 5, below).

Other sources of law of a constitutional nature are constitutional conventions and constitutional practices. The former are customs of constitutional status and therefore superior to, and binding upon, ordinary legislation. Such constitutional customs, however, can only be *praeter Constitutionem*, and not *contra* or *secundum constitutionem*, for the Constitution does not acknowledge the existence of custom. Constitutional practices are not legal norms because they lack the subjective element necessary to qualify them as custom (see p 83, below).

(*ii*) *The primary sources of law.* These include:

(a) ORDINARY PARLIAMENTARY LEGISLATION. This is the source of law *par excellence* both because of its importance and its frequency of application. Ordinary legislation comprises the Codes and so-called 'special legislation'. There are five Codes in force at present: the Civil Code, the Code of Civil Procedure, the Navigation Code (which regulates both internal and international sea and air transport), the Criminal Code, and the Code of Criminal Procedure. The first three became effective in 1942, and the last two in 1931. The Codes, being the product of systematisation carried out according to doctrine, are pitched at a higher level of abstraction than is necessary for the solution of a concrete case; their norms are general and theoretically broad enough to encompass all of the practical problems likely to arise in the future. Increasingly, the Codes have been expanded and supplemented by so-called special legislation, which has been voluminous and extensive, covering every sector of the law, e g divorce, landlord and tenant, employment, companies, public administration, health, and urban development. The nineteenth century ideal of consolidating all of the law into a single text has never become a reality so that, and in particular nowadays, a knowledge of special legislation is indispensable to a complete picture of the law. Special legislation has not only dealt with new subjects and subjects not completely regulated by the Codes, but it has also introduced new legislative values and ideals, so that the Codes can no longer be considered the sole source of the general principles to which reference must be made either to interpret the law or to fill its lacunae. It has been rightly observed, in short, that this is the age of 'decodification'. In contrast to the Codes, the style of the individual norm contained in special legislation ranges from the same degree of abstraction as that of the Codes to more specific legislative provisions, depending upon the subject matter of the legislation.

(b) LEGISLATIVE DECREES (DECRETI-LEGGE). These are issued by the Executive in cases of urgency and necessity but which only temporarily have the force and effect of legislation, that is, if parliament fails to convert a decree into law within 60 days of its publication, it becomes retrospectively ineffective.

(c) THE CONSTITUTIONS OF THE ORDINARY REGIONS. These take the form of ordinary national legislation (see ch 5 below).

(d) THE DELEGATED LEGISLATION WITH WHICH EFFECT IS GIVEN TO THE CONSTITUTIONS OF THE SPECIAL REGIONS. In other words, the decrees that the national Government is authorised by constitutional legislation to issue for the purpose of giving effect to the constitutions of the Special Regions.

(e) REGIONAL LEGISLATION. This is made pursuant to the legislative powers granted to the Regions under A.117 C.

(f) THE LEGISLATION OF THE PROVINCES OF TRENTO AND BOLZANO. These provinces enjoy a special legislative autonomy.

There are two further sources of law which, although coming within the category of primary legislation, are of an inferior status to the types listed above. First, regional legislation on matters which come within State jurisdiction but which have been delegated to the Regions. The validity of such legislation is dependent upon the ordinary State legislation that delegated the relevant power. Second, ordinary delegated legislation made by the national government pursuant to delegation from the parliament. The validity of this type of delegated legislation is, again, dependent upon the primary source of law which authorised it. In short, although all of the primary sources of law are formally on a level of parity, their actual effect is limited by the reciprocal relationships which exist amongst them.

(iii) The secondary sources of law. These comprise the normative acts of both the national administration (e g the government, ministers, and prefects) and the other public entities (e g municipalities, regions, and provinces). They are formal administrative acts which may take the form of regulations, ordinances, or the constitutions of minor administrative entities. Regulations are the typical normative acts of the Executive. Ordinances are atypical administrative measures comprising administrative orders issued in cases of urgency or necessity but having a temporary validity limited to the duration of the urgent or necessary circumstances which gave rise to them. The constitutions of minor entities, finally, are acts which contain the general principles governing the organisation and operation of the minor public entities. They have the formal validity of an administrative act and generally an effect which is only internal to the organisation in question.

All secondary sources of law, being mere administrative acts, are inferior to legislation and all other acts having the force of legislation. It follows that secondary sources of law cannot modify or conflict with either constitutional norms or any primary source of law. They can only modify ordinary legislation where the Executive has been delegated the right to make norms having the same force and effect as legislation.

(iv) Custom. Custom is the typical source of unwritten law. Article 8 dp provides that in the case of subjects dealt with by legislation or regulation, custom is only admissible to the extent contemplated by the written law. It has been said that custom is merely a subsidiary or complementary source of law vis-à-vis legislation and regulations and, moreover, can become operative only insofar as it is admitted in the manner expressly envisaged by A.8 dp. This approach would seem to lead to the conclusion that whilst custom has retained its position as an autonomous source of law in certain spheres (e g in international, Canon, constitutional, and administrative law), it has not done so in the private law. However, even after the introduction of A.8 dp by the 1942 Civil Code there has still remained a certain sphere of application for custom, including in the area of private law.

The 1942 Code, by adopting the term 'usage' in lieu of the traditional term 'custom', initially created a certain perplexity which has been overcome by the distinction drawn by the case law between normative and interpretative usages. The former, according to Cassation, are relevant to, and constitute, a true subsidiary source of law in subjects where there is a lack of legislative or administrative regulation; the latter concern subjects governed by legislation or regulation and are therefore only relevant if expressly admitted by the written law. Interpretative usages are a means of interpreting the intent of the parties to a transaction where that intent is ambiguous; they incorporate habitual practices into a contract, thereby converting them into contractual provisions which, it is presumed, would have been intended by the parties to the transaction. The Civil Code contains numerous references to both normative and interpretative usages, although normative usages have a more important function in public rather than in private law, e g in constitutional and administrative law.

Custom, therefore, may be said to be of three types, depending upon its relationship to legislation and the other sources of law: *secundum legem*, *praeter legem*, and *contra legem*. It is *secundum legem* where it is expressly referred to or recalled by legislation, in which case it is complementary to, and interpretative of, the latter. It is *praeter legem* where it regulates subjects which are not dealt with by the written law, although it can never be a source of criminal law, which can only be created by legislation: '*nullem crimen sine lege*'. Finally, custom can never be *contra legem* as A.15 dp expressly provides that legislation may only be expressly or impliedly repealed by later legislation.

The three elements necessary for the existence of a normative usage or custom are: first, the objective or external element, which consists of a uniform, general, and constant behaviour in a given situation; second, the subjective element, which consists of a belief that the observance of a defined behaviour corresponds with the law; and finally, the acquiescence of the law in the existence of the custom. In general, the onus of proving the existence of a custom lies on the party affirming it, unless its existence is acknowledged by judicial notice.

C. THE RELATIONSHIP BETWEEN THE SOURCES OF LAW

There are three fundamental rules concerning the relationship between the various sources of law: a norm of inferior status cannot modify or abrogate a norm of superior status; conversely, a norm of superior status can always modify or eliminate a norm of inferior status; and finally, a later norm modifies or abrogates an earlier norm of equal status. Cases of equal status are relatively rare because most parallel sources have some differentiating element which avoids their conflict, e g a different legislative competence. The clarification and emphasis of the relationships and priorities which exist amongst the various types of law illustrate how the work of the doctrine in the elaboration of the sources of law has also had a practical utility.

D. THE INDIRECT SOURCES OF LAW

There are three indirect sources of law:

(*i*) *The case law (giurisprudenza).* An evaluation of the role of case law in Italy involves a consideration of a complex set of related factors. First, the relationship between case law and legislation, which is a fixed datum and constitutes itself as authoritative. This is the area of the interpretation of legislation in its application to concrete cases. Second, the relationship between case law and doctrine, which also concerns itself with the search for and interpretation of the law. And finally, the internal aspects of the authority of judicial precedent. The theoretical views on the role of case law range from the traditional standpoint to the exactly opposite view. However, the actual position is somewhere in between, namely, notwithstanding that the legislative system continues to occupy its fundamental position, it is undeniable that there is an evolutive case law.

The basis of the traditional position is the separation of powers doctrine and its corollary, the self-sufficiency of the legislative system. It is traditionally said that the legislative system has no lacunae. Legislation provides an a priori system of general, abstract, and hypothetical norms encompassing every factual situation which can possibly arise. The written law is complete and prescient. It follows that the legal system consists of a large number of legislative compartments, each giving the answer to a certain type of fact situation, and the work of the judge is simply to fit the concrete facts into one of these abstract categories, which will automatically give the solution. This is the logical mechanism embodied in the syllogism in which the major premise is the legislative norm and the minor premise is the facts: it is enough that the facts coincide with a legislative provision for the conclusion to come out of its own accord.

Article 12(1) dp, in fact, prohibits the interpretation of an unclear norm other than in accordance with the clear meaning of its words, considered in their legislative context (literal interpretation), and its legislative intent (logical interpretation). The interpretor, in determining the meaning of a norm, may have recourse to the following criteria. First, the reasons for which the norm was introduced (the historical criterion). These reasons may be gleaned from a consideration of the norm's antecedents, including the parliamentary and committee deliberations which preceded the introduction of the norm into the legislative system. Second, the relationship of the subject norm to the other norms in the legislative system (the systematic criterion).

And third, the correlation of the norm with its object or function (the teleological criterion). Depending upon the extent to which the literal interpretation of a norm coincides with its logical interpretation, the result of the interpretative process may be merely declaratory, extensive, or restrictive.

Apart from the case of an ambiguous norm, it is apparent that notwithstanding the infinite number of abstract legal situations, or compartments, contemplated by legislation, it may happen that fact situations arise which do not exactly correspond to, or even resemble, any existing legislative provision. Article 12(2) dp, which deals with legislative 'lacunae', provides that such cases are to be decided by reference to similar or analogous provisions and, if still doubtful, by reference to the general principles inherent in the legislative system. Recourse to similar cases or subjects (the analogical method) is only admissible if the following conditions are satisfied: first, the case in question is not covered by a particular legislative norm; second, there is a similarity between the situation provided for and that not provided for; and third, the element of similarity between the two situations must imply a justification for the same legislative solution ('*eadem ratio*'). However, the application of a legislative norm by analogy finds some limits in the legislative system, e g a criminal norm cannot be applied by analogy if it is unfavourable to the accused and, similarly, a norm which constitutes an exception to a general legislative provision or other law cannot be applied by analogy (A.14 dp).

Thus even A.12 dp admits that there may be fact situations which do not exactly correspond to abstract legislative provisions, and in such cases the matter is left to case law for resolution. The judge cannot dismiss a case for the want of law: if the solution is unclear, he must decide it by interpreting the available norm; if, instead, there is a lacuna, he must resort to either analogous principles or the general principles of the legal system. But this addendum to the law through case decisions has been traditionally regarded as interpretation and not as the creation of law, that is, as the extraction from general and abstract legislation of something which already existed by virtue of the will of the legislature and not as the creation of something new. Therefore, the application of the law to the practical case is primarily one of interpretation, that is, of the discovery within a norm of other norms which, although of a less abstract nature, nonetheless resemble the norm from which they are derived. Thus, even though those derived norms or maxims are less abstract, they are not pitched at the level of the individual case but remain general rules suitable for application to future cases. This is the traditional 'conceptual' as distinct from the 'creative' approach to the case law. In practice, when a lawyer is organising a defence, he seeks out the legislative norm appropriate to the situation and those maxims in the case law that best support his case. In this way, those case law maxims which are confirmed by other cases eventually acquire a de facto authority similar to legislation: they become the so-called consolidated maxims (*massime consolidate*). The traditional controversy between the supporters of the conceptual and creative approaches to the case law is very old and coincides with the debate between the certainty of law and the equity or justice of the individual case.

The legal system cannot provide in detail for every practical situation that may arise and thus, even in a legislative system, every norm leaves a certain margin of discretion through its interpretation and application, as a result of which the judge may create law. Notwithstanding the theoretical assertion that the judge is no more than an interpretor of the law, his normal interpretative powers are such as to allow a certain space for creativity. The legislative system, therefore, does not eliminate the judicial creation of law; it merely reduces and rationalises it within the categories provided for it by the legislative system. Even when an Italian judge decides a case according to that discretion permitted by law, it is not admitted that the decision is individual to that case; there dominates a need to announce a general principle, or maxim, which is somehow suitable for application to all similar cases in the future. In other words, the judge does not admit that the decision is based on facts unique to the case; rather, the decision is translated into the typical terms of legal logic by extracting from the case the general principle which lies at the basis of the decision. Thus the individual decision is transformed into general and abstract terms. The negative aspects of this process materialise when the maxim becomes consolidated and takes on an independent existence. At that point it imposes itself upon cases which are formally, but not substantively, like that which gave rise to it, thereby sacrificing the justice of the individual case. In other words, a maxim born out of the equitable considerations in a particular situation is in future applied because of its formal applicability to cases in which equity would require a different and even opposite conclusion.

This very process highlights the persuasive authority of judicial precedent in Italy. Under the formal position, legislation is the source of law and the courts are limited to its 'interpretation'. It follows that decisions of courts are only binding on the parties to the relevant proceedings and do not become binding precedents. That is to say, the case law cannot be a source of law as this would be contrary to a strict separation of powers and would have the effect of making legislators of the judges. In reality, the interpretative effect of a decision goes beyond the case at hand and creates a precedent. The repeated application of a maxim establishes a 'constant case law' which satisfies the need of certainty in the law. In practice, the Italian courts cite and apply case decisions, or at least the maxims from them, and only very rarely do they depart from an established precedent. On the other hand, the absence of a formal *stare decisis* enables the courts to render justice in the individual case as well as adapting to new demands through recourse to evolutive interpretation, analogy, and general principles. Whether the courts in fact keep abreast of changing conditions or entangle themselves in their own web of maxims is a much debated issue.

The importance of judicial precedent in Italy is manifest in certain other factors. For instance, the creation of a single Court of Cassation, which replaced the previous five decentralised Courts of Cassation, with the object of ensuring a 'uniform interpretation of legislation' and 'the unity of national law'. In practice, very few courts would knowingly adopt an interpretation different to that of Cassation notwithstanding that the decisions of the latter are not theoretically binding. Another factor testifying to the importance of case law is the existence of various law reports and collections of maxims.

The creative and evolutive nature of Italian case law is particularly evident in the decisions of the Constitutional Court, which has the function of deciding the constitutional legitimacy of legislation. Although only those decisions of the Constitutional Court that declare legislation unconstitutional formally bind third parties (in the sense that such decisions eliminate the unconstitutional legislation from the statute books), it is apparent that the mere interpretative decisions of the Court (that is, decisions which adopt an interpretation rendering the relevant legislative provision consistent with the Constitution rather than declaring it unconstitutional) are also authoritative and contribute to a continuous adaptation of the law to current socio-economic conditions. Notwithstanding that the ordinary courts, unlike the Constitutional Court, are more restricted in terms of their interpretative techniques and cannot eliminate a norm by either not applying it or declaring it invalid, they may nonetheless adapt the values inherent in a norm to modern conditions, e g the court may impose modern health requisites for factories through the adaptation of an old norm which sought to guarantee a healthy work environment by the provision of air and light. This interpretative or 'evolutive' process will vary, depending upon the sector of the law, and the detail and stability of the values inherent in the relevant legislation. In this way there has been an interesting and important evolution of case law in areas such as labour, environment, commercial, and administrative law, and in certain sectors of the private law such as in civil responsibility.

In other areas of the law, as in procedure, where the inherent legislative values are uniform and rigid, the courts have been less able to adapt the rules to modern needs, e g the inability to adapt the law of procedure for the protection of diffused interests. However, the courts possess a vast network of legislative values which can be utilised in adapting the law to modern requirements and through which they can make a clear 'creative' contribution to the law. But such creativity, which always remains within the framework of the norm by adapting its inherent values to present needs and conditions, continues to be described as 'interpretation'. This approach fits the creative activity of the courts into the traditional framework and justifies it. The extreme theoretical view that creative interpretation is not a permissible judicial function has been repudiated and the issue became not one of its legitimacy, but a question of its nature.

There is little practical difference between the strict observance of the persuasive authority of precedents, as is the case in Italy, and a situation in which formally binding authority is avoided by various techniques such as 'distinguishing' and interpreting precedents, both of which are variously utilised in common law countries. Formally, it remains true that the case law has no binding authority and thus cannot be considered a source of law equal in status to legislation. At the same time, it is also true that the case law has an evolutive or creative function, irrespective of whether it is classified as 'interpretation' or not. This is manifest in the fact that the practical solution of a problem necessitates a consideration of both the legislation and case law on the point. Moreover, it is also formally true that legislation remains the fundamental factor and provides the framework within which the creative activity of Italian judges takes place. Therefore judicial contributions to the evolution of the legal system never result in a formal denial of the existence or application of a legal norm, nor in the creation of a new source of law independent of legislation.

(ii) The doctrine (la dottrina). The doctrine encompasses the writings of academic lawyers. It is not a formal source of law, although it exerts considerable influence on the legal system, an influence which is generally commensurate with the standing of the author. As a source of law it is not as important as the case law: the courts generally refer to doctrine where there is either a lack of case law or the latter is conflicting; where the case law is settled, the courts rarely refer to doctrine. Even where the courts do refer to doctrine, they do not necessarily adopt its views: in this respect, not only is the prestige of the author important, but also the extent to which the courts can be persuaded. In many instances where the case law has adopted its own view, doctrine has generally adapted by restricting itself to an explanation and criticism of the case law. Certainly the legal scholar enjoys a higher status than in common law countries, but although sometimes prolonged and persuasive criticism by eminent scholars succeeds in influencing the development of the law, this process is not commonplace and its importance must not be overstated.

Doctrine also influences the development of the law in that scholars generally participate in the expert commissions formed to draft new codes and legislation. New legislation often gives effect to doctrinal developments and teachings. Finally, it must be remembered that all judges and lawyers have experienced the influence and teachings of doctrine: the method, style, and attitudes of doctrine have been imparted to them at the beginning of their studies, and this is a culture which they carry with them throughout their professional lives.

(iii) Equity (equità). The civil law does not have anything resembling the distinction in English law between equity and common law. There is in Italian law no separate body of law known as equity. Equity, in Italian law, is used to express the value of 'justice in the individual case'. Understood in this way, equity can be relevant as a source of law in either a 'strict' or an 'indirect' sense. It is a source of law in a 'strict' sense where it is expressly contemplated by law. This arises in exceptional cases only (e g A.1374 cc) as it cuts across the principle of 'certainty in the law'. It constitutes a source of law in an 'indirect' sense because it expresses the general tendency of applying the otherwise general and abstract provisions of the law with 'substantial equality'.

The basic transformation of the Italian legal system

The traditional doctrine has not altered its formal position to reflect the profound changes which have affected the Italian legal system. Rather, it has generally responded by either refuting those changes or adapting and incorporating them within its traditional framework. The reality of the situation is that the Italian legal system has undergone a profound transformation in several respects. First, there has been increasing governmental intervention in every area of the law combined with a corresponding restriction of private autonomy—a phenomenon sometimes referred to as the 'publicisation' of the law—placing the traditional dichotomy between public and private law in crisis. Second, there has been a steady departure from its position as a 'codified system' because the enormous volume of special legislation has dwarfed the codes. This process has led to the assertion that the system is now in a process of 'decodification'. The dramatic increase in special legislation has had the function of supplementing the codes by dealing with subjects which were either non-existent or underdeveloped at the time when the codification process took place. Moreover, the provisions of the codes themselves have undergone profound modification in various areas as a result of either recognised changes in social attitudes or an intensive interpretation of static legislative provisions within the context of a changing socio-economic environment. Finally, there has arisen a complex relationship amongst the various sources of law. The traditional view, based on a strict separation of powers and the self-sufficiency of the codes, namely, that legislation is the sole source of law, is unrealistic; the case law through evolutive interpretation has had to fill gaps, co-ordinate legislation, and adapt static texts to new socio-economic conditions. Although traditional doctrine rationalises this process as the 'interpretation' of legislative texts, the case law constitutes a de facto source of law and has given rise to a system of precedent which, although not formally binding, is strictly observed. However, all these factors do not mean a breakdown of the Romano-Germanic tradition, to which the Italian legal system belongs; the basic framework, attitudes, and methods of the Romano-Germanic family always survive. All it means is that the system is in a state of evolution. No less important than any of the above factors is also the deep and widespread effect of that omnipotent body, the Constitutional Court, which has been instrumental in introducing and giving effect to the ideals of the Republican Constitution of 1948. In toto the Italian legal system is at an important and interesting stage of its development.

The spatial extent of Italian law—the rules of private international law

A. INTRODUCTION

The basic principle regulating the spatial application of Italian law is that of territoriality, which, however, may be affected by the rules of private international law. The Italian conflict rules relate almost exclusively to private law relations; generally speaking, conflict issues concerning public law either fall outside the interests of the State or are dealt with specifically by norms of internal law. This state of affairs with respect to public law is clearly seen in the case of the criminal law.

B. THE CRIMINAL LAW AND THE PRINCIPLE OF TERRITORIALITY

The general principle governing the spatial extent of Italian criminal law is territoriality, according to which Italian law is applicable to all crimes committed by either Italian or foreign nationals on Italian territory (A.28 dp). In particular circumstances Italian law is also applicable to certain crimes committed abroad by either Italian or foreign nationals, viz, in the case of certain crimes committed by either citizens or foreigners against either the Italian State or Italian citizens (Artt.7, 8, 10(1) cp); in the case of certain classes of crimes committed abroad by Italian citizens (A.9 cp); and in the case of crimes committed abroad by a foreigner against either a foreign state or a foreigner, although such proceedings may only be brought at the request of the Minister of Justice and provided always that the accused is on Italian territory, has committed a delict punishable with no less than three year's imprisonment, and has not been extradited (A.10(2) cp). In the end, the principle of territoriality is limited to two classes of crimes: contraventions (see ch 7, below) and crimes punishable by fine.

C. FOREIGN CRIMINAL LAW AND ITALIAN PROCEEDINGS

Foreign criminal law can only be relevant to Italian proceedings if it is expressly referred to by a specific norm. This arises in two cases only. First, extraditions, which are only granted where the following requisites are fulfilled: the alleged crime also constitutes a crime under Italian law; the crime is not one for which extradition is expressly prohibited by international convention; and the fugitive is not an Italian citizen unless the extradition is nonetheless expressly required by international convention (A.13 cp). Extradition is not available for political crimes (Artt. 10 and 26 C), except for genocide, nor is it available for reasons of race, religion, or nationality. The extradition procedure is regulated by Artt. 661–671 cpp (see ch 6, below). Second, in proceedings for the recognition of a foreign criminal judgment pursuant to A.12 cp which enables recognition where the foreign judgment either produces defined consequences under Italian law or gives rise to damages or other civil effects (A.12 cp) (see ch 6, below).

D. THE TRADITIONAL CONFLICT RULES

The general conflict rules are contained in Artt. 17–31 dp, although they are modified and supplemented in various ways. First, by the conflict rules concerning navigation contained in Artt. 1–14 of the Navigation Code. Second, by specific rules applicable to particular subjects, e g authorship rights (the law of 22 April 1942 n.633), marriage (Artt.85, 86, 87 nos. 1, 2 and 4, 88, 89 and 116 cc), and commercial companies (Artt.2505–2510 cc). And finally, by special rules applicable to certain subjects by reason of international treaty or uniform law, e g the Hague Conventions of 1902 relating to marriage, divorce, separation, and the protection of minors, the Hague Conventions of 1905 relating to the personal and property effects of marriage, interdiction and other protective measures, the Geneva Conventions of 1930–1931 on bills of exchange and cheques, and the Hague Convention of 1955 on sales.

E. THE JURISDICTION OF ITALIAN COURTS

One of the first issues in any matter involving foreign elements is whether the court has jurisdiction which depends upon the connection between the dispute and the State. The jurisdiction of Italian courts may be deduced primarily from A.4 cpc, which defines the situations in which a foreigner may be made a defendant to proceedings. Jurisdiction always exists in relation to a national, whether as plaintiff or defendant. A foreigner may only be a defendant if he is connected to the State in a manner defined in A.4 cpc, whilst he may always be a plaintiff provided that the state of the foreigner's nationality concedes a reciprocal right to an Italian plaintiff (A.16 dp). In the latter situation, if the defendant is also a foreigner, jurisdiction again depends upon the defendant's connection with the State in accordance with A.4 cpc.

According to A.4 cpc, a foreigner is sufficiently connected with Italy to be made a defendant to Italian proceedings in the following cases:

(a) if he is resident or domiciled in Italy, has accepted Italian jurisdiction, or is represented within the jurisdiction by an agent who is authorised to bring or defend proceedings;
(b) if the proceedings concern property located within the jurisdiction, the estate of a deceased national, or a succession which was 'opened' in Italy;
(c) if the proceedings concern obligations 'arising or to be performed in Italy', irrespective of whether the part of the transaction in dispute is connected with the jurisdiction;
(d) if the proceedings are connected with litigation which is already pending before the courts, or concern provisional remedies which, if granted, are to be executed in Italy; and
(e) if, in the absence of any of the above bases for jurisdiction, an Italian plaintiff could be made a defendant to similar proceedings before a court of the defendant's nationality (that is, reciprocity): this basis for jurisdiction is only applicable where the plaintiff is an Italian national.

There is nothing in Italian law to prevent Italian litigants from bringing proceedings in a foreign court and later having the foreign judgment recognised in Italy (provided that the judgment complies with certain requirements). All that Italian law refuses to enforce is an agreement to oust its jurisdiction, although this is mitigated by the effect of certain arbitration clauses which are valid because of international convention.

F. DETERMINATION OF THE APPLICABLE LAW

Once jurisdiction is established, reference must be made to the conflict rules to determine the applicable law. Because the conflict rules deal with abstract legal categories (e g obligations, succession and donation), the facts before the court must be classified into a particular category to identify the relevant conflict rule. This preliminary classification is made according to the *lex fori* and therefore the abstract legal categories must be given their normal meaning according to Italian law. Once the relevant legal category or conflict rule is identified, the latter defines the applicable law through the indication of an inherent circumstance or connection of the facts with a foreign state. In some cases a conflict rule may indicate more than one connecting criteria which may be either successive, which consists of a principal and a subsidiary criteria, e g A.29 dp which adopts the criterion of residence as subsidiary to nationality where the facts concern a stateless person, or concurrent, which consists of several simultaneous connecting factors, thereby necessitating the definition of how they are to be co-ordinated amongst themselves, e g A.26(1) dp which adopts three concurrent criteria and provides that priority must be given to that criterion which identifies the law most favourable to the formal validity of the act in question. The determination of the connection is according to the *lex fori*, unless the conflict rule necessarily makes it dependent upon foreign law, e g nationality, as the *lex fori* can only regulate the acquisition of Italian nationality.

The various connecting criteria adopted by the Italian conflict rules are as follows. First, nationality, which is the basic criterion utilised by Italian private international law. If, in a case of dual nationality, one of the nationalities is Italian, the conflict rules are inapplicable and Italian law regulates the situation in question. If both components of a dual nationality are foreign, then the nationality which is based on principles closer to Italian law with respect to the grant of citizenship in analogous circumstances determines the applicable law. Second, residence and domicile, both of which are technical notions defined by A.43 cc: residence is the locality where a person habitually resides whilst domicile is the locality in which a person has established the principal seat of his affairs. Third, the location of property. Fourth, the location of either the cause or effect of a legal transaction. As the most important element of a non-contractual obligation is considered to be its subjective element, the applicable law in such a case is generally that of the locality where the facts which gave rise to the obligation took place. On the other hand, the applicable law in the case of a contractual obligation is generally that of the locality where the contract was formed (that is, usually where the offeror receives notice of acceptance). Fifth, the locality where the obligation is to be performed, although this criterion is only applicable in certain cases defined by international convention, e g the Geneva Convention on bills of exchange and cheques. Sixth, the law validly selected by the parties to a transaction. Where such right of selection is allowed, it is completely free of restrictions (A.25 (1) dp, Artt.9 and 10 cn). Finally, the nationality of the ship or aircraft, in the case of legal relations concerning or related to a ship or aircraft.

A conflict rule, once it has identified the applicable law, exhausts its function and the foreign law then regulates the situation in question. Accordingly, the preliminary classification of the facts by the *lex fori* to determine the applicable conflict rule also becomes irrelevant; once the foreign legal system is identified, the latter classifies (or re-classifies) the facts to determine which norms in the foreign legal system are applicable to the problem at hand. Moreover, the reference to a foreign legal system does not take account of the conflict rules in that system, as a result of which there is no *renvoi* (A.30 dp), except in certain defined cases in which Italian law had to adapt to international convention, e g the Hague Convention on marriage and the Geneva Conventions on bills of exchange and cheques.

The conflict rules may find certain specific or general obstacles to their application. A specific obstacle which sometimes finds application is the requirement of reciprocity, i e that the applicable foreign legal system contains a conflict rule which applies Italian law in the reverse situation, e g A.5(2) cn which applies the law of the flag in relation to acts executed on board a ship or aeroplane, but only if the state of the flag applies Italian law to acts performed on Italian ships or aeroplanes whilst in the course of navigation. A general limit, on the other hand, to the operation of the conflict rules is the requirement of public order (*ordine pubblico*) (A.31 dp), which avoids a reference to foreign law where the latter is based upon principles which conflict with the fundamental principles of the *lex fori* in that subject, e g foreign laws which allow polygamy. The public order referred to in A.31 dp, sometimes called 'international public order', is to be kept distinct from the general concept of 'internal public order' which means that certain substantive norms cannot be contractually excluded from a given transaction.

G. THE ITALIAN CONFLICT RULES

(*i*) *Legal personality.* The commencement or end of the legal personality of natural persons is always determined by Italian law as there is no conflict rule on the subject (see ch 8, below). The formation of companies is subject to Italian law whenever a company is connected with the Italian State in any of the following ways: first, where it is formed in Italy notwithstanding that it may operate abroad (A.2509 cc); second, where it has its administrative seat or principal activities in Italy, even if it was formed abroad (A.2505 cc); and finally, where it has one or more secondary seats in Italy with a permanent representation, wherever it was formed (A.2506 cc). Therefore, only those companies which are not connected with Italy in any of the above ways, may have their foreign legal personality automatically recognised in Italy without the necessity of complying with local law.

(*ii*) *Status and capacity (A.17 dp).* According to A.17(1) dp, the status and capacity of persons are regulated by the law of the nationality.

Status, for the purposes of A.17(1), concerns personal status and not a status which depends upon a relationship with another subject, such as marital or filial status. Moreover, capacity in this context does not mean capacity in the sense of the general theory of law, that is, equivalent to legal personality, but the capacity to act or to execute legal acts (see ch 1, above). Article 17(2) dp qualifies the general principle in A.17(1) with respect to capacity by providing, in effect, that the more favourable of either the law of the nationality or Italian law is applicable unless the transaction in question concerns family relationships, devolution on death, donations, or the disposal of an immovable situated abroad.

(iii) The protection of incapable persons (A.21 dp). Apart from 'parental authority', which is specifically dealt with by A.20 dp, all other institutions for the protection of minors (guardianship, trusteeship, emancipation, and affiliation) and persons who have attained their majority but are totally or partially incapable are regulated by A.21 dp, which applies the law of the nationality of the incapable person.

(iv) Family relationships (A.17 dp)

(a) PROMISE TO MARRY. A promise to marry, under Italian law, falls into the category of family relationships and is therefore regulated by A.17 dp, which applies the law of the nationality of the parties. Where the parties are of different nationalities, the two laws must be harmonised and the solution, subject always to the overriding factor of public order, must satisfy both laws.

(b) THE SUBSTANTIVE VALIDITY OF A MARRIAGE. The capacity of the parties and all other substantive requirements for the celebration of a marriage are regulated by the law of the nationality of each spouse. In other words, when the spouses have different nationalities the marriage, to be valid, must comply with both laws. Article 15 cc repeats the same rule in relation to an Italian citizen who contracts marriage abroad, as a result of which the marriage must also comply with Italian law. However, the rule is modified by A.116 cc in relation to a foreigner contracting marriage in Italy, in which case the foreigner need only comply with the law of his nationality and those Italian provisions specified in A.116(2) cc. It must be remembered that in this area the general limitations imposed by the principle of public order may become important. It must be noted, further, that within the scope of the Hague Convention on marriage, the provisions of the Convention take precedence over the above norms, although the Convention, like Italian law, adopts the law of the nationality subject, however, to the application of the doctrine of *renvoi*, which is inapplicable in Italian conflicts law.

(c) THE FORMAL VALIDITY OF A MARRIAGE. The formal requirements for a valid marriage are regulated by the general conflict rule on form, namely, A.26(1) dp which, of the law of the place where the marriage is celebrated, the law of the nationality of the parties, if common, and the law which regulates the substantive validity of the marriage, applies that which is most favourable to the formal validity of the marriage.

(d) THE MARRIAGE RELATIONSHIP. The Italian conflict rules distinguish between personal and patrimonial aspects of the marriage relationship. Personal relationships between spouses are regulated by A.17 dp, that is, by the law of the the nationality of the spouses. However, A.18 dp proceeds to specifically deal with the situation where the spouses have different nationalities. It provides that the law of the last common nationality during the marriage is applicable or if there has never been a common nationality during the marriage then the law of the husband's nationality at the date of the celebration of the marriage (although the latter rule has been varied in those cases affected by the Hague Convention of 1905). Therefore, separation, which modifies the personal relationship between spouses, is regulated by either A.17, if the spouses' nationalities are the same, or by A.18, if their nationalities are different. However, in the case of divorce the matter is surrounded by some doubt. Prior to the law of 1 December 1970 n.898, which introduced divorce into Italian law, the negation of divorce was based upon the principle of public order as a result of which the Italian courts never pronounced a divorce, not even between foreigners. Since 1970, the question of the conflict rule which is applicable to divorce has not been specifically resolved. The question is whether divorce is regulated by A.17 only or by both Artt.17 and 18. The result would be the same in either case if both spouses have the same nationality at the date of the divorce, but in every other case the results would be different. The general approach is to apply A.17 only with the result that divorce is regulated by the common nationality of the parties; if the nationalities of the parties are different, then a divorce can only be pronounced if it is permitted by both laws. Finally, it must be noted that all procedural aspects concerning the enforcement of any rights or obligations are regulated by A.27 dp, which is the general conflict rule concerning procedure and which provides that all proceedings are regulated by the *lex fori*. Therefore, only those proceedings and remedies permitted by Italian law may be initiated.

The patrimonial aspects of the marriage relationship are regulated by A.19 dp, which applies the law of the husband's nationality at the date of the celebration of the marriage. Where, however, there has been an express agreement as to the property regime applicable to the marriage and that agreement was entered into after both the marriage and a change in nationality resulting in a common nationality between the spouses, the common nationality regulates the agreement. It may be noted that the latter rule differs from the position taken by the Hague Convention. Article 19 only deals with the substantive situation; the capacity to enter into the agreement is regulated by A.17(1) dp and the form of the agreement by A.26(1) dp.

(e) THE RELATIONSHIP BETWEEN PARENT AND CHILD. Everything pertinent to establishing the relationship between parent and child comes within A.17 dp, which deals with family relationships generally. Therefore, the law of the nationality of the persons whose relationship is in question is applicable. If the nationalities are different, then the solution must comply with both laws, although this aspect is not entirely settled. Some authors maintain that in such a situation only selective parts of either law are applicable so that the law of the child's nationality is only relevant so far as the child's status is concerned and the law of the parent's nationality is only relevant so far as the status of the latter is concerned. This approach could lead to conflicts, although it is said that this may be resolved by the application of a single law: that designated by A.20(1) dp which can be applied by analogy. Once a relationship is established, it is regulated by the law designated by A.20(1) dp. This provision states that the relationship of a child with both parents is regulated by the law of the father's nationality, but if maternity alone has been established or a child has only been legitimated by the mother, then the law of the mother's nationality regulates the relationship. Similarly, the establishment of a parent-child relationship by adoption is regulated by A.17 dp, whose application is subject to the same doubts as those just described for filiation, but once the adoption has been granted it is regulated by the law designated in A.20(2) dp, viz, the nationality of the adopting parent at the date of the adoption.

(v) *Devolution on death (A.23 dp).* Devolution on death is regulated by the law of the nationality of the deceased at the date of his death irrespective of the location or nature of the assets. In the case of testate succession, testamentary capacity and the formal validity of wills are regulated by Artt.17(1) dp and 26(1) dp respectively. It follows that capacity is not invariably regulated by the law of the deceased's nationality at the date of his death, and that a will is formally valid if it complies with the law of the place where it is made, the law of the nationality of the deceased at the date of the will, or the law of the deceased's nationality at the date of his death. It must also be noted that the validity of certain testamentary dispositions, the publicity of the homologation of wills, the transmission or extinguishment of rights over property, and matters relating to the possession and division of property are regulated by the *lex rei sitae*, as all of these matters concern real rights and their validity vis-à-vis third parties rather than the law of succession.

(vi) Donations (A.24 dp). Donations, or gifts inter vivos, are regulated by the law of the nationality of the donor as at the date of the donation. Again, the capacity to donate and the necessary form are regulated by Artt.17 dp and 26(1) dp respectively.

(vii) Possession and Real Rights (A.22 dp). Article 22 dp provides that possession, ownership, and other real rights over moveables or immoveables are regulated by the *lex situs*. However, the classification of rights as real rights depends upon the *lex fori*. It follows that neither rights classified as obligations, which are regulated by A.25 dp, nor privileges (liens and priorities) which are considered by Italian law as procedural matters regulated by A.27 dp, come within the scope of A.22 dp. Moreover, the capacity of the parties, the form of the transaction, and its registration are regulated by Artt.17 dp, 26(1) dp and 26(2) dp respectively.

(viii) Obligations. Article 25 dp, which deals with obligations, makes a distinction between 'obligations arising out of contract' (A.25(1) dp) and 'non-contractual obligations' (A.25(2) dp). Article 25(1) provides that all contractual obligations, except donations which are dealt with by A.24 dp, are regulated as follows: first, by the law designated by the parties; second, in the absence of such designation, by the law of the nationality if it is the same for both parties; or, finally, by the law of the place where the contract was concluded. Article 25(1) dp regulates the requisites (except for capacity which depends upon A.17 dp and form which depends on A.26(1) dp), effects and interpretation of a contract.

Non-contractual obligations, which not only include tortious but also other extra-contractual obligations, are generally regulated by A.25(2) dp, which applies the law of the place where the facts that have given rise to the obligation have occurred. The majority of the doctrine takes the view that this means the place where the cause occurred, whilst others maintain that it is the place in which the damaging event, or effect, occurred.

(ix) Formalities. As already noted several times, the formal validity of a transaction is regulated by the law designated in A.26(1) dp, that is, the law most favourable to formal validity amongst the following: the law of the place where the act was carried out (*locus regit actum*), the law designated by the conflict rule which regulates the substance of the transaction, and the law of the nationality of the author or parties to the transaction provided that it is common to all of the parties in the case of a bilateral or plurilateral transaction. Thus a transaction is formally valid if it is valid according to any one of the laws referred to by A.26(1) dp.

(x) Procedure. Article 27 dp provides that competence and procedure

are to be regulated by the law of the place in which the proceedings take place. Therefore all proceedings in Italy are exclusively regulated by Italian law, as a result of which the courts may only grant remedies of the types and upon the conditions stipulated by Italian law. For example, there cannot be the bankruptcy of any person who is not an entrepreneur conducting a commercial activity even though the bankruptcy of that person would be allowed by the law of the nationality of either the debtor or creditor; a foreign bill of exchange may only be self-executing in Italy if it contains the essential requisites of both Italian law and the law of the place in which it was issued to give it that effect; foreign judgments which have been recognised in Italy also give rise to judicial mortgages (*l'ipoteca giudiziale*), even if such institution is unknown to the original jurisdiction.

The temporal extent of the law

A legislative norm becomes effective after both publication in the official gazette and the lapse of a certain period of time from the date of publication known as the *vacatio legis*, which is normally of 15 days' duration. This period of *vacatio* is designed to enable those to whom the law is addressed to acquaint themselves with it, after which the law becomes binding and the ignorance of its existence can be no excuse. On the other hand, a law ceases to be effective by its express repeal, by its implied repeal through incompatibility with subsequent legislation, by its repeal through a popular referendum (A.75 C; see ch 5, below), by expiration of time where the legislation was to have a limited life only, or upon a decision of the Constitutional Court declaring it unconstitutional. Moreover, legislation cannot be retrospective (A.11 dp), although there are certain exceptions to this principle: legislation expressly made so, criminal laws favourable to an accused or convicted person (A.2 cp), interpretative norms, and legislation which concerns public order and protects the fundamental interests of the State. Generally speaking, only legislation favourable to its addressees may have retrospective effect.

Part II
Public law

Chapter 4

The Italian State and foreign relations law

The Italian Republic

The Italian Republic is a unitary state divided into various decentralised districts, the most important being the regions which have a limited legislative, administrative, and financial autonomy. Without entering into the difficulties of defining a 'State', doctrine identifies its three constituent elements as follows: population, territory, and an organisational element which is variously defined but, broadly, may be said to be the legal structure. Part of the doctrine considers this third element to be 'sovereignty', but the majority of the doctrine more properly considers sovereignty a characteristic rather than an element of the State.

Population

Although the population of a state may be said to comprise all individuals subject to its rule, viz, all citizens, aliens, and stateless persons within its territory, it more generally means all individuals connected to the state by citizenship. Citizenship may be based on one or both of two basic criteria: first, *jus sanguinis* which means that citizenship is dependent upon the citizenship of the father or, in the case of an illegitimate child, that of the mother, at the date of the child's birth; and second, *jus soli* which means that citizenship depends upon the place of birth. Because different states adopt different criteria, this often gives rise to dual citizenship, e g the child of an Italian immigrant born in Australia is an Italian citizen so far as Italian law is concerned and an Australian citizen so far as Australian law is concerned. The dual citizenship often resolves itself when the subject is called upon to exercise certain civic or political rights of a given country, because most legal systems connect the loss of citizenship with the exercise of the civic or political rights of another country. Italian citizenship is basically regulated by the law of 13 June 1912 n.555 which embodies three basic principles: the acquisition of citizenship by *jus sanguinis*; the loss of citizenship upon the acquisition of a foreign civil status; and, subject to certain exceptions, a single citizenship for the family unit.

Italian citizenship may be acquired in five different ways. First, by *jus sanguinis*. Second, by *jus soli* limited to those cases where a person born on Italian territory is of unknown or stateless parents, or of parents belonging to a state which does not grant citizenship by *jus sanguinis*. Third, by naturalisation, which may normally be granted in the following cases: service to the State for at least three years; residence in Italy for at least five years; residence in Italy for at least two years and either notable service to the State or marriage to an Italian citizen; or residence of six months in the case of persons otherwise entitled to citizenship but who have failed to apply within the prescribed time. Citizenship by naturalisation may be exceptionally conceded by the government in the absence of any of these requisites. Fourth, by election, in the following cases: foreigners who, in certain circumstances, have had their filiation to an Italian citizen acknowledged; foreigners either born in Italy or born of foreign parents who were resident in Italy for more than ten years as at the date of their birth; and, in certain circumstances, descendants of Italian citizens by birth. Finally, by *communicatio* where a foreign woman marries an Italian man. Similarly, non-emancipated minors of a person who acquires or re-acquires Italian citizenship normally become Italian citizens as well. Although the 1912 legislation does not specifically deal with cases of legitimation, affiliation, and adoption, some of these have been brought within the legislation by extensive interpretation. Moreover, the law of 5 June 1967 n.431, which introduced 'special adoptions' into Italian law, specifically provides that a minor of foreign nationality adopted by Italian parents acquires Italian citizenship as of right.

Italian citizenship may be lost as follows: first, by the voluntary acquisition of a foreign citizenship and residence; second, by accepting the employment or military service of a foreign state and its continuance notwithstanding intimation by the Italian government that such employment or service should be abandoned within a given time; third, by choice, that is, where an Italian citizen with dual citizenship opts for the foreign one; finally, where Italian territory is transferred to a foreign state. It ought be noted that as a result of the recent changes in family law, introduced by the law of 19 May 1975 n.151, an Italian woman retains her Italian nationality, unless expressly renounced, where either she marries a foreigner or her husband changes nationality (A.143 *ter* cc). The 1975 legislation has also provided for the re-acquisition of Italian citizenship where it was lost in such cases prior to 1975.

A former citizen reacquires citizenship as follows: first, by rendering military service or accepting public employment in Italy; second, by renouncing foreign citizenship, foreign employment, or foreign military service and resuming residence in Italy; and third, by residing in Italy for two years where the loss of citizenship was the result of the acquisition of a foreign nationality.

Italy is also party to certain international treaties which affect citizenship. Those of a general nature include the 1948 Universal Declaration of Human Rights, and the 1966 Covenant on Civil and Political Rights (both of which proclaim citizenship as a right of every person and child), the 1954 Convention on the Status of Stateless Persons (which facilitates the naturalisation of stateless persons resident in the contracting states) and the 1967 European Convention on the Adoption of Minors (which facilitates the acquisition of citizenship by foreign minors adopted by citizens of the contracting states). More specific, but of limited practical application, are the rules relating to the acquisition of citizenship annexed to the 1961 and 1963 Vienna Conventions on diplomatic and consular relations respectively (both prohibit contracting states from automatically attributing their citizenship to members of foreign diplomatic or consular missions). The only other significant multilateral treaty to which Italy is party is the 1963 European Convention relating to the reduction of plural citizenship, although Italian law already generally coincided with its provisions. Italy is party to a number of bilateral treaties seeking to rationalise the problems arising from dual citizenship.

The national territory

The spatial or material element of the State consists of its *territory*, which comprises three elements. The first two, the *terrafirma* and the territorial sea, are subject to the absolute sovereignty of the State. The law of 24 August 1974 n.359, in accordance with customary international law, modified A.2 cn by extending the territorial sea from its previous six-mile to the present 12-mile limit. With regard to the delineation of the territorial sea, Italy has adopted, with the dPR 26 April 1977 n.816, the straight baseline method. However, the decree of 1977 is of doubtful validity both on the domestic and international plane: domestically, because notwithstanding that it is an administrative measure only it has purported to repeal a legislative provision (viz, A.2 cn which utilised the low-water mark to delimit the territorial sea) and, internationally, because it has resulted in the closure of, inter alia, the entire Gulf of Taranto which is a true and proper bay in the sense of A.7 of the 1958 Geneva Convention on the territorial sea.

The state has the same powers over the territorial sea as it has in relation to the *terrafirma*, subject to two limits. First, the right of the innocent passage by foreign vessels, and second, a limited criminal jurisdiction over foreign ships. Italian case law, in accordance with generally observed international practice, draws a distinction between facts which are purely internal to the affairs of the ship, and facts which have an external repercussion or, in other words, affect the normal course of life in the territorial community. This distinction is also applied to ships in port, even if in such cases it is more difficult to find crimes which have no external repercussions, e g disciplinary infractions by crew members. There are several Italian decisions on the point, e g that of the Naples Tribunal of 7 February 1974 which denied jurisdiction as to the crime of mere possession of drugs on board a foreign ship in an Italian port.

The exploitation of resources on the continental shelf is regulated by the 1958 Geneva Convention on the continental shelf, which defines the shelf as

'the seabed and subsoil of the submarine areas adjacent to the coast outside the area of the territorial sea, to a depth of 200 metres or, beyond that limit, to where the depth of the superjacent waters admits of the exploitation of the natural resources of the said areas.'

Italy faces the problem of the division of a common continental shelf with other states, a problem to which the Geneva Convention applies the criterion of equidistance, which, however, can be varied by agreement as was the case in, for example, the agreements between Italy and Yugoslavia of 8 January 1968 and Italy and Tunisia of 20 August 1971.

In addition to the continental shelf, there has been the further cumulation of rights over marine resources in the so-called 'exclusive economic zone'. These rights, laid down in the 1982 UN Convention on the Law of the Sea, have been given legislative effect by Italy. The economic zone may extend up to 200 nautical miles from the base line of the territorial sea and gives the coastal state exclusive control over all biological and mineral resources, whether on or in the seabed or in the waters, including fishing. Within this zone, other states continue to have the freedom of sea and air navigation and the right to lay submarine pipelines and cables.

State sovereignty extends to airspace to the extent that the state has a concrete interest. Foremost, it involves the right to regulate flight in the airspace above the *terrafirma* and the territorial sea, although this has become less important after the introduction of high velocity aircraft and the creation of 'identification zones' extending hundreds of miles in the airspace above the high seas surrounding the coastlines. In the case of the upper atmosphere there is the complete freedom of flight, and state jurisdiction is limited to projectiles belonging to the launching state. The cosmos has been the object of various multilateral treaties promoted by the United Nations including that of 27 January 1967, which has been ratified by Italy, relating to the exploration and use of outer space, the moon, and other celestial bodies. Finally, the territory of a state includes its fluctuating or floating territory, in particular merchant ships whilst on the high seas, as well as aircraft whilst in flight, unless they are in the territory of another state. Military ships and aircraft, wherever situated, are always considered part of the 'national territory' although this theory has become so tenuous that even warships and military aircraft are no longer considered to be 'fragments of national territory'.

Territorial sovereignty and its erosion by treaty

Territorial sovereignty, according to international law, means that each state has the right to govern independently its territorial community, that is, the individuals and property within its territory. Exceptionally, international law imposes certain limits as to the treatment of foreigners and their property, foreign states, and international organisations whenever these are present or operative within state territory. Moreover, there are numerous treaties or conventions with which the state assumes obligations in relation to the treatment of its own subjects and thereby limits its own territorial sovereignty, e g in the human rights area in which, apart from the European Convention for the Protection of Human Rights and Fundamental Freedoms, Italy has ratified, with certain reservations, the 1966 UN covenants relating to economic, social and cultural rights, and civil and political rights (see *l* 25 October 1977 n.881). However, in contrast to the European Convention on Human Rights, these two covenants do not establish effective international controls. Other collective agreements for the protection of human rights to which Italy is party include the 1951 Convention and 1967 Protocol on Refugees (see *l* 24 July 1954 n.722 and *l* 14 February 1970 n.95 respectively), the 1952 Convention on the Political Rights of Women (see *l* 24 April 1967 n.326), the 1954 Convention on Stateless Persons (see *l* 1 February 1962 n.306), the 1965 Convention on the Elimination of All Forms of Racial Discrimination (see *l* 13 October 1975 n.654), and the European Social Charter of 1961 (see *l* 3 July 1965 n.929). It is apparent that the broad domestic jurisdiction recognised by customary international law is becoming more restricted as a result of various international conventions and treaties. This progressive erosion of the customary position is evident not only in the human rights area but also in the case of economic relations.

The treatment of foreigners

The position of a foreigner in Italy is primarily regulated by those constitutional norms on fundamental rights expressly applicable to citizens and foreigners, viz, those constitutional norms which either refer to 'all persons' as distinct from 'citizens' or are, at least, expressed in an impersonal form. Moreover, two decisions of the Constitutional

Court (nos. 120/1967 and 104/1969) have held that notwithstanding that the principle of equality contained in A.3 C refers to 'citizens', it is also applicable to foreigners where the protection of inviolable human rights are involved as such an approach would create a state of affairs consistent with the international legal order. None of this, however, prevents the differential treatment of foreigners where justified through the existence of particular conditions.

In particular, the position of foreigners in Italy is dealt with by A.10 C and Artt.16ff dp and may be summarised as follows. First, foreigners, like residents, are subject to the local criminal and police laws and enjoy the same civil rights as citizens irrespective of reciprocal treatment by the foreigners' state (A.16 dp and A.10 C). Second, foreigners may remain in Italy by merely fulfilling their obligation of making a 'visitor's declaration' to the police authorities, although the right of movement and sojourn may be restricted. Third, foreigners may be refused entry when they are unable to provide 'personal details' or are 'without means', and they may be required to leave the national territory if convicted of a crime or for reasons of public order, although never for political reasons. In regard to the admission or expulsion of foreigners the state has, under customary international law, full territorial sovereignty which enables it to freely admit or expel foreigners from its territory, subject only to international treaty, e g the free movement of persons within the European Community. If there is a violation of international law, a foreigner is often better protected by having recourse to the local courts rather than relying upon his own state through diplomatic protection, which is often conditioned by political motives based on international relations. This is particularly so where the local courts, as in Italy, strictly and impartially apply the law and operate in a climate in which the observance of international law is guaranteed. Fourth, a foreigner who is 'impeded in his own country from the effective exercise of the democratic liberties guaranteed by the Italian Constitution has the right of political asylum in Italy' (A.10(3) C). Fifth, a foreigner, like a citizen, cannot be extradited for political crimes (Artt.10 C and 26 C), except genocide (C*l* 21 June 1967 n. 1). Finally, a stateless person is obliged to give military service (A.14 of *l* 13 June 1912 n.555) and is subject to Italian law in all cases in which, according to private international law, the law of the nationality is applicable.

The treatment of diplomatic agents: diplomatic and consular relations

Certain limits to the power of government over the national territory arise from customary international law relating to diplomatic agents or, more specifically, from so-called diplomatic immunities. The subject is regulated by various international treaties, to which Italy is a party, as well as domestic law including first, the law of 9 August 1967 n.804 which authorised the Head of State to ratify the 1961 Vienna Convention on Diplomatic Relations and the 1963 Vienna Convention on Consular Relations together with their respective Protocols, as well as providing for their total incorporation into domestic law, and second, the law of 13 July 1966 n.891 which delegated to the government the task of reorganising the Department of Foreign Affairs. This led to the dPR 5 January 1967 n.18 which introduced a new and organic discipline of both the central institutions of the Italian diplomatic service and its external organisation (embassies, consulates, permanent representations at international organisations, and special missions).

Diplomatic status gives rise to a particular treatment comprised of four aspects. First, the diplomatic immunities in a strict sense, the non-treaty matters enjoyed by diplomatic agents personally as distinct from the immunities conferred by diplomatic law upon the diplomatic mission as such, e g immunity from civil or criminal process, immunity from direct taxation, the inviolability of private residences, and customs duty exemptions. These immunities apply to official and private acts and extend to all diplomatic personnel and their families. Second, privileges enabling the performance of acts from which foreigners are generally excluded. Third, prerogatives which enable diplomatic agents to make requests, of a type that cannot be made by other persons, of the accrediting state. And finally, various facilitations and honours which are extended to diplomatic agents.

There has developed in the doctrine over recent decades a tendency towards a unitary concept of diplomatic-consular law. However, although consular agents have a similar basis and structure to diplomatic missions, they nonetheless have particular functions which justify a separate and detailed normative regulation. Hence the expression 'diplomatic-consular law'. On the plane of international law, moreover, the 1963 Vienna Convention has codified the norms regulating consular relations. This confirmed the continuing existence of the conceptual and technical distinction between consular and diplomatic relations. Consular relations presuppose a mutual trust and co-operation manifest in the concession by the receiving state of various internal law functions to consulates; functions that in the absence of a consulate would have had to be performed by the territorial state. To enable consular officials to carry out their functions with the necessary freedom and decorum, there exists a consular status which varies, depending upon the type of consular office established.

Consular law has undergone important normative developments in Italian domestic law. Two Italian legislative acts have operated this reform. The first is the dPR 5 January 1967 n.18, referred to above, which reorganised the entire foreign service. It regulates the relationships between diplomatic missions and consular offices. It entrusts the co-ordination and supervision of consular offices located in a given foreign state to the diplomatic mission located in that state. These co-ordinative and supervisory roles of a diplomatic mission do not affect those functions which specifically come within the competence of a consular office. Nonetheless the diplomatic mission becomes part of the Italian consular system not only because of its co-ordinative and supervisory functions, but also because it can itself exercise consular functions in three defined situations: where there are no consular offices; where it is specifically given consular functions by the Ministry of Foreign Affairs for the reason that the relevant consular office can no longer function; and where it is permanently given consular functions through the establishment of a consular section in the mission. The second piece of Italian domestic legislation on consular law is the dPR 5 January 1967 n.200 which contains the provisions on consular functions and powers. It is based upon, and further develops, the provisions of the first piece of legislation.

The recent reforms in consular law reflect not only the modern requirements of states and individuals but also aim at establishing and regulating international relations by emphasising reciprocal collaboration. Although the system of international relations created by consular agreements is analogous and closely connected with the system of diplomatic relations, it is nonetheless different to the latter because first, it is based on bilateral accords, second, it has a different content, third, it may be established where diplomatic relations have not yet been instituted or have been interrupted, and finally, it may not exist or cease to do so where diplomatic relations exist.

The consular conventions concluded after 1963 manifest an evolution in diplomatic-consular law in a double sense: whilst, on the one hand, they highlight the distinction between the two systems of international relations, on the other hand, they draw the two systems closer together under various aspects. In particular, diplomatic and consular law are drawing closer in that consular status is approaching diplomatic status. Although this increasing similarity in status is limited insofar as consular functionaries are personally concerned (where only the taxation exemptions of diplomatic agents is applicable), it is more complete in the case of consular offices as such.

Finally, it may be noted that the bilateral consular conventions confirm the duty of the local authorities to inform a consul, within a reasonable time, of the arrest or detention of co-nationals, irrespective of the prior consensus of the detainee. The conventions also confirm the power of a consul to visit co-nationals in gaol, again without the necessity of the prior consent of the interested party. The conventions, by eliminating the need for prior consensus in either case, exceed the Vienna Convention according to which consensus is generally required.

However, at the ratification of the Vienna Convention, the Italian government declared that it did not consider the right of a consular functionary to visit and assist detained co-nationals as being subject to renunciation by the detainee insofar as the right is part of general international law and that the Italian government would therefore act accordingly, subject only to reciprocity.

The treatment of foreign states

The principal problem in this area is whether it is possible to exercise civil jurisdiction over foreign states. Until World War I the universal theory was that of the absolute immunity of foreign states from civil process. It was the Italian and Belgian case law after the First World War that led to the theory of restricted or relative immunity which is the theory commonly accepted today. According to this theory, foreign states are exempt from civil jurisdiction in relation to the exercise of public state functions only and not as to acts of a private nature. This distinction, which reflects the same uncertainties as those inherent in the distinction between public and private law, is not always easy to apply and leaves a certain margin for judicial discretion. In cases of doubt, Italian case law is inclined to immunity rather than subjection as the latter is considered to be a sort of exception to the former. This tendency widens rather than restricts the sphere of immunity.

An area in which the problem of state immunity frequently arises, and in which the distinction between public and private state functions is difficult, if not impossible, is that of labour disputes. These generally involve actions brought by local nationals employed by foreign delegations. The court must determine which aspects of the labour relationship are to be taken into account in order to qualify it as either public or private. Italian case law generally refers to the duties performed under the employment contract and regards the foreign state as immune if there is a participation by the employee in the exercise of 'sovereign functions' or, in any event, the 'public law activities' of the foreign state. By taking this approach, the Italian courts have given immunity a wide application, e g librarians (Cass Sez Un 25 November 1971 n.3441), secretaries, telephonists, accountants (Cass Sez Un 23 November 1974 n.3803), and auxiliary staff (Cass Sez Un 26 May 1979 n.3063). However, the above criterion for attracting local jurisdiction has been criticised and various others have been suggested. The criterion adopted by the European Convention on State Immunity, not as yet ratified by Italy, is a combination of the nationality of the employee and the place of employment. Some reference to the European Convention was made by Cassation in its decision Sez Un 21 October 1977 n.4502 which concerned the immunity of international organisations. Notwithstanding that the judgment regarded the European Convention, although not ratified by Italy, as a 'document recognising the evolution of customary international law', and acknowledged the difficulty of the dichotomy between public and private acts, it applied the usual criterion.

The same theory of restrictive immunity is applicable to execution against property belonging to a foreign state, with the result that it is only admissible against property not destined for public functions. Italy has enacted special legislation on the point: DL 30 August 1925 n.1629 which became the law of 15 July 1926 n.1263 according to which the prior authorisation of the Minister of Justice is in every event necessary, although this requirement applies to states which give reciprocal treatment only. The legislation used to provide that there was no judicial or administrative appeal against a ministerial decree refusing authorisation, but this was declared unconstitutional by the Constitutional Court in judgment no. 135/1963.

The treatment of International Organisations and their functionaries

The final limit to Italian territorial sovereignty arises from the presence of certain international organisations within its national territory, e g FAO and the institutions of the European Communities. Although there is no customary international law which requires states to concede any particular immunities, least of all diplomatic immunity, to the functionaries of such organisations, the matter is covered by convention. The Treaty on the FAO headquarters, for instance, makes the distinction between a total immunity from criminal and civil proceedings in the case of the Director-General and the principal resident representatives, who have the status of ambassadors (Artt.11 and 13 of the Treaty), and a limited jurisdictional immunity for acts performed in the exercise of official functions in the case of certain other state representatives and international functionaries defined in Articles 12, 13 and 14 of the Treaty. The immunities of the functionaries of the European Communities, to take another example, are contained in the Protocols on immunities and privileges annexed to each Treaty and are similar to the immunities enjoyed by the functionaries of the United Nations.

The host state of an international functionary of foreign nationality is bound to give him the same protection as that required by customary international law in the case of any other foreigner. The obligation of the host state is vis-à-vis the state of the functionary's nationality and its violation therefore gives rise to diplomatic protection. Whether the same obligation also exists vis-à-vis the organisation, which could then also exercise diplomatic protection, is not clear. It appears that the diplomatic protection of international organisations is limited to the damages caused to an official function and not to the individual as such, unlike diplomatic protection proper.

International organisations are subject to the same limits as foreign states, immune from the civil jurisdiction of the territorial state. The Italian courts have several times, within the context of employment disputes, declared the immunity of international organisations, and the comments made above with respect to the immunity of states are equally applicable here. Some of the most important international organisations expressly regulate their employment relationships and define the court which is competent to resolve any such disputes, e g in the case of the European Communities all labour disputes come within the competence of the Community Court.

International subjects with powers to limit territorial sovereignty

Apart from substantive rules, treaties may contain procedural provisions which enable the creation of norms or decisions which are binding on member states whose sovereignty is thereby limited by reason of their adhesion to the treaty. The most important example of such voluntary limitation of sovereignty in the case of Italy is that in favour of certain international organisations, viz, the European Communities.

A. THE EUROPEAN COMMUNITIES

Amongst all the international organisations, the three European Communities (EEC, CECA, & Euratom) have the strongest decisional powers vis-à-vis member states. Community measures go beyond mere recommendations and also include binding decisions.

The three Communities were created at different times: CECA in 1951 and the EEC and Euratom in 1957. Although they are separate and distinct, they operate through common organs, the most important of which are the Council and the Commission. CECA is a sectional organisation in that it is directed to achieving a common market (e g by abolishing custom barriers, unifying prices and rationalising production) in the coal and steel industries. The EEC, on the other hand, is concerned with the totality of the socio-economic life of member states. It provides for the free circulation of goods, persons (including labour), services, and capital. Apart from these four fundamental freedoms, the Treaty of Rome provides for free competition (Artt.85ff which contain the general principles of Community anti-trust law), the achievement of a common transport policy, the regulation of assistance and incentives to enterprises, the regulation of social welfare, and other specific aims. Also of importance are the powers attributed to Community organs to facilitate the movement towards uniform legislation amongst member states (Artt.100–102 EEC Treaty).

For these reasons the European Communities are often referred to as being supranational, and not merely international, organisations. This emphasises that the Communities, in contrast to other international organisations, have extensive decisional powers and occupy themselves with many relationships which are purely internal to individual member states thereby substituting the latter in the regulation of those relationships. The contrast with other international organisations is of a quantitative rather than a qualitative nature because the Communities, unlike many other international organisations, do not have decisional powers which are restricted to determinate and limited situations only.

The principal organs of the EEC are the Commission, the Council, the Assembly (or European Parliament) and the Court of Justice. The Commission consists of individuals, not states, appointed upon the consensus of all of the member states. The members of the Commission serve in their personal capacities and are not to receive instructions from their respective governments as they are to pursue the interests of the Community and not those of individual member states. Unlike the Commission, which generally has powers of initiative only, the Council is the effective decision-making organ and comprises the representatives, in the form of different ministers of state depending upon the agenda, of the member states. It is the organ which emanates Community legislation. Although it can decide by majority, an understanding, reached amongst the member states to overcome the crisis provoked by De Gaulle in the 1960s, binds them to making every attempt at reaching unanimous decisions. The European Council, which consists of the heads of state, the heads of government and the ministers for foreign affairs of the member states, has superimposed itself above the Council. The European Council deals with general Community problems and aims at achieving political co-operation. It is not a Community organ issuing formal Community measures but a diplomatic conference which is held three times a year to seek agreement amongst member states. Even if informal, its decisions condition the activities of the Commission and the Council and provide the framework within which those organs may operate. It is the decisions of the European Council that either encourage or arrest European integration. It should be noted, finally, that in the case of CECA the roles of the organs are reversed: the Commission is the decision-making organ and the Council is the consultative organ.

The Assembly (or European Parliament) which, since 1979, has been elected by universal suffrage, does not have any decision-making powers. Apart from its powers with respect to the budget and the right to pass motions of no confidence in the Commission thereby provoking the dismissal of the latter, its powers are limited to expressing opinions and putting questions to other Community organs. The lack of effective power in the Parliament, and the related concentration of power in the Council, are the most controversial issues on the question of European integration.

The European Court of Justice, finally, is more like an internal than an international tribunal because, unlike the latter, the exercise of its jurisdiction is not dependent upon the voluntary submission of the respondent. The Court consists of six judges who are appointed by common accord of the governments of the member states and hold office, on a staggered basis, for a term of six years with eligibility for reappointment. The jurisdiction of the Court, limiting the discussion to the EEC Treaty, apart from its arbitral function in disputes between member states where such disputes are voluntarily submitted to the Court, may be said to fall into three categories. First, jurisdiction over proceedings brought by either the Commission or any member state for violation of the Treaty by a member state. Second, jurisdiction over proceedings brought by a minister of state, the Council, the Commission or, in the case of decisions, by any interested party, against binding Community measures on the grounds of legitimacy available in French administrative proceedings, viz, lack of competence, infringement of an essential procedural requirement, infringement of the Treaty or of any rules of law relating to its application, and misuse of powers. Finally, the jurisdiction over so-called 'prejudicial questions' pursuant to A.177 of the EEC Treaty which provides that where a question relating to the interpretation of the Treaty or a question relating to the validity or interpretation of a Community measure comes before a national court, the court *may*, unless it is a court of last instance in which case it *must*, suspend the proceedings and seek an opinion from the European Court. The opinion has an immediate effect on the national proceedings and will be utilised in all other member states until the European Court is asked to change it in a subsequent case. The object of this unique jurisdiction is to ensure a uniform interpretation of Community law in the various member states.

The measures issued by Community organs may be either binding or non-binding and, especially the former, manifest the acceptance by member states of the authority of Community 'legislation'. Article 189 of the EEC Treaty provides for three types of binding measures, viz, regulations, decisions and directives, and two non-binding measures, viz, recommendations and opinions. Regulations, which are directly applicable in member states, are the most important and comprehensive of the Community measures and replace inconsistent national legislation. Decisions, unlike regulations, are not general and abstract but specific measures addressed to either a member state or an individual or enterprise operating within the Community. The distinction, which is difficult in practice, between general and specific measures is dependent upon the substance and not the form of the measure. Whilst regulations and decisions are binding in every detail, directives, on the other hand, are binding as to their purpose only so that member states remain free as to the form and means of their implementation. From the text of the Treaty, directives ought to limit themselves to the definition of general principles. Yet, in practice, the tendency is always towards more detailed directives which, in some instances, merely give member states a discretion as to the form (legislative or administrative) with which they are to be internally implemented. Although detailed directives are probably valid where the Community organ was also free to regulate the subject in the form of regulations or decisions, where, instead, the Community organ is limited to acting through directives then, in principle, a detailed directive ought be regarded as invalid. Nor, it appears, can it be argued that detailed directives are valid as a result of a newly established custom because it is doubtful that a custom can modify statutory norms. However, it can be argued that once a member state has internally given effect to a detailed directive, it has thereby renounced its right to select the form and means of its implementation.

The Community, moreover, has the power under various specific or general provisions to enter into international treaties which become binding on member states. The general treaty-making power of the EEC is subject in every case to a preliminary decision of the Court of Justice as to the compatibility of the proposed treaty with the EEC Treaty (A.228 of the EEC Treaty). The EEC has an exclusive power to enter into treaties whenever such treaty-making power is specifically contemplated by the Treaty. Since 1971, the European Court has consistently held that the Community also has an implied power to enter into treaties in relation to any subject in which it is competent to make internal Community legislation and that such external power becomes exclusive to the Community when the latter acts in a given subject either internally or externally. Needless to say, this approach has created many uncertainties which still remain unresolved.

B. THE COUNCIL OF EUROPE AND THE PROTECTION OF HUMAN RIGHTS

The Council of Europe, whose membership includes, inter alia, the present member states of the EEC, was one of the first international organisations directed to the protection of human rights. The Council was responsible for the European Convention for the Protection of Human Rights and Fundamental Freedoms, as well as various protocols which have increased the number of recognised rights. All of the members of the Council of Europe have adhered to the Convention (although not always in toto). The Italian ratification was authorised by the law of 4 August 1955 n.848. The first and most important part of the Convention (Artt. 1–18) contains the substantive provisions, that is, the list of rights and fundamental freedoms which every contracting state recognises in favour of all persons within its jurisdiction, whether citizens, aliens, or stateless persons. The second, or procedural part of the Convention (Artt. 19–56) establishes two organs, the Commission and the European Court of Human Rights which, together with the Committee of Ministers of the Council of Europe, are to guarantee, on an international plane, compliance with the Treaty.

The Commission, which comprises one member from each of the contracting states, is charged with the investigation and conciliation of complaints against a state brought by another state or directly by an individual or group of individuals for the violation of the Convention. However, direct recourse by individuals is only available if this type of jurisdiction has been accepted for either an unlimited or limited period by the particular state. Where a complaint cannot be entertained (e g, because the available internal recourses have not been exhausted or the complaint is anonymous or manifestly unfounded) the Commission nonetheless seeks to arrive at an amicable solution inspired by a respect for human rights. In any event, the only remedy which is available from the Commission is the conciliation of the parties. If this fails, the Commission must make a report to the Committee of Ministers of the Council of Europe, which comprises the foreign ministers, or their nominees, of each member state, after which the matter may proceed either before the Court or the Committee of Ministers.

The jurisdiction of the Court, composed of a number of judges equal to the number of members on the Council of Europe and selected from 'jurisconsults of recognised competence', may be invoked by the Committee of Ministers upon receiving a report from the Commission, the state which brought the complaint before the Commission, the state of the injured person's nationality, or the state accused of the violation, but in no case does the injured person have locus standi. Moreover, the jurisdiction of the Court is subject to its prior acceptance by the accused state. Where none of the states having the right to invoke the Court's jurisdiction have done so within a period of three months from the date of the Commission's report to the Committee of Ministers or where the Court is unable to act because the accused state has not accepted its jurisdiction, then the Committee of Ministers may decide, by a two-thirds majority of its members, whether there has been a violation of the Convention and prescribe a term within which the violation must be remedied. Italy first accepted the jurisdiction of the Court in 1973 for an initial term of two years, renewable for terms of three years.

C. THE ROMAN CATHOLIC CHURCH

(*i*) *The relationship between State and Church.* The Catholic Church has been regarded, almost from its inception, as a subject of international law equal in status to other states. For this reason relations between State and Catholic Church have always been regarded as appurtenant to international law whenever they have formed the object of an agreement. Modern relations between State and Catholic Church may be of two basic types. First, separatism, which is characteristic of the 'non-Confessional State'. In such a system the State is totally disinterested in the Church and considers religion as a private matter: the State limits itself to guaranteeing the freedom of religion and does not grant the Church any privilege vis-à-vis other religions or churches. Second, concordat, according to which State and Church come to an agreement in relation to those matters which are of mutual interest. The study of the latter type of relationship between State and Church falls within ecclesiastical law.

The present relationship between the Italian State and Catholic Church is of the concordat type. It dates to the Lateran Pacts made between Mussolini and Pope Pius XI on 11 February 1929. The Lateran Pacts are soon to be replaced by the new Concordat made between the State and Church on 18 February 1984, effective upon the exchange of ratification instruments (A.13), which is to take place six months from the date of execution of the Concordat subject, however, first, to the approval of the new Concordat by both Houses of Parliament and second, the settlement, by a joint State-Church Commission, of certain questions relating to State-Church financial relations and the recognition of ecclesiastical bodies.

(*ii*) *The 1929 Concordat and the evolution of State-Church relations.* The 1929 Pacts comprise three documents. First, the Treaty which resolved the question of the recognition and independence of the Vatican City, subject to the exclusive sovereignty of the Pontiff, and established the *Sacra Rota*, which has jurisdiction over the nullity of Italian marriages. Second, the Concordat which regulates State-Church relations. And finally, the Financial Convention which deals with issues arising out of the confiscation of the Church's temporal property in the nineteenth century. The Pacts had the effect of placing the Catholic Church in a position of privilege vis-à-vis other religions. The Pacts seriously compromised three matters. First, the equality between religious cults because the Treaty declared Catholicism to be the State religion (A.1 of the Treaty). Second, the freedom of thought because the State undertook not to employ, or to continue to employ, in any teaching or other position involving contact with the public, any priest who had abandoned his vows or had been censured by the Church (A.5

Concordat). And finally, State jurisdiction over the nullity of marriages that had been totally abdicated in favour of the Church and Canon law (A.34 Concordat).

Notwithstanding these defects, the concordat system survived the changed circumstances of the postwar period. The Republican Constitution of 1948, by expressly safeguarding the Lateran Pacts, confirmed the judgment of the Constitutional Fathers that the concordat system was compatible with the new political formula. Article 7 C declares, first, that the State and Catholic Church are, in their respective spheres, independent and sovereign; second, that relations between them are to be regulated by the Lateran Pacts; and third, that any modification in the Pacts accepted by both parties does not require the observance of the special procedure for constitutional revision.

The effect of the Pacts' incorporation into the Constitution has been the subject of much debate. According to some writers, A.7 C intended to elevate the basic principles of the Lateran Treaties to fundamental constitutional principles which both place a limit upon ordinary legislation and require the concurrence of the Holy See in any proposed legislative changes. However, the practical aspect of the debate centred on the problem of the conflict between the provisions in the Pacts and the Constitution. This conflict, which became apparent soon after the introduction of the Constitution, affected, on the one hand, the equality of religious cults as such and the freedom of religion (Artt. 8 and 19 C) and, on the other hand, the principle of 'confessional' jurisdictionalism characteristic of the Lateran Pacts, made at a time when both the State and Church found themselves in different circumstances.

Although the Council of State and the Court of Cassation had often held that the Pacts prevailed over the Constitution, the Constitutional Court has recently taken the opposite approach. It has repeatedly held that the binding principles arising out of either a bilateral agreement of the State, as in the case of the Concordat, or from obligations of a more properly international nature, such as the EEC Treaty, can never violate the fundamental principles of the Italian Constitutional system (see judgments 23 December 1965 n.98, 1 March 1971 nos. 30 & 31, 30 November 1971 n.190, and 27 December 1973 n.183). This is regarded as being particularly applicable to State-Church relations as A.7 C expressly acknowledges that the State and Church are mutually independent and sovereign so that A.7 cannot, even impliedly, be regarded as compromising the supreme principles of the constitutional system. Notwithstanding this, the Constitutional Court has never held any norm of the Concordat unconstitutional even though it has been asked to do so in several cases. Rather, when the Constitutional Court was faced with the conflict between the marriage provision of the Concordat and the new civil institution of dissolution of marriage, it avoided the real problem by interpreting A.34 of the Concordat, in one of its most superficial judgments, to mean that it did not preclude the introduction of the dissolution of Concordat marriages within the civil system.

Nonetheless, the conflict between the Pacts and the Constitution led to the need to revise the former to make them consistent with the new constitutional system and its religious freedoms. This need to revise the Pacts was felt as far back as 1967 when parliament passed a motion calling upon the government to bring to the attention of the Holy See the need for a 'bilateral revision of certain norms of the Concordat' having regard to the 'evolution of the times' and the 'developments in the democratic life' of the nation. Soon after the government appointed a Commission with which the Holy See signified its willingness to make contact. This Commission's report in 1969 recommending the revision of the Concordat was to form the basis for all future parliamentary debates on the issue. Some time later the Vatican established a corresponding Committee, but negotiations between the two Committees were fraught with many difficulties, viz, the approach of the Constitutional Court to the concordat marriage and its interpretation of A.34 of the Concordat, the legislative reforms relating to marriage and family law, including the introduction of divorce and its application to the concordat marriage, and the introduction of the new abortion law. In the light of this background and several abortive drafts of a new Concordat it appeared that a definitive solution was far from realisation. However, the State and Church finally reached agreement on a new Concordat whose terms were not publicised until after its execution by the parties on 18 February 1984.

The general opinion, whether well-founded or not, on the eve of the new Concordat was that the 1929 Concordat could no longer survive, notwithstanding the definite and positive judgment in its favour by the Constitutional Fathers, because it contained many renunciations of State sovereignty, several violations of the principle of equality between citizens, and various other iniquities. One current of opinion had it that the Concordat was too paternalistic and thus the need for a new accord that would expunge all its defects. A more radical current believed that the time had come to put an end to concordat politics. However, although it was for some time doubtful, recent events have shown that the direction of State-Church relations in Italy appears to be firmly set on the concordat path.

(iii) The privileges of the Catholic Church under the 1929 Pacts. The 1929 Pacts placed the Catholic Church in a position of privilege in various spheres. First, in the matrimonial field, through its exclusive jurisdiction in relation to the nullity and dissolution of religious marriages which, moreover, by virtue of the Pacts, are to have the same effects as a civil marriage. Second, in the criminal law, through the

crimes defined by Artt. 402–404 cp (public contempt of the State religion and the public offence of religion through the contempt of persons or things) which place the Church in a privileged position vis-à-vis other religions. This particular disparity of treatment has been upheld by the Constitutional Court (see judgment nos. 125/1957 and 39/1965) on the basis that the Catholic religion is the religion of nearly the entire Italian population and therefore these criminal norms protect the religious sentiment of the majority of citizens. Third, in Italian politics, by the right of intervention through various means and organisations, e g the *Azione Cattolica*. Fourth, in scholastic matters, through A.26 of the Concordat which affirms that Catholic doctrine forms the basis and fulfilment of all Italian public education. This led, in primary schools, to its synthesis with all other subjects so that it cannot be avoided by non-Catholics; in secondary schools, to the teaching of catechism on the same basis as any other subject; and in the Catholic university, to the requirement of the antimodernistic oath on the part of all lecturers, who can only be appointed with the consensus of the Holy See (A.38 Concordat). Finally, in the patrimonial sphere, in which the Church was granted various privileges by the Concordat, especially of a taxation nature. All of these privileges conflict with the various Constitutional provisions which guarantee equality and the freedom of religion, expression, thought, and instruction. In addition, there has been the question of the constitutionality of A.5 of the Concordat (see p 118, above) which, having regard to the Constitutional case law, would appear to be unconstitutional for violation of Artt. 2 and 51 C, which guarantee personal fulfilment and access to public offices respectively.

(iv) The equality between religions. The same problems of compatibility with the Constitution arise in the case of equal freedom before the law of all religious confessions (A.8(1) C). However, from the combined effect of Artt. 3, 8 and 19 C, it appears that although the Constitution provides for a perfect and total equality between individuals with respect to religious belief and its extrinsic manifestation, whether individually or collectively, it limits the equality between various religious confessions as such to their freedom only (i e they are 'equally free before the law', not 'equal before the law'). In fact, the Catholic Church enjoys a sovereign position, as already described, whilst the non-Catholic religions are subject to the limitations arising out of A.8 C, viz, first, their organisation and external activities must not conflict with the Italian legal system (A.8(2) C), and second, their relationships with the State are to be regulated by legislation based upon 'understandings' reached between each religious cult and the State (A.8(3) C). These 'understandings', which take the form of ordinary legislation, will have a different status than the accords

between the State and Catholic Church as the latter cannot be unilaterally modified by the State except under certain circumstances. A further common limit upon all religions, but of practical application to non-Catholic confessions only, is the requirement that their rites conform to good custom (A.19 C).

Whilst the new Concordat was being negotiated, the State also commenced negotiations on the 'understandings' contemplated by A.8(3) C with the non-Catholic confessions. Some of the 'understandings' have already been concluded and the Government approved the first of these 'understandings', namely, that reached with the Waldensian and Methodist Church, on the day prior to the execution of the 1984 Concordat. It follows that, upon approval of the various 'understandings' the unitary regulation of the non-Catholic confessions dating from 1929–30 will become defunct.

(v) The 1984 Concordat and State-Church relations. The new Concordat is much shorter than its 1929 counterpart, which indicates a simplification of State-Church relations. It consists of 14 articles and an 'additional protocol' which contains more specific provisions with respect to the subject matter of certain articles and postpones defined matters to 'subsequent understandings'. Although the Concordat is prefaced by the statement that it is a consensual modification of the Lateran Concordat, it is, in reality, a totally new and comprehensive Concordat. It seeks to establish a situation in State-Church relations which is compatible, on the one hand, with the Constitution and the fundamental principles of the Italian legal system and, on the other hand, with the significant changes that have come about in civil society since the 1929 Concordat. Therefore, the new Concordat, together with all of the 'understandings' that will eventually be concluded with the various non-Catholic religions, is to give full effect to the Constitutional provisions concerning religion. The Concordat basically seeks to eliminate the privileges previously accorded to the Church as well as every vestige of jurisdictionalism by either the State or Church in each others affairs. It therefore has, at least formally, brought about significant changes; formally, because, in substance, most of the changes it contained had already come about through practice, the decisions of the Constitutional Court, or the introduction of recent legislative reforms. But notwithstanding that the State had little to gain in practice from entering into a new Concordat, it was concluded primarily in recognition of the social role played by the Catholic Church, whose membership comprises the majority of the Italian population.

Some of the most significant changes contained in the new Concordat are as follows. First, the declaration that the State and Church are mutually independent and sovereign, including the express repeal of the provision in the 1929 Concordat that made Catholicism the sole religion of the Italian State. Second, the renunciation by the State of every residue of jurisdictionalism, that is, of any pretence of political or administrative control over internal Church matters so that the Church regains full freedom of internal government. The State no longer requires a reduction in the number of dioceses to make them coincide with the provinces, the advance notification of the nomination of bishops so as to enable objections of a political nature, or the swearing in of new bishops in the presence of the President. Third, the introduction of a new regime concerning the status of clerics, including the repeal of A.5 of the previous Concordat (see p 118, above) that restricted State employment of clerics who had either renounced their vows or had been censured by the Church. Moreover, the general exemption of clerics from military service and other civic duties, such as jury service, are repealed as, too, the prohibitions in A.43 of the 1929 Concordat which prevented clerics from joining or participating in political parties and prevented the pressure group, *Azione Cattolica*, from carrying out its activities within the framework of any political party. Fourth, the renunciation by the Church of every vestige of its 'secular arm' or civil authority in various fields such as education, marriage, and the regulation of non-religious Church activities. Fifth, the establishment of a new regime as to both the recognition of Church bodies and State-Church financial relations. The definition of the new regime in these matters has been delegated to a joint State-Church Commission established at the execution of the new Concordat. The joint Commission is, in particular, required to establish the provisions and procedures concerning State recognition of ecclesiastical bodies which had until now been almost automatically recognised, review State financial obligations and devise a modern system of State financial assistance for Church bodies, and determine a new regulation of ecclesiastical bodies whose non-religious activities are to become subject to the ordinary taxation system. Sixth, the acknowledgement by the Church of the existence of certain restrictions upon the civil recognition of religious marriages and judgments of Church tribunals declaring the nullity of marriage. Therefore, the civil registration of a religious marriage may in future take place only where the civil law requisites concerning capacity and the absence of any impediments to the celebration of the marriage have been satisfied. Similarly, a judgment of a Church tribunal declaring a marriage null is now subject to the same procedure as for the recognition of foreign judgments so that it is no longer automatically recognised as was the case under the old Concordat. Seventh, the acceptance by the Church that religious instruction in schools may only be imparted to persons expressly requesting it. There is no longer a different regime applicable to primary and secondary schools and in both cases a student may at the beginning of each year elect, without any consequent discrimination, whether or not to receive religious instruction.

The reception of international law into municipal law

A. ORDINARY AND SPECIAL RECEPTION PROCEDURES

The basic distinction between the means with which international law is nationalised or introduced into the municipal system is that between ordinary and special reception procedures. The ordinary reception procedure consists of the mere conversion of international law into municipal law through the normal internal law-making processes, that is, by the creation of internal norms which correspond to international norms, e g A.2 of the Navigation Code extending the territorial sea to the 12-mile limit. In the case of special procedures, on the other hand, the international norm is not converted into an internal norm but the competent domestic organ limits itself to stipulating the observance of the international norm: the legislative or administrative organ simply operates a *renvoi* to the international norm which thereby assumes full force and effect in the municipal system, e g A.10(1) C which operates a general reception of the 'generally recognised norms of international law', and 'execution orders' which incorporate treaties into municipal law. It follows that where an international norm is received into domestic law through the ordinary procedure, the norm continues to exist in the domestic system as a rule of substantive internal law even if the international norm ceases to exist, whilst where an international norm is received through a special procedure, the existence of the norm within the municipal system is dependent upon the existence of the norm on the international plane. In whatever manner an international norm is introduced into municipal law, Italian case law at all levels is consistent in holding that the norm binds all public and private subjects operating within the State in the same manner as if it were a norm of national origin. Moreover, once an international norm has been introduced into municipal law it assumes, as a general rule, the same status as the norm with which it was introduced into the municipal system. Thus, for example, if an international norm is introduced into the municipal system through the operation of A.10(1) C, it takes the status of a constitutional norm.

B. THE RECEPTION OF CUSTOMARY INTERNATIONAL LAW

General international law is automatically incorporated into Italian municipal law through the operation of A.10(1) C which provides that 'the Italian legal system shall conform to the generally recognised norms of international law'. Article 10(1) C therefore operates as a 'permanent transformer' converting general international law into internal law by means of a general *renvoi*. It follows that in such cases the municipal judge must resolve all of the problems pertinent to the existence, content, and identification of general international law. Moreover, as general international law is incorporated into municipal law by a Constitutional norm, it assumes a status equal to a constitutional norm within the municipal system. Therefore where ordinary legislation conflicts with customary international law, the former is unconstitutional because it indirectly violates A.10 C and may therefore be nullified by the Constitutional Court. However, although this is the approach taken by the Constitutional Court, it has not as yet held any ordinary legislation unconstitutional on this ground.

Part of the doctrine maintains that although A.10 C gives general international law a pre-eminent status, it is implicit that A.10(1) does not incorporate into domestic law a general international norm which is contrary to the fundamental values which inspired the Constitution. The Constitutional Court has partially taken this approach in its judgment of 18 June 1979 n.48 when, apparently without justification according to the doctrine, the Court distinguished between those international customs which were in existence at the date of the introduction of the new Republican Constitution and those which came into existence at a date subsequent to the Constitution. The former, said the Court, would prevail over every constitutional norm, whilst in relation to the latter it held that the automatic mechanism of A.10 C could not operate to violate the fundamental principles of the constitutional system which is based upon popular sovereignty and a rigid constitution.

C. THE RATIFICATION AND RECEPTION OF TREATY LAW

The case law puts it beyond doubt that A.10(1) C does not apply to treaty law which, instead, is normally incorporated into municipal law by an execution order, usually made with the same legislation that authorises the ratification of the treaty. The execution order does not ordinarily repeat the contents of a treaty but simply incorporates it into municipal law by *renvoi*.

Normally, the signature of the plenipoteniaries at the conclusion of treaty negotiations does not bind the state, but only authenticates the final text of the agreement. The state binds itself in the successive ratification phase, regulated by the internal law of the individual state. In Italy, A.87(8) C provides that the President of the Republic is to ratify international treaties subject, where necessary, to the prior authorisation of Parliament. Article 80 C specifies that the legislative authorisation of Parliament is necessary where a treaty is of a political nature, concerns arbitrations or judicial procedures, varies the national territory, or requires financial burdens or the modification of existing legislation. Moreoever, these two provisions are to be read in conjunction with A.89 C, which provides that no act of the President is valid unless countersigned by the responsible minister. It is generally considered that, if requested by the government, the President cannot refuse to ratify a treaty so that the power of the President is, in effect, limited to forcing a re-examination prior to his signature. Therefore, in Italy, the power of ratification essentially lies with the Executive, except in the subjects noted above in which case it lies with both the Executive and Parliament. It is controversial in the doctrine whether the intervention of the President is part of the formation process of a treaty or whether it merely consists of a control function comprising the possibility of requiring a re-examination of the treaty. In any event, once an instrument is ratified through the appropriate method, the treaty is concluded with the exchange or deposit, as the case may be, of the ratification.

Subsequent to the ratification of a treaty, its reception into municipal law depends upon an ad hoc measure known as the 'execution order' which, like the automatic reception process under A.10(1) C, is a special procedure and incorporates the treaty by *renvoi*. In other words, the execution order limits itself to the expression of an intent that the treaty become internally effective without repeating it in the form of internal legislation. The execution order is normally made by ordinary legislation, usually the same legislation that authorised the Head of State to ratify the treaty. In such event the execution order precedes the date of the treaty which, depending upon its nature, is formed either at the exchange of ratifications or upon deposit of a certain number of ratifications.

In the absence of an execution order, the case law is unanimous in holding that a treaty is of no effect in the internal legal system, e g Cass Sez Un 867/1972, 1196/1972, and 1773/1972, in all of which the full Court of Cassation held that certain favoured treatment for imports was of no effect because the agreement had not been made internally effective by an execution order and furthermore that this was so notwithstanding that it rendered the Italian Government internationally responsible for violation of its contractual obligations under the agreement in question. As Cassation clearly pointed out in judgment no. 1196/1972, when an international treaty is put into existence by the competent organ representing the state in its international relations, the treaty is not ipso facto incorporated into the internal legal system but remains effective on the international plane only. Its incorporation into the internal system arises at a subsequent and distinct point as a result of a measure called an execution order made either by legislation, where the subject matter of the treaty is internally exclusive to the legislative power, or by an administrative act, where the subject matter comes within the power of the public administration. In the absence of an execution order, the internal legal system remains unchanged and therefore the international treaty does not affect the legal position of individuals in the way contemplated by the treaty.

The general rule that international norms acquire an internal status equivalent to that of the norm incorporating them into municipal law is also applicable to treaty law. Therefore, a treaty provision acquires the same status as the normative act which makes the execution order, e g if the execution order is contained in ordinary legislation, the treaty provisions acquire an internal status equal to ordinary legislation. Nonetheless, the case law has ascribed, for various and sometimes weak reasons, special characteristics to treaty provisions introduced by execution orders made with ordinary legislation and has thereby rendered them immutable by subsequent legislation unless the execution order itself is revoked or suspended. It was in this way that, for instance, the Italian courts have held that the Code of Civil Procedure did not motify certain prior international treaties. Finally, the case law of the Constitutional Court takes the view that because treaty provisions form part of the normal internal hierarchy of norms upon their incorporation into municipal law by execution orders, they become subject to constitutional review in the normal way and may, therefore, be held void for unconstitutionality by the Court.

The final aspect of the reception of treaty law is whether its reception also implies the obligatory reception of ulterior norms arising from sources provided for in the treaty, e g the decisions of an international organisation created by the treaty. There can be no doubt that this is the case where the treaty expressly provides for the direct application in member states of decisions taken by treaty organs, e g Community regulations. Where the treaty is silent, it appears that the matter depends upon the internal legal system rather than the treaty, and Italian practice tends towards the individual reception (usually in ordinary form) of each decision taken by an international treaty organ. However, this practice cannot be taken as conclusively supporting the view that prior to the emanation of specific reception measures the decisions of international treaty organs are of no value in the Italian legal system. Part of the doctrine supports the view that the general execution order of a treaty creating a given international organisation also covers that part of the treaty which empowers that organ to issue binding decisions which therefore, without more, have full internal effect. The emanation of individual reception measures in the ordinary form are formally superfluous and can only serve the purpose of conferring a greater certainty on the decision in question or of integrating its content.

D. THE RECEPTION OF COMMUNITY LAW

(*i*) *General*. The Treaties setting up the European Communities were received in the usual manner, viz, an execution order made by ordinary legislation. This, combined with the fact that the Communities are international organisations, ought to lead to the conclusion that, so far as municipal law is concerned, the Treaties and Community legislation are no different from other treaties and the norms deriving from them. Nor would this conclusion give rise to any inconvenience because treaties, in practice, are given a privileged position vis-à-vis both ordinary legislation and the Constitution: generally through inter-pretative means in the case of the former, and through a cautious application by the Constitutional Court of the principle that received treaty law is subject to constitutional control in the case of the latter.

However, in reality, the position is different because, under the influence of a European philosophy, there has been an attempt to differentiate between Community law and conventional international law in order to give the former an absolute precedence over all internal law, including Constitutional law, with the result that those internal norms which conflict with Community law can be said to be non-existent. The generally approved basis for this approach maintains that there has been a partial transfer of legislative and judicial competence from member states to the Community; a transfer that in the case of Italy can be justified under A.11 C, which provides that Italy may consent to necessary limitations of sovereignty in favour of a system which ensures international peace and justice and that it promotes and favours inter-national organisations with such objectives. However, part of the doctrine does not accept that A.11 C can lead to the proposition that the European Treaties and Community legislation are free from any control when applied by the national courts and can therefore even take priority over fundamental Constitutional provisions. Nonetheless, although not accepting the extreme position adopted by those taking a European philosophy, the Italian Constitutional Court has recently taken the approach which favours a differentiation between Community law and the conventional law of treaties thereby placing the former in a privileged position in the domestic sphere.

(*ii*) *The reception of the various Community measures*. There is little doubt that the execution order which received the EEC Treaty automatically extends to Community regulations. This is the clear result of both the express terms of A.189 EEC Treaty which provides that regulations are 'directly applicable' in member states and the fact that the execution order unequivocally included A.189. Moreover, the automatic application of regulations in Italy is not contrary to the Constitution: there are many instances in which Italian law permanently refers to the law of another legal system, as in the case of the rules of private international law, and therefore a *renvoi* must be understood as being impliedly permissible under the Constitution. In any event, the automatic application of regulations can be supported by following the theory adopted by the Constitutional Court, viz, that A.11 C allows a 'limitation of sovereignty' in favour of international organisations. These observations necessarily refer to the *formal* reception of regulations because in many instances their practical reception will require their specific execution and integration by member states. But the end result is that Community regulations necessarily take precedence over internal legislative acts. On the other hand, because A.189 EEC Treaty relates to the direct applicability of regulations only, the general opinion is that Community directives and decisions are not automatically applicable by virtue of the execution order of the Treaty but must be received on an ad hoc basis. In practice, this is done by the ordinary reception procedure, viz, their adoption by repeating them in internal legislative or administrative measures.

Part of the doctrine is of the view that regulations, directives, and decisions are all directly applicable and that ad hoc internal reception measures are only necessary where the regulation, directive, or decision is incomplete. It follows that in the case of directives, because they are incomplete by definition, only those effects which are consistent with the obligation of achieving a particular result have a direct and immediate application whilst those effects which are dependent upon the definition of their manner and form by national organs can only produce their effects upon the emanation of internal execution measures.

(iii) The relationship between Community norms and ordinary domestic legislation. The relationship between those Community norms which are automatically and directly applicable and ordinary internal legislation was first dealt with by the Constitutional Court in 1964 (judgment no. 14/1964), when it held that the legislation receiving Community Treaties, like any other execution order, was subject to the normal principles of legislative succession and could thus be abrogated or modified by subsequent internal norms. In 1975, with a radical change in approach consistent with a Community spirit, the Court held (judgment no. 232/1975), specifically with reference to regulations but in a judgment which is equally applicable to other forms of directly applicable Community norms, that the violation of Community law by subsequent internal legislation is an indirect violation of A.11 C and therefore renders the conflicting internal legislation constitutionally invalid. The Court even went so far as to say that internal legislation which simply reproduced a directly applicable Community norm violates Community law and must therefore be held constitutionally

invalid. This was, inter alia, because its reproduction could give the reproduced norm an 'internal' significance different from that attributed to it by the Community Court on a Community level.

The approach of the Constitutional Court ensures the priority of Community law vis-à-vis internal legislation through the device of constitutional control which, however, in Italy necessitates recourse to the Constitutional Court. Although based on a Community approach, this does not satisfy the European Court of Justice, which in the *Simmenthal* case (106/1977) maintained that internal legislation in conflict with Community law must be considered as 'not having been validly formed', in which event it can be automatically disapplied without the need to have recourse to the Constitutional Court. Notwithstanding that the latter approach may be justifiable from a Community point of view, it is difficult to reconcile with the internal legal system. In practice, the approach taken by the Constitutional Court certainly gives rise to absurd effects, e g a norm of internal law which is incompatible with a Community norm or which merely reproduces a preceding EEC regulation cannot be disapplied by the ordinary municipal courts in favour of the Community norm until the internal norm is declared invalid by the Constitutional Court whose judgment, moreover, does not have retrospective effect.

A part of the doctrine argues that if the Constitutional Court desires to give an effective European significance to A.11 C, it ought to intervene only in cases of effective, unequivocal, and deliberate conflicts between internal and Community law, that is, in those cases in which the legislative provision has the clear object of wholly or partially suspending the application of the Community Treaties; in all other cases of conflict it ought to be left to the ordinary courts, through interpretative measures, to give priority to Community law. The relevant interpretative measure would simply be that which has always been used by the Italian case law in the relationship between internal law and international treaties, viz, the more specific nature of treaties. A move in this direction is evident in the recent case law of the Constitutional Court (judgment nos. 176 and 177/1981) in which the Court has been more inclined to resolving conflicts between internal and Community legislation through the adoption of an interpretation of the internal legislation that is consistent with the observance of the Treaty and the norms deriving from it.

(iv) The relationship between Community law and constitutional norms. Again, the Constitutional Court was initially cautious. In an early judgment (98/1965), the clear assumption was that Community legislation was subject to constitutional review. In 1973 the Court radically changed its approach by adopting a European philosophy. In its judgment no. 183/1973, it held that Community law (whose

introduction into Italy was constitutionally legitimate because A.11 C permits limitations of sovereignty) and internal law are separate, although related, systems of law; that Community law, which is not international, foreign, or domestic law, must have a complete, obligatory, and direct application in all member states so that it can have a uniform application; that the Community system is character-ised by its own statutory and judicial guarantees; and that as Community regulations belong to this autonomous Community system they are not subject to constitutional review, which is limited under A.134 C to State and regional legislation. This renunciation of constitutional review by the Court is in contrast with its approach toward treaties generally, in which case, although exercised cautiously, constitutional review has always been said to be available for the safeguard of fundamental constitutional provisions. The approach of the Court, therefore, creates a discrimination between Community law and the general law of treaties to the advantage of the former.

The Regions and international treaties

There is no doubt that the Regions can neither conclude nor negotiate international agreements as there is no basis whatsoever in the Constitution. The Constitutional Court has taken the lack of regional competence in international relations so far as to prohibit agreements of friendship and collaboration with bodies in other systems, although this has been criticised by the doctrine as excessive. The matter is expressly regulated by A.4 dPR 24 July 1977 n.616 which reserves to the State all functions pertinent to international relations in those subjects which come within regional competence and, moreoever, prohibits the regions from undertaking promotional activities abroad without the prior consent of the national government.

Once an international agreement is ratified, the majority of the doctrine and the Constitutional Court (see judgment no. 46/1961) are unequivocally of the view that the State has the exclusive right to incorporate treaty provisions into the municipal system. Moreover, once a norm of international origin is incorporated into municipal law, it is settled that the Regions must conform with it. Thus regional legislation which conflicts with binding international norms of any kind is constitutionally invalid (Constitutional Court judgments nos. 49/1963 and 120/1969).

Given that the State has the exclusive rights of ratifying and then incorporating international obligations into the municipal system, and that the regions are bound to comply with these obligations, part of the doctrine maintains that there are no other limitations upon the normal legislative and administrative powers of the regions. In other words, whilst the State has an exclusive right to make execution orders, the regions remain competent to adopt, in the subjects within their jurisdiction, the norms necessary to integrate and give effect to the relevant treaty provisions. In those subjects in which the regions have a concurrent competence with the State, the latter may, in accordance with A.117(1) C, define the general principles with which regional legislation must comply.

However, another part of the doctrine, with which the Constitutional Court is in agreement, takes an approach based on the idea that the application of international law concerns the subject of 'foreign affairs', which is within the exclusive competence of the State. More particularly, the Court takes the view that international obligations not only give rise to a negative effect, that is, a limitation upon the competence of the regions in issuing legislative or administrative measures, but also a positive effect in the sense that they give rise to an exclusive State competence in relation to all of the legislative and administrative measures necessary to give effect to the relevant international or Community law. This, according to the Court, is necessary in order to prevent the State incurring a responsibility for the failure to give effect to its international obligations. Such an approach may have the effect of divesting the regions of their competence, although the Court has conceded that the regions may participate in the execution of international or Community law provided that it is in a manner which ensures that the State retains a controlling or substitutional power. The approach taken by the Court has been criticised because the limitations imposed through a need to respect international or Community obligations has had the effect, in the absence of express Constitutional provisions on the point, of converting negative limits upon regional competence into positive ones which defeat that jurisdiction expressly given to the regions by the Constitution.

The basic regulation of foreign trade

A. GENERAL

The evolution of foreign trade policy has been influenced by a range of factors, such as the establishment of the Common Market, the reduction in tariff barriers consequent to various multilateral agreements made within the ambit of GATT, the establishment of favoured trade agreements between the Community and third states, the creation of free trade zones embracing the Community, the establishment of the general system of preferences in favour of developing countries, and the competition generated by newly industrialised countries. The present phase in the regulation of foreign trade must be examined in the light of both the transfer of trade policy to the Community and the principle of the free movement of goods within the latter.

B. THE REGULATION OF TRADE BETWEEN MEMBER STATES OF THE EEC: THE FREE CIRCULATION OF GOODS

Trade with other member states of the EEC is based upon the principle of free circulation irrespective of whether it concerns goods originating from within the Community or goods imported from third countries. The principle of free circulation implies not only the abolition of all custom duties and other taxes on imports and exports, but also the abolition of all quantitative restrictions and other measures having an effect equivalent to the latter (Artt. 30ff EEC Treaty). The notion of 'quantitative restrictions' has not given rise to any definitional problems and simply comprise any measure which wholly or partially restricts the quantity or value of exports and imports. On the other hand, the notion of 'measures equivalent to a quantitative restriction' has caused definitional difficulties largely overcome as a result of EEC Directive 70/50/CEE of 22/12/1969, which contains both a general definition of the notion and a specific list of examples, and the interpretation of the notion by the European Court. In short, 'measures equivalent to a quantitative restriction' comprise measures which discriminate between national and imported products with the result that they obstruct imports, and include those measures which make the import of goods more difficult or onerous than trade in national products. The Community Court has held that no measure must directly or indirectly nor actually or potentially obstruct intra-Community trade and that this freedom of trade must be protected by the national courts.

However, the general principle contained in A.30 is mitigated by Artt. 36, 115 and 223 of the Treaty, all of which are given a restrictive interpretation. Article 36 enables the imposition of prohibitions and restrictions on imports and exports for reasons of public morality, public order, public security, the protection of human and animal health and the preservation of flora, the protection of artistic, historical and archeological property, and the protection of industrial and commercial property. Article 115 is, instead, directed to avoiding market problems arising from differing import policies in the case of products which, although cannot be freely imported into the Community, are not yet subject to a common trade policy. In other words, A.115 is directed to the situation that arises from the fact that, until a common import policy is devised for imports into the Community from third states, imports into a member state with a more liberal policy may then be re-exported to a member state with a more restrictive import policy because of the principle of free circulation. In such a case, A.115 enables a member state to exclude goods originating from defined third states. Finally, A.223 enables every member state to regulate freely its own production and trade in armaments, ammunition and military hardware, all of which are related to national security. There are also other Treaty provisions (Artt. 103, 107, 108, 109 and 224) which enable the mitigation of the principle of free circulation.

C. THE REGULATION OF TRADE BETWEEN THE EEC AND THIRD STATES

The basis of EEC foreign trade policy, arising out of A.113 of the Treaty, is its uniform regulation, especially with respect to tariffs, tariff and trade agreements, the standardisation of liberalising policies, export policies, and the measures in defence of trade including dumping and subsidies. The EEC Treaty therefore transferred jurisdiction in foreign trade policy from member states to the Community, giving the latter the exclusive right to negotiate and conclude trade agreements. In delimiting Community jurisdiction it is thus important to define 'trade policy', but whatever its meaning it certainly comprises exports and imports. Consequently there is a progressive standardisation of trade relations between member states and third states at the instance of the Community.

D. THE UNIFORM EEC TRADE POLICY WITH THIRD STATES

EEC trade policy with third states distinguishes between market economies, non-market economies except China, and China. Moreover, it provides for a preferential trade treatment in the case of developing countries, and certain other schemes for Mediterranean countries and countries belonging to the European Free Trade Association. Insofar as imports are concerned, the general principle is one of prohibition except for a defined list of products whose import is free from any quantitative restriction (the so-called positive list). This list, which in any event varies depending upon the origin of the products, may be altered by the addition of further products provided that there is no risk of a situation which would justify the application of protective measures. Such a risk exists where goods are imported in such quantities or under such conditions so as to cause or threaten to cause serious prejudice to the producers of similar products within the Community or where circumstances are such so as to require the protection of Community interests. In such a case, the Commission may, at the request of a member state or of its own motion, require import authorisations. Moreover, according to EEC Regulation 1439/1974, a member state may, in similar circumstances and as a protective measure, subject a product which has been placed on the positive list to a national authorisation.

The present regulation of imports is a step towards the more advanced harmonisation of import policy which is to be progressively achieved through Community trade agreements. Pending such harmonisation member states are free to impose two types of restriction. First, to stipulate that both the exporting state and the state of origin of a product be states to which the common import policy of the EEC is applicable, unless the product has already been subjected by Community regulation to the sole restriction as to its origin. Second, to restrict the validity of the import documentation stipulated by the Community (and which would therefore be normally valid in all member states) to the confines of the member state which released or authenticated it. Moreover, Italy is free to impose particular conditions on imports from Egypt, Yugoslavia and Hong Kong, and generally on the import of all agricultural products.

Exports from the Community, on the other hand, are totally free. The basic principle is freedom from quantitative restrictions except in the case of defined products (the negative list). However, even in the case of exports, protective measures may be adopted by the Community either where there is a need to prevent or remedy critical shortages of essential products, or where such measures are required in the Community interest. In such cases the Commission may, of its own motion or at the request of a member state, subject the export of given products to authorisations which may either delimit the destination or origin of exports. Where similar situations to those just described affect a member state only, the latter may, as a precautionary measure, subject exports to national authorisations. It may be noted, finally, that import and export quotas are administered on a Community level and are fixed by the Community either autonomously or by agreement.

E. ITALIAN NATIONAL TRADE POLICY WITH THIRD STATES

National provisions concerning trade also include supervisory and control measures over imports and, to a lesser extent, exports necessitated by the establishment of trade relations between the Community and third states. Leaving aside such supervisory and control measures, the primary object of this section is to consider the national regulation of imports and exports insofar as this is still compatible with the jurisdiction of the Community over the subject.

The national regulation of imports is restricted to those goods which are to remain within the national territory. On the other hand, the temporary import of goods, the definitive import of goods which have been previously temporarily imported and the re-importation of goods which were temporarily exported, all remain outside the general system of controls and are, instead, subject to a system of authorisations. The principal characteristic of the national regulation of imports is the division of countries into three groups, viz, zones 'A', 'B' and 'C'. Zone 'A' is sub-divided into zones 'A1', 'A2' and 'A3' which distinguish the different levels of free trade existent with the various countries within Zone 'A': 'A1' comprises those countries with which trade is absolutely free (member states of the Community); zone 'A2' comprises those countries with which trade is semi-free (including countries which have concluded agreements for preferential treatment with the Community); and zone 'A3' comprises all other countries except states with a non-market economy (which comprise zone 'B') and Japan (which is zone 'C'). The economic treatment of imports, therefore, depends upon the zones or sub-zones from which the goods originate. The origin of the goods is determined having regard to the definition of 'origin' in Community Regulation n.802/1968, its definition in the agreements made between the Community and third states and any special provisions applicable to the relevent product or sector. The present system contemplates three import regimes. First, merchandise whose importation is free from any quantitative restrictions. In this case the Customs authorities are permitted to immediately consent to the definitive import of any merchandise not included in the negative list annexed to the DM of 6/5/1976, as amended, as well as any merchandise which although listed, is not subject to an import authorisation because of the zone from which the subject merchandise originates. What is relevant in this category is the country of origin of the goods, and not the country of export, except for goods originating from zone 'B', Egypt and Yugoslavia in which cases the exporting country must coincide with the country of origin. Second, merchandise which can only be imported pursuant to a prior and particular authorisation. This relates to the definitive import of those goods which are both on the negative list annexed to DM 6/5/1976 and marked with the letter 'A' which marking depends upon the zone to which the country of origin of the subject merchandise belongs. Finally, goods which may be imported upon the observance of certain formalities. This category comprises merchandise whose import is free from quantitative restrictions yet subject to certain supervisory or control measures for precautionary reasons. The list of such merchandise, and the supervisory and control measures, are set out in circular n.22/1976 of the Ministry of Foreign Trade. For practical reasons such list also comprises agricultural products regulated at the Community level. The three measures which are utilised comprise import declarations, endorsements by the National Institute of Foreign Trade, and the automatic release of authorisations.

The regulation of exports is dealt with by DM 10/1/1975. The general principle is that the Customs authorities may directly authorise the definitive export of any merchandise not contained in the 'Export' table annexed to the above decree. The export of merchandise in a second list annexed to the same decree is subject to the observance of certain prescribed formalities whilst the export of goods in the 'Esport' list is subject to ministerial authorisation. The same observations which have been made in relation to temporary imports are also applicable to temporary exports.

It must be observed, finally, that Italy is bound to conform not only with autonomous Community provisions which restrict exports of certain goods to third states, but also those restrictions adopted by the Community pursuant to its adherence to International Agreements (e g the International Coffee Agreement) which may prescribe either quantitative restrictions or particular formalities concerning imports and exports.

F. TRADE IN AGRICULTURAL PRODUCTS

All imports and exports between the Community and third countries in agricultural products which are subject to a common marketing organisation (e g rice, sugar, milk, meat), require licences. In Italy, these licences are issued by various ministries in conjunction with the Ministry of Foreign Trade (collectively known as the issuing authority) pursuant to Community law which provides for an issuing authority in each member state. The import or export licence respectively authorises and obliges the import or export of a net quantity of the subject product during the licence period. Moreover, the licences limit trade to the country or group of countries indicated by either the licence or the Community regulations concerning the particular product sector.

Chapter 5

The constitutional system

Introduction

Italy has a written constitution, the Republican Constitution of 1948, which contains numerous fundamental guarantees and cannot be modified by ordinary legislation. It established a democratic parliamentary republic in which Parliament occupies a dominant position. Although the Executive (or more precisely, the Cabinet) formulates political policy, the latter may be overturned by the Parliament through its withdrawal of confidence in the government. Supervision over the application of the Constitution has been given to an organ which is both independent of the three branches of government and specifically created for the purpose, viz, the Constitutional Court.

Although the Constitution sought to retain a strict separation of powers, the principle has undergone such an evolution under the force of various political practices that it can no longer be said clearly to exist. Each branch of government now exercises diverse functions. Thus the government, which traditionally exercises the executive function, also exercises certain legislative functions by making delegated legislation (*leggi delegate*) and legislative decrees (*decreti-legge*); the Parliament, which under the traditional doctrine exercises the legislative function, also creates detailed measures typical of the executive power (*leggi-provvedimenti*) and the judiciary, which ought only supervise the observance and application of the law, also exercises functions of an executive type, e g the voluntary jurisdiction of the civil courts. Moreover, there has appeared a further function or power in addition to the traditional three, viz, the political function which is the determination of the objects to be pursued by the State at any given time and which is exercised, to a varying degree, by all of the constituent organs as well as numerous local organs (Regions, provinces, communes and district councils) and community groups (political parties, unions, professional bodies and the like). Moreover, many organs defy classification according to the traditional trichotomy of powers. Therefore, the doctrine has resorted to the more fruitful concept of State powers, which may be defined as those organs enjoying a qualified autonomy in the Italian constitutional system. In other words, those organs which are subject only to constitutional review by the

Constitutional Court or the President of the Republic, or financial supervision by the Court of Accounts.

The Italian constitutional system comprises the following organs of State power: the President of the Republic, the Parliament (both as a whole and the two Houses severally), the government, the Constitutional Court, the judicial power which is headed by the Court of Cassation, the Superior Magisterial Council which is separate from the judicial power as it is the superior administrative organ of the latter, the National Economic and Labour Council, the Court of Accounts, and the Council of State together with the local organs of administrative justice (the *Tribunali Amministrativi Regionali* or TARs).

Those State powers which participate in the political function are known as constitutional organs. The main characteristic of a constitutional organ is that, together with the other constitutional organs, it defines the form of government which would alter even if a single constitutional organ were to be suppressed or operate in a way different to that contemplated by the Constitution. Thus, the constitutional organs are: the electorate, the President of the Republic, the House of Deputies, the Senate, the government, the Constitutional Court and the Regions which are representative of local autonomy. On the other hand, those organs which do not have a political function nor are essential to the constitutional structure of the State, but which are nonetheless contemplated by the Constitution, are known as organs of constitutional importance. They are the National Economic and Labour Council (CNEL), the Court of Accounts, the Council of State, the Superior Magisterial Council and the Supreme Defence Council.

The electorate

Article 1 C sanctions the principle of popular sovereignty, exercised both indirectly, through elected representatives, and directly, through the vote, referendum, and legislative initiative. Popular participation in the political life of the country may also take place through the formation of social groups specifically recognised and protected by A.2 C, the most important of which are the political parties and industrial unions.

The constitutional basis of the political parties are Artt. 18 and 49 C. Article 18 C declares the right of citizens to freely associate provided that its purpose is not prohibited by the criminal law, and A.49 C provides that all citizens may freely associate in political parties with the object of competing democratically in the determination of national policy. The rider that political contest must be 'democratic' implies an absolute prohibition on any form of physical or moral violence with the object of imposing party politics, although it does not appear to imply an effectively democratic structure within the individual parties in the sense of equal participation by members. However, part of the doctrine maintains that the Constitution enables the registration and supervision of political parties to ensure an internal democratic structure, the legitimate election of office-bearers, and the regular pre-selection of candidates in public elections. In any event, the ideological control of political parties is permitted under Art. XII of the transitional provisions of the Constitution mainly to impede the re-establishment of the fascist party.

In Italy, suffrage is universal, secret, and obligatory. Every person who has attained the age of majority and is unaffected by any form of electoral incapacity must exercise his right to vote. Electoral incapacity exists in the case of civilly incapable persons, bankrupts, persons subject to precautionary measures under the criminal law, and persons convicted of certain crimes. The only sanction applicable for a failure to exercise the right to vote is a notation of the elector's personal record which may have important consequences in various instances such as public employment.

The institutions of direct democracy

There are three forms of direct democracy. First, the introduction of proposed legislation in Parliament by at least 50,000 electors eligible to vote for the Lower House (A.71(2) C). The proposed legislation, which cannot concern those subjects excluded from an abrogative referendum (see below), *must* be considered by the Parliament. Second, the right of any citizen to petition Parliament requesting it to examine or regulate a particular matter (A.50 C). In this case, Parliament is free to decide whether or not it will consider a petition or take legislative action. The right of petition is more readily accessible than the right to introduce legislation because, first, it is available to 'citizens' and not merely 'electors'; second, there are no formal requirements except the authentication of the proponent's signature; third, it may be exercised by a single person or any number of persons; and finally, there is no need to put the proposal into the form of draft legislation.

The final and most important form of direct democracy is the referendum, of which there are three types. First, the abrogative referendum, a popular referendum held at the request of 500,000 electors or five regional Parliaments to determine the total or partial abrogation of legislation (A.75 C). An abrogative referendum may not relate to the budget, amnesties and general pardons, the ratification of international treaties, or taxation. All electors eligible to vote for the Lower House may vote in the referendum, which successfully repeals the subject legislation if approved by a majority of valid votes provided that a majority of those entitled to vote have done so. Second, the suspensive referendum, which concerns legislation amending the Constitution (A.138 C). Where a proposed constitutional amendment has been approved by *less* than a two-thirds majority at the second reading in either House of Parliament, the legislation must remain in suspense for three months from the date of its passage, during which time a referendum may be called by one-fifth of the members of either House of Parliament, 500,000 electors, or five Regional Parliaments. If a referendum is called and the legislation is not approved by a majority of valid votes, the constitutional legislation cannot become law. Finally, the regional referendum, which is restricted to the relevant regional electorate and concerns the approval of variations to the regional territory (A.132 C), the abrogation of regional legislation or regulations (A.123 C), or the consultation of the regional electorate in relation to the creation of new communues or other local matters of regional interest.

Parliament

The bicameral Parliament comprises the House of Deputies and the Senate. Both Houses of Parliament are popularly elected and have identical powers placing them in a position of complete parity. This is clearly contemplated by the Constitution, which provides not only that the legislative function is to be exercised collectively by both Houses (A.70 C), but also that the government must enjoy the confidence of each House (A.94 C). It follows that because the government is equally responsible to both Houses, it can fall through a vote of no confidence in either House; a situation which has been criticised by part of the doctrine because it compromises political stability, especially where the two Houses have different political compositions. Moreover, the Constitution does not make any provision for the resolution of conflicts between the two Houses. These have been overcome by mediation by the President or consultation amongst representatives of the various political groups and the Speakers of each House. If a conflict between the two Houses cannot be resolved, the President may dissolve both Houses and call new elections.

Notwithstanding that the two Houses are in a position of parity, there are several differences between them. First, whilst all persons who have attained the age of majority (18) are eligible electors for the House of Deputies, in the case of the Senate the minimum age is 25. Second, the minimum age for candidature in elections is 25 in the case of the House of Deputies and 40 for the Senate. Third, the House of Deputies has 630 members whilst the Senate has half this number. Fourth, the electoral system is different for each House. Broadly speaking, the electoral system for the House of Deputies is a proportional representation system whereas in the case of the Senate it is a combination of a weighted majority system and proportional representation. Finally, the Senate has two categories of non-elected members: a maximum of five life Senators who are Presidential appointees and all former Presidents of the Republic who become life Senators as of right.

Each House of Parliament has certain prerogatives or privileges, including the power of self-regulation, self-control over its finances, the inviolability of its premises by police authorities, its protection by the criminal law (hence the crimes of impediment of the House in the exercise of its functions (A.289 cp) and contempt of the House (A.290 cp)) and self-control over the eligibility of members and electoral disputes which are decided by the Electoral Committee and the relevant House. There are also the privileges of individual members. These privileges are not personal but are directed to protecting the independence of members and the proper exercise of their functions. They are: first, immunity from criminal process, arrest or search unless authorised by the House, except in the event of apprehension during the commission of a crime. Second, immunity from process for statements or votes made in the exercise of a member's functions (A.68 C), although this does not exonerate a member from disciplinary sanctions imposed by the House. Part of the doctrine maintains that this privilege also extends to statements made in meetings and interviews outside the Parliament as a member also exercises his functions outside the House. Finally, members of Parliament are assured economic independence through a fixed income and travelling expenses.

Article 67 C, which provides that 'Every member of Parliament represents the Nation and exercises his functions free from any binding mandate', seeks to protect the independence of members. This provision combines the notion of national representative which frees individual members from the local electoral colleges that elected them, and *prohibits members from accepting a binding mandate or giving an undertaking* to any person whatsoever. A practical obstacle to this prohibition is the bond which exists between members and their political parties. It has been argued, although denied by part of the doctrine, that this political bond has been legitimatised by usage.

Both Houses contain various internal organs. On the one hand, there are instrumental bodies such as the Temporary President who chairs the first meeting of a new Parliament, the Permanent Presidency which comprises a president, four vice-presidents, eight secretaries, three police officers and several councillors, the Permanent Committees which deal with parliamentary regulations and procedures, and the Electoral Committee which examines electoral disputes in the first instance and then submits them to the House for decision. On the other hand, there are the important operative organs which exercise parliamentary functions. First, the Parliamentary Commissions which, by express provision of the Constitution, examine proposed legislation for the purpose of either making a report to the House or, in defined cases, approving it in lieu of the House. The composition of the Commissions reflect the political divisions in the House. There are corresponding Commissions in each House and they may work either separately or jointly. There are 11 permanent Commissions in the Senate and 14 in the House of Deputies, as well as several temporary or special ones set up to deal with ad hoc matters. Second, Parliamentary Committees, which also reflect the political composition of the relevant House, but have non-legislative consultative functions only, e g the European Communities Committee which gives advice on the application of the European Treaties. Finally, the Parliamentary Groups which are associations of Deputies or Senators formed to more effectively exercise political pressure. Within two days of the first sitting of a new Parliament, members must declare with which group they will enrol, otherwise they are deemed to belong to a mixed group. Each House also has representative organs which represent the House abroad or at official ceremonies.

When the Parliament meets in joint sitting it constitutes a separate institution to the individual Houses, and in such cases the rules and Presidency of the House of Deputies are applicable (A.63 C). A joint sitting may only take place in the cases exhaustively listed in the Constitution (A.55 C), namely, for the election and swearing-in of the President of the Republic (Artt. 83 and 91 C), the indictment of the President, Prime Minister or ministers of State (Artt. 90 and 96 C), the election of one-third of the members of the Superior Magisterial Council (A.104 C; see ch 2 above), the election of one-third of the judges of the Constitutional Court (A.135 C), and the compilation of the list of citizens from which lay judges are drawn for any proceedings brought upon indictment against the President, Prime Minister or ministers before the Constitutional Court (A.135 C).

The Parliament is elected for five years (A.60 C), subject to its sooner dissolution or extension in certain circumstances. The Houses may be jointly or severally dissolved by the President, except in the last six months of the parliamentary term (A.88 C). The doctrine maintains that, according to the constitutional practices of parliamentary regimes, there are three cases in which a dissolution may take place: when the Parliament is no longer representative of the actual political forces in the country; when it is impossible to form a stable parliamentary majority; and when there is an irremediable political conflict between the two Houses. On the other hand, the life of the Parliament may be extended beyond five years in two cases only. First, by the temporary extension of powers according to A.61 C which provides that until a new Parliament meets the powers of the preceding one are extended. The prorogation of powers cannot be indefinite because A.61 C provides that the President must call new elections which are to take place within 70 days of the expiration of the previous term and that the new Parliament must meet within 20 days of its election. Second, by the voluntary act of Parliament in times of war (A.60 C), but only for an additional term.

As a result of certain limits, not all eligible voters are entitled to seek election to Parliament. For election to Parliament a candidate must have been validly elected (the determination of which rests exclusively with the Parliament) and must not be affected by incapacity, ineligibility, or incompatibility. The causes for incapacity are the same as those which exclude the right to vote (see p 140). Ineligibility, instead, arises where the candidate is under the age of 25 in the case of the House of Deputies or 40 in the case of the Senate, holds certain public or administrative offices unless relinquished more than 180 days prior to the end of the previous Parliament, holds an office abroad (e g in foreign embassies), or holds an office in an enterprise which has contractual relationships with the State. Ineligibility gives rise to the invalidity of a member's election if the cause existed at the time of the elections, or forfeiture if the cause arose after his election. Incompatibility, finally, prevents the accumulation of offices. The major categories of incompatible occupations are: constitutional offices (e g member of the other House, President of the Superior Magisterial Council, and judge of the Constitutional Court), offices held as a government appointee in public or private entities, offices in entities dependent upon or subsidised by the State, and offices in banking or financial institutions.

The ordinary legislative process comprises three distinct phases: the preparatory phase which comprises the introduction and instruction phases, the deliberative phase and the execution phase. The introduction phase consists of the initiation of the legislative process by the introduction of a Bill in either House by the government, a member of Parliament, the CNEL, which has the power to introduce Bills on economic and labour matters, the electorate except in the case of certain subjects (see p 140), or the Regional governments, in those subjects of direct interest to them. Once a Bill is introduced, the House is *obliged* to come to a decision upon it. This leads to the instruction phase which has the object of facilitating an informative debate by the House. This phase consists of a preliminary examination of the Bill by the competent Parliamentary Commission which makes a report on the proposed legislation to the House. The report, which includes any dissenting views, invites the House to either adopt or reject the Bill and nominates a sub-committee responsible for considering any amendments proposed by the House.

The deliberative phase may take any of four different procedures. First, the ordinary procedure which is obligatory in cases of constitutional and electoral issues, the delegation of legislation, the ratification of international treaties, and the approval of the budget. According to this procedure, after the reading of the Commission's report, there is a debate and vote upon each article of the Bill as formulated by the Commission. Any proposed amendments are to be considered by the Commission's sub-committee before their final approval by the House. After each article in the Bill has been individually approved, a vote is taken on the Bill as a whole. It is clear that in this procedure the competent Commission has a mere consultative role. Second, the abbreviated procedure which is the same as the ordinary procedure except that all of the times stipulated by the parliamentary regulations have halved. This procedure is utilised for legislation declared by the House, on a show of hands, to be urgent (A.72 C). Third, the decentralised or Commission procedure (A.72(3) C) according to which the legislative process is entirely carried out by the relevant permanent Parliamentary Commission which, in this case, also acts in a deliberative capacity. In the case of the Senate, its President has the sole discretion as to which Bills are to be assigned to the Commission procedure whilst in the case of the House of Deputies, the regulations both limit the powers of the President of the House in this regard and confer a right in the House to oppose any such delegation. There are several guarantees against the abuse of the Commission procedure: the distribution of summaries of all deliberative proceedings of the Commissions to members of the House; the provision of audiovisual equipment to enable the public and the media to follow all deliberative sittings of the Commissions; and a power in the government, one-tenth of the members of the House or one-fifth of the members of the Commission to require a remission of the whole or part of the deliberative phase to the House. Finally, the intermediate procedure which is a compromise between the ordinary and decentralised procedures and in which both the House and the relevant Commission participate in the deliberative process. The House reserves to itself either the vote on the Bill as a whole or the right to determine the general direction that the legislation is to take.

Each step in the legislative process examined thus far must be repeated in the opposite House, although each House is free to follow whatever deliberative procedure it desires. Where, however, a Bill is rejected by either House, it cannot be re-introduced into the same House until the expiration of six months from the date of its rejection.

Once the same text of a Bill is approved by both Houses, it passes into the final legislative phase in which first, it receives the Presidential assent which, in effect, constitutes a check on its validity, both as to legitimacy and the merits; second, it is sealed by the Minister of Grace and Justice who must ascertain that the Bill is formally valid; and third, it is published in the Official Gazette. However, the law does not become binding and operative until the expiration of a period of grace which is normally 15 days from the publication of the legislation.

In accordance with a strict doctrine of the separation of powers, the government or Executive branch of government may only make administrative or secondary norms. However, with the consent of the Parliament the government may sometimes exercise the legislative function. This consent may arise in either of two forms. First, by the delegation of legislative powers. The delegation, which may, in fact, be made in favour of the government only, must conform to certain strict limits. In accordance with A.76 C, the delegation must contain general guidelines, impose temporal limits and relate to a defined subject. The aim of these limitations is to prevent the government from accumulating both executive and legislative functions at the expense of the principle of the separation of powers. Second, by the subsequent ratification or *conversion* of the legislative decrees issued by the government, upon its own motion, in urgent and necessary circumstances. The conversion of a decree into legislation by the Parliament has a dual effect: apart from the substitution and confirmation of the decree it absolves the government of responsibility for its issue. The ratification is retrospective to the date of the decree in the same way that a failure by Parliament to confirm the decree renders it invalid ab initio. The conversion must be sought by the government on the same day that the decree is published and Parliament must within five days, even if it has been dissolved, convene to examine the decree whose ratification must take place within 60 days from its publication otherwise it becomes null and void. It follows therefore that all decrees must necessarily be converted into legislation through the abbreviated legislative process.

A special legislative procedure is necessary to modify the Constitution (A.138 C). The legislation resulting from such procedure is known as constitutional legislation. The revision procedure is a special adaptation of the ordinary legislative process. Whilst the preparatory phase in the revision procedure differs from the ordinary legislative process to the extent only that the CNEL cannot introduce constitutional Bills, the deliberative phase differs in several respects. First the decentralised procedure is not permitted and thus a Bill must be deliberated upon both article by article and as a whole by each House. The Commission procedure is therefore restricted to its consultative function, that is, to the presentation of a report, in this instance, by the Constitutional Affairs Commission. Second, there must be two successive deliberations of the same text in each House separated by an interval of at least three months. If the text is amended between the first and second readings, the procedure must be recommenced. Although a strict interpretation would require an affirmative vote in two consecutive readings before a Bill can pass to the opposite House, in order to speed up the process, if a Bill has been approved in the first reading it can immediately proceed to the first reading in the opposite House. A Bill must be approved at the second reading in each House by at least an absolute majority (that is, a majority of members), whilst a simple majority (that is, a majority of those voting) is sufficient at the first readings. Moreover, if a Bill has been approved by a two-thirds majority at the second reading in each House, the President may proceed to promulgate the legislation, unless he utilises his suspensive veto. If, on the other hand, a Bill has only been approved by an absolute majority in each House, although the legislation is still published it must remain in suspense for a period of three months within which time a suspensive referendum (see p 141, below) may be requisitioned by one-fifth of the members of either House, 500,000 electors or five Regional Parliaments. If a popular referendum is in fact requisitioned the legislation must be approved by a simple majority whereupon the legislation is promulgated by the President. If the referendum fails the legislation does not come into existence.

Constitutional revision is not only subject to formal limitations but also to certain substantive limitations. Constitutional revision cannot, first, alter the republican structure of the State (A.139 C) or, more particularly, convert the State into a monarchy; second, violate the fundamental principles protected by the Constitution, for instance, those principles described by the Constitution as 'inviolable'; and finally, subvert the existing constitutional system by creating, in effect a new Constitution rather than merely revising or integrating it, although the dividing line between the two situations is not clear.

Finally, it must be remembered that, apart from dictating the procedural requirements of the ordinary legislative process, the Constitution also imposes substantive limitations upon the ordinary legislative powers of Parliament. Whilst ordinary legislation must generally comply with the Constitution, a couple of the more important specific requisites with which the legislature must comply are that incriminating norms cannot have retrospective effect and that certain subjects *must* be regulated exclusively by legislation. The latter requisite is of particular interest. The restriction of a given subject to legislative action may be either absolute or relative. Where it is absolute the whole subject must be dealt with by legislation, except for minor details which may be regulated by secondary norms, e g the judicial system (Artt. 25 and 108 C), the criminal law (A.25 C), limitations on personal liberty (A.13 C), the right to strike (A.40 C), limitations to private ownership (A.42 C), and the organisation of the government (A.95 C). The qualified reservation of a subject to legislative action, on the other hand, means that legislation need only fix the general principles and the rest may be left to secondary sources of law, e g the organisation of the public service (A.97 C). In yet other subjects, the Constitution restricts legislative action even further by requiring constitutional legislation, e g the adoption of the Constitution of a Special Region (A.116 C) and the fusion or creation of new Regions.

The government

The principal organs of the government, at the apex of the Executive power, are the Prime Minister, ministers, and Cabinet. There are certain less important elements, such as ministers without portfolio, interministerial committees, and under-secretaries. The basic functions of the government are the formulation and execution of political policy for which it is responsible to Parliament. The government must, therefore, retire on a formal vote of no confidence from the Parliament, although it need not do so in the case of an implied vote of no confidence manifested through the rejection of a government proposal (A.94 C). Apart from its normal political and administrative functions, the government exceptionally has legislative and judicial functions. Of these its legislative function is of a more practical importance and includes the issue of delegated legislation and legislative decrees (see p 146, above).

The Head of State nominates and appoints the Prime Minister and, on the recommendations of the latter, the ministers of State (A.92 C) but once appointed they cannot be removed by the President unless they refuse to resign consequent to a vote of no confidence in the Parliament. Neither the Prime Minister nor his ministers need be members of Parliament (A.64(4) C).

The Prime Minister is undoubtedly in a superior position vis-à-vis his ministers. He recommends their nomination, directs and co-ordinates the political and administrative policy of the various ministries and is responsible for government policy as a whole, as a result of which his resignation causes the resignation of the whole government. Moreover, he ensures that his ministers promptly carry out Cabinet decisions, endorses all important Presidential measures, temporarily assumes any vacant ministry, manages the Cabinet Secretariat, may intervene in proceedings before the Constitutional Court concerning the constitutional validity of legislation, presides over the Interministerial Committee for Economic Policy and is head of the police forces. However, his supremacy, unlike most English systems, is not a perfect hierarchical one nor one of absolute pre-eminence.

Individual ministers, on the other hand, are the politico-administrative heads of their respective ministries, although, according to a now well-established practice, there are a number of ministers without portfolio who therefore have mere political duties. Ministerial functions include the right to introduce Bills into Parliament, the indorsement of Presidential measures which originated from them, participation in Cabinet activities, the issue of regulations and other administrative measures, and the exercise of all other activities relevant to the administration and organisation of their ministries. Each minister is responsible both to Parliament and the Prime Minister and, depending upon whether a measure is a Cabinet or ministerial one, their responsibility may be either collegiate or individual.

The Cabinet comprises all of the ministers, including those without portfolio. When it considers issues relevant to a Special Region, the President of the interested Region may also participate in the meeting. However, of the Special Regions, the President of the Sicilian Region only has a voting right; all others have a mere consultative role. The Cabinet determines the nation's political and administrative policy, the government's legislative programme and decides, after hearing the opinion of the Council of State, whether to adopt those regulations which take the form of Presidential Decrees. Ministerial regulations or decrees, on the other hand, come within the jurisdiction of the individual ministers and are only subject to their prior communication to the Prime Minister who ensures that they are compatible with the politico-administrative policy of the government. The Cabinet also has various other secondary functions.

The remaining government organs worthy of brief mention are the interministerial committees and under-secretaries. The former co-ordinate the activities of two or more ministries, one of the most important being the Interministerial Committee for Economic Planning. The latter, on the other hand, are merely temporary delegates of the ministers and their nomination constitutes one of the first acts of a new government. They assist and represent their respective minister who may delegate various functions and duties to them.

The public administration and administrative law

A. INTRODUCTION

The contemporary doctrine has abandoned any attempt to define administrative law upon the basis of its content or substance and has, instead, resorted to its definition upon the basis of the necessary party to the administrative law relationship, viz, the public administration. Therefore administrative law may be defined as that body of norms which regulate the organisation and activities of the public administration and its legal relationships with other subjects. The doctrine identifies four main characteristics of administrative law. First, it is internal public law because it derives from the will of the State and regulates relationships in which one of the parties is always the State or a public entity (viz, the public administration) which exercises administrative activities. Second, it is autonomous because it is based upon its own principles which are different to those of any other branch of law. Third, it is a common law because it is applicable to all legal subjects and not only to certain categories of them. Finally, it has a variable content because the public administration has differing aims at different historical periods.

Administrative law differs from both the private law which regulates relationships between private subjects and the criminal law which does not concern the organisation of the State in a strict sense but rather public order. Although there may be a certain similarity with the criminal law insofar as the violation of an administrative norm also results in the imposition of a sanction, the administrative sanction is different to a criminal 'penalty' because the latter may only be imposed by a judicial authority consequent to a trial. Moreover, administrative law also differs from constitutional law because, although they are both branches of internal public law, the former strictly concerns the exercise of the State's administrative function, whilst the latter studies the fundamental structure of the State.

B. THE EVOLUTION OF ADMINISTRATIVE JUSTICE IN ITALY

The structure of Italian administrative justice has undergone a gradual evolution since 1865 so that the present system reflects the cumulative results of successive reforms. Before unification and until 1865, in accordance with a strict concept of the separation of powers, many Italian states had a system in which controversies between citizen and public administration were resolved by administrative boards of review composed of judges drawn from the administration itself. The law of 20 March 1865 n.2248 annexure E abolished the boards of review and invested the ordinary courts with jurisdiction over all disputes which concerned the public administration and involved private or public subjective rights. This left a serious gap in administrative law because the ordinary courts did not have any jurisdiction over the violation of so-called legitimate interests which could henceforth only receive protection by recourse to the administrative superiors of the wrongdoing body. This inadequate protection of legitimate interests was remedied by the laws of 31 March 1889 n.5992 (*legge Crispi*) and 1 May 1890 n.6837. The former established, for the first time, a true administrative court in the shape of the IV judicial section of the Council of State which had a general jurisdiction over the legitimacy and, exceptionally, the merits of administrative measures. The latter realised a system of decentralised administrative justice by conferring upon bodies known as the *Giunte provinciali amministrative* a jurisdiction of first instance in recourses against certain measures adopted by local administrative bodies. It was in this way that the division of jurisdiction between the ordinary and administrative courts came to depend, as it still does today, upon the dichotomy between 'subjective rights' and 'legitimate interests' (see pp 20 ff, above as to these concepts). This is a distinction which is difficult in practice and in which therefore the case law is important. However, even the case law fails to provide all of the answers, and it is not uncommon that an aggrieved subject is still today faced with the problem of which jurisdiction to choose. In order to overcome part of the difficulty in distinguishing between subjective rights and legitimate interests, and hence of ascertaining the appropriate court, RD 30 December 1923 n.2840, gave to the administrative courts an exclusive jurisdiction over certain subjects, including public employment in which it was often particularly difficult to discern whether the issue in dispute involved a legitimate interest or a subjective right.

The introduction of the Republican Constitution in 1948 gave rise to a new set of norms which guaranteed the independence of the judiciary, including the administrative judges, and the judicial protection of subjective rights and legitimate interests. These constitutional guarantees led to the declaration by the Constitutional Court in the late 1960s that the various local organs of administrative justice, including the *giunte provinciali amministrative*, were unconstitutional because they did not enjoy an effective independence from the administration. Consequently, the law of 6 December 1971 n.1034, intended to overcome the defects raised by the Constitutional Court, created the *Tribunali Amministrativi Regionali* (TARs), the new administrative courts of first instance, and retained the Council of State as the administrative court of appeal. At about the same time, DPR 24 November 1971 n.1199, effected a comprehensive reform of all administrative recourses to the administration itself, thereby replacing the previous numerous and fragmentary texts on the subject.

C. THE PATHOLOGY OF ADMINISTRATIVE MEASURES

(*i*) *Introduction.* An administrative measure may be afflicted by various defects. First, non-existence, which arises where an element essential to the existence of a measure is lacking. Part of the doctrine regards non-existence as synonymous with the nullity of an administrative measure (see p 35, above). Second, invalidity, arising where there is a defect in one of the elements or requisites of the subject measure which, according to the seriousness of the defect, may be either void or voidable. Third, imperfection which arises where the formation process of the relevant measure has not been concluded. Fourth, inefficacy which occurs where the measure has not yet either been subjected to the necessary controls or communicated to the legal subjects to whom it is directed, both being necessary for the effectiveness of the measure. Finally, irregularity, a defect which does not have any negative consequences for the measure but merely gives rise to an administrative sanction against the agent who put the measure into existence.

(*ii*) *The invalidity of administrative measures.* An administrative act is invalid when it fails to conform with a norm which supports it. Consequently, there are two major categories of defects which may affect an administrative measure: if the norm is a legal one, then the resultant defect is one of legitimacy and the resultant illegitimate act is either void or voidable; if, the norm is a non-legal one, that is, one which comes within the ambit of good administration, then the resultant defect is one on the merits and the measure is said to be 'inopportune'.

The grounds upon which an administrative act is void or non- existent are as follows. First, non-existence of the administrative agent, that is, where the agent who put the measure into existence either does not have or has never been validly conferred the status of a public official. Second, absolute incompetence which arises where an administrative organ: (a) issues a measure which falls within the jurisdiction of another power of State so that the measure is legally non-existent; (b) issues a measure which is within the competence of a completely different administrative sector so that the measure is again non-existent; or (c) issues a measure which is within the territorial competence of another administrative organ in which case although the measure exists it is null. Third, the non-existence of the object of a measure because it is impossible, illegal or uncertain. Fourth, the natural incapacity (A.428 cc) of the agent issuing the measure on behalf of the administrative. Fifth, the failure to define the persons to whom the measure is directed. Finally, the failure to comply with the essential formalities required for the particular measure.

Article 26 of RD 26 June 1924 n.1054, refers to three grounds of voidability: incompetence, excess of power and violation of law. Incompetence, in this context, means relative incompetence, that is, where an administrative organ invades the sphere of competence of another administrative organ which belongs to the same administrative sector or entity. An excess of power, the most important of the grounds for voidability, may arise in various circumstances: (a) a misuse of powers (*sviamento di potere*) where the administration either uses its discretionary power for an end different to that for which the power was conferred or pursues the public interest with a power different from that conferred for the purpose; (b) a misconstruction and erroneous evaluation of the facts where the administration has erroneously regarded a non-existent fact as existent, or vice versa, or where it has given an erroneous, illogical, or irrational significance to the facts; (c) an illogical or contradictory measure; that is to say, where the reasoning is illogical or contradictory, or where the reasoning is in conflict with the decision; (d) an insufficient or incongruous reasoning; it is insufficient where it fails to consider a relevant matter and incongruous where it is based upon or gives weight to irrelevant or insufficient elements; (e) a conflict between several measures dealing with the same matter; (f) a failure to observe circulars, thereby giving rise to a conflict between the intent in the immediate case and the general intent contained in the circular; (g) an unequal treatment; and (h) a manifest injustice, although this arises rarely because it generally relates to the merits (opportunity or convenience) of a measure rather than its legitimacy. The ground of violation of law is a residual category comprising all legal defects which do not come within the other two grounds; 'law' here does not include 'circulars', which merely give rise to internal administrative norms within the ground of excess power.

An administrative measure may in certain circumstances be attacked on the merits. The basis for such action is not the violation of a legal norm but of the principle of good administration (A.97 C) which requires the administration to act in the most suitable manner having regard to the means and ends. It concerns, therefore, the violation of non-legal norms (rules of opportuneness, equity, economy and expediency) and the invalidation of discretionary administrative measures only.

C. REMEDIES AGAINST INVALID OR INOPPORTUNE MEASURES

The challenge of illegitimate and inopportune administrative measures by either recourse to the administrative or ordinary courts or review within the administrative structure itself is dealt with in ch 6 below. A defective administrative measure may also be dealt with in certain other ways which may result in either its abrogation or remedy: first, by the spontaneous withdrawal of the defective measure by the relevant administrative authority; second, by the 'rectification' of the defective measure through its repetition by the issue of a new and valid measure, its ratification by the competent branch of the administration, or its subsequent perfection where the original measure was imperfect; and finally, by the 'conservation' of the measure through the existence of a certain state of affairs which prevents its attack, viz, by acquiescence in the measure, its consolidation by the lapse of time, its conversion into another type of measure whose essential elements have been satisfied, or its confirmation.

The President of the Republic

The President is an impartial power with basically supervisory and guarantee functions. He polices the observance of the Constitution and arbitrates between the political parties. This position is confirmed by A.87 C which describes the President as head of state and representative of national unity. The President must be an Italian citizen, aged at least 50, in possession of all his civil and political rights and unrelated to the Royal House of Savoy. The office, moreover, is incompatible with any other office whatsoever (A.84(2) C). The President, elected for a term of seven years by the Parliament sitting in joint session together with representatives of the Regions, is eligible for re-election. The Constitution does not create an office of Vice-President, providing that the President of the Senate temporarily exercise the functions of President when the latter cannot do so personally. Apart from death, resignation, and normal expiration of the term of office, the Presidential term may come to an end for either permanent impediment or dismissal pursuant to a conviction by the Constitutional Court for high treason or violation of the Constitution. In order to prevent any prorogation of the President's powers, the Constitution provides that the President of the House of Deputies is to call new Presidential elections within the 30 days prior to the expiration of the current term of office.

The President is not politically responsible for the executive or legislative measures which he originates or promulgates. Political responsibility always rests with the Prime Minister or minister who countersigns the measure as the President is not part of the Executive and only formally participates in the legislative process. Political responsibility for strict Presidential measures is limited to serious matters leading to either his indictment before the Constitutional Court (for high treason or violation of the Constitution) or non re-appointment at the expiration of his term; he cannot otherwise be dismissed or invited to resign by Parliament. The President enjoys immunity from civil or criminal process for matters connected with the execution of his duties.

The President has numerous functions and powers spanning the legislative, executive, and judicial branches of government, as well as certain special functions of an administrative and ecclesiastical nature. His powers connected with the legislative branch of government include calling new elections; communicating messages to Parliament; authorising the introduction of government Bills into Parliament; calling extraordinary meetings of Parliament or of either House; dissolution of Parliament or of either House except in the last six months of their term; promulgation of legislation, decrees and regulations; exercise of the suspensive veto in relation to legislation forwarded for promulgation by requesting its re-examination; calling popular referendums where provided for by the Constitution; and nomination of life Senators whose number may not at any one time exceed five. Presidential functions of an executive nature include nomination of the Prime Minister and, on the latter's recommendation, the ministers of State; formal nomination of certain State functionaries such as the President and Councillors of the Court of Accounts and the President of the Council of State; nomination of the eight experts of CNEL; countersignature of ministerial measures which formally issue as Presidential Decrees; declaration of a state of war after its decision by Parliament; command of the armed forces; presidency of the Supreme Defence Council; ratification of international treaties; accreditation and reception of diplomats; conferral of State honours; and dissolution of Regional Parliaments. Functions connected with the judicial branch of government include the nomination of one-third of the judges of the Constitutional Court; presidency of the Superior Magisterial Council (see ch 2, above); and the grant of individual and general pardons, amnesties, and commutation of convictions.

The Constitutional Court

The basic function of the Court, which is independent of the three traditional branches of government including the ordinary judiciary, is the judicial review of legislation. The Constitutional Court is the organ created by the Constitution to check the legislative power which must conform to Constitutional principles. Under the strict application of the separation of powers doctrine it was considered inappropriate to grant the judicial review of legislation to the ordinary judiciary and it was therefore given to the exclusive jurisdiction of the Constitutional Court.

The Court normally comprises 15 judges, although it may sit with quorum of 11 members. Five members of the bench are nominated by the senior judiciary from their own ranks, five by Parliament in joint sitting, and five by personal nomination of the President. The parliamentary and Presidential nominees must be magistrates of the superior courts (even if already retired), attorneys of at least 20 year's standing, or full university law professors. Members of the Court hold office for a term of nine years and are not eligible for immediate reappointment. The composition of the Court incorporates features characteristic of both judicial and parliamentary organs. This is the result of the intent to create a body which reflects the dual aims of the institution, namely, the guarantee of fundamental rights, and the arbitration of conflicts between State organs or between the State and Regions. The tripartite method of nominating members is also clearly connected with the Court's arbitration role. When the Court sits as a criminal court, that is, in proceedings against the President or ministers of State, the bench is augmented by 16 lay judges selected by Parliament from a list which is periodically prepared by the latter.

The Court has three judicial functions. First, the judicial review of 'legislation and . . . acts having the force of State and Regional legislation' (A.134(1) C). It follows from this provision that the measures subject to judicial review are Constitutional legislation (for formal defects only), ordinary State legislation, the legislative measures of the government (that is, legislative decrees and delegated legislation but not regulations which are mere executive or administrative measures), Regional legislation and the Regional Constitutions which take the form of State legislation or Presidential Decrees. The Court's jurisdiction, limited to 'constitutional legitimacy' and not the merits, comprises both formal and substantive defects. The former concerns procedural defects and incompetence for the violation of the division of legislative powers between the State and Regions, and the latter, the violation of Constitutional principles. Second, the resolution of jurisdictional conflicts between State constitutional bodies (e g the government and President), between State bodies and the Regions, and between Regions (A.134(2) C). Third, a criminal jurisdiction, which extends to the merits, limited to proceedings against the President for high treason or violation of the Constitution and the ministers of State for crimes of a political nature committed in the exercise of their ministerial duties. All other crimes fall within the jurisdiction of the ordinary courts. The Court also has certain other powers, including administrative functions (viz, the preliminary check on the admissibility of abrogative referendums and the authorisation of proceedings against a member of the Court), judicial-administrative functions limited to the employment relationship of its employees, and inherent powers of internal self-organisation.

Proceedings for judicial review may take the form of either direct or indirect review. The latter is the normal procedure, originating from proceedings pending before any judicial authority. In particular, where a constitutional issue arises in the course of proceedings before any ordinary or administrative court, the judge remits the issue to the Constitutional Court and suspends the original proceedings pending the resolution of the issue. The issue may be raised by any party to the original proceedings or by the court of its own motion. However, as a condition for the submission of the issue to the Constitutional Court, the original court must be satisfied that the resolution of the issue is significant to the resolution of the original proceedings and that the issue is not manifestly unfounded. If the Constitutional Court confirms the significance and foundation of the issue, the President of the Court appoints an examining judge who prepares a report for the Court's consideration. In the proceedings before the Constitutional Court, apart from the original parties, the Prime Minister (through the State Attorney) or Regional President, whichever is relevant, may appear to defend the legislation whose validity is being challenged. The decision of the Court is made in camera and remitted to the original court, the Minister of Grace and Justice or Regional President, whichever is relevant, and to the State or Regional Parliament, as the case may be, for appropriate action. There is no appeal from the Court's decision.

The Court, in reaching its decision, is limited to the grounds or constitutional provisions made out in the application. Moreover, the scope of the proceedings is limited to the provision under attack; the only instance in which the Court may go beyond the scope of the application is to also declare unconstitutional any other legislative provision which becomes illegitimate as a consequence of the Court's decision.

The result of proceedings before the Constitutional Court is either the grant or the rejection of the reference. The grant of a reference means that the Court declares the norm in question totally or partially unconstitutional with the immediate consequence that the norm therefore totally or partially disappears from the statute books. On the other hand, when the Court rejects a reference this does not affirm the validity of the challenged provision but rather rejects the grounds upon which the provision was challenged. Moreover, a rejection judgment does not have any binding effect beyond the immediate case and does not therefore prevent the question being again put to the Court in other proceedings, even if between the same parties. On many occasions, however, the decision of the Court is not simply a grant or a rejection of the reference but rather an 'adaptation' process. For instance, the so-called 'interpretative judgments' in which although the Court rejects the interpretation advanced in the reference it does not invalidate the subject legislative provision, the understanding being that if the courts in future insist on that interpretation the Court will next time grant the reference and thereby invalidate the norm altogether. Similarly in the case of so-called 'additive' or 'creative' judgments in which the Court introduces interpretative modifications to the legislation in question in order to make it compatible with the Constitution.

The other form of judicial review is direct review which is the direct and immediate recourse to the Constitutional Court independent of any other dispute or proceedings. The right to bring proceedings for the constitutional review of legislation directly to the Constitutional Court is limited to defined applicants: the State government in the case of a challenge to Regional legislation; the Regional governments in the case of a challenge to either State legislation or the legislation of other Regions; and finally, the Provinces of Trento and Bolzano in relation to a challenge to State or Regional legislation, including the legislation of their own Region, Trentino-Alto Adige.

Other bodies of special constitutional importance

A. THE COURT OF ACCOUNTS

This Court had its origins in the need for an organ to supervise and control the financial activities of State, but it has since evolved into a general supervisory organ over defined administrative measures as well as a judicial organ over certain matters. It is an independent and autonomous State body whose functions may be said to fall into three broad categories: supervisory and control functions; judicial functions, principally in relation to accounting and pension matters; and administrative and consultative functions. The Court of Accounts is the highest organ of administrative review as well as the supreme judicial organ in matters of public accounts.

Its supervisory or control functions, as defined by A.100(2) C, comprise the preliminary control over the validity of government measures; the subsequent check on the management of the State budget; a participation, in certain cases and circumstances, in the supervision of the financial management of entities financed in the ordinary way by the State; and the direct report of its findings to Parliament. Its preliminary control relates to nearly all Presidential decrees, ministerial measures and the measures of certain other bodies. The Court reviews the validity of these measures on the traditional administrative law grounds (incompetence, excess of power, and violation of law) and if found valid, 'registers' them. Only exceptionally does a negative finding by the Court ipso facto determine the invalidity of a measure; in the majority of cases the government may nonetheless issue the measure and request its 'reserved registration' by the Court in which case the government takes political responsibility for the measure. It is left to Parliament, after the Court's periodical submission of a list of such measures, to exercise political control over the government's conduct.

The Court's *ex post facto* control over the administration of the State budget is undertaken at the close of every financial period and relates to the financial statement of every State administration as well as the general State Balance which together with the Court's report is submitted to Parliament. The object of the Court's review, extending to both legitimacy and the merits, is to ensure that the management of public funds conforms with the law relating to public finances.

The Court's judicial functions fall into three broad categories: disputes regarding the administration of State funds and property; pensions; and the employment disputes of its own personnel. The Court's jurisdiction is exclusive as it extends to both subjective rights and legitimate interests.

The Court's consultative functions concern the necessity for its opinion in relation to any legislation which modifies or enlarges the functions of the Court, as well as in relation to any legislation which modifies the existing law on public finance. Finally, the Court's administrative functions relate to the appointment, career, and salary of its own employees.

B. THE COUNCIL OF STATE

The Council of State, like the Court of Accounts, is not a government organ. Article 100(3) C guarantees the independence of both the Council of State and the Court of Accounts from the Government. Consisting of six sections, the Council of State has both judicial and consultative functions. Its judicial functions are exercised by the IV, V and VI sections and by the Plenary Assembly, composed of the President and four judges from each judicial section. Its consultative functions are exercised by the first three sections and by the General Assembly, composed of the President and all the judges of the Council of State.

The consultative function of the Council basically comprises the expression of opinions on the legitimacy and merits of various administrative activities. The consultation of the Council may be either discretionary, in which case the public administration is never bound by the Council's opinion, or mandatory in which case the Council's opinion may or may not be binding on the administration. Some instances in which the opinion of the General Assembly must be sought are: the proposed issue by Cabinet, in the form of a Presidential Decree, of regulations; extraordinary recourse to the President against definitive administrative measures (see ch 6, below); and proposed legislation modifying or enlarging the functions of the Council of State. The mandatory opinion of a consultative section, rather than the General Assembly, is required in a large number of instances.

The judicial function of the Council has undergone recent changes with the reform of the administrative justice system and the establishment of the Regional Administrative Tribunals (*Tribunali Amministrativi Regionali*, or TARs). The law of 6 December 1971 n.1034, made the Council the administrative court of second instance. Apart from its appeal jurisdiction, the Council also has an exclusive jurisdiction at first instance over certain matters, e g enforcement proceedings taken to compel the public administration to conform with the judgments of the ordinary or administrative courts.

C. THE SUPERIOR MAGISTERIAL COUNCIL (see ch 2, above)

The Republican Constitution radically reformed this institution, established in 1907; it seeks to guarantee that the judiciary enjoy a functional and organisational autonomy and independence from all other powers of State (Artt. 101 and 104 C). As already noted, the functions of the Superior Magisterial Council include: the allocation of magistrates to their respective seats and duties; promotions, transfers and all other measures relating to the status of magistrates; the nomination of professors and attorneys as magistrates; the appointment and removal of 'honorary' magistrates and the 'lay' judges of the various specialised sections of the courts; and the expression of opinions, at the request of the Minister of Grace and Justice, on proposed legislation relating to the administration and organisation of justice. The Constitution does not make any provision for the dissolution of the Superior Magisterial Council. Despite doubt that this lacuna can be filled with ordinary legislation, a law of 1958 provides for its dissolution by the President in circumstances where it can no longer function. Its dissolution by the President is in his capacity as President of the Republic, an office characterised by its impartiality, and not as President of the Council.

D. THE NATIONAL ECONOMIC AND LABOUR COUNCIL (CNEL)

The Council exercises functions accessory to those of the government and Parliament. Established in order to benefit from the experience and expertise of its members, they represent the various forces involved in national production, in the determination of economic policy. It consists of a President and 79 members, of which 59 represent industry, agriculture, the professions, and State enterprises and 20 are experts in the social and economic sciences.

CNEL was to be primarily a *consultative* body to the government and Parliament in labour and economic matters. This role has degenerated from that of an effective representative college comprising various socio-economic interests to that of a research centre. Its opinions need not be sought and, in any event, are never obligatory nor need even be considered. It also has various other functions, including the right, subject to certain exceptions, of introducing Bills into Parliament on labour and economic matters; the right, within certain limits, of making its contribution to economic and social legislation; the right to undertake studies either on its own initiative or at the request of Parliament or the government; and it may give opinions to Regional governments at their request.

E. THE SUPREME DEFENCE COUNCIL

This is, in substance, an interministerial organ with consultative and decision-making powers. It comprises the President, Prime Minister, Treasurer, ministers for Foreign Affairs, Internal Affairs, Defence, and Industry and Commerce, and the Head of the Defence Staff, although other ministers of State and commissioners may be invited to participate in its meetings. It examines general political and technical problems pertinent to national defence, and fixes the principles and guidelines for the organisation and co-ordination of the military activities of the State. Its powers are not unlimited, but meet the restrictions imposed by analogous functions in other defence organs, e g the Ministry of Defence and the Military Staff. The doctrine defines it as an interministerial organ with both consultative and co-ordination functions aimed at better ensuring the national defence.

The judicial branch of government

A. THE ORGANISATION OF JUSTICE

In Italy the judicial function does not repose in a unitary jurisdiction or court system but is divided between the ordinary jurisdiction and several special jurisdictions. The ordinary jurisdiction encompasses all disputes other than those attributed by law to the special jurisdictions and comprises the civil and criminal jurisdictions. The criminal jurisdiction has several particular characteristics: it concerns the violation of norms which apply a criminal sanction; the criminal process is always initiated by a public or State functionary, the *pubblico ministero*; and the criminal trial aims, in the interests of the collectivity, at the *ascertainment of the 'objective' truth*. The civil jurisdiction concerns the legal protection of private rights. The civil process, in contrast to the criminal process, depends upon the initiative of an interested private party and is essentially a party process. It is not, therefore, directed to ascertaining the 'objective' truth in the interests of the collectivity but merely the foundation (truth and correctness) of the plaintiff's claims in the exclusive interest of the latter.

The various special jurisdictions comprise the following. First, the administrative jurisdiction, concerning all disputes between various organs of the public administration or between the public administration and private subjects, unless the dispute relates to subjective rights in which case it comes within the jurisdiction of the ordinary courts. Only exceptionally do the administrative courts have the jurisdiction to adjudicate on a subjective right. The administrative courts of first instance are the *Tribunali Amministrativi Regionali* (TARs) and the court of second instance is the Council of State. Second, the accounts jurisdiction, exercised exclusively by the Court of Accounts (see p 158, above). Third, the jurisdiction over public waters, exercised at first instance by the Regional Tribunals of Public Waters and at second instance by the Superior Tribunal of Public Waters. Some writers consider that the former are specialised sections of the ordinary courts and the latter a special court of an administrative nature. Fourth, the military jurisdiction, exercised by the military courts pursuant to A.103(3) C. In peacetime their jurisdiction is limited to military crimes committed by members of the armed forces. Finally, the constitutional jurisdiction, exercised by the Constitutional Court (see p 155, above).

B. THE CONSTITUTIONAL PRINCIPLES RELATING TO THE JUDICIAL POWER

The basic constitutional principles on judicial power are contained in either that part of the Constitution which deals with the fundamental rights and duties of citizens or that part which deals with the judiciary, and include the following: (a) The principle of equality (A.3 C). Article 3 C is one of the most important provisions of the Constitution and provides that 'all citizens have equal social dignity and are equal before the law, without distinction of sex, race, language, religion, political opinion, and personal and social conditions'. It also extends to foreigners and stateless persons whilst on Italian soil. (b) The right to the judicial protection of subjective rights and legitimate interests (Artts. 24 and 113 C). Article 24 C sanctions the right to proceed judicially for the protection of rights and legitimate interests (see ch 1, above for the definition of these concepts). This general right is confirmed by A.113 C with specific reference to the violation of rights and legitimate interests by the public administration. Article 24 C renders judicial protection effective by providing that the 'right of defence is inviolable at every stage and grade of proceedings'. The right of defence implies, in particular, the right to legal representation and therefore the provision of legal aid for the impecunious (A.24(3) C) and the right to a trial. Through these provisions the Constitutional Court has invalidated a large number of legislative provisions in both the criminal and civil law fields. (c) The right to be adjudicated by a pre-defined court (A.25 C). This means that the jurisdiction of the courts must be objectively defined by legislation prior to its concrete application. In other words, the criteria for selecting the competent court cannot be defined after the commission of the event to be adjudicated. This principle is also another aspect of the autonomy, independence, and impartiality of the judiciary. (d) Justice is to be administered in the name of the people (A.101 C). This principle emphasises that the judicial function is to be exercised impartially, or *super partes*, and independent of any other State body. (e) The prohibition against the institution of extraordinary or special courts (A.102 C). This principle, which is amongst the provisions dealing with the judiciary (Title IV, Artts. 101–103 C), is connected with the principles of equality and the right to a pre-defined court. This principle is designed to prevent the constitution of a court for a specific controversy, thereby conditioning the results of the proceedings. (f) The judiciary is subject to law only (A.101 C). This provision protects the impartiality of the judiciary who is to be guided in its decisions by legislation and the lawful measures of the public administration only. (g) The independence of the judiciary (A.104 C). The declaration in A.104 C, viz, that the judiciary is autonomous and independent from every other power, is guaranteed by the establishment of the Superior Magisterial Council, which administers every aspect of the judicial career and isolates the judiciary from every external control or influence. To guarantee freedom of action, every judge enjoys a territorial and functional irremovability, subject only to his request or consent, or pursuant to disciplinary action by the Superior Magisterial Council (see p 74, above). (h) The obligation to reason every judicial measure (A.111 C). This guarantees that the judge properly applies the law, and thus emphasises both judicial responsibility and the validity of judicial decisions. (i) The overriding supervision of the Court of Cassation in matters of personal liberty (A.111 C). Article 111 C provides that recourse to Cassation is always available for the violation of law by the ordinary and special courts in matters of personal liberty. The only exception relates to the decisions of military tribunals in times of war. (j) The obligation of the *pubblico ministero* to initiate the criminal process (A.112 C) (see ch 6, below). (k) The non-retrospectivity of incriminating legislation (A.25 C). (l) The inadmissibility of extraditions for political reasons, except for genocide (A.26 C).

The Regions

A. INTRODUCTION

The Italian State is divided into some 20 Regions, five of which have special autonomy (the so-called Regions with Special Constitutions or Special Regions) and the remainder an ordinary autonomy (the so-called Regions with Ordinary Constitutions or Ordinary Regions). Although the Regions are divided into progressively smaller territorial divisions, namely, Provinces and Communes, only the Regions have a limited legislative, administrative and financial autonomy, the Provinces and Communes being mere territorial divisions of the State administrative structure.

The recognised need at the time of unification to create a national consciousness amongst the heterogeneous States which formed the Italian State led to the predominance of a centralist philosophy and the consequent establishment of a unitary system. These centralist tendencies attained their apex during the fascist regime. The economic and cultural differences between the Regions had accentuated themselves and consequently, after the fall of fascism and at the formulation of the new Republican Constitution, a regional State was established as a compromise between the previous unitary State, which was too centralised, and a federal State, which would have been too decentralised. The Italian Constitution, therefore, although it declares the Republic to be 'one and indivisible', recognises and promotes local autonomy and confers certain rights and powers upon the Regions. For political, ethnic, and economic reasons, the Constituent Assembly conceded a particular position to the so-called Special Regions (Sicily, Sardegna, Trentino-Alto Adige, Friuli-Venezia Giulia and Valle d'Aosta, all of which, except Friuli-Venezia Giulia, were established in 1948. Friuli-Venezia Giulia was given its Special Constitution in 1963, after settlement with Yugoslavia of the political question of Trieste. The establishment of the Ordinary Regions and the transfer of functions assigned to them by the Constitution commenced in 1970 and was not completed until 1975.

B. THE CONSTITUTIONS OF THE REGIONS

The Constitutions of the Special Regions take the form of constitutional legislation passed by the national Parliament. Unlike the Ordinary Regions, the Constitutions were prepared by the national government, it being said in the doctrine that the Special Regions have had, in this way, their powers and autonomy improperly diminished. As constitutional legislation, the Constitutions of the Special Regions prevail over ordinary national legislation and the general constitutional provisions relating to Regions, although not the constitutional provisions relating to the rights and duties of the citizen and the organisational structure of the State. Even though the Constitutions of the Special Regions have a narrower ambit than those of the Ordinary Regions, they confer a broader autonomy over those subjects contained in them in contrast to the Constitutions of the Ordinary Regions.

The Constitutions of the Ordinary Regions take the form of ordinary national legislation. However, their formulation comes within the jurisdiction of the Regional Parliaments; they are only sent for their approval and passage to the national Parliament, which has no power to introduce amendments but only to withhold approval. They are in substance Regional normative acts but, in form, ordinary national legislation. This does not mean that the Regional Parliaments have an unlimited power in drafting their Constitutions. Apart from those subjects falling outside Regional competence, A.123 C imposes a general limitation to the effect that the Regional Constitutions must, in any event, be in 'harmony with the Constitution and national legislation'. Whilst there was never any doubt that the Regional Constitutions must not conflict with the Constitution, there has been disagreement as to the significance of the requirement that they must be in harmony with 'national legislation'. According to an authoritative part of the doctrine, it merely means that the Regional Constitutions must comply with the general principles of the State legal system, although the Regions must be regarded as having the statutory power to give effect to their particular political choices and to adopt varying solutions necessitated by local differences. However, a State law of 1953 (*legge Scelba*) took a restrictive approach and provided that the Regions had to adhere to the general principles established by State legislation. This meant that the Regions had mere integrative powers. Although clearly unconstitutional, the matter did not come to a head until 1970, when the Ordinary Regions were established. At that time, in the light of an open conflict threatening the emerging State-Region relationship, the question was put to an end by legislation repealing those provisions of the *legge Scelba* that dealt with subjects reserved by the Constitution to the Regions. In any event, Title V of the Constitution specifies the general principles regulating the internal organisation and functions of the Regions.

C. THE LEGISLATIVE AUTONOMY OF THE REGIONS

Article 117 C confers upon the Regions certain legislative powers over defined subjects which may be said to fall into four broad categories: the administrative system and its organisation, public and social services, economic development, and the administration and utilisation of territorial assets. The legislative powers of the Regions may be of three types: exclusive powers; complementary powers which only enable the Regions to legislate within the scope and general principles dictated by the State; and adaptation powers which limit the Regions to adapting existing State legislation to their particular needs and circumstances. The Special Regions have been given, to a varying degree in different subjects, all of these types of legislative power. On the other hand, according to the formula contained in A.117 C, the Ordinary Regions have only a complementary competence with the State. The Ordinary Regions are restricted in their legislative powers by the fundamental or guiding principles fixed by State legislation. These principles, peculiar to every subject of Regional competence, are not to be confused with the more general principles of the State legal system constituting an overall limit to Regional constitutional and legislative autonomy.

The legislative autonomy of the Regions has several limits, the foremost being that the legislative competence of the Regions is restricted to those subjects which are exhaustively defined in A.117 C. However, even there Regional competence is subject to certain overriding principles and interests, viz, the fundamental principles fixed by national legislation in each subject, the national interest and the interest of other Regions. The fundamental principles need not be expressly defined by the national legislature but may arise by implication from existing legislation in the subject. Furthermore, various other limits within those subjects listed in A.117 C arise out of the case law of the Constitutional Court concerning State-Regional relationships, e g the Regions are incompetent in matters affecting private law relationships, the law of procedure, the legal system, and the criminal law, and their legislation cannot interfere with national defence or economic policy. The difficulty in defining the exact content of Regional competence by referring to the list of subjects contained in A.117 C has been alleviated by recent legislation transferring apposite functions to the Regions upon the basis of organic sectors; the re-elaboration of Regional competence in terms of function rather than subject matter has facilitated a more realistic determination of Regional competence.

Other limitations upon Regional competence are as follows: (a) The territorial limit according to which each Region may only legislate for its own territory. (b) Conformity with the international obligations assumed by the State and the national legislation which gives effect to them. (c) Compliance with the general principles of the State legal system, that is, according to the Constitutional Court, those principles of a general and fundamental nature that can be deduced from the norms which at any given historical point constitute the fabric of the existing system, e g the legality of administrative action and the non-retrospectivity of criminal laws. This limitation upon Regional competence is linked with the maintenance of a unified legal and political system as sanctioned by A.5 C. (d) Compliance with the Constitution. (e) The obligation of financing all expenditures resulting from Regional legislation (A.81 C). (f) The prohibition on creating obstacles to the free circulation of persons and things between the Regions (A.120 C). The Regional legislative power cannot be delegated to the Regional Executive or Junta, which precludes the emanation of delegated legislation or legislative decrees, although doubts exist as to the latter issued in cases of urgency.

All existing national legislation remains effective until the Regional legislature replaces it with fresh legislation or 'adopts' the existing State legislation in the subject. Until the Regional legislature intervenes, the preferable view is that the State may continue to regulate the subject.

D. THE ADMINISTRATIVE AUTONOMY OF THE REGIONS

The administrative autonomy of the Ordinary Regions is primarily based upon A.118 C. However, depending upon their source, three types of regional administrative functions may be individuated. First, the true and proper administrative functions of the Regions that represents their administrative autonomy. This is the administrative power given to the Regions by A.118(1) C over all of those subjects coming within their legislative competence under A.117 C. However,

A.118(1) C is subject to the rider that the State may confer upon the provinces, communes, or other local entities administrative functions in the subjects listed in A.117 C where the subject is one of purely local interest. Second, administrative functions exercised by the Regions as delegates of the State. Article 118(2) C provides that the State may delegate its own administrative functions to the Regions which exercise them on behalf of the State. Finally, administrative functions complementary to subjects, other than those listed in A.117 C, in which legislative competence has been delegated by the State to the Regions pursuant to A.117(3) C. The latter two types of administrative function do not form part of the Regions' administrative autonomy.

It appears from an examination of the legislative and administrative functions of the Regions, and the subjects in which they are exercised, that there exists a 'parallelism' between the two functions. From this premise it follows that the administrative activities of the Regions meet the same limits as exist in their respective legislative activities. Therefore it appears that there is not a complete and exclusive administrative competence but rather an administrative autonomy which follows the outcome or which, in other words, is dependent upon the validity, efficacy and limits of the normative powers of the Regions.

The initial transfer of administrative functions from the State to the Regions, in 1972, led to major demarcation conflicts between the Regional and Central Administrations. These conflicts paralysed the whole system and were not only the result of a non-organic transfer of administrative functions but also an attempt by the Central Administration to re-appropriate powers already transferred to the Regions. This situation led in 1975 to new legislation that dealt generally with the regional system and the organisation of the public administration and delegated to the government, which acted accordingly in 1977, the power: first, to finalise the transfer to the Regions of all of those administrative functions relevant to the subjects listed in A.117 C; second, to delegate to the Regions, pursuant to A.118(2) C, such State administrative functions as were necessary for the fulfilment of Regional administrative functions in the subjects listed in A.117 C; and third, to transfer to the Regions those offices and personnel that had not yet been transferred, thereby reducing the State administrative network.

Notwithstanding the transfer of administrative functions from the State to the Regions, there still exists the Financial Law of 1970 which reserves to the State the right to formulate policy and co-ordinate activities in those subjects affecting the unitary nature of the State. This reservation has been held valid by the Constitutional Court as being in the national interest. As a result, the State and Regional Administrations must keep each other informed, through a Government Commissioner located in each Region, of all matters relevant to the exercise of their respective functions.

Two further matters concerning Regional administrative functions must be mentioned. First, A.130 C provides that a Regional body, established in the form specified by State legislation, is to exercise control over the legitimacy and, where stipulated, the merits of measures issued by the provinces, communes and other local entities. It follows that although these control bodies are Regional organs, they fall outside the normative powers of the Regions because they are set up by national legislation. The control function is in fact exercised by a Provincial Control Committee (*Comitato di Controllo sulle Province*) established in each Regional capital. The Committee, which is dependent upon the Regional Parliament, comprises three experts in administrative law elected by the Regional Parliament, a member nominated by the relevant Government Commissioner and a judge of the Regional Administrative Tribunal nominated by its President. Apart from provincial measures, the Committee may control communal measures unless a Communal Control Committee has also been established. Second, notwithstanding that there also exists a 'parallelism' between legislative and administrative functions in the case of the Special Regions, two factors relating to the legislative-administrative powers of the Special Regions distinguish the latter from the Ordinary Regions. These factors, which have in fact exerted a negative influence upon the development of the Special Regions, are: first, the two functions were not simultaneously conferred upon the Special Regions; and second, because the Special Regions received their powers at a time when Regional policy was still in its infancy, their competence was compromised and restricted.

E. THE FINANCIAL AUTONOMY OF THE REGIONS

Article 119 C provides that the Regions are to enjoy financial autonomy in the forms and within the limits fixed by national legislation which is to co-ordinate State, provincial and communal finances. The financial autonomy of the Regions is limited as Regional finances are strictly regulated by State legislation, and the Regions cannot generally introduce new forms of taxation nor regulate existing taxes.

The financial autonomy of the Ordinary Regions is, in effect, a mere autonomy of budget and expenditure, a direct administration of the income fixed by State legislation. The revenue sources of the Ordinary Regions comprise Regional taxes, a proportion of the public revenue collected by the national Treasury (which constitutes the major income of the Ordinary Regions), and special grants made by the national government for defined projects. However, the various Regional taxes are levied and minutely regulated (except, generally, for the rate of taxation) by national legislation which then surrenders their yield to the respective Regions, e g motor vehicle registrations.

The Special Regions have a more marked financial autonomy. This is not to say that the general limits upon Regional legislative and administrative powers are not applicable. Every form of Regional taxation must be in harmony with the State taxation system and not interfere with the taxation system extant in the remainder of the national territory. The actual tax regime and its regulation in the various Special Regions are dealt with by the relevant Regional Constitutions and vary from Region to Region.

F. THE STRUCTURE OF REGIONAL GOVERMENT

Article 121 C provides that the organs of Regional government are the Regional Parliament, the Junta and the Regional President (corresponding roughly to the Parliament, government and President of the Republic on the national level), and defines in general terms their principal functions. However, there are many detailed differences amongst the various Regions, mainly because the constitutional provisions on the subject are framed in very general terms. Certain other variations amongst the Regions may be explained by the different origins of their Constitutions; the Constitutions of the Special Regions originated from the State whereas those of the Ordinary Regions originated from the relevant Regional Parliament. In general, the Special Regions are all structured along the lines of parliamentary governments, whereas the majority of Ordinary Regions have an assembly system mitigated with certain elements of a parliamentary form of government.

The Regional Parliaments, being unicameral, exercise both the legislative and regulation-making functions of their respective Regions as well as any other functions conferred upon them, including administrative functions. However, in the Special Regions the regulation-making function is, in practice, conferred upon the Junta or executive power.

The Regional Junta or executive organ, unlike the State Executive, is elected by the Regional Parliament. Moreover, and again unlike the State Executive, its degree of subjection to the Regional Parliament varies from Region to Region. It has a general administrative competence except, as already noted, in relation to the regulation-making power. It has the right to introduce Bills into the Regional Parliament but cannot, unlike the State government, make legislative decrees. In the case of the Special Regions the members of the Junta, like the ministers of State, are true and proper governmental organs with external powers. The members of the Junta in an Ordinary Region do not have any autonomous powers and may only act collegiately as part of the Junta.

The Regional President combines the functions performed by the

Head of State and Prime Minister in the national government. This combination of functions makes him very similar to a President in a presidential republic. The Regional President is elected, together with the Junta, by the Regional Parliament. In his capacity as President of both the Junta and the Region, apart from his normal executive functions, he promulgates Regional legislation and regulations, superintends the administrative functions delegated to the Regions by the State, and represents the Region. He is the Regional spokesman in dealings with the Government Commissioner.

The establishment of a regional administrative structure is generally limited to the extent necessary for the exercise of high administration and the political and legislative functions of government; the creation of a more extensive Regional bureaucracy to implement Regional decisions is expressly prohibited. Article 118(3) C, in order to avoid that the Regional system lead to the creation of a new bureaucratic structure, provides that the Regions are to exercise normally their administrative functions through the provinces, communes, or other local authorities by availing itself of the existing bureaucracies of these minor territorial authorities.

On the whole, in the Special Regions, the fundamental division of power is between the Regional Parliament which exercises the legislative function and the Junta which exercises the executive function including, usually, and unlike the Ordinary Regions, the regulation-making function. The Junta is dependent on the Regional Parliament, which both elects the individual members of the Junta and may provoke a government crisis by withdrawing its confidence in the Junta. The relationship between the Regional Parliament and the Junta is not dissimilar to that between the State Parliament and government and is therefore substantially a parliamentary form of government. On the contrary, the system of government in the Ordinary Regions is characterised by a certain prevalence of the Regional Parliament; a feature typical of an assembly system of government. The normative and organisational features which support this characterisation of the Ordinary Regions are: the powers of the Regional Parliament in determining political and administrative policy; the exercise of certain administrative functions by the Regional Parliament rather than the Junta; the power of the Regional Parliament in certain circumstances to intervene directly in the executive functions of the Junta; and the direct election by the Regional Parliament of individual members of the Junta, including the President, thereby bestowing its confidence which can be revoked at any time.

G. STATE CONTROL OVER THE REGIONS

(*i*) *Introduction.* State control over the activities of the Regions is exercised through a Government Commissioner located in every

Region. The Commissioners, appointed by the Cabinet, are part of the peripheral State bureaucracy. As already noted, the Commissioners supervise State administrative functions and co-ordinate them with the administrative functions exercised by the Regions. The Commissioners have the powers to challenge Regional legislation before the Constitutional Court and to invite the national government to dissolve a Regional Parliament for persistent violation of the local Constitution.

(ii) Controls over Regional administrative measures. According to A.125 C, Regional administrative measures are subject to the control of a State organ to be established by national legislation. In 1953 there was established in the Regional capital of every Ordinary Region a Control Commission comprising the Government Commissioner, who presides, a judge of the Court of Accounts, three State functionaries, and two experts in administrative matters nominated by the Regional Parliament. In order to preserve a uniform approach amongst the various Control Commissions, the Regions have been given certain rights of appeal, namely, to the TAR in the first instance and then to the Council of State. The supervision of the Commissions extends not only to the legitimacy of Regional administrative measures but also, in defined cases, to their merits. A Regional measure becomes fully effective if it has not, within 20 days of its communication to the Commission, been annulled or returned to the Regional authority for re-examination. In the latter instance, if the measure is confirmed by the Regional authority, the Commission may only annul the measure on the ground of the formal regularity of the confirmation procedure, again within 20 days of the communiction of the measure to the Commission. In the Special Regions the control over administrative measures is exercised by the Court of Accounts, except in the case of Valle d'Aosta which has a Co-ordination Commission. The control of the Court of Accounts is limited to legitimacy and is exercised in the normal way, that is, by the 'registration' of valid measures (see p 158, above).

(iii) Control over Regional legislative measures. According to A.127 C, the State government is to exercise a preliminary check on Regional legislation. The Regional legislative process is analogous to the State process and comprises the same three fundamental phases: the preparatory, deliberative, and execution phases. In the final phase, a Regional Bill is sent, through the Government Commissioner, to the State for review. If the State government considers that the proposed legislation is legitimate and in harmony with State socio-economic policies, it is returned to the Commissioner for approval; otherwise, it is returned to the Regional Parliament, through the Government Commissioner, for re-examination on the points on which it is regarded illegitimate or inopportune. If the Regional Parliament complies with

the view of the State government, the amended Bill is again communicated to the State for approval. If, instead, the Regional Parliament confirms the Bill in its original version with an absolute majority of its members, the State government may either acquiesce or, within 15 days, bring the Regional Bill before the Constitutional Court, if its legitimacy is in question, or the Parliament, if the merits are in question. Where the Constitutional Court or the Parliament, whichever the case, confirms the view of the State government, the Bill cannot be promulgated. If instead, the Bill is not affected by any vitiating factor it is communicated to the Government Commissioner who must approve it, after which it is promulgated by the Regional President and published in the Regional Gazette. Unlike the national President, a Regional President does not have a power of veto over legislation because control over Regional legislation is exercised by the State through the procedure just set out.

(*iv*) *State control over Regional parliaments.* A Regional Parliament may be dissolved by the national government in various circumstances: where it acts contrary to the Constitution or commits a serious violation of law; where it fails to respond to a government invitation to replace its President or the Junta in the event that these have committed acts or violations analogous to those just described; where it cannot function for the lack of a working majority; and finally, for reasons of national security. The procedure for the dissolution of a Regional Parliament includes the opinion of the national Parliamentary Commission on Regional Affairs, a motion by the Prime Minister, the decision of Cabinet, and a reasoned Presidential Decree which also appoints three administrators who are to call new elections within three months and, in the meantime, carry out the ordinary administration of the Region. In accordance with A.113 C, a decree dissolving a Regional Parliament may be challenged before the 'judicial authorities' which, according to the doctrine, must, in this instance, be the Constitutional Court rather than the TAR. Special provisions apply for the dissolution of the Sicilian Regional Parliament.

The minor territorial authorities

Apart from the Regions, which are autonomous constitutional entities, there are other autonomous territorial entities of a non-constitutional nature, viz, the communes and provinces. The former are the smallest of the territorial entities and consist of a popularly elected council, a junta which is elected by the council and has executive functions, a mayor who not only represents the council but is also a government official, and a secretary who is a government functionary. The commune performs both functions of its own and those delegated to it by the State. Its own functions cover local police, health, public works, social services and town planning as well as other optional activities. The functions delegated by the State include the maintenance of the civil registry and military call-up lists, and the concession of licences to operate public transport. Furthermore, it must exercise those functions delegated to it by the Regions, it must participate in certain State services, and has the power to impose and administer local taxes. Control over communal activities is exercised by the Regions through appropriate Control Commissions (see p 168, above). By virtue of the law of 8 April 1976 n.278, communes may be further divided into districts comprising an elected council and a president. However, they are optional and usually availed of only in larger communes. The districts are not autonomous territorial entities nor do they have any general functions. Their principal powers are to represent the needs of residents, express opinions on local affairs and services, convene public meetings and formulate proposals in areas of communal competence. They may also exercise deliberative functions in matters of public works and communal services pertinent to their respective districts upon delegation from the commune.

The provinces are fundamental administrative districts which realise a bureaucratic decentralisation of State activity and comprise the territory of several communes. They consist of an elected council which has deliberative functions, a junta which has executive functions, and a president who presides over both the council and junta and represents the province. The functions of the province are generally defined by State legislation and comprise obligatory institutional functions of its own (generally health and hygiene, public works and services, social services and auxiliary staff for secondary educational institutions), optional functions (such as public transport), functions delegated to it by the State (e g fishing, hunting and railway concessions), and functions delegated to it by the Regions.

The citizen and the State: the Constitutional Declarations

A. GENERAL CONCEPTS

A significant part of the Italian Constitution is dedicated to the protection of human rights and fundamental freedoms: the first two Parts of the Constitution, comprising 54 articles. Part I is entitled 'Fundamental Principles' and contains 12 articles; Part 2, entitled 'Rights and Duties of Citizens', comprises Artt. 13 to 54 and is subdivided into four Titles, viz, 'Civil Relations', 'Ethical-Social Relations',

'Economic Relations', and 'Political Relations'. It must be remembered that a significant role in giving effect to the Constitutional Declarations belongs to the Constitutional Court. Some three-quarters of all proceedings before the Court relate to the constitutional validity of legislation at the point where the rights of the citizen are involved. In some areas, the decisions of the Court have led to a complete renewal of the law, particularly in relation to the criminal process and family law, but also in subjects such as labour law and Community law.

The emphasis on the rights of the citizens is manifest from the debate concerning the status of the fundamental rights and, in particular, as to whether they are limited to those expressly contained in the Constitution. Some writers maintain that the expression 'inviolable rights' in A.2 C, which provides that 'The Republic recognises and guarantees the inviolable rights of man', infers that the rights guaranteed by the Constitution are an open list capable of extension not only through interpretation but also by reason of social progress. It has been argued that the Constitution also protects fundamental rights which have not been expressly included in it, such as privacy, conscientious objection, and political demonstration. This expansionist approach is to some extent vindicated by the case law of the Constitutional Court which has sometimes discovered rights that have no Constitutional basis in Italy. For instance, the Court has utilised various international declarations to discover analogous rights under the Italian Constitution. However, the Constitutional Court has oscillated in its approach and in some instances taken the opposite and restrictive approach of maintaining that the fundamental rights are exhaustively defined by the Constitution.

The Constitutional Declarations are only exceptionally of immediate application. Generally, they merely have the effect of restraining the use of the legislative power or of prescribing a programme to be implemented by the ordinary legislature. However, the fulfilment of many constitutional provisions has proceeded very slowly and, in some cases, have even remained a dead letter. The fulfilment of the fundamental principles and personal freedoms have thus far been left almost entirely to the Constitutional Court with no or minimal legislative intervention.

B. THE PRINCIPLE OF EQUALITY

The interpretation and application of the principle of equality contained in A.3 C are central to the protection of fundamental rights. Article 3 has, indeed, become the key provision of the Constitution and provides in A.3(1) that 'all citizens have equal social dignity and are equal before the law, without distinction of sex, race, language, religion, political opinion, and personal and social conditions'. Article 3(1) embodies the principle of the *legal* equality of citizens whilst

A.3(2) deals with their *actual* equality placing upon the State the duty of removing all economic and social obstacles which limit the liberty and equality of citizens and impede both the total development of the human person and the participation of all working people in the political, economic, and social organisation of the State. At first, the Constitutional Court took a restrictive interpretation of A.3: it was not only limited to the heads of discrimination specifically mentioned in the article, but it was also limited to cases of disparate treatment only. Later the Court began to base its decisions on the 'rationality' of the discrimination in question, and broadened the application of A.3 by including comparable fact situations (e g the extension of A.3 to include 'foreigners'), permitting a differential treatment where the circumstances justified it, and extending the types of discrimination caught by A.3. In relation to the last aspect, the Court at first extended A.3 to only those types of discrimination which could be deduced from the text, but then applied it to those types arising out of the 'predominant social conscience of the national community', so that now the types of discrimination caught by A.3 may be said to be unlimited.

The principle of equality means, in practice, the equal subjection of all citizens to the law and the jurisdiction of the State, the equal enjoyment of private and public rights, equal opportunity, equal subjection to public duties (e g military service and taxes), equal protection before the law, and equal subjection to penalties, irrespective of the economic and social status of the accused. It requires the impartial exercise of State functions vis-à-vis private individuals; a principle which is confirmed in A.97 C in relation to the administrative function and in A.101 C in relation to the judicial function.

C. THE 'INVIOLABILITY' OF HUMAN RIGHTS

Article 2 C provides that the Republic recognises and guarantees the inviolable rights of man both as an individual and in the social organisations in which he manifests his personality, and requires the performance of the unrenounceable duties of political, economic, and social solidarity. This general affirmation of 'inviolability', more specifically recalled in Artt. 13ff C, refers to all 'natural' or fundamental human rights. The term 'inviolable' not only signifies the essential nature of the constitutional provisions which concern these rights but also that these rights cannot be curtailed by constitutional amendment. By making reference to 'social organisations', the inviolability affirmed by A.2 extends beyond individuals rights to include the rights of all types of social formations as such, viz, the family, associations, political parties, unions and all other intermediate communities, as well as the rights of individuals within these formations. On the other hand, A.2 also declares that certain duties are unrenounceable which, in this context, means that no one may be exempt from them. These duties are the defence of the State and, accordingly, the obligation to perform military service within the limits and methods fixed by legislation (A.52 C), contribution by foreigners and citizens alike to the public expenditure (A.53 C), and loyalty to the Republic, its Constitution and laws (A.54 C).

D. CIVIL RELATIONS

Adopting the classification of part of the doctrine, the rights connected with civil relations may be divided into four categories: rights of status, such as legal capacity and citizenship, neither of which may be denied for political reasons (A.22 C); the right to external signs distinguishing the human person, such as name which, moreover, cannot be denied for political reasons (A.22 C); the right to the physical integrity of the person; and civil liberties, which shall occupy the rest of this section.

The most important civil liberty is personal freedom, protected by A.13 C, which provides that no form of personal detention, inspection or search nor any other restriction of personal freedom is permitted except pursuant to a reasoned judicial measure and even then only in the cases and in accordance with the means defined by law. The general principle in A.13(1) C, is mitigated by A.13(2) C which provides that the legislature may strictly define any exceptional cases of necessity and urgency in which the police authorities may temporarily adopt measures restrictive of personal freedom, but all such measures must be communicated to the judicial authorities within 48 hours and unless confirmed by the latter within the next 48 hours, are to be deemed revoked and of no effect. The exceptional cases so far defined by legislation comprise arrest in flagrance (Artt. 235–237ff cpp; see ch 6, p 239, below), restraint of suspects (A.238 cpp; see ch 6, p 239, below) and the detention of persons for a time strictly necessary to ascertain their identity where a person either refuses to disclose his identity or there are sufficient reasons to believe that his identification is false (*l* 19 May 1978 n.191). Some writers take the view that the last exception is unconstitutional. Moreover, pursuant to A.13(5) C, which provides that the ordinary legislature is to define the maximum periods of preventive detention, the law of 11 April 1974 n.99 (*legge Valpreda*) prescribes, on a sliding scale, the maximum periods for which a person who has been lawfully arrested and awaiting trial may be detained. If such time limits are exceeded the accused must be immediately released. In 1980 the prescribed limits were increased by one-third in relation to the crimes of terrorism and subversion of the democratic system.

A complementary right to that of personal freedom is the freedom of domicile, declared by A.14 C to be inviolable. Article 14 prohibits any domiciliary search, inspection or sequestration except in the cases and in the manner provided for by law but always subject to the same grounds as prescribed by A.13 C for personal freedom. Any evidence procured contrary to A.14 C cannot be used in legal proceedings. However, A.14(2) C creates certain exceptions as to investigations concerning health, public safety, or economic and fiscal matters. A further mitigation of A.14 was created in 1977 to enable the judicial authorities to provide for the search of immovables suspected of being havens for terrorists. To facilitate the discovery of such havens, landlords are required to submit declarations to the police authorities concerning the tenancy of their premises.

The freedom and secrecy of expression of thought, and of its communication, is protected by A.15 C, which provides that their limitation may only arise through a reasoned judicial measure. This provision, which extends to every form of correspondence, also protects telephonic communications and therefore necessitated the recent modification of A.226 cpp which used to allow police interception of telephone conversations without prior judicial authority. The present position in relation to telephonic interceptions is regulated by the law of 8 April 1974 n.98 as modified by the so-called decreto-legge Moro of 21 March 1978 n.59. Telephonic interceptions must now be previously authorised by a member of the judiciary and may only take place in the investigation of certain defined crimes. In cases of urgency and necessity judicial authorisation may be given orally and then confirmed in writing as soon as possible. The authorisation may be for up to 15 days but can be extended for further periods of 15 days, provided that the pre-requisites for the authorisation continue to exist. To enable judicial supervision, all interceptions are to be carried out from the offices of the *Procura della Repubblica*, except in urgent situations in which case a judicial authorisation may be obtained to carry out the interception from the offices of the judicial police. Where certain serious crimes are involved, the evidence obtained from such interceptions may be used in proceedings other than those for which the interception was being carried out. Moreover, the law of 1978 referred to above introduced the so-called 'preventive interception' aimed at preventing the commission of serious crimes, but any information derived therefrom cannot be used in evidence in any proceedings. This exclusion of evidence is an obvious admission that this institution is a gross violation of the Constitution.

It was in connection with the protection of the individual freedoms that the question as to the existence of a right to privacy has arisen. The doctrine and case law had for a long time oscillated on the point. The Court of Cassation had recently, in substance, admitted the existence of such a right by including it within the wider concept of the protection of the person, although it denied the formal existence of an autonomous right to that effect. It was only with the legislation of 8 April 1974 n.98 that the right to privacy has been regulated by generally providing, first, that an illicit interference in private lives, the interception of communications and the like by private parties amount to crimes and second, where such interferences are carried out by the police, they must be authorised by the judiciary.

Article 16 C guarantees the freedom of movement which comprises three principles: first, the freedom of movement within the national territory; second, the freedom to establish residence anywhere; and third, the freedom to temporarily or permanently leave and re-enter the national territory. In addition, A.120 C prevents the Regions from creating obstacles to the free movement of persons or things between Regions. The freedom of movement may only be limited for 'health and security' reasons.

The freedom of assembly and association are guaranteed by Artt. 17 C and 18 C respectively. The former is the right of persons to assemble temporarily and voluntarily for pre-determined purposes, e g public meetings, processions, demonstrations, and the like. This right has two limits: a general one, namely, that meetings must be peaceful and unarmed, and a particular one, namely, that public meetings must be authorised. Subject to these limits, the authorities may only prevent meetings for proven reasons of security and public safety, the general possibility of a public disturbance not being a sufficient ground. The right of association is different to the right of assembly because of its permanent nature, it being characterised by the existence of a stable organisation and a permanent tie with members. The Constitution more particularly recognises this right in the political (A.49 C), industrial (A.39 C), and religious (A.19 C) fields. However, associations to commit crime (A.116 cp), secret associations (A.18(2) C) and military associations (A.18(2) C) are prohibited.

Article 19 C guarantees the freedom of religion, subject to the requirement that religious practices are not to be contrary to good custom or public order. The freedom in A.19 is a guarantee in favour of the *individual* who therefore enjoys a perfect equality and freedom of religion with the corollary that religion cannot be a reason for discrimination. Article 8 C, also dealing with religion, proclaims the equal freedom of all religious cults as such before the law. However, the relations between State and Catholic Church under the 1929 Lateran Pacts were such as to place the Catholic Church in a predominant and privileged position vis-à-vis other Churches and therefore seriously compromised the equality between religious cults contemplated by the Constitution. Notwithstanding that the Constitutional Fathers, by expressly safeguarding the Lateran Pacts under A.7 C, apparently regarded the 1929 Concordat system as compatible with the new political formula under the Republican Constitution, the conflict between the Pacts and the Constitution quickly became apparent, as a result of which, after protracted negotiations with the Holy See, the new Concordat of February 1984 was settled. The new Concordat, which revised the relationships between State and Catholic Church, together with the 'understandings' that, as contemplated by the Constitution, are to be concluded with all of the non-Catholic religions, is to create a system compatible with the Constitution and modern social developments (see ch 4, above for a more detailed treatment of State-Church relations).

Article 21 C protects the freedom of thought and its public expression by any means whatsoever, e g press, radio, and television. This right of public expression, which differentiates A.21 C from A.15 C, includes the right of information in a double sense, viz, the right to inform the public and the right of the public to be informed. However, A.21 C is limited by other Constitutional principles such as the privacy of the individual, good custom, and the proper administration of justice. The most important manifestation of the freedom to disseminate thought is the freedom of the press, on which A.21 C sets out various principles. First, the press cannot be subjected to authorisations, as a result of which the present system is limited to requiring the registration of all periodicals at the *Tribunale* of the district in which they are published. Second, the exclusion of any form of preliminary censorship. Third, seizure can only take place pursuant to a reasoned judicial measure in cases of either a crime expressly provided for by law or for the failure to identify the responsible editor. In a case of urgency any seizure by the judicial police must be referred to the judiciary within 24 hours and confirmed by the latter within the successive 24 hours. Finally, the legislature may provide for the disclosure of the financial means of the periodical press and adopt measures to prevent the violation of good custom. The 'responsible editor' (whose appointment is obligatory in the case of the periodical press) has the duty to see that the numerous limitations upon the freedom of the press are not violated. Article 57 cp provides that where a responsible editor fails to exercise the necessary control over the contents of a publication so as to prevent the commission of a crime by the press, he is personally punishable, with a reduction in penalty of one-third, for the same crime as is committed by the press. Non-periodical publications must at least indicate the name and address of the publisher.

Radio and television transmissions were orginally subject to an uncontrolled monopoly of the Executive, notwithstanding several challenges to its constitutional validity. In 1974, although the Constitutional Court continued to affirm the validity of State control, because of various reasons, including the limited availability of frequency range, it imposed two conditions: that there be an impartial and general access to radio and television transmissions by all political, religious and cultural groups, and that the management of the media be free from the domination of the Executive power. These suggestions of the Court were incorporated into certain 1975 legislative reforms which, inter alia, shifted State control from the government to the Parliament. Nonetheless, and to some extent operating a reversal on its earlier decisions, the Constitutional Court in 1976 declared the State monopoly over *local*, although not national, radio and television transmissions unconstitutional in recognition of the fact that there were sufficient frequencies to permit a complete freedom of private initiative. Subject to regular authorisation, anyone may now conduct radio or television transmissions provided that these are limited to a local area.

E. ETHICAL-SOCIAL RELATIONS

The Constitution contains numerous general principles in three broad categories appertaining to ethical-social relations. First, family relations and the legal status of the family unit, understood as a natural association founded upon marriage (Artt. 29–31 C), e g the moral and legal equality of spouses, the protection and guarantee of the family unit, and the rights and duties of parents vis-à-vis their children. Family law has been the subject of numerous decisions of the Constitutional Court as from 1970, when divorce was introduced into Italy. It was the legislature which, with the legislation of 19 May 1975 n.151, profoundly modified the law on family relations, giving full effect to even those principles which were only implicit in the Constitution. The law of 1975 recognised the complete legal and moral equality of the spouses, e g the abolition of the notion that the male was the head of the family and that he exercised sole authority over the children, and the introduction of the community of property between spouses. Moreover, it introduced a substantive equality between legitimate and illegitimate children, including in matters of succession. These innovations in family law have been followed by further legislative reforms which have established equal work opportunities as between the sexes and the equality of treatment in relation to social welfare assistance and social security.

Second, education (Artt. 33 and 34 C), considered of equal importance to the family in the development of the person. From the education provisions in the Constitution there arise principles such as academic freedom, the freedom to establish private schools, the complete equalisation of State and private schools, the establishment of State institutions at every educational level, the freedom of access without discrimination to scholastic institutions, the admission to various educational levels upon examination, the admission to professional occupations after examination, compulsory and gratuitous education, and the right of capable but impecunious persons to tertiary education.

Third, the protection of health both as a fundamental individual right and in the collective interest, including the guarantee of the gratuitous treatment of the needy (A.32 C). The same Constitutional provision provides that no person can be obliged to undergo any given treatment, unless provided for by law, nor can the law in any case violate the inherent limits dictated by human dignity. An important step in fulfilling A.32 C has been the law of 23 December 1978 n.833 establishing the National Health Service, which encompasses all of the functions, organisations, services and activities relating to the promotion, maintenance and recuperation of physical and psychiatric health.

F. ECONOMIC RELATIONS

The economic relations protected by the Constitution generally relate to labour relations and private ownership. The Constitution considers 'labour' as the most important social phenomenon. Labour, according to A.1 C, is not an end in itself nor a mere means of livelihood, but as a necessary means of fulfilling individual personality. Labour, under the Constitution is a right-duty. Article 4(1) C provides that the Republic recognises the right to work and shall promote the conditions necessary to render this right effective. Article 4(1) is a mere policy provision and does not create a perfect right enforceable by the individual; it does not guarantee the right to obtain employment, nor the right to retain a position. However, according to the case law of the Constitutional Court, it is to be interpreted as favouring stability of employment through a rigorous discipline over dismissals. This provision has been used by the Constitutional Court to restrict the right of employers to withdraw from the employment relationship and, in particular, to affirm the validity of various provisions of the 1970 Labour Law: the judicial right to order the reinstatement of an employee who has been improperly dismissed; the State monopoly over the conduct of employment offices; the prohibition on employers making nominative requests for employees; and the requirement that enterprises employ given proportions of certain classes of person, e g blind and invalid persons. The right to work in A.4(1) also includes entrepreneurial activities which are more specifically recognised and protected in A.41 C which guarantees the freedom of private enterprise. Article 4(2) C provides that every citizen has a duty to perform an activity or function which contributes to the material or spiritual progress of society. However, this is only a moral and *not* a legal duty.

Apart from the general provisions of Artt. 1 and 4 C, there are many specific constitutional provisions relating to the employment relationship, unionism, and collective contracts. The provisions relating to the employment relationship include the right to remuneration in proportion to the quantity and quality of labour but in any case sufficient to ensure the employee and his family a free and dignified existence (A.36(1)C), the irrevocable right to weekly rest and paid annual holidays (A.36(3)C), equal rights for equal work (A.37(1)C), which has led to the law of 9 December 1977 n.903 entitled 'Equal treatment of men and women in labour matters', the harmonisation of maternity with the equal right to work (A.37(1)C), equal payment for minors and the regulation of child labour (A.37(3) C), the duty of the ordinary legislature to determine the maximum length of the working day and the minimum age for salaried work (Artt. 36(2), 37(2) C), the right of persons incapable of work to social services (A.38(1) C), the right to all forms of social security (A.38(2) C), and the right of minors and incapable persons to education and professional training (A.38(3) C). These principles constitute the minimum rights of all workers, including non-unionists and, with appropriate modification, self-employed persons. The Labour Law of 20 May 1970 n.300 has gone a considerable way towards fulfilling and broadening all the Constitutional provisions on labour relations (see also ch 10, below).

The Constitutional system acknowledges the right of workers to protect their economic and legal position vis-à-vis the employer through the recognition of two important institutions: the freedom of forming industrial associations, that is, the right to unionism (A.39 C), including the correlative right of stipulating collective contracts binding on all workers in a particular category independent of their membership of the relevant union (A.39(3) C), and the right to strike (A.40 C). According to A.39 C, the only obligation that can be imposed on unions is registration, which gives them both legal personality and the capacity to stipulate collective contracts. Under the Constitution, a condition for the registration of unions is that they have a democratic structure, although it is probable that other conditions may be required. However, as the legislature has not yet implemented the provisions of A.39 C, the unions are not at present required to register nor do they have legal personality. They merely constitute unincorporated associations as defined by the general provisions of the Civil Code (Artt. 36ff). The freedom of unionism guaranteed by A.39 C includes the freedom to form more than one union for the same category of workers, except in defined cases (magistrates and the armed forces), the freedom of individuals to choose amongst available unions or not to join any of them, the freedom from State interference in their organisation and activity, as well as in the formation of federations and confederations on a local, national, or international level, and the freedom to exercise union rights, even in the workplace, provided that no damage is caused to the employer, who is prohibited from taking any anti-union activity.

The collective agreements bind all members of the employment categories referred to in the particular agreement. As registered unions do not yet exist, the collective agreements presently in existence, as normal contracts, bind only the parties to the contract, that is, the members of the stipulating union. To prevent disparate treatment these collective agreements have been extended, at least in relation to the determination of remuneration, to all workers in a given category on the basis of the principle contained in A.36 C relating to proportional and sufficient remuneration.

In general, there has evolved in labour law a system which is in conformity with the constitutional provisions on the subject. The Labour Law of 1970 has introduced various provisions protecting the freedom and dignity of employees, the freedom of unionism, and the freedom of union activity in the workplace. Also introduced is a new procedure for the resolution of labour disputes characterised by its orality, speed, and concentration, as well as the very wide investigative powers conferred on the court in relation to the facts. The right to strike has been extended by the Constitutional Court from strikes with mere economic ends to the political strike.

Private ownership, which together with public ownership is expressly recognised by A.42 C, is 'guaranteed by the law' which, the article immediately adds, is to determine 'the manner of its acquisition and enjoyment and its limits with the object of assuring its social function and of making it accessible to all'. Article 42 not only in this way destroys the traditional notion of ownership but it goes on to provide that private property may, in the cases provided for by law, be expropriated in the general interest subject to indemnity. It follows that private property is subject to various limitations. First, as to its content or enjoyment, which may be compromised as a result of the social function of ownership. Second, as to its ownership, which may be compromised by its expropriation not only in the collective interest (e g public works and hygiene) but also for its 'public utility', that is, by the nationalisation of enterprises which concern essential public services, sources of energy or a monopoly in an individual economic sector (A.43 C). And finally, as to its extension, which may be limited in order to ensure a more rational use of land and to establish more equitable social relations (A.44 C). Private property may also be subject to various public servitudes.

G. POLITICAL RELATIONS

Political relations generally concern the rights and duties inherent in participation in the political life of the country. The basic political right, or the franchise, is dealt with in A.48 C (see p 140, above). Article 49 C guarantees the right of all citizens (not foreigners or stateless persons) to freely associate in political parties so as to compete democratically in the determination of national policy. Articles 50 and 51 C protect certain general political rights inherent in the exercise of either political functions vis-à-vis elected bodies or public functions pertinent to a public office, namely, the right to petition the Houses of Parliament as a means of direct democracy (A.50 C), the right to compete freely and equally for elected or non-elected public office (A.51(1) C), and the right of persons elected to public office to be allowed the necessary time for the performance of their functions without jeopardy to their employment (A.51(3) C). In the last case the employment relationship is temporarily suspended.

Articles 52, 53, and 54 C prescribe a series of public duties appertaining to both citizens and non-citizens as a consequence of their citizenship, permanent residence, or conduct of economic activities within the State. These duties are all necessary consequences of A.2 C, which requires the performance of the unrenounceable duties of political, economic, and social solidarity. The principal duties are as follows: first, the duty to exercise the franchise; second, the duty of military service (A.52 C) which has only recently been mitigated by the substitution of civil service for conscientious objectors (*l* 15 December 1972 n.772, as modified by *l* 24 December 1974, n.695); third, the duty to contribute to the public expenditure by the payment of taxes in accordance with the capacity to contribute; fourth, the duty of allegiance to the Republic and the observance of the Constitution and the law (A.54(1) C) and finally, the duty of citizens who hold public office to perform their duties in accordance with the law and in a befitting and honourable manner, taking where required an oath of office (A.54(2) C).

Chapter 6

The resolution of disputes: civil, criminal, and administrative procedure

Introduction

The law of procedure is that part of public law which regulates the exercise of the judicial function. Italian law does not have a unitary law of procedure, but rather a law of procedures corresponding to the various types of jurisdiction (see ch 5, p 161, above). The ordinary jurisdiction comprises the law of criminal procedure which regulates the criminal process or, in other words, that activity of the State directed to the application of the substantive criminal law, and the law of civil procedure which regulates the civil process or, in other words, the jurisdictional protection of rights. Generally, the former is regulated by the Code of Criminal Procedure (1930), and the latter by the Code of Civil Procedure (1940), although many provisions applicable to both types of procedure are also to be found in the Constitution (see ch 5, p 162, above) and in various special legislation.

Where the public administration is a party to civil proceedings, the division between the civil and administrative jurisdictions becomes relevant. Administrative justice in Italy is organised along the lines of a double jurisdiction: where subjective rights (see ch 1, p 20, above) are involved, the competent courts are the ordinary courts whose power vis-à-vis an administrative measure is limited to declaring it illegitimate and not applying it to the immediate case; where legitimate interests (see ch 1, p 23, above) are involved, the competent courts are the administrative courts, which have a power to annul illegitimate administrative measures. Whilst proceedings before the ordinary civil courts concerning the public administration are, like civil proceedings generally, regulated by the Code of Civil Procedure, proceedings before the administrative courts of first instance have, because it was anticipated at the date of their establishment that there will be enacted a codified law on administrative procedure, been made subject to the same provisions as are applicable to proceedings before the administrative court of second instance, the Council of State. Because this expediency has given rise to many lacunae in the regulation of the administrative process, the provisions of the Code of Civil Procedure have been applied by analogy. This has led to a particular relationship between civil and administrative procedure, namely, the law of administrative procedure constitutes a specific law which is supplemented, insofar as compatible with the administrative process, by the more general codified law of civil procedure.

The civil jurisdiction

Italian civil procedure has four basic characteristics, the first three highlighting that it is a party process and not, as is commonly thought, an 'inquisitorial' procedure. First, the proceedings are dependent upon party initiative (Artt. 99, 112 cpc, A.2907 cc). In contrast to criminal proceedings, the onus of initiating civil proceedings lies with the party who is seeking to have his rights recognised. This onus pervades the whole process so that if party impulse is lacking at the various points during the proceedings at which it must be renewed, the proceedings are extinguished. Second, the decision of the court is limited by the plaint (A.112 cpc). The court cannot of its own motion raise a claim or defence which has not been adduced by the parties and must restrict its decision to the claims and defences made out by the parties. Third, subject to special exceptions defined by law, the court must base its decision upon the evidence adduced by the parties (A.115 cpc). This characteristic, a consequence of party initiative, places the onus on the parties of adducing the evidence in support of their allegations. Another evidentiary consequence of the principle of party initiative is that the court, in contrast to criminal proceedings, is not required to ascertain the material truth but merely to decide which party, having regard to the party evidence, acted correctly and justly in the circumstances. Exceptionally, the court is given broader investigatory powers, e g in labour and family law matters. Fourth, the requirement of a trial. Article 101 cpc sanctions the principle that the court cannot make a decision unless the opposite party has been given an opportunity of appearing. This is generally satisfied by the service of the citation upon the opposite party, whereupon the court is still restricted to deciding those causes in which the plaintiff insists on a decision.

The civil courts and their structure

A basic feature of the Italian court system in general is the presence of both monocratic and collegiate-type courts. The debate as to which form is more desirable is of long standing. A collegiate decision, which involves an examination and discussion of the issues by several judges, is said to embody major guarantees, especially where new or controversial issues are involved. A collegiate decision means that the majority of the judges were convinced as to its correctness. From a practical point of view, a monocratic court has the advantages of rendering a speedier and more complete decision; speedier because its procedures are shorter and simpler and more complete because the judge is intimately familiar with the proof-taking and instruction phase of the proceedings which, unlike in the case of a college, he has himself generally conducted or supervised. Consequently, many writers prefer a mixed system, viz, a monocratic court at first instance and a collegiate structure at any subsequent stage of the proceedings. Such a system combines the advantages of both types of court structure without their corresponding disadvantages: the proof-taking phase is carried out by a monocratic court at first instance and there remain the guarantees inherent in a collegiate re-examination of the issues where the parties are dissatisfied with the decision at first instance.

The Italian civil courts, in decreasing order of importance are: the *Corte di cassazione* (Court of Cassation), the *Corti d'appello* (the Courts of Appeal), the *Tribunali* (the Tribunals), the *Preture* and the *Conciliatori*. Only the *Conciliatori* and *Preture* are monocratic courts; all of the remainder are collegiate organs. The *Tribunali* and Courts of Appeal each have a bench comprising three judges, and the Court of Cassation consists of five judges, unless it sits as a full court, when the bench is increased to nine.

The jurisdiction and competence of the civil courts

The Italian doctrine distinguishes between jurisdiction and competence. Jurisdiction describes the distribution of the judicial power to take cognizance of disputes amongst the various general court systems. Therefore, one can distinguish between the 'jurisdiction' of the Italian and foreign courts, of the ordinary and special courts, or of the civil and criminal courts. On the other hand, competence describes that part of the jurisdiction of a general court system that belongs to the individual courts within that jurisdiction. For instance, the Code of Civil Procedure divides the civil jurisdiction amongst the various civil courts listed above according to various criteria: value; subject matter; territory; and, although only impliedly mentioned by the Code, function. It follows that there may arise conflicts as to either jurisdiction or competence. Jurisdictional conflicts may relate to the question of Italian jurisdiction vis-à-vis a foreigner (see ch 3, above), a conflict between the ordinary courts and the public administration, a conflict between the ordinary and special courts, or a conflict amongst special courts belonging to different jurisdictions. Conflicts as to competence, on the other hand, may arise either between the ordinary courts or between special courts belonging to the same jurisdiction.

As far as competence is concerned, the Code deals with value and subject matter jointly, and territoriality separately. This bipartite treatment of the subject corresponds to the procedure in identifying the competent court: the subject matter and value of the cause together determine the competent grade of court within the court hierarchy, whilst territoriality determines which particular court within that grade is competent to deal with the cause.

The competence of the civil courts in terms of value and subject matter is as follows:

A. THE CONCILIATORI

The *Conciliatori*, who have both decisory and conciliatory functions, have their decisory competence limited to causes which are of a value of no more than Lit. 50,000 and concern movables (unless the particular subject matter falls within the competence of another court), eviction of tenants or other matters related to the lease of immovables (A.7 cpc).

B. THE PRETURE

The *Preture* have a competence at first instance in all causes with a value of more than Lit. 50,000 but not exceeding Lit. 750,000. Moreover, they have an exclusive jurisdiction, irrespective of value, in two broad classes of proceedings. First, in relation to possessory actions, proceedings for certain provisional remedies, boundary disputes, certain eviction proceedings, and disputes concerning the use of services in co-owned houses (A.8 cpc). Second, in certain enforcement and attachment proceedings, including the recovery and delivery of things, the attachment of movables, ejectment proceedings and the enforcement of mandatory and restraining orders (A.16 cpc). Moreover, the *Preture* are the courts of appeal from the decisions of the *Conciliatori*.

C. THE TRIBUNALI

The *Tribunali* have a residual competence at first instance encompassing all causes which do not come within the competence of either the *Preture* or *Conciliatori* (A.9(1) cpc). They have an exclusive competence in matters of taxation, the status and capacity of persons, honorific rights, special proceedings involving the authenticity of documents (*querela di falso*) and any cause with an indeterminable value (A.9(2) cpc) as well as in proceedings concerning the attachment of immovables or movables which are contained within an immovable which is itself subject to attachment (A.16 cpc). The *Tribunali* are the courts of appeal from the decisions of the *Preture*.

D. THE COURTS OF APPEAL

The Courts of Appeal have only an exceptional competence at first instance, e g proceedings for the recognition of foreign judgments (A.796 cpc). Their principal function is as courts of appeal from the decisions of the *Tribunali*.

E. THE COURT OF CASSATION

The Court of Cassation has a competence limited to the review of questions of law. It is a unitary court at the apex of the court hierarchy charged with the duty of ensuring the exact observance and uniform interpretation of the law and thereby of maintaining national unity in the substantive law. It is also competent to resolve conflicts in jurisdiction and competence.

In contrast to earlier times when there were itinerant justices with no territorial limits to their competence, the present Italian system divides the national territory into judicial districts (*circoscrizioni giudiziarie*) which define the territorial competence of each court. The district of each court in the judicial hierarchy contains the districts of several immediately inferior courts. In particular, the territorial competence of each court, in decreasing order, is as follows: the Court of Cassation, which is a unitary court situated in Rome, is competent over the whole of the national territory, and is the only court with an unlimited territorial competence; the Courts of Appeal are competent in their respective *distretto*; the *Tribunali* are competent in their respective *circondario*; the *Preture* are competent in their respective *mandamento*; and the *Conciliatori* are competent in their respective *comune*.

THE CIVIL COURTS

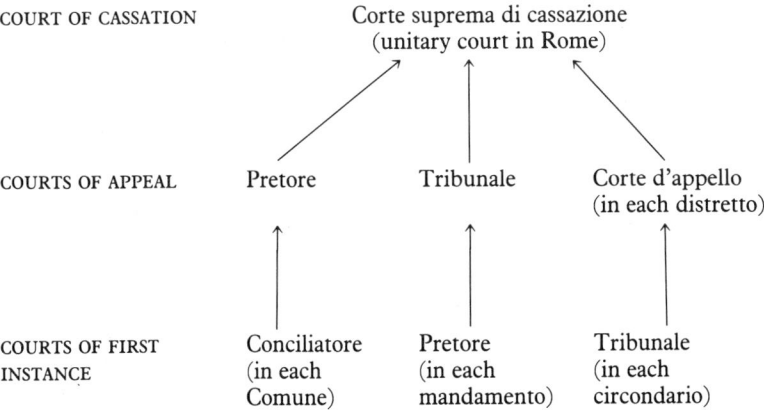

COURT OF CASSATION	Corte suprema di cassazione (unitary court in Rome)		
COURTS OF APPEAL	Pretore	Tribunale	Corte d'appello (in each distretto)
COURTS OF FIRST INSTANCE	Conciliatore (in each Comune)	Pretore (in each mandamento)	Tribunale (in each circondario)

The general territorial forum is where the defendant has his residence, domicile or, if these are unknown, his place of abode. If even his abode is unknown, or where he has a foreign residence, domicile or abode, then the general forum is where the plaintiff resides (A.18 cpc). In the case of legal persons, the forum is where the legal person has its seat, branch or an authorised representative for legal proceedings (A.19 cpc). The Code also provides specific rules for defined causes. However, as territorial competence is prescribed in the interests of the parties, the forum may, except in defined cases, be varied by agreement between the parties (Artt. 28 and 29 cpc). One case in which the forum cannot be varied is where the State is a party to the proceedings, as the competent court is that in whose territory the relevant State Attorney's Office, which represents the State, is located. Moreover, the forum may, as in the case of the other rules on competence, be affected by the joinder, incorporation or connexion of causes.

An issue of *jurisdiction* may be raised for the first time at any stage or grade of the proceedings by either a party or the court of its own motion (A.37 cpc). As an exception to this rule, a foreigner cannot raise the issue once he has expressly or impliedly accepted Italian jurisdiction. One way in which a foreigner will be taken to have accepted Italian jurisdiction is if he has failed 'timely' to raise the issue. Where the proceedings relate to immovables situated abroad or the defendant fails to appear, the court must raise the issue of its own motion (A.37(2) cpc). The court before which the issue of jurisdiction arises immediately decides the issue by judgment which is then subject to appeal which may be either taken immediately, through the normal appellate channels including final review by the Court of Cassation, or reserved until the final disposition of the case. An alternative procedure, known as *regolamento di giurisdizione*, is contained in A.41 cpc which enables an interested party to seek the direct and preliminary decision of the jurisdiction issue by the Court of Cassation at any time during the course of the proceedings at first instance. In such a case, the court of first instance must suspend the proceedings pending the decision of the jurisdiction issue by the Court of Cassation. This procedure enables a speedy and conclusive determination of the issue without the need for a prior decision of the issue by the court before which the original proceedings are pending.

The point in time at which an issue of *competence* may be raised varies depending upon its type: incompetence for subject matter may be raised by the parties or the court of its own motion at any stage or grade of the proceedings; incompetence for value may again be raised by either the parties or the court of its own motion, but only during the proceedings at first instance; and territorial incompetence, which may, subject to certain exceptions, be challenged by the parties only, must be raised in the plaintiff's appearance or in the initial answer of the defendant. The Code distinguishes two methods of challenging competence. First, at the instance of a party subsequent to a decision of the issue by the court before which the proceedings are pending. In this case the procedure differs depending upon whether the court of first instance has only decided the issue of competence or the merits as well. In the former case, the only means of attack is directly before the Court of Cassation (A.42 cpc); in the latter case, the party may choose to go directly to Cassation on the issue of competence (A.43 cpc) or follow the normal appellate channels. Second, at the instance of the court (Artt. 45 and 47(4) cpc) which arises when one court considers itself incompetent and remits the case to another court that also considers itself incompetent, whereupon the second court is obliged to remit the issue to Cassation for decision.

The classification of civil actions

Classical Roman law began as a formulary system in which actions were classified according to the rights and interests they sought to protect and the facts upon which they were based. The formulary system and its classification of actions denoted the form of action for a given factual situation and the available relief as each formula specified the appropriate remedy. Even after the formulary system was abandoned, the classification of actions continued to depend upon the legal rights and facts in question. This meant that the substantive issues often determined the relevant procedural rules and gave rise to a procedural system with many technical pitfalls. The Italian Codes have generally abandoned this system of classification, and therefore the modern doctrine classifies actions according to their typical relief rather than the factual situations or legal rights upon which they are based.

The doctrine classifies actions into three main divisions. First, *le azioni di cognizione* (cognitive actions), actions that require the adjudication of substantive rights. It is the archetype of civil proceedings because it is the type through which subjective rights are realised. Cognitive actions are, in turn, divided into three types depending upon the relief granted:

A. AZIONI DI MERO ACCERTAMENTO (DECLARATORY JUDGMENTS)

Declaratory judgments merely confirm the existence or non existence of uncertain or controversial legal relationships, e g the capacity and status of persons, the authenticity or falsity of private writings, the nullity of acts and the like.

B. AZIONI DI CONDANNA (ACTIONS SEEKING COERCIVE RELIEF AGAINST
THE LOSING PARTY)

These actions result in judgments that, apart from resolving a
controversial issue, are immediately enforceable or self-executing.
They are actions which result in an order for the performance or
non-performance of a specified act, or the payment of a sum of money.

C. AZIONI COSTITUTIVI (ACTIONS AFFECTING A LEGAL RELATIONSHIP OR
STATUS)

These actions result in judgments that create, modify, or extinguish
legal relationships. These judgments differ from declaratory judgments
because they create or alter a legal relationship rather than judicially
confirm a pre-existing situation.

Second, *azioni esecutivi* (enforcement proceedings), brought to
enforce a judgment or any instrument having the legal force of a
judgment such as a negotiable instrument. Judgments neither
voluntarily obeyed nor self-executing must be enforced through
enforcement proceedings. In other words, whilst a cognitive action
aims at ascertaining the sum or thing due and orders the debtor to
deliver the sum or thing, an enforcement action satisfies the judgment
by materially obtaining the sum or thing or, if it is not possible to
obtain them, by expropriating the property of the debtor and obtaining
the cash equivalent of what is due. In these proceedings the judge
carries out the operations necessary to satisfy the creditor. Italian law
provides three forms of execution: first, forced liquidation of assets,
which consists of the sale of the debtor's property to obtain what is
owing to the creditor; second, dispossession, the seizure of the thing
owing to the creditor and its transfer to the latter; and third, substitution, consisting of the performance, at the debtor's expense, of that
which the debtor should have performed pursuant to an obligation to
perform, or the destruction, again at the debtor's expense, of that
which the debtor performed in violation of an obligation not to
perform.

Third, *azioni cautelari* (provisional proceedings) which are accessory
or subsidiary to principal proceedings. As there is some delay in
obtaining a definitive judgment, provisional proceedings enable both
the temporary protection of the rights claimed in the principal
proceedings and the grant of temporary measures necessary for the
effective conduct of the principal proceedings. Provisional remedies are
generally available in three situations: to preserve evidence; to ensure
that the final judgment will not remain unsatisfied; and to safeguard the
rights of the parties and provide them with interim relief pending the
conclusion of the principal proceedings. They may give rise to either
autonomous proceedings or auxiliary orders granted during the course

of the principal proceedings. The necessary pre-requisites for a provisional remedy are the possible existence of the right claimed in the principal proceedings, and a well-founded fear that before the conclusion of the principal proceedings the circumstances favourable to the enforcement of the alleged right will disappear. The provisional remedies are divided into three broad types:

A. THE SO-CALLED SPECIFIC REMEDIES

These, in turn, comprise three types:

(*i*) *Sequestration* consisting of placing property in the custody of a third person or a party and forbidding its disposition. Sequestration may be judicial sequestration granted where the ownership or possession of property is in dispute or for the preservation of documentary or other tangible evidence; conservative sequestration granted to ensure satisfaction of a future judgment; or liberating sequestration granted where property or money has been tendered but refused by the creditor, thus unburdening the debtor of the custody of items which he acknowledges are owing.

(*ii*) *Denuncia di nuova opera* (*complaint of new work*) *and denuncia di danno temuto* (*complaint of feared damage*), both being directed to safeguard property against physical damage caused by either work in progress on adjoining premises or the physical condition of the latter and may take the form of restraining orders, mandatory injunctions, or orders to post bonds.

(*iii*) *Istruzione preventiva* (*preliminary instruction*) consisting of taking evidence or carrying out inspections either before an action is begun or by anticipating them during the course of the action when it is feared that the evidence may not later be available.

B. PROVVEDIMENTI D'URGENZA (URGENT RELIEF)

This permits the court, in cases of imminent and irreparable injury and where there are no specific provisional remedies available, to grant appropriate provisional relief in order to render effective any future judgment on the merits (A.700 cpc).

C. ADDITIONAL FORMS OF PROVISIONAL RELIEF

Scattered throughout the Codes and special legislation are many additional forms of provisional relief not specifically labelled as such.

The civil process

Book 2 of the Code of Civil Procedure deals in detail with the civil process before the *Tribunale*. This process constitutes the general model applicable to all other civil courts as to which the Code restricts itself to stipulating variations only. Broadly speaking, civil proceedings before the *Tribunale* unfold in three distinct phases: first, the introductory phase characterised by the initiation of the proceedings by the interested party; second, the instruction phase comprising two aspects: the procedural preparation of the case (*trattazione*) comprising all of those activities concerned with establishing or settling the pleadings, and the *evidentiary phase* (*istruzione probatoria*) comprising the taking of the evidence; and third, the decision-making phase characterised by the issue of the court's judgment. The fundamental characteristic of the proceedings is the clear division between its instruction, which is conducted by a single judge, the so-called examining judge, and its decision, made by a college of three judges. Although quite distinct the two phases are connected through the examining judge who forms part of the college and acts as rapporteur.

The civil process under the 1865 Code was a written one and excluded the examining judge from membership of the adjudicating panel. Due to strong doctrinal pressures, the present 1942 Code introduced several radical changes. The civil process was to be principally oral, concentrated into a few proximate audiences, and immediate through the participation of the examining judge as a member of the adjudicating panel. The Code limited the review of interlocutory decisions so as to coincide chronologically with the review of the principal judgment and increased the powers of the court. But, for practical reasons, certain amendments introduced in 1950 led to the erosion of the principle of orality and the civil process being returned to being a primarily written process. The instruction phase is in fact characterised by the exchange of written memoranda and the oral part of the proceedings have degenerated into mere formalities. Attorneys generally attend only when important oral evidence is offered or at the final oral argument, leaving the rest to their juniors. The principle of concentration has, in practice, not been applied as a result of the broad powers granted to the parties during the instruction phase. Today, civil proceedings are long and comprise a number of disconnected audiences.

The introductory phase

The most authoritative doctrine considers the commencement of the proceedings to be at the point of serving the summons upon the defendant. The summons, apart from indicating the court and the particulars of the parties and their legal representatives, must contain a statement of the relief sought (*petitum*) together with the facts and rules of law giving rise to the claim (*causa petendi*), an indication of the evidence that will be relied upon to prove the allegations, an invitation to the defendant to enter an appearance, and the subscription (A.163 cpc). There are no rules which prohibit the inclusion of irrelevant or inadmissible allegations, and although claims may usually be modified up until the conclusion of the instruction phase, further claims may not normally be introduced. Before the 1950 amendments, in order to avoid surprise and to force the parties to reveal their positions at the outset, only the evidence mentioned in the summons or statement of defence was admissible. It is now permissible to introduce new evidence during the course of the proceedings, and there is no effective sanction against withholding evidence until late in the proceedings except for the possibility of imposing costs for violation of the duty of 'probity and fairness'. Service is effected by the court bailiff and may be personal or, if to be effected outside the commune of the bailiff's residence, by mail.

The commencement of the proceedings may be ineffectual either because the summons is void for non-compliance with certain requisites listed in A.163 cpc or because the service is void. In accordance with the general principle that nullity for mere failure to observe form depends upon whether the act in question has in any event achieved its object, all of the above defects will be cured by the appearance of the defendant. This general principle is an attempt to discourage reliance upon procedural formalities, and manifests itself through the three broad principles contained in A.156 cpc: first, the mere failure to observe a procedural formality can only give rise to nullity if expressly provided for by law; second, nullity may, in any event, be declared where an act lacks a formal requisite indispensable to the achievement of its purpose; and finally, nullity can never be declared, even where expressly provided for by law, if the act has achieved its purpose. Other provisions which discourage procedural formalism include: first, A.157 cpc which contains four principles, viz, the court may not of its own motion, unless provided otherwise by law, declare a procedural act void; only the party whose interest the procedural formality seeks to protect may raise the nullity of an act; the nullity must be raised immediately upon its occurence or notice thereof, otherwise it shall be deemed to have been waived; and a null act may not be relied upon by the party who either caused it or expressly or impliedly waived it; second, A.159 cpc which provides that the nullity of an act does not avoid any preceding or subsequent act which is not dependent upon the void act and, similarly, that the partial nullity of an act does not invalidate the whole act where the valid part is independent of the invalid part; and finally, A.162 cpc which provides that the court must, wherever possible, order the renewal of a null act.

Where one party only enters a formal appearance, the other party may appear at any time until the first audience, or remain in default: if the defendant has failed to appear, the case continues; however, if the plaintiff fails to appear, he is declared to be in default and the proceedings immediately discontinued unless the defendant requests that the proceedings be permitted to proceed. Where neither party enters a formal appearance then, unless the proceedings are re-activated within one year by the service of a notice on the opposite party, the proceedings are discontinued.

In Italy there is no concept of a limited appearance. Thus, as the court must of its own motion examine the summons and its service where the defendant fails to appear, if there is a defect the defendant has no alternative but not to appear and hope that the court will discover it for if he appears the defendant will ipso facto waive any reliance upon the defect. However, some courts allow attorneys informally to point out defects even though no appearance has been entered. In the introductory phase, moreover, there may be the voluntary or involuntary joinder of third parties and the consolidation of causes.

At the time of appearance each party must deposit a file containing his documents; any subsequent documents will also be filed in it. When one of the parties, usually the plaintiff at the time of his appearance, files a notice for listing, the court clerk opens the official file which is sent to the president of the court who designates the examining judge who will have the conduct of the instruction phase. The appointment of the latter marks the close of the introductory phase.

The instruction phase

A. INTRODUCTION

In a broad sense, the instruction is that phase in which all of the material necessary for a decision is collected: the examining judge brings the instruction phase to its conclusion and then passes the matter to the tripartite adjudicating college, which includes himself, for decision. According to A.175 cpc, the examining judge has all of the powers necessary for the prompt and fair conduct of the instruction proceedings: he can fix the dates of the successive hearings and the times within which the parties must comply with certain procedural matters, decide all claims and defences raised by the parties, and arrange to take the evidence. The proceedings are generally informal and closed to the public except for the parties and their legal representatives. The two aspects of this phase are first, the settlement of the pleadings and other procedural matters and second, the taking of the evidence which may, of course, not always be necessary, e g where the only issue is one of law. However, in practice the separation between these two aspects of the instruction phase is of little importance and many of the audiences at various stages during the instruction phase deal with either or both aspects.

B. THE PROCEDURAL ASPECTS OF THE INSTRUCTION PHASE

At the first audience the examining judge is required to investigate the regularity of the proceedings and the formal and actual appearance of the parties (Artt. 181, 182 cpc). Article 181 cpc deals with the absence from the first audience of either or both of the parties in the case in which both parties had entered formal appearances. If both are absent, the examining judge sets a new date, and if both are again absent from the second audience the case is struck from the list and the proceedings discontinued unless re-activated within one year. If the defendant is absent, the proceedings may nonetheless continue. If, however, the plaintiff is absent, the proceedings may only continue at the request of the defendant; otherwise the judge fixes a new date and if the plaintiff is again absent the case is struck from the list and the proceedings immediately discontinued. According to A.182 cpc, the judge is required to examine ex officio the regularity of the formal appearances and the compliance with any mandatory requirement for legal representation; if there are any defects in these matters he must fix a time within which they are to be regularised. If a party to the proceedings has failed to make a formal appearance (see p 196, above) by this stage, the examining judge on verifying the regular service of the summons declares him to be in default. A defaulting party may, however, make a formal appearance at any time before the case is remitted to the college, but he must accept the proceedings as he finds them at the point at which he appears subject only to the right at the first audience of denying the authenticity of any private writings produced against him. He may nonetheless seek consent to perform those instruction activities from which he would by that stage be precluded from exercising.

Article 183 cpc provides that at the first audience the parties may clarify and, where necessary *modify* their claims, defences or sub-missions. This used to be complemented by A.184 cpc which precluded such modifications in any successive hearings. However, since the 1950 amendments the new formulation of A.184 cpc permits, at 'any time until the matter is remitted to the college', the modification of claims, defences, and other submissions, the production of new documents, the request that new evidence be admitted, and the submission of new defences. But 'modification' does not mean 'change' and therefore, it must be emphasised, it is well settled in Italian law that a claim cannot be changed. Finally, according to A.185 cpc the judge must at the first audience seek to reconcile the parties, although such an attempt may again take place at any stage of the instruction proceedings.

The instruction phase consists of a number of separate hearings stretching, very often, over a long period of time. Once the case is ready for decision, the examining judge remits the case to the adjudicating panel. However, if during the course of the instruction phase, any preliminary or prejudicial issue arises, e g jurisdiction, the examining judge may at his discretion either remit the issue to the panel for a separate decision or postpone the issue until the whole case is passed to the panel for final disposition. Similarly, in relation to the evidence, the examining judge may separately remit issues of admissibility or significance of evidence, as too, if he considers it opportune, the actual assumption of that evidence which can only be taken by the panel. On the other hand, the panel has a general control over the orders of the examining judge. In fact, once the case passes to the college, it re-examines all of the orders made by the examining judge and may even come to a different conclusion. Moreover, the panel also has the right to immediately decide issues of admissibility or significance of the evidence upon either an application by a party or reference by the examining judge when the latter does not desire to personally decide the issue.

C. EVIDENTIARY ASPECTS OF THE INSTRUCTION PHASE

The collection of the evidence in this procedural phase is one of the most important aspects of the civil process mainly because, in practice, the evidence is rarely re-taken in the decision-making phase notwithstanding that the panel has the right to re-hear any part of the evidence which was taken by the examining judge. Apart from documentary evidence, which is usually attached to the pleadings, the evidence is taken pursuant to orders (*ordinanze*) of the court normally made after a party motion requesting that the evidence in question be taken. The orders are made by the examining judge except in the rare cases in which only the panel may make the order to receive the particular type of evidence.

The rules of evidence are not only to be found in the Code of Civil Procedure; those rules which regulate the substantive aspects of the evidence are to be found in the Civil Code (Book VI, Title II). A simultaneous consideration of the evidentiary rules in both Codes will make it abundantly apparent that the Italian system places a greater importance on documentary evidence and the evidence of court appointed experts than on testimonial evidence. It is the distrust of the latter, combined with the abstract nature of the Codes and Italian legal education generally, that partly explain the tendency of Italian courts and lawyers to overrate issues of law at the expense of the facts.

The onus of proving a claim or defence generally lies on the party asserting it (A.2697 cc). In certain cases the substantive law reverses the onus of proof, e g there is a presumption at law that a debtor is at fault for the non-performance of an obligation. Therefore the plaintiff never need prove the fault of the debtor who in this instance bears the onus of proving that the performance of the obligation was impossible for a reason not imputable to him (A.1218 cc). The onus of proof may be varied by agreement provided that the contract does not involve non-disposable rights nor make it excessively onerous for a party to exercise his rights (A.2698 cc).

The procedural regulation of the onus of proof is dealt with in A.115 cpc which states that, unless provided otherwise, the court must base its decision upon the evidence adduced by the parties or the *pubblico ministero*. It follows that the court may only rely on the evidence offered by the parties and therefore, as a general rule, the court cannot investigate facts which, although important, have not been adduced by them. The court may seek clarifications and explanations inherent in the facts or matters which arise, even incidentally, from the instruction of the case. A major exception to this general position is that the inferior courts (the *Preture* and *Conciliatori*) may of their own motion call as witnesses persons who are referred to by the parties and appear to be in a 'position to know the truth' (A.317(1) cpc). Other general exceptions include the power to require the testimony of persons referred to by a witness as having knowledge of the facts (A.257 cpc), the power to appoint expert consultants (Artt. 61 and 191 cpc), the right to order inspections of persons, places or things (A.118 cpc), the right to administer an informal interrogatory of the parties (A.117 cpc), and the right to put supplementary oaths. Although important exceptions exist, Italian courts do not have broad powers to take evidence of their own motion. However, no evidence is required of undisputed facts, rules of law which may only be ascertained and applied by the court, and notorious facts of which the court has judicial notice (A.115(2) cpc). On the other hand, the courts exercise a control over the evidence which is adduced by the parties as it must be significant to the decision of the case.

The general rule as to the probative value of evidence is that the judge may freely evaluate it 'according to his prudent judgment', subject to any express provision to the contrary (A.116(1) cpc). This does not mean that the court can weigh the evidence arbitrarily; it must explain the use of the evidence in its judgment and any insufficient or contradictory explanation gives rise to grounds for review. Nonetheless, for practical reasons, there have remained in Italian law certain forms of legal proof, that is, certain forms of evidence in relation to which the Code assigns defined and binding effects. The court, in these cases, does not have any evaluative functions but must merely assign the defined effects to the evidence. Examples of legal proof are confessions and oaths. Moreover, it is important to note that although the law provides that certain forms of evidence cannot be relied upon by the court (called 'inadmissible' by the Codes), in many cases such evidence nonetheless comes to the attention of the court. For instance, documentary evidence which is filed with the court clerk and therefore comes before the court without any test as to its admissibility. In fact, a party has the duty to produce preconstituted forms of evidence by either its inclusion in the file or its presentation at the audience, although this only goes to its production and not admissibility. Moreover, the mere taking of inadmissible testimonial evidence does not constitute a ground for error. The only consequence of the inadmissibility of the evidence is that the court cannot place formal reliance upon it.

D. THE PRINCIPAL FORMS OF CIVIL EVIDENCE

(*i*) *Expert evidence* (Artt. 191ff cpc). The technical consultant is considered by Italian law as an auxiliary court official rather than a witness. Nonetheless, the court is free to evaluate the expert evidence and may even reject it. The technical consultant is appointed by the examining judge or panel at either the instance of the court or at the request of a party. The consultant is generally selected from persons on the relevant list of experts kept by the court. In the same order appointing a consultant, the court assigns a time within which the parties may nominate their own expert, known as a party expert, who may assist the court appointed expert and present his own written reports. The usual situation is that the judge entrusts the consultant with the conduct of a defined inquiry which is to be performed without the intervention of the court. The consultant may be authorised to request clarifications of the parties, to obtain information from third persons and to draw up plans, calculations and surveys. The president of the court may invite the consultant to assist at the trial and to express his opinion in camera when the court is considering its decision.

(*ii*) *Documentary evidence*. Italian law distinguishes between public acts and private writings. A public act (A.2699 cc) is a document drawn, in conformity with the prescribed formalities, by a notary or some other public official who confers public faith upon it. It constitutes conclusive evidence, until *querala di falso* (see p 188, above), of two matters, namely, of its source, that is, that the public official who prepared the document was its author; and of the declarations and events that the public official declares were made or performed, respectively, either in his presence or by him (A.2700 cc). A private writing is one which is drawn and subscribed by a party to the proceedings without the assistance of a public functionary. It constitutes conclusive evidence, until *querela di falso*, that the person who subscribed it was the author of the statements contained in it, but it only has this effect if either the person against whom the writing is produced acknowledges that the subscription is his or the subscription has been authenticated by a notary (A.2703 cc). If the subscription is acknowledged or authenticated, then the private writing has the same probative value as a public act. It must be stressed that neither type of document constitutes conclusive evidence of the *truth* of the statements contained in them, although they may nonetheless contain admissions which often do constitute conclusive evidence (see p 202, below). Exceptionally, the law attributes the same value as private writings to documents without a subscription, eg telegrams where the original delivered to the telegraph office has been either signed by the sender or delivered to the telegraph office by the latter or at his request (A.2705 cc) and books of account kept by commercial enterprises.

As already noted, a private writing does not per se constitute evidence of its authenticity unless it has been authenticated by a notary. The proof of authenticity is facilitated by placing the onus of its denial upon the person against whom the document is produced. The denial must be made either at the first audience or with the first document which is filed after the production of the disputed writing. If the person who produced the document still desires to avail himself of it, he must request its verification by commencing separate or incidental proceedings to ascertain the authenticity of the writing. If the court finds that the document is genuine, it may impose a pecuniary penalty on its author for denying its authenticity.

Querela di falso is different from verification proceedings because in the latter the party who produced the document bears the onus of verifying it whilst in the former the onus of showing that the document is false is borne by the party alleging it. A *querala di falso* may be initiated at any stage or grade of the proceedings and may take the form of incidental or principal proceedings. If the proceedings on the document are unsuccessful, mention of the judgment is made on the document itself and a pecuniary fine may be imposed on the proponent of the proceedings.

Traditionally, the writings of third persons were inadmissible as evidence on the ground that any information within the knowledge of third persons ought to be given orally. However, as it was often impossible to obtain testimony from such persons because of the rules applying to testimonial evidence much relevant, even if hearsay, evidence was excluded. Consequently, Cassation has repeatedly held that the writings of third persons may be admitted into evidence. Such writings do not constitute conclusive but merely circumstantial evidence which cannot, without other evidence, support a judgment. Moreover, their authenticity may be challenged by any form of evidence.

(iii) Production of tangible evidence and inspections. The production and inspection of evidence are related because often the production of tangible evidence is a pre-requisite for its inspection. A party may voluntarily produce a document or other tangible evidence either with the pleadings or at a later stage. However, if a document or other tangible evidence which is necessary for the decision of the cause is in the possession of a third person or another party to the proceedings, including the public administration, and it is not voluntarily produced, its production may be ordered by the court if the following requisites are satisfied (Artt. 118 and 210ff cpc): the motion for production originates from a party; the evidence to be produced is in the possession or control of the person to whom the order is addressed; the production appears indispensible to the decision of the cause; the production does not seriously damage the party or third person to whom the order is addressed nor give rise to the violation of professional privilege or official secrecy; and the proponent advances the costs that will be incurred to effectuate the production. The person ordered to make the production may move to have the order set aside. The court, however, is free to draw the appropriate inferences where there is an unjustified refusal to produce the evidence pursuant to a court order.

An inspection (Artt. 258–262 cpc) may relate to persons or things (whether movable or immovable) and is ordered by the examining judge who may proceed to carry out the inspection personally, even if it is to take place outside the *circondario* of the court, or through an expert consultant who may be entrusted to carry out the inspection either alone or together with the judge. Whereas production may only be ordered on the motion of a party, an inspection may also be ordered at the instance of the court.

(iv) Admissions (Artt. 2730–2735 cc; Artt. 228ff cpc). An admission (or confession) is defined by A.2730 cc as a 'statement made by a party as to the truth of facts unfavourable to him and favourable to his adversary'. It is a form of legal proof and as such the judge cannot freely evaluate the admission but must accept the confessed facts as true. The person making the statement must have the capacity to dispose of the rights in issue and if the author of the statement is only an agent, the statement is only effective if it is made within the limits of the agent's authority. An admission must concern facts only and, to constitute conclusive evidence, it must concern immediate and certain facts which

create, impede, or extinguish the disputed relationship and avoids the need for further evidence on the matter.

An admission made outside the scope of the proceedings to an adversary, or to an agent of the latter, has the same probative value as an admission made within the proceedings, viz, it constitutes conclusive evidence but only in relation to the proceedings as to which it has been made. If, the admission is made to a third person, is contained in a will, or is made in different proceedings, it may be freely evaluated by the court.

An admission made within the scope of the proceedings may be either spontaneous, that is, contained in any procedural document signed by a party, or provoked, that is, obtained through a formal interrogatory.

(v) Formal interrogatories (Artt. 230–232 cpc). The formal interrogatory is the means expressly provided for by law to provoke admissions from an adversary. As a party is not a competent witness, his knowledge of the facts may only be obtained through spontaneous admissions, formal interrogatories (that is, provoked admissions), party oaths, and informal interrogatories. However, the formal interrogatory is not frequently availed of as it seldom produces the admissions sought, particularly as the adversary knows the questions beforehand and is not examined under oath. The party who intends to have his adversary interrogated must formulate separate and specific questions to be put to the adversary by the examining judge. The examining judge may not go beyond the questions unless either agreed to by the parties or by way of clarification of the answers given. If the party fails to appear at the hearing fixed for his formal interrogation or refuses to answer without just cause, the court may, having regard to all of the other evidence, regard the facts which were to be deduced from the interrogatory as admitted.

(vi) Informal interrogatories. In contrast to formal interrogatories, free or informal interrogatories are at the disposal of the court only. The court, according to A.117 cpc, may at any stage or grade of the proceedings, order the personal appearance of both parties so as to confront and freely interrogate them at the same time on the facts of the case. The parties may request the presence of their legal representatives at the interrogatory. The informal interrogatory is primarily aimed at assisting the interrogated party by clarifying his claims or defences. Although this institution had the potential of developing into a form of party testimony, it has not done so, unlike the case in France. However, the court may draw inferences from the answers given and the behaviour of the parties during the interrogation (A.116 cpc). There are two differences between formal and informal interrogatories with respect to the probative value of the answers given: first,

admissions against interest made during the course of an informal interrogatory do not constitute conclusive evidence but may be freely weighed by the court; and second, whilst, in a formal interrogatory, only those answers which contain admissions constitute evidence, answers to informal interrogatories constitute evidence irrespective of whether they are favourable or unfavourable to the party making them, although the tendency is to give answers to informal interrogatories very little weight thereby highlighting the courts' distrust of the institution which is infrequently utilised.

(vii) Party oaths. This is the most extreme example of the rules of legal proof which exist in the Italian law of civil procedure today. A party oath is a solemn declaration of the truth of a fact favourable to the declarant. Once sworn, the fact is considered conclusively proven and cannot be challenged by any means whatsoever. If the declarant has perjured himself he is liable to criminal prosecution (A.371 cp) and, after conviction, civil proceedings for damages at the instance of his adversary, even though the original judgment cannot be set aside. The onerous criminal and civil consequences of perjury in this instance explains why the institution is resorted to so frequently.

There are two types of party oath. First, the decisory oath (A.2736(1) cc) taken by one party upon a challenge made by his adversary on a matter decisive of the whole or part of the proceedings. The decisory oath may be put at any stage of the instruction phase. The party making the challenge must formulate the facts, the truth of which he wishes his adversary to swear, in separate statements. The party to whom the oath is put may refer it back to the proponent who must then swear the facts favourable to him. For example, if the plaintiff maintains that the contract in dispute was made on 1 January 1982 whereas the defendant maintains that it was made on 1 January 1983, if all of the pre-requisites necessary for a decisory oath are satisfied, the plaintiff may challenge the defendant to swear that the date of the contract was 1 January 1983. However, the defendant may refer the challenge back to the plaintiff who must then swear that the date was 1 January 1982. The failure to appear, like a refusal to either swear or refer back the oath, is conclusive proof of the truth of the adversary's allegations. Second, the supplementary oath (A.2736(2) cc) which is put, at the instance of the court, to one of the parties with the object of deciding a case where the claims or defences are not fully proved but are not totally without proof. Only the adjudicatory panel and not the examining judge may ask a party to take the supplemental oath. The oath may be put to any party, not necessarily that which has the burden of proof, and it cannot be referred back to the adversary.

(viii) Presumptions. Italian law considers circumstantial evidence as a

form of presumption. This is logical, for both are a means by which an unknown fact may be deduced from a known but indirectly relevant fact. Therefore Italian law distinguishes between two types of presumptions: legal presumptions and simple presumptions. The former, like common law presumptions, are defined by law and may be either conclusive or rebuttable presumptions. The latter are simply situations in which the court may infer, from common experience or science, a certain consequence from a known fact.

(ix) Testimony. In Italian law testimony may be defined as the oral narration of evidence by third persons. Italian law distrusts testimony as a form of proof and places serious limitations upon its admissibility, yet, once admitted, both the testimony and the credibility of witnesses may be freely evaluated by the court.

All persons who have an interest in the action are incompetent as witnesses (A.246 cpc), as, too, are the spouse and all lineal relatives of the parties unless the cause concerns status, personal separation, or family relations (A.247 cpc). However, the Constitutional Court has held A.247 cpc to be constitutionally invalid and therefore the persons listed in the provision must now be considered competent, even if not compellable witnesses. Similarly, witnesses who enjoy professional or State privilege are competent but not compellable witnesses. In the case of State privilege (A.249 cpc; Artt. 351 and 352 cpp), the court may require the Prime Minister to investigate the basis of a claim for privilege by a witness who must nonetheless submit to examination unless the Prime Minister confirms the claim for privilege within 60 days of the court's request.

There are also a number of substantive law rules in the Civil Code that limit the admissibility of testimony. First, oral evidence is inadmissible where the dispute relates to a legal act which must be in writing for its validity. Where, however, a contracting party has without his fault lost the document, oral testimony is admissible to prove that the legal act was made in the form required by law (A.2725 cc). Second, testimony is not admissible to prove any contract or payment of a value exceeding Lit. 5,000. This provision is of little practical importance as the court may in its discretion, having regard to the nature of the parties and the contract and any other circumstance of the case, admit testimonial evidence (A.2721 cc). Third, oral evidence is never admissible if it goes to prove the existence of additional or collateral agreements or agreements in conflict with the contents of a document when such agreements were made prior to or simultaneously with the document; when, however, the relevant agreement is consequent to the document, the court may in its discretion, again having regard to the nature of the parties and the contract and any other circumstance of the case, admit the oral evidence (A.2723 cc). On the other hand, testimonial evidence is *always* admissible in the cases defined by A.2724 cc, i e where there is a beginning of written evidence, where there is a moral or material impossibility of procuring written evidence, and where a party has without his fault lost the document constituting the written evidence.

Certain other limitations upon the admissibility of oral evidence arise from the procedural rules relating to the taking of testimony. Each party must submit a list of persons who are to be called as witnesses as well as the facts on which each witness must be examined. Although the court does not generally have the power to call additional witnesses of its own motion, it has the power to refuse to hear any witnesses considered to be superfluous. The opposite party must then indicate in his first reply the witnesses he desires to call either in mere rebuttal or for the deposition of new facts and, in the latter case, the facts on which the witnesses are to be examined. Witnesses are questioned by the judge who cannot depart from the matters specified in writing by the party calling the witness unless it is to seek a clarification of the answers or facts. The parties and their legal representatives are specifically forbidden from the examination or cross-examination of witnesses. This has often been criticised as removing the spontaneity and penetration of questioning that, instead, would result from an examination of witnesses by the parties or their legal representatives, who not only have a better knowledge of the facts but are also stimulated by personal interest. The Italian procedure of examining witnesses, on the other hand, has been defended on the very basis of the impartiality of the judge who avoids framing questions in a manner which would confuse or badger witnesses. Witnesses are heard separately and under oath, and, in practice, their evidence is not taken down verbatim but in the form of summaries dictated to the court clerk by the judge. The written depositions are then signed by the witnesses.

The court also has certain ex officio powers concerning testimonial evidence. First, when a witness refers to other persons, the court may require that they also be called as witnesses. Second, the court may later call as witnesses persons whom it had earlier either allowed to withdraw from giving evidence or considered to be superfluous. Third, the court may require that a witness be heard again or confronted with other witnesses. Finally, if a witness fails to appear for examination, he may be forcibly brought before the court and, in any event, ordered to pay a pecuniary penalty and the costs of any necessary adjournment.

The decision-making phase

When all of the necessary evidence has been collected and the parties have made their submissions, the examining judge remits the case to the college for decision. The proceedings before the college are public and may be broadly divided into four parts. First, the examining judge gives a report setting out the undisputed facts, the history of the proceedings and the issues of fact and law which are in dispute. After the report, in the second part of this phase, the president invites the parties to read their submissions and to address the court. In practice, these first two sub-phases are normally expedited since in the majority of cases the parties renounce their right of address and merely request that the matter pass for decision. Third, the decision by the college which is made in camera. The college comes to its decision by majority. It first considers any prejudicial questions and then passes on to the merits of the case. The rapporteur, who normally is the examining judge, always votes first, then the other puisne judge and finally the president. At the close of the voting, the president draws up and subscribes the orders and then generally leaves it to the rapporteur to draw up the judgment. Finally, there is the delivery of the judgment which is by means of its deposit in the court registry. The Code provides that this take place within 30 days of the hearing but the term is hardly ever complied with.

Exceptionally, a decision may be made in accordance with *equità*, that is, according to principles of justice and equity rather than law. All cases before the *Conciliatori* of a value not exceeding Lit. 20,000 must be decided according to equity (A.113(2) cpc). In all other proceedings, whether at first or second instance, the courts may only decide according to equity if requested to do so by both parties and even then only if the proceedings involve a right which may be freely disposed of by the parties (A.114 cpc). However, this is an uncommon situation as litigants generally prefer to put such a request to arbitrators rather than the courts.

A judgment may not be enforced during the time in which an appeal may be commenced nor during the course of any appellate proceedings. However, the court at first instance may, in defined cases, provide for the provisional enforcement of a judgment as between the parties to the cause, e g where the success of the claim was based on strong evidence such as a public document, an acknowledged private writing or a res judicata judgment; and where delay may render enforcement impossible, difficult or futile. Judgments of appellate courts are immediately enforceable unless suspended by the court.

A judgment becomes res judicata when it is no longer subject to appeal, review by Cassation, regulation for competence or to revocation on the grounds contained in paras (4) and (5) of A.395 cpc (A.324 cpc). Unless the judgment is served on the adversary or his legal representative, in which event the time within which the judgment may be attacked will commence to run from the date of the service, the judgment will only become res judicata one year after its publication provided that it is not challenged. These provisions embody the conflicting principles of the necessity for certainty in legal relations and the need for better justice. Certain exceptional defects are considered to be so serious that they may even be raised after the judgment becomes res judicata. It is for this reason that res judicata is said to be 'relative'. Consequently, judgments which have become res judicata nonetheless remain subject to revision, revocation, and third party opposition; methods of review which are therefore known as 'extraordinary' as opposed to the 'ordinary' methods of review which are not available after a judgment becomes res judicata.

Proceedings before the Preture and Conciliatori

In accordance with the general approach adopted by the Code (see A.311 cpc), in the absence of any specific provisions, the procedure prescribed for the *Tribunale* is also applicable to these courts. In fact, the particular provisions concerning these courts are generally restricted to their monocratic composition, social function and limited competence. The basic differentiating characteristics of the *Pretura* are: the amalgamation in the person of the *Pretore* of the functions performed by both the examining and trial judges in the case of the Tribunale; the simplification of formalities; speedier proceedings; and wider instruction powers such as the right of the judge to raise ex officio any lacunae or irregularity in the evidence and the power to call witnesses. The provisions applicable to the *Pretura* are also applicable to the *Conciliatori*. Moreover, in proceedings before the latter a party may be represented by a non-lawyer or not all. Furthermore, the *Conciliatori* not only have a statutory duty to attempt a conciliation of the parties to any proceedings, but they also have a pure conciliatory function unrelated to formal proceedings. The latter function may even be initiated upon a verbal application.

The judicial review of civil decisions

A. INTRODUCTION

There are in Italian law three grades of jurisdiction: first instance which is the proceedings on the merits; second instance, known as appeal; and third instance which is restricted to a review of errors of law. Therefore, a judgment at first instance may give rise to two consecutive grades in the proceedings: first, an appeal which in Italian law means a new trial on any question of fact or law that the appellant desires to have re-examined at second instance; and second, recourse to Cassation which is the review of any errors of law in the proceedings at second instance.

More particularly, the various types of review, apart from regulation of competence, are appeal, review by Cassation, revocation, and third party opposition (A.323 cpc). However, there are notable differences which distinguish an appeal from the other types of review. First, an appeal is a total re-examination of the dispute and is always available to the losing party. Therefore, unlike the other forms of review, no specific grounds for appeal are required. Second, unless there has been an order for provisional enforcement, the right of appeal has a suspensive effect because the judgment at first instance cannot be enforced until the time for lodging an appeal has expired, whereas the other forms of review do not suspend the enforcement of a judgment, unless specifically ordered by the court to avoid serious and irreparable damage. Third, in an appeal, it is the relationship in question which devolves upon the appellate court which then gives a new judgment replacing, rather than reforming or revoking, that of the court of first instance. Unlike the other forms of review an appeal is not based on the existence of a given defect which limits the scope of the review. Fourth, an appeal, unlike the other forms of review, does not give rise to new proceedings but it is a continuation of the proceedings at first instance supplemented by a new decision-making phase. Finally, both the proceedings at first instance and the appeal are known as proceedings on the merits because it is only in these that the merits may be considered in toto.

B. APPEAL

It follows that an appeal is conceded to a party merely for having failed at first instance so that there is a complete re-examination of the dispute without its restriction to the alleged defects in the judgment of first instance. However, certain judgments cannot be appealed, namely, judgments of the *Conciliatori* concerning disputes of a value of less than Lit. 20,000, unless the appeal relates to competence or jurisdiction; judgments made in accordance with *equità*; judgments in relation to which the parties had voluntarily agreed to omit an appeal (A.360(2) cpc); and judgments concerning individual employment disputes or social welfare benefits of a value not exceeding Lit. 50,000.

An appeal may be brought within the following times from the service of the subject judgment by the adversary: ten days in the case of a judgment of the *Conciliatori* and 30 days in the case of judgments of the *Pretori* or *Tribunali*. If the judgment is not served on the party by his adversary, appeal may be brought at any time within one year from the publication of the judgment. Although new claims are inadmissible in an appeal, the parties may raise new defences (which, however, must have been admissible at first instance), produce new documents, and request the admission of new evidence (which, however, if available at the time of the proceedings at first instance, may affect the award of costs). The proceedings before a court of appeal are also divided between an instruction phase, conducted by an examining councillor who has powers analogous to those of the examining judge, and a decision-making phase. In certain cases, the court of appeal remits the case to the court of first instance for its final disposition (Artt. 353 and 354 cpc).

C. REVIEW BY CASSATION

The functions of the Court of Cassation are statutorily defined as ensuring the exact observance and uniform interpretation of the law, the unity of the substantive law, and compliance with jurisdictional limits, as well as the regulation of any conflicts in competence and any other functions which are conferred upon it by law. Review may be sought by either an aggrieved party or the *pubblico ministero* in the event of inaction by the former. The right of the *pubblico ministero* is based upon the general interest, namely, the facilitation of the interpretation of the law by the Court of Cassation in the interests of the certainty of law. The review must be brought within 60 days of the service of the judgment by the adversary or, where the judgment is not served, within one year of its publication. The right of the *pubblico ministero* is without time limitation as, too, in the case of review on the ground of jurisdiction. Only appeal and non-appealable judgments (except the non-appealable judgments of the *Conciliatori*) may be reviewed by Cassation. Therefore, in the absence of an appeal, a judgment of first instance can never be reviewed by Cassation. However, where the parties had agreed to omit an appeal, the Court of Cassation may review the judgment of first instance but only for the violation or erroneous application of a rule of law. Moreover, an appeal or a non-appealable judgment of the special courts may also be reviewed by Cassation except for judgments of the Council of State and the Court of Accounts, in relation to both of which the Court of Cassation is only entitled to review issues of jurisdiction. In short, review by Cassation is, in essence, restricted to errors of law (A.360 cpc) which are traditionally divided into procedural and substantive errors.

The principal object of Cassation proceedings is to have the judgment under attack quashed and thereby pave the way for a fresh examination of the matter. If the application for review is dismissed, the judgment under attack becomes res judicata. If the reasoning only of the judgment under review was erroneous, Cassation will simply correct the reasoning without vacating the judgment (A.384 cpc). When an application for review is successful, the Court will quash the judgment and remit the case for its final disposition to a court different, but of equal grade, to that which made the quashed judgment, except in those cases in which the parties had agreed to omit an appeal when the court may remit the matter to the court which would have been competent to decide the appeal. The court to which the case is remitted is bound to follow the rules of law announced by Cassation. Exceptionally, Cassation may simply quash a judgment without remittance to another court, e g where no Italian court had jurisdiction, where there was no right to bring the action at all, or where there was no right of review (A.382(3) cpc).

When a case is remitted for final disposition, it must be recommenced by the parties through the issue of a new summons. If the case is not re-activated within one year, the proceedings are extinguished and the only remaining effect is the quashing by Cassation. Upon the re-activation of the proceedings, apart from the right of the parties to put a decisory oath, no new submissions may be made unless necessitated by the judgment of Cassation. The remand court is limited to the examination of that part of the judgment which has been quashed as to which it remains free subject to the binding effect of the judgment of Cassation. However, the remand court has the power to interpret the judgment of Cassation and, moreover, the quashing of the judgment does not necessarily mean that the new decision will come to a different conclusion.

D. REVOCATION

This form of review is only available against appellate and non-appealable judgments. The grounds upon which a revocation may be sought may be conveniently divided between the grounds for *ordinary* and *extraordinary* revocation. The grounds for ordinary revocation are that the judgment in question contains errors of fact patent from the court records or is inconsistent with an existing res judicata judgment (A.395(4) and (5) cpc). An application for ordinary revocation must be brought within 30 days of the service of the judgment. On the other hand, the grounds for an extraordinary revocation may appear after the expiry of the time for the ordinary appeal of the judgment in which case the revocation proceedings may be brought within 30 days of the discovery of the ground. The grounds for extraordinary revocation are: that the fraud of a party affected the judgment; that the judgment was based on evidence which was recognised or declared to be false after the judgment was given; the discovery of decisive documentary evidence which was not available at the date of the proceedings because of either *forza maggiore* or the behaviour of the adversary; and that the judgment was the product of judicial fraud which has been found in other proceedings which have since become res judicata (A.395(1), (2), (3) and (6) cpc).

The application for revocation is made to the same court which pronounced the judgment under attack. Where the application is granted, the judgment in question is revoked leading to a second phase in the proceedings in which the merits of the original cause are redetermined. The new judgment pronounced pursuant to revocation proceedings cannot itself, however, be the subject of further attack by revocation but only by the other forms of review which were available against the original judgment. Revocation is never available against decisions of Cassation. When the *pubblico ministero* is a party to the original proceedings, he may seek revocation on the same grounds as any other party. Where, however, he was not a party to the original proceedings, he may only seek revocation in those cases in which his intervention was obligatory and, even then, only on two grounds: that he was not made a party to the proceedings, or that the judgment was affected by the collusion of the parties (A.397 cpc).

E. THIRD PARTY OPPOSITION

Third party opposition may only be brought by a stranger to the proceedings. To prevent the multiplicity of suits, a third person may intervene in proceedings which are still pending. However, in the failure of an intervention, to avoid the initiation of another action, a third person who is prejudiced by a judgment is given the right to bring a third party opposition even if the judgment has already become res judicata between its parties. This extraordinary remedy is of two types. First, ordinary or simple opposition available to third parties who are prejudiced by the existence of an enforceable or res judicata judgment. This type of opposition may be brought at any time. Second, revocatory opposition which is available to the creditors and successors in interest of a party to proceedings in which the judgment is affected by either the collusion of the parties or the fraud of one of them. It must be brought within ten days, in the case of a judgment of the *Conciliatori*, or within 30 days, in the case of a judgment of the *Pretore* or *Tribunale*, of the discovery of the collusion or fraud.

The judgment which is attacked must be res judicata between the parties and enforceable. Judgments of first instance which do not provide for provisional enforcement, and judgments of second instance in which enforcement has been suspended, cannot be opposed. The opposition must be brought before the court which pronounced the judgment being opposed. Where the opposition is granted, the opposed judgment becomes ineffective and unenforceable vis-à-vis the third person opponent. However, the judgment continues to exist and to produce its effects as between its parties but only insofar as it does not prejudice the third person.

Special civil proceedings

A. INTRODUCTION

The various types of special proceedings are dealt with in Book IV of the Code of Civil Procedure. The only characteristic common to all of these proceedings is that their procedures differ from ordinary proceedings. Nonetheless, they may be classified into several categories. First, summary proceedings which comprise those proceedings characterised by an abbreviated adjudicative process. They are summary ex parte proceedings (*procedimento di ingiunzione*), eviction proceedings (*procedimento per convalide di sfratto*), proceedings for provisional remedies (*procedimenti cautelari;* see p 192, above), and possessory proceedings (*procedimenti possessori*). Second, non-contentious proceedings (*giurisdizione volontaria*). Third, proceedings relating to the issue of copies or the inspection of public records. Fourth, proceedings for the partition of property and the release of immovable property from mortgage or lien. Fifth, proceedings for the recognition of foreign judgments. And finally, arbitrations. It is opportune to refer briefly to some of these special proceedings.

B. SUMMARY EX PARTE PROCEEDINGS

These proceedings are characterised by the substitution of a two-party procedure with a summary ex parte procedure. The rationale is to speed up proceedings in those cases in which there is unequivocal evidence of non-performance so that the ordinary adjudicatory process would be superfluous. The procedure is available in claims for liquidated sums or a determinate quantity of fungible things, for the delivery of defined movables, and for the recovery of professional or trade fees which are determined according to a lawfully approved scale for the services rendered. The application must contain the evidence supporting the claim and if successful the ex parte order, which takes the form of a decree, is served on the debtor who may oppose it within 20 days, or any greater or lesser period fixed by the court, in which event the normal adjudicative process takes place.

C. NON-CONTENTIOUS PROCEEDINGS

A basic distinction drawn in Italian procedural law is that between contentious and non-contentious proceedings. The latter are traditionally said to constitute the so-called voluntary jurisdiction (*giurisdizione volontaria*). Although it is difficult to define 'voluntary jurisdiction', it can be said to comprise all of those proceedings necessary to give effect to various types of private law relationships which would be ineffective in the absence of judicial intervention. The

Code, on the other hand, uses the term 'voluntary jurisdiction' in relation to the recognition of foreign judgments only. It speaks, instead, of 'provisions on proceedings in chambers' which include certain contentious proceedings.

The non-contentious procedure is simpler and speedier than ordinary contentious proceedings. It is initiated by an application to the competent court. In certain cases the court must hear the opinion of certain officials. The court has, in contrast to contentious proceedings, very broad powers to act of its own motion: it has very broad investigatory or inquisitorial powers and may order that any interested person be heard. The court rules on the application by a decree made in chambers without holding a trial. A party or the *pubblico ministero* may, within ten days, attack the decree before the next highest court by a form of appeal known as *reclamo*. Examples of voluntary proceedings are the consensual separation of spouses, decrees declaring the interdiction or incapacity of persons, declarations of absence and presumed death, measures regulating the affairs of minors and incapable persons, and measures taken in relation to deceased estates.

D. THE RECOGNITION OF FOREIGN JUDGMENTS

The recognition and enforcement of foreign judgments is achieved through a special procedure known as *delibazione*. Once a foreign judgment is recognised it becomes enforceable and produces any other consequences which generally flow from an Italian judgment. The conditions necessary for the recognition of a foreign judgment are (A.797 cpc): that the foreign court was competent according to Italian principles on jurisdiction; that the decision was the result of a normal trial according to the foreign law; that the judgment has become res judicata; that there is no conflicting domestic decision in the same dispute nor any pending domestic proceedings which were commenced prior to the foreign judgment becoming res judicata; and that the foreign judgment does not contain any orders contrary to public order as understood in Italian law. The application is by summons addressed to the Court of Appeal of the district in which the judgment is to be enforced (A.796 cpc). The intervention of the *pubblico ministero* is necessary in all proceedings for the recognition of a foreign judgment. Generally, the court cannot examine the merits of a foreign judgment and must limit itself to verifying the conditions stipulated in A.797 cpc. An examination of the merits takes place, exceptionally and at the instance of the defendant, where the foreign judgment is either a default judgment or one which is affected by a defect which could give rise to a revocation under A.395(1), (2), (3), (4) or (6) cpc. The decision of the court is given by judgment, which can be reviewed in the same way as any other judgment. The delibazione procedure is applicable to awards made in foreign arbitrations (A.800 cpc), and to foreign decisions which are equivalent to the measures issued under the Italian voluntary jurisdiction (A.801 cpc).

E. ARBITRATION

Article 2 cpc provides that Italian jurisdiction cannot be avoided by private agreement in favour of a foreign jurisdiction or arbitrators unless it is in respect of a matter between aliens or between an alien and a citizen who is neither resident nor domiciled in Italy and the agreement is in writing. This provision would seem to prohibit arbitration agreements and clauses. However, there are both a number of Conventions relating to international arbitrations and a number of statutory exceptions.

Domestic arbitrations may be either formal or informal. Formal arbitrations are those which conform with the provisions of the Code of Civil Procedure (Artt. 806ff) and are therefore eligible to receive the same status as a judicial decision. An agreement to submit a dispute to formal arbitration must be in writing and must define the scope of the arbitration, that is, the subject matter of the dispute. There cannot be an arbitration in respect of individual employment disputes, questions of personal status, separation of spouses, and matters which cannot lawfully form the object of a transaction. Arbitration clauses as to future disputes must be in writing (A.808 cpc) and must either nominate the arbitrators or define their number and method of nomination (A.809 cpc). The arbitrators must decide according to law unless the parties have authorised them to decide according to equity. The award is filed with the *Pretore* who, after controlling its formal validity, declares it to be enforceable thereby giving it the same effects as a judgment. This is a typical example of voluntary jurisdiction.

An informal arbitration arises where the parties submit a dispute to private arbitrators, but without observing the formalities prescribed by law. The resulting award becomes binding in contract only, in the same way as any other consensual agreement, and not because of its formal judicial recognition. The award may only be attacked on general contractual principles and not in accordance with the provisions that govern the validity of arbitration awards. In any event, informal arbitration awards have been readily enforced by the courts as contracts.

Enforcement proceedings

A. GENERAL

In Italy, the enforcement of a judgment involves further and separate proceedings to those in which the judgment to be enforced was obtained. As there is nothing like our civil contempt of court, nor anything like the French system of astreintes, the judgment debtor may simply refuse to comply with the judgment. Therefore, in those cases in which the judgment debtor fails to spontaneously comply with the judgment, the judgment creditor must take enforcement proceedings which are conducted by a single judge assisted, where necessary, by the court bailiff and the judicial police. Apart from the enforcement of judgments which are based on a prior action on the merits, a number of non-judicial instruments, such as negotiable instruments, may be enforced without the necessity for any such action on the merits. These instruments are considered by Italian law to have such probative value that no preliminary adjudication is necessary for their enforcement.

Enforcement proceedings are regulated by Book 3 (Artt. 474–632) of the Code of Civil Procedure and comprise three fundamental types of enforcement. First, forced liquidation of assets (*espropriazione forzata*) which is regulated differently depending upon whether the liquidation relates to movables in the possession of the debtor (Artt. 513–542 cpc), assets in the possession of third persons (Artt. 543–554 cpc), immovables (Artt. 555–598 cpc), jointly owned property (Artt. 599–601 cpc), or property belonging to third persons (Artt. 602–604 cpc). Second, specific enforcement of judgments which order the delivery of movables or the release of immovables (*esecuzione per consegna o rilascio*) (Artt. 605–611 cpc). Specific enforcement is only available to effectuate the delivery of specific property and not for the enforcement of a claim for unspecified fungible goods or chattels. The court bailiff enforces the judgment at the expiration of the time specified in the precept or notice served on the judgment debtor without the need for any further judicial intervention or proceedings. Any problems arising during the enforcement of the judgment are dealt with by the *Pretore*. Third, enforcement of mandatory and restraining orders (Artt. 612–614 cpc). The subject matter of a mandatory order must be the performance of fungible things and not the performance of non-fungibles such as the painting of a portrait. They are enforced specifically by ordering a court appointed substitute to act for the debtor. On the other hand, restraining orders concern something which has been performed contrary to an obligation but will only be granted if it is possible to destroy what has been built or done in violation of the debtor's obligation.

All enforcment proceedings must be preceded by the service of both the judgment, or other instrument which is to be enforced, and the precept upon the debtor (A.479 cpc). The service of the judgment or instrument to be enforced normally precedes the service of the precept, although they may be served together. The precept is a notice which requires performance in no less than ten days and contains a warning to the effect that enforcement proceedings will follow in the absence of performance. Enforcement proceedings must commence within 90 days of the service of the precept.

B. FORCED LIQUIDATION OF ASSETS

The court, or *giudice dell'esecuzione*, which supervises the liquidation proceedings depends upon the type of liquidation: the competent court is the *Tribunale* in the case of immovables and the *Pretore* in the case of movables irrespective of whether the latter are in the possession of the debtor or third parties. There are four broad stages in liquidation proceedings. First, the attachment of the debtor's goods thereby removing them from his dispositive powers. Part of the doctrine, in fact, regards the attachment as a provisional measure rather than part of the enforcement proceedings. The attachment either affects determined property within the debtor's estate or property belonging to a third party who either guaranteed the debt or acquired the property through an act which has been revoked because it prejudiced the creditor. Certain property cannot be attached (see generally Artt. 514, 545 cpc). The creditor may freely select the property to be attached in the case of immovables and credits, and may generally freely select in the case of movables. However, the creditor's right of selection is limited by the fact that he cannot attach other property without also attaching any property over which he has a mortgage or other charge (A.2911 cc). The attachment does not affect the ownership of the property which always remains in the debtor; it merely renders any disposition by the debtor ineffective vis-à-vis the creditor subject always to the operation of the principle of possession in good faith of unregistrable movables (Artt. 2913ff cc). This is a relative inefficacy because any alienation by the judgment debtor will be valid in the event that the enforcement proceedings are discontinued. The attached property is then entrusted to a custodian who may even be the debtor himself depending upon the type of property. The debtor may avoid attachment by payment to the bailiff of the sum claimed and costs. The application for the sale of the attached property must be made within 90 days of the attachment.

Second, the intervention of other creditors. In contrast to bankruptcy proceedings, which are always concoursual proceedings, enforcement proceedings may be either individual or concoursual. Where several creditors intend to satisfy themselves in the same enforcement proceedings, the creditor who initiated the proceedings is known as the proceeding creditor. In such a case the Code specifies the following general propositions: only one enforcement proceeding against the same property is permitted; an intervening creditor who holds an enforceable instrument may provoke the liquidation of any attached asset in the case of the inertia of the proceeding creditor; and finally, as to the distribution of the proceeds, all creditors, except for secured creditors who always enjoy their priority, are in a position of equality subject to the provisions on tardy intervenors. The particular consequences of intervention are: first, secured creditors retain their priority irrespective of when they intervene; second, unsecured creditors in possession of an enforceable instrument, if they intervene prior to the hearing which determines whether the sale is to be authorised, become joint claimants with the attaching creditor and may even provoke the execution; if they intervene tardily, they only share in the sum left over after the satisfaction of secured creditors and unsecured creditors whose intervention was timely; and third, unsecured creditors without an enforceable instrument, if their intervention was timely, participate in the distribution of the proceeds of sale or, if they intervene tardily but always before the settlement of the proposed distribution of the proceeds, share in the sum left over after satisfaction of all other creditors. In any event unsecured creditors without an enforceable instrument may be precluded from receiving payment upon the protest of the debtor.

The third stage in the forced liquidation procedure is the sale or assignment of the attached property. The creditor is allowed a choice between sale and assignment in two situations: first, in the case of movables which have a determinate value; and second, in the case of any type of property subsequent to a futile attempt at its sale. The final stage in the proceedings is the distribution of the proceeds of sale in the order of priority agreed upon by the creditors and approved by the judge. Any residual sum is returned to the debtor or third person suffering the enforcement proceedings.

All the above rules are common to all types of forced liquidation of assets. Certain special rules are applicable depending upon the nature of the property involved, that is, whether it is movable, immovable or credits, and its status, that is, whether it is co-owned or already attached, in which event their liquidation could injure third persons.

C. OPPOSITION TO ENFORCEMENT PROCEEDINGS

The Code of Civil Procedure distinguishes between two forms of opposition. First, opposition brought by persons suffering the execution, whether the debtor or a third person. This type of opposition may challenge either the right to bring the enforcement proceedings at all (Artt. 615 and 616 cpc) or only a particular aspect of the proceedings (Artt. 617 and 618 cpc). The rationale of this form of opposition is that, because the enforcement proceedings are ex parte, the debtor would be, in the absence of any remedy, at the mercy of the creditor where the enforcement proceedings are unjustly commenced or carried out. An opposition to the right to bring enforcement proceedings may relate to the existence of the title upon which the purported right of enforcement is based, the locus standi of the parties to the enforcement proceedings, or the attachability of the subject property, i e that the property is of a type not subject to attachment or belongs to a third person. If the enforcement proceedings are based upon a judicial instrument, the opposition cannot relate to the formation of the instrument (already res judicata), but only as to its effect, e g payment of the debt after the judgment; if the enforcement proceedings are based on a non-judicial instrument, the opposition may relate to the formation of the instrument, subject to any special legislative provisions.

An opposition to a particular aspect of the enforcement proceedings, on the other hand, is based upon form rather than merits, that is, it is an opposition to a particular act in the enforcment process rather than the right to bring the enforcement proceedings at all. Thus it may relate to the formal regularity of the enforcement procedures, e g of the precept, or the expediency of the particular type of enforcement measure. However, the doctrine treats an opposition by a third person who is himself subject to the enforcement proceedings as an opposition on the merits, which in this case concerns only a particular enforcement measure. It may relate to the order of priority, the existence of the credit or its amount, or the fraudulent character of the obligation from which the purported credit arose.

The second type of opposition is that brought by third persons, or strangers to the enforcement proceedings, who claim rights in the property being attached (Artt. 619–622 cpc). This type of opposition is directed to protecting third persons regarded by law as having rights superior to the subject creditor over the attached property. These rights may include total ownership, a real right of enjoyment over the property, a pledge (a secured creditor always being able to protect his rights against unsecured creditors), a right over incorporeals (e g a trade mark), or possession in good faith.

The criminal jurisdiction

A. THE NATURE OF THE ITALIAN CRIMINAL PROCESS

The strict accusatory system is essentially a party process characterised by a two-sided contest between prosecution and defence before an impartial moderator, the judge. This fundamental characteristic of the accusatory system gives rise to various distinctive features: first, the public, oral and antithetical nature of the trial; second, the participation of three distinct organs—prosecution, defence and judge; third, the inability of the judicial organ to initiate the criminal process; and finally, the obligation of the judge to decide according to the evidence presented by the parties without any power to seek out other or further evidence. The accusatory system was the criminal process of the Roman law. The strict inquisitorial system, on the other hand, is characterised by, first, the absence of orality and publicity—it is a secret and written process; second, the existence of a public prosecutor; third, the pre-eminent role of the judge who has the right to initiate the criminal process and is not restricted by the views of either party in relation to the search for evidence; and finally, the existence of various limitations upon the defence of the accused. It was exemplified by the Canon law process. The Italian criminal process consists of an osmosis of these two systems through dividing the criminal process into two parts: the instruction phase, dominated by the principle of secrecy, and the trial phase, characterised by its publicity.

B. THE BASIC CHARACTERISTICS OF CRIMINAL PROCEDURE

The primary characteristic of the Italian criminal process is that, in contrast to civil procedure, it aims not at ascertaining whether the prosecution is right or wrong in its assertions, but rather to ascertain the truth. In contrast to civil procedure, it is a process which strives towards a complete and factual judicial enquiry rather than mere procedural truth. The criminal process is not a party process in which the judge must decide exclusively upon the evidence adduced by the parties and find in favour of the party who more adequately reasons and proves his case. Rather, it is a process embodying the principle of the free persuasion of the judge that manifests itself in the judge's power-duty to ascertain the truth; this, in turn, implies that he is not to be restricted by the evidence adduced by the parties and is free to evaluate it without any limitation. Italian civil procedure, like the common law generally, seeks truth as the product of the collaboration between the parties; Italian criminal procedure, on the other hand, places the pursuit of the objective truth in the complete control of the judge who is given the necessary powers to collect and evaluate the evidence required to decide the matter, without being limited to the evidence tendered by the parties: therefore, the judge also, in a criminal trial, is a source of evidence which may be either favourable or unfavourable to the accused; and the parties cannot restrict the judge who is free to utilise any form of evidence he considers opportune and orientate the investigations in the direction he considers necessary.

The other basic characteristics of Italian criminal procedure are:

(*i*) *The necessary implementation of the criminal process for the infliction of a criminal sanction.* No provision of the substantive criminal law or any precautionary measure may be inflicted unless pursuant to the explication of the criminal process.

(*ii*) *The judge cannot initiate the criminal process of his own motion.* The separation of judge and prosecutor, which is an element of the accusatory system, protects the individual against excesses of the judicial power. The initiation of the criminal process is the duty of a separate and distinct subject, normally the *pubblico ministero*. The judge cannot proceed of his own motion for a crime other than that for which the *pubblico ministero* has initiated the criminal process, nor proceed at his own instance for concurrent crimes or aggravating circumstances which become evident during the proceedings. Moreover, this principle is adhered to in the special procedure before the *Pretore*, who accumulates the functions of both *pubblico ministero* and judge, as it is considered that the *Pretore* initiates the criminal process in his capacity as *pubblico ministero*.

(*iii*) *The criminal process is public.* The *pubblico ministero*, who is a public functionary, has a monopoly over criminal prosecutions. Only the State, as representative of the public interest, has the right to enforce the criminal law. It follows that in Italian law there is no provision for private prosecutions.

(*iv*) *The obligatory initiation of the criminal process.* The *pubblico ministero* is bound to initiate ex officio the criminal process in every instance in which a breach of the criminal law comes to his notice (A.112 C, A.74 cpp). As a corollary, once the criminal process is put into motion, it is *irretractable*, that is, it cannot be suspended, interrupted or terminated except in the manner prescribed by law (A.75 cpp). There is in Italian law no discretion as to whether the criminal process should be put in motion. In practice this means that in every case in which the *pubblico ministero* receives a *notitia criminis*, he has the power and the duty to initiate the criminal process, even if he considers the complaint to be unfounded, in which case the criminal process is merely initiated to request the archivation of the complaint. The application for archivation is the means through which the judiciary reviews a decision of the *pubblico ministero* that the matter is unfounded and no proceedings are called for. Similarly, the *pubblico ministero* cannot discontinue proceedings already on foot. This characteristic of the criminal process means, so far as the defendant is concerned, that he cannot accept a penalty outside the scope of the criminal process nor bind the court with his requests. On the other hand, so far as the court is concerned, it means: first, that it must close the criminal process with a judgment;

second, that it is free from the desires of the parties as to the collection of the evidence; and third, that it is not bound by the requests of the parties as to the conviction or acquittal of the accused so that it also remains free either to convict where the *pubblico ministero* seeks an acquittal or to acquit where the accused has confessed or requested his own conviction. It follows from this principle that plea bargaining is never a possibility in Italian law. However, the obligatory nature of the criminal process does not apply to proceedings beyond first instance, at which point the parties are at liberty to bring or withdraw further proceedings.

In some instances there are certain procedural prerequisites in the absence of which the *pubblico ministero* cannot initiate, or sometimes continue, the criminal process. Of these requisites, those relevant to the initiation of the criminal process are as follows. First, the *querela* (or complaint) which, in essence, subordinates the public interest to the private interest. The *querela* is the act with which the passive subject of a criminal situation removes the obstacle to the initiation of the criminal process in the case of those crimes in relation to which the *pubblico ministero* cannot commence the criminal process of his own motion. The rationale of the *querela* is that in certain cases the expediency of initiating the criminal process is left to the judgment of the injured person. Such situations fall into two broad categories: crimes of slight value; and crimes which, although of a certain gravity, may, through the publicity inherent in the criminal process, cause the injured person greater damage than already inflicted by the commission of the crime. Second, the request to proceed which is a public right inherent in the Minister of Grace and Justice who makes the request through an administrative measure which removes the obstacle to the initiation of the criminal process. It is required in the case of political crimes committed abroad, crimes committed abroad from the national territory by Italian citizens when the crime is punishable with imprisonment of not less than three years, and crimes against the freedom and honour of foreign heads of state. Third, the instance which is a public subjective right of the person injured by the crime to request the punishment of certain crimes which were committed abroad but if committed within the national territory would have been prosecuted at the instance of the *pubblico ministero*.

There are two procedural conditions relevant to the continuation of the criminal process. First, those cases in which an authorisation to proceed must be obtained from the relevant authority as a result of the status or situation of the accused, e g crimes committed by members of Parliament and judges of the Constitutional Court. Second, the lapse of the time fixed for the administrative conciliation of certain crimes, which are not punishable by detention, relating to trade practices.

In short, therefore, the criminal process *must* be initiated by the *pubblico ministero* upon receipt of a *notitia criminis* in all those cases where there is no need for a *querela*, request or instance. The *notitia criminis* may consist of any report, reference, declaration or any other form of notice through which the *pubblico ministero* or *Pretore* (in his capacity as *pubblico ministero*) obtains knowledge about a fact which constitutes a crime. The police are required to pass regularly all reports and complaints to the *pubblico ministero* for action.

(v) The criminal process is indivisible. This means that the criminal process must be initiated against every person who participated in the crime in question. Thus a complaint against one co-criminal extends automatically to the others. Similarly, a remission in favour of one extinguishes the crime vis-à-vis the others.

(vi) The presumptions of freedom and innocence. The disposition of the legal system towards the personal freedom of the accused is manifested through the prohibition on resorting by analogy to general principles which have the effect of restricting personal freedom, as well as the obligation on the judiciary to restore personal freedom as soon as the circumstances which justified its restriction have ceased. The presumption of innocence embodies the prevalence of the interests of the accused as against the punitive interests of the State and manifests itself in the acquittal of the accused for insufficiency of evidence or the failure to satisfy the burden of proof.

(vii) The requirement of reasoned judgments. This is a requisite which is directly related to the principle of the 'intimate conviction' of the court. The more liberal the latter principle, the greater the necessity for the court to explain the reasons upon which it is convinced of the correctness of its judgment. The obligation to give reasoned decisions is now guaranteed by A.111 C and serves two basic functions: it subjects the decision and its reasoning to public opinion and enables a court of appeal to evaluate the reasons at the basis of the judgment.

(viii) The right of defence. This is embodied in A.24 C (see p 49, above). Recent reforms, instigated by the decisions of the Constitutional Court, have brought the right of defence back to the pre-instruction phase conducted by the judicial police. The two aspects of the right of defence are a substantive right which comprises the right of the suspect to an immediate communication of the existence of enquiries against him (given by means of a 'judicial communication'), the right to attend and directly participate in various investigatory measures, the right to the knowledge of the charge, and the right to make applications and produce evidence at any point in the criminal process; and a formal right which comprises the right to legal representation.

(ix) A two-sided debate or altercation. This consists, in substance, of the contemporaneous participation of the parties in the proceedings. The principle is only partially fulfilled in the pre-judicial (or pre-instruction) and instruction phases, whilst it is fully realised in the trial phase.

(x) The principle of dualism applicable to the non-public instruction phase. This principle, guaranteeing that the proceedings are as objective as possible and the protection of the accused, requires the presence of two or more subjects during the performance of defined instruction measures which could prejudice the accused, e g the defendant has the right to the presence of his legal representative during his own interrogation and also during the examination of witnesses.

(xi) The principles of continuity and immediacy. The former aims at avoiding the dispersion of the evidence and its loss by lapse of memory. It finds its strongest expression in A.431 cpp which requires very brief intervals between adjournments where a case cannot be concluded in a single audience. The principle of immediacy, on the other hand, is inspired by the desirability that the judgment result from the trial judge's personal perceptions of the evidence (see A.472 cpp).

(xii) The principle of parity between the prosecution and defence.

The criminal courts and their structure, jurisdiction and competence

A. GENERAL.

The criminal jurisdiction is exercised by the ordinary courts which are the *Pretore*, the *Tribunale*, the *Corte d'assise*, the *Corte d'appello*, the *Corte d'assise d'appello*, the *Tribunale per i minorenni* (the minors tribunal), and the Court of Cassation. Certain special courts exceptionally have jurisdiction in defined criminal matters, namely, the Constitutional Court, whose criminal jurisdiction relates to certain crimes committed by the President and ministers of State in the course of their duties (see ch 5, p 156, above), and the military courts, which have a limited peacetime jurisdiction in relation to military crimes committed by members of the armed forces. The Constitution specifically excludes the creation of any other extraordinary court (A.102 C) because of the right of each person to be tried by the competent ordinary court as predefined by law (A.25 C) (see ch 5, p 162, above).

The criminal jurisdiction is divided amongst the various criminal courts according to three criteria: territory, subject matter and function. The manner in which these criteria divide the criminal jurisdiction between its three possible grades or levels and the courts within each grade is as follows: territory and subject matter individuate the competent court of first instance which, in turn, automatically identifies the relevant court of appeal, that is, the court of second instance; the court of third instance is always the Court of Cassation. Moreover, subject matter competence, by individuating the relevant court of first instance (*Pretore*, *Tribunale* or *Corte d'assise*), also determines which of the three respective forms of trial is applicable.

B. THE STRUCTURE AND SUBJECT MATTER COMPETENCE OF THE CRIMINAL COURTS

The courts of first instance, their subject matter competence and their respective courts of appeal are as follows:

(*i*) *The Pretore.* The *Pretore* is a single career judge, although there is also provision for the appointment of honorary lay *Pretori*. The *Preture* are the lowest criminal court with a territorial jurisdiction limited to their respective district, known as *mandamento*. The *Pretore* has a general subject matter competence over all crimes which have either a maximum penalty of three years imprisonment or a pecuniary penalty, or both (A.31 cpp), except for certain defined crimes which fall within the exclusive jurisdiction of the other criminal courts of first instance. An appeal lies from the decision of the *Pretore* to the territorially competent *Tribunale* (see p 226, below).

(*ii*) *The Corte d'assise.* This is composed of a bench of eight judges: the President (who is a judge of the Court of Appeal) and one other judge (who is a judge of the *Tribunale*) are career judges; the other six judges are lay persons selected from citizens, aged between 30 and 65, of good moral conduct and with at least a basic secondary education. It has a territorial competence restricted to its respective district, known as the *circolo* which is defined without relation to the other judicial districts. Its subject matter competence is limited to certain defined serious crimes including crimes against the State. An appeal lies from the *Corte d'assise* to the *Corte d'assise d'appello*, there being one *Corte d'assise d'appello* in every *circolo*. The latter court is composed of a President, who is a judge of Cassation, a puisne career judge, who is a judge of Appeal, and six lay judges with at least a full secondary education. In both the *Corte d'assise* and the *Corte d'assise d'appello* the career and lay judges form a unitary bench and together decide law and fact; the lay and career judges are in a position of complete parity in the exercise of all judicial powers. The jury, in the form known in the common law, is regarded as inadmissible in Italy because the unreasoned verdict of the traditional jury would fail to comply with the Constitutional requirement that all judicial decisions must be reasoned.

(*iii*) *The Tribunale*. The *Tribunale* consisting of three career judges with a territorial competence limited to its respective *circondario* which comprises several *mandamenti*, has a residual competence in relation to all crimes which do not fall within the competence of the *Pretore* and the *Corte d'assise* as well as an exclusive competence over certain defined crimes such as financial crimes, crimes committed by the press and the contraventions contained in Artt. 134–141 cc. Appeals against decisions of the *Tribunale* may be taken to the territorially competent Court of Appeal, also composed of three career judges.

(*iv*) *The Tribunale per i minorenni*. Located at every *Corte d'appello* (Court of Appeal) is a *Tribunale per i minorenni*, which consists of a judge of the Court of Appeal, a judge of the *Tribunale* and two lay judges selected amongst social workers possessing certain professional qualifications and who are at least 30 years of age. It has jurisdiction over crimes committed by persons aged under 18 (but over the age of 14). Appeals from the *Tribunale per i minorenni* are heard by a specialised section of the territorially competent Court of Appeal composed of two lay experts and three career judges.

The court of third instance, the Court of Cassation, is the supreme criminal court and comprises five career judges when sitting as an ordinary section, or nine career judges when sitting as a full court. Its competence is limited to the review of errors of law and procedure (see p 189, above).

THE CRIMINAL COURTS

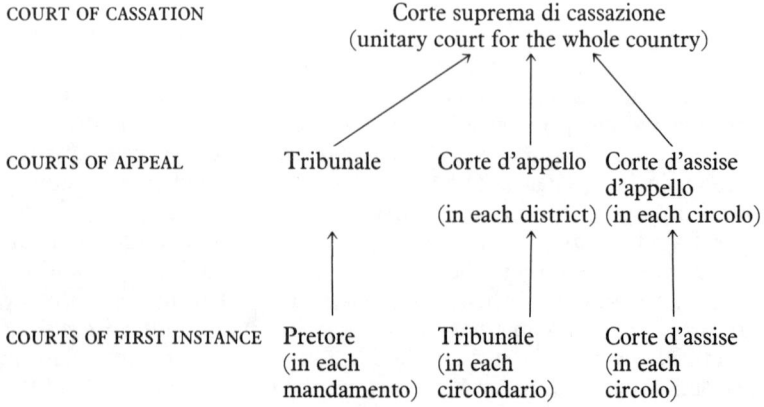

COURT OF CASSATION	Corte suprema di cassazione (unitary court for the whole country)		
COURTS OF APPEAL	Tribunale	Corte d'appello (in each district)	Corte d'assise d'appello (in each circolo)
COURTS OF FIRST INSTANCE	Pretore (in each mandamento)	Tribunale (in each circondario)	Corte d'assise (in each circolo)

C. THE NON-OBSERVANCE OF SUBJECT MATTER COMPETENCE

The failure to observe the limitations imposed on subject matter competence will result in the *nullity* of the proceedings before the incompetent court, except for those acts which cannot be repeated (A.34(1) cpp). The only exception to this general provision is that contained in A.34(2) cpp which provides that a superior court may, with the consent of the parties, deal with a crime falling within the competence of an inferior court. The issue of subject matter competence may be raised by either the parties or the court ex officio at any stage or grade of the proceedings.

D. THE DETERMINATION OF TERRITORIAL COMPETENCE AND ITS NON-OBSERVANCE

Territorial competence depends upon the place where the crime was committed. The criteria to determine the location of the crime distinguishes between crimes committed within the State and crimes committed abroad. In the case of crimes committed within the State, the primary criteria for establishing the *forum delicti* are: the place of consummation in the case of consummated crimes; the location of the last act directed to the commission of the crime in the case of attempts; the place where the consummation began in the case of permanent crimes; and the place of the most serious crime or, when of equal gravity, where the first crime was committed in the case of continuing crimes. Where the primary criteria cannot be applied, certain subsidiary criteria are applied, in the following order: the place where part of the act or ommission occurred; the locality of the arrest; the place where the warrant for arrest was issued; the place where a summons to appear has been issued; or the place where the first act in the criminal process took place. If even the subsidiary criteria cannot be applied, then the residence, abode or domicile of the accused determines the territorially competent court. In the case of crimes committed abroad, where the crime was committed partly within the territory and partly abroad, the court of the place where the crime was consummated or that where the last act or omission, if this only occurred within the State, is territorially competent. If the crime has been entirely consummated abroad, then territorial competence is determined in the following order: the residence, abode or domicile of the accused, the place of arrest, or the place at which the accused is delivered by the foreign authorities in the case of an extradition.

There are certain exceptional variations to the rules of territorial competence, for instance, in the case of crimes committed aboard ships or aircraft, in which case the territorially competent court is the court of the place where the ship or aircraft first lands, and in the case of financial crimes in which case territorial competence depends upon where the crime was discovered, that is, where the enquiries took place and the evidence was collected.

In contrast to incompetence for subject matter, territorial incompetence does not nullify any instruction act which has been performed prior to the issue being raised. Territorial incompetence may be raised, at first instance, at any stage of the instruction phase or at the first audience of the trial phase, at which point the matter is transferred to the competent court. It may only be raised on appeal or in Cassation if the issue was raised at first instance and is included as one of the grounds for appeal or review.

E. VARIATIONS TO THE NORMAL RULES ON COMPETENCY

A variation of the rules on territorial and subject matter competence may arise from the joinder (Artt. 45ff cpp) or removal of proceedings (Artt. 55ff cpp). The joinder of criminal proceedings is much more frequent in Italian law than in the common law. There is joinder when the same person is charged with several crimes, when several persons have acted either in unison or to their reciprocal injury or when there is either a probative or instrumental connection between different crimes (A.45 cpp). These general rules on joinder have, however, been limited by A.2 of the law of 8 August 1977 n.533 which permits the separation of crimes when they have been committed flagrantly or when the evidence is apparent, and the law of 22 December 1980 n.879, which adopted an analogous position in relation to proceedings in which a magistrate is the suspect, accused, or victim of a crime. Prior to these changes, the rules on joinder prevented the speedy disposition of that part of the proceedings which concerned those defendants whose position was self-evident.

The removal of proceedings from the court which is normally competent to another court arises when there exist 'serious reasons of public order', a legitimate reason to believe that the proceedings will not be conducted in a regular manner, or when the suspect, accused or victim of the crime was or is a member of the competent court. In such cases, the court of Cassation decides whether the prerequisites for 'removal' exist and, if so, to which court the matter should be removed.

F. CONFLICTS IN JURISDICTION AND COMPETENCE

In the criminal law there are certain procedural guarantees for the resolution of conflicts regarding competence. As in civil procedure, the conflict may arise between the ordinary and special courts (that is, conflicts in jurisdiction) or between two ordinary courts (that is, conflicts in competence). These conflicts may be eliminated either temporarily by one of the courts declaring itself competent or incompetent, as the case may be, or definitively by referral of the issue to the Court of Cassation by either the judge, when he has the right to raise the issue ex officio, or, in any event, at the instance of the *pubblico ministero*, the accused or one of the other parties to the proceedings. The Court of Cassation decides conflicts in competence in chambers and conflicts in jurisdiction by a decision of the full court. The decision of Cassation also indicates the proper court and the extent to which the prior proceedings remain valid.

The Parties to Criminal Proceedings

The necessary subjects to criminal proceedings are the *pubblico ministero*, or prosecutor, (see p 221, above, and ch 2), the judge who must be impartial vis-à-vis the parties and independent from any other power of State (see p 163, above), and the accused. However, two other procedural relationships, both of a civil nature, may arise within the context of criminal proceedings. First, the intervention of the so-called civil party who seeks damages for the civil wrong arising from the accused's actions thereby giving rise to a procedural relationship amongst the civil party, the accused, perhaps a civilly responsible party (who is civilly answerable for the accused) and the judge (see p 265, below). Second, the joinder or intervention of a subject known as the person civilly liable for the fine (that is, a party who is civilly and secondarily liable for the fine because of his relationship with the accused when the latter is insolvent and has been convicted of a fine for the commission of a contravention) thereby giving rise to a procedural relationship amongst the *pubblico ministero*, the personal civilly liable for the fine and the judge (see p 266, below).

The Situation of the Accused

The accused in the Italian non-accusatorial process is not without procedural rights or guarantees. Although this will become evident through a closer examination of the criminal process, it is important to stress at the outset that, contrary to common belief, the presumption of innocence operates in two senses: first, in the sense of the burden of proof requiring that, in cases of doubt, the accused must be acquitted for insufficiency of evidence; and second, in the sense of status: the accused must 'not be considered guilty until definitive conviction' (A.27 C).

A person becomes an accused person either upon arrest, when he is placed at the disposal of the judicial authorities, or at the point of his identification or suspicion consequent to any report, reference, information, complaint, request, instance or any other disclosure of the crime. Because a person under suspicion of a crime must be considered an 'accused' person and therefore entitled to remain silent, it follows that if a suspicion arises during an activity of the judicial police in the pre-instruction phase involving the suspect, the judicial police, like the judicial authorities, are bound to caution the suspect that he has the right to remain silent.

A person who, pursuant to a *notitia criminis*, becomes a suspect first learns of the charge or suspicion at one of the following points in time: at his arrest; at his interrogation by the judicial police or judicial authorities; upon service of the so-called 'judicial communication' (*communicazione giudiziaria*); or during his interrogation other than as a suspect when there arises a suspicion in regard to him, whereupon the *pubblico ministero* or examining judge must issue a caution that anything he may say could be used in evidence against him and adjourn the interrogation to a later date when, if the accused has failed to appoint a defence lawyer, the court will nominate one ex officio.

The function of the 'judicial communication' is to ensure that no criminal process can be initiated or continued without the knowledge of the accused. In cases of pre-instruction investigations conducted by the *pubblico ministero* and summary instructions, the 'judicial communication' must be served on the accused prior to the first act of the *pubblico ministero*, unlike the initial pre-instruction investigations carried out by the judicial police. It follows that only pre-instruction activities carried out by the judicial police prior to passing the matter on to the *pubblico ministero* for judicial investigation can be secret from the accused. In the case of a formal instruction, carried out by an examining judge, if the *pubblico ministero* has not already carried out any pre-instruction activities, the 'judicial communication' must be given to the accused before any instruction act is performed. The 'judicial communication' must indicate the proceedings, the accused, the charge including the norm alleged to have been violated and the date of the facts, and the office which is conducting the instruction. Moreover, it must contain an invitation to nominate a defence lawyer. The 'judicial communication' is also sent to anyone who could be interested in the proceedings as a private party. It is obvious that certain other acts that contain the above information are equivalent to a 'judicial communication', which is therefore not necessary, although the accused must nonetheless be charged.

The right of the accused to know of the existence of a criminal process against him is an essential element of his right of defence as, too, are the rights to dispute the charge, make submissions, introduce evidence, participate in the procedural activities within the limits fixed by law, and legal representation (see ch 2, above). The right of defence is so essential to the whole of the proceedings that the failure to observe any provision relating to the defence of the accused leads to the absolute nullity of the proceedings (A.185(1)n.3 cpp).

The ordinary criminal process

The ordinary criminal process may be divided into three phases: the pre-instruction, instruction, and trial phases.

A. THE PRE-INSTRUCTION PHASE

The criminal process proper is generally preceded by a phase of preliminary enquiries comprising a summary investigation of the *notitia criminis*. This phase consists of the investigations carried out autonomously by the judicial police, as well as any preliminary activities carried out by the *pubblico ministero*, with the object of ascertaining whether the *notitia criminis* discloses the elements of a crime so that the criminal process may be initiated against the suspect. It follows that this phase is *not* a necessary phase in that its necessity depends upon whether the *notitia criminis* per se discloses the elements of a crime and the direction which the investigations will need to take in the next phase. The pre-instruction phase concludes with either a decision that the *notitia criminis* discloses a breach of the criminal law, in which case the criminal process proper is initiated and the matter passes into the next phase, or a decision that the *notitia criminis* has no basis in the criminal law, in which case an order to that effect, so-called archivation, must be sought from an examining judge before the matter can be closed. The archivation procedure constitutes the judicial control over the decision that the *notitia criminis* does not disclose a breach of the criminal law, that is, a check to ensure that the *pubblico ministero* complies with his obligation to initiate the criminal process in every case where it is justified.

The pre-instruction activities mainly comprise all those preliminary police activities directed toward the discovery of crime, individuating suspects, collecting the immediate evidence and everything else that may be necessary to the application of the criminal law, and to prevent any ulterior consequences to the commission of a crime, such as the destruction of the evidence (A.219 cpp). The activities of the judicial police may include measures restrictive of personal liberty, e g the arrest of persons apprehended during the commission of a crime, the restraint of suspects, the seizure of property connected with the commission of a crime, and personal and domiciliary searches in cases of flagrant crimes or abscondence, all of which must be reported to the judicial authorities within 48 hours for their ratification and validation (see ch 5, pp 176 ff, above). Many activities are performed on the previous authority or instruction of the *pubblico ministero* or examining judge, e g telephonic interceptions (see ch 5, p 177, above). However, the role of the police is more limited in Italian criminal procedure than in English jurisdictions; although it is more marked in this phase, it is limited to the brief preliminary investigations to determine whether there is a breach of the criminal law, the ulterior investigations being left to an independent and impartial judicial officer in the instruction phase of the criminal process.

An important consequence of the distinction between activities carried out by the judicial police and activities carried out by the *pubblico ministero* in this phase is that as soon as some activity is carried out by the latter there must be the service of a 'judicial communication', whilst this is not required so long as all of these activities are merely carried out at the instance of the judicial police (A.390 cpp).

B. THE INSTRUCTION PHASE

(i) *General.* This phase, which is part of the judicial proceedings, has in practice become the most important phase in the criminal process. It is in essence a prima facie examination of the *notitia criminis* through a judicial investigation and collection of all the evidence, culminating in a decision as to whether there is sufficient evidence to warrant placing the accused on trial, that is, whether or not to initiate the third and final phase of the criminal process. This phase serves a double function: it avoids subjecting the accused to harmful publicity, in itself a form of punishment, and it avoids the initiation of futile trial proceedings. The traditional and fundamental characteristics of the instruction phase are that it is written and secret, in contrast to the oral and public trial phase. These distinctive characteristics arise from the different object of the two phases: the instruction phase is concerned with the protection of society whereas the trial phase is concerned with the guarantee of individual rights; in other words, the two phases combine the two fundamental but conflicting aspects of the criminal law. However, it must be immediately particularised that the Code contains two types of secrecy: internal and external. The latter eliminates knowledge of the instruction measures by persons external to the proceedings. The former eliminates party knowledge of certain instruction measures on the basis that it would endanger the evidence. The Constitutional Court has, through its numerous and wide-ranging judgments, removed the most restrictive of the rules which excluded the presence of defence counsel during instruction proceedings so that today there are basically four types of instruction proceedings which remain secret from the defence: testimony which is not of future record, that is, testimony which can be re-taken in future, although it is unclear why secrecy still prevails in relation to this; sequestrations, which are mainly acts of surprise; bodily and domiciliary searches, for obvious reasons; and confrontations between witnesses or between a witness and the accused. A knowledge of the existence of the criminal process at a very early stage, combined with access to most instruction proceedings, realises the right of the accused to take immediate steps in the preparation and assertion of his defence in an attempt to bring the proceedings to a close before they gain the publicity inherent in a trial.

The instruction may be either formal or summary. A summary instruction is held first, where the accused has been apprehended during the commission of a crime, that is to say, where the evidence is apparent; second, where the crime was committed by the accused whilst under arrest or detention; third, where a confession makes further investigations appear unneccessary; and finally, in all crimes within the jurisdiction of the *Pretura*, that is, in those cases in which the investigations will be rapid and uncomplicated. In every other case the instruction is formal. A summary instruction is carried out by the *pubblico ministero* who, in the case of the *Pretura*, is the *Pretore* himself. A formal instruction is conducted by an examining judge, a member of the strict judiciary. A summary instruction must be brief, although no time limit is set. Where the accused is under detention and the instruction exceeds 40 days, it automatically becomes a formal one. Further, a summary instruction may be converted into a formal one in certain instances which are incompatible with the speed and simplicity inherent to a summary instruction. Furthermore, the accused in a summary instruction is given the right to require its conversion into a formal instruction. As this implies an admission on the part of the accused that the allegations against him are not short and simple, it is rarely availed of in practice.

Whilst a summary instruction is brief and simple, a formal instruction may comprise the most varied of procedural measures directed toward the discovery and collection of every type of evidence. The essential object of a formal instruction is the collection of the evidence necessary to ascertain the truth. The characteristics and objects of a formal instruction, and, indeed, of instruction phases generally, arise from A.299 cpp which provides that the examining judge has the duty to promptly carry out those measures which, according to the elements of the case and the development of the instruction, appear necessary to the ascertainment of the truth. It emerges from the formulation in A.299 cpp that first, the object of the instruction is to ascertain the truth; second, this object must be carried out equitably, objectively, and impartially because the examining judge has a duty not only to carry out investigations directed to ascertain the guilt of the accused but also those investigations which prove his innocence; and third, the instruction must conform to the criteria of speed and significance in that the examining judge must promptly carry out 'all and only' those investigations necessary to ascertain the truth. The examining judge therefore enjoys a complete initiative and control over the collection of the evidence and may embark on any investigation necessary to unearth the evidence required to ascertain the truth.

The central figure in the instruction phase is the examining judge, the descendant of the inquisitor. Whilst in a pure inquisitorial system the inquisitor combines the functions of prosecutor, defence and judge, its modern equivalent, in the form of the examining judge, preserves only traces of its forerunner. Although the examining judge is the dominant figure in the instruction, that is, in the collection of the evidence, which is a typically inquisitorial function, his activities are always increasingly tempered by the participation of the parties or their legal representatives who, although still excluded from participating in certain instruction measures (e g the taking of testimonial evidence which is not of future record), may, since the reforms of 1955 and 1971, immediately participate in certain other instruction measures (e g the interrogation of the accused and expert investigations) and have the right to know the results of yet other instruction measures upon their conclusion (e g corporal inspections and sequestrations).

(ii) The instruction measures. Whilst the instruction phase is primarily concerned with the performance of measures necessary to determining the foundation of the *notitia criminis* (the so-called instruction measures in a strict sense: the collection of the evidence), various other activities of a procedural nature not strictly related to the primary object of this phase are dealt with during the instruction (e g the imposition of penalties, the imposition of temporary precautionary measures, and the joinder of the civil party). A particularly important measure belonging to this latter category is, as already noted, the service of the 'judicial communication'.

(iii) Criminal evidence. In contrast to civil procedure, dominated by the system of legal proof, the operative principle in criminal procedure is that of free proof, and its corollary, the free evaluation of evidence. Article 308 cpp expressly provides that the limitations applicable to civil evidence (Artt. 2699–2739 cc) are inapplicable in criminal proceedings. The judge may freely decide upon the admissibility of evidence and, once admitted, freely evaluate it according to his 'prudent judgment'. These principles are the modern derivatives of the principle that developed from the French Revolution, viz, the 'intimate conviction' of the court.

Again in contrast to civil procedure where the parties control the evidence which is to be presented to the court, in criminal proceedings, as a direct consequence of the principle of the 'free and intimate conviction' of the court, the judge has a complete control over the discovery and collection of the evidence including the decision as to the direction which the investigations should take. This power to initiate the discovery of the evidence which the court believes necessary for the decision of a case is an inquisitorial feature of the criminal process. It follows that one cannot speak of a formal burden of proof in the sense of the introduction of the evidence as the inquisitorial principle places this power in the court; evidence both favourable and unfavourable to the defendant originates at the instance of the court. Consequently, one can only speak of the substantive burden of proof in the sense of evaluation of the evidence; in other words, in the sense that the court must be fully convinced as to the guilt of the defendant.

The power of the court to search freely for, and evaluate, the evidence includes the right of the court to take judicial notice of maxims of experience (e g natural laws) and notorious facts (e g an earthquake) subject to the obligation of bringing their use by the court to the attention of the parties who may challenge their existence. Circumstantial or indirect evidence may be utilised by the court, but *only* in the absence of direct evidence. Circumstantial evidence must be evaluated with caution and only be used to support a conviction if it gives rise to 'a convincement which does not leave any reasonable doubt'. Therefore, it must be certain, consistent and consequently logical and precise.

Some writers maintain that the principles of free proof and material truth mean that the court has a freedom to receive any form or type of evidence, even if it is of a type which is not specifically envisaged by the Code of Criminal Procedure. Others argue with a certain degree of logic that the principle of the 'free convincement of the court' cannot imply such freedom: the fact that the court looks to ascertain the truth does not imply that the exclusion of atypical forms of evidence is unnecessary, nor that there are no restrictions upon the typical forms of evidence expressly recognised by the Code. In fact, whilst there are no general exclusionary rules of evidence (such as the hearsay rule) in Italian law, the Code contains many specific rules placing limitations upon the admissibility of evidence, e g A.349 cpp which prevents a witness expressing personal opinions or appraisals as to the moral character of the accused or other persons; A.348 cpp which places certain restrictions on taking evidence from accomplices; and A.141 cpp which excludes, subject to certain exceptions, the use of anonymous writings. The Italian judiciary has in practice utilised the principle of the free evaluation of evidence both to justify a probing into any form of evidence, even if of a type not expressly recognised by the Code, and to ignore any express restrictions on the admissibility of the types of evidence generally recognised by the Code. Taking the principle of free evaluation to its logical but extreme conclusion, the courts contend that even if the collection of certain evidence does not comply with certain procedures or other requirements stipulated by the Code, it may nonetheless utilise the evidence and evaluate and convince itself of its probative value, e g the Code of Criminal Procedure provides that before admitting evidence of identification pursuant to a line-up, the court must ascertain if the witness has previously seen a photograph of the person to be identified. However, the Court of Cassation has often held that the court is free to convince itself of the weight to be given to such evidence, even if it is excluded by some provision of the Code. In the end result, the only practical bar to the admissibility of evidence arises from the general requirement that it *must* be relevant and significant: the court may always refuse the admission of evidence which it regards irrelevant or insignificant, with the object of avoiding superfluous and futile procedural activities.

(iv) The individual types of criminal evidence. The various types of evidence envisaged and regulated by the Code of Criminal Procedure are: inspections, judicial experiments, expert evidence, translations from foreign or dialectal languages, searches, sequestrations, testimony, identifications, confrontations, telephonic interceptions, and, imperfectly, the interrogation of the accused. As already noted, all the evidence is written, and oral testimony is reduced into summary depositions dictated by the examining judge to his clerk. Several

reservations have been expressed in relation to this system of drawing the depositions because the dictation of the summary by the judge often removes the immediate and spontaneous response of the witness through the judge's interpretation of the testimony.

(a) THE INTERROGATION OF THE ACCUSED. This is an instruction measure of fundamental importance. However, the doctrine is in disagreement as to its precise nature, basically because the various writers emphasise different aspects. Nonetheless, its several functions are clear: it is the means of identifying the accused; it is the means of joining issue on the charge; it guarantees the right of defence because a precise definition of the charge enables the accused to make whatever submissions he considers appropriate; and finally, it is a source of evidence because, notwithstanding that the object of the institution is not to elicit evidence, the court may nonetheless draw favourable or unfavourable inferences. Prior to the interrogation, the accused must be advised that he may remain silent, except in relation to certain personal details such as his name. The accused is then asked to name or proceed to appoint a legal representative who is entitled to be present at the interrogation. If the accused fails to do so, the court ex officio appoints a legal representative. If the accused chooses to answer questions in relation to the charge, he is under no obligation to tell the truth as he is not under oath. The interrogation must be conducted without the exertion of any physical or moral pressures, and if a confession is the result of any means which affects the mental freedom of the accused not only is the confession invalid but its extraction also constitutes a crime. It is clear from the Code, furthermore, that a confession per se is not sufficient to support a conviction for which a confession must be corroborated by some other objective *indicia* that confirms its veracity, genuineness and spontaneity.

(b) TESTIMONY. The examining judge or *pubblico ministero* conducting an instruction has the duty to examine all witnesses who have a knowledge of the facts pertaining to the case in question and who are considered useful in ascertaining the truth (A.348(1) cpp). It follows that first, witnesses mean all persons having knowledge of the subject facts; second, the object of testimony—and of criminal proceedings generally—is to ascertain the truth; and third, the judge has an obligation to examine all persons having knowledge of the subject facts, except those witnesses whom he considers futile to the proceedings. Persons who are incompetent as witnesses are the accused, whether of the subject proceedings or of a connected crime, the judge, the *pubblico ministero* and the court clerks connected with the proceedings. The only exception to the principle that a party to the proceedings cannot be heard as a witness is the civil party (see p 265, below). Competent but not compellable witnesses must be advised of their right to abstain from giving testimony and include first, the proximate relatives of the accused or of a co-accused of the same crime (A.350 cpp); second, ministers of recognised religions, attorneys, procurators, technical or expert consultants, notaries, and persons involved in health (e g doctors, pharmacists, midwives) (A.351(1) cpp); and third, public officials and public employees who have a knowledge of the facts through their office or who are bound by State privilege or secrecy (A.351(2) cpp). This last category of persons are obliged to abstain from giving evidence as to matters coming within State privilege, and the court is likewise prohibited from interrogating them on what is covered by that privilege (A.352 cpp). Witnesses, in the instruction phase, do not normally give evidence under oath (A.357 cpp) unless the testimony relates to the identification of persons or things (A.363 cpp) or facts relating to inspections and judicial experiments (A.313 cpp). However, the examining judge must take testimony under oath when he envisages that for some reason the witness cannot appear at the trial, i e testimony of future record (A.357 cpp), in which case the legal representative of the accused is entitled to be present at the hearing. At the trial testimony must always be on oath, if not already sworn, except in the case of children under the age of 14 (A.449 cpp). Various sanctions apply to false testimony and to witnesses who fail to appear or are unwilling to answer questions.

(c) EXPERT EVIDENCE. Where investigations which require a specific expertise are necessary, the judge may enlist the assistance of an expert. This power becomes a *duty* when an investigation is of a technical nature or of such difficulty that it cannot come within the normal cognitive abilities of the judge (A.314 cpp). The expert, in contrast to a witness who introduces new probative elements, interprets, explains and illustrates a pre-existing probative element. They are regarded as collaborators with the judge rather than witnesses. In a formal instruction the expert investigation is ordered by the judge ex officio or at the instance of the *pubblico ministero* or one of the private parties. In a summary instruction, which theoretically ought to be brief and simple, the *pubblico ministero* may seek the assistance of an expert provided that the expert investigation is itself brief and simple; otherwise the *pubblico ministero* must transmit the matter to an examining judge who proceeds by formal instruction. Expert investigations may also be ordered during the trial phase. Notice of the order appointing an expert is given to the parties who are entitled to be present at all of the audiences and investigations with which the expert is concerned. The expert must, on his appointment, take the oath and may either give an immediate oral report, which is taken in the form of a deposition, or, if impossible, the court will fix a time within which a written report is to be given. The parties may, at their own expense, appoint private expert consultants who may attend the investigations carried out by the court appointed expert and make any observations and submissions.

(d) INSPECTIONS. Judicial inspections are the direct and immediate means through which the judge discovers the clues and other material effects of a crime (A.309 cpp). Inspections may be made of persons (bodily or corporal inspections which may be carried out by the judge personally or through an expert nominated by him, e g autopsies), localities or things.

(e) JUDICIAL EXPERIMENTS. These are the re-enactment or reconstruction of given situations to establish the veracity or similarity of a fact.

(f) SEARCHES. Searches, personal or domiciliary, are conducted either by the judge personally (with the assistance of the police) or by delegating them to the judical police pursuant to a reasoned decree. Bodily searches are conducted when the judge has a justifiable belief that things pertaining to the crime are hidden on the person. It can be made of any person except diplomats and members of Parliament unless these are caught in flagrance. The defence has a right to know of the results of a bodily search but not of being advised that it will be carried out. A domiciliary search is ordered where there is a justifiable belief that a thing pertinent to the crime, the accused, a suspect or a fugitive is to be found at the location. It is subject to various restrictions arising out of international law (e g property belonging to the Holy See or diplomats), constitutional law (the residences of members of Parliament), and temporal rules (except in cases of urgency, it cannot be effected earlier than an hour after sunrise nor later than an hour after sunset: A.333 cpp). Again, although the parties are entitled to know of its results, they are not entitled to notice that the search is to be carried out.

(g) SEQUESTRATION. A sequestration consists of the seizure of property relevant to a crime and usually arises consequent to a search. It has the object of acquiring for the purpose of the proceedings the instrument or product of the crime, e g a pistol or forged banknotes, and generally all other things pertinent to the crime and which, even indirectly, assist in establishing the existence of the crime, a fact, or the identity of the accused. Certain things are not subject to seizure, namely, things concerning political or military secrets, things concerning professional or State privilege, and documents in the possession of either legal representatives or technical consultants. A seizure made during the instruction phase is always pursuant to a reasoned decree of the judge who may either carry out the seizure personally or through the judicial police.

(h) IDENTIFICATION OF PERSONS OR THINGS. The latter concerns the identification of inanimate things (A.361 cpp), whereas the former generally arises where the judge believes that a person is able to identify the accused, in which case he may order a line-up (A.360 cpp). All the parties are entitled to be present and must be given notice of the proceedings. To ensure the objectivity of either type of identification, the Code prescribes various formalities and precautions.

(i) CONFRONTATIONS. Where there are discrepancies in relation to facts or circumstances important to the decision of the case, the examining judge may order a confrontation (A.346 cpp). It consists of a direct dialogue between a witness and the accused, between witnesses, or between co-accused, in the presence of the *pubblico ministero*, with the object of ascertaining the truth as amongst the conflicting declarations. The defendant's legal representative is not entitled to be present at a confrontation held during the instruction phase.

(j) TELEPHONIC INTERCEPTIONS (see p 177, above).

(*v*) *The personal liberty of the accused in the criminal process.* The criminal process represents the focal point of two fundamental but conflicting principles: the interests of the State in protecting society through the enforcement of the substantive criminal law, on the one hand, and individual freedom, protected by A.13 C (see ch 5, p 176, above), on the other. The various institutions of ordinary law which affect personal liberty are:

(a) ARREST WITHOUT A WARRANT. This comprises, in substance, the so-called police measures. They have the object of ensuring that the accused does not escape or avoid the proceedings. Arrest without warrant may occur in two situations:

1 arrest in 'flagrance' (*arresto in flagranza*: Artt. 235–237 cpp) which is arrest during, immediately before, or immediately after the commission of a crime (A.237 cpp). The arrest of persons apprehended in flagrance is mandatory in the case of certain categories of criminals (such as professionals) and in the case of crimes which carry a maximum penalty of not less than one year. In all other cases, arrest is discretionary. The arrest is subject to control by the *pubblico ministero* through the interrogation of the accused that must take place not later than three days from the arrest, thereby complying with the time limits prescribed by A.13 C.

2 restraint of suspects (*fermo di indiziati di reato*: A.238 cpp). Where there has been a *notitia criminis*, A.238 cpp provides that, apart from cases of flagrance, the police may detain persons reasonably suspected of being fugitives provided that there are sufficient indicia of guilt of either a crime punishable with a maximum penalty of not less than six years' imprisonment or a crime concerning arms or explosive materials. The judicial authorities must be immediately notified of

the arrest and advised within 48 hours of its basis and the results of any summary investigations. The judicial authorities must then, within the next 48 hours, proceed to interrogate the detainee and, if the arrest is considered to be well-founded, ratify the detention by the issue of a reasoned decree. This institution is an example of the exception contained in A.13(2) C concerning urgent and necessary measures affecting personal freedom.

(b) JUDICIAL MEASURES

1 *General*. The judicial measures restrictive of personal freedom are detention (*cattura*), arrest (*arresto*), summons (*comparizione*), and accompaniment (*accompagnamento*). These measures may issue from the judiciary in a strict sense, when the relevant measure is prefixed by the term '*mandato*' or from the *pubblico ministero*, when the relevant measure is prefixed by the term '*ordine*'. The essential pre-requisite for the issue of any of these measures is the existence of a sufficient indicia of guilt. Defendants normally come before the criminal courts pursuant to a judicial measure; it is only in a minority of cases that defendants appear pursuant to police measures (see p 239, above) which constitute a provisional restriction on personal freedom and which, if ratified by the judicial authorities, lead to preventive detention. Therefore, the majority of defendants appear before the criminal courts either in a state of freedom pursuant to a summons, or in a state of custody pursuant to a warrant issued by the judicial authorities.

2 *Warrants issued by the judicial authorities*. The two forms of judicial warrant are first, a warrant for detention (i e either a *mandato* or *ordine di cattura*) which is a judicial order that the accused be taken into custody and placed at the disposal of the judicial authorities. Its issue is obligatory in the case of the crimes defined by A.253 cpp and discretionary in the case of the crimes defined by A.254 cpp. A warrant for detention cannot be issued in the case of a crime not listed in either of these two provisions. Second, a warrant for arrest (*mandato* or *ordine di arresto*) which is identical to a warrant for detention except that it is a temporary measure issued in a case of urgency by a judicial authority not having the competence to deal with the matter. As soon as the warrant is executed, the arrested person must be placed at the disposal of the competent judicial authority which must, within 20 days, either issue a warrant for detention or convict the accused if proceeding according to the procedure known as *procedimento direttissimo* (see p 246, below); otherwise the warrant loses its effect.

3 *Appearances in a state of freedom*. As already noted, the accused may appear before the court in a state of freedom. This may be either

pursuant to a summons (*mandato* or *ordine di comparizione*) which requires an appearance before the proceeding authority or, if the summons is not obeyed, pursuant to a warrant for accompaniment (*mandato* or *ordine di accompagnamento*) into which a summons may be converted and which directs the judicial police to forcibly conduct the accused, without making an arrest, before the court.

(c) PROVISIONAL LIBERTY OR BAIL (*libertà provisoria*). The bail provisions, like many other provisions of the Italian criminal process that affect personal liberty, have undergone changes depending upon the state of public order. Although previously bail was not available in the case of crimes which attracted the mandatory issue of a warrant for detention, in 1972 the so-called *legge Valpreda* extended the bail provisions to these crimes as well. However, the institution was again altered pursuant to the law of 22 May 1975 n.152 (the so-called law on public order) that sets out a list of crimes in which bail is not available unless the accused is in such a state of ill health that necessary medical treatment cannot be administered, in which event the judge is given a discretion as to whether bail should be granted. In every other case, bail may be granted at any stage or grade of the proceedings. In granting bail, the court must have regard to the probability of the accused, having regard to the circumstances of the case and the accused's character, committing further crimes and the extent that it is still necessary to avoid any interference with the evidence.

(d) RELEASE (SCARCERAZIONE) FOR THE LACK OF SUFFICIENT INDICIA OF GUILT OR BECAUSE OF THE LAPSE OF THE STATUTORY PERIODS OF MAXIMUM DETENTION. Provisional detention may cease because there is either no longer a sufficient indicia of guilt or because of the lapse of the maximum statutory periods for preventive custody. The latter is a response to the constitutional obligation contained in A.135 C statutorily to impose maximum periods of preventive detention to protect persons who have been lawfully arrested and are awaiting process. At the expiration of the relevant period the detainee must be automatically released notwithstanding that the proceedings against him are still pending. This institution prevents an excessively long instruction becoming a burden upon the accused and also serves as an incentive for the speedy conclusion of the investigations. The various maximum periods of preventive detention vary according to a sliding scale depending upon the court before which the proceedings are pending and the stage and grade of the proceedings.

(e) THE REVIEW OF MEASURES AFFECTING PERSONAL LIBERTY—THE TRIBUNALE DELLA LIBERTÀ. The recent reforms implemented by the law of 12 August 1982 n.532 sought to organically regulate the review of measures affecting personal liberty. The 1982 legislation has introduced a unitary procedure for the review of four categories of measures which affect personal liberty: first, the review, at the instance of the *pubblico ministero*, of the refusal of an application by the *pubblico ministero* for the issue of a warrant for detention, the imposition of measures alternative to detention, or the revocation of a warrant (A.263(1) and (2) cpp); second, subject to certain exceptions, the review, at the instance of the accused, of warrants for detention or arrest, the imposition of alternative measures, or the revocation of measures imposed in lieu of preventive detention (A.263 *bis* cpp); third, the review, at the instance of either the *pubblico ministero* or the accused, of decisions relating to *release* from detention (A.272 *bis* cpp); and finally, the review, again at the instance of either the *pubblico ministero* or the accused, of measures concerning provisional liberty (A.281 cpp). In all of these cases the review concerns a re-examination of the decision, including the merits.

The competent court is the *Tribunale* in the capital of the province in which the authority that issued the measure under attack is located. Thus only one *Tribunale* in each province is competent to deal with all of the measures issued in that province concerning personal liberty. Therefore, of some 159 *Tribunali* and 899 *Preture* in all, there are only 95 *Tribunali della liberta'*. The procedure is that as soon as an application for review is received by the body which issued the measure, the application and the file must immediately, and in any event within 24 hours, be forwarded to the competent *Tribunale*. The *Tribunale* must then within three days, which may be extended to six days in complex cases, confirm or revoke the measure appealed against. If the *Tribunale* fails to decide within the prescribed time, the relevant measure will cease to have any effect. The *Tribunale* makes an *ex novo* decision on the personal liberty of the accused and its decision is subject to further review by Cassation on the ground of violation of law. The proceedings before the *Tribunale* have been criticised because an effective dialogue between the parties is hindered by the secrecy of many instruction measures in the principal proceedings (see p 232, above). The effectiveness of the institution is therefore restricted by the inquisitorial framework into which it has been introduced.

Measures which affect personal liberty but are not subject to review by the *Tribunale della libertà*, e g a measure made at second instance consequent to an appeal by the *pubblico ministero* against the decision of an examining judge or a measure made by the instruction section of the Court of Appeal, are reviewable, on the ground of violation of law, by the Court of Cassation. Generally, furthermore, review by Cassation of measures affecting personal liberty is always available after the expiration of every other available form of review (A.111 C).

(vi) The closure of the instruction phase. The examining judge or *pubblico ministero* will normally close the instruction phase at the point at which all the relevant and significant evidence has been gathered. The body that makes the relevant order at the conclusion of the instruction phase depends upon whether the instruction was a formal or summary one. In the case of a summary instruction this will, in turn, depend upon whether the instruction was conducted by the *Pretore* or the *pubblico ministero*. In the former case the *Pretore* himself issues either a judgment acquitting the accused or a decree of citation for trial. If the instruction was conducted by the *pubblico ministero*, the two possible orders originate from different bodies: if the *pubblico ministero* seeks an acquittal the competent body is the examining judge, who may refuse the application and initiate a formal instruction against the accused; if the *pubblico ministero* decides that there is sufficient evidence to put the accused on trial, the relevant order must be sought from the trial court. In the case of a *formal instruction* the examining judge either decides that there is sufficient evidence to put the accused on trial and orders accordingly or acquits the accused.

C. THE TRIAL PHASE

The trial phase may be divided into three phases: acts preliminary to the trial; the trial; and matters subsequent to the trial. The preliminary phase is essentially a preparatory phase whose object is to ensure that the parties are in a position to conduct their cases, e g a preparatory activity of particular importance is the filing and admission of the list of witnesses whom the parties wish to call: not only must the list be filed timely, to avoid the loss of the right to call witnesses, but the court also has a very wide and often criticised discretion over the number of witnesses it wishes to hear.

The trial is characterised by various features. First, it is, theoretically, characterised by its orality and immediacy, although in practice it has degenerated into a mere formal reception of the written summaries of the evidence collected in the instruction phase. Therefore the trial phase is largely dominated by, and has become a formal confirmation of, the previous instruction phase. This seriously compromises the principles of orality and immediacy because, on one hand, unlike civil proceedings, the examining judge who conducts the instruction phase does not form part of the adjudicatory panel as a result of which no member of the panel has had the opportunity of taking cognizance of the demeanour of the witnesses and, on the other hand, the written summaries taken in the instruction phase must necessarily embody the interpretative and filtering processes of their author. The various phases of the criminal process therefore constitute a continuum; a continuous series of phases in which each phase leads into and becomes cumulative with the next, and all of which are utilized in reaching the final decision of the case. The trial phase ultimately does not have that primacy which the principles of orality and immediacy ought to have given it. Second, the trial is characterised by the contestation of the charge and an altercation between the parties. The contestation of the charge is through the notification of the order remitting the case to trial. The order contains both an indication of the competent court and the specification of the charge. The altercation between the parties is assured through their joinder in the trial. Finally, the trial phase is public as opposed to the secret instruction phase. Nonetheless, the trial may be closed to the public for certain reasons: State security, public order, morality, precipitation of excessive curiosity, disturbance of the serenity of the trial, for public intemperance, and public hygiene. All trials in the minors tribunal are closed to the public.

The trial procedure has been devised with the object of ascertaining the truth and may be divided into three parts. First, the opening formalities which concern the appearance of the parties, witnesses, experts and interpreters, and the reading of the charge. After these formalities, the *Pretore* or President of the court declares the trial open, at which point there is the appearance of the civil party, the summons of the civilly responsible party and his intervention, the resolution of any preliminary questions, that is, questions relating to the procedural regularity of the proceedings, and the resolution of any incidental questions raised by any party at the trial itself. Second, the trial instruction phase which comprises the laying of the charge which is read in court, the interrogation of the accused, the taking of the general evidence (that is, carrying out inspections and receiving the reports of experts), the taking of specific evidence (that is, the examination of witnesses), and the laying of charges for concurrent and continuing crimes or for new crimes committed during the trial. As in civil procedure, the witnesses are examined by the judge and there is no cross-examination. Depositions are prepared of all of the trial proceedings by the court clerk who works under the direction of the judge. These depositions are not verbatim but only summaries of the declarations made by the parties and witnesses or of the oral conclusions stated by the court appointed experts and technical consultants. Third, the closing addresses by the various parties, in the following order: the civil party, the *pubblico ministero*, the civilly responsible party, the party civilly liable for the fine, and the accused. The *pubblico ministero* and the legal representatives of all the parties may have one reply only but, in any event, the legal representative of the accused, and the accused himself if he so requests, must be heard last (A.468 cpp).

The proceedings then pass into the post trial phase consisting, in essence, of the court's judgment. The verdict, reached in camera, must be delivered in open court immediately after the close of the trial: this requirement, ensuring that a decision is taken whilst the evidence is fresh, does not include the delivery of the reasoning which is prepared later. Thus the decision process consists of the following: a verdict reached in camera; the delivery of the verdict which may consist of an acquittal, a penalty, the imposition of a precautionary measure (see ch 7, p 301, below), and any order for costs, damages or restitution; the preparation of the reasoning; and the deposit of the reasoning in the court Registry. Once the reasoning is deposited in the Registry, it is communicated to the accused at which point the time within which an appeal may be lodged begins to run.

Variations of the ordinary criminal process

The ordinary or typical criminal process described above, although it remains substantially unvaried, in some cases takes on special features due to the particular structure or needs of the court in question. This arises in the following cases: the *procedimento d'assise* (the procedure before the courts of assizes. See p 225, above), the *procedimento pretorile* (the procedure before the *Pretura*), and the *procedimento minorile* (the procedure before the minors' court).

The *procedimento pretorile* consists of the ordinary procedure except that the *Pretore* dominates the whole process; he initiates the criminal process (i e he is the prosecutor), conducts the instruction, and eventually decides the case. The procedure therefore comes close to a pure inquisitorial system. First, there is no distinction between prosecutor and decision-maker. As already noted, in the *Pretura*, the functions of the *pubblico ministero* are exercised by the *Pretore* himself who in his capacity as such initiates the criminal process and, because the instruction is always a summary instruction, also conducts the instruction although at the very beginning of the instruction phase he is required to serve upon the accused a 'judicial communication' which defines the charge and invites the latter to nominate a legal representative. Second, the *Pretore* enjoys all of the usual powers in relation to the collection of the evidence, that is, the *Pretore* is not restricted to the evidence presented by the parties. Third, the *Pretore* decides the case but in this phase the functions of the *pubblico ministero* are exercised by one of various other defined persons (e g probationary judges, vice-*pretori*, attorneys, mayors, or town clerks). Nonetheless, the laying of any extra charges arising out of a concurrent crime or an aggravating factor is always done by the *Pretore*. The *procedimento pretorile* has been the subject of many criticisms, especially in relation to the significant powers of the *Pretore* that therefore enable the imposition of a certain political or social philosophy. The requirement of the impartiality of the bench has several times been raised before the Constitutional Court which, because of practical and economic reasons, has not invalidated this form of procedure.

The procedure before the Minors' Court (see p 226, above), is the ordinary procedure with certain variations. It has a more flexible instruction phase and its trial phase varies from the ordinary procedure as follows: the citation for trial must be brought to the knowledge of the person having the lawful custody of the minor; the trial is not public; the court may order that the minor leave the court for any part of the proceedings considered harmful to his welfare; special reports are obtained in relation to the minor's criminal and familial precedents; and only attorneys registered on a special 'roll' may represent a minor.

The special procedures

Apart from the ordinary or typical procedure, the Code prescribes various atypical or special procedures. These comprise default proceedings, characterised by the absence of any debate with the accused; the *procedimento direttissimo* which lacks an instruction phase; and the *procedimento per decreto* which lacks a trial phase.

Default proceedings (Artt. 498–501 cpp) arise where an accused person fails to appear at the commencement of the trial. An accused person may only be declared in default if he has been regularly summoned and there is no legitimate reason for his failure to appear. Moreover, the accused cannot be declared in default until his legal representative or, if he fails to appoint one, the legal representative appointed ex officio by the court to represent him, is heard. Once the accused is declared to be in default, the proceedings are conducted normally with the legal representative acting, wherever posssible, for the accused. If the accused appears before the final address, the declaration of default is revoked but the accused must accept the proceedings as at the stage or grade they have reached when he appears.

The *procedimento direttissimo* (Artt. 502–505 cpp), which enables a speedy conclusion of criminal proceedings, has since 1974 been given broader application, mainly as a manifestation of the State's readiness to act swiftly in dealing with certain types of criminality. The procedure is available first, where the accused is arrested during or immediately before or after the commission of a crime or where he commits a crime whilst in the state of arrest; second, where the accused is arrested pursuant to a warrant for detention issued within 30 days of the commission of the crime; and finally, in the case of certain defined serious crimes. The common element to all these situations is the lack of a need for an instruction, even of a summary type. This procedure represents the only example of a pure accusatorial process in the Italian legal system. The result of the proceedings may be a definitive judgment, a decision that the proceedings are not yet ready for decision and therefore a formal instruction is required, or that the case was not one to which the *procedimento direttissimo* was applicable, in which event the matter is referred to the *pubblico ministero* to be dealt with according to the ordinary procedure.

The *procedimento per decreto* (Artt. 506–510 cpp), regarded by some writers as the strongest example of an inquisitorial procedure, omits, as an economy measure, the trial phase of the proceedings. It is only applicable to crimes which first, come within the competence of the *Pretura*, second, may be prosecuted ex officio, and third, are punishable with either a fine or a fine and detention but remitted to a fine only in the instant case. In the case of such crimes, at the close of the instruction phase, the *Pretore* may enter a conviction by decree without proceeding to a trial. The decree, which must have the same content as a judgment, is communicated to the defendant who may, if he considers the decision unjust or illegal, within five days of its communication oppose the decree by personally appearing at the court Registry, after which a trial is held in the normal way. If the accused fails to appear at the trial, the judgment becomes res judicata. This procedure, and the requirement that the accused personally appear at the Registry to make the opposition, has been attacked as infringing the constitutional right of defence. However, the Constitutional Court has held, basically on the ground that there exists a right to require a trial, that the procedure is constitutionally valid.

Extradition proceedings (Artt. 661–671 cpp)

A person whose extradition is sought may be arrested pursuant to a warrant for detention issued by the *pubblico ministero* upon request of the Minister of Grace and Justice. The arrest cannot extend beyond 60 days if the State requesting the extradition is in Europe, or 90 days in any other case. The ultimate decision rests with the government which, can never order an extradition without a favourable opinion of the instruction section of the Court of Appeal of the district in which the person is held or was arrested. The decision of the Court is merely a declaratory judgment subject to review by Cassation, in this case, on the merits as well.

Proceedings for the recognition of foreign criminal judgments (Artt. 672–675 cpp)

An application for the recognition of a foreign criminal judgment may be made either by the *pubblico ministero* or any person who is entitled to restitution, damages or any other civil remedy consequent upon the foreign judgment. The recognition of the judgment does not depend on a review of the decision of the foreign court, but only on certain formal matters and the observation by the foreign court of various guarantees. The necessary requisites for recognition are: first, that the foreign judgment has become res judicata; second, that the convicted person was summoned to appear in court and represented by a lawyer; third, that the foreign judgment does not contain any orders contrary to the general principles of the Italian legal system; and finally, that there exists an extradition treaty between Italy and the State in which the subject judgment was made. The recognition of foreign judgments is determined by the Court of Appeal whose decision is subject to review by Cassation at the instance of the *pubblico ministero* or the convicted person.

The review of criminal judgments

A criminal judgment may be reviewed as to fact or law, or both. The review of a criminal judgment is characterised by certain basic features. First, in contrast to the obligation of the *pubblico ministero* to initiate the criminal process upon receipt of a *notitia criminis* the parties to the proceedings have a complete discretion as to the initiation of any further proceedings for the review of the decision of first instance and may, moreover, even withdraw any review proceedings they had already initiated. Second, where the accused only seeks a review of the judgment, the superior court cannot alter the judgment in a manner unfavourable to the accused. Article 515(3) cpp, expressly prohibits, subject to the exception contained in that provision, the infliction of a heavier penalty or the revocation of any benefits conceded by the inferior court (e g suspended sentence or non-recording of the offence) in such cases. Third, the review of a criminal judgment has certain extensive effects: on one hand, there is a right in any person who did not initiate the review but who has an identical or connected interest, to participate in the proceedings; and, on the other hand, the judgment extends in certain cases to a party who has not sought a review of the decision. These extensive effects arise where there are several authors to a crime, where there is the joinder of proceedings, or where the review is initiated by the civilly responsible or civilly liable party in which case the decision may affect the accused. The review of a judgment at the instance of one co-accused suspends the execution of the judgment vis-à-vis every other co-accused, whereas a review initiated by a civil party can be of no benefit to the other parties, as too, in the case of an appeal by the *pubblico ministero* limited to one of the co-accused.

There are three basic forms of review. First, appeal. An appeal may concern law or fact and the whole or part of the decision at first instance. An appeal takes the form of a *de novo* trial and may be brought against decisions of a *Pretore*, *Tribunale* or *Corte d'assise*. It consists of three phases: pre-trial, trial, and post-trial. The pre-trial phase begins with a preliminary examination by the court of first instance of the admissibility of the appeal, the transmission of the file to the appeal court, and an examination of the matter by the President of the appeal court. If the President finds either a cause for the inadmissibility of the appeal or a ground for the acquittal of the convicted person, he convenes the court for the pronouncement of the appropriate order. Otherwise he issues a decree ordering the summons of all parties to the appeal. The basic distinguishing factor of the trial phase in an appeal is an even greater limitation of the principle of orality as extensive use is made of written evidence. However, oral proceedings may arise where the matter cannot be decided without a total or partial renewal of the trial; where a measure carried out at first instance has been declared null and needs to be renewed; or where, and in this case the renewal of the trial is obligatory, the court at first instance erroneously declared that the crime in question was extinguished or that the proceedings could not have been initiated at all.

Second, review by Cassation. This form of review is only available in relation to judgments not subject to appeal and appellate judgments; not, therefore, judgments which could, but have not been, appealed. Review by Cassation, moreover, is limited to errors of law (whether of substance or procedure); only exceptionally does the Court have the right to review the merits of a decision. Apart from declaring the inadmissibility of the proceedings, the only orders that the Court may make are either to dismiss the application or, where the application is allowed, quash the whole or part of the judgment under attack. Where the Court quashes a judgment, given that its jurisdiction is limited to issues of law, it may be necessary to remit the matter to the court competent on the merits for final disposition. The latter court is, however, bound by the decision of Cassation on the issues of law and any further review by Cassation is limited to issues which have not already been reviewed. The proceedings before the court to which the matter is remitted are part of the review procedure.

Third, revision. This is an extraordinary means of review aimed at the elimination of a conviction which has already become res judicata (that is, where no other form of review is possible) and its substitution with an acquittal or, in the case of certain types of homicide, with a conviction for a different crime because supervening matters have rendered the original conviction unjust. Revision may be sought notwithstanding that the penalty has been served or extinguished, or that the convicted person has died. It may be brought by the convicted person himself; a close relative, tutor, or heir of the convicted person; or by the *pubblico ministero* ex officio, or at the request of the Minister of

Grace and Justice. Revision is only available on the grounds defined by A.554 cpp: first, where the facts at the basis of the conviction are irreconcilable with those in another criminal judgment, whenever made; second, where the criminal conviction was consequent to a civil or administrative judgment since revoked; third, where there is supervening or new evidence which either alone or together with the existing evidence shows that the convicted person ought to be acquitted on certain grounds; fourth, where the conviction was the result of either false evidence or a fact which constitutes a crime; and finally, where, after conviction for homicide, there is supervening or new evidence which either alone or together with the existing evidence shows that the death of the victim had not occurred. Revision is sought from the Court of Cassation which, exceptionally, carries out all of the necessary inquiries and investigations. At the close of such instruction procedures the Court either declares the application inadmissible on the grounds defined in A.555 cpp or grants the application. In the latter event it may either quash the conviction without more (where the innocence of the convicted person is evident) or quash the conviction and order a new trial. Persons who are found by Cassation or at the new trial to have been unjustly convicted are entitled to reparation for judicial error provided that they had not, either intentionally or with serious fault, given rise or contributed to the judicial error. If the convicted person is deceased, then the right of reparation belongs to certain proximate relatives.

The review of instruction decisions

There are three types of review of instruction decisions. First, appeal. The decision 'not to proceed' with the criminal proceedings made by an examining judge at the close of the instruction phase conducted before a *Tribunale* is subject to appeal to the instruction section of the Court of Appeal; a similar decision by the *Pretore* in instruction proceedings before the *Pretura* is subject to appeal to an examining judge of the *Tribunale*.

Second, review by Cassation. It may be sought by the *pubblico ministero* against either an appellate decision made by the instruction section of the Court of Appeal to acquit the accused or a non appealable decision to that effect made by an examining judge of the *Tribunale* or a *Pretore*. Similarly, the accused may seek the review of an acquittal made on appeal by either the instruction section of the Court of Appeal or an examining judge of the *Tribunale*, as too, against a non-appealable acquittal made by the *Pretore*. It may appear strange that the accused would seek the review of an acquittal, but this can be understood against the background of many qualified forms of acquittal which can be made in Italian law at the close of the instruction phase, e g an 'acquittal for insufficient evidence' (Artt. 378 and 479 cpp). It may therefore happen that the accused is entitled to a more favourable form of acquittal or even an unqualified acquittal.

Third, the re-opening of the instruction phase. This is an extraordinary form of attack of an instruction decision, analogous to the revision of a criminal judgment, based upon the discovery of new evidence. It may arise in two cases (A.402 cpp): on the one hand, upon application of the *pubblico ministero* where new evidence is discovered against a person who was previously acquitted and, on the other hand, upon application of a person who was acquitted for 'insufficient evidence' where new and favourable evidence is discovered. The application is made to the court which had pronounced the acquittal. The decision of the court must be reasoned and, when it orders the re-opening of the instruction, it is subject to review by Cassation on error of law if it prejudices the freedom of the accused. The re-opening of an instruction in any of the above circumstances concerns an acquittal which was previously made in the instruction phase. This is to be distinguished from a case which had proceeded to trial in which event there is a res judicata judgment which, according to A.90 cpp that embodies the double jeopardy rule, prevents the initiation of further criminal proceedings against the same person for the same facts.

Administrative justice

A. INTRODUCTION

Administrative justice concerns the remedies available to an individual for his protection against the activities of the public administration. The Italian administrative justice system is independent from the ordinary judicial system. Its autonomous nature is the consequence of the co-existence of three fundamental principles: first, the extension of the judicial protection of rights and interests against the public administration (A.24(1) C); second, the autonomy of the Executive power of State; and third, the compliance, as determined by the judicial authorities, of administrative action with the law (A.101 C). In Italy, administrative review may be of two broad types: review within the administrative structure itself and judicial review. The latter is, in turn, divided between the ordinary and administrative courts depending upon whether a subjective right or a legitimate interest respectively has been violated (as to these concepts see ch 1, pp 20 ff and ch 5, p 151, above). Any conflicts in jurisdiction between the ordinary and administrative courts are resolved by the Court of Cassation sitting as a full court.

A relatively new institution in Italian administrative law is the Ombudsman, recently introduced into certain Regions (Liguria, Toscana and Lazio). It represents a new form of review for administrative acts of the Regions. In the relatively few Regions in which it has been introduced, the Ombudsman has not been given any decisional functions, merely a power to request information on the progress of administrative matters and a right to copies of any relevant documentation. The only other power of the Ombudsman is that of initiating disciplinary actions against officers who hinder his functions. The institution therefore has few substantive powers against negligent administrative organs and for this reason is likely to become a mere information and complaint office for the Regional administrations. The limited powers of the Ombudsman also reflect a lack of conviction on the part of the Regions as to the utility of the institution.

B. THE ADMINISTRATIVE REVIEW OF ADMINISTRATIVE DECISIONS: REVIEW WITHIN THE ADMINISTRATIVE STRUCTURE ITSELF

This form of review does not involve any judicial intervention. It gives the administration an opportunity to resolve any dispute arising out of its activities, through the pronouncement of a definitive decision made pursuant to an application by an interested person, before the matter proceeds to the judicial sphere. This form of administrative review constitutes a legal remedy, which may result in the annulment or modification of the administrative act in question. The administration is bound to decide an application for the review of a decision within 90 days, in the absence of which there is a presumption that the application has been rejected whereupon the applicant may proceed before the administrative courts. An application for administrative review gives rise to administrative contentious proceedings whose decision is in the form of an administrative measure, usually a decree, which must be reasoned.

Administrative review may be divided into three broad types: ordinary review, the general type of administrative review and comprises hierarchical review; exceptional review, available in defined cases only and comprises the form of review known as opposition; and extraordinary review, administrative review by recourse to the Head of State and alternative to judicial review by the administrative courts. The availability of the various types of administrative review depends upon whether the administrative decision is definitive or non-definitive. An administrative decision may be definitive first, by reason of the nature of the body which issues the decision: namely, a body without a superior in the administrative hierarchy, a collegial body which, by definition, can have no superior, or a public entity which does not form part of an administrative hierarchy; second, by operation of law, namely, where law attributes a definitive nature to defined decisions; and third, by implication, namely, where the power to make an administrative decision is *exclusively* conferred upon an inferior body.

The review of definitive administrative measures is limited to either extraordinary administrative review by the Head of State or, alternatively, judicial review by the administrative courts. Exceptionally, the law provides for an improper form of hierarchical review, that is, although a particular administrative body has no superior in a strict or technical sense the law nonetheless expressly provides for the 'hierarchical' review of its measures by some other defined administrative organ. This makes available the additional advantage inherent in a hierarchical review, namely, that the latter, unlike, generally, judicial review by the administrative courts, also encompasses a review of the merits of an administrative decision.

A non-definitive administrative measure is subject to either hierarchical review or, alternatively, judicial review by the administrative courts. It is to be noted carefully that the hierarchical review of a non-definitive measure does not preclude the subsequent judicial review by the administrative courts of the definitive administrative decision which results from the hierarchical review: the only restriction in this case is that the applicant, before seeking judicial review, must await the expiration of the 90 day period within which the administration is required to come to a decision in the hierarchical review of the non-definitive decision. If the administration fails to make a decision within that time, there is a presumption that it has tacitly rejected the hierarchical appeal by the applicant, who is therefore free to bring an application for the judicial review of the presumed definitive decision of the administration.

Administrative review may be sought by either natural or legal (whether public or private) persons who must have an interest in the annulment of the administrative measure. The necessary interest must consist of the actual and concrete violation of either a subjective right or a legitimate or (simple) interest (see chs 1 and 5 above). Administrative review may relate to either the merits or the legitimacy of an administrative decision, except in the case of extraordinary review by the Head of State which is limited to the legitimacy of an administrative measure. The time within which administrative review may be sought is 30 days, in the case of hierarchical review and oppositions, and 120 days, in the case of extraordinary review by the Head of State, from the date of communication of an individual measure or from the date of publication in the case of an administrative measure of general application.

The administrative review process consists of the instruction and decision phases. The instruction phase is both a preparatory and probative phase. In accordance with the general procedural principle of the effective debate of the issues, the applicant must also give notice of his application to persons who have an interest in supporting the measure under attack so that the latter may present any counter-arguments to the applicant's case: in the case of an extraordinary review the onus is on the applicant to give notice of the proceedings to at least one 'counter-interested' party whilst in the case of hierarchical review the administration bears the onus of giving such notice in the event that the applicant has not done so. This notice may be given by publication in a gazette. The evidence in the proceedings is collected by the administrative authority hearing the application and, in accordance with the inquisitorial principle, it is free to effectuate whatever investigations it considers opportune. There is no exhaustive list of the types of evidence which may be utilised in administrative proceedings, but A.13 of the DPR 24 November 1971 n.1199 on administrative review (DPR ra), in relation to extraordinary review, refers to the three typical forms of evidence in administrative proceedings: request for documents, request for clarifications, and verifications conducted during the ebate between the parties. The instruction must be concluded within 90 days of the commencement of the proceedings in the case of hierarchical review and within 120 days of the date fixed for the filing of submissions by the 'counter-interested' parties in the case of extraordinary review. The decision is in the form of an administrative decree which must contain a sufficient and complete reasoning. The decision may be based upon either prejudicial matters, which render the application inadmissible, or the merits of the application. A decision on the merits may only be based upon the grounds adduced in the application and may concern either legitimacy or the facts. The consequences of a successful application for review are: in the case of legitimacy, the annulment of the administrative measure subject, of course, to the right of the administrative body to emanate a new measure, and in the case of the facts, which may only be reviewed in a hierarchical review, the revocation or modification of the measure under review resulting in a new administrative measure which is attributable to the reviewing body and which must be in conformity with the public interest, expediency and equity.

The three types of administrative review may be described as follows:

(i) Hierarchical review. This is the typical or general remedy available against every non-definitive administrative decision. It consists of the review of an administrative decision by a hierarchically superior administrative body. The doctrine distinguishes between hierarchical review in a strict sense, which arises where the administrative organ which issued the measure is subordinate to that to which the review is addressed, and an improper hierarchical review which is the review of

an administrative measure by a superior organ not in a strict hierarchical relationship to that which issued the measure. The latter is an exceptional remedy (like oppositions) available only in cases defined by law. Hierarchical review is available *once* only, even if there are several hierarchically superior administrative bodies to that which issued the measure. The decision resulting from a hierarchical review is a definitive administrative decision which, as already noted, is only subject to extraordinary review by the Head of State or, alternatively, judicial review by the administrative courts.

(ii) Opposition. This is an atypical type of administrative review available only in those cases defined by law. It is addressed to the same authority which emanated the measure under review and not to its hierarchical superior. The same procedure as for hierarchical review is applicable to oppositions and, like the former, oppositions may be brought for either legitimacy or on the facts, and for the violation of either legitimate and simple interests or subjective rights. An opposition must generally be brought within 30 days of the date of communication of the measure under attack.

(iii) Extraordinary review by the Head of State. This is a general remedy available against all definitive administrative measures. Although, like the other forms of administrative review, it is available against violations of either legitimate and simple interests or subjective rights, unlike the other types of administrative review, it may only be brought on the grounds of legitimacy and not for a review of the facts. It is alternative to judicial review by the administrative courts so that if either procedure has been availed of, the other is not available. Moreover, as judicial review offers better guarantees, the 'counter-interested' party may require that the matter be dealt with by the administrative courts rather than the Head of State. Thus, if the applicant has initiated an extraordinary review by the Head of State, the 'counter-interested' party may either adhere to the applicant's selection or request, through an opposition made within 60 days of the notification of the proceedings, that the matter be transferred to the administrative courts. The decision of an extraordinary review is in the form of a Presidential Decree issued on the advice of the competent minister of State after receiving the opinion of the Council of State. The opinion of the Council of State is binding on the minister who, to depart from it, must put the matter to the Council of Ministers (Cabinet). There are two forms of appeal against a Presidential Decree: revocation, on the same grounds as in A.395 cpc (see p 211, above) and review by the administrative courts for formal or procedural defects.

C. THE JUDICIAL REVIEW OF ADMINISTRATIVE DECISIONS: THE PROTEC-
TION AFFORDED BY THE ORDINARY COURTS AGAINST THE ACTS OF THE
ADMINISTRATION.

According to A.2 of the law of 20 March 1865 n.2248 annexure E, the
ordinary courts have jurisdiction over all violations of the criminal law
and all matters relating to the existence or violation of subjective rights
notwithstanding that the issue arises out of an Executive or administrative measure and irrespective of whether the administration is
interested as plaintiff or defendant. The jurisdiction of the ordinary
courts over subjective rights is subject to the limitations inherent in the
grant of an exclusive jurisdiction over defined subjects to certain special
courts, e g the jurisdiction of the Court of Accounts in relation to
pensions, the jurisdiction of the Taxation Commissions, and the
jurisdiction of the administrative courts in relation to public
employment.

The powers of the ordinary courts in relation to administrative
measures are as follows. First, the jurisdiction of the ordinary courts is
limited to the mere legitimacy of an administrative measure and not its
merits; not, that is, to the expediency of the measure. Even in cases of
legitimacy, the ordinary courts are limited to the extrinsic defects of a
measure, that is, incompetence and violation of law. Second, the
ordinary courts cannot interfere with an administrative measure itself,
even if illegitimate. In other words, the ordinary courts cannot revoke
or annul an administrative measure nor act in the place of the public
administration by, for instance, modifying an administrative decision.
This is a direct consequence of the separation of powers as any
revocation, annulment or modification of an administrative measure by
the ordinary judicial authorities would constitute an interference with
the Executive Power. This restriction relates to administrative
measures only, and not to measures which the administration creates in
its private capacity, e g contracts. Third, the powers of the ordinary
courts vis-à-vis an administrative measure are restricted to declaring
the measure illegitimate and not applying it in the immediate case.
Fourth, it follows that a judgment of the ordinary courts, as regards an
administrative measure, is limited to the relevance of the measure to the
case in question. Finally, the ordinary courts may award damages
against the public administration (A.2043 cc), or make any other order
concerning the payment of moneys to the plaintiff.

Where the public administration is a party to civil proceedings, the
ordinary civil process is nonetheless applicable. Because the administration is represented by the State Attorney in all cases in which the
former acts in its private capacity, the rules for determining the
territorially competent court differ: territorial competence depends
upon the location of the particular office of the State Attorney upon

which the originating process must be served (see ch 2, p 52, above). Moreover, the procedure for the enforcement of judgments differs depending upon whether the judgment is a declaratory judgment or a judgment for damages. In the former case if the public administration fails to conform to the judgment, the interested party may apply to the administrative courts for its enforcement. In the case of judgments for damages, on the other hand, the normal enforcement procedure is applicable subject to the following: first, only the disposable State patrimony may be attached and not the public demesne nor the inalienable State patrimony; second, only the private law credits (e g rents) and not public law credits of the public entity, may be attached; finally, attachment is limited to the funds which have been paid into the general revenue of the relevant public entity provided that the funds have not been allocated to a specific purpose.

D. THE JUDICIAL REVIEW OF ADMINISTRATIVE DECISIONS: THE PROTECTION AFFORDED BY THE ADMINISTRATIVE COURTS AGAINST THE ACTS OF THE ADMINISTRATION

(*i*) *General.* Although the administrative courts are, in accordance with A.103 C, judicial organs, they differ from the ordinary judiciary for various reasons. First, they are formally part of the administrative branch of government. They are said to be only formally part of the latter branch of government because they enjoy the same autonomy and independence from the administration that distinguishes judicial organs of State. Second, the administration is a necessary party to all administrative proceedings which involve either the public administration and a private person, or two public administrations. And third, the jurisdiction of the administrative courts is limited to legitimate interests except in defined subjects over which they have been given an exclusive jurisdiction, that is, a jurisdiction over both subjective rights and legitimate interests. The ordinary administrative courts comprise the *Tribunali Amministrativi Regionali* (referred to as TARs) which are the courts of first instance, and the Council of State, which is the court of appeal against the decisions of the TARs (except for the Sicilian TAR, from which appeals lie to the Council of Administrative Justice for the Sicilian Region). There are also special administrative courts which have a particular jurisdiction defined by law, e g the Court of Accounts, the Tribunals for Public Waters, and the Taxation Commissions.

(*ii*) *The Tribunali Amministrativi Regionali (TARs).* Although the TARs are not Regional organs, they are called Regional Administrative Tribunals because their territorial competence is defined on a Regional basis. There is a TAR in each Regional capital, although in the case of some Regions the court also has decentralised sections in other major centres. The TAR located at the national capital, the TAR of the Lazio Region, apart from its decentralised sections, has three sections because of the heavy workload of the central administration in Rome. The courts are staffed by a career judiciary. Each TAR has a President and at least five administrative judges. The court exercises its judicial function as a collegiate organ consisting of three judges. The TAR has three species of jurisdiction: first, a general jurisdiction over the legitimacy of administrative measures; second, a jurisdiction on the merits in defined subjects; and third, an exclusive jurisdiction in defined subjects.

The general jurisdiction of the administrative courts on legitimacy concerns any dispute as to the legitimacy of an administrative measure that violates a legitimate interest. It is a residual jurisdiction in the sense that the protection of any legitimate interest not expressly reserved to the jurisdiction of a special administrative court falls within the jurisdiction of the TARs. The general jurisdiction of the administrative courts is restricted to illegitimacy on three specific grounds: incompetence, violation of law, and excess of power. It follows that the court cannot investigate the merits of a case except insofar as is necessary to determine the grounds for illegitimacy adduced by the party. The TARs, moreover, may only review the 'acts and measures' of administrative bodies, that is, measures which are administrative both in form and substance. The administrative courts cannot entertain attacks upon the administrative acts of non-administrative organs, such as parliamentary, political or judicial administrative measures, or the non-administrative measures of administrative organs.

It may be noted here that although regulations are, in abstract, administrative acts and therefore subject to attack before the TARs, in practice they are rarely subject to challenge because the applicant generally lacks the necessary interest to bring the proceedings. The necessary interest, analogous to that for civil proceedings, depends upon the usefulness of the proceedings to the applicant, that is, there must be first, an effective material or moral injury to the individual interests of the applicant caused by the administrative measure in question, and second, a potential advantage from the annulment of the measure. Although the TARs do not normally have jurisdiction over subjective rights, they may nonetheless decide a subjective right where it is incidental to the resolution of a dispute concerning a legitimate interest, unless the subjective right concerns personal status or capacity which, in every event, remain exclusive to the ordinary courts. The effects of an incidental decision of a subjective right by a TAR is limited to the administrative judgment. An administrative court, finally, may make the following orders in proceedings concerning the legitimacy of an administrative measure: first, the annulment of the measure and a reference back to the competent authority in cases of incompetence; second, the total or partial annulment of the measure in cases of either excess of power or violation of law; and third, the payment of costs by the administration.

The jurisdiction on the merits enables the review of a measure not only on legitimacy (that is, its conformity with legal norms), but also as to its expediency (that is, its conformity with the norms of good administration). It is a cumulative jurisdiction in that it is always additional to and never exclusive of the court's jurisdiction over the legitimacy of a measure. However, it is an exceptional jurisdiction as it is only available in defined cases.

The most important part of the jurisdiction on the merits is the enforcement of judgments against the public administration. As already noted, the ordinary courts cannot annul, revoke, or modify an administrative measure nor can they order specific performance against the administration. Therefore an interested party is dependent upon the public administration voluntarily conforming to a judgment of the ordinary courts, as required under A.4 *l*20 March 1865 n.2248, Annexure E. Where the public administration fails to do so the interested party may bring enforcement proceedings in the administrative courts to enforce the judgment of the ordinary courts. The legislation which introduced the TARs (*l* 6 December 1971 n.1034; *l* TAR) extended their enforcement jurisdiction to include judgments of the administrative courts as well. In particular, A.37 *l* TAR confers upon the Council of State a jurisdiction at first instance in relation to the enforcement of the following judgments: judgments of the ordinary courts where the administrative authority in question exercises its activities beyond a single Region; and judgments of the Council of State, unless they are merely confirmatory of the judgment of a TAR. In every other case, the enforcement jurisdiction belongs to the TARs.

The powers of the TARs in relation to their jurisdiction on the merits are: first, the annulment of a measure on the grounds of illegitimacy; second, the total or partial revision of a measure; third, the substitution of an administrative measure with that formulated by the court; and finally, orders for costs against the public administration when the latter is unsuccessful.

Like the jurisdiction on the merits, the exclusive jurisdiction of the TARs is exceptional and limited to certain subjects defined by law. As the exclusive jurisdiction of the TARs in these subjects is not concurrent with any other court, the distinction between legitimate interests and subjective rights is irrelevant and it was, in fact, because of the difficulty of this distinction in certain subjects that the exclusive jurisdiction of the TARs was created, e g in the subject of public employment which is an important part of the exclusive jurisdiction. Even in the case of exclusive jurisdiction certain matters fall outside the decisory powers of the TARs: questions relating to the status and capacity of natural persons; questions as to the authenticity of documents; and the patrimonial consequences (or damages) flowing from judgments holding an administrative measure void. These matters always remain within the jurisdiction of the ordinary courts.

(iii) The Council of State. The Council of State, after the reforms of 1971, has become the court of appeal from the decisions of the TARs. It has an exclusive jurisdiction at first instance over defined matters and a residual jurisdiction over all administrative disputes which do not come within the jurisdiction of either the TARs or any of the other subordinate special administrative courts. The judicial functions of the Council of State are exercised by its IV, V and VI sections and its Plenary Assembly. The judicial business of the Council is allocated amongst the three sections according to the ministries from which the measure under attack has originated. Each section is comprised of a president, a vice-president, seven councillors and a certain number of referees, and exercises its judicial functions through a collegiate bench of seven magistrates.

The Plenary Assembly consists of four councillors from each of the three sections and the President of the Council of State. Thus all decisions of the Plenary Assembly are made by a collegiate bench of 13. Its basic function is to resolve any conflicts in the case law amongst the judicial sections of the Council. The Plenary Assembly is also a court of appeal from certain decisions of the Council of Administrative Justice for the Sicilian Region. This latter Council has a tripartite jurisdiction: it is the court of appeal from the decisions of the Sicilian TAR; it has an exclusive jurisdiction, from which there is no appeal, in relation to petitions against definitive measures adopted by the Regional administration; and finally, it has a jurisdiction at first instance in relation to petitions against measures concerning Regional matters issued by State authorities having their seat in the Region. An appeal lies from these latter decisions of the Sicilian Council to the Council of State.

(iv) The administrative process. The administrative process is essentially a party process. The general principles which characterise the administrative process may be summarised as follows. First, party initiative according to which administrative proceedings, like civil proceedings, are commenced at the discretion of the interested party. Second, party impulse upon which, as a corollary to the first principle, the continuation of administrative proceedings depend. Thus the inertia of the parties for two consecutive years will result in the discontinuance of the proceedings. Similarly, a failure to resume the proceedings after their interruption for a proper cause will result in their

forfeiture if the matter is raised by a party to the proceedings. Third, an effective debate which requires that notice of the proceedings be served upon 'counter-interested' parties. Fourth, the free or intimate conviction of the court as a consequence of which the President of the court may order whatever instruction measures he deems necessary to better understand the issues. However, the instruction powers of the administrative courts are much more limited than those of the civil courts. Fifth, the concentration of the proceedings according to which the matter must, as far as possible, be dealt with at a single audience. Sixth, the orality of administrative proceedings. And finally, as in civil procedure, the decision of the court is restricted by the grounds deduced by the parties. Therefore, if the grounds raised by the applicant fail, the court cannot ex officio raise any other vitiating factor which will annul the administrative measure but must simply dismiss the application.

An application for the review of an administrative measure by the court must be served upon the public administration which issued the measure or the State Attorney, whichever is relevant (see ch 2, p 52, above), and at least one of the 'counter-interested' parties, if there are more than one such parties, within 60 days of the communication of the measure to the applicant. The procedural phases consist of the instruction and decision-making phases. In the instruction phase the President orders whatever measures are necessary to procure the necessary certainty of the factual elements at the basis of the application. The instruction is not a necessary phase and is only utilised where the documentation produced by the parties is incomplete or where there is a conflict between the measure under attack and the documentation produced in the proceedings. The usual instruction measures are a request for documents directed to either the public administration or the private parties, a request for clarification which may be directed to the public administration only, and an order to carry out new verifications.

(v) The review of the decisions of the Tribunali Amministrativi Regionali. The decisions of the TARs are subject to revocation and appeal (A.28 *l* TAR). In relation to the former, Artt. 395 and 396 cpc (see p 211, above) concerning revocation have been made applicable to the decisions of the administrative courts. An application for revocation must be made within 30 days of the notification of the judgment to the applicant if the grounds of the revocation are res judicata or judicial fraud, or 30 days from the discovery of the ground in the case of any other cause for revocation.

An appeal to the Council of State must be brought within 60 days of the notification of the judgment to the applicant. The availability of an appeal means that the judicial review of administrative measures is a double jurisdiction. An appeal to the Council of State has the following characteristics. First, it is a process of second instance. Second, it results in the annulment of the decision of first instance which is replaced with a new decision on the merits, without any reference back to the court of first instance. The matter is only referred back to the TAR where an appeal is allowed on the basis of procedural defects, formal defects in the judgment made at first instance, or where the TAR erroneously declared itself incompetent. Third, the whole question is transferred to the Council of State on an appeal. In other words, the scope of the appeal is parallel to the proceedings at first instance, both as to jurisdiction (which may, therefore, be limited to the legitimacy of an administrative measure, extend to its merits also, or even encompass subjective rights if the jurisdiction at first instance was an exclusive one) and decision-making powers. Finally, the appeal does not suspend the enforceability of the decision at first instance. However, the Council of State may, at the motion of a party, suspend the enforceability of the decision made at first instance where its immediate enforcement could give rise to serious and irreperable damage.

There are two possible remedies against an appeal judgment of the Council of State: first, revocation (see p 261, above), and second, review by Cassation but only on the grounds of jurisdiction (A.362 cpc). The jurisdictional grounds may concern an absolute defect in jurisdiction because the matter belonged to another power of State; a defect in jurisdiction vis-à-vis the ordinary courts; or a defect in jurisdiction vis-à-vis the other special administrative courts, e g the Court of Accounts.

The relationship between the civil, criminal, administrative and constitutional jurisdictions

The relationship between the various jurisdictions concern three major issues: the predominance of the criminal jurisdiction; the problem of prejudicial issues; and the joinder of a civil action to criminal proceedings.

A. THE RELATIONSHIP BETWEEN THE CRIMINAL AND CIVIL JURISDICTIONS

The Italian legal system places a major importance upon criminal proceedings. This is manifest through, first, the absolute precedence of criminal proceedings vis-à-vis civil proceedings; second, the binding effect of criminal judgments on civil proceedings; and third, the utilisation in civil or administrative trials of the evidence collected in criminal trials. The basis for this natural predominance of the criminal process is that the inquisitorial nature of criminal proceedings gives it an advantage vis-à-vis the civil party process for arriving at the truth. This approach is embodied in A.3 cpp which provides that where, in the course of civil or administrative proceedings, there appears the elements of a crime which may be prosecuted ex officio or of a crime which may only be prosecuted upon complaint, request or instance but there has been such complaint, request or instance, then the civil or administrative judge must immediately refer the matter to the *pubblico ministero*. If, pursuant to the reference, a criminal process is initiated and its resolution would influence the outcome of the civil or administrative proceedings, the latter must be suspended, unless provided otherwise by law, pending the decision of the criminal proceedings.

The judgment of a criminal court may be binding on civil or administrative proceedings. This arises in three cases. First, A.25 cpp precludes the initiation, continuation, or recommencement of civil proceedings which seek restitution or damages where there is a criminal judgment which acquitted the defendant on any of the following grounds: that the fact did not occur; that the fact was performed in the fulfilment of a duty or in the exercise of a lawful power; that the accused did not commit the fact; or that there is insufficient evidence to prove that the fact occurred or that it was committed by the accused. However, the Constitutional Court held, in its judgment of 26 June 1975 n.165, that A.25 cpp is unconstitutional to the extent that it purports to preclude the initiation of civil proceedings by a person who was not party to the criminal action either because he was ineligible to participate as a civil party or because, in any event, he was not in a position to take part in the criminal proceedings. Second, A.27 cpp provides that a criminal judgment which convicts the accused is binding on civil or administrative proceedings brought for restitution or damages but only 'as to the existence of the criminal act, its illegality and the responsibility of the convicted person'. The Constitutional Court held, in judgment no. 99 of 27 June 1973, that A.27 is un- constitutional to the extent that it applies to civil proceedings against the civilly responsible party who did not or was not in a position to participate in the criminal proceedings. Finally, A.28 cpp provides that a criminal judgment which either acquits or convicts is binding in civil proceedings, other than those seeking restitution or damages, that concern any right whose existence depends upon the ascertainment of facts which formed the object of the criminal proceedings provided always that the civil law does not impose some limitation upon the proof of the disputed right. The Constitutional Court, in judgment no. 55 of 22 March 1971, declared A.28 unconstitutional to the extent that it binds persons who were not in a position to become parties to the criminal proceedings. A fourth situation, which is not dealt with by the Code, is the question of the effect of evidence collected in criminal proceedings upon civil or administrative proceedings. It is now universally accepted, because it is consistent with the above scheme, that evidence collected in criminal proceedings has the same effect as if it were collected in the relevant civil or administrative proceedings.

B. PREJUDICIAL QUESTIONS

This arises where the decision of one case is affected by the decision of another. This may arise in four different situations. First, where the resolution of one criminal process depends upon the resolution of another criminal process (A.18 cpp). This is dealt with by either the joinder of proceedings (where the joinder is both permitted by A.413 cpp and convenient) or by adjournment of the dependent proceedings pending the decision of the principal cause (where the joinder is either not possible or inconvenient). Second, where a question of personal status arises during criminal proceedings. In such a case, the criminal proceedings *must* be suspended pending the resolution of the question of personal status by the civil courts. To overcome any inertia by the civil parties, the *pubblico ministero* may initiate or continue the relevant civil proceedings to have the status issue resolved. A judgment of the civil courts on personal status is unconditionally binding on the criminal trial (A.21(1) cpp). Third, where a prejudicial issue, other than status, that falls within the jurisdiction of the civil courts arises during criminal proceedings. In such cases the criminal court has discretion: it may either decide the prejudicial issue itself; or remit the issue to the civil courts either ex officio or upon a motion of the parties. However, the reference of an issue to the civil courts is subject to three conditions: the existence of the crime must be dependent upon the civil issue; the resolution of the civil issue must *not be easy*; and the civil law must not impose any probative limitations upon the resolution of the civil issue as such evidence would be in any event admissible in the criminal trial which is based upon the system of free proof. Where an issue is referred to the civil courts, if it remains unresolved at the expiration of the term, including any extension, fixed by the criminal court, then the latter may decide the prejudicial issue itself. A civil judgment which has become res judicata between the same parties to the criminal proceedings is always binding upon the criminal court. Finally, where the constitutional legitimacy of a substantive or procedural criminal or civil norm is raised by either the court ex officio or by a party to the proceedings. In such cases, provided that the constitutional issue is not manifestly unfounded, the proceedings are suspended and the issue referred to the Constitutional Court (see ch 5, above).

C. CIVIL ACTIONS TAKEN WITHIN CRIMINAL PROCEEDINGS

A criminal act may constitute a civil wrong which gives rise to a civil liability in the accused for restitution and/or damages (A.185 cp). It has already been noted how in Italian law the primacy of criminal proceedings means first, that a civil action cannot be commenced or, if already commenced, must be suspended pending the conclusion of any criminal proceedings upon which the former is dependent; and second, that a criminal judgment has a binding value in civil proceedings. In accordance with the primacy of criminal proceedings, the law of procedure provides that within certain limits the civil liability of a defendant may be determined together with the criminal issues (A.22 cpp). This takes place through the intervention of the civil party (*parte civile*) in the criminal proceedings and gives rise to a civil action, which seeks restitution and damages from the author of the crime, within the framework of the criminal proceedings. This action by the civil party or person injured by the crime against the accused and/or a responsible third party for restitution or damages is a true and proper civil action commenced within or transferred to the criminal proceedings; only if the proceedings cannot be joined, must they proceed separately. The result is that the civil party seeks damages whilst the *pubblico ministero* seeks the imposition of a criminal sanction against the accused. The incorporation of civil proceedings within the criminal process has several advantages, e g it avoids duplicate proceedings and conflicting decisions, but its basic justification is that the inquisitorial nature of criminal proceedings makes the latter more apt than the party process operative in civil procedure for arriving at the truth and thereby gives the criminal proceedings a natural predominance over civil proceedings. However, the presence of a civil party has negative repercussions on the right of defence as the civil party assists and encourages the prosecution in obtaining a conviction. The intervention of a civil party may be opposed by the accused, the civilly responsible party (see below) or the *pubblico ministero*, on either substantive or procedural grounds.

Normally the intervening civil party seeks damages from the accused only. However, apart from the accused, the so-called civilly responsible party (*il responsabile civile*) who, under the civil law, is answerable for the actions of the accused, is also liable to the civil party (A.185(2) cp). This liability may only arise in those cases, and within the limits, strictly defined by law (A.185(2) cp), e g the responsibility of parents and tutors (A.2048 cc), the vicarious responsibility of owners and employers for their domestic staff and employees (A.2049 cc), and the responsibility of owners of motor vehicles (A.2054 cc). The civilly responsible party is summoned by the court at the instance of the civil party. Notice of his summons is communicated to the *pubblico ministero* and the accused both of whom may oppose his joinder. Moreover, the civilly responsible party may voluntarily intervene provided that he has an interest in the proceedings and there is a civil party.

Another possible party to criminal proceedings is the party civilly liable for the fine (*il civilmente obbligato per l'ammenda*) who, like the civilly responsible party, bears a civil responsibility only. The party civilly liable for the fine is responsible for the payment of the fine imposed upon the defendant where the latter is insolvent. This subsidiary liability of the party civilly liable for the fine arises only in the case of those legal relationships between the party civilly liable for the fine and the accused defined by Artt. 196 and 197 cp. However, the responsibility of the party civilly liable for the fine depends first, on the imposition of a fine upon the directly responsible person for the commission of a contravention (see ch 7, p 273, below), and second, the failure of the directly responsible party to pay the fine for reasons of insolvency only. The party civilly liable for the fine becomes party to the proceedings either pursuant to a summons issued at the instance of the *pubblico ministero* or voluntarily.

Chapter 7

Criminal law

The sources of criminal law

The criminal law has fewer sources than other categories of law because of a fundamental principle which requires that the criminal law is to be created exclusively by legislation (A.25 C and Artt. 1 and 199 cp) which, as the Constitutional Court has often emphasised, is a law-making instrument within the exclusive power of the State. However, the Constitutional Court has often said that although this principle applies strictly in relation to the penalty of a crime, it has a qualified application in relation to the definition of the facts which constitute a crime notwithstanding that it has never specified the extent of the qualification. Cassation, taking a similar approach, has held that laws substantially legislative in character, such as regulations, may specify and integrate those elements of a crime already outlined by legislation. As far as the doctrine is concerned, some writers adhere to the view that there exists a strict and absolute 'legislative monopoly' in the criminal law, whilst others argue that the term 'legislation' is not used in a strict sense, but only to indicate all sources which are legislative in nature, such as ordinances. In the end result, however, the consequences of the principle of 'legislative monopoly' are: first, that a fact cannot constitute a crime, nor be made subject to a penalty or police measure, unless it is classified as such by 'legislation' in existence at the date of the commission of the fact; second, that all penalties and police measures must be expressly defined by legislation; and third, that a penalty cannot be imposed by analogy to a different fact situation. The practical consequences of the principle are first, that a judge cannot apply an extensive interpretation to a criminal norm nor impose a sanction by analogy, and second, that the only source of the criminal law is the 'positive legislative order' or, in other words, any act having the force and effect of legislation. The political consequence of the principle is that it protects citizens from punishment, other than in accordance with a legislative disposition, and thereby prevents the arbitrary application of criminal sanctions by the State apparatus.

The term 'legislation' therefore limits the sources of the criminal law to constitutional legislation, ordinary legislation, delegated legislation, legislative decrees, and governmental decrees in times of war. The following, on the other hand, cannot generally contain criminal norms: regional and provincial legislation, urgent ordinances, regulations, collective labour contracts, and circulars. It follows that the role of custom as a source of the criminal law is very limited: it certainly cannot create nor render inapplicable the criminal law. Where there is a legislative vacuum, however, the doctrine is in disagreement as to the role of custom: part of the doctrine maintains that in such a case it can only operate when favourable to the accused. It seems, nevertheless, that the only positive role for custom in the criminal law is an integrative one where expressly sanctioned by legislation. As a consequence, the judiciary has a power-duty to supervise the validity of the criminal law in terms of its source. Therefore the court must, in cases of legislative incompetence, defects in the legislative process, or conflict with the Constitution, raise ex officio the constitutional validity of the criminal provision and refer it to the Constitutional Court. This 'closed system' characteristic of Italian criminal law finds a corollary in the limited application of analogy in the interpretation of the criminal law (A.14 dp). The limitation in A.14 dp certainly applies with respect to incriminating norms and norms which integrate them, both of which restrict the rights of the individual, although the doctrine is not in agreement in relation to provisions which do not pejorate the situation of the accused.

The fundamental source of the criminal law is the Criminal Code of 1930, known as the Codice Rocco, which became effective on 1 July 1931. It contains 734 articles divided into three books: Book 1 contains the general principles of the criminal law (Artt. 1–240) whilst Books 2 and 3, in accordance with the principle of 'legislative monopoly' applicable to the criminal law, define the individual types of crime. Book 2 deals with delicts (Artt. 241–649) which are classified into 13 Titles as follows:

1 Delicts against the State, e g espionage and offences against the President.
2 Delicts against the public administration, e g corruption and disclosure of official secrets.
3 Delicts against the administration of justice, e g perjury and the failure to refer a *notitia criminis* to the judicial authorities in the case of crimes whose prosecution is obligatory.
4 Delicts against religious sentiments and piety for the dead, e g desecration of church property and cemeteries and the illegal use of a corpse.
5 Delicts against public order, e g an instigation to commit crime or disobey the law and a conspiracy to commit crime.

6 Delicts against public safety, e g arson and the adulteration of food.
7 Delicts against public faith, e g forgery of currency or documents.
8 Delicts against the public economy, industry, and commerce, e g causing the destruction of raw materials.
9 Delicts against public morality and good custom, e g carnal violence and obscenity.
10 Delicts against the integrity and health of issue, e g abortion.
11 Delicts against the family, e g bigamy and incest.
12 Delicts against the person, e g homicide and defamation.
13 Delicts against property, e g robbery, larceny and extortion.

The third book deals with contraventions (Artt. 650–734) and is divided into two Titles: police contraventions, and contraventions concerning social and administrative activities, e g truancy, the damage of the archaeological, historical, or artistic wealth of the nation, and the destruction and spoiling of the natural environment. However, the Code has undergone notable modification over the years and a significant part of it has fallen into disuse. Thus the importance of the so-called complementary criminal law which is contained in an infinite number of special laws which create new criminal norms, especially in the case of contraventions.

The non-retroactivity of the criminal law

Another fundamental principle of the criminal law is its non-retroactivity (A.25 C, A.11 dp, A.1 cp). This is complemented by A.2 cp which provides that amongst chronologically successive criminal laws, the most favourable to the accused is applicable. In particular, A.2 cp contains three distinct principles: first, incriminating legislation cannot have retrospective effect (see also A.25(2) C); second, legislation which repeals an incriminating norm applies retrospectively in favour of an accused person, irrespective of whether the accused has already been convicted; and third, where the law is only modified after the commission of a crime, the most favourable law is applied unless the accused has already been irrevocably convicted. The principle of the retroactivity of laws favourable to the accused, however, is not applicable in cases of temporary, exceptional (i e, concerning abnormal situations such as wars, epidemics or earthquakes) or financial legislation: in these cases the applicable law is that in force at the date of the commission of the crime.

The nature and elements of crime: the general theory of criminal law

A. DEFINITION OF CRIME

According to the prevalent doctrine, the difference between criminal and civil wrongs is a purely formal one depending upon the nature of the sanction: those illicit acts punishable with a criminal sanction are crimes, whilst those which result in an obligation to make compensation are civil wrongs. In addition there are administrative wrongs which are characterised by a disciplinary sanction which is either of a pecuniary or police nature. The administrative, in contrast to the criminal, pecuniary sanction cannot become a detentive penalty in the case of the insolvency of the transgressor. In general, therefore, a crime is defined as every fact to which the legal system attaches a penalty as its consequence.

In order to fit the study of criminal law and its definition into the general scheme provided by the general theory of law (see ch 1, pp 18 ff), it may be conveniently observed at this point that a crime comes within the general category of 'legal facts' (see p 27, above), that is, of events which produce legal consequences which, in the case of the criminal law, are generally penalties but may also be, for instance, precautionary measures, restitution and damages. One class of legal facts, it will be recalled, are 'legal acts' which are determined by voluntary human conduct. Legal acts may be either licit or illicit depending upon whether they conform with the legal system; and criminal acts, like civil wrongs, form a category of illicit legal acts.

The doctrine has, as in other branches of the law, elaborated a general theory of the criminal law with the same conceptual and systematising style as that of the more general theory of law studied in chapter 1. The general theory of criminal law consists of both a synthetical and analytical study of the criminal law.

B. THE SYNTHETICAL STUDY OF CRIMINAL LAW: THE COMMON FEATURES OF CRIMES

Every crime has an active subject (*soggetto attivo*) or person who commits the illicit act. Depending upon whether a crime may be committed by any subject or only a subject with particular characteristics (e g a public official), crimes are divided between common and special crimes.

A criminal norm, by prohibiting and punishing a given behaviour, aims at protecting a legal asset (*bene giuridico*) which would be violated by that behaviour. The object of a crime, therefore, is the legal asset, that is, the material or immaterial value which is protected by the criminal norm, e g the criminal norm which punishes homicide protects the legal asset of 'life'. Closely connected with the concept of the legal asset is the concept of criminal damage (*danno penale*) which is the harm caused to the legal asset. Harm constitutes the legal event (*evento giuridico*) which occurs on every occasion that a crime is committed. The harm (or legal event) caused by a crime may be either an injury or a peril depending upon whether the legal asset has actually been injured (e g a homicide in which the asset 'life' is injured) or merely threatened (e g attempted homicide). The notion of 'legal asset' is, in fact, central to the general part of the Code in which many provisions refer to the 'protected asset'. Some of the concepts which depend upon this notion are: the legal event; the passive subject of the crime; the consent of the person entitled to a right; the illegality of the fact; and the consummation of the crime.

The passive subject of the crime is the owner of the asset or interest protected by the criminal norm; this is the subject who is injured through the commission of the crime. The Code speaks of the passive subject as the 'person harmed by the crime' (*persona offesa dal reato*), e g the person harmed by the crime of robbery is the possessor of the thing stolen. However, the passive subject of the crime must be distinguished from the passive subject of the conduct (*soggetto passivo della condotta*), that is, the person upon which the criminal conduct is immediately inflicted. Sometimes the two concepts coincide, as in homicide, where the passive subject of both the crime and the conduct is the deceased victim. In other cases the two subjects are different, e g in the case of self-mutilation to avoid military service, the passive subject of the conduct is the same person as the active subject who mutilated himself whilst the passive subject of the crime is the State which is the owner of the interest that all citizens perform military service. Furthermore, the passive subject of the crime must be distinguished from the damaged subject (*il danneggiato*), that is, the person who suffered a civil injury and therefore entitled to compensation, even if he is not the owner of the legally protected asset. The concept of the owner of the legally protected asset (the passive subject of the crime) is important because this person is entitled, where permitted by law, to consent to the commission of the crime and, where necessary to the initiation of the criminal process, to lay the complaint. The damaged subject, on the other hand, may only bring a civil action for damages.

C. THE ANALYTICAL STUDY OF CRIMINAL LAW: THE ELEMENTS OF CRIMES

The general theory of criminal law makes a distinction between the essential (or constituent) and accessory elements of a crime. Although a crime cannot exist in the absence of the former, the latter do not affect the existence of the crime but only its seriousness and penalty. The essential elements are in turn divided into general elements, which are common to all crimes and are regulated by the general part of the Criminal Code, and special elements which are additional elements which together with the general elements go to define and differentiate the individual types of crime.

This chapter is mainly concerned with the general elements of a crime and not with specific crimes. The first Book of the Criminal Code, however, does not define, in a general manner, the essential elements of a crime; rather, the doctrine has done so in its elaboration of the general theory of crime.

The traditional bipartite theory still adhered to by some writers (e g Antolisei) individuates two fundamental elements of a crime: the objective element (or fact) which consists of an act or omission and a causal relationship between the conduct and the event; and the subjective element or blameworthiness (*colpevolezza*) which is the psychological element required for the commission of a given crime and may consist of intent (*dolo*), fault (*colpa*) or extra-intent (*preter-intenzione*).

The more recent and dominant doctrine has adopted a tripartite theory which individuates three essential elements of a crime: fact (*fatto*), illegality (*antigiuridicità*), and blameworthiness (*colpevolezza*). Fact is a composite category comprising the objective element of a crime, that is, conduct, event and causal relationship, which are the typical objective elements, or typical facts, defined by a given criminal norm. Illegality, on a formal plane, is the discordance between the fact and a normative command which prohibits it or, on a substantive plane, the harm inherent in a crime, that is, the injury to the legal asset protected by the criminal norm which has been violated. Finally, blameworthiness, according to the 'psychological' conception, is the mental relationship between the author and the fact and coincides with the subjective element of the bipartite theory or, according to a 'normative' conception, is the disobedience of the imperative force of the norm, that is, an intent which is contrary to the obligation contained in the norm.

The principle difference between the bipartite and tripartite theories is the differing importance attributed to the element of illegality. The followers of the bipartite theory maintain that illegality is not a constituent element of a crime but the qualification of the fact considered as a whole; it is inherent in the nature of all crimes which consist of conduct contrary to law. The followers of the tripartite theory, on the other hand, do not consider illegality as a general characteristic of crime but as one of its elements which could be absent and which consists of an injury to the legal asset protected by the criminal norm. Thus for the followers of the bipartite theory, a crime is a fact comprising both objective and subjective elements which are contrary to law; for the followers of the tripartite theory, instead, a crime is a typical, illegal, and blameworthy fact and if any of these three elements are missing there cannot be a crime.

Classification of crimes

The most important general classification of crimes is that which is expressly adopted by the Code, namely, the division between delicts (*delitti*) and contraventions (*contravenzioni*). Because the substantive differences between the two types of crime are doctrinally controversial, the most convenient distinguishing criterion is the formal one contained in the Code itself, namely, the type of penalty (A.39 cp). Article 17 cp specifies that the principal types of penalty applicable to delicts are life imprisonment (*ergastolo*), imprisonment (*reclusione*) and fine (*multa*) and in the case of contraventions, arrest (*arresto*) and making amends (*ammenda*). This distinction has certain important consequences defined by the Code, for instance, first, unless provided otherwise, contraventions are punishable irrespective of whether the subjective element of their author is intent or fault (Artt. 42 and 43 cp); second, an attempt may only be committed in the case of a delict (A.56 cp); third, certain aggravating circumstances are applicable to delicts only (e g Artt. 61, n.3, 7, and 8 cp); fourth, all crimes which are committed abroad but punishable within the national territory, subject to the exception contained in A.7 n.5 cp, are delicts; and finally, 'political crimes' are always delicts (A.8 cp).

The objective element of a crime

A. CONDUCT

This element of a crime signifies the human behaviour which constitutes a crime: A.42(1) cp provides that 'no one can be punished for an act or omission defined by law as a crime unless the act or omission is conscious and voluntary'. Whilst an act is a simple voluntary muscular movement consciously directed to the commission of a crime, an omission is a purely legislative concept comprising a failure to act in those cases in which a legislative command obliges an action. Although a majority of the doctrine examines the conscious and voluntary nature of an act or omission under the head of the subjective elements of a crime, it must be remembered that this element is so intricately connected with the objective element of a crime that, in the absence of a conscious and voluntary act, there is no 'conduct'.

The problem of what constitutes a conscious and voluntary act has been resolved by Antolisei whose approach has been accepted and followed by both the case law and the dominant doctrine. He emphasised how acts which can be avoided by an exertion of the will are nonetheless attributable to the will of their agent. The only acts falling outside the sphere of a voluntary act are those which cannot in any way be prevented by the subject. It follows that not only acts which are the result of conscious impulses but also those which the subject, through the exertion of the will, could but does not avoid are attributable to the wilful conduct of the subject. The attribution of the latter to the volition of the subject derives from the fact that the legal order may not only expect a certain positive behaviour from subjects, but may also command them to do everything possible so that a defined event does not arise.

B. EVENT

An event is defined, according to a naturalistic approach, as the effect (whether physical or psychological) of a human action. It is the natural effect of the external conduct of man; an effect which is consiered relevant by the law insofar as the law connects certain legal consequences to it. However, this conception of an event gives rise to certain implications: first, an event is not an indispensible element of crime, e g the crime of escape in which a mere action, without an event, is sufficient; second, that certain crimes are characterised by a plurality of events as in the case of the so-called 'composite' crimes, e g robbery which is composed of larceny and violence; and finally, that certain crimes are aggravated by an event, e g abortion which is aggravated by death. The supporters of the normative conception of an event, on the other hand, observe that the criminal law is indifferent to the naturalistic concept because the criminal law is only concerned with particular or defined 'events', that is, the harm (an injury or peril) of an interest protected by the law, that which Antolisei calls 'criminal damage'.

The concept of 'event' has enabled the construction of several significant classifications of crimes. First, crimes of pure conduct and crimes of event. The former are the so-called formal crimes which, according to the naturalistic conception, consist of a certain conduct only, without any event, although, according to the normative conception, they are said to have a legal or defined event. The latter, or the so-called material crimes, are those crimes which, according to the naturalistic conception, comprise an act or omission and the happening of an event or, according to the normative conception, comprise, in addition to a legal or defined event (which can never be absent), a material or natural event. Second, proper and improper omissive crimes. The former are those in which the simple negative conduct of their author is necessary and sufficient without the need for any ulterior effect from such conduct. The latter are those in which the omission must cause a given event for the existence of the crime. Third, crimes of injury and crimes of peril. This distinction depends upon whether the event is an actual 'injury' or merely a 'threat' to the asset protected by the law. Crimes of peril, or threats, must be kept distinct from attempts which require the performance of that minimum necessary for an actual 'injury' to the legally protected asset and not its mere exposure to danger. As the criminal law is not only concerned with injury but also threats, the latter is variously said to be a 'possibility of injury' or, more commonly, the 'probability of a feared event'. Finally, instantaneous and permanent crimes. In the former, the relevant event is instantaneous, e g death, whilst in the latter the relevant event endures for a certain time, as in a kidnap.

C. CAUSATION

The perfection of a crime in its objective element requires, apart from the conduct (positive or negative) of the agent and an event, a third factor, namely, a causal nexus between the conduct and its consequences. This requirement arises out of A.40 cp which provides that no one can be considered the author of a crime unless the injury or threat (the event) is a consequence of his conduct. The causal nexus need not consist of a circumstance which autonomously gives rise to the event but may also consist of a contributory factor or even a circumstance which has a mere tendency towards the realisation of the event.

According to Antolisei, the causal relationship consists of both a positive element, namely, the creation of a condition of the event or, in other words, an antecedent without which the event would not have happened, and a negative element, namely, the event must *not* result from the concurrence of exceptional intervening circumstances. The positive element is contained in A.41(1) and (3) cp which provide that every condition without which the event would not have happened, is a cause of the event. The extent of the negative element, on the other hand, depends upon the interpretation of A.41(2) cp which, according to some writers, only excludes the causal nexus in the case of a supervening circumstance that would result in the event independently of the original cause. Other writers point out that this situation would, in any event, be excluded by A.40 cp so that A.41(2) must operate, in accordance with the view of Antolisei, to exclude causation in the case of a supervening cause which, although not connected to the original cause, is related to it in the sense that the event would not have happened had it not been for the original cause, e g death caused by the collision of an ambulance carrying a person injured by an aggressor.

The same two elements are relevant in relation to causation in the case of omissive crimes (A.40(1) cp). However, as the doctrine points out, causation in the case of omissive crimes is always of a normative character, that is, it is always defined by the relevant criminal norm because an omissive crime cannot have a causal relationship in a natural sense as an omission can never cause anything in a physical sense. Article 40(2) cp provides that the failure to impede an event where there is a legal obligation to do so is equivalent to causing the event. The characteristics of such an obligation are: first, the obligation must be imposed by law, which need not be the criminal law and may even be a contractual obligation; second, the obligation may arise out of one's own antecedent conduct, e g the failure to put out a fire which was lit in a dangerous place; and finally, punishability in such cases depends upon the psychological element which motivates the person guilty of the omission.

Illegality (*antigiuridicità*) as an element of crime

As mentioned earlier, the dominant part of the modern doctrine, which adheres to the tripartite rather than the bipartite theory of the elements of a crime, considers that crime also comprises a third element, namely, illegality. Illegality in this sense designates the contrast between the actual fact and the legislative norm. It consists of an evaluation by the court in ascertaining the injurious character of human conduct. Criminal illegality, in other words, concerns a comparison between the fact to be adjudicated and the relevant criminal norm and arises where there is a conflict between these two elements. The supporters of the bipartite theory do not consider illegality as an element of a crime but rather as the essence of crime itself. The opposite current of thought argues that it is punishability which is the essence of crime and not illegality which, instead, is one of its elements. A fact is 'criminally illegal' where (a) it conforms to a typical fact situation contained in a criminal norm (the so-called positive aspect of illegality), and (b) there is the absence of a 'justifying cause', that is, although the fact corresponds in abstract to a criminal norm it is nonetheless not subject to a criminal sanction (the so-called negative aspect of illegality). This latter aspect shall now be examined.

The objective grounds excluding criminal liability

The mere correspondence between a fact and an abstract criminal norm is often insufficient to classify the fact as illegal and, therefore, criminal. In some instances the law itself provides objective grounds for the exclusion of criminality by authorising or even obliging the fact which would otherwise constitute a crime. However, it is unsettled in both the doctrine and the case law as to whether the court must convict or acquit where there is doubt as to the existence of a justifying ground. According to Cassation, the accused bears the onus of fully proving the existence of a justifying ground, in the absence of which the court must convict. However, the prevalent approach taken by the courts of first instance, and sometimes accepted by Cassation, is that the accused does not bear the onus of conclusively proving the justifying ground because it is the court, according to the principle that it must ascertain the truth, that must evaluate the results of the evidence to ascertain the existence of the exemption. Thus, where it is ascertained that the accused committed the alleged fact but the court remains in doubt as to a ground excluding punishability, it must concede the qualified acquittal of 'insufficiency of evidence'.

The various grounds precluding criminality are:

A. CONSENT (A.50 cp)

The Code provides, in A.50, that a person who injures or threatens a right cannot be punished if the person entitled to dispose of the right has given his consent. The following requisites are inherent in this provision: the consent must be forthcoming from either the owner or the person who can validly dispose of the protected asset or right; the protected asset must be alienable and not, therefore, either belong to the collectivity or constitute an inalienable asset for reasons of public policy; the person whose consent is required must have the capacity to act which may not only depend upon age, which is not always fixed at 18, but also other requisites which may be stipulated by the particular criminal norm; the person giving his consent must also have the capacity freely to determine and understand his act; the consent must be voluntary; the consent must be given for a lawful purpose and not for one which is contrary to good custom or obscene; the consent must exist at the date of the commission of the subject act; and the consent need not be in any particular form. Consent may not only be express or implied, but also putative or presumed: it is putative where the actor regards the consent as existent in which case, although the fact is unlawful, the actor is not regarded as having acted fraudulently; and it is presumed where the actor knows that consent has not been given but believes that it would have been forthcoming had the owner of the asset known of the circumstances.

B. THE EXERCISE OF A RIGHT RECOGNISED BY LAW (A.51 cp)

The exercise of a right recognised by the legal system cannot constitute an unlawful fact. The elements of this ground are the existence of a recognised right, irrespective of its source, that is, any legitimate power whether deriving from law, custom, contract, administrative act, or judicial decision; and the ownership of the right by the actor. The exercise of the right is not without limit but must be in conformity with the limits inherent in its source. Examples of such rights are journalistic activites, family discipline, and the defence of property.

C. PERFORMANCE OF A LEGAL DUTY (A.51 cp)

A legal duty may arise from a written or customary law, or the superior orders of a public authority. Although the responsibility for an illegitimate superior order always rests with the public official issuing it (A.51(2) cp), the person executing the order is also responsible unless either he believed, as a result of an error of fact, that he was obeying a legitimate order, or the law fails to provide any means for the review of the legitimacy of the superior order in question. It follows that a review on the merits is irrelevant, so that a person carrying out the order need only ascertain its formal validity.

D. THE LEGITIMATE USE OF WEAPONS (A.53 cp)

The doctrine is divided as to whether this is an autonomous ground or forms part of the broader exemption contained in A.51 cp relating to the performance of a legal duty pursuant to a legislative norm. Because the Code deals with it separately and defines particular prerequisites for its application, the preferred view is that it forms a distinct ground. The exemption is only available to public officials and persons who are lawfully requested to assist a public official. The application of the exemption is limited to the exercise of official duties pursuant to a necessity to repress violence, overcome resistance or prevent the commission of those crimes defined by A.53 cp. Article 53(3) cp defines the remaining cases in which the use of weapons or other means of physical coercion is permissible. These include the enforcement of police measures where the relevant party fails to submit voluntarily, the policing of national boundaries to prevent illegal passage and smuggling, and the policing of the prison system.

E. LEGITIMATE DEFENCE (A.52 cp)

An act of defence is legitimate if it is necessary to repel the *actual* threat to a right where the resulting injury to the right would be contrary to law. Moreover, the act of defence must be proportional to the threatened injury.

F. NECESSITY (A.54 cp)

This comprises acts necessary to save oneself or another from serious personal injury in the face of an actual danger which is neither voluntarily brought about by the actor nor otherwise avoidable provided that such acts of necessity are proportional to the danger, e g a mountain climber who, to save himself, cuts the rope supporting another climber or a shipwrecked person who assaults another to seize a one-man lifeboat. The necessity must, therefore, concern an actual or probable danger of serious personal injury to the actor who must not have caused the dangerous situation nor occupy a position which carries the duty to expose himself to such danger. Moreover, the act must be absolutely necessary to save oneself from the apprehended injury and must be proportional to the danger. Article 54(3) provides that a state of necessity also exists in cases where a subject is required, under threat from another subject, to perform an otherwise illegal act, e g a threat to kill the actor unless the latter agrees to steal. However, to raise the defence the threat must create a true and proper state of necessity in the actor and satisfy all of the normal requisites examined above. In any event, the person issuing the threat will be responsible for the act of the threatened person.

G. NON-CODIFIED GROUNDS EXCLUDING CRIMINALITY

The question of the extension by analogy of the legislative grounds excluding criminal liability is controversial: part of the doctrine denies such a possibility because the operation of the criminal law is limited to defined situations, whilst another part of the doctrine supports the analogical method in this situation because the principle requiring a strict interpretation and application of the criminal law is only applicable to provisions which are unfavourable to the accused and which are themselves exceptions to a general rule. The most important non-codified grounds of justification are: the supply of commercial information notwithstanding that such information injures reputation; surgical treatment which is always lawful where there is an express or presumed consent of the patient coupled with a necessity for surgical intervention, and sporting injuries which are caused notwithstanding a compliance with the rules of the game. A general principle applicable in the area of non-codified exemptions is that which provides that the exercise of an activity authorised by the State in the public interest cannot give rise to criminal liability provided that the rules regulating the activity are observed. This principle is based upon the balance of interests notion devised by the German doctrine.

H. EXCESS AND ERROR IN A GROUND EXCLUDING CRIMINAL LIABILITY

It may be that the circumstances, which prima facie constitute a justifying cause, are affected by the excessive or erroneous reaction of the actor. An excessive reaction arises where the limits inherent in a defined justifying cause are surpassed, e g the victim of an assault uses a pistol to defend himself whereas a baton would have been sufficient (See A.55 cp, p 282, below). An erroneous reaction arises where the actor erroneously regards as existent the necessary conditions for a justifying cause, e g the victim of a slight injury erroneously believed that he was faced with a threat of serious personal injury (see A.59(3) cp, p 282, below).

The subjective element of a crime: blameworthiness (*colpevolezza*)

A. GENERAL

Another essential element of a crime is volition (*volontà*). The doctrine defines this requisite, or the subjective element of a crime, as blameworthiness (*colpevolezza*) or blameworthy volition (*volontà colpevole*). Blameworthiness may be of two fundamental types: fraud (*dolo*) or fault (*colpa*) depending upon the volition of the actor. Blameworthiness may be defined as an improper form of volition which provokes the material facts required for the existence of the crime.

B. FRAUD (DOLO)

Dolo is a typical form of blameworthy volition. *Dolo*, according to A.43(1) cp, exists where the event, or consequences of the criminal conduct, is both foreseeable and intended. However, this is only a prima facie definition as the existence of *dolo* depends upon the cumulative effect of A.43(1) cp and certain other provisions of the Criminal Code, e g A.59(3) cp which provides that there is no *dolo* in the case of an error as to the existence of a justifying cause as, for instance, where the actor takes possession of an object in the belief that there is the consensus of the owner. It is clear from the definition of *dolo* in A.43(1) cp that it has a dual structure: first, an intellectual aspect which requires that the actor anticipate all of the factual elements which constitute the particular crime, and second, a volitive aspect which is directed to the realisation of the conduct and its consequential event. The intensity of the *dolo* determines the seriousness of a crime and depends upon a series of factors: the duration of the criminal idea, the major or minor knowledge of the anti-social nature of the action, and the formation of the volitive element in relation to which, for instance, direct *dolo* (where all of the results of the crime were intended) is more serious than indirect *dolo* (where the actor proceeded notwithstanding an acknowledged risk of the possibility of the consequences of his action).

Dolo must be distinguished from certain other concepts. First and foremost, it should be noted that premeditation does not constitute a particular category of *dolo* and is, indeed, considered as falling entirely outside the subject of *dolo*. Rather, it is considered to be a special aggravating circumstance in the case of certain delicts which involve personal injury, e g homicide and bodily harm. Premeditation consists of a decision (as distinct from a deliberation which is a stage preliminary to a decision) which has remained constant, and a lapse of a significant interval of time ending with the execution of the act. Premeditation is also different to the preparatory activity to commit a crime, as the former may exist without the latter. *Dolo* must also be distinguished from the motives of a crime. Even where the law makes the existence of a crime dependent upon a certain motive, so that the latter becomes a constituent element of the crime, it does not modify the notion of intention or *dolo*. Moreover, the particular *modus operandi* contemplated by the actor is irrelevant in ascertaining the existence of *dolo*.

C. FAULT (COLPA)

Article 43(1) cp provides that a delict is unintentional (*colposo*) when the event, even if foreseen, was not intended but arose out of negligence, imprudence, lack of professionalism or because of the inobservance of legislation, regulations, orders or disciplinary provisions. It follows that the elements of an unintentional delict are: first, unintentional conduct; second, the absence of a volition, characteristic of *dolo*, that would render the event intentional; and third, an event which was due to negligence (that is, the unwise or inattentive execution of the act or omission which constituted the crime), imprudence (that is, acting without opportune precautions or restraint), lack of professionalism (that is, a general or specific professional ineptitude or inadequacy known to but ignored by the actor), or the inobservance of legislation, regulations, orders or disciplinary provisions (all of which have the object of preventing, or prescribing precautions concerning, the very results caused by the actor) although it must be remembered that the observance of such specific norms does not, however, prevent fault arising from a failure to observe rules dictated by experience.

Fault (*colpa*) may be either so-called general or specific negligence depending upon its basis. General negligence arises from the failure to observe social usages and depends upon a combination of foreseeability (which is a subjective test) and avoidability. Consequently an actor cannot be held responsible for facts or events which are beyond his control. Specific negligence derives from the inobservance of legislation, regulations, orders, or disciplinary provisions. Specific negligence, therefore, depends upon the failure to observe a norm, e g the failure of a motorist to observe a stop sign.

A brief examination of the various types of fault indicates the breadth of the concept. One distinction drawn by the doctrine is that between conscious (or foreseeable) fault and unconscious fault. Conscious (or foreseeable) *colpa* arises where the event was foreseen but unintended by the actor and borders on indirect *dolo*. However, it is different to the latter because the actor was relying on the certainty that the foreseen event would not eventuate. In any event, foreseeability constitutes an aggravating circumstance in the case of unintentional delicts (*delitti colposi*) and therefore results in a higher penalty (A.61 n.3 cp). Unconscious fault, on the other hand, arises where the event was not even foreseen by the actor.

Another distinction drawn by the doctrine is that between proper and improper fault. The former category comprises the normal cases of fault, namely, cases in which the result or event was unintentional. The latter category, instead, comprises certain exceptional cases defined by law in which, although the event was intentional, the actor is only answerable for an unintentional crime. There are three such exceptional cases. First, a blameworthy excess in the case of an objective ground which would have excluded criminal liability (A.55 cp; see pp 279–80, above). Article 55 cp provides that where, in the case of an unintentional delict, the limits imposed by legislation, superior orders or a state of necessity are unintentionally exceeded in cases of the exercise of a right or duty (A.51 cp), legitimate defence (A.52 cp), the legitimate use of weapons (A.53 cp) or necessity (A.54 cp), the provisions concerning unintentional crimes are applicable, e g if X surprises and injures a thief with a gun where he could have driven the thief away with a baton, X is answerable for an unintentional injury even though he intended the event. It may be noted how blameworthy excess is not expressly extended by A.55 cp to cases of consent by the owner of a right (A.50 cp) although part of the doctrine maintains that A.55 cp may be extended to his case of justification as well. Second, an erroneous belief as to the existence of an objective ground excluding criminal liability. Article 59(3) cp provides that if the actor erroneously believes that there exists circumstances which preclude punishment, these are to be evaluated in his favour although it adds that, where the belief was induced by the actor's own fault, he is nonetheless criminally responsible where the fact constitutes an unintentional delict, e g where X, who is in a state of trepidation because he happens to be in an infamous area inhabited by criminals, erroneously believes that he is about to be assaulted and kills his presumed aggressor. Here, too, the actor is answerable for an unintentional crime although the result was intended. Article 59(3) cp is different to A.55 cp as A.59(3) concerns a situation in which there is a total absence of a justifying cause excluding criminal liability whereas A.55 concerns a situation where the actor exceeds the limits of an existing justifying cause beyond which the justification becomes inoperative. Finally, an error of fact due to the fault of the actor. An error as to one or more essential elements of a crime excludes intent or fraud (*dolo*). However, it is nonetheless an inexcusable error, so that the actor remains criminally responsible, where the facts constitute an unintentional delict (A.47 cp) e g X is nonetheless responsible for unintentional arson where he burns down a garage in an isolated location in the erroneous belief that he is its owner.

D. STRICT LIABILITY

Article 42(3) cp deals with strict liability which arises where a fact is attributable to a subject on the mere basis of a causal nexus. In such cases the subject is responsible even in the absence of the slightest fault. However, although the subjective element of the crime is irrelevant, the act or omission must nonetheless be conscious and voluntary. Thus, strict or objective responsibility may be said to have four characteristics: a conduct and an event connected by a causal nexus and corresponding to the elements of a crime; the irrelevance of fault or fraud; the attribution of the facts to the actor on the mere basis of a causal nexus; and a voluntary conduct on the part of the actor, in the terms of A.42(1) cp. The most important examples of strict liability in the Criminal Code are the super-intentional delict (*il delitto preterintenzionale*) and delicts aggravated by the event (*delitti aggravati dall' evento*). Article 43(2) cp provides that a delict is super-intentional, or beyond that intended, where an injury or peril more serious than that intended by the actor results from the act or omission. The only instance of a super-intentional crime in the Code is super-intentional homicide (A.584 cp) in which case, although the actor had only intended a personal injury, his act resulted in the death of the victim. This example of strict liability as a super-intentional homicide is attributable to the actor on the mere basis of a causal relationship independent of any enquiry of a subjective nature. Delicts aggravated by the event are those crimes which are punishable with a heavier penalty because some ulterior injury or peril, over and above that necessary for the existence of the crime, has arisen. The responsibility for this ulterior event is imposed upon the actor for the sole reason that it is causally related to the actor's criminal behaviour and it is therefore independent of any blameworthy conduct in the actor, e g A.549 cp concerning the death or injury of a woman pursuant to an abortion.

E. THE SUBJECTIVE ELEMENT IN THE CASE OF CONTRAVENTIONS

Article 42(4) cp provides that in the case of contraventions, the actor is responsible for his conscious and voluntary acts and omissions irrespective of whether they are the result of fraud or fault. Although this provision has been subject to conflicting interpretations, the modern doctrine and recent case law interprets the norm as first, requiring at least fault in the actor, and second, as raising a rebuttable presumption of fault in the actor for the commission of the contravention. Therefore, the court need not ascertain fault as the onus is on the accused to show his good faith, although recent doctrine includes an occasional writer who is critical of this presumption which is contrary to the general presumption of innocence applicable to criminal procedure. Merely because the minimal subjective element for a contravention is fault, it must not be thought, however, that contraventions comprise only crimes whose subjective element is fault. On the contrary, many contraventions require fraud for their existence.

Accepting the theory that there must be at least fault for the existence of a contravention, it follows that wherever a subject is able to prove his good faith, and therefore the absence of fault, he must be acquitted. However, according to the most recent approach taken by Cassation, good faith cannot exist where there is blameworthy error in the actor, ignorance of the law, or the erroneous belief that the behaviour was legal, but must be based upon the objective circumstances of each case.

The subjective grounds excluding criminal liability

There are two broad categories of subjective grounds which exclude criminality: first, those grounds which are based upon the absence of the requirement of a conscious and voluntary act or omission (A.42(1) cp) and second, those grounds which are based upon the absence of the subjective element of the crime, that is blameworthiness (whether fraud or fault). The former category includes unconsciousness, as distinct from voluntariness (although this is more commonly dealt with in the discussion on conduct which is part of the objective element of a crime), *forza maggiore* and physical constraint. The latter category includes fortuitous circumstances and error. Not all of the doctrine, however, classifies the subjective grounds excluding criminal liability in the same way.

Forza maggiore is every superior external force which necessarily and inevitably causes a positive or negative act which is against the will of the actor, e g a painter who is blown off a ladder by a gust of wind and falls upon and kills a child. It is controversial in the doctrine whether *forza maggiore* must relate to natural phenomenon only or whether it may also include human factors. Fortuitous circumstances, instead, concern unforeseen and unforeseeable circumstances which are beyond the limits of prudence and human attention. Physical constraint, dealt with in A.46 cp, excludes criminal liability for facts committed under physical force, or the threat of physical violence, which the actor cannot escape or avoid. As is evident, the actor in such cases is only the means or instrument of another subject who is regarded as being responsible for the crime, e g where the author physically forced the actor to pull the trigger. Physical constraint is to be kept distinct from cases of mental constraint which were dealt with earlier and are regulated by A.54(3) cp (see p 279, above).

Error may intervene in either the formative process of a criminal intent, in which case the prevailing doctrine maintains that it excludes any fraud (*dolo*), or in the execution of the crime giving rise to the so-called aberrant crime (see p 288, below). The former situation only shall be examined here. An error in the formative process of a criminal intent may be based upon either fact or law. The question of an error of law may be immediately disposed of as A.5 cp clearly provides that ignorance of the law can never be invoked.

An error of fact, on the other hand, is more complex. In accordance with A.47 cp an 'essential error', that is, an error affecting an essential element of the crime, is an excusable error and excludes punishability provided that the actor erred without any fault on his part, e g where a person carries away a thing believing, without fault, that the thing is his cannot be punished as larceny because an element of the crime is knowledge that the thing belongs to someone else. However, error is inexcusable when it is determined by the actor through his own fault, e g through negligence or imprudence, in which case the actor remains criminally responsible whenever the act, in abstract, constitutes an unintentional crime, e g if X shoots at a shadow killing a man, the error is inexcusable because it is due to the negligence of X. Article 47(2) cp, however, contains the rider that an error as to a fact which constitutes a given crime, does not exclude punishment for a different crime, e g if X did not know that his victim was a public official, then although he is not responsible for an offence against a public official, he will nonetheless remain responsible for an affront. In the case of contraventions, excusable error always excludes criminal responsibility, whilst inexcusable error always preserves it.

An error as to the circumstances, as distinct from an error as to an essential element of the crime, is irrelevant and does not affect the criminal responsibility of the actor: the circumstances are objectively evaluated for or against the accused, even if he was ignorant of their existence. Thus if the actor erroneously believed the existence of an aggravating or attenuating circumstance, this is irrelevant to his criminal responsibility unless expressly made relevant by A.60 cp.

A similar discipline as provided for in the case of an essential error is applicable to an erroneous belief as to the existence of an objective ground excluding criminal liability. Article 59(3) cp, as already noted, provides that an error as to the existence of circumstances excluding punishment are evaluated in favour of the accused, unless the error was due to the fault of the accused in which case he remains liable if the fact constitutes an unintentional delict. However, it is necessary to remember that only errors of fact are relevant. Thus in the case of A.51 cp (the defence that the actor was performing a right or duty) it is not enough that the actor believes that he is exercising a legitimate right or duty but the right or duty must effectively exist, that is, the error may only relate to the circumstances which give rise to the right or duty and not as to the existence of the right or duty. For instance, the owner of a bee hive enters land which is fenced and owned by another person (such entry in the absence of necessity being a crime under A.637 cp) pursuant to the right which is in fact conceded by A.924 cc (the right to follow escaped swarms), erroneously believing that the swarm entered such land.

According to A.47(3) cp an error as to a non-criminal law will exonerate the accused where it causes an error in relation to an element of a crime. Thus, if as a result of an error in civil law, a thief believes that the stolen item belonged to A whilst, in fact, it belonged to B, the error is irrelevant as it does not affect an element of the crime. If, however, X erroneously believed that the thing he took belonged to him, the error results in the elimination of the crime because it affects an element of the crime of larceny, that is, separate ownership. The error referred to in A.47(3) cp is different to that in the first two paragraphs of A.47 cp. The latter involve an error as to the existence of a fact, whilst A.47(3) concerns the erroneous interpretation and evaluation, through an error of law, of an existent fact.

The types of crime

A. THE CONSUMMATED CRIME (IL REATO CONSUMATO)

The various stages in the commission of a crime may be divided into three successive phases. First, the formation of an intent to commit a crime, that is, the formulation of a design or purpose. This phase can only arise in the case of intentional crimes (*reati dolosi*) characterised by the intention to commit them. The mere intent to commit a crime is never punishable as punishment requires some external behaviour prohibited by the criminal law. Only where there is an agreement between several persons to commit a crime does the criminal law become relevant in this phase, and even so, for the purpose of applying precautionary measures only and not penalties (A.115 cp). Second, the execution phase, which consists of carrying out the criminal purpose, that is, the realisation of the contemplated conduct which is prohibited by the criminal law. This phase may be divided into a preparatory phase and the actual *execution* of the criminal conduct. Finally, the consummation of the crime, which is the bringing of the criminal conduct to its conclusion. The consummation of the crime coincides with the point at which the legally protected asset is injured. In some cases the necessary conduct to bring a crime to its completion is interrupted either by some factor external to the actor or by the will of the actor himself. Moreover, consummation may not arise because of the existence of an objective or subjective ground excluding criminal liability (see above).

B. ATTEMPT (IL DELITTO TENTATO)

Article 56(1) cp deals with attempts, that is, the commission of appropriate acts unequivocally directed to the commission of a delict which is not brought to completion. An attempt is something less than a consummated delict and differs from the latter because the object of the crime is not brought to completion with the result that the legally protected asset is not injured but merely placed in peril. The crime of attempt is the result of a combination of two norms: the principal or specific criminal norm regulating the crime which has not been brought to completion, and the so-called secondary or extensive norm, that is, A.56 cp which concerns the performance of acts unequivocally directed to realising the crime in the principal norm.

An attempt consists of three elements. First, the intention to commit a defined delict. This intention must not remain a mere 'proposal'; it must be externally manifested. Second, the fulfilment of suitable acts unequivocally directed to the commission of a delict. Therefore, preliminary or preparatory acts, as distinct from executory acts, are irrelevant because of their uncertain significance. It is to avoid the difficulty of distinguishing between preparatory and executory acts that the Code has adopted the test of acts unequivocally directed to the commission of a delict. This is gleaned from the objective character of the act and the manner in which it is performed. Thus, an act is objectively unequivocal if it clearly evidences the purpose to which it was directed and it has reached a point which does not leave any serious doubt that the author would have brought the purpose to its conclusion. A suitable act, on the other hand, means an act capable of fulfilling the purpose. Third, the non-occurrence of the event or purpose because of the interruption of the executory acts through circumstances external to the will of the actor.

An attempt is inapplicable in a number of instances, for example, attempts are applicable to delicts only, not contraventions, and are inconceivable in the case of unintentional crimes. An attempt is punished with a lesser penalty than that prescribed for the consummated crime: by imprisonment of not less than 12 years where the penalty for the consummated crime is life imprisonment, and by a reduction of between one-third and two-thirds of the penalty prescribed for the consummated crime in every other case (A.56(2) cp). Where the accused voluntarily desists from bringing the criminal purpose to its conclusion, he is only responsible for the conduct actually carried into effect if it per se constitutes a crime (A.56(3) cp). Where, however, the accused has brought the criminal conduct to its conclusion but then seeks to avoid its consequence by acting to impede it, he remains guilty of an attempt but the penalty prescribed for the consummated crime is reduced by between one-third and one-half, e g where the accused throws a victim into a river with the intent of drowning him but then rescues him.

C. THE IMPOSSIBLE CRIME (IL REATO IMPOSSIBILE)

According to A.49(2) cp, a crime is impossible where the conduct is inappropriate to the commission of the crime (e g where X intends to kill with a toy pistol), or the object (whether a person or thing) of the crime is non-existent. According to a majority of the doctrine, the person or thing must be non-existent at the time at which the author sets about his criminal plan: if at that point the presence of the object appears improbable, the crime is impossible; in every other case the conduct is criminal, e g if X shoots at an empty bed which is usually occupied by the person whose murder was intended. Article 49(3) cp, however, provides that if the conduct contains the elements of a different crime, the penalty for the crime effectively committed is applied. Where a person is acquitted for impossibility, the court has the power to apply the precautionary measure of supervised freedom if the conduct of the accused indicates that he is socially dangerous.

D. THE ABERRANT CRIME (IL REATO ABERRANTE)

The expression 'aberrant crime' concerns those cases in which the actor, through an error, realises a crime different from that which was intended or commits it against the wrong person. In both cases the error does not affect the intent but only the execution of the crime. The Code deals with both types of aberrant crime. First, the so-called *aberratio ictus* (A.82 cp) which concerns an exchange of victim. This type of error is irrelevant and the author is punished as if he had committed the crime against the intended victim, subject to any aggravating or attenuating circumstances stipulated by A.60 cp (see p 292, below). Where both the erroneous and intended victims are offended, the accused suffers the penalty for the more serious crime increased by up to one-half. Second, the so-called *aberratio delicti* (A.83 cp) which comprises, excluding the situation contemplated by A.82 cp, any event different from that which was intended. In such cases, the accused is responsible for an unintentional act only provided that his conduct constitutes an unintentional crime, e g if X intends to kill Y but the projectile misses and hits an inflammable substance causing a fire, X is responsible for unintentional arson. If, however, he had only broken a window, he would not be liable for property damage because such crime is an intentional delict. Where the accused also caused the intended event, then the rules on concurrent crimes are applicable.

The doctrine has created a third type of *aberratio*, namely, *aberratio causae* which arises where a causal process other than that which was intended comes about through some error in the consummation phase, e g where it was intended to drown the victim who, instead, died from a head injury upon being hurled into a river. The erroneous causal process is always irrelevant, although it must be kept distinct from the situation where the accused erroneously believes to have caused an event which he then brings about by a subsequent act, e g X assaults Y and erroneously believing him dead buries him and Y then dies from suffocation. The dominant approach is that in the latter case there is both an attempt and an unintentional crime (unintentional homicide in the example just given).

E. THE CIRCUMSTANTIAL CRIME (REATO CIRCOSTANZIATO)

(*i*) *Definition*. As already noted, a crime is composed of both essential and accessory elements. Although the former are essential to the existence of a crime, the latter are not and are known as circumstances which merely affect the seriousness and penalty of a crime. A fact may be either a constituent or a circumstantial element, depending upon its function. Consequently, a fact may be such as to distinguish one crime from another, in which case it is a constituent element of the crime and may even give rise to a special crime, e g if the ulterior fact is the consent of the victim in a homicide it gives rise to a special crime as distinct from the base crime of common homicide; on the other hand, if the fact is not indispensible to the base crime, then it is a mere circumstance which transforms the simple (or base) crime into a circumstantial crime. Whether an additional fact is a circumstance (circumstantial crime) or a constituent element of an autonomous crime (special crime) is, of course, important in relation to penalty.

(*ii*) *Classification of circumstances*. Circumstances may be classified in different ways. First, as aggravating or attenuating circumstances depending upon whether they result in an increase or decrease in penalty whose variation may be either quantitative or qualitative. Second, as objective and subjective circumstances (A.70 cp). The objective circumstances include: the nature, object, means, species, time, place, and any other aspect of the act; the seriousness of the injury or peril caused by the crime; and the personal conditions or characteristics of the victim. The subjective circumstances include: the degree of fraud (*dolo*) or fault (*colpa*); the personal conditions or characteristics of the accused; and the relationship between the accused and the victim. Third, as real and personal circumstances. The former are circumstances which generally affect the seriousness of the crime, whilst the latter are circumstances which augment or attenuate the penalty in relation to the particular defendant. Fourth, as common and special circumstances. The former are circumstances applicable to all crimes and dealt with in the general part of the Code, whilst the latter are circumstances relevant to particular crimes only. Finally, as antecedent, concomitant and successive circumstances, depending upon whether the circumstance precedes, accompanies or is subsequent to the conduct and event.

(iii) The common aggravating circumstances. These are defined in A.61 cp and are:

1 contemptible or trifling motives for the crime (A.61 n.1 cp);
2 the commission of a crime for the purpose of carrying out or concealing another crime, or for the purpose of ensuring for oneself or another the product, profit, price or non-punishability of another crime (A.61 n.2 cp),
3 the foreseeability of the event in the case of unintentional delicts (A.61 n.3 cp), that is, so-called conscious fault;
4 the use of torture or cruelty (A.61 n.4 cp);
5 having taken advantage of circumstances of tie, place, or person in such a manner as to hinder the public or private defence (A.61 n.5 cp);
6 the commission of a crime during a period of time in which the accused had voluntarily evaded the enforcement of a warrant for arrest, detention or imprisonment issued in relation to a previous crime (A.61 n.6 cp);
7 the cause of a significant patrimonial loss to the victims of crimes against property or crimes motivated by reason of profit (A.61 n.7 cp);
8 the aggravation or attempt to aggravate the consequences of a crime, eg the hinder of the emergency treatment of a victim (A.61 n.8 cp);
9 the commission of a crime which involves an abuse of power or the violation of duties inherent in the exercise of a public function or the functions of a minister of religion (A.61 n.9 cp);

10 the commission of a crime against a public official, a minister of the Catholic or other religion recognised by the State, or a foreign diplomatic or consular agent in connection with the exercise of their functions or services (A.61 n.10 cp); and

11 the commission of a crime pursuant to an abuse of authority or of a domestic or official relationship, or through the abuse of a relationship based upon employment, cohabitation, or hospitality (A.61 n.11 cp). This aggravating circumstance comprises all of those abuses of authority which do not come within para 9, above.

(iv) The common attenuating circumstances. These are defined in A.62 cp and are:

1 motivation through moral or social values (A.62 n.1 cp), e g patriotism. However, the following have been held not to constitute motives of a moral or social value: jealousy, so-called reasons of honour (as modern morals do not approve of the killing of an unfaithful spouse: Cass 23/4/1971), and the intent to limit the birth rate by abortion (Cass 19/6/1974);

2 provocation (A.62 n.2 cp). Provocation requires an uncontrollable emotive impulse (not vindication) in response to an unjust act. The provocative act is unjust if it constitutes an attack against an interest, expectation, opinion or behaviour which the social conscience regards worthy of protection (Cass 9/10/1970). It follows, therefore, that what constitutes an unjust act is an objective test. The reaction to an unjust act need not be immediate but may follow after some time, e g after an event which reawakens or revives the memory of the wrong suffered (Cass 2/2/1971);

3 a reaction to the suggestion of a crowd in turmoil (A.62 n.3 cp);

4 a particularly slight loss in the case of crimes against property (A.62 n.4 cp);

5 a person harmed by the crime contributed, through his own fault, to the event (A.62 n.5 cp); and

6 there has been, prior to judgment, a complete compensation of damages or, where possible, restitution; or, again prior to judgment, and apart from the situation contemplated in A.56(4) cp concerning attempts, there has been a spontaneous and effective attempt at avoiding or attenuating the injury or peril consequent to the commission of a crime (A.62 n.6 cp).

(v) General attentuating circumstances. Article 62 *bis* cp provides that the court may take into account any circumstances, other than those listed in A.62 cp, that justify a diminution of the penalty. This provision introduces the possibility of mitigating the penalty as a result of circumstances not expressly contemplated by A.62 cp.

(vi) The evaluation of circumstances. The attenuating or aggravating circumstances are applicable as a result of their objective existence, the knowledge of the accused being irrelevant. It follows that errors as to circumstances do not affect the position of the accused, e g the increase in penalty stipulated in A.61 n.7 cp is not applied to a thief who thought that he was stealing a valuable original painting which was, instead, a poor imitation. The position is different in relation to error as to the identity of the person harmed by the crime, that is, a situation in which, e g. A intends to kill B but because it is dark he kills C instead. This is different to *aberratio ictus* (see p 288, above) in which there is no confusion as to the identity of the victim, but, through an error, the projectile hits a different target. In the case of erroneous identity, A.60 cp provides first, that aggravating circumstances concerning the condition or status of the person harmed through the error are not to be applied against the author of the crime, and second, that the attenuating circumstances which are erroneously supposed to exist are nonetheless applied in favour of the accused.

Where there is a concurrence of several homogeneous circumstances (that is, all attenuating or all aggravating circumstances) the increase or decrease in penalty, with certain exceptions, is proportional to the number of circumstances. Where, however, the concurrent circumstances are heterogeneous, the court decides the prevalence or equivalence of the aggravating and attenuating circumstances. This evaluation by the court is not subject to review.

F. CONCOURSAL CRIMES: ACCOMPLICES

These arise where several persons are involved in the commission of the same crime. The matter is dealt with by A.110 cp which provides that where several persons are involved in the commission of the same crime, each person suffers the penalty fixed for the crime, subject to certain exceptions. Two such exceptions are to be found in Artt. 112 and 114 cp which prescribe certain aggravating and attenuating circumstances which operate to increase or decrease the penalty of certain accomplices to a crime. The aggravating circumstances enumerated in A.112 cp are: the collaboration of five or more persons in the commission of a crime; the promotion, organisation or direction of the criminal activities; the use of authority to induce subordinates to commit a crime; and the inducement of a minor or a mentally infirm or retarded person to commit a crime. The attenuating circumstances prescribed by A.114 cp are: a participation of minimal importance in the preparation or execution of the crime; a participation through reverence to a superior; and participation by minors or mentally infirm or retarded persons who were induced to participate in the crime.

The unitary nature of a crime which involves a number of

accomplices results in their similar treatment comprising the following effects. First, all of the accomplices answer for the same crime, even if the type of crime changes as a result of the status or condition of one of the accomplices or because of the relationship between an accomplice and the person harmed (A.117 cp). However, the communication of the new crime depends upon two factors: the activity of the communicant must per se constitute a crime; and, although this requirement is not considered relevant by all of the writers, the communicant must be aware of the status of the communicator who thereby alters the nature of the crime. Second, the effect of a subjective ground excluding criminal liability is limited to the relevant accomplice whilst the existence of an objective ground excluding criminal liability extends its effect to all of the accomplices (A.119 cp). Third, the objective circumstances of a crime affect all of the accomplices, even if they are unaware of the circumstances, whereas, except in certain exceptional cases, subjective circumstances (e g premeditation) and circumstances personal to an accomplice (e g habituality) are not communicated to the others (A.118 cp). Fourth, the voluntary interruption or withdrawal from a criminal activity, or repentance followed by positive conduct to avoid the consequences of a crime, operate for the benefit of the relevant accomplice only. Finally, the time and place of the commission of the crime is presumed to be the same for all of the accomplices.

Article 116 cp deals with the situation where a crime different to that intended by some of the accomplices is committed, e g A and B agree to commit a larceny, but A introduces violence into the commission thereby converting it into robbery. An accomplice who intended a less serious crime is responsible for the more serious one if the latter was committed in the fulfilment of the criminal purpose and is the consequence of his acts or omissions, although the penalty may be reduced by up to one-third in his regard. The basis of the responsibility for the more serious crime, notwithstanding any reduction in penalty, is that it is a foreseeable consequence of the criminal purpose; A.116 cp is based upon the imprudence in trusting another person in the realisation of the criminal purpose.

Article 113 cp specifically deals with concurrent liability in the case of unintentional delicts: it provides that where the event is caused by the concurrence of several persons, each is liable for the total penalty applicable to the delict, although in certain cases it is increased with respect to an accomplice who induced certain categories of person to participate in the delict.

G. MULTIPLE CRIMES

This arises where an individual violates the criminal law more than once in which case he becomes liable for several crimes. The legislative regulation of multiplicity has the object of limiting the accumulation of the penalties stipulated for the several crimes. Multiplicity does not arise, however, where a criminal norm combines several otherwise independent crimes (e g robbery which comprises larceny and private violence). Rather, the latter type of legislative unification of crimes gives rise to the so-called continuing, composite and compound crimes (see below). Multiple crimes may be either material or formal. The former arises where an individual violates one or more criminal norms through a plurality of acts or omissions, e g where X kills and then steals. The general principle adopted by the Italian Criminal Code in the case of material multiplicity is the material accumulation (or arithmetical sum) of the penalties applicable to each crime committed by the accused subject, however, to certain mitigating factors the most important of which is the stipulation of certain maximum limits (Artt. 78 and 79 cp). Formal multiplicity arises where several crimes are committed pursuant to a single act or omission of the accused, e g where X injures several persons with a single utterance. The reforms of 1974 extended the penalty system applicable to continuing crimes to cases of formal multiplicity (A.81 cp), namely, the so-called legal accumulation of penalties which consists of the application of the most serious penalty increased by a defined proportion rather than the arithmetical accumulation of penalties corresponding to the number of infractions.

H. THE CONTINUING CRIME

This involves several violations of the same or different criminal norms, whether at the same or different times, by several acts or omissions directed to the same criminal design. The continuing crime is one of the major exceptions to the general provisions on multiplicity. The various acts which comprise the so-called continuing crime are treated as a unit, not only in the determination of the penalty (A.81(3) cp, see above) but also for the purposes of determining limitation periods, determining habituality or professionalism, identifying the territorially competent court, applying general pardons, and determining applications for the conditional suspension of penalties and conditional liberty. However, in relation to the determination of penalty, the case law has generally not applied A.81 cp in cases of continuing crimes comprising both delicts and contraventions on the basis that the heterogeneous nature of the penalties makes it impossible to proportionally increase the most serious penalty. A rigorous application of this approach would also exclude the application of the continuation concept in the case of delicts which carry heterogeneous penalties, e g imprisonment and fine. The case law is, in fact, divided on the issue although it generally regards A.81 cp as being applicable to cases of homogeneous penalties only.

Antolisei favours a more general application provided that it results in an advantage for the defendant.

I. THE COMPOSITE CRIME

The substantive characteristic of the composite crime is the legislative unification of several crimes into a single one. Such unification may consist of either first, the unification of several independent crimes as constituent elements of a new or different crime or second, the unification of two crimes, one as a constitutent element and the other as an aggravating circumstance thereby leaving the former or base crime unaltered. In either event, A.84 cp provides that in all such cases of 'apparent multiplicity' the provisions on multiplicity are inapplicable. It should be noted that A.170 cp provides that a ground which extinguishes a crime which is either a constituent element or an aggravating circumstance of a composite crime does not also extinguish the latter.

J. THE COMPOUND CRIME

In contrast to the composite crime, which consists of the union of two or more serious crimes, the compound crime is a crime that necessarily embodies a less serious crime. The minor crime remains within the major crime and is not separately punished. The basis for this category of crime is not A.84 cp but the general principle contained in A.15 cp according to which where several provisions deal with the same matter, a more specific provision overrides a more general one, viz, the compound crime is more specific vis-à-vis the minor crime.

K. PERMANENT CRIMES

These are crimes in which the event, and thus its consummation, lasts for a certain period of time, e g kidnap with the object of extortion. The notion is important in relation to the determination of the location of the crime, the definition of the territorially competent court, the existence of 'flagrance', the lapse of any limitation period, the lapse of any period for laying a complaint, and the application of amnesties.

The accused

A. GENERAL

In Italian law the author of a crime must necessarily be a natural person; a legal person, not having a will of its own, cannot attract criminal liability. The fact that individual will lies at the basis of criminal responsibility is confirmed by A.197 cp, which merely imposes upon a legal person the civil obligation to guarantee the performance of a criminal obligation assumed by its representatives. Antolisei observes that because the Criminal Code centres on the accused rather than crime, it can be said that Italian criminal law takes a subjective orientation. The Code has supported the principle of individual responsibility by making the application of a penalty dependent upon imputing responsibility to the accused. However, the Code has also created a concept of criminal propensity, that is, the inclination of an individual to commit crime, which gives rise to the application of various precautionary measures (see ch 1, p 41, above).

B. CRIMINAL RESPONSIBILITY (L'IMPUTABILITÀ)

Criminal responsibility requires the capacity to understand and intend (A.85 cp). The former represents the capacity to appreciate the social value of the act, whilst the latter is the aptitude of self-determination. The substance of the capacity to understand and intend is mental maturity and health. Article 85 cp does not, it should be emphasised, repeat the same requirements that are contained in Artt. 42 and 43 cp. Article 42 cp, which requires a conscious and voluntary act, concerns the nature of the criminal conduct and is clearly different to the concept in A.85 cp: an individual may well be responsible yet his conduct be unconscious or involuntary, e g in the case of *forza maggiore*. Furthermore, the voluntariness referred to in A.43 cp, which distinguishes between unintentional, intentional and super-intentional delicts, is again different to the concept in A.85 cp and concerns the *causal* nexus between conduct and event. The capacity to understand and intend contained in A.85 cp, which goes to imputability, concerns, as distinct from both Artt. 42 and 43 cp, the subject of the crime and, in particular, his state (considered objectively) at the time of the commission of the crime.

C. GROUNDS EXCLUDING CRIMINAL RESPONSIBILITY

Criminal responsibility, or the capacity to understand and intend, may be excluded or diminished because of various physical or mental conditions specified in Artt. 88ff cp. The prevalent doctrine has it that the grounds excluding criminal capacity cannot be extended by analogy, although Antolisei is of the contrary view as extension by analogy in this case would always be to the advantage of the defendant. The various grounds set out in the Code are:

(*i*) *Minority* (Artt. 97 and 98 cp). There is an absolute presumption that children under the age of 14 lack the capacity to understand and intend (A.97 cp). However, in relation to children between the ages of 14 and

18 there is no presumption either way and the court must ascertain capacity in the individual case (A.98 cp). An incapable minor must be acquitted and no penalty can be imposed. However, if he is considered to be socially dangerous the court may impose precautionary measures which may be either of a reformatory or supervisory nature. Minors between the ages of 14 and 18 who are found to have capacity are subject to the imposition of a reduced penalty and, perhaps, precautionary measures which are applied subsequent to the penalty where the minor is considered to be socially dangerous. No penalty imposed upon a minor must have the object of punishment but only of social prevention and rehabilitation.

(ii) Infirmity of the mind (Artt. 88 and 89 cp). Infirmity of the mind consists of a mental defect consequent upon a disease. It must be a pathological state which disturbs the mind. The infirmity need not be permanent provided that it existed at the date of the commission of the crime. This form of incapacity results in an acquittal and the application of the precautionary measure of recovery in a legal asylum or, where the incapacity is merely partial, a reduced penalty together with the imposition of appropriate precautionary measures which take effect at the expiration of the penalty. In order to remove any doubt as to the mental states of emotion and passion, A.90 cp expressly provides that these do not exclude or diminish capacity, although they may constitute attenuating circumstances (see A.62 nos. 2 and 3 cp, p 291, above).

(iii) Deaf and dumb (A.96 cp). Although the Code acknowledges that a defect in *both* hearing and speech may hinder the mental development of a subject, it does not give a definitive solution, leaving capacity in such cases to be determined in the individual case. Therefore, if the court finds total capacity, the subject is regarded normally; if, instead, it finds total or partial incapacity, then the deaf-dumb is equated to a person who is suffering from a total or partial mental incapacity.

(iv) Drunkenness. The Code distinguishes drunkenness from chronic intoxication. The Code specifies four categories of drunkenness:

(a) INCIDENTAL DRUNKENNESS (A.91 cp) which arises where the state of drunkenness is not due to the fault of the agent, e g an employee of a distillery who becomes drunk from inhaling fumes, or inebriation as a result of a trick by friends. If there is a total drunkenness in such cases, the subject lacks capacity; if, instead, there is a partial capacity, there is a reduction in penalty without the imposition of any precautionary measures.

(b) VOLUNTARY DRUNKENNESS (A.92(1) cp) which arises where the agent either intended to become drunk or did so out of imprudence or negligence. This type of drunkenness does not exclude or diminish capacity, although there have been proposals for the introduction of a discretion to enable a reduction in penalty in such cases of between one-third and one-half.

(c) PREMEDITATED DRUNKENNESS (A.92(2) cp) which is drunkenness that is voluntarily induced with the object of preparing an excuse for the commission of a crime. This type of drunkenness, again, does not exclude or diminish capacity.

(d) HABITUAL DRUNKENNESS (A.94 cp) which results in an increased penalty and the application of the precautionary measure of rehabilitation, although recent proposals have suggested the repeal of the former in such cases.

(*v*) *Chronic intoxication* (A.95 cp). Criminal acts committed in a state of chronic intoxication, which represents the final stage of alcoholism and gives rise to certain associated mental diseases, are regulated by Artt. 88 and 89 cp in the same way as crimes committed by persons suffering from total or partial mental infirmity.

(*vi*) *Drugs*. The Code equates the consequences of intoxicating drugs with the various forms of alcoholism described above (Artt. 93, 94 and 95 cp).

Finally, A.87 cp provides generally that A.85(1) cp is not applicable to persons who place themselves in a state of incapacity to understand and intend with the object of committing a crime or preparing an excuse. A specific application of this general provision has already been seen in the case of alcoholism and drugs (see Artt. 92(2) and 93 cp).

D. CRIMINAL POTENTIAL AND CRIMINAL PROPENSITY (CAPACITÀ CRIMINALE AND PERICOLOSITÀ CRIMINALE)

The concept of criminal potential (*capacità criminale*) or the inclination to commit crime is contained in A.133 cp which provides that the court is not only to take into account the seriousness of the crime in exercising any discretion when determining the penalty, but also the criminal potential of the accused having regard to the nature of the crime, the motives of the accused, the antecedents of the accused, the behaviour of the accused both before and after the commission of the crime, the character of the accused, and the accused's environment. Whilst criminal potential signifies a possibility that the actor will commit a crime, the ulterior notion of criminal propensity (*pericolosità criminale*) signifies that there is a probability that he will do so. The latter notion is a more intense and specific form of the inclination to commit crime and is ascertained from the same elements used to determine criminal potential. The quality of 'criminal propensity' constitutes a special status which is expressly adopted by A.203 cp which provides that a person is to be considered 'socially dangerous', even if he is not imputable or punishable, where it is probable that he will commit further criminal acts. Criminal propensity or dangerousness is an important concept in the present law as it is directly related to the application of precautionary measures, the determination of the quantity and quality of punitive measures, and the forfeiture of both the conditional suspension of sentences and judicial pardons. The Code distinguishes four types of dangerousness: repetition (*recidiva*), criminal habit (*abitualità criminosa*), professionalism (*professionalità nel reato*), and the tendency to commit crime (*tendenza a delinquere*). Repetition (A.99 cp) may be simple (the commission of a further but different crime), aggravated (the commission of a similar kind of crime within five years of the preceding conviction) or iterative (the commission of a further crime where the author had already fallen into a simple or aggravated repetition). All types of repetition result in a proportional increase in the base penalty for the new crime. Criminal habit constitutes a personal status indicative of a notable aptitude to commit crime and arises either where an individual has received a certain number of defined convictions within a given period or upon declaration by the court where certain conditions exist. The consequences flowing from the status of 'habitual criminal' are: the application of precautionary measures, ineligibility for public office, unavailability of a conditional suspension of sentence, the inapplicability of amnesties and general pardons unless the decree provides otherwise, the inapplicability of the limitation period which applies to penalties for delicts, and the doubling of the period fixed for rehabilitation. Professionalism (A.105 cp) and the tendency to commit crime (A.108 cp) involve more serious situations than habitualism resulting, in addition, in the imposition of precautionary detentive measures.

The penal consequences of a crime

The penal consequences of a crime may be said to fall into three broad categories: *penalties, precautionary measures*, and *alternative measures*.

A. PENALTIES

A penalty is the sanction imposed by a legal norm for the violation of the criminal law and its essential character is that it inflicts a true and proper suffering upon the subject threatened with the sanction. It is always applied by a judicial authority upon the conclusion of the criminal process. The penalty has, under Italian law, continued to retain its nature as a form of punishment both because of its afflictive nature and because it is directly proportional to the seriousness of the crime. However, it also combines functions of deterrence and rehabilitation.

The principal types of penalty are detentive, pecuniary and accessory penalties. The detentive penalties comprise life imprisonment, imprisonment (which ranges from 15 days to 24 years and, like life imprisonment, is applicable to delicts only) and arrest (which ranges from five days to three years, is applicable to contraventions only and is served in particular institutions). The death penalty has been almost totally abolished; the only case in which it is still applicable is for military crimes committed during times of war. The pecuniary penalties are the fine (which ranges from Lit. 2,000 to Lit. 2,000,000 and is applicable to delicts only) and the amend (which ranges from Lit. 800 to Lit. 400,000 and is applicable to contraventions only). There are also a number of accessory penalties which are applicable in defined instances, e g permanent or temporary disqualification from public office (Artt. 28 and 29 cp), disqualification from a profession or trade for a period of between one month and five years (A.30 cp), and the loss of legal capacity (A.32 cp), including the loss of the capacity of testation and the nullification of any will made prior to a conviction (A.32 cp).

Normally, penalties are not fixed but, within certain limits defined by legislation, left to the discretion of the court (A.132 cp). The court, in determining a penalty, must take into account two basic factors. First, the seriousness of the crime (A.133(1) cp), which is deduced from the following factors: the nature and specie of the crime as well as the modus, motives, time, place and other circumstances related to its commission; the seriousness of the injury or peril caused to the person harmed; and the intensity of the fraud (*dolo*) or fault (*colpa*) in the author of the crime. Second, the propensity of the accused to commit crime (A.133(2) cp, see p 298, above). Therefore, every penalty reflects a double evaluation: the seriousness of the crime and criminal propensity. The penalty is also subject to increase or decrease depending upon the existence of any aggravating or attenuating circumstances (Artt. 63–68 cp, see p 292, above). Although it follows that a basic principle applicable to penalties is their proportionality to the seriousness of the crime, the provisions relating to repetition and criminal propensity obviously constitute two exceptions to the general rule.

The Code defines the various ways in which a penalty may be extinguished or, in other words, totally or partially waived. First, death which extinguishes the crime and, depending upon whether the death occurs before or after conviction, the penalty. In any event, the civil obligations arising out of the crime survive as a burden upon the heirs. Second, amnesty, the means with which the State waives the application of a penalty in defined categories of crime. It is a general or impersonal measure which may relate to either proceedings still on foot or existing convictions. Amnesties are frequently granted in Italy and this is the reason why defendants often protract criminal proceedings. However, a defendant is always entitled to renounce the benefit of an amnesty as the law must allow a person the opportunity of being acquitted as innocent. Third, general pardon which affects the principal penalty only, and not any accessory penalties. Like an amnesty, it is granted by the President upon delegation from the Parliament (A.79 C). Fourth, pardon, which is an act of clemency issued by the President (A.87 C). It is always directed to a particular person after his conviction and relates to the principal penalty only. Fifth, prescription, which does not apply to crimes which carry the death penalty or life imprisonment, and may extinguish either the crime or the penalty alone provided that the penalty has not been served. In both cases the prescriptive period varies on a sliding scale depending upon the penalty fixed for the crime in question. Sixth, oblation (A.162 cp) which is the voluntary payment of a given sum in the case of contraventions punishable by amend. The payment extinguishes the crime and downgrades the act to an administrative wrong. Seventh, judicial pardon of minors which enables the extinguishment of crimes committed by minors so as to facilitate rehabilitation. It may be granted at the discretion of the court but is limited to first offenders under the age of 18 and to crimes which are not serious. Eighth, conditional suspension of sentence, granted to first offenders of minor crimes provided that they do not have a criminal propensity. If the convicted person commits another crime within a certain period, he is sentenced for both crimes. Ninth, parole, which suspends that part of the penalty which remains to be served and is granted where the conditions in Artt. 163–168 cp are satisfied. Tenth, rehabilitation (A.178 cp) which extinguishes both accessory penalties and every other penal effect of the conviction. It is granted after the expiration of a defined period from the date of conviction where certain conditions are satisfied. Finally, non-notation of the criminal record (A.175 cp) which, although left to the discretion of the court, is only available to first offenders of crimes punishable with modest penalties. The concession of this benefit is revoked if the accused later commits a delict.

B. PRECAUTIONARY MEASURES

These are measures which are intended to rehabilitate the accused and, in any event, to place him in a position such that he cannot commit further crimes. They are intended to complement the traditional system of penalties and are applied where a penalty is either inapplicable or, even if applicable, inappropriate to prevent further criminality. Their introduction into the present Code represented one of the principal innovations of the criminal law at that time. A precautionary measure is different from a penalty because it is not a sanction: as it is exclusively directed to the future, it is not proportional to the seriousness of the crime in question but only to the dangerousness of the accused which is the factor justifying its application. This gives rise to two important corollaries: first, precautionary measures, in contrast to the fixed nature of penalties, are indeterminate because they endure for the duration of the dangerousness of the accused; and second, and again in contast to penalties, they are also applicable to non-imputable persons, such as minors and persons suffering from mental infirmity.

However, the modern doctrine is critical of the institution. It regards precautionary measures as being equivalent to criminal sanctions for the following reasons: first, they presuppose a crime; second, like penalties, they are regulated by the Criminal Code; and third, they are both a means of combating crime and constitute a legal consequence of its commission. Moreover, as Antolisei notes, this attitude is consistent with their application forming part of the judicial function, as is evidenced by the following factors: their application is entrusted to the judicial authorities and requires an impartiality which distinguishes that jurisdiction; their application is subject to the principle of legality (A.199 cp), that is, they may only be applied in the cases strictly defined by legislation; they are regulated by the Code of Criminal Procedure in a manner and form characteristic of judicial proceedings; their revocability does not remove their judicial nature as the recent doctrine denies that revocability is a characteristic exclusive to administrative measures; and finally, the execution and service of the measures are subject to judicial supervision by the so-called supervisory judge.

There are two requisites for the application of precautionary measures. First, the commission of an act which constitutes a crime. However, precautionary measures are also applicable in two exceptional cases in which there has not been the commission of a crime and which the doctrine denominates as quasi-crimes, that is, impossible crimes (A.49 cp) and agreements to commit crime (A.115 cp). Second, the dangerousness of the accused.

Precautionary measures are ordered by the court with the same judgment with which it convicts or acquits the accused. At the expiration of the minimum statutory period for which the relevant precautionary measure could have been imposed in the particular case, the court re-examines the dangerousness of the subject and either revokes the measure or continues it for further terms until the element of danger disappears. Precautionary measures may also be imposed for the first time at a point subsequent to a conviction or acquittal, that is, by order of the supervisory judge, as follows: in the case of a conviction, at any time during the service of the penalty or during the time in which the offender has voluntarily avoided the penalty; in the case of an acquittal, where the state of social danger arises by presumption of law and a term equivalent to the minimum applicable to the relevant precautionary measure has not yet lapsed; and finally, at any time whatsoever in the cases expressly defined by law.

Precautionary measures may be divided into two broad categories: personal measures (either detentive or non-detentive), and patrimonial measures. The personal detentive precautionary measures are: assignment to an agricultural or labour colony (Artt. 216–218 cp), assignment to a home of care and custody (Artt. 219–221 cp), rehabilitation in a legal asylum (A.222 cp), and rehabilitation of minors in a legal reformatory (Artt. 223–227 cp). The personal non-detentive precautionary measures are: supervised or conditional freedom (Artt. 228–232 cp), prohibition from travel to certain communes or provinces (A.233 cp), prohibition from frequenting taverns and other public places dealing in alcoholic beverages (A.234 cp), and the expulsion of aliens from the national territory (A.235 cp). There are two patrimonial precautionary measures (Artt. 237–240 cp), namely, entry into good behaviour bonds by the lodgment of cash or security and the confiscation of property which was either used in the commission of the crime or constituted the profit or product of the crime.

C. ALTERNATIVE MEASURES

The so-called alternative measures are regulated by the law of 26 July 1975 n.354 which enables their substitution for a detentive penalty in defined situations. There are four types of alternative measures: probation, daily release for work or education, advance release, and leave.

Probation consists of the release of persons sentenced to short detentive penalties into the custody and control of a social welfare organisation for the period which otherwise remains to be served in detention. The necessary conditions for the grant of probation are: first, a conviction of no more than two and a half years or, in the case of persons aged under 21 or over 70, of no more than three years; second, the absence of any precautionary detentive measure which is to take effect at the termination of the penalty; third, the absence of any previous conviction for a delict of the same nature as that in question; fourth, that the crime in question is not one amongst certain serious crimes; and finally, a satisfactory report on the detainee's behaviour in the relevant institution over a period of at least three months. It is granted by the Supervisory Section of the Courts of Appeal and the probationer must comply with various conditions and remain under the control of a social worker.

Daily release consists of the concession to either a convicted person or a person subject to precautionary detentive measures of the right to spend part of the day outside the subject institution for work, education, or other social activities appropriate to social re-integration. Daily release is granted by the Supervisory Section and may, depending upon the circumstances, be automatic or discretionary. As in the case of probation, it is not available where the person has been previously convicted of either a delict of the same nature or certain serious crimes. The measure may be suspended or revoked by the Supervisory Section where the conduct of the releasee is unsatisfactory.

Advance release consists of a reduction in penalty at the rate of 20 days per semester of the time actually served and is granted by the Supervisory Section to convicted persons who, through their conduct, have given proof of their successful participation in rehabilitation programmes. It is a discretionary measure and may be granted for any type of crime. The time which is discounted is considered for all purposes as having been served. The benefit may only be revoked if the subject commits an intentional delict during the period for which he was originally convicted.

Leave, which before 1975 was only available to persons who were subject to precautionary detentive measures, has since then been extended to convicted persons who are admitted to the daily release scheme. The latter persons may be granted by the supervisory judge, by way of reward, one or more periods of leave not exceeding in toto 45 days per year. During any period of leave, the releasee is subject to the same conditions as are applicable to the precautionary non-detentive measure of supervised freedom. Persons who are merely subject to precautionary detentive measures may be granted much more extensive periods of leave.

Amongst the alternative measures there are two further institutions worthy of mention. First, the remission of the debt that a detainee (whether a convicted person or a person detained pursuant to a precautionary measure) owes to the State for his maintenance in gaol. The benefit of such remission is granted to detainees who are suffering economic hardship and have had a good record during their incarceration. Second, conditional release which is not regulated by the Penal Law of July 1975 but by the law of 12 February 1975 n.6. Like the alternative measures, this institution modifies the enforcement of a penalty. It is granted to convicted persons who demonstrate, through their good behaviour whilst in detention, that they have reformed. It can only be granted after the service of part of the term, except in the case of minors in which case it may be granted at any time. Moreover, the convicted person must have fulfilled all of his civil obligations arising out of the crime, unless their performance is impossible. The grant of conditional release is discretionary and made by the Court of Appeal. Where granted, the same conditions as for the precautionary measure of supervised freedom are applied. The measure may be revoked if the releasee either fails to comply with the obligations inherent in his release or commits another delict or contravention of the same nature. Conditional release merely suspends the service of the balance of the detentive sentence although at the expiration of the original sentence the penalty is totally extinguished if the measure has not in the meantime been revoked. All other effects of the conviction, including accessory penalties, survive.

It follows that in Italy the penal phase of the criminal process has been judicialised. Judicial intervention ensures impartiality, objectivity, and diligence in the application of the law. The judicialisation of the penal phase has meant, in practice, that all of the administrative and judicial functions of this phase are carried out by either the supervisory judge or the Supervisory Section. The supervisory judge is the organ which supervises all precautionary and penal institutions; reports to the Minister of Grace and Justice on the needs of the various services and, in particular, in relation to the achievement of the rehabilitation process; and has the duty of ensuring that the custody of accused persons is in conformity with the relevant laws and regulations. The Supervisory Section, on the other hand, which exists in every Court of Appeal, has complete jurisdiction over alternative measures and the revocation of precautionary measures. It is a collegiate organ comprising a supervisory judge of the status of a judge of Appeal, who presides over the Section, a puisne supervisory judge of the status of a judge of *Tribunale*, and two social workers

The civil consequences of crime

A. INTRODUCTION

The same act may constitute both a crime and an illegal act of a different kind, such as a civil, administrative, or disciplinary wrong and therefore give rise to legal consequences other than those typical of the criminal law. Many crimes also constitute a civil wrong under A.2034 cc which gives rise to civil sanctions. In some cases a civil norm itself provides a civil sanction for a criminal illegality, e g A.463 cc which provides that homicide renders the author of the crime 'unworthy' in the succession of his victim. The most important civil consequences of an act, however, are those contained in Title VII of

Book I of the Criminal Code, the most significant of which are: restitution, damages, reimbursement of maintenance expenses to the State, and the civil obligation to pay the amend.

B. RESTITUTION

Article 185(1) cp provides that every crime gives rise to an obligation of restitution in accordance with the civil law. Restitution in this context is not only the restitution of the ill-gotten gain but also so-called *restitutio in integrum*, that is, the reinstatement of the situation that existed prior to the crime. The obligation, obviously, arises only in those cases in which a restitution in the above sense is naturally and legally possible.

C. DAMAGES

Article 185(2) cp provides that every crime which causes either a patrimonial or a non-patrimonial damage renders the party at fault, or the persons responsible for him, liable in damages. Patrimonial damages comprise the injury of a patrimonial interest and include both consequential damages and loss of profit. Non-patrimonial damages, sometimes also referred to as moral damages, comprise physical and psychological pain, e g pain, suffering, distress, resentment, and anguish. It is controversial whether non-patrimonial damages are a civil or a criminal sanction. The general principle regarding non-patrimonial damages contained in A.2059 cc provides that liability for non-patrimonial damages arises only in the cases and in the forms defined by law. As the only instance of liability for non-patrimonial damages is that contained in A.185 cp, it can be said that the only compensatable non-patrimonial damages are those arising out of a crime. Because of this non-patrimonial damages have a dual nature: they are a civil sanction from the point of view of their content, i e they give rise to a pecuniary obligation, whilst they are a criminal sanction having regard to the fact that they only arise in the case of crimes. Both patrimonial and non-patrimonial damages must bear an immediate relationship with the criminal act, i e they must be connected by a strict causal relationship (see too A.1223 cc). The passive subject (debtor), or subject liable for the compensation, is the offender and where there are several offenders they are jointly and severally liable (A.187(2) cp). Moreover, if in the circumstances there is a civilly responsible party, he is jointly and severally liable with the offender. The active subject (creditor) is the so-called damaged party (*danneggiato*) who may be different to the passive subject of the crime, e g in a homicide the damaged party is the heir of the victim. Finally, the offender is also liable for the publication of the judgment convicting him where its publication is a means of repairing the non-patrimonial injury caused by the crime (Artt. 186 and 187 cp).

D. THE OBLIGATION OF CONVICTED PERSONS TO REIMBURSE THE STATE
FOR COSTS OF MAINTENANCE

According to A.188 cp a convicted person is liable, with all of his movable and immovable estate, to reimburse the Treasury for up to two-thirds of the real cost of his maintenance in penal institutions. However, this obligation does not extend to either the person civilly liable to pay the amend nor the heirs of the convicted person.

E. THE CIVIL OBLIGATION TO PAY THE AMEND

Article 196 cp imposes an obligation on the person who had the authority or supervision over the person convicted of a contravention to pay an amount equal to the pecuniary penalty or amend in the event of the insolvency of the convicted person. The prerequisite for such liability is the violation of a norm whose observance the person in authority should have ensured and for which, however, he is not personally answerable under the criminal law. Article 197 cp imposes a similar liability on legal persons (except for the State, provinces or communes) in relation to their representatives or administrators where the commission of a contravention by the latter concerns a violation of an obligation inherent in the office of the offender who, however, is unable because of insolvency to pay the amend. These two provisions do not contravene the principle of the personal nature of criminal sanctions as the obligation to pay an amend is not a penal sanction but a mere civil guarantee for the performance of a penal obligation; the liability in the case of both Artt. 196 and 197 cp arises only in the case of the insolvency of the convicted person and is therefore only a secondary liability.

F. THE EXTINGUISHMENT AND GUARANTEE OF CIVIL LIABILITY

Article 198 cp provides that the extinguishment of the crime, or of its penalty, does not extinguish the civil obligations arising out of the crime except for the civil obligation to pay the amend contained in Artt. 196 and 197 cp. The logic of A.198 cp is clear: the extinguishment of the crime or penalty eliminates criminal illegality, but not any other form of illegality. However, as the civil obligation to pay the amend is a guarantee for the criminal liability, it follows that it too must be extinguished because the object of the obligation which is guaranteed disappears.

Articles 189 and 195 cp contain a series of provisions aimed at ensuring performance by the accused of his civil obligations. These include an *ipso iure* mortgage in favour of the State over the assets of the accused and the civilly responsible party to secure the obligations defined in A.189 cp; conservative sequestration of the movable assets of the accused to guarantee performance of the *ipso iure* mortgage where there is a founded reason to fear that the property will not be available; security which may be given by the accused to avoid the mortgage or sequestration; and penal revocatory actions which are available to set aside gratuitous or onerous dispositions of property which are alleged to have been carried out to defraud the creditors.

Administrative criminal law

This is a comparatively modern notion connected with the problem of decriminalisation. The broad category of punitive law does not only include the criminal law in a strict sense but also administrative punitive law, now generally called administrative criminal law, which designates those administrative norms having sanctions of a punitive nature. Administrative criminal law must, however, be kept distinct from administrative preventive measures as well as administrative disciplinary law. Administrative criminal law has become increasingly important as it has recently been extensively utilised by State and regional legislation which often either impose administrative sanctions ab initio or utilises them in the so-called decriminalisation process. This kind of sanction has become the modern answer to those punitive requirements of the law that cannot be appropriately resolved by the application of the criminal law and the criminal process.

With the passage from a police State to the rule of law after the fall of fascism, there was an extensive transformation of administrative illegalities into crimes, generally contraventions, with the object that they would then become subject to the guarantees of the criminal process. This, together with the propensity of the legislature to attach criminal penalties to its norms, had led to such an increase in the number of crimes so as to suffocate the criminal law and its administration. There are two solutions to such an abnormal situation. First, the simplification of the substantive and procedural provisions relating to contraventions, although this solution remains wholly within the sphere of the criminal law itself. This has been the French solution where, ever since the Revolution, decriminalisation has been refuted for the fear that it would endanger the rights and guarantees of the citizen. This solution therefore leads to a widening of the sphere of contraventions. Second, decriminalisation, that is, the downgrading of criminal illegalities into administrative illegalities, thereby reversing the criminalisation process initiated at the end of the eighteenth century, and at the same time improving the guarantees and procedures of the administrative process. This has been the solution adopted by Germany, Austria, Switzerland, and, recently, Italy which has introduced a series of decriminalising laws, the latest being the law of 24 November 1981 n.689.

The generally felt need for the rationalisation and organic discipline of the substantive and procedural aspects of administrative illegalities has led to a kind of general theory of administrative punitive law which has, to a certain extent, already been codified by German and Italian legislation. The subject, generally neglected by administrative and criminal writers alike, has recently formed an area of separate study within the criminal law. In fact, and particularly in the case of the decriminalising administrative legislation, the structure and regulation of criminal and administrative sanctions have converged; depending upon the extent of the particular legislation, the administrative criminal norm increasingly resembles the criminal model. This is evident, for example, in the case of the 1981 decriminalising legislation which provides for the 'administrative sanction of the payment of a sum of money'. Administrative criminal law, like the criminal law, has come to centre on the principle of legality which comprises three underlying principles: the exclusiveness of legislation as the source of administrative criminal law, the so-called 'legislative reserve'; the non-retroactivity of law; and the exhaustive definition of illicit situations which means, in effect, the statutory definition of the elements of an administrative wrong and the prohibition against any extension of the law by analogy where this operates to the disadvantage of the offender.

Two major problems have been identified with respect to administrative illegalities: first, the determination of the criteria with which to distinguish between criminal and administrative illegalities; a matter which is also important in guiding future decriminalisation programmes. The Italian tendency, at least until 1981, has been to primarily utilise the external criterion of the patrimonial nature of the sanction imposed for the crime to be decriminalised. However, this approach risks downgrading behaviour which endangers the primary assets of 'life' and 'physical safety', e g motor vehicle accidents. In particular, whilst the law of 3 May 1967 n.317 expressly defined the crimes to be decriminalised, the law of 24 December 1975 n.706 took a more general approach by decriminalising all contraventions punishable by amend only, except for those contained in the Criminal Code and those relating to the following subjects: labour, health, environment, construction, and drugs. The legislation of 24 November 1981 n.689 extended the decriminalisation to delicts punishable by fine except for those contained in the Criminal Code and, because of their social or ideological importance, those contained in certain pieces of special legislation dealing with abortion, weapons, pollution, the peaceful use of nuclear energy, town planning and construction, foodstuffs, worker safety, and electoral matters.

The second problem concerning administrative offences has been that of defining their structure. The gradual tendency towards affirming the same elements as a contravention (legality-typicality and blameworthiness), necessitated by constitutional and guarantistic requirements, has been expressly confirmed and codified by the 1981 legislation. In particular, an administrative offence incorporates both the objective and subjective element of a contravention. The 1981 legislation, moreover, by expressly incorporating the formula contained in A.42 cp concerning the subjective element of a contravention, has eliminated any possibility of administrative criminal norms giving rise to a strict liability. However, unlike the criminal law, punishability in the case of criminal administrative law is based solely upon the responsibility of the offender (that is, the capacity to understand and intend) and *not* also on the propensity to commit offences.

In relation to the question of sanctions, the doctrine has had to face a dual problem. First, that of the types of administrative sanctions. The 1981 legislation provides for two types of sanction. The first is the administrative pecuniary penalty, ranging from Lit. 4,000 to Lit. 20,000. This range is only applicable to offences originally created as administrative offences. In the case of decriminalised offences, where the decriminalisation is general the legislation usually applies the amounts of the original amend or fine, and where crimes are specifically decriminalised the legislation generally defines afresh the amount of the pecuniary penalty. An unsatisfied administrative pecuniary penalty, unlike a criminal penalty, cannot be converted into a detentive penalty nor can it produce any other criminal effect. The other category of sanctions envisaged by the 1981 legislation is accessory administrative sanctions such as confiscation.

In determining the size of a pecuniary penalty and the applicability of the accessory penalties, the 1981 legislation provides that the following factors must be taken into account: the seriousness of the offence; any act of the offender taken in an attempt to eliminate or attenuate the consequences of the offence; the character of the offender; and the offender's economic conditions. In the case of pecuniary sanctions, the interested party may apply to pay by instalments. There is, moreover, a prescriptive period of five years from the date of the commission of the offence for the collection of any pecuniary penalty. The 1981 legislation also introduced a civil obligation for the administrative pecuniary sanction (already provided for in the 1967 and 1975 legislation but more limited in scope) which makes the following persons jointly and severally liable with the offender: the owner, usufructuary or other person entitled to the enjoyment of the thing used to commit the violation, unless the thing was used against their will; the person having the authority, supervision, or direction over an offender incapable of understanding or intending his act, unless the act could not, in any event, have been avoided; and any legal person, entity or entrepreneur where the offence is committed by one of its dependents or representatives in connection with their duties. Unlike the civil obligation for a criminal pecuniary penalty, the civil obligation for an administrative pecuniary penalty is not a secondary but a primary and joint and several liability. By affirming, finally, that the obligation to pay does not devolve upon the heirs of the offender, the legislation adheres to the principle of personal responsibility characteristic of the criminal law.

The second problem concerning sanctions arises because the same fact may constitute both a criminal and an administrative offence and there is therefore a need to avoid that the same behaviour can be prosecuted under both branches of the law where these have the same punitive objectives. Where the criminal and administrative norms are heterogeneous, in the sense that their respective sanctions have a different objective (e g punitive and compensatory), both norms are applicable because neither of them alone totally vindicates the negative aspects of the act which is prohibited by the norms. Where the criminal and administrative norms are of a homogeneous nature, there is a direct conflict with the general principle that no one may be punished more than once for the same fact. However, the problem is resolved through normal interpretative principles, and foremost, the principle that the more particular norm prevails over a more general one. The approach specifically adopted by the 1981 legislation is based on three propositions: first, the applicability of the more specific norm, irrespective of whether it is the criminal or administrative one; second, and as an exception to the first proposition, the priority of criminal norms vis-à-vis concurrent administrative norms of the Regions and the autonomous provinces of Trento and Bolzano, unless the criminal norm is only applicable in the absence of other provisions in which case the administrative norm is exclusively applicable; and third, the priority of certain general criminal norms in the subject of foodstuffs.

Part III
Private law

Chapter 8

Civil law

The content of the private law

The private law is that complex of norms which regulate the relationships between private citizens. It comprises civil and commercial law. Unlike most countries belonging to the Romano-Germanic system of laws, civil and commercial law are today, in Italy, dealt with by a single Code: the 1942 Civil Code which became effective on 21 April 1942 and replaced the hitherto separate regulation of civil and commercial law by the 1865 Civil Code and the 1882 Commercial Code respectively. The 1942 Code is technical in nature rather than doctrinal. It consists of an Introductory Part and six Books. The Introductory Part comprises 31 articles and is entitled General Provisions on the Law (the so-called 'preliminary provisions of the Civil Code'). It deals with the sources of law and the law's spatial and temporal efficacy (see ch 3, above). The First Book (Artt. 1–455) deals with persons and domestic relations; the Second Book (Artt. 456–809) with succession and gratuitous inter vivos transactions; the Third Book (Artt. 810–1172) with ownership, possession and other real rights; the Fourth Book (Artt. 1173–2059) with obligations; the Fifth Book (Artt. 2060–2642) with labour relations and associations; and the Sixth Book (Artt. 2643–2969) with the protection of rights.

Persons

Legal subjects, in Italian law, are of three types: natural persons, legal persons, and de facto entities.

A. NATURAL PERSONS AND THEIR CAPACITY

Every human being is a legal subject capable of both holding and exercising legal rights and duties. Moreover, every natural person is the holder of a series of status' or legal qualities which concern the individual per se (*status personae*), his appurtenance to a family (*status familiae*), and his appurtenance to the State (*status civitatis*), the combination of which go to constitute his personality. However, the question of the status of a person is usually connected with that of his legal capacity and his capacity to act. Legal capacity is the ability to be a holder of rights and duties and is always acquired at birth. Exceptionally, the law, through its rules on the remoteness of vesting, grants a limited capacity to persons who are either not yet conceived or conceived but not yet born. The former class concerns gifts to the children of persons who are living at the date of the death of the testator or at the date of the gift inter vivos, whichever is relevant (Artt. 462(3) and 784 cc). The latter class receives a more definite protection in both the criminal and civil law, e g through the crime of abortion and the capacity to receive in a succession. In various situations the legal capacity of natural persons is subject to certain limitations depending upon age, sex, health, and criminal conviction.

Legal capacity is extinguished at death upon which all personal rights and certain property rights (e g usufruct) are also extinguished and the succession to the deceased is 'opened'. Where more than one person dies in a situation in which the order of deaths cannot be ascertained, there is a rebuttable presumption that the deaths occurred at the same instant (A.4 cc). Where, however, the death or existence of a person is uncertain, the consequences vary depending upon which of three institutions are applicable. First, disappearance which arises where a person leaves his last domicile or residence and his whereabouts are unknown. The legal consequences of a 'disappearance' are that the subject can no longer acquire rights by inheritance or otherwise and that a curator may be appointed to preserve his patrimony. However, a declaration of disappearance does *not* modify the legal position of the subject. Second, absence whose declaration may be sought where the absent subject has been unheard of for a period of two years. An application for such a declaration may be brought by any person who would have a right in the property of the absent subject upon the death of the latter. Such a declaration does not affect personal rights, e g it does not dissolve a marriage, but only patrimonial rights which, however, are only temporarily affected, e g the temporary possession and administration of property by the absent person's heirs and the temporary exoneration from performing obligations. This state of affairs comes to an end by proof of death, a declaration of presumed death, or proof that the absent person is alive. Third, presumption of death which may be declared in the following cases: where the subject has been unheard of for ten years; where the disappearance was connected with an event which makes it probable that the subject is dead; or where the disappearance was connected with the politico-military situation which existed between 1940 and 1945. The declaration gives rise to the same effects as in a situation of ascertained death and therefore affects both patrimonial and personal rights. If the subject is subsequently found to be alive, the effects of the declaration will cease with the consequences that the subject regains his property, although in the state in which he finds it, and any marriage contracted by his spouse subsequent to his disappearance becomes invalid.

Whilst legal capacity confers an abstract capacity to hold rights and duties, the capacity to act is the capacity of the subject to autonomously determine his own legal position. The capacity to act assumes that the subject is capable of administering his own affairs and enables him to give effect to a legal transaction without the concurrence of any other subject. The capacity to act is generally acquired at the age of 18 and endures until death. A limited capacity to act may arise in the case of a person under the age of 18 through his emancipation by reason of marriage. A person over the age of 18 may find that his capacity to act may be either totally or partially restricted as a result of certain circumstances which affect his capacity.

Emancipation arises where a minor over the age of 16 has, with the appropriate permission, contracted marriage. The principal effects of emancipation are first, the substitution of parental authority with the authority of a curator who may even be the other spouse if the latter is over the age of 18; and second, the acquisition of the capacity to act which, however, is restricted to acts of ordinary administration. If, moreover, the *Tribunale* authorises an emancipated minor to conduct a commercial enterprise, he acquires a total capacity in patrimonial matters except in relation to gifts inter vivos.

There are four institutions for the protection of incapable persons over the age of 18. First, judicial interdiction (Artt. 414ff cc) which is a judicial declaration to the effect that a person who is suffering from a *permanent* infirmity of the mind is incapable of administering his own affairs. It results first, in a total incapacity to act in transactions of either a patrimonial or a personal nature and second, the appointment of a tutor. Any transaction entered into by an interdict may be avoided at the instance of the tutor, the interdict himself, or any heir or other person who has a right through the interdict without having to prove the infirmity of the mind in the instant case. The interdiction may be either revoked or transformed into so-called disability.

Second, disability which is a partial incapacity which is not serious enough to give rise to interdiction. It results in a limited capacity analogous to that of an emancipated minor, that is, the incapable may autonomously perform acts of ordinary administration but he requires the authorisation of the protective judge and the consensus of his curator for acts of extraordinary administration or the authorisation of the *Tribunale* and the intervention of the curator in the case of those transactions defined in A.375 cc. Any act which does not comply with the appropriate formalities is voidable at the instance of the incapable, his heirs or any person having a right through him.

Third, legislative interdiction which is an anomalous institution as, rather than having the object of protecting the subject, it is an accessory punishment consequent upon a criminal conviction of imprisonment for a period of not less than five years (A.32 cp). This form of incapacity, however, is limited to transactions of a patrimonial nature which are voidable at the instance of any interested party.

Fourth, natural or de facto incapacity (A.428 cc) which is the inability of a normally capable subject to freely understand and intend his act at the point of its execution as a result of any cause whatsoever, even if only of a transitory nature. Unlike the cases of legal incapacity examined so far, natural incapacity is not presumed *ipso iure* but must be shown to exist in the individual case. Such acts are *voidable* at any time within five years of the execution of the act. However, in order to balance the interests of the incapable person with those of any other party dealing with him, the following rules apply: in the case of a unilateral act, the act is voidable whenever it is prejudicial to the incapable; in the case of a contract, its invalidity depends upon the existence of both a prejudice to the incapable and bad faith on the part of the other contracting party; and in the case of a marriage, will or gift inter vivos, the proof of natural incapacity is sufficient per se to invalidate the transaction.

B. ABODE, RESIDENCE AND DOMICILE OF PERSONS

The legal location of persons has several important consequences in Italian law which utilises three different concepts for this purpose. First, abode (*dimora*) which is the place where a subject occasionally resides. It is legally irrelevant except for the service of certain documents where the residence of the subject is unknown (A.139 cpc). Second, residence (*residenza*) which describes the effective and habitual location of a person. Residence may be freely selected and changed, although it *must* be declared in the manner prescribed by law. A person, moreover, may have more than one residence if he habitually resides in more than one place. Residence is relevant in relation to the publication of notices, the celebration of marriages, and adoptions. Third, domicile which is the principal location of a person's affairs and interests (A.43 cc). Domicile is deduced from both objective and subjective elements: the former concerns the location of the principal economic interests of the subject and the latter comprises the intent of the subject to set up the centre of his affairs in a given location. Domicile, unlike the concepts of abode and residence, is concerned with the economic and social activities of a person; the domicile of a subject need not, in fact, correspond with the place in which he lives. A subject may only have *one* domicile which is relevant to matters such as succession (A.456 cc), and the bankruptcy of entrepreneurs (A.9 of the Bankruptcy Law). The notion of domicile corresponds to the seat of a legal person.

C. LEGAL PERSONS AND THEIR CAPACITY

Legal personality has two basic advantages: first, patrimonial autonomy as a result of which the property of the legal entity is distinct from that of its members and second, the limited liability of members so that the members of a legal entity are not liable for the latter's debts and vice versa. Legal persons may be divided into corporations and institutions (see ch 1, p 25, above). The constituent elements of a corporation are a plurality of members (at least two) and a common object which must be determinable and lawful. The patrimony of the entity, although necessary because it is expressly required by law (A.33 cc), is not a constituent element of a corporation but only a means of achieving its object. The constituent elements of an institution, on the other hand, are a patrimony and an object which is determinable and lawful. In the case of either type of legal person, the acquisition of legal personality requires a further formal element: State recognition which may be of three types. First, express or 'by concession' which is the general case and is granted by decree. Second, normative or general which is exceptional and applicable to commercial companies only. According to this form of recognition, legal personality is automatically acquired upon entry of the entity on the register of enterprises. Third, by registration which is the form specified by the Constitution (A.39) for the recognition of industrial unions, although this provision has not yet been implemented.

Legal persons have a limited legal capacity, both in relation to personal and patrimonial transactions. In relation to the former, legal persons, because of their particular nature, exceptionally enjoy personal rights, e g they have a right to a name but not to any rights of a domestic or family nature. In relation to patrimonial rights, the principal limitation arises from the need for a governmental authority (A.17 cc) in relation to the acquisition of immovables, whether for value or not, the acceptance of an inheritance, and the receipt of legacies. The purpose of this provision is to provide a means for the prevention of an excessive accumulation of property by legal persons and the consequent removal of property from the market. The same purpose lies behind A.979 cc which limits an usufruct in favour of a legal person to a maximum duration of 30 years.

Legal persons manifest their intent and enter into legal relations with other subjects through their administrators who, together with the assembly of members, which is the deliberative organ, constitute the two fundamental organs of legal persons. The seat of a legal person is where it carries out its principal activites and must be specified both in its constitution and in the registry of legal persons. The fundamental affairs of a legal person must be publicised by the administrators through the lodgment of certain documents in the appropriate registry located at the *Tribunale* of the relevant provincial capital. This publicity has the object of keeping third parties who are about to enter into legal relations with the legal entity informed about the affairs of the latter. The failure to publicise a relevant matter in the registry results first, in the criminal liability of the administrators, second, a joint and several liability of the administrators with the legal entity for the obligations assumed by the latter, and finally, the inability to raise notice of the matter against a third party who was not otherwise aware of it.

A legal person ceases to exist either for a cause contained in its constitution (e g a time limit) or because of the supervening impossibility or fulfilment of its object. In addition, an association may be extinguished because of a fall in the requisite membership or on the motion of its assembly or the government. Moreover, the winding-up of any type of legal person also requires a governmental authority which may be sought at the instance of either an interested person or the government itself. This leads to the liquidation of the legal person whose assets are distributed in accordance with the provisions contained in its constitution or, in the absence of such provisions, to an entity with analogous objects.

Family law

A. INTRODUCTION

Family law concerns the status of the individual members of the family and the relationships between them. It differs from the other areas of private law for two reasons: first, because it is concerned with the collective interest of the family unit rather than the interests of individual members; and second, because it is regulated by many provisions which cannot be varied by agreement, thereby imposing a limit upon the freedom of contract characteristic of the private law. This area of the law has undergone certain major changes. First, through the introduction of divorce by the law of 1 December 1970 n.898 which provoked so much controversy as to culminate in a popular referendum in 1974 that confirmed the new legislation by a large majority. Second, the law of 19 May 1975 n.151 which significantly reformed family law through the application of the constitutional principle of the legal equality between spouses (A.29 C). The 1975 reforms introduced a complete legal parity between spouses, gave natural children the same rights on succession as legitimate children, gave the judiciary (through the *Pretore* and the Minors' Court) an active role in family matters, introduced the community of property between spouses, replaced paternal authority with parental authority, and gave the surviving spouse absolute property rights on succession rather than the previous mere rights in usufruct.

B. MARRIAGE

(*i*) *General.* The first Civil 'Code of united Italy (1865) completely secularised marriage so that a civil marriage only produced any legal effects. Since the majority of the population, by reason of both religious conviction and a long tradition, continued to remain faithful to the religious form of marriage, the majority of Italians celebrated marriage in both the religious and civil forms. This position endured until 1929 when, as a result of the Concordat between Italy and the Holy See of 11 February 1929, introduced into municipal law by the law of 27 May 1929 n.810, the religious marriage was no longer legally irrelevant but, subject to certain conditions, produced civil effects. Therefore the present position, not in substance affected by the 1984 Concordat, is that there are three types of marriage: the civil marriage celebrated before State Officials, the concordat marriage celebrated before a Catholic priest and then transcribed in the civil registry, and marriages celebrated before non-Catholic ministers although these are, in practice, regarded as normal civil marriages.

(*ii*) *The applicable law.* Whilst civil marriages are totally regulated by the provisions of the Civil Code, in the case of concordat marriages it is necessary to distinguish between the marriage act and the matrimonial relationship. The marriage act, viz, its celebration and validity, is subject to canon law but, to produce civil effects, first, the marriage must, as it always had to do, satisfy certain formal requisites of the civil law, e g the publication of the marriage according to the forms of the civil law, the reading of certain provisions in the Civil Code during the marriage ceremony and the transmission of the documentation to the Civil Registry for registration, and second, although the substantive validity of the Catholic marriage is, under the 1929 Concordat, exclusively subject to canon law, when the 1984 Concordat becomes operative the Catholic marriage must also comply with certain substantive requisites of the civil law, e g in relation to the capacity to contract marriage and the impediments to a valid marriage (see ch 4, p 123, above). Moreover, although the 1984 Concordat preserves the exclusive jurisdiction of the Ecclesiastical Courts over the nullity of Catholic marriages, the 1984 Concordat, confirming an already established practice, provides that the judgments of the Ecclesiastical Courts may only be recognised in the civil law after their subjection to the same procedure as that for the recognition of foreign judgments. The matrimonial relationship is exclusively subject to the Civil Code which regulates the rights and duties arising out of the marriage, separation, and the dissolution of marriage (divorce). The choice between a civil or a concordat marriage is of considerable practical importance because of the various conditions necessary for the substantive validity of the marriage: as the conditions are substantially greater in the case of religious marriages it makes a declaration of nullity available in a larger number of cases. If the parties to the marriage are non-Catholic, the Registry may, upon request, consent to the marriage being celebrated before a minister of that religion. However, in contrast to Catholic marriages, they are wholly regulated by the Civil Code. The remainder of the section on family law shall be concerned with the civil marriage only.

(iii) Promise of marriage. A promise of marriage has, in Italian law, little relevance. It does not oblige the parties to contract the marriage nor to perform any penalty stipulated by the agreement in the event of its breach. However, a promise of marriage is not totally without effect. A party may, within one year of a refusal by the opposite party to celebrate the marriage, request the restitution of gifts made as a consequence of the promise of marriage. Moreover, the party who unjustly (that is, without cause) refuses to contract the marriage is liable in damages for the expenses and obligations assumed by the opposite party in contemplation of the marriage.

(iv) The conditions of marriage. There are several 'impediments' to the celebration of a valid marriage. First, a minimum age of 18 which, however, may be reduced to 16 by the Minors' Court in serious cases. Second, mental capacity as a result of which judicial interdicts cannot contract marriage. Third, the absence of an existing marriage. Fourth, the absence of certain relationships, whether by blood or affinity, between the intending spouses, that is, the so-called prohibited degrees (A.87 cc). Fifth, the absence of certain relationships arising from an adoption or affiliation. Sixth, the absence of the so-called 'criminal impediment' according to which marriage is prohibited between a person convicted of homicide or attempted homicide and the spouse of the victim. And finally, the lapse of 300 days from the cessation of a prior marriage in the case of a woman who desires to re-marry. This last condition aims at avoiding the birth, during a subsequent marriage, of children belonging to an earlier marriage. The presence of an impediment renders the marriage either voidable or merely irregular although the *Tribunale* may dispense with compliance with certain of the impediments listed above.

(v) Celebration of marriage. The necessary formalities for the valid celebration of a marriage include first, the affixing of a notice (giving the general details of the parties who intend to contract the marriage and an indication of the place where the marriage is to take place) for a period of eight days in the town hall of the commune where the parties

have their residence and second, the celebration of the marriage by a State functionary in the presence of two witnesses (A.107 cc). The law exceptionally allows marriage by proxy, namely, where one of the parties resides abroad or in times of war (A.111 cc).

(vi) Nullity of marriage. The Civil Code deals with the invalidity of marriages under the head of 'nullity', which is an imprecise term as invalid marriages also include those which are merely voidable. The various forms of invalidity (see ch 1, p 35, above) are: first, non-existence, e g a marriage between two persons of the same sex; second, nullity, e g where there is the absence of the requisite celebration or declaration of intent; and third, voidability which may be either absolute or relative. Absolute voidability refers to those marriages which can be annulled at the instance of *any* interested party, namely, in the case of marriages which are voidable for reasons of prior marriage, prohibited degrees, and criminal impediment. Relative voidability, on the other hand, refers to those marriages which may be annulled at the instance of defined persons only, that is, in the case of marriages voidable because of age, interdiction for infirmity of the mind, natural incapacity at the date of the marriage, lack of consent as a result of moral violence, lack of consent as a result of an error as to either the identity of the other spouse (which can only arise in proxy marriages) or his personal characteristics (A.122 cc), permanent impotence which predated the marriage, and simulation which is a pre-marital agreement not to perform the rights and obligations arising out of the marriage.

(vii) The putative marriage. The annulment of a marriage operates retrospectively to eliminate all of its effects. This would also mean, therefore, that any children of the union would become illegitimate. However, the Code has mitigated the effects of a void marriage according to the bona fides of the parties. Where both parties contracted the marriage in good faith or its celebration was the result of violence or threats by other than a party to the marriage, its annulment does not have any retrospective effect. If only one spouse acted bona fide, the retrospective effect of the annulment does not affect the bona fide spouse nor the children born to the marriage. Finally, where both parties to the marriage acted in bad faith, the marriage nonetheless produces the effects of a valid marriage vis-à-vis any children born or conceived during the union unless the nullity arises out of bigamy or incest. In the case of a putative marriage the court may order that either spouse make periodical payments to the other for a period of not more than three years where the latter does not have an independent income and does not contract a new marriage. Moreover, a spouse who acted in

good faith is entitled to receive from the other spouse (or a third party) who is held responsible for the nullity, an indemnity equivalent to maintenance for at least three years.

C. THE EFFECTS OF MARRIAGE AS BETWEEN THE SPOUSES

Article 29(2) C provides that marriage is based upon the moral and legal equality of the spouses, subject to the limitations necessary for the preservation of family unity. The Civil Code, through the 1975 reforms, gives effect to the constitutional precept by removing the husband as the head of the family and attributing equal rights and duties to both spouses. They together decide and give effect to family policy and, subject to their separate needs, together determine the family residence. In the case of disagreement, either spouse may approach the court which, on hearing the parties and any children over the age of 16 cohabiting with the parties, seeks to reach a compromise solution. If a compromise is not possible, the court may make a definitive decision by adopting that solution which it considers most appropriate to the preservation of the family unit. Judicial intervention in such disputes has been justified because of the need to reconcile the equality of the spouses with the concept of family unity. It follows from the principle of equality that the spouses have reciprocal rights and duties which are: fidelity, moral and material assistance, collaboration in the interests of the family, and cohabitation. A further consequence of marriage is that the wife adds her husband's surname to her own and retains it until re-marriage unless the parties divorce whereupon the wife is not entitled to retain her ex-husband's surname.

D. SEPARATION

The reciprocal duties incumbent upon the spouses are attenuated in the case of separation. The obligations of cohabitation and fidelity cease and that of assistance retains a purely economic aspect in the form of periodical maintenance payments which are to be made to a spouse left without an independent income (A.156 cc). Separation may be either judicial or consensual.

Judicial separation is granted at the request of one of the spouses where supervening factors, even if independent of the violation of one or both spouses, are such as to render cohabitation either intolerable or injurious to the education of the children (A.151(1) cc). In making an order for separation the court may, upon request, declare which party is at fault having regard to the violation of the duties inherent in marriage. The party at fault is not entitled to maintenance but only to alimental support. The court, when making an order for separation, also decides which spouse is to have the custody of the children, the extent to which the other spouse must provide for their maintenance, and which spouse is to remain in the family home (A.155 cc). The custody of the children is exclusively determined according to their moral and material interests and, therefore, the issue of which spouse is at fault for the separation is irrelevant to the question of custody. The spouse who is given custody has the exclusive parental authority over the children, although major decisions must still be taken by both spouses.

Consensual separation, on the other hand, is that separation mutually agreed amongst the parties, who may also determine the issues of custody and the maintenance of the children or either spouse. The agreement becomes effective upon confirmation by the *Tribunale* which may require any modifications necessitated in the interests of the children. Consensual separation, like judicial separation, comes to an end either by formal agreement or by implied reconciliation through the resumption of cohabitation.

E. THE DISSOLUTION OF MARRIAGE

A marriage is dissolved either by the death of a party to the marriage or by divorce. Divorce not only determines a civil marriage but also the civil effects of a religious marriage (A.149 cc). Dissolution relates to the marriage relationship and therefore produces its effects as from the moment at which the cause of the dissolution occurs (i e from the date of death or the date of notation of a divorce in the civil registry). It differs to a declaration of nullity which relates to the validity of the marriage and therefore eliminates *ab initio* all of the effects of the marriage (except for the effects of a putative marriage, including the status of any children to the union: see p 323, above).

There are four principal grounds upon which divorce may be granted. First, separation, whether judicial or consensual, for five years but increased to six years where the opposite party in the case of a consensual separation opposes the divorce and seven years where the party seeking the divorce was held to be at fault for the separation. Where both parties to the separation were held to be at fault, the period remains at five years. Second, conviction of the respondent spouse for either certain defined crimes or an intentional delict which carries a penalty of more than 15 years imprisonment, even if the crime in question was committed prior to the marriage. Third, non-consummation of the marriage. And finally, where the other spouse, who is a foreign national, has obtained a foreign annulment or dissolution of marriage and has contracted a new marriage abroad. In every case the court must first attempt to reconcile the parties and, moreover, be satisfied that the 'spiritual and material communion between the spouses can no longer be maintained or re-established'. In practice, the impossibility of re-establishing the 'communion' between the parties is the automatic consequence of an unsuccessful attempt at reconciliation.

The court, on pronouncing a divorce, also determines which party is to have the custody of any children (determined according to the children's 'moral and material interests') and the extent to which the other spouse must provide for their maintenance. The court may also order that either spouse make periodical payments to the other. These payments, however, will cease upon the re-marriage of the spouse receiving them. The court utilises three criteria in determining both whether to order such payments and, if so, their quantum: the economic conditions of the spouses (or assistance element), the reasons which led to the dissolution (or punitive element) and the personal and economic contributions of each spouse to the running of the family and the formation of the family patrimony (or compensation element). Where there is a risk that the debtor will not fulfill the obligation to assist and maintain either or both the spouse and children, the court may order an appropriate form of security, including a mortgage. A usual measure is an order for the direct payment of a share of income or salary to the obligee. The court, finally, may review the custody and financial arrangements in the event of any supervening circumstances.

The death of the obligor in the above circumstances has never substantially affected the rights of the children who have always been entitled to certain guaranteed rights on succession. However, the rights of a surviving divorcee to the deceased's pension and other periodical allowances were much more tenuous and it was only through certain amendments introduced in 1978 that these rights have been better regulated and protected.

F. THE PROPERTY REGIME BETWEEN SPOUSES

The normal property regime, which applies automatically by operation of law, between husband and wife is that of the communion of property, yet another manifestation of the principle of equality applicable to the marriage relationship. Although the parties to a marriage remain free to adopt a different property regime, such as the separation of property, unless such an agreement is made, the communion of property automatically applies.

Four broad categories of property fall into the communion. First, all joint and several acquisitions made during the marriage. This does not include property acquired by the spouses prior to their marriage nor personal property which includes property acquired after the marriage by gift or succession, property of a strict personal nature, property used in the practise of a profession, property in the form of compensation for damages, and property acquired with the proceeds of sale of personal property, or its exchange, provided that this is expressly declared in the instrument of acquisition. Second, the fruits of the personal property of each spouse received during the marriage or communion and unconsumed as at the date of the dissolution of the communion. Third, the proceeds of the separate activities of the spouses received during the marriage or communion and unconsumed as at the date of the dissolution of the communion. Finally, any business established during the marriage and managed by both spouses. It is apparent from these categories that three patrimonial masses may be identified. First, the actual communion, viz, the assets which go to form part of the communion during the marriage (the first and fourth classes described above). Second, the potential communion which comprises so much of the fruits and proceeds referred to in the second and third classes described above as remain in existence as at the date of the dissolution of the communion. This is sometimes also called the residual communion. Finally, the personal patrimony which does not form part of the communion.

Although the ordinary administration of the assets falling into the communion may be exercised severally by each spouse, their extraordinary administration must be exercised jointly (A.180 cc). In the case of any disagreement between the spouses, either of them may approach the court (A.181 cc). Where an act is performed without the necessary consent of the other spouse, the act is voidable at the instance of the latter within one year of the knowledge of such act but this remedy is limited to transactions concerning immovables or registrable movables. In the case of all other movables, the transaction remains valid although the spouse who acted without authority must compensate the common mass (A.184 cc). The regulation of the subject represents a compromise between two conflicting objects: the prevention of one spouse performing acts of extraordinary administration without the knowledge of the other and the security of title in the circulation of property.

The rationale behind the establishment of the communion of property was the maintenance of the family and the instruction and education of the children; in other words, the collective interest of the family takes precedence over the individual interests of its members. This object is guaranteed through a limited protection of the common fund from creditors. The Code distinguishes, for this purpose, between two sets of creditors: first, creditors whose rights arose from obligations which were either entered into in the interests of the family or connected with the administration of the common property; and second, the personal creditors of the individual spouses. The first set of creditors may satisfy themselves from the common fund (A.186 cc). However, once it is exhausted they may proceed against the personal assets of each spouse for half of the debt (A.190 cc). This gives rise, in substance, to a limited responsibility in each spouse where the other spouse has no personal assets. The second set of creditors, or personal creditors, must first proceed against the personal assets of the debtor spouse and only if these assets are insufficient they may proceed (but always after the debtors of the communion) against the share of the debtor in the communion (A.189(2) cc).

The communion between the spouses is dissolved, giving rise to an equal division of the assets (A.194 cc), in the following cases: the annulment of the marriage; the dissolution of the marriage through either the death of one of the spouses (including cases of absence and presumed death) or divorce; the separation of the spouses; an agreement to convert to the separation of property; the separation of property pursuant to a court order made at the instance of one of the spouses on the grounds set out in A.193 cc (e g the interdiction, natural incapacity, or maladministration of a spouse); and the bankruptcy of one of the spouses (A.191 cc). It ought to be noted that in the case of the death of one of the spouses, the surviving spouse not only takes half of the community as a result of its dissolution but also the relevant share by succession in the deceased's half of the community.

Where the spouses have elected, at the date of the marriage or at any subsequent point of time, to adopt the separation of property, then each spouse retains both the exclusive title to any property acquired separately during the marriage and its exclusive enjoyment and administration subject, of course, to the general matrimonial obligation of assistance vis-à-vis the other spouse and the children. An election in favour of the separation of property may be declared either at the celebration of the marriage and annotated in the margin of the marriage documents or by notarised deed.

Apart from the communion or separation of property, the spouses may also adopt some atypical form of property regime, for instance, by expanding or restricting the property which forms part of the communion. Not only may the matrimonial property regime be stipulated at any time, but it may also be freely changed during the marriage, subject to the consent of all of the original parties to the agreement or their heirs (A.163 cc). The matrimonial property agreement is a contract and therefore subject to all of the requirements relating to contracts generally. It must, moreover, on the pain of nullity, be in the form of a notarised deed.

G. THE FAMILY ENTERPRISE

Another aspect of patrimonial family relations is the family enterprise, also introduced by the 1975 family law reforms. It is an enterprise in which certain relatives of the entrepreneur contribute a continuous service. This is not to say that the labour of the family must prevail over that of strangers (although the latter may only be employees and not partners) nor that the enterprise must necessarily be a small one. A family enterprise automatically comes into existence upon admission to the enterprise of even a single person amongst certain defined relatives of the entrepreneur (namely, the spouse, a blood relative of up to the third degree, or a relative by affinity of up to the second degree) and without the need for any written act or formality. The entrepreneur alone has the power and freedom to admit members of the family into the enterprise but once a member of the family participates in the enterprise he becomes entitled to a series of rights collectively known as participation rights. These rights, of an economic and administrative nature, comprise the following. First, a right to maintenance according to the patrimonial condition of the family. This right, therfore, also exists after the family member is not otherwise entitled to maintenance, e g a son over the age of majority. Second, a right to share in the profits according to the quantity and quality of work contributed to the enterprise. Third, a right to share, in the same proportion as above, in any property which is acquired with the retained profits of the enterprise. Fourth, a right to share, again in the same proportion, in the expansion of the firm as from the date of admission.

The members of the family who participate in the enterprise share in the profits and losses of the enterprise. In the case of a loss, the risk of participating family members is limited to first, the loss of remuneration and second, the loss of any rights which had accrued in the assets of the enterprise. Only the entrepreneur is personally liable for the debts of the enterprise and therefore subject to bankruptcy.

The entrepreneur is entitled to make all decisions concerning the ordinary management of the enterprise and the direction of employees, including family members. However, all decisions concerning the employment of the profits and capital gains of the enterprise, extraordinary administration and policy, and the winding-up of the enterprise require a majority decision of all participating family members. In the case of a dead-lock, the decision must be referred to the competent court.

A family member ceases to have membership of the family enterprise in the following cases: voluntary withdrawal, withdrawal for just cause, exclusion by the entrepreneur where the member is a negative element for the enterprise, and the loss of the 'status' of family member, e g because of divorce, nullity of marriage or separation of the spouses. In each case the entrepreneur must immediately liquidate the rights of the outgoing member. The family enterprise itself may cease because of the decision of the entrepreneur, the alienation of the business, the bankruptcy of the entrepreneur, or the death of the latter in which case the heirs succeed to the ownership of the business.

H. THE CONJUGAL ENTERPRISE

The involvement of the spouses in an enterprise as a consequence of the community of property has given rise to the institution of the so-called conjugal enterprise which arises in two situations. First, where an enterprise is formed after the marriage and is managed by both spouses. Second, where an enterprise was formed and belonged to one of the spouses prior to the marriage but is managed by both spouses after the marriage in which case, although the original owner remains its proprietor, both spouses are entitled to manage the enterprise and enjoy its profits which immediately form part of the communion. In both situations, the spouses are considered to be entrepreneurs and there is a de facto partnership. Where, on the other hand, the enterprise belonged to one of the spouses prior to the marriage and continues to be managed by that spouse alone after the marriage, the communion is limited to the proceeds of the enterprise in existence and unconsumed as at the date of the dissolution of the communion. In this situation the owner or manager only is an entrepreneur and there is no conjugal enterprise. It follows that the conjugal enterprise is made up exclusively of both spouses and must be kept distinct from the family enterprise which is characterised by the participation of family members other than the spouses.

I. FILIATION

A child may be legitimate, natural (as illegitimate children are known), incestuous, or adopted. A legitimate child is one conceived by parents who are united in wedlock. There are two presumptions concerning legitimacy. First, the rebuttable presumption of paternity, based upon the conjugal fidelity of the wife, according to which the law presumes that the husband is the father of any child born during the marriage. The husband may rebut the presumption and disown the child in the cases expressly defined by A.235 cc. The action must be brought within one year of the birth and, since the new family law, may also be brought by the mother or a third party. Second, the presumption of conception, that children born not before 180 days of the celebration of the marriage and not more than 300 days after its dissolution, annulment or cessation are irrebuttably presumed to have been conceived during the marriage and are therefore legitimate. However, a birth within 180 days of the marriage does not automatically give rise to illegitimacy which can only arise pursuant to a disavowal. Similarly, a child born more than 300 days after the cessation of the marriage may be considered legitimate if each spouse proves that it was conceived during the marriage. In any event, the child itself may bring an action to claim a legitimate status. The two presumptions are interdependent in that in the absence of one of them, the other alone is not sufficient to prove a legitimate status.

A legitimate status gives rise to certain reciprocal duties between parent and child. The parents have, first, an obligation, according to their material possibilities (A.148 cc), to maintain, instruct, and educate their children (A.147 cc) and second, the right to exercise their parental authority (or joint authority) over them. If a parent neglects his duties or abuses his authority to the prejudice of a child, the court may deprive that parent of any authority and order the removal of the child from the family residence. In the case of any disagreement between the parents on an important issue, either parent may appeal to the court which may also hear the child if he is over the age of 14. However, the father may, in the meantime, take any urgent and necessary measures. The court in such cases does not make an order but merely suggests a solution. If the conflict continues, the court attributes the power of decision to the parent it regards as best suited to care for the interests of the child. The parents also legally represent their minor children and as such may continue to run a commercial enterprise of which the minor is proprietor. The parents, furthermore, have a right of usufruct over their childrens' property, except for property acquired by the children with the proceeds of their own labour, but the fruits which the parents receive in this way must be utilised in the maintenance of the family and the instruction and education of the children (A.324 cc). The children must obey their parents and, if cohabiting with their family, contribute to the maintenance of the latter with any independent means and income (A.315 cc). The children cannot leave the family home without their parents' permission, in relation to which the parents may have recourse to the protective court.

A natural child is one born out of wedlock but recognised by one or both parents. There is a distinction between a recognisable natural child who is one born to either unmarried persons or persons who are already married but not to each other as at the date of conception and an unrecognisable natural child who is one born to persons within the prohibited degrees, though such child may nonetheless be recognised where either the parents were unaware of their relationship (although if one parent only was in good faith then that parent may recognise the child) or, where the relationship is one of affinity only, the marriage upon which that relationship depended has been declared null (A.251 cc).

Recognition is a declaration by one or both parents that a given person is his or their natural child whereupon the child acquires the status of 'natural' child. The recognition, which dates retrospectively from the birth, gives rise to lesser rights than in the case of legitimate status. The consequences of a recognition are as follows: first, recognition does not per se entitle the child to become part of the legitimate family of his parent. This may only arise pursuant to an order of the Minors' Court provided always that the order is not contrary to the interests of the minor and there is the consensus of the other spouse and any legitimate children over the age of 16. Second, the recognising parents have the same rights and duties over the child as in the case of a legitimate child. Third, the natural child has equal rights with the legitimate children on succession. Finally, the natural child does not acquire any relationship with the relatives of the recognising parent.

Where a child has not been recognised, the child may institute proceedings to have his maternity or paternity recognised. Where such action is not available, the child may, in any event, seek provision for his maintenance, instruction, and education and, notwithstanding that he may have attained his majority, aliment should he be in need of support (A.279 cc).

Finally, a recognised or an unrecognisable natural child may be legitimatised in one of two ways: first, by the subsequent marriage of his parents or second, by court order where there is the impossibility or a serious obstacle to the celebration of his parents' marriage (see A.284 cc).

J. ADOPTION

The common features of every type of adoption are that an adopted child takes the surname of the adopting parent who acquires parental authority over the child together with all of its concomitant rights and duties. The adopted child, has, moreover, in every case, the same rights of succession to the adopting parent as a legitimate child. In other respects, however, the effects of an adoption may vary depending upon its type. There are two types of adoption under Italian law: ordinary adoption, the traditional form, and special adoption, introduced by the law of 5 June 1967 n.431.

(i) Ordinary adoption. Under an ordinary adoption, the adopted child does not become related to the relatives of the adopting parent nor does the adopting parent acquire any rights of succession to the adopted child. The necessary conditions for an ordinary adoption are: the adopting parent must not have any legitimate or legitimated children as the object of the institution is to enable a childless person to have a descendant; there must be an age difference of 18 years between the adopting parent and the child; the adopting parent must be at least 35 years of age (reduced to 30 in special circumstances); the adopted child cannot be the natural child of the adopting parent (A.293 cc); and there must be the consensus of the adopting parent and the child, as well as the consent of the parents of the adopted child, if known, and the spouse of the adopting parent. An adoption may be revoked for the 'unworthiness' (see p 371, below) of either the adopting parent or the adopted child, or for reasons of good custom which may be raised by the *pubblico ministero*.

(ii) Special adoption. A special adoption has the object of enabling married couples of more than five years' standing, even if they have children of their own, to adopt minors of under the age of eight who are in need of moral and material assistance. The adopting parent must not be separated and must exceed the age of the adopted child by at least 20 and not more than 45 years. The effects of such an adoption are that the child acquires the same status as a legitimate child of the adopting parents and that all of his relationships with his family of origin cease, except in relation to any norms connected with marriage and the criminal law. The adopted child does not acquire any relationship with the collateral relatives of the adopting parents.

K. AFFILIATION

Affiliation is distinct from adoption and produces lesser consequences. It may be sought by anyone who has raised a foundling for at least three years. The child acquires the surname of the affiliated parent, the latter acquiring both parental authority over the child and the duty to maintain, educate and instruct the child who, however, does not acquire any rights of succession to the affiliated parent. An incestuous child cannot be affiliated.

L. THE ALIMENTARY OBLIGATION

Amongst the most important patrimonial obligations arising out of domestic relations is the alimentary obligation. This obligation arises by operation of law between certain related persons and consists of the support of a needy person by another member of the family who is in a position to provide that support. There are two necessary preconditions for the obligation to arise: first, a relationship constituted by blood, affinity, adoption or previous donation; and second, a state of need accompanied by both an impossibility for the person in need of providing for himself and the possibility of the obliged person to provide support. The obligation is commensurate to the needs and social position of the person in need and the economic conditions of the obliged person. It comprises not only ordinary needs but also other fundamental requirements which vary with the circumstances. The mode of payment is at the option of the obligor and may consist of periodic payments or taking the obligee in and providing for him. The classes of related persons bound by the alimentary obligation are listed in A.433 cc in decreasing order of family tie. Where there is more than one obligor in the same category, each is bound in proportion to his economic condition.

Prescription

The lapse of time may give rise to either the acquisition or extinction of a subjective right. The former is known as 'acquisitive prescription' or *usucapione* (see p 344, below) and the latter as 'extinctive prescription'. Only the latter shall be dealt with in this section. Extinctive prescription is the loss of a right because of the inertia or non-user by the owner of the right for a certain period of time defined by law. The ordinary prescriptive or limitation period is ten years except for real rights in which case it is 20 years. There are various specific limitation periods which are shorter, the most important of which are: five years for claims in damages arising out of an illicit act (tort or crime), two years for claims in damages arising out of motor vehicle accidents, and five years in the case of claims concerning periodical payments. A special characteristic of the shorter limitation periods is that enforcement proceedings taken to enforce a res judicata judgment obtained in an action subject to a short limitation period are subject to the ordinary limitation period of ten years.

A limitation period may be either suspended or interrupted. It is suspended where the inertia of the holder of a right is due to circumstances expressly defined by law. In such cases the period during which a cause for suspension exists is not taken into account in determining the limitation of period. On the other hand, a limitation period is interrupted where the owner of the right performs an act in exercise of his right (e g by putting the debtor in 'delay' or making use of a right of way) or where the right itself is acknowledged by the passive subject of the legal relationship (e g by the acknowledgment or part payment of a debt). In such cases, because the very cause of the institution is lacking (that is, inertia), the whole limitation period must run again before the right can be extinguished. Interruptory acts, however, may have either an instantaneous effect, in which event the new limitation period will immediately commence to run, or a prolonged effect in which event the new limitation period will not commence to run until after some time, e g the initiation of an action will prevent the commencement of the new limitation period until the judgment in the action becomes res judicata.

Italian law also contains the concept of so-called presumptive prescriptions which, however, do not give rise to limitation periods in a strict sense. They, instead, give rise to a rebuttable presumption that the obligations arising from everyday informal transactions are extinguished after the lapse of a defined period, e g the obligation to pay the price for meat purchased from a butcher who does not normally issue receipts. The prescriptive presumption does not operate to extinguish the right, but merely gives rise to a presumption that the debt was paid and thus extinguished: it goes to questions of proof only and not to substantive rights. The presumptive limitation periods are six months, one year or three years, depending upon the relationship in question (Artt. 2954–2956 cc). The only way in which a creditor may rebut the presumption is by issuing a challenge to the debtor to take a decisory oath (see ch 6, p 204, above), that is, to challenge the debtor to swear that the debt was paid. If the debtor takes the oath, the matter is closed, subject to any action for perjury; if the debtor refuses to swear the oath, then the presumption is rebutted and the creditor acquires the right to prove that the debt is unpaid.

Italian law draws a distinction between prescription and forfeiture (*decadenza*). There are two basic differences between these two institutions. First, although prescription is based upon a subjective element, that is, the inertia of the holder of a right, forfeiture concerns the loss of a possibility of exercising a right because of an objective element, that is, the failure to perform a given act within the peremptory term prescribed by law. All subjective elements are irrelevant to forfeiture which depends upon a sole objective factor: the lapse of the prescribed time. Therefore, unlike prescription, there can be no suspension or interruption of the defined time. Second, whilst prescription concerns the loss of an existing right, forfeiture impedes the acquisition of a new right. As the two notions are different, it is clear that a right may be subject to both forfeiture and prescription, e g in the case of sales, A.1495(1) cc provides that an action for the breach of warranty against latent defects is forfeited if the purchaser fails to notify the vendor of a latent defect within eight days of its discovery, yet, in accordance with A.1495(3) cc the limitation period for the action is one year from the consignment of the article. Forfeiture may be prescribed by law or by agreement, but in the latter case it must relate to a disposable right and must not render the exercise of the right too burdensome.

Property (*beni*) and real rights

A. GENERAL CONCEPTS RELEVANT TO PROPERTY

Although the word things (*cose*) will be used liberally, it is clear that the concept of property (*beni*) is narrower than that of 'things' as A.810 cc states that property comprises only those things which can form the object of rights, that is, only those things which have an economic interest and not, e g sun and air.

Things may be classified in various ways, some of the most important classifications being as follows. First, specific and general things: the former are things which may be individuated by reference to their own particular characteristics whilst the latter are things which belong to a genus or class. This distinction is important for several reasons: title to specific things passes at the date of contract whilst title to general things passes at the moment of their individuation, generally at consignment; the risk in general things remains with the vendor and does not pass until consignment; and an obligation to consign a given quantity of a general thing cannot become impossible. Second, fungible and non-fungible things. Third, consumable and non-consumable things. Fourth, divisible and indivisible things. This distinction depends upon whether the thing is divisible into homogenous fractions without destroying its economic value. Indivisibility may arise from the nature of the thing itself, by agreement, or by definition of law (eg the minimum cultivable unit (A.846 cc) and the common property in a condiminium).

However, the most important classification is that between movables and immovables. Immovables are defined by A.812 cc and may be divided into two categories. First, immovables by nature which are those things which normally cannot be moved from one place to another without altering their structure and nature. The Code enumerates them as the soil, springs, water courses, trees, buildings (even if only temporarily affixed to the soil) and, in general, everything which is naturally or artificially attached to the soil (A.812(1) cc). Second, those things which are specifically deemed to be immovables by A.812(2) cc. Movables, on the other hand, are defined by exclusion, namely, as all things which are not immovables (A.812(3) cc). The classification between movables and immovables is important for various reasons. First, in relation to form as all transactions concerning immovables must be in writing. Second, in relation to notice which in the case of immovables is through the registration of the transaction in the relevant registry and in the case of movables through possession. Third, in relation to the creation of secured charges which in the case of immovables is by hypothec and in the case of movables by pledge. Finally, in relation to the special protection afforded to immovables through the 'possessory actions'. Certain movables, however, are equated to immovables with respect to the form and notice of any transaction concerning them, namely, the so-called registrable movables which generally comprise objects of transport, eg ships, aircraft and motor vehicles (A.815 cc).

Things may also be classified, according to their mutual connection, into simple things (which arise where the elements of a thing are mutually interpenetrated to such an extent that they cannot be separated without altering the nature of the thing), compound things (which consist of a combination of several complementary things giving rise to an economic function and value different to the individual things which go to make it up) and connected things (which comprise several things which are related to each other in such a manner as to enable the identification of a principal thing and one or more accessory things). In the last case the connection may be either an incorporation or an appurtenance. Incorporation arises where a movable (the accessory thing) is naturally or artificially interpenetrated with an immovable (the principal thing). The movable loses its individuality and follows the legal destiny of the immovable into which it has been incorporated. The two things must belong to the same person, otherwise there will be mere accession through which the owner of the principal thing will also become the owner of the accessory thing, subject to various other rights in the parties. An appurtenance, on the other hand, is a 'thing utilised in the service or ornament of another thing'. Appurtenances also follow the title of the principal thing so that, in the absence of a contrary intention, a sale of the principal thing also includes appurtenances notwithstanding that they are capable of forming the object of an independent legal relationship. Appurtenance, unlike incorporation, may also concern the relationship between two movables.

Two important concepts relevant to property law are patrimony and fruits. Patrimony is the sum total of the active and passive relationships (that is, rights and obligations) of an individual. Thus, technically, a person has a patrimony even if he has debts only as these are passive legal relations. The concept of fruits is related to the distinction between productive and non-productive things. Fruits derive from productive things, or capital, whose nature is not thereby altered. Fruits are considered to be future things when they form the object of a contract prior to their accrual or collection, in which case they may form the object of an obligation only and not a real relationship which requires an immediate power over a thing. Fruits may be either natural, e g the fruit of a tree, or civil which constitute a counter-prestation for the enjoyment of the thing by another person, e g interest and rents.

Things may be owned by either the State and other public entities or private subjects: public things, or the public demesne, include both the State demesne (A.822 cc) and the inalienable patrimony (A.826 cc).

B. THE NATURE OF REAL RIGHTS

Real rights are nominate and defined rights which give an immediate and absolute power over a thing. It follows that real rights have four basic characteristics: first, immediacy which signifies that they give a direct and independent domination over a thing; second, absoluteness which signifies that they can be enforced against all persons who have a corresponding negative duty to abstain from any interference with the right; third, typicalness which means that they are expressly defined by law as a result of which new types cannot be contractually created by analogy or otherwise; and finally, they give their holder a power to follow the relevant thing and to regain it from an unlawful possessor.

Notwithstanding the significant differences between ownership and the other types of real rights, real rights constitute a unitary category. The unitary concept of real rights is a result of the ideology of the French Revolution which affirmed the principle of unfettered ownership rather than the hitherto feudal concept of property and its associated restrictions on the enjoyment of ownership. Therefore, ownership, the widest available right over property, became the general rule and all other real rights constituted exceptions precisely limited to defined types. This distinction still exists today in the division between real rights over one's own property (that is, ownership) and real rights over the property of another. The latter are in turn divided into real rights of enjoyment (which restrict the powers of enjoyment of an owner of property and comprise *superficie, enfiteusi*, usufruct, usage, habitation, and servitudes) and real rights of guarantee (which restrict the powers of disposition of an owner of property as they are accessory to and guarantee a right of credit and comprise the pledge and the hypothec).

Real rights are distinct from rights of credit (or obligations), the essential differences being as follows: first, a real right is characterised by its immediacy whilst the realisation of a right of credit depends upon the co-operation of the debtor; second, real rights are absolute, that is, enforceable against all persons, whilst rights of credit are relative rights only; third, the rules of priority apply to the acquisition of inconsistent interests over real rights (*prior tempore potior iure*, subject to the effects of registration where applicable) whilst the general principle of *par condicio creditorum* applies to rights of credit; fourth, possession is a typical characteristic of real rights whilst it is inconceivable in the case of rights of credit which cannot, therefore, be acquired by long user; fifth, real rights generally prevail over rights of credit, subject to the exception in A.1599 cc; and finally, real rights generally endure in perpetuity (except for usufruct, usage and habitation) in contrast to the temporary nature of rights of credit.

C. OWNERSHIP

The right of ownership is *complete* in that, according to A.832 cc, an owner may make any lawful use of his property. The breadth of this right includes a complete right of enjoyment and disposition. Even where the right of ownership is limited by the grant to another person of some minor real right (e g usufruct), the right of ownership (called the 'nude ownership') remains potentially complete because as soon as the charge is extinguished the ownership regains its former completeness. The right of ownership, unlike the other real rights, does not give rise to any parallel right in some other person. However, the right of ownership is not unlimited but meets several restrictions which derive from both the public and private interest. Restrictions based upon the public interest comprise expropriation for public purposes (A.42 C, A.834 cc) and requisitions. Restrictions based upon the private interest concern the regulation of relationships between proximate owners and include: the distance between buildings; an owner's right to air and light and the protection of his neighbour's privacy; the ownership of private waters; and emissions such as smoke, heat and noise from property. Moreover, A.833 cc limits the power of ownership by prohibiting 'emulative acts' which cause damage to others without any corresponding benefit to the owner who performs the acts. The institution comprises two elements: an objective element which is the lack of utility to the owner and a subjective element which part of the doctrine considers to be an *intent* to harm or cause an injury, whilst another part of the doctrine considers to be mere *knowledge* of the harm or nuisance.

Theoretically vertical ownership to immovables extends upwards infinitely into space and downwards to the centre of the earth. However, the positive law limits this right to that part of the land which can be usefully exploited so that an owner cannot prevent the activity of a stranger at either a depth or a height at which there can be no interest in excluding the latter (A.840 cc). Horizontal ownership, which extends to the boundaries of the immovable, is subject to the limitations that the owner must permit access to his land for hunting (if safe to the existing user of the land), the performance of necessary works to adjoining properties, and the retrieval of things or animals which accidentally come onto the property.

Traditionally, ownership is acquired through either an original title, that is, where title is independent of prior ownership (e g title in the spoils of fishing, title by long user, title by the possession of movables acquired in good faith, and title by finding) or a derivative title which is where ownership depends upon the existence of the right in the preceding owner (e g contracts for sale and succession on death).

The actions available for the protection of ownership fall into two major categories. First, proprietary actions (Artt. 948–951 cc) which are given to the owner as such to enable the ascertainment and assertion of ownership against whomsoever either directly disputes his ownership (by its challenge) or indirectly does so (through the claim of a real right over a thing). Second, possessory actions which assist a possessor, even if he is not owner, to temporarily and rapidly protect his possession against disturbance. They are, in contrast to proprietary actions which provide a definitive protection, only provisional remedies.

The most important of the proprietary actions is the action of *rivendicazione* (A.948 cc) with which an owner may claim his property from whomsoever wrongfully possesses or detains it. The basis of the action is the right to follow property; a right which is innate to the right of ownership. The action, therefore, not only enables the establishment of ownership but also the recuperation of the property. There is no limitation period and the action is available in the case of all things which may form the object of ownership. However, the action is not available in the case of movables which were acquired in good faith at the time of their consignment (A.1153 cc) nor negotiable instruments acquired in good faith (A.1994 cc). A person who wrongfully detains a thing must give restitution of the thing and its fruits. However, if he acted in good faith he need only restitute the fruits falling due after the commencement of the action, that is, the fruits which he would have obtained after that time if he had used the normal diligence of a good paterfamilias; if, instead, he acted in bad faith he must restitute all of the fruits which he could have obtained as from the date of his possession if he had used the normal diligence of a good paterfamilias. In either event, however, he is entitled to be reimbursed for all expenditures incurred on extraordinary repairs and the amelioration of the property and, for the period over which he is required to restitute the fruits, all expenditures incurred on ordinary repairs and the expenses in accruing the fruits. A possessor in good faith, furthermore, is entitled to retain the property to protect his right of reimbursement.

Other proprietary actions include: *l'azione negatoria* through which an owner may have a claim which prejudices or disturbs his right of ownership declared non-existent; the action to settle boundaries which is available to adjacent owners when a boundary is objectively uncertain; and the action to have a common boundary, which is objectively certain, physically marked or restored at joint expense. There are also several other types of action available to protect the right of ownership such as the possessory actions, the actions for new work or feared damage (Artt.1171 and 1172 cc; see ch 6, p 193, above), judicial sequestration (A.670 cpc), the actions for the delivery of movables or release of immovables (Artt. 605–611 cpc) and the action of restitution referred to earlier.

D. COMMUNION

Communion is the broadest form of co-ownership. Each co-owner in a communion has a right to the use and enjoyment of the thing as a whole and is only limited by the existence of similar rights in the other co-owners. A co-owner may freely dispose of his quota, enjoy any profits in the proportion of his quota and request a partition (unless excluded by reason of express agreement or legislative prohibition) whereupon he is entitled to participate in the division in the same proportion as his interest in the communion. A communion may arise either voluntarily or by operation of law. The latter comprises the most important and complex form of communion, viz, the condominium of buildings which is an obligatory and perpetual form of communion over the common areas of buildings: the individual co-owner, apart from being the exclusive owner of his apartment, is necessarily a co-owner of the common property. The condominium consists of a general assembly, which is the deliberative organ, and an administrator, who is the executive organ that represents the condominium both externally and procedurally.

E. SUPERFICIE (EDIFICE)

This real right constitutes an exception to the principle of accession according to which everything that is annexed to the land belongs to the owner of the land. This real right derives from the right of an owner of land to either grant a right to construct and maintain a building on his land to another person who thereby acquires the ownership of the building or to alienate an existing building separately from the land upon which it is erected (A.952 cc). Therefore, the right of *superficie* is the right of a grantee to construct and maintain a building on the land of the grantor or a right of maintenance only where there is an alienation of an existing building which stands on the land of the grantor. The grantor is thereafter limited to the enjoyment of the sub-soil but only insofar as it does not endanger the building. The interest of the grantee may be alienated or hypothecated and, although the Civil Code does not provide for the payment of rent by the grantee, this may be required by agreement. The right of *superficie*, which can only be created by the owner of the land, may be perpetual or for a limited period only in which case the owner of the land also becomes the owner of the building at the expiration of the limited period. The right of *superficie* is, furthermore, subject to extinguishment by prescription.

F. ENFITEUSI

This is a real right which confers upon the grantee the same rights of enjoyment as the owner of the property subject, however, to the obligations of the grantee to improve the property and to pay a periodical rent. It is, therefore, the broadest of the limited real rights as it confers powers which are almost analogous to those of ownership. Apart from certain binding statutory provisions, the only situation in which the *enfiteusi* becomes subject to statutory regulation is in the absence of an agreement to the contrary between the parties (A.957 cc). The right may come into existence by long user, will or agreement. It may be perpetual or for a limited period in which case it cannot be for less than 20 years. The grantee has three fundamental obligations: the improvement of the property, the payment of a periodical rent, whether in cash or in kind, and the avoidance of any deterioration in the property. The grantee may alienate his interest, either inter vivos or by will, but cannot sub-*enfiteusi*. In the case of a proposed sale of the right, the grantor has a right of pre-emption at the same price. Moreover, by certain recent amendments, the grantee has been given the right to acquire absolute ownership upon the payment of a sum calculated by capitalising the annual rent. On the other hand, in the event of a breach of the grantee's obligations, the owner has been given the right to regain the property, although this is subject to the overriding right of the grantee to purchase the ownership. The *enfiteusi* may also be extinguished by its non-user for 20 years by the grantee.

G. USUFRUCT

The right of usufruct, similar to a life estate, gives the grantee the right to enjoy the property, including its fruits, with a corresponding obligation not to change its economic nature (A.981 cc). This right, in contrast to the other real rights, cannot exceed the lifetime of the grantee or 30 years where the grantee is a legal person. An usufruct may be created over both immovables and other forms of property such as movables, credits and negotiable instruments. However, in general it must concern infungibles and unconsumable property because of the obligation to return the property to the grantor at the end of the usufruct. However, A.995 cc provides for the quasi-usufruct of consumable things giving rise to an obligation to restitute either their value or property of an equivalent species and quantity. An usufruct may arise by operation of law (e g the usufruct of parents over their children's property), contract, will or long user. The rights of the grantee are: possession of the property; the receipt of the fruits of the property for the duration of the usufruct; the alienation of the usufruct for the remainder of its duration; the lease of the property; an indemnity, payable at the termination of the usufruct, for improvements made by the grantee but limited to the lesser of the expenditure in making the improvements or the resulting benefit to the property as a result of the improvements; the removal of 'additions' where this does not affect the economic value of the property unless the grantor opts to retain them upon paying adequate compensation; and the mortgage of the interest. The grantee also has various duties, all of which are related to the fundamental obligation of restituting the property at the expiration of the usufruct, e g the exercise of all rights with the diligence of a good paterfamilias; the burden of all expenses connected with the custody, administration and ordinary maintenance of the property; the payment of the annual outgoings; and making the owner aware of all violations against the property by third persons as well as sharing the costs of any litigation concerning the property. The grantor, on the other hand, must bear all expenses connected with extraordinary repairs and outgoings of a non-annual nature.

H. USAGE AND HABITATION

These are restricted forms of usufruct. Usage enables the utilisation of a thing and, if productive of fruits, the right to such fruits as are necessary for the personal consumption of the grantee and his family. Habitation merely gives the right to inhabit a house, but again limited to the personal needs of the grantee and his family. Neither right may be alienated.

I. SERVITUDES

Servitudes are analogous to easements and are defined as a burden imposed upon an immovable (the so-called servient tenement) for the benefit of another immovable (the so-called dominant tenement) which is in a different ownership. A servitude cannot be personal to the owners; its function is to give the dominant tenement some particular benefit which is possessed by the servient tenement (e g a right of way) with a corresponding restriction upon the latter. There are four basic principles applicable to servitudes. First, the servient and dominant tenements must be in different ownership, the only exception being where the dominant owner is also co-owner of the servient tenement. Second, servitudes cannot comprise a positive duty on the part of the servient tenement but only a negative duty or a toleration. Nonetheless, the servient owner may oblige himself to a given conduct which, however, may only be accessory to the servitude. Third, although the two tenements need not be adjacent to each other, they need to be sufficiently close to support the relationship. Finally, the servitude becomes an inseparable aspect of the immovable and cannot, therefore, be separately alienated.

Servitudes may arise expressly pursuant to either an agreement or will; by either long user or implication in the case of apparent (that is, permanent and visible) servitudes; or by operation of law in specifically defined cases (the so-called coercive servitudes, e g in the case of a land-locked property). On the other hand, servitudes are extinguished by common ownership, non-user for 20 years, the lapse of a term or the satisfaction of a condition stipulated by agreement, or by abandonment of the servient tenement.

J. POSSESSION

Possession is the exercise of ownership or some other real right over a thing and consists of both an objective and a subjective element, that is, an act accompanied by an intent to exercise ownership or some other real right over the thing. The advantages flowing from possession are: the acquisition of real rights by long user; the procedural advantages arising from the possessor's position as defendant in any proprietary action of *rivendicazione* as the plaintiff-owner bears the onus and burden of proving his title; and the right to take possessory actions which ensure a ready, even if only temporary, protection.

Possession, however, must be distinguished from detention which is the mere intent to hold a thing for a lawful purpose and without any intent of exercising real rights over it. However, as it is difficult to determine whether there is an *animus possidendi* or an *animus detinendi*, there is a general presumption in favour of possession unless it can be shown that the possessor commenced to exercise the power over the thing as a detainer only. A detention cannot convert itself into possession unless either a third party claims to be owner and transfers the property in the thing to the detainer or the detainer notifies the owner of his intent to continue to hold the thing on his own account.

The distinction between detention and possession is important as a possessor only (and not a detainer) may acquire ownership by long user, provided that the owner of the property has not, in the meantime, brought an action of *rivendicazione* against the possessor for the restitution of the property together with its fruits. As noted earlier, in such an event, the obligation of the possessor to restitute the fruits depends upon his bona fides (see p 340, above). However, there is one situation in which a possessor acquires immediate title. Article 1153(1) cc provides that the alienee of a movable (not being a registrable movable) acquires title by possession from an alienor without title provided that the alienee was in good faith at the date of delivery and the transaction was otherwise valid and abstractedly suitable for the transfer of ownership. Article 1153, therefore, equates possession with title. Moreover, A.1155 cc provides that where an alienor contracts to sell the same thing to several persons, possession gives priority to a subsequent purchaser provided that at the date of delivery he was in good faith, that is, without notice of the earlier agreement as a result of which the alienor no longer had any title. The effect of these provisions is that, on the one hand, the effective owner of the thing loses his title and cannot obtain restitution, and on the other hand, the alienee acquires title free from any interest not shown in the transfer.

K. LONG USER (*usucapione*)

Usucapione is the acquisition of ownership or any other real right over a thing by possession for a given period. Acquisition of title by long user requires a continued and uninterrupted possession which is not violent nor clandestine and which endures for a certain period of time. The ordinary periods of long user, except for ordinary movables, are: 20 years for immovables and a universality of movables; ten years for registrable movables; and 15 years in the case of improved rural properties. These periods may be shortened where certain additional requisites are satisfied, namely: good faith at the date upon which possession was received, a transfer which was valid and abstractedly suitable to pass title, and the registration of the title, from when, in fact, time commences to run. Where these additional requisites are satisfied, the periods of long user are reduced as follows: ten years for immovables and a universality of movables; three years for registrable movables; and five years in the case of improved rural properties. In the case of ordinary movables, on the other hand, where the transfer is abstractedly suitable to pass title, title is acquired immediately (A.1153 cc); where, instead, there is the lack of an abstractedly suitable transfer, then the prescriptive period is ten years if the possession was acquired in good faith or 20 years if it was acquired in bad faith (A.1161 cc).

Obligations

A. NATURE AND DEFINITION

Although the Civil Code does not define the concept of 'obligation', the doctrine has deduced its definition from an interpretation of all of the norms regulating it. An obligation, therefore, has been defined as a relationship between two parties as a result of which one party (the debtor) is bound to a certain conduct (or prestation) in favour of the other (the creditor). According to classical theory the difference with real rights is that the latter are absolute rights (that is, enforceable against everybody) whereas obligations are relative rights (that is, enforceable against certain persons only). A more recent distinction is that obligations require the 'co-operation of the debtor' if the purpose of the transaction is to be achieved.

Obligations may arise by agreement, as a consequence of the freedom of contract, from unlawful acts, or from any other fact or act capable of producing obligations 'according to the legal system' (A.1173 cc). It is clear that the civil law of obligations comprises both, in common law terms, contract and tort.

An obligation, as is evident from its definition comprises two basic elements. First, at least two identifiable subjects: an active subject or creditor and a passive subject or debtor. Second, an object which is the prestation or conduct that the debtor is bound to perform. Whilst the prestation must have a patrimonial character (that is, capable of monetary valuation), the interest of the creditor may be merely scientific, cultural, idealistic or affectionate provided that it is 'socially valuable' and therefore worthy of legal protection. Moreover, the object must be possible, although a mere temporary impossibility does not impede the existence of an obligation so that, for instance, an obligation to deliver future property is valid (A.1348 cc). Furthermore, the object must be lawful, that is, not contrary to imperative norms, public order or good custom, and must be determined or determinable.

The debtor and creditor, alike, have a duty 'to conduct themselves according to the rules of propriety' (A.1175 cc). The tendency of both the doctrine and the case law has been to assimilate this ethical duty, thereby converting it into a legal duty, with the concept of good faith. Cassation has described the duty as requiring each party to behave in a manner that does not injure the interests of the other party beyond that necessitated by the legitimate protection of individual interests.

Although non-legal obligations are generally irrelevant to the law, A.2034 cc sets out two situations in which social or moral obligations may acquire a legal significance. First, A.2034(1) stipulates the general rule that restitution is not available in the case of a spontaneous payment made pursuant to a moral or social duty which is to be interpreted according to the current social conscience. Second, A.2034(2) specifically provides that restitution is not available in three cases:

(a) The spontaneous performance of a fiduciary disposition (A.627 cc). This rule is the direct consequence of the formal non-existence of the 'trust' in Italian law. Therefore, although a beneficiary cannot take proceedings to enforce a trust, if the fiduciary or trustee spontaneously performs it, the trustee cannot later seek restitution of the property.
(b) The spontaneous payment of a gambling debt.
(c) The spontaneous payment of a statute-barred debt.

B. THE PRINCIPAL TYPES OF OBLIGATIONS

An important type of obligation is that with a plurality of active or passive subjects. Such obligations give rise to two questions: first, whether a debt may be discharged by the payment of the whole of the debt to one only of several co-creditors or whether it must be paid to each creditor proportionately; and second, whether each co-debtor is liable for the whole or only his proportionate share of the debt. As to the former, there is no general presumption in favour of the joint and several discharge of debts as a result of which a debtor may only discharge a debt by payment of the whole of the debt to one only of several co-creditors where such joint and several discharge is expressly provided for by law or by agreement. On the other hand, although co-debtors are jointly and severally liable only where this is stipulated by law or by agreement, there is a general presumption in A.1294 cc that co-debtors are jointly and severally liable for the whole of the debt unless provided otherwise by law or by agreement. An exception to the general presumption is the liability of heirs for their testator's debts in which case each heir is liable in the proportion of his interest in the inheritance, unless provided otherwise by the testator (A.754 cc).

Where a co-debtor has paid the entire debt, he may proceed through the so-called action of regression against his co-debtors for reimbursement of their respective shares. Similarly, a co-creditor who has collected the whole debt must pay the appropriate shares to his co-creditors. Any act prejudicial to one co-debtor or co-creditor does not extend to the others, e g the effect of placing one co-debtor in delay does not extend to the others (A.1308 cc). However, an act favourable to one co-debtor or co-creditor does extend for the benefit of the others, e g the payment of a debt by one co-debtor completely extinguishes the obligation.

Several important consequences in the law of obligations are dependent upon the distinction, based upon the nature of the object of an obligation, between generic obligations (where the object of the obligation is a generic thing or a certain quantity of a fungible thing) and specific obligations (where the object of the obligation is a specific thing). First, A.1178 cc provides that in the case of a generic obligation the debtor must deliver a thing belonging to the genre agreed upon and of a quality not inferior to the average. Second, a generic obligation cannot be extinguished by reason of supervening impossibility because the genre never disappears. Third, whilst title passes at the date of agreement in the case of specific obligations, it passes at the date of the individuation of the object in the case of generic obligations.

A particular group of generic obligations is the pecuniary obligations (Artt. 1277–1281 cc) which have as their object a sum of money. The pecuniary obligations, under the nominalistic principle (A.1277 cc), are extinguished by the payment of the sum due irrespective of its effective value. The case law has restricted the nominalistic principle to those obligations which have a pecuniary sum as their object as from the date of their formation (the so-called monetary obligations) and not to those obligations whose original object is something other than cash so that any monetary considerations necessarily arise subsequent to their formation (the so-called value obligations), e g if A is obliged to deliver a vehicle and he fails to perform, the nominalistic principle is inapplicable in determining damages because the monetary issue arises at a point subsequent to the formation of the obligation. Where a pecuniary obligation is expressed in foreign currency, the debtor may pay in either the foreign or national currency, but if he pays in national currency then the relevant exchange rate is that applicable to the day and place of payment. The parties to an agreement are free to expressly oust the nominalistic principle.

A specific type of pecuniary obligation is the obligation to pay interest. This obligation, always accessory to a pecuniary obligation, may arise either by operation of law or by agreement. The former, or the so-called obligation to pay legal interest, which is fixed at 5% per annum, automatically applies to all pecuniary obligations which are liquid and whose payment are not subject to any terms or conditions. In such event legal interest runs without the prior need to demand payment and irrespective of whether there is delay in performance (A.1282 cc). This provision satisfies the principle of unjust enrichment by restoring an equilibrium between the parties, that is, by counter-balancing the debtor's enjoyment of the capital at the expense of the creditor. The obligation to pay interest arises, in any event, as a form of damages, from the date of delay in performance of the principal obligation and in such case the same rate of interest, if it was higher than the legal rate, as that which was payable before the delay is applicable (A.1224 cc). An obligation to pay interest arising out of an express agreement, on the other hand, may stipulate a rate of interest other than the legal rate, provided that the agreement is in writing and that the rate of interest is not usurious (A.1284 cc). Finally, it must be noted that interest is not payable on interest which is already due. Compound interest may only arise in two cases: from the date of legal proceedings specifically directed to seeking interest on interest which is already due; and where there exists a custom in favour of compound interest (A.1283 cc).

Obligations may be divided into two basic types depending upon the type of prestation in question. First, positive obligations whose object is some positive conduct on the part of the debtor, that is, an obligation to deliver a thing, an obligation to do, or a combination of the two. Second, negative obligations which comprise an obligation not to do or a toleration by the debtor.

C. EXTINCTION OF OBLIGATIONS

The extinction of obligations may be divided into two broad categories: satisfactory extinction which either directly or indirectly gives to the creditor the prestation which was due to him and includes perform-ance, set-off and fusion; and unsatisfactory extinction in which case, although the debtor is freed of the obligation, the creditor does not receive the prestation to which he was entitled and includes novation, release and supervening impossibility.

Performance (Artt. 1176–1200 cc) of an obligation is the exact execution of the prestation stipulated in the agreement and thereby extinguishes the obligation of the debtor and the right of the creditor. Article 1176 cc requires the diligence of a good paterfamilias in order to avoid contractual responsibility in the performance of an obligation. The absence of diligence in performing an obligation may result in *culpa levis* (slight or average fault) which is that relevant to A.1176 cc and arises where there is a violation of the average diligence of a good paterfamilias, *culpa lata* (serious fault) which arises where there is a violation of that minimum diligence required of everybody and not only of a good paterfamilias and which is equivalent to *dolo* (fraud or intent), and *culpa levissima* (very slight fault) which arises where a greater than average diligence is required either by law or by agreement. Article 1229 cc, in fact, provides that every agreement which excludes or limits the debtor's responsibility for *dolo* (ie the intention not to perform) or serious fault is null because this would render the obligation meaningless as it would be dependent upon the arbitrariness of the debtor. The remaining forms of extinction may be briefly described as follows. Set-off (Artt. 1241–1252 cc), which arises where there is a reciprocal indebtedness between the parties to an obligation, is the extinction, through the operation of law (A.1243 cc), of the common amount of the reciprocal obligations with the result that the residue only remains as an obligation. Fusion (Artt. 1253–1255 cc) extinguishes an obligation where, owing to some event subsequent to the formation of the obligation, the debtor and creditor become the one and same person. Novation (Artt. 1230–1235 cc) is an agreement between the debtor and creditor as a result of which the original obligation is extinguished and replaced with a new obligation or agreement. The novation may relate to either the parties or the object of the agreement. Release (Artt. 1236–1240 cc) is the total or partial remission of the debt by the creditor. Finally, as to supervening impossibility, see p 350 below.

D. NON-PERFORMANCE AND DELAY

(*i*) *Introduction.* The ordinary remedy in Italian law for the breach of an obligation is damages. However, the award of damages is not only dependent upon a suffering of damage by the plaintiff which is imputable to the defendant but also, in most cases of contractual obligations, on placing the defendant in delay (*mora*).

(*ii*) *Non-performance.* Both a total failure to perform and an irregular performance of an obligation amount to non-performance. Article 1218 cc provides that a debtor who does not exactly perform the prestation which is due under an obligation is liable in damages unless he can prove that the non-performance or delay was due to an impossibility of performance for a cause which was not imputable to him. The responsibility contemplated by A.1218 cc is a contractual responsibility as distinct from a responsibility for an illicit fact (that is, an extra-contractual or so-called *aquiliana* responsibility). The latter involves the actual violation of a duty to respect the legal sphere of another and is not dependent upon the violation of a specific obligation between two subjects to a defined legal relationship.

A central concept in the responsibility of the debtor is the imputability to him of the cause resulting in the non-performance. To escape this responsibility, the debtor must prove that the non-performance was due to an objective external cause, namely, fortuitous circumstances or *forza maggiore*. If the cause is imputable to the debtor, then the intensity of the intent in the debtor is relevant in distinguishing between *dolo* which is the premeditated intent not to perform and *colpa* which is negligence or disregard in the performance of an obligation.

The debtor is imputable for non-performance in the following cases: first, absolute non-performance which arises where either performance is impossible due to a cause imputable to the debtor (either as a result of his *dolo* or *colpa*) or because of the lapse of an essential term within which the obligation was to be performed; and second, relative non-performance or delay which is an unjustified delay in performance. The debtor, on the other hand, is not imputable for non-performance if two elements are present: the impossibility to perform (the objective element) and the non-imputability of the impossibility to the debtor (the subjective element). Impossibility, if it is not to be imputable to the debtor, must be supervening, insurmountable (which means that the impossibility which impedes the performance of the debtor must arise from fortuitous circumstances or *forza maggiore*), objective and indefinite. A temporary impossibility does not extinguish the obligation where there is no essential term for performance and the creditor still has an interest in receiving it. In the case of a partial impossibility (A.1258 cc), the debtor is released from the obligation by performing that which has remained possible. This is an exception to the rule that the creditor can refuse a partial performance; a rule only applicable where the partial performance is unjustifiable.

(iii) Delay. Delay, an unjustified postponement of performance by the debtor, is the most frequent instance of inexact performance. Where a debtor delays in the performance of an obligation, it is unknown whether he is merely late or whether he does not intend to perform at all. In cases of doubt, the rules on delay may be applied to determine a state of non-performance. Where the obligation either expressly or impliedly as a result of its nature contains a condition which requires performance within a term which is of the essence, delay without more constitutes non-performance.

A debtor is in delay and therefore deemed guilty of non-performance if the following circumstances are satisfied: the time for performance has elapsed; the delay is imputable to the debtor; and the debtor has been placed in delay. The debtor may be placed in delay in two ways. First, by operation of law in which case the debtor may incur delay without a need for the creditor to do anything. It arises where the obligation must be performed within a time which has elapsed, where the debt arises out of an illicit act, and where the debtor declares in writing that he does not intend to perform. Second, delay pursuant to the service of a formal notice requiring performance, which notice may be either an official notice served through the court bailiff or a simple private notice. The notice must be given whenever a debt is payable by the debtor but no term was fixed for performance nor did the creditor have a term fixed by the court. Three consequences follow from placing a debtor in delay. First, the risk of supervening impossibility is transferred to the debtor, who becomes liable to the creditor even in a case of *forza maggiore*. The only way in which the debtor can avoid this responsibility is by showing that the object of the performance would have, in any event, disappeared from the hands of the creditor. Second, the debtor becomes responsible for the delay and is therefore liable in damages. Finally, the prescriptive period is interrupted (A.2943 cc).

(iv) Delay by the creditor. This arises where the creditor, without legitimate reason, either refuses to receive the performance of the debtor or omits to complete the preparatory acts necessary to receive the prestation. The delay of a creditor, unlike that of a debtor, does not constitute the violation of an obligation as there is no legal duty to accept a performance. Therefore, the only consequences of a delay by the creditor are: the risk of an impossibility of performance remains with the creditor; the debtor must be compensated for any damages resulting from the delay; interest is no longer due; and the expenses of storage and custody pending delivery must be paid by the creditor. In order to place a creditor in delay, the debtor must make an offer to perform which must be made in a solemn form, that is, served by a public official in accordance with A.1208 cc. An offer to perform which is not in a solemn form is not totally without effect: although it does not put the creditor in delay, it avoids both the possibility of the debtor being put in delay and the latter's contractual liability for the same. If the creditor fails to accept the offer or fails to receive the things offered in a solemn notice, the debtor may free himself of the obligation by the deposit of the goods in the manner stipulated in A.1212 cc.

(v) Damage. The prejudice suffered by the creditor through non-performance or delay, called 'patrimonial damage', comprises the effective loss arising out of non-performance, e g the sum paid for goods which have not been received, and the loss of profits as a result of the non-utilisation of the prestation, e g the profit in reselling the goods. Both forms of damage, in order to give rise to compensation, must first, be a direct and immediate consequence of the non-performance, that is, there must be a causal connection between the non-performance and the damage, and second, be foreseeable as at the time that the obligation arose unless the non-performance is intentional (or with *dolo*) in which case the debtor is also liable for unforeseeable damage. The

measure of compensation payable for the damage, however, is limited or reduced if the creditor was party to the debtor's fault in failing to perform or where the damage has been aggravated by the creditor.

E. THE RIGHTS OF CREDITORS

A debtor has an unlimited liability towards his creditors. Therefore, the totality of the debtor's property, irrespective of whether it was acquired before or after his obligations arose, is available for the satisfaction of creditors (A.2740 cc). This general and unlimited liability of the debtor is known as the 'general guarantee'. Because the security offered by the general guarantee is limited to that property still within the debtor's patrimony as at the date of execution, a creditor's rights may be affected by either a diminution of the debtor's estate (although a creditor may take certain precautionary measures in this regard: see p 354, below) or an insufficiency of the debtor's assets to meet all of his liabilities in which events the creditor is only entitled to a pro rata payment.

To protect against such events, a creditor may avail himself of certain specific guarantees which reinforce his security. The specific guarantees, the first two of which also confer a priority over other creditors, are: first, privileges (A.2745 cc) which arise by operation of law (that is, independent of the volition of the parties) as a consequence of the nature of the credit in question; second, the real guarantees which consist of the express creation of real rights over the specific property of the debtor, viz, the pledge and the hypothec; third, the grant of a personal guarantee by a third person whose patrimony also becomes available for the satisfaction of the creditor's rights; and fourth, the payment of an advance on the performance of an obligation such as a deposit which, like a penalty clause, reinforces the creditor's rights to damages.

Privileges may be either general or special. General privileges, which relate to movables only, give priority to certain liabilities payable from the proceeds of the forced liquidation of the debtor's movable estate. The obligations guaranteed by general privilege are defined by Artt. 2751–2754 cc, e g professional fees, alimental credits, funeral expenses, and an employer's social welfare contributions for his employees. Special privileges relating to either movables or immovables secure certain credits against specific assets of the debtor and arise as a result of the particular nexus which exists between the asset and the credit, e g the legal costs incurred in procedings for the preservation or realisation of a given asset in the debtor's estate, and the rates and direct taxes payable on a given property. In the absence of a legislative provision to the contrary, a special privilege gives rise to a right to follow the property. The order of priority in cases of conflict between the various privileged credits is defined by Artt. 2777–2783 cc. Whilst in the case of movables, a special privilege cannot generally take priority over a credit guaranteed by pledge against the same movable, in the case of immovables a special privilege generally has priority over a credit guaranteed by hypothec against the same immovable.

The real rights of guarantee (pledge and hypothec) also constitute secured debts and give rise to priority. They are absolute rights which can be immediately enforced and give rise to a right to follow the property. They are securities against specific property. If the security perishes or deteriorates the creditor may request that the security be given over other property and if the request is refused, it makes the credit immediately payable (A.2743 cc). There is a prohibition against any agreement to the effect that the title to the security pass to the creditor upon a failure to pay the debt.

The pledge relates to non-registrable movables only whilst the hypothec is applicable to immovables and registrable movables. In the case of the pledge the object of the security is physically transferred to the creditor as security for the payment of the debt thereby denying the debtor of its enjoyment. In the case of the hypothec, the object of the security, and hence its enjoyment, remains with the owner as the security is constituted by registration. The salient characteristic of the pledge and the hypothec is that they give the creditor a priority in the proceeds of the sale of the security.

A hypothec may arise in three ways: by operation of law; pursuant to a judgment; or by agreement. A hypothec arises by operation of law, without the concurrence of the debtor, in the cases listed in A.2817 cc, e g in favour of an alienor over the alienated property as a guarantee for the obligations to be performed under the contract. A person who obtains a favourable judgment for the payment of a sum of money, damages, or the performance of any other obligation, has the right to register a hypothec (Artt. 2818–2820 cc). Priority amongst several registered hypothecs depends upon the date of registration, not the date of the transaction. Although the right to a hypothec is not subject to a limitation period, the effects of its registration is limited to 20 years so that registration must be renewed every 20 years for its continued effect.

A creditor may also secure his credit by taking a so-called simple or personal guarantee from a third party. This form of security is unrelated to a particular thing and consists of the creation of a new obligation accessory to the principal obligation, which is therefore reinforced by the additional security arising out of the availability of the patrimony of the guarantor. The various forms of personal guarantee are the *fideiussione*, the mandate of credit and the *avall*.

The *fideiussione* is constituted by a contract with which a third party personally guarantees the obligation of another person. The guarantor thereby becomes jointly and severally liable with the debtor, although the agreement may provide that there must be a prior execution against the estate of the principal debtor (A.1944 cc). A guarantor who has paid the debt is subrogated to the same rights, including any guarantees, that the creditor had against the debtor. Apart from the right of subrogation, the guarantor has a special action, called the action of regression (*azione di regresso*), against the debtor for the sum paid to the creditor.

The mandate of credit is a contract with which one person (A) obligates himself to another person (B) to give a credit to a third person (C). The person requesting that the credit be made available to the third party (B) becomes a guarantor of the future debt which will be assumed by (C). Notwithstanding its name, it is unrelated to the mandate.

The *avall*, finally, is the guarantee of a negotiable instrument on behalf of one of the persons obligated on the bill (drawer, promissor or indorsee). It is an autonomous obligation; that is, whilst a guarantee is generally accessory to the principal obligation and therefore follows its outcome, the *avall* is independent of the validity of the obligation upon which the bill is founded and thus the guarantor cannot raise any defences which are available against the creditor at the instance of the person guaranteed. Since the guarantor on a bill is jointly and severally liable with the person guaranteed, the holder of a bill may demand payment directly from the guarantor. The guarantee must be written on the bill itself (see ch 10, p 412, below).

F. THE PRESERVATION OF THE PATRIMONIAL GUARANTEE

Creditors have an obvious interest in ensuring that their debtor does not diminish his patrimony, and therefore jeopardise their security, through negligence or fraud. Consequently, the law provides creditors with several devices to ensure the 'preservation' of their patrimonial guarantee over the debtor's property.

First, the action of substitution (A.2900 cc) which enables the substitution of the debtor with the creditor in individual activities so as to prevent a prejudice to the creditor's expectations through the inertia of the debtor in the management of his patrimony.

Second, the revocatory (or Paulian) action (Artt. 2901–2904 cc) which is an action available to a creditor where the debtor knowingly seeks to prejudice the creditor by divesting himself of property thereby putting it outside the reach of the creditor. The action does not *invalidate* the subject transaction but merely renders it *ineffective* vis-à-vis the creditor who took the action. However, the rights of a bona fide purchaser for value are protected from the effects of a revocatory action. The action must be brought within five years of the date of the transaction under attack. Revocatory actions are also available in the criminal and bankruptcy spheres although these differ to the ordinary revocatory action dealt with here. The object of the bankruptcy revocatory action is to re-integrate the bankrupt's estate and invalidate any acts prejudicial to the creditors. It differs from ordinary revocation because first, it benefits *all* of the creditors of the bankrupt, unlike an ordinary revocation which only benefits the plaintiff creditor, as a result of which, moreover, it may only be brought by the curator, and second, it only strikes at the following transactions: gratuitous transactions made within two years of the bankruptcy; transactions for value which raise a suspicion of fraud because of their abnormality (e g the payment of statute-barred debts) unless the third party can show that he acted in good faith; and regular transactions for value where the curator can show that the third party had notice of the insolvency.

Third, the action of conservative sequestration (Artt. 2905–2906 cc) which is a precautionary measure whereby a creditor may, prior to the determination of a controversy, impede the disposition of property by the debtor where he has a founded fear that the debtor will act in that way to the prejudice of his security for the credit in question.

G. INDIVIDUAL AND COLLECTIVE ENFORCEMENT PROCEEDINGS

A creditor may have the property of his debtor, or of a third party guarantor, realised for the satisfaction of his credit. The realisation of the creditor's rights may affect any part of the debtor's estate: immovables, movables, credits or any other rights. In general it involves three phases: first, attachment; second, forced liquidation or forced assignment; and third, the payment of the proceeds to the creditor or their division where there are several co-creditors. The exact procedure varies depending upon the object of the execution. This procedure (see ch 6, p 215, above) must be distinguished from what is called 'collective enforcement' or bankruptcy which applies to commercial entrepreneurs only (see ch 10, p 415, below).

The individual sources of obligations: A. Contract

A. DEFINITION

A contract is a 'legal transaction' (*negozio giuridico*) encompassing all of the essential and incidental elements of the latter. Article 1325 cc defines the essential elements of contract as follows: agreement or consensus of the parties (which results from a union of wills); cause; object or prestation (which must be possible, lawful, and determinate or determinable); and form (which is only exceptionally necessary for the validity of a transaction) (see ch 1, p 32, above). Moreover, a prerequisite for the existence of a contract is the capacity to contract.

The normative regulation of contractual relationships may arise from three sources: law, agreement, and custom (see ch 3, pp 79ff, above).

B. CLASSIFICATION OF CONTRACTS

There is no single classification of contracts but several classifications depending upon the criterion adopted for the purpose. Some of the most important classifications drawn by the doctrine are:

(i) *Typical (or nominate) and atypical (or innominate) contracts.* The former are contracts which are specifically contemplated and regulated by the Code and therefore have a typical cause; the latter, instead, are those types of contract which are not specifically defined by the Code and are therefore said to have an atypical cause (see ch 1, p 33, above).

(ii) *Onerous and gratuitous contracts:* (see ch 1, p 31, above.) This classification, like the first one, is a general one applicable to all kinds of legal transactions, whereas the other classifications referred to below are all exclusive to contracts.

(iii) *Consensual and real contracts.* This is a classification which is based upon the formation of contracts: consensual contracts, which represent the majority of contracts, are formed upon a mere consensus of the parties whilst real contracts also require the delivery of the object for their formation.

(iv) *Transmissible and obligatory contracts.* This distinction is based upon the effects of a contract. The former are contracts which effect a passage of title upon formation: they are consensual contracts wherein title passes upon agreement without a need for delivery, which is only useful because of the effects of possession. Obligatory contracts do not pass title but only give rise to personal obligations, e g the contracts of lease and deposit. This distinction is important in the case of sales. A sale may be either a transmissible contract, as is the general rule, in which case title passes on formation (A.1376 cc) or an obligatory contract in which case the contract does not pass title but merely imposes an obligation upon the vendor to procure the transfer of title to the purchaser. The obligatory sale arises in three situations: the alternative sale in which case title passes when the purchaser makes the selection as to the object of the sale; the future sale in which case title passes when the object of the sale comes into existence; and the sale of generic things in which case title passes at the moment when the object of the sale is individuated. In all of these cases, the passage of the risk to the purchaser for a fortuitous loss of the object of the sale is delayed to coincide with the passage of title (A.1476 cc).

(v) Bilateral and unilateral contracts. The former are characterised by their reciprocal prestations which are interdependent in that if one party fails to perform the other party is not bound to perform either. Unilateral contracts are those which impose an obligation to perform upon one only of the parties to the contract, e g the contract of donation.

(vi) Commutative and aleatory contracts. These are both bilateral contracts but in the former case the parties know as from formation the extent of the advantage and sacrifice imposed by the contract whilst in the latter case these are unknown at the date of stipulation.

C. FORMATION OF CONTRACTS

The Civil Code does not dictate a general set of rules applicable to the formation of all types of legal transaction but rather limits itself to regulating the formation of contracts. A contract arises through a union of wills which is reached across an offer and an acceptance. A contract may be formed instantly, although it generally arises through negotiations which are of a mere preparatory nature and will only become relevant in the event that agreement is reached. However, even in the absence of an agreement, the negotiations are not without legal relevance as A.1337 cc imposes an obligation upon the parties to act in good faith during the negotiations, that is, an obligation to act honestly and fairly. This obligation is violated where a party ceases negotiations without just cause or fails to inform the opposite party of the existence of a cause for invalidity which would be discoverable with normal diligence. The violation of the obligation gives rise to damages for pre-contractual responsibility or *culpa in contrahendo*. However, the quantum of damages is less than for non-performance and is limited to first, the expenses and losses strictly connected with the negotiations, e g costs of travel and correspondence, and second, the advantage that the party could have achieved through negotiations with others, i e loss of profits.

D. OFFER

An offer must be complete, that is, it must contain all of the essential elements of the proposed contract. An offer may be revoked at any time before its acceptance. Moreover, an offer becomes ineffective, thereby freeing the offeror, where the acceptance does not take place within the time fixed by the offeror or by custom or within the time ordinarily considered necessary. An offer may be made to more than one person or to the public at large. If made to the public, it may be revoked in the same manner in which it was made even if it does not come to the attention of all who had notice of the offer (A.1336 cc).

In the case of adhesion contracts, which seek to eliminate the negotiation phase, the weaker contracting party (that is, the offeree) receives a special protection under A.1341 cc which provides: first, that the general conditions of the contract as predetermined by the offeror are only valid if the other contracting party, at the point of formation, 'knew or could have known of them using ordinary diligence' (A.1341(1) cc), and second, that *onerous* conditions must be approved separately and in writing so that the attention of the opposite party may be expressly drawn to them. The onerous conditions coming within this requirement are listed in A.1341(2) cc.

E. ACCEPTANCE

A contract is formed at the point at which the acceptance of an offer is communicated to the offeror. The acceptance must be timely and coincide exactly with the offer, otherwise it will constitute a counter-offer (A.1326 cc). The acceptance must be in the same form as is required for the proposed contract. An acceptance may be revoked (or withdrawn) provided that the revocation reaches the offeror before the acceptance (A.1328(2) cc). An acceptance may be tacit in those cases in which the offer, the nature of the transaction, or custom contemplate that acceptance may take the form of a commencement in performance.

Where the parties to the negotiations are separated by distance, the various theoretical possibilities as to the point at which the contract is formed are: at the emission of the acceptance (emission theory); at the despatch of the acceptance (postal theory); at the receipt of the acceptance by the offeror (reception theory); or upon effective knowledge of the acceptance by the offeror (communication theory). The Italian solution in this case is a compromise between the arrival of the acceptance (reception theory) and its effective knowledge by the offeror (communication theory): the communication theory (A.1326(1) cc) has been mitigated with a rebuttable presumption that the acceptance is within the knowlege of the offeror when it arrives at the offeror's address (reception theory: A.1335 cc). The presumption in A.1335 cc may be rebutted if the offeror proves that, through no fault of his own, he had in fact no knowledge of the acceptance.

F. INTERPRETATION OF CONTRACTS

The legal norms concerning the interpretation of contracts may be divided into several categories some of which form a certain hierarchy as to the order of their application.

(i) The strict interpretative norms (Artt. 1362–1365 cc) take absolute priority; their purport is that the common intention of the parties (A.1362 cc) must prevail over the literal sense of the words used in the contract. They ensure a prevalence of the intent rather than the declarations of the parties and therefore the negotiations and the manner in which the contract has been performed may be utilised as interpretative tools.

(ii) The interpretative-integrative norms (Artt. 1366–1370 cc) are utilised where the subjective search for the meaning of the contract was fruitless. These norms involve an objective interpretation directed to ascertaining the presumed intent of the parties. Foremost amongst these norms is the general and fundamental principle that a contract must be interpreted according to good faith (A.1366 cc) which, in this context, is to be understood not in a subjective sense but as the faithful behaviour of the parties according to the average social conscience. The more specific canons of interpretation in this category include: the so-called principle of the preservation of the contract according to which that interpretation which gives some effect to the contract is to be preferred (A.1367 cc); the interpretation of ambiguous provisions according to the general practices of the place where the contract was concluded (A.1368 cc); the adoption, amongst several possible meanings, of that most convenient to the nature and object of the contract (A.1369 cc); and the interpretation of printed forms, in cases of doubt, against their author (A.1370 cc).

(iii) The interpretation of the so-called 'obscure' contract. Where a contract remains obscure notwithstanding the application of the interpretative and interpretative-integrative norms, A.1371 cc provides that gratuitous contracts are to be interpreted in a manner least burdensome to the obligor, whilst onerous contracts are to be interpreted so as to equitably balance the interests of the parties.

(iv) The integration of contracts. Finally, A.1374 cc provides, in effect, that any lacunae in a contract is to be filled by resorting, in the first instance, to any legislative provision which regulates the matter or, in its absence, to custom and equity. Although A.1374 cc, like the interpretative-integrative norms, is concerned with the presumed intent of the parties, it differs from the latter because it concerns the integration of contracts with specific norms which expressly regulate the matter which has not been dealt with by the contract.

G. THE EFFECTS OF CONTRACTS

The general rule is that the effects of a contract, which has the force of law, extends to the parties only (A.1372 cc). There are two exceptions to the rule. First, the effects of a contract generally extend to either the universal successors (or heirs) of the contracting parties or to the particular or individual successor (or legatee) of the rights in question. Second, the Civil Code contemplates contracts for the benefit of third parties (Artt. 1411–1413 cc). The stipulator must have an interest, even if only moral, in conferring an advantage upon the third party. The consequences of such contracts are: first, the third party acquires an enforceable right against the obligor as from the date of the stipulation; second, the stipulator may only revoke or modity the stipulation before the third party has declared his intent to benefit from the contract; and third, the obligor may only raise defences founded upon the contract against the third party and not any defences subsequently arising between him and the stipulator.

H. THE OBLIGATIONS OF BUYER AND SELLER

The principal obligations of the seller are: first, the delivery of the thing sold to the buyer; second, in the case of obligatory contracts, the transfer of title to the buyer; and finally, the warranties against eviction and latent defects. The principal obligation of the buyer is the payment of the contract price.

A breach of the seller's warranty against eviction arises where the buyer loses his right over the object of the sale as a result of a judgment which finds in favour of a third party because of a defect in the seller's rights. Where there is a total eviction, the seller must restitute the price, reimburse the buyer's costs in entering into the contract, and make good any successive costs and the cost of any improvements made to the object of the sale. Where there is a partial eviction, the buyer is only entitled to a reduction in price and damages although the rules on total eviction will be applicable if, in all of the circumstances, it appears that the buyer would not have entered into the contract unless he obtained title to the total object of the sale. The warranty against eviction is an implied warranty which may be excluded or made less onerous by the parties although an exclusion clause will be ineffective if it is the consequence of the fraud or serious fault of the seller.

The warranty against latent defects concerns defects which either render the object of the sale unsuitable for the purpose for which it was intended or appreciably reduces its value. The warranty is limited to latent defects, viz, defects which, at the point of purchase, were unknown to the buyer and could not have been discovered by the latter through the exercise of normal diligence. The breach of the warranty gives rise to rescission or reduction in price and, in either case, damages. A defect must be notified to the seller within eight days of its discovery to avoid forfeiture of the right of action which is subject to a limitation period of one year from the date of delivery of the object of the sale.

I. THE SALE OF IMMOVABLES

Such sales are subject to a particular regime in relation to the following matters: form in relation to which the contract must be in writing; publicity which is achieved through registration, as in the case of registrable movables (see p 336, above); and the security of debts which in the case of immovables is by hypothec.

J. REMEDIES FOR BREACH OF CONTRACT

(i) General. Apart from cases of void and voidable transactions (see ch 1, p 35, above), the Civil Code provides that a contract may come to an end by either rescission or termination both of which are related to a defect in the nexus between the counter-prestations of the contract.

(ii) Rescission (Artt. 1447–1452 cc). Rescission is available in two situations. First, in the case of a contract concluded in a state of peril (A.1447 cc). The necessary requisites for rescission in this case are: one of the parties to the contract was, at the date of its formation, in a state of peril (that is, in actual danger of serious personal injury) known to the other contracting party; and the inequity of the conditions to which the subject had to succumb in order to avoid the state of peril. Second, in the case of lesion (A.1448 cc) which arises where the following elements coexist: a disproportion between the counter-prestations, that is, the prestation of the injured party must be double the value of the counter-prestation; the injured party was in a state of need which may also be of a non-economic nature; and the knowledge of the state of need by the opposite party accompanied by an intent to extract an immoderate profit in the circumstances. Rescission for lesion may be avoided by an offer of an increase in the counter-prestation thereby restoring an equilibrium between the prestations. Moreover, the action is not available either where the disequilibrium does not subsist at the date of the commencement of the proceedings or in the case of aleatory contracts in which a disproportionate outcome is inherent in the very nature of the contract.

(iii) Termination. Termination arises in three circumstances:

(a) TERMINATION FOR NON-PERFORMANCE (Artt. 1453–1462 cc). Where a party fails to perform, the opposite party may seek either specific performance or termination and, in either case, damages (A.1453 cc). Once a contract is terminated, specific performance is no longer available. A contract may be terminated without recourse to the courts in the following cases: first, where the contract contains an express provision for termination in the event that the contract is not performed in the manner stipulated; second, by the service, after the date for performance, of a notice of no less than 15 days calling for performance and a failure to comply with the notice; and finally, after the lapse of the term contained in a time of the essence provision unless the party entitled to the performance declares within three days that performance is nonetheless required. In every other case, termination must be sought from the court. However, in both cases termination is only available where two conditions are satisfied: first, the non-performing party's fault is essential even in the case of a time of the essence provision; and second, the non-performance must not be of a slight importance, although this requirement is inapplicable in cases of an express termination clause and the violation of a time of the essence provision. Termination is a termination *ab initio* although this does not prejudice a third party who acquired rights prior to the termination. There are two defences to an action for non-performance or delay: first, that the plaintiff failed either to perform or to offer to perform contemporaneously with the defendant (A.1460 cc); and second, that the patrimonial conditions of the plaintiff are such as to make the performance of the counter-prestation doubtful. However, a contract may contain a provision to the effect that a party cannot raise any defence with the object of avoiding or delaying performance but, because such a provision is an onerous one, it must be specifically agreed to in writing.

(b) TERMINATION FOR SUPERVENING IMPOSSIBILITY. As already noted, supervening impossibility extinguishes an obligation as a result of which the party who is freed from the obligation as a result of the impossibility cannot require performance of the counter-prestation (A.1463 cc). On the other hand, where there is only a partial impossibility, there is a partial extinction of the contract with a corresponding reduction in the obligation of the opposite party who may nevertheless terminate the contract if he has no appreciable interest in the partial performance.

(c) TERMINATION FOR EXCESSIVE ONEROUSNESS. Termination may also be sought where a contract has become excessively onerous through supervening factors which have brought about a disequilibrium between the respective prestations, eg a contract for the sale of an object whose price radically increases because of an unforeseen event such as war. However, in order to avoid a termination in every case in which a prestation becomes more onerous, it is only available where the following conditions subsist: first, the contract must provide for future performance; second, the onerousness must have arisen subsequent to the formation of the contract; and third, the onerousness must be due to an extraordinary and unforeseen event thereby eliminating the possibility of a termination of aleatory or speculative contracts. The defendant may avoid termination by offering to make an equitable modification of the conditions of the contract.

The individual sources of obligations: B. Unilateral acts

Unilateral promises, or unilateral legal transactions, comprise a closed class of typical or nominate obligations. A unilateral legal transaction has the following characteristics: the promise constitutes an obligation to perform even in the absence of, or before, an acceptance by the beneficiary; it is irrevocable; and there is no counter-prestation as performance is unrelated to a quid pro quo. The unilateral legal transactions are the promise to pay (A.1988 cc), an acknowledgment of debt (A.1988 cc), a promise to the public (A.1989 cc), negotiable instruments (Artt. 1992–2027 cc), the endowment of a foundation, the grant of a hypothec (A.2821 cc), and the creation of an *inter vivos* annuity.

The individual sources of obligations: C. Obligations arising by operation of law

These concern implied obligations which automatically bind a subject who finds himself in defined circumstances. An implied obligation arises in three cases:

A. THE MANAGEMENT OF ANOTHER PERSON'S AFFAIRS (Artt. 2028–2032 cc)

This arises where one subject (the manager) spontaneously (that is, without any request or obligation to do so) assumes the administration of the patrimonial affairs of another subject whereupon the law automatically imposes certain obligations upon both the manager and the interested party. This institution, however, can only arise where the interested party is not capable of administering his own affairs.

B. MONEY HAD AND RECEIVED (Artt. 2033–2040 cc)

The payment of a non-existent debt gives rise to an obligation for restitution which must, however, be sought within the ordinary limitation period of ten years. The extent of the restitution depends upon the good faith and capacity of the recipient: if the recipient was in good faith, he must return the money had and received and its fruits as from the date of the commencement of the proceedings; if in bad faith, he must also return the fruits received prior to the commencement of the proceedings; if, however, the recipient was an incapable, he need only restitute that which was converted to his advantage or enrichment (A.2039 cc).

C. UNJUST ENRICHMENT (L'ARRICHIMENTO SENZA CAUSA) (Artt. 2041–2042 cc)

Unjust enrichment arises where one subject, in the absence of a justifying cause, converts the property or activity of another subject to his own profit or advantage to the damage of the latter. The essence of the institution is not to avoid an enrichment but rather the impoverishment of a subject at the unjust profit of another. The result is an obligation on the part of the enriched party to indemnify the impoverished party who is given the special action of unjust enrichment. It follows that the elements of the action are: the enrichment of a subject; the diminution of the patrimony of another subject; a strict causal nexus between the diminution and the enrichment; and the absence of a justifying cause for the enrichment and the corresponding diminution. The defendant is required, whenever possible, to make restitution, in the absence of which the plaintiff is entitled to an indemnity equal to the lesser of the impoverishment suffered by him or the corresponding enrichment of the defendant. If, however, the defendant was in bad faith, then this limit upon the quantum of the indemnity is inapplicable and the defendant is fully liable in damages, even if they exceed the extent of the enrichment. The action of unjust enrichment is only available if the plaintiff has no other remedy.

The individual sources of obligations: D. Civil wrongs (Torts) (Artt. 2043–2059 cc)

A. INTRODUCTION

Obligations arising out of civilly illicit acts (or torts in the English sense) also form part of the general category of legal obligations. Therefore, civilly unlawful acts, like obligations generally, clothe the obligor with a responsibility resulting in a liability for damages.

It may be that an unlawful act gives rise to both criminal and civil responsibility. However, civil responsibility differs from criminal responsibility because: first, criminally illicit acts are repressed for reasons of a higher order, such as social defence, whilst civilly illicit acts are repressed to protect individual patrimonial interests; second, criminally illicit acts must be expressly and specifically defined by legislation (A.25 C; see p 267, above) whereas civilly illicit acts are defined generically: A.2043 cc defines them as 'any fact . . . which causes an unjust damage . . .'; and finally, the imputability of the fact is evaluated differently in the civil and criminal law.

Moreover, the phrase 'civilly illicit acts' is here used to denote extra-contractual responsibility and must therefore be distinguished from contractual responsibility. The latter arises from the violation of a specific duty arising out of an obligatory relationship of the parties, whilst the former involves the violation of a general duty not to injure the legal sphere of another subject. There are certain differences between the two types of responsibility. First, extra-contractual responsibility requires a mere natural capacity, that is, a capacity to understand and intend (see ch 7, p 296, above), whilst contractual responsibility requires the specific capacity to obligate oneself, that is, the capacity to act (see ch 1, p 25, above). Second, in the case of extra-contractual responsibility, the plaintiff must prove both the fact giving rise to the obligation and its imputability to the defendant, whereas in contractual responsibility the plaintiff need only prove the fact because its imputability to the defendant is presumed. Third, only in the case of extra-contractual responsibility are unforeseen damages recoverable. Finally, contractual responsibility is subject to the ordinary limitation period whereas extra-contractual responsibility is subject to a shorter limitation period (A.2947 cc). The case law has affirmed that both forms of responsibility may arise at the same time, in which case the plaintiff must elect between them.

B. THE ELEMENTS OF A CIVILLY ILLICIT ACT

The following elements of a 'tort' or civilly illicit act may be deduced from its definition in A.2043 cc:

(*i*) *The fact* which may be either an act or an omission.

(*ii*) *The capacity to understand and intend.* The damage arising out of a civilly illicit act must be caused by a fact which is imputable (that is, referable) to the defendant. The fact cannot be imputable to the defendant unless it is voluntary, that is, unless it is an act of a subject who is capable of understanding and intending the fact. Thus the actor must not be in a state of unconsciousness nor lack the powers of discernment, unless he put himself into that psychological state through his own fault or intent (A.2046 cc). A person responsible for the supervision of an incapable subject must answer for the acts of the latter unless he can show that he could not have avoided the fact (A.2047 cc).

(*iii*) Blameworthiness (*colpevolezza*) which may be either fault (*colpa*) or intent (*dolo*). As these notions are not defined in the Civil Code, their definition must be drawn from the Criminal Code (see ch 7, p 280ff, above). *Dolo* (intent) consists of a voluntary or intentional transgression of a legal duty. *Colpa* (fault), on the other hand, is the violation of a duty of diligence, care or prudence and can be *colpa lieve* which is a lack of the diligence of an average man (the *bonus paterfamilias*), *colpa grave* which is a serious lack of diligence and is equated with intent, or *colpa minima* which is only a minimal lack of diligence. The degree of fault relevant to extra-contractual responsibility is that of *colpa lieve*. *Colpa minima* is only relevant where expressly made so by law.

However, there are also many instances of strict liability in which responsibility is unrelated to either fault or intent but rather to the causal nexus between the act and the damage. Messineo considers this form of responsibility to be based upon the notion that a subject who exercises certain activities or utilises certain things assumes complete responsibility for all of the consequences. The most frequent cases of objective or strict responsibility are: first, the responsibility of employers for the illicit acts committed by their employees in the performance of their duties (A.2049 cc); second, the responsibility for damage caused by things or animals in the custody of the defendant (Artt.2051–2052 cc) unless he can prove fortuitous circumstances (that is, that the fact causing the damage could not have been prevented with ordinary means), *forza maggiore*, that the fact was attributable to a third party, or that the fact was the exclusive fault of the injured party; third, the responsibility for damage caused through the disrepair of buildings (A.2053 cc) unless the owner can show that the disrepair was not due to either a lack of maintenance or a defect in construction; fourth, the responsibility for damage arising out of the exercise of a dangerous activity unless the actor can show that he adopted all of the suitable measures necessary to avoid the damage; fifth, the responsibility for damage caused by the circulation of motor vehicles insofar as the owner of a vehicle is jointly and severally liable with the driver unless the owner can show that the use of the vehicle was contrary to his will (A.2054(3) cc); and finally, the responsibility of parents, tutors, instructors and teachers for the damage resulting from an illicit act of a person in their care unless the person in authority could not have impeded the fact (A.2048 cc). However, the prevalent doctrine is of the view that the second and final cases are not examples of a strict liability for the conduct of others but a liability for the defendant's own behaviour in failing to exercise his duty of supervision.

(*iv*) *Damage* which is the injury of a legally protected interest and gives rise to a liability for compensation of damages because the injury is a consequence of the violation of the legal sphere of the injured subject. The doctrine has devised various classifications of damage. First, direct and indirect damages, the former being the immediate and direct consequences, and the latter the mediate or indirect consequences, of the injurious fact. According to the literal wording of the Civil Code only the former may be compensated, although the recent case law has extended compensation to indirect damage in those cases in which the injurious fact has given rise to a state of affairs without which the indirect damage would not have come about. Second, foreseeable and unforeseeable damages both of which are subject to compensation. This is in contrast to contractual responsibility which is limited to foreseeable damage only. Third, present and future damages, which is a distinction that depends upon the certainty and existence of the damage as at the date of the proceedings. Present damage may always be compensated whilst future damage may only be compensated if its existence is certain, notwithstanding that it may be uncertain in amount. Fourth, actual and consequential damages, the latter being a loss of profit as a result of the civil wrong, both of which may be compensated. Finally, patrimonial and non-patrimonial damages. The former is a prejudice to the patrimonial interests of a subject, that is, losses measurable in money terms, and comprises both actual economic losses and loss of profits. Patrimonial damages is generally subject to compensation. Non-patrimonial or moral damages comprises physical and psychological injury (e g injury to the physical person, injury to a person's honour, the loss of liberty, the invasion of privacy and mental suffering on the loss of a loved one). Non-patrimonial damages may only be compensated in those cases expressly defined by law (A.2059 cc) which primarily restricts compensation to moral damages connected with the commission of a crime (see ch 7, p 306, above).

(v) An unjust damage. The injustice of an act depends upon its illegality: in other words, the damage is unjust and results in compensation where it arises through the illegitimate injury of the legal sphere of another subject. In certain instances, illegality is excluded, e g in the case of a legitimate defence (A.2044 cc) which arises where an act is committed through a necessity to defend a personal right or the right of another from an actual threat of an unjust injury provided, however, that the defence is proportional to the threatened injury; likewise, in the case of an act committed in a state of necessity (A.2045 cc), that is, an act which is committed to save oneself or another from an actual and serious personal injury provided that such state of necessity was not voluntarily brought about by the defendant.

(vi) Causation which is the nexus between cause (imputable fact) and effect (damage). According to the dominant case law, the necessary nexus does not exist where the damage is the result of an abnormal and fortuitous combination of extraneous circumstances, but only where the damage is the result of the natural order of things.

C. THE CONSEQUENCE OF CIVIL RESPONSIBILITY: COMPENSATION FOR
DAMAGE

Damages generally comprise a sum of money equivalent to the
patrimonial damage suffered by the plaintiff, that is, actual losses, loss
of profits and future damages. The plaintiff may, in addition, seek a
'restitutio in integrum' or specific restitution (A.2058 cc), eg the plaintiff
may request the restitution of the thing which he lost, the restoration of
property to its previous condition, or the destruction of an indiscreet
photograph. Generally, specific restitution is either inadequate to
eliminate the effective damage suffered by the plaintiff or impossible:
in such cases, the plaintiff will obtain damages, which is the general
remedy, either alone or together with specific restitution. It should be
noted that the dominant doctrine excludes the possibility of specific
restitution in the case of contractual responsibility.

It must be re-emphasised that in Italian law there is no general rule
which permits compensation for the injury or loss of rights of a
personal nature which are not measurable in money terms; in other
words, injuries comprising physical and psychological suffering. In
Italian law moral damages are only available in the cases defined by law
(A.2059 cc) and it so happens that all such cases relate to damage
suffered pursuant to a crime. One consequence of this restrictive
approach is that it generally excludes compensation for damages in
cases of violations of privacy because such violations do not constitute a
crime unless they are committed through some illegal means such as
telephonic interceptions. Therefore, as a violation of privacy does not
normally involve patrimonial damages, it follows that the defendant
generally avoids any kind of sanction. This is, therefore, an area in
which the doctrine has urged legislative intervention.

Succession

A. GENERAL PRINCIPLES

Italian law, like the common law, is concerned to achieve a system of
devolution of property on death such that the patrimony of the
deceased does not remain ownerless between the death of the deceased
and its acquisition by the beneficiaries. Italian law, according to the
Roman tradition, achieves this through the principle of continuity, that
is, the continuity of all of the deceased's active and passive legal
relationships in his successors. It is for this reason that the effects of the
acquisition of the quality of successor or the acquisition of rights in
property, even where these arise subsequent to the opening of the

succession, relate back to the moment of death. Therefore, the concept of the continuity of the legal personality of the deceased and its corollary, the concept of universal succession, operate a passage of title whereby the heir succeeds not only to the deceased's wealth but also to his obligations. Italian law, unlike English law, does not have the concept whereby the deceased's patrimony becomes a legal entity which, under the supervision of a court, pays debts, duties and legacies and is subsequently distributed.

Succession may be either by universal title or by particular title. Universal succession arises where the beneficiary succeeds indistinctly to the whole or a fraction of the deceased's patrimony. In this case the beneficiary is known as 'heir', and his entitlement as 'inheritance'. Particular succession arises where the beneficiary succeeds to one or more specific real rights or relationships in such a manner that the benefit cannot be regarded as a fraction or quota of the deceased's patrimony. In this case the beneficiary is known as 'legatee' and his benefit as 'legacy'.

The distinction between heir and legatee has several important consequences. First, an heir, as a universal successor to the active and passive relationships of the deceased, substitutes the deceased as to possession which continues in the heir, as from the opening of the succession, with the same nature that it had in the deceased, e g in good or bad faith. A legatee does not substitute the deceased but begins a new possession to which he may join the deceased in order to reap its benefits. Second, as the heir substitutes the deceased in all his active and passive relationships, the heir becomes personally liable for all of the debts of the deceased and is therefore liable beyond the value of the assets received in the inheritance unless he accepted the inheritance with the benefit of inventory. A legatee, because he succeeds to a specific active relationship only, is not liable for debts unless the legacy was expressly charged with debts by the deceased. Third, the acquisition of an inheritance requires an acceptance by the heir (A.459 cc) whereas in the case of a particular succession the legatee acquires the legacy *ipso iure* subject to a right of renunciation.

It follows that universal succession is a necessary phenomenon; whilst particular succession is optional, universal succession is necessary because the system requires that at the death of every individual there *must* be an heir. If the deceased disposes of the whole of his estate by legacy, then the quality of heir is attributed to those legatees who would be heirs under a distribution on intestacy. As a universal succession becomes effective as from the death of the deceased, it cannot be limited to take effect from a later date and once accepted cannot be revoked. Furthermore, where the beneficiaries (under a will or an intestacy) do not immediately accept, the court may, in order to avoid the patrimony remaining in abeyance and without protection pending acceptance, nominate a curator who has the duty to care for the interests of the inheritance until either its acceptance or its devolution to the State where an acceptance is not forthcoming (A.528 cc). The curator must proceed to make an inventory and account to the court, and may pay debts and liabilities with the previous authority of the court. The recent doctrine considers that the institution of the curator gives rise to an autonomous patrimony pending either its disappearance upon an acceptance or its becoming a 'separate patrimony' upon an acceptance with the benefit of inventory.

Italian law prohibits all agreements created outside a will concerning the devolution of an estate (A.458 cc). Agreements with such an objective generally fall into three broad types: contracts as to dispositions by will, the alienation of an expectation in a future estate, and the renunciation of rights in a future succession. Moreover, in the same vein, Italian law refuses to enforce any fiduciary dispositions contained in a will, that is, dispositions with which the testator gives property to an apparent beneficiary on the understanding that the latter will transfer the property to a third person. Article 627(1) cc prohibits any legal action to require the apparent beneficiary to perform the trust although, according to A.627(2) cc, if the fiduciary spontaneously performs the trust and transfers the property to the person designated by the testator, the apparent beneficiary cannot later claim restitution of the property. Even if spontaneously performed, the secret beneficiary does not become an heir but merely takes by virtue of an *inter vivos* transaction with the fiduciary. In any event, nothing in A.627 cc prevents the proof and consequently the reversal of the effects of a trust which has the object of making a gift through a fiduciary to a person incapable of receiving by will (Artt. 627(3) and 599(1) cc).

Notwithstanding the designation by law or by will of a person as a beneficiary, the right of that person to succeed is dependent upon two further factors: the capacity to receive and unworthiness. The capacity of natural persons to receive is expressed in the general principle that only persons born or conceived as at the opening of the succession are capable of receiving. For this purpose, all persons born within 300 days of the opening of the succession are, subject to any evidence to the contrary, presumed to have been conceived at the opening of the succession. The capacity to receive is broader in the case of testamentary succession because of the rule on future interests, viz, the rule that a gift may be made to the unborn children of a person living at the opening of the succession even if the beneficiaries have not yet been conceived. Certain persons are, in any event, incapable of receiving by will: a tutor or a pro-tutor of the testator if the will was drawn at a time when the former exercised their protective functions; the notary or other official receiving the will; and the witnesses and interpreters assisting in the making of the will. Recognised legal persons also have the capacity to receive but unrecognised legal persons must make an application for their recognition pending which their testamentary benefit remains in suspense.

Unworthiness is a cause for the exclusion of a beneficiary from the succession. The causes of unworthiness, set out in A.463 cc, may be conveniently grouped into two broad categories: first, acts against the person of the deceased; and second, certain serious acts against the testator's freedom of testation or the will itself. If the unworthiness is ascertained at the opening of the succession, then the unworthy person cannot claim his inheritance or legacy; if, instead, it is discovered at a subsequent time, the unworthy person must restitute the property and its fruits. An unworthy person may be 'rehabilitated' by the deceased either making a gift to the unworthy person in the knowledge of the cause of the unworthiness or expressly rehabilitating the unworthy person by will or by public deed.

Where an heir or legatee is unable (e g because he is unworthy or because he has predeceased the testator) or unwilling (e g because he renounced the gift) to accept an inheritance or legacy, then the devolution of the object of the benefit is determined according to three institutions: substitutional gifts, representation, and accruer. Substitutional gifts, which are only relevant in the case of testamentary succession, take priority over both representation and accruer. Where there is no substitutional gift, because either the will does not contain one or the succession is an intestacy, then representation is applicable (Artt. 467–469 cc). This institution provides that where a child (legitimate, natural, legitimated or adopted under a special adoption) or a brother or sister of the deceased is entitled under a will or an intestacy and that person is unable or unwilling to accept the entitlement, then that person's descendants take in substitution upon a *per stirpes* basis. Finally, accruer arises where several persons take jointly and one of them is unable or unwilling to accept his share in which case that share accrues for the benefit of the others. Accruer cannot take place where the testator has either expressed a contrary intention or made a substitutional gift nor where representation is applicable. In the case of an intestacy, this means that accruer takes place where several persons in the same category are entitled and one of them is unable or unwilling to accept, unless, of course, representation is applicable (A.522 cc). In the case of a will, where there is no substitutional gift and the institutions of representation and accruer are inapplicable, the lapsed share passes on intestacy.

A person can only become an heir upon acceptance. The right of acceptance is subject to the ordinary limitation period of ten years which commences from the opening of the succession (A.480 cc). That right may be forfeited prior to the expiration of the limitation period where the court, at the instance of an interested party, fixes a shorter period within which the beneficiary must either accept or refuse the inheritance (A.481 cc). Where a person dies without exercising the right of acceptance, it is transmitted to his heirs. Once made, an acceptance relates back to the opening of the succession, thereby preventing any interruption in title to the deceased's relationships. An acceptance may be either pure and simple or with the benefit of inventory. In the former case there is a fusion of the patrimonies of the deceased and the heir as a result of which the heir becomes personally liable for the deceased's debts and hereditary legacies, even if their value extends beyond the value of the deceased's estate. On the other hand, an acceptance with the benefit of inventory prevents a fusion of the patrimonies of the deceased and the heir and therefore limits the heir's liability for the obligations of the deceased to the value of the deceased's estate. A person entitled as heir in a succession will be presumed to have accepted purely and simply where he takes possession of the hereditary property unless he completes an inventory within three months of the opening of the succession and then within a further 40 days elects whether to renounce or accept the inheritance.

One consequence of an acceptance with the benefit of inventory is that the deceased's creditors and legatees acquire a priority over the deceased's patrimony for the satisfaction of their debts and legacies. Where an acceptance is pure and simple, the creditors of both the deceased and the heir and the legatees of the deceased have recourse to the joint patrimonies of the deceased and the heir as a single fund for the satisfaction of their debts and legacies. It follows that the deceased's creditors fall into a disadvantage if a heavily indebted heir either accepts an inheritance purely and simply or forfeits the benefit of inventory. In such cases the creditors and legatees of the deceased are entitled to seek a separation of the patrimonies, whereupon the 'separated' creditors and legatees take priority against the creditors of the heir and the non-separated creditors and legatees of the deceased in having their claims satisfied from the hereditary property.

An heir, as already noted, may renounce an inheritance, in which case he remains isolated from the succession and no creditor of the deceased may seek payment of hereditary debts from him. As a result of the prohibition against agreements concerning succession, a renunciation may only be validly made after the opening of the succession. Moreover, the renunciation must be in a solemn form received by either a notary or the clerk of the territorially competent court. A renunciation, however, may obviously operate to the disadvantage of the creditors of the renouncing heir in which case the creditors may seek an authorisation from the court to accept the inheritance in the name and stead of the renouncing heir but solely for the purpose of satisfying their claims out of the inheritance. A renunciation, finally, may be revoked within the ordinary limitation period provided that there has not been an acceptance by other heirs in the interim. In any event the revocation of the renunciation does not prejudice any third parties who have acquired rights over the hereditary mass in the meantime.

B. INTESTACY

The Civil Code lists the following categories of persons as eligibile to succeed in an intestacy: the surviving spouse, the legitimate and natural descendants, the legitimate ascendants, the brothers and sisters, the parents of a natural child, other relatives up to the sixth degree, and the State (A.565 cc).

The surviving spouse has the following entitlements in the deceased's patrimony: one-half where the deceased leaves one child only (A.581 cc); one-third where the deceased leaves more than one child (A.581 cc); and two-thirds where the deceased leaves no children but only legitimate ascendants or brothers and sisters (A.582 cc). Where the deceased is not survived by any of the relatives mentioned in Artt. 581 and 582 cc, the surviving spouse takes the entire estate. A divorced spouse has no rights in the succession of his ex-spouse. In the case of a separation only the surviving spouse retains the normal rights on succession unless he was held to be at fault in the separation proceedings in which case there is only a right to a life annuity provided that at the opening of the succession the surviving spouse was in fact receiving aliment from the deceased. The size of the annuity depends upon the size of the estate and the number and categories of legitimate heirs but must not, in any event, exceed the quantum of the alimentary assistance which was previously enjoyed (A.585 cc).

The remaining persons entitled on intestacy may be divided into three categories. First, the legitimate, natural, legitimated and adopted children, and their respective descendants, all of whom exclude any participation in the deceased's patrimony by the ascendants or collateral relatives of the deceased (but not of the surviving spouse). Second, the ascendants, the brothers and sisters, and the descendants of the latter. As to ascendants, the rule is that the more proximate ascendants exclude the remoter ones. If there are several ascendants of the same degree, the paternal and maternal lines take half each irrespective of the number in each line (Artt. 569 and 571 cc). As to brothers and sisters, those of the half-blood take half of the share taken by the brothers and sisters of the full-blood (A.570 cc). Third, the collateral relatives, ranging from the third to the sixth degrees, who are only entitled if there are no relatives in the other classes mentioned above. Again, a more proximate degree excludes a remoter one and all of those of the same degree share equally.

Unrecognisable natural children (a category which is today effectively limited to children born of an incestuous relationship or of a marriage which is null because of consanguinity) are only entitled to an annuity equal to the income on that share of the inheritance to which they would have been entitled had their filiation been declared or recognised. The annuity may be capitalised at the request of the child (A.580 cc).

In the absence of any person in the above categories, the patrimony of the deceased passes to the State (A.586 cc) by operation of law. The right operates without the need for an acceptance by the State and cannot be renounced. However, the liability of the State for the hereditary debts and legacies cannot in any event exceed the value of the patrimony received.

C. TESTAMENTARY SUCCESSION

The legislative definition of a will, namely, 'a revocable act with which one may dispose of all or part of his assets mortis causa', emphasises the typical or dispositive nature of a will. However, a will may contain provisions of a non-patrimonial nature which comprise the atypical contents of a will, eg the recognition of a natural child and the appointment of a testamentary executor.

Although the duty of giving effect to the will of a testator is normally left to the heirs, the law nonetheless allows a testator to nominate by will a testamentary executor who takes the place of the heirs in ensuring the execution of the provisions contained in the will. The office is of indefinite duration and gratuitous although the testator may provide for the remuneration of the executor. The person nominated as executor is free to refuse the office but if he accepts it he has several duties. First, the administration of the hereditary mass including the possession of the property comprising it. Such possession cannot normally exceed one year although it may be extended for a further year by order of the court. Second, the procedural representation of the inheritance. Third, the compilation of an inventory of the hereditary property. And finally, the render of accounts either at the close of his duties or, if his duties extend beyond a year, both one year from the testator's death and at the close of his duties.

A will is a solemn act, that is, it must be made in one of the forms prescribed by law, all of which require writing. The Civil Code distinguishes between ordinary and special wills. Ordinary wills may be either holograph or notarial wills and the latter are, in turn, divided into public and secret wills.

Special or privileged wills (Artt. 609–619 cc) are a species of public wills which can be made in certain special and exceptional situations as a result of which the ordinary formalities are relaxed. However, unlike common law privileged wills, they require certain minimum formalities, namely, the declaration of the testamentary intentions before a public official or permitted substitute and the reduction of the will into writing by that official, as well as certain other formalities depending upon the particular situation. The situations in which a special will may be made are: in cases of epidemics or public disasters when normal facilities are not available; on board a ship or aeroplane; and by military or assimilated personnel. However, again unlike the common law, a special will becomes ineffective at the expiration of three months from the return to normal conditions.

A holograph will (A.602 cc) must be entirely written, dated and subscribed in the hand of the testator. This form of will is only available to a testator who is able to write; if unable to write, a testator must have recourse to one of the alternative forms.

The notarial or public will (A.603 cc) is one drawn by a notary, according to the prescribed formalities, in the presence of at least two witnesses.

The secret or mystic will (A.604 cc) comprises the solemn delivery to a notary of a paper containing the testator's testamentary wishes, which paper remains in the custody of the notary. The secret will therefore comprises two elements: first, the will which may, unlike a holograph will, be written either by a third person or by mechanical means; and second, the formal delivery of the will, in a sealed cover, to a notary in the presence of two witnesses. The secret will has advantages over both the public will, because its contents remain secret, and the holograph will, because it avoids loss or forgery. At the death of the testator, the secret will, like a holograph will, must be registered so that third parties may learn of the contents of the will.

A will may be either void or voidable as a result of a defect in either testamentary capacity or form. The following persons lack testamentary capacity: persons under the age of 18; persons who have been declared interdicts for infirmity of the mind; and persons suffering of 'natural incapacity', that is, persons who at the date of the will, lack the capacity to understand and intend the effects of their act. In all of these cases the will is voidable and the onus of proving the incapacity lies upon the person who alleges it. Moreover, persons sentenced to imprisonment for a period of at least five years lose their testamentary capacity and any existing will is automatically revoked (A.32 cp).

A formal defect may result in the total or partial nullity or voidability of a will depending upon the seriousness of the defect (A.606 cc); the serious defects which give rise to nullity concern formalities whose absence would cast doubt on the authenticity of the will. However, what appears to be a null will may be valid if it satisfies all of the formal requirements of another type of will, e g a secret will which has been improperly received by the notary may nonetheless be valid if the will satisfies all of the requirements for a holograph will. Moreover, A.590 cc provides that a person cannot raise the nullity of a testamentary provision if that person, after the death of the testator, confirmed or voluntarily executed the provision in the knowledge of the defect. However, this apparently wide formulation of A.590 cc does not apply to a revoked or forged will, nor to testamentary dispositions which are either contrary to the principles of public order or determined by an illicit motive or condition.

A will may always be freely revoked by the testator during his lifetime. A revocation may arise either voluntarily, in which case it may be either express or implied, or by operation of law. An express revocation may be contained in a notarial instrument drawn in the presence of two witnesses or in a subsequent and valid will. An implied revocation may arise in the following ways: by a subsequent will which, although not containing an express revocation clause, is incompatible with an earlier will; by the withdrawal of a secret will; by the destruction, tearing or cancellation of a holograph will; and by the alienation or transformation of a thing which was the object of a legacy. A will is not, unlike English law, revoked by the subsequent marriage of the testator. However, it is revoked *ipso iure* by the following events or circumstances: the birth of a legitimate child or descendant of the testator, even if posthumously; the legitimation or adoption of a child by the testator; the recognition by the testator of a natural child; and the testator's ignorance at the date of the will of the existence of a child or a descendant.

D. FORCED INHERITANCE

The rules on forced inheritance attribute to certain defined relatives an intangible right to a particular share in a deceased's patrimony. The total portion of a deceased's patrimony to which the favoured beneficiaries are entitled is called the 'reserve'. The rights to the reserve therefore limit the freedom of testation and, moreover, correct or neutralise the effects of both testamentary dispositions and gifts *inter vivos* which violate those rights. Notwithstanding that it is a controversial issue, it appears that forced inheritance (which resembles intestacy because it applies by operation of law) is not a separate form of succession but rather operates as a corrective to either testamentary or intestate succession where the benefits under either of these violate the reserve or the individual forced shares of the favoured beneficiaries.

The favoured beneficiaries are the surviving spouse, the children of the testator, whether legitimate, legitimated, adopted or natural, including their descendants when these are entitled by representation, and the legitimate ascendants (A.536 cc). A favoured beneficiary is an heir and therefore becomes personally liable for the obligations of the deceased, unless he accepts his interest with the benefit of inventory.

The intangibility of a forced share means first, that neither the deceased nor any other person may violate the rights of a favoured beneficiary (A.457(3) cc) and second, that the testator may not impose any burden, charge or other condition upon a forced share. Moreover, the intangibility of a forced share is to be understood in a quantitative and not a qualitative sense with the consequence that the favoured beneficiaries are entitled to a certain value only and not to any particular composition of the share. However, this does not mean that the rights of a favoured beneficiary are mere rights of credit against other beneficiaries; they are, rather, absolute rights over the hereditary property thereby giving rise to a right to follow the property which constitutes the forced share.

The presence of favoured beneficiaries means that the deceased's patrimony is divisible into two parts: first, the disposable quota (*la quota disponibile*) which is that part of the deceased's patrimony that can be freely disposed of by the deceased either by gift *inter vivos* or by will; and second, the reserve (*la quota legittima o riserva*), which is that part of the deceased's patrimony that cannot be freely disposed of but which must necessarily devolve upon the favoured beneficiaries. The size of the reserve is calculated as follows. First, the determination of the hereditary mass, which consists of the total value of the property belonging to the deceased at the date of death (that is, the actual estate, or *relictum*) minus debts. Second, the sum of the net value of the hereditary mass (the *relictum*) and the value of all property disposed of by the deceased by gift *inter vivos* (the *donatum*). Finally, the determination of the reserve by aggregating the entitlement of each favoured beneficiary in the fund constituted by the sum total of the *relictum* and the *donatum*. The entitlement of each favoured beneficiary, the size of which depends upon the classes and number of favoured beneficiaries in the particular case, is defined by the Civil Code (Artt. 537–548 cc). The balance of the sum of the *relictum* and the *donatum*, after the deduction of the reserve, constitutes the disposable quota of the deceased's patrimony.

If the calculation of the reserve reveals that the forced share of a favoured beneficiary has been violated, the favoured beneficiary may vindicate his rights by the reduction of testamentary dispositions and, if necessary, gifts *inter vivos* by the amounts necessary to re-integrate his entitlement; that is, by the reduction of the offending dispositions in an amount by which they exceeded that which the testator could have freely disposed of. This is known as the action of reduction (Artt. 553ff cc). There are two requisites to the action: first, the favoured beneficiary must bring into hotchpot any gift *inter vivos* or legacy received from the deceased, unless expressly exempted from doing so, and second, the favoured beneficiary must accept the inheritance with the *benefit of inventory* (A.564 cc). The action must be brought within the ordinary limitation period of ten years and if successful the reduction of the offending dispositions commence with the last one in point of time and then retrospectively in chronological order until the favoured beneficiary has re-integrated his entitlement: that is to say, first, all offending testamentary dispositions are reduced proportionately (subject to a different order of reduction stipulated by the testator) and, if this is not sufficient to re-integrate the entitlement of the favoured beneficiary, second, gifts *inter vivos* are reduced individually commencing with the last one in point of time. The reverse order of reduction is attributed to the later act of liberality aggravating the violation of the reserve.

The consequence of a successful action of reduction is that an injurious disposition is declared invalid and the donee or beneficiary of such disposition must give restitution in kind free from any charge or burden (A.561 cc). It is apparent that restitution in kind may operate to the prejudice of a third party acquiring title from a donee or beneficiary. However, the favoured beneficiary must first execute against the donee or beneficiary of the offending disposition and because the latter is personally liable with all of his own property it is only where such an execution is in vain that the favoured beneficiary may seek restitution from a third party. Only in the case of movables may a bona fide third party resist a challenge to his title by a favoured beneficiary (A.563 cc). In any event, a third party who is bound to make restitution in kind may always avoid doing so by paying an equivalent money sum (A.563 cc). Bearing in mind the effects of the action of reduction, a person who acquires an immovable must proceed cautiously where it was the object of a gift which was made by a person who had favoured beneficiaries. Such an acquisition is only unassailable after a lapse of ten years from the death of the donor. Moreover, it is of no avail to obtain a deed of release from all future heirs of the donor as such a renunciation of rights is invalid if made during the donor's lifetime (A.557 cc).

E. THE DIVISION OF LIABILITIES AND HOTCHPOT

The general rule is that debts are divided proportionately amongst the heirs, subject to any contrary provision by the testator who may charge the debts against one co-heir only or divide them in unequal proportions. Any variation of the general rule merely affects the co-heirs as amongst themselves as the creditors may always proceed against an heir for his proportional share of the liabilities as defined by the general rule. There are certain exceptions to the general rule as, for example, where a debt is charged on a particular property in which case the heir entitled to that property is solely liable for the debt. Hereditary burdens, i e liabilities arising in consequence of the death of the deceased (e g succession duties, costs of administration and funeral expenses), and legacies are divisible amongst the heirs in the same way as debts.

A general principle applicable to the distribution of a deceased estate is that of hotchpot (Artt. 737ff cc). The basis of the principle is that where a deceased has made a gift *inter vivos* to his legitimate or natural children, his descendants, or to his spouse, the law presumes that the deceased did not thereby intend to alter their benefits as prescribed by the will or intestacy but to merely make an advance on the future succession. Therefore any gift *inter vivos* which is made to any of the persons specified above must be brought into hotchpot which aims at maintaining the proportionality established amongst the heirs by the will or intestacy. The testator is free to dispense with the requirement of hotchpot. Moreover, certain gifts *inter vivos* defined by A.742 cc are not subject to hotchpot.

Donations

Book Two of the Civil Code not only deals with succession but also with gifts *inter vivos* (*donazioni*). It may appear strange that donations, which are considered by the civil law to be contracts (A.769 cc), are dealt with in the same Book as succession. The explanation lies in the close relationship, as noted above, between donations and forced inheritance. Because a contract of donation does not involve a quid pro quo, acceptance by the donee is not only a requisite for its efficacy but also a constituent element of the transaction (except in the case of gifts in anticipation of marriage) until which either the donor or donee may revoke the declaration of liberality. Furthermore, because of the enrichment inherent in a donation, the donee becomes obligated to give aliment to the donor if the latter becomes needy unless the donation was made in remuneration for past services or in anticipation of marriage. However, the alimentary obligation does not extend beyond the value of the donation which is still existent from time to time in the donee's patrimony. A contract for donation is a solemn act and must therefore be made in the form prescribed by law, that is, by notarised deed (A.782 cc).

Registration of deeds

The system of registration in Italy is generally that of registration of deeds and not registration of titles. The basic function of registration is, therefore, simply one of placing third parties on notice as to the present status of immovables and registrable movables. Registration serves the purpose of resolving a conflict between two or more persons who have acquired inconsistent interests through separate instruments from a common vendor. The acquisition of title is not dependent on registration which only assists in making and retaining priority. This is clear from A.2644(1) cc which confers priority not according to the date of the instrument but rather according to the date of registration. The only instance in which registration is also a constituent element in acquiring title is in the case of hypothecs (A.2808 cc), in which case the failure to register prevents the creation of a hypothec between the parties. Moreover, registration does not overcome any defect in the transaction giving rise to the registration. Only exceptionally may a purchaser who relies upon the faith of the validity of a registered instrument overcome any defect in his vendor's title by registration, e g a purchaser from a donee is only safe from the claim of a favoured beneficiary of the donor after ten years from the death of the latter provided, however, that, after the expiration of that time, the purchaser has registered prior to the registration of the proceedings brought by the favoured beneficiary.

Registration does not affect the application of the general law principle of *prior tempore potior iure*, or priority according to the date of acquisition, in the following situations: first, where there is a conflict between an original title (that is, a title which is not dependent upon its transmission from another subject) and a derivative title; second, where the conflict arises between persons acquiring title from different vendors; and finally, where neither party has effected registration. Furthermore, where there is a conflict between a real right and a right of credit, the real right prevails even if it is not registered.

In order to effectively rely upon registration as a means of priority it is also necessary that there be a continuous chain of registration which is not to be confused with the chain of title. This requirement arises from the very object of the doctrine of notice connected with registration, namely, the necessity that the register put third parties on notice of the present status of given property, that is, of the ownership and charges affecting the subject property. An isolated registration, in fact, cannot ensure that third parties will be made aware of all of the successive interests in an immovable because of the very manner in which the registries of immovables are generally kept: that is, registrations are not recorded with reference to the immovable itself but according to an index of vendors and purchasers. Therefore, A.2650 cc provides that where the registration of an instrument is available, all successive registrations dependent upon it will be ineffective if that prior instrument in the chain of title remains unregistered. However, the registration by a purchaser from a vendor who had not registered his instrument of acquisition (so that the registration is fragmentary, isolated and unconnected with a chain of registration) is not completely futile as the registration operates as a reservation. In fact A.2650(2) cc provides that when an antecedent instrument is registered, the later registrations take full effect retrospectively as from the dates on which they were actually registered and not as from the date on which the antecedent unregistered instrument is registered. The breach in the chain of registrations is completely and retrospectively overcome. Moreover, as between two purchasers from a common unregistered vendor, the first purchaser to register takes priority because the second purchaser would have been able to ascertain from the state of the register the fact that the property had already been transferred to the first registered (or reserved) purchaser. The reservation will not as is evident from the saving in A.2650 cc, operate retrospectively to prejudice the rights of a person (and his successors in title) who registers, prior to the registration of the antecedent unregistered instrument, a transaction entered into with the last registered link in the continuous chain of registrations as such person could not have been aware, because of the breach in the chain of registrations, of the reserved registrant and his registered successors in title. It is apparent that the purchaser of an immovable may only be certain of taking priority if both his purchase and all of the preceding instruments of transfer relating to the same property have been registered.

Generally, all instruments which involve immovables (A.2643 cc) and registrable movables (Artt. 2683–2684 cc) may be registered. Registrable movables comprise ships, aeroplanes and automobiles. In all of these cases registration serves its primary or original function of resolving conflicts between more than one alienee from a common alienor.

However, registration has also been given certain exceptional functions in individual cases. These arise in the registration of the following transactions: partitions of property (A.2646 cc), whose registration aims at protecting third parties who had acquired rights over the undivided property; the establishment of a patrimonial fund as between spouses and instruments concerning the separation of property between spouses (A.2647 cc), the registration of which enable the patrimonial status to be raised as a defence against third parties who ought to have been aware of it; the acceptance of inheritances and the acquisition of legacies (A.2648 cc), the registration of which merely aim at maintaining the continuity of the chain of registration of the subject property; judgments which give rise to prescription or usucapion (A.2651 cc), whose registration is required for fiscal purposes; and the registration of the commencement of proceedings whose registration, under procedural law, gives a judgment granting an application a restrospective effect to the date of the registration of the proceedings.

Chapter 9

Commercial law

Introduction

Historically, the increasing diffusion of trade stimulated by new geographical discoveries was accompanied by the development of a separate and special commercial law, the law merchant, adapted to the particular needs of trade. The applicability of this specialised commercial law was originally determined by membership of commercial guilds or corporations. The determining nexus eventually became an objective one, namely, the nature of the individual transaction. In accordance with this development, the Napoleonic Commercial Code of 1808 adopted the criterion of *acte de commerce* as the factor or nexus which determined the applicability of commercial law to any given transaction. The advent of the era of the commercial code, moreover, signified the period in which commercial and civil law were regulated by separate codes; it was the period of separate commercial and civil jurisdictions.

The first Italian commercial code followed the principles of the French Code which had, in any event, been introduced into Italy with the Napoleonic wars. In a separatist system, many institutions, such as the sale, are sometimes regulated by the Civil Code and sometimes by the Commercial Code depending upon the presence of certain requisites which qualify the transaction as either commercial or civil. Commercial law, therefore, constituted an autonomous system of specialised norms which prevailed over the more general private law. With the continuing expansion of commerce, there was a progressive widening of the applicability of the principles and institutions of commercial law which became more and more a 'common law'. This tendency towards the 'commercialisation' of private law culminated in the unified Civil Code of 1942 which, in repudiating the idea of separate civil and commercial codes, unified the law of obligations and adopted the notion of the 'commercial entrepreneur' as the sole criterion for differentiating commercial activities.

The modern commercial law of Italy is said to be characterised by three broad principles: first, it no longer constitutes a specialised body of law qualifying the ordinary civil law but is rather on a level of parity with the latter, as the norms of commercial law have the same formal value as any other norm of the general private law; second, it constitutes a particular branch of the private law in that it is regulated by the Civil Code and is not therefore subject to regulation by an autonomous body of law; and finally, it is the object of certain supranational norms because Italy, as a member of the EEC, is bound to adapt to and comply with Community norms on the subject.

The concepts of 'entrepreneur' and 'enterprise'

The legal concept of 'entrepreneur', introduced by the Civil Code of 1942, comprises the former and narrower concept of 'merchant' adopted by the repealed Commercial Code of 1882. Article 2082 cc defines an entrepreneur as one who professionally conducts an organised economic activity whose object is the production or exchange of goods and services. The qualification of a natural or legal person as an 'entrepreneur' gives rise to various rights, duties and responsibilities where that person exercises an entrepreneurial activity; in particular, the management of the enterprise, the obligation of providing appropriate working conditions by adopting all necessary measures to safeguard the physical and moral well being of his dependants, and a strict subjection to regulation. However, as shall become evident, practical considerations necessitated a less rigorous formal regulation of economic activities of a more limited scale.

Although the Civil Code does not define an enterprise, the prevalent doctrine maintains that its definition is implied in the definition of entrepreneur. It may, therefore, be defined as the professional conduct of an organised economic activity which has the object of either production or the exchange of goods and services. An enterprise, however, is not a subject nor an object of the law, nor can it be identified with a business (*azienda*). Rather, it is that activity which is directed to the organisation of the means of production.

An entrepreneurial activity has the following characteristics, deduced from the definition of 'entrepreneur':

A. ECONOMIC ACTIVITY

According to the dominant doctrine this means not only the creation of new wealth (that is, the production or exchange of goods and services, as the legislature puts it) but also the assumption of economic risk by the entrepreneur. In short, economic activity is that which, in the creation of new wealth, exposes existing wealth to the risk of loss. As a result of this element, it is clear that whilst agriculturalists and theatrical managers may be considered entrepreneurs, the mere enjoyment of property (e g the owner of a rural property, even if he obtains rent from it), mere speculation (that is, the acquisition of value through the lapse of time) and the activities of intellectual professionals and artisans do not qualify as entrepreneurial activities. It should be noted that whilst the doctrine is in agreement as to the exclusion of intellectual professionals and artisans from the category of entrepreneurs, not all of the doctrine excludes them upon the basis that they do not assume an economic risk. That part of the doctrine which relies upon the risk aspect emphasises that, because professionals and artisans have only an obligation to render a means and not a result, as a consequence of which they are entitled to remuneration irrespective of the result, the risk remains with the other party to the obligation. Other writers rely upon either the lack of 'organisational activity', which will be explained below, or the nature of the activity which, it is argued, is neither a good nor a service in the sense that these terms are used in A.2082 cc.

B. ORGANISATIONAL ACTIVITY

According to the dominant doctrine, this means the mediation of labour and capital. Thus notwithstanding that an independent professional conducts an economic activity, he cannot be considered to be an entrepreneur because the conduct of a professional activity does not involve any mediation factor.

C. PROFESSIONALISM

Professionalism is the systematic and permanent exercise of related activities which are directed to a defined end. Thus entrepreneurial activity must be habitual and continual, not merely occasional. A controversial aspect of the characteristic of professionalism relates to the profit motive. The majority of the doctrine is today of the view that the profit motive is not an essential element of entrepreneurial activity but only an incidental element. Although it is present in the majority of cases, there are many instances in which the profit motive is not part of the objects of an enterprise, e g co-operatives and those public corporations whose object is not profit. The essential aspect of an enterprise is rather the object of profitable management, that is, the capacity to cover the costs of production. A final aspect of professionalism is that the organised economic activity of an enterprise must be directed to the market and realise an exchange of goods or services. Therefore an entrepreneur who lives off his own production without offering it on the market cannot be an entrepreneur in a legal sense.

D. PERSONAL CONDUCT OF THE ECONOMIC ACTIVITY

The economic activity must be exercised by the entrepreneur on his own behalf. This leads to the assumption of risk which differentiates an autonomous worker from a subordinate.

Types of entrepreneurs

A. INTRODUCTION

The concept of entrepreneur as defined by A.2082 cc is very broad and comprises every form of organised productive activity, whatever its nature, size or object. Because of the very breadth of the concept, the Code itself contains three different criteria for the classification of entrepreneurs, each of which has important consequences. First, a qualitative criterion according to which entrepreneurs may be divided between agricultural and commercial entrepreneurs; second, a quantitiative criterion according to which entrepreneurial activities are divided between small and large entrepreneurs, depending upon their size; and finally, a personal criterion which is dependent upon the number of persons conducting and managing the enterprise and according to which entrepreneurs are divided between sole entre- preneurs (who may, nonetheless, have dependants) and collective entrepreneurs or companies.

B. THE AGRICULTURAL ENTREPRENEUR

Although the definition of entrepreneur is sufficiently wide to include agriculturalists, the latter have nonetheless retained certain privileges which they enjoyed under the previous system, namely, exemption from both maintaining written accounts and registration in the register of enterprises, and their exclusion from the purview of the law of bankruptcy and certain other aspects of insolvency. The agricultural entrepreneur is not subject to the norms applicable to commercial entrepreneurs and is, instead, regulated by special legislation and the relatively few norms on the subject contained in the Civil Code itself. The definition of the agricultural entrepreneur (and, therefore, of an agricultural enterprise) is contained in A.2135 cc which distinguishes between principal and connected agricultural enterprises. The general definition in A.2135(1) cc provides that an agricultural entrepreneur is one whose activity involves the cultivation of land, the production of timber, or the breeding of animals (the so-called principal agricultural enterprises) as well as any other activity connected with them (the so-called connected agricultural enterprises). Article 2135(2) cc then proceeds to define specifically connected activities as those activities which are directed to the transformation or alienation of agricultural products when such activities come within the normal conduct of agriculture. The definition in A.2135(2) cc has given rise to several interpretative problems, including the question of whether it is an exhaustive or merely exemplary definition of 'connected agricultural activities' although in this respect the dominant doctrine takes the latter approach.

C. THE COMMERCIAL ENTREPRENEUR

The commercial entrepreneur is defined by exclusion as comprising all of those entrepreneurs who do not exercise agricultural activities. In particular, according to A.2195 cc, commercial entrepreneurs include those conducting the following: industrial activities concerned with the production of goods and services; intermediary activities concerning the circulation of goods (e g distribution and finance); land, water and air transport; banking and insurance; and all other activities accessory to any of the foregoing. The majority of the doctrine maintains that this dichotomy between agricultural and commercial enterprises is exhaustive and there cannot be any intermediate or *tertium genus*, as some writers contend, in the form of a civil enterprise. It should be noted, moreover, that navigational enterprises are regulated by the Navigation Code and that banking and insurance are regulated by numerous special laws.

D. THE SMALL ENTREPRENEUR; THE CRITERION OF SIZE

The distinction between small and large entrepreneurs is important as notable consequences attach to this distinction. The small entrepreneur, like the agricultural entrepreneur, is exonerated from both keeping accounts and registration in the register of enterprises and excluded from the purview of the law of bankruptcy and certain other aspects of insolvency. Small entrepreneurs are defined in A.2083 cc as direct cultivators, artisans, small merchants and those who exercise a professional activity organised primarily with their own labour or that of their family. The definition specifically identifies three of the most common types of small entrepreneur and in its last part provides a general criterion for the identification of other categories, namely, the prevalence of individual or family labour over outside labour and capital. Certain problems in relation to the effect of A.2083 cc have arisen because of the existence of other inconsistent definitions of the small entrepreneur contained in various pieces of special legislation. However, the approach taken by Cassation, and part of the doctrine, has been that the effect of the somewhat restrictive and specific definitions contained in the various pieces of special legislation must be limited to the purposes of the relevant legislation and that for every other purpose the definition in A.2083 cc remains applicable. Other writers, instead, maintain that the particular definitions contained in the special legislation qualify the general definition contained in the Civil Code.

The legal consequences arising from the status of commercial entrepreneur

The status of commercial entrepreneur is acquired through the substantive requirement of exercising professionally an economic activity of a non-agricultural nature and is not dependent upon any formal requirement relating to registration which has a mere declaratory function. Conversely, such status is lost with the cessation of economic activity independent of cancellation from the register of enterprises. Entrepreneurial status arises as from the performance of the first extrinsic preparatory act which permits the individuation of the object and commercial nature of an enterprise. In the case of a company it arises at the date of the company's constitution even though it has not yet effectively initiated any commercial activities. Entrepreneurial status thereafter endures until the enterprise is liquidated.

Where one party to a contractual relationship is an entrepreneur certain consequences follow. First, an offer or an acceptance made by an entrepreneur in the course of his enterprise remains effective notwithstanding that the entrepreneur dies or becomes incapable prior to the conclusion of the contract unless the entrepreneur is a small entrepreneur or a contrary intent is evinced from either the circumstances or the nature of the transaction (A.1330 cc). Second, A.1341 cc, which concerns standardised contractual conditions, is generally applicable. The rationale of this article is the existence of an organisation of notable size which gives rise to the concept of the 'stronger contractual party'. Finally, in relation to the interpretation of contracts, ambiguous clauses are interpreted according to the general practices of the place where the enterprise has its seat (A.1368(2) cc).

As the conduct of an enterprise involves both risk and recourse to credit, persons having legal relations with an enterprise are protected through the regulation of the capacity to conduct commercial enterprises. An absolutely incapable person (that is, unemancipated minors and interdicts) can never commence a commercial enterprise, although he may, as in the case of ordinary incapacity, continue, after authorisation by the *Tribunale*, an enterprise acquired through gift or succession. Persons affected by disability (see ch 8, p 317, above), on the other hand, may, likewise, only continue and not commence an enterprise, subject to authorisation by the court, although an emancipated minor may, in addition, seek authorisation to commence a new commercial enterprise.

Article 2188 cc contemplates the institution of a registry of enterprises which has the object of publicising the affairs of both collective enterprises (that is, companies) and sole commercial entrepreneurs so that all persons who anticipate dealing with an enterprise may assess the security and value of the proposed transaction. The Civil Code imposes an obligation upon all entrepreneurs (except small entrepreneurs), public entities exercising economic activities, and commercial companies (except the simple partnership) to register thereby disclosing all of the more important matters concerning the life and activity of the enterprise. Registration has a dual effect: a positive effect as a result of which no person can raise his ignorance of a registered fact of which he is presumed to have notice; and a negative effect as a result of which a non-registered fact cannot be raised by an enterprise against a person dealing with it unless the enterprise can show that the person had actual knowledge of the fact. The main purpose of registration is merely that of notice; only exceptionally does registration also have a constituent effect, e g share companies which can only acquire legal personality upon registration. However, the registry of enterprises has not yet been established and a transitional system only is in operation according to which sole entrepreneurs and public entities are exonerated from registration and, therefore, from publicising their affairs. Under this transitional system it is only commercial companies and consortiums which have external activities that are required to register and make general disclosures. Moreover, an authorisation granted to an incapable person to conduct an enterprise, or its revocation, as well as any instrument appointing an attorney must also be registered.

However, two special and additional requisites as to the publication of commercial affairs have been recently introduced. The first, which is a consequence of the EEC Directive of 9 March 1968 n.151, requires publication in an official gazette (the so-called B.U.S.A.R.L.) of various matters concerning private and public share companies. This is additional to both any other registration requirement and the deposit of documents in the registry of enterprises. The importance of this form of publication is that all acts which must, in addition to registration or deposit in the registry of enterprises, be published in the B.U.S.A.R.L. may only be raised against any person dealing with the company after their publication unless the company proves that that person had, in any event, notice of the act (A.2457 *ter* cc). This provision, therefore, introduces an absolute presumption of notice of all matters published in the B.U.S.A.R.L. subject to a certain exception for transactions executed within 15 days of the publication where there was an impossibility of acquiring notice in the circumstances. The second innovation is the requirement that various matters concerning co-operative societies must be published in the B.U.S.C. However, unlike the B.U.S.A.R.L. it does not give rise to an absolute presumption of notice.

Another important obligation upon certain commercial enterprises is the maintenance of various records in accordance with defined formalities, including certain requisites as to audit and accounting procedures. Every commercial entrepreneur, except small and agricultural entrepreneurs, is required to keep the following records: a journal in which all daily operations must be recorded chronologically and immediately; a book of accounts, comprising inventories of the active and passive relationships of the enterprise, that must be prepared at the commencement of operations and thenceforth annually, concluding in each case with a balance sheet and a profit and loss account; and finally, all correspondence, contracts and invoices which, like the book of accounts, must be kept for ten years. Certain other books and registers must also be kept depending upon the nature and size of the enterprise. The records which must be kept by entrepreneurs constitute an important means of evidence. Their evidentiary value may be summarised in two basic propositions. On the one hand, that all records may *always* constitute proof against the entrepreneur, irrespective of whether they have been kept in the manner prescribed by law. However, once admitted into evidence, their evidentiary value extends to the whole of their contents including entries unfavourable to the person seeking to rely upon them (A.2709 cc). On the other hand, however, the tender of records by an entrepreneur in his favour is subject to the following conditions: (a) the records must have been audited; (b) the records must have been kept in the manner prescribed by law; and (c) the proceedings in question must be between persons who are obliged to maintain their records (that is, entrepreneurs) and concern the conduct of their enterprises (A.2710 cc).

The business or concern

A business is defined as a combination of various items of property organised by an entrepreneur for the conduct of an enterprise (A.2555 cc). The various property components are not necessarily owned by the entrepreneur but may be co-ordinated by him in virtue of rights other than ownership. Therefore the doctrine speaks of a 'holder of the business' in the sense that the entrepreneur is the holder of rights (not necessarily ownership) which enables a functional co-ordination and complete utilisation of the individual property components for the conduct of the enterprise. Furthermore, a business also involves contracts, credits, and debts, all of which are directly related to the entrepreneur. However, although related to the latter they are distinct from and extrinsic to the business. Thus there are three distinct concepts: the business (*l'azienda*) which is the composite whole of organised property; the enterprise (*l'impresa*) which is the economic activity conducted through the composite whole of organised property; and the business patrimony (*il patrimonio aziendale*) which is the totality of the legal relationships appertaining to the entrepreneur for the conduct of the enterprise.

The goodwill of a business consists of the increased value that individual items of property acquire through their combined organisation into a business. The goodwill of a business is expressly recognised by the Civil Code (A.2427 cc) and the recent law of 27 July 1978 n.392 relating to tenancies. The goodwill of a business is protected both directly and indirectly; directly by the law of 1978 which protects a lessee entrepreneur vis-à-vis the lessor through a presumption of the loss of goodwill by an outgoing tenant who must be indemnified for the loss by the lessor who must, moreover, make an additional indemnity if the premises are re-leased to a similar business as that conducted by the outgoing tenant; and indirectly through, e g the repression of unfair competition and the protection of distinctive marks.

The transfer of a business must be in writing, although this requirement generally relates to evidentiary purposes only unless the transfer of the business also includes an item of property whose valid transfer necessitates writing, e g an immovable. The transfer of a business, which concerns the various items of property that comprise the business, is different to the usufruct or lease of a business which, on the other hand, concerns the business in a unitary sense. The usufructuary or lessee of a business has two basic obligations: first, to manage the business without modifying its objects, and second, to replace both alienated stock and that plant which has deteriorated through use.

The assignee of a business automatically succeeds to all contracts, other than those of a personal nature, which were entered into for the conduct of the business (e g contracts of employment and leasing agreements), subject, however, to any agreement to the contrary. The succession to these contracts is independent of the consensus of the other contracting party who may only withdraw from the contract for just cause within three months of notice of the transfer (A.2558(2) cc).

As a general rule the debts and credits of a business pass to the assignee. A business credit passes to the assignee of a business either from the date of notification of the assignment to the debtor or from the date of the debtor's acceptance. In the case of a failure to give notice of the assignment of the business to a debtor, the debt is nonetheless validly discharged if it is paid in good faith to the alienor of the business, that is, provided that the debtor did not in fact know of the transfer of the business. As far as the debts of the business are concerned, although, as between the parties to the transfer of the business, they pass to the assignee, subject, of course, to any agreement to the contrary, both the assignor and the assignee of the business remain liable to the business creditors for the debts evidenced in the compulsory books of account and for any entitlements due to employees.

Article 2557 cc prevents the alienor of a business from initiating, within five years of the sale of the business or for the duration of its lease or usufruct, a new enterprise which because of its objects, location or other circumstances is capable of diverting the clientele of the business which has been alienated. The restraint of trade, however, may be varied provided that it does not operate to impede every professional activity of the alienor.

Certain of the provisions concerning businesses referred to thus far are not applicable to agricultural enterprises, viz, the need for written evidence of the transfer of a business, which is a requirement that is only applicable to enterprises which are subject to registration; the cumulative liability of the alienor and the alienee for the debts of a business, which is a provision that is only applicable to large commercial businesses which are required to keep business records; and the restraint of trade provision, which is only applicable to connected agricultural enterprises.

Moreover, none of the Code provisions relating to businesses are applicable to professional practices as professionals are not entrepreneurs. Therefore, the transfer of a professional practice is regulated by the general Code provisions and not the specific provisions concerning businesses contained in Artt. 2555ff cc.

The various distinctive marks of a business comprise its business name, insignia and trade mark. The business name must contain at least the surname or initials of the entrepreneur in deference to the principle of truth which requires that economic activity be conducted in the entrepreneur's own name. Moreover, the business name must not be such as to create a confusion with another enterprise which has the same object and operates in the same locality. A business name may only be transferred together with the relevant business. A business may also have an insignia, which is distinctive of the locality in which the enterprise conducts its activity and is subject to a similar regulation as for business names, and trade mark, which are distinctive of its products. The exclusive use of a trade mark may be acquired in two ways. First, by patent (the so-called registered trade mark: A.2569 cc) granted by the Central Patents' Office. The right then endures for 20 years subject to further extension. Moreover, if the trade mark is registered in Geneva it also acquires protection in all of the member countries of the Paris Convention of 1883 and the Madrid Convention of 1891. Second, by usage (the so-called unregistered trade mark: A.2571 cc) or, in other words, by general notoriety acquired prior to an application for registration of the same mark by another business. Of course, registration is to be preferred as it gives rise to an absolute presumption of ownership of the mark and its effects extend to the whole of the national territory whilst, on the other hand, a business relying upon usage must prove its ownership of the mark and even then the protection of the mark is limited to the extent of its prior use. A trade mark cannot be transferred separately from the business or one of its branches (A.2573 cc).

Competition

A. GENERAL

The principle of free competition is a corollary of the principle of the freedom of economic initiative contained in A.41 C. In reality, however, the Italian economy is characterised by monopolistic and oligopolistic structures, economic concentration, and industrial understandings, all of which impede free competition. Nonetheless, the Civil Code, strangely, proceeds from a presumption of free competition which the Code states must be exercised consistently with the protection of the national interest and within the limits fixed by law (A.2595 cc).

Other restrictions on free competition may arise either by operation of law or by agreement. Examples of the latter include: (a) agreements restricting competition which must be evidenced in writing and are only valid if limited to a given area or activity for a period not exceeding five years (A.2596 cc); (b) cartels which must also be evidenced in writing and may concern marketing, prices or contractual conditions; (c) sole agency agreements; and (d) preferential supply agreements (A.1566 cc). The limitations arising by operation of law may be directed to either: (a) the protection of a given entrepreneur and include restraint of trade (A.2557 cc) and the prohibition against an employee trading on his own account or on account of a third party in competition with his employer (A.2105 cc); or (b) the protection of all entrepreneurs conducting similar economic activities and include first, the concession of monopolies (usually in favour of the State or a public entity) for the exercise of certain economic activities, e g postal services and railways, although such exclusive position is counterbalanced by the obligation imposed on the monopolist to contract on the same terms and conditions with whomsoever requires his services (A.2597 cc), and second, the obligation to abstain from certain forms of competition which produce defined types of prejudice, that is, unfair competition.

B. UNFAIR COMPETITION

Unfair competition is defined as the violation of the norms of professional fairness with the object of deriving an advantage through the deviation of the clientele of other enterprises. Not withstanding that such illicit conduct is specifically dealt with by the Civil Code (Artt. 2598–2601), it also comes within the more general sphere of a civil wrong (tort). On the international level, unfair competition is regulated by various conventions which have been ratified by Italy.

The individual instances of unfair competition include drawing advantages from competitors through the use of similar names, insignias, and other devices apt to confuse (A.2598(1) cc), the discredit of the products of others or the false attribution of particular characteristics to one's own products (A.2598(2) cc), and all other forms of conduct representing a departure from the principles of professional fairness (A.2598(3) cc). Article 2598 is, moreover, complemented by the Paris Convention of 1883, as subsequently modified, which includes as unfair competition all competitive acts contrary to honest usages in the industrial and commercial areas. The available remedies against unfair competition are extensive and include declaratory judgments, prohibition, mandatory injunctions and damages. The defendant bears the burden of proving the absence of fault as he is affected by a presumption of responsibility.

Free and fair competition is also protected on the Community level by the EEC and ECSC Treaties, the most important provisions in this regard being Artt. 85 and 86 of the EEC Treaty. The former prohibits and nullifies agreements made between enterprises that have as their object the impediment, restriction, or falsification of competition within the Common Market. Article 86 prohibits the abusive exploitation of a dominant position within the whole or a substantial part of the Common Market. Abusive practices include the imposition of unjust prices and conditions of sale, limitations on production to the disadvantage of consumers, and the application of dissimilar conditions in contracts for equivalent prestations. An offender may be ordered to put an end to the infraction and to pay penalties and fines for delay. Both Treaties have a wide range of exceptions and also contemplate authorisations for activities which, although affecting competition, nonetheless contribute to the amelioration of production and distribution and the promotion of technical and economic progress. Finally, it must be noted that the operation of the Treaty provisions is limited to that conduct which is capable of prejudicing free competition between member States.

Co-operation between enterprises

A. CONSORTIUMS

(*i*) *Introduction.* A consortium arises where several enterprises form a group with the object of establishing a common organisation for the co-ordination of production and distribution. It may arise by agreement (through consortium contracts), by order of a public authority (so-called compulsory consortiums), or by legislation (so-called coercive consortiums, e g the Office for the Sale of Italian Sulphur). Although the object of a consortium contract is to achieve a more efficient economic structure for participating members, it is also capable of lending itself to the regulation of competition. Therefore, consortium contracts are subject to government approval and, moreover, once established, the consortium's activities are subject to various governmental controls.

(ii) Voluntary consortiums. The object of a consortium is always an economic one comprising that advantage which individual members intend to achieve through their association, e g saving costs or increasing profits. It is open to entrepreneurs only and it is irrelevant that they may exercise diverse economic activities. It must have a common organisation for the regulation of those activities subject to the consortium contract beyond which each enterprise remains completely independent and autonomous. The consortium may only come into existence pursuant to a written contract which must set out the following matters: the objects of the consortium; its duration which in the absence of any provision on the subject cannot exceed ten years unless it limits competition between its members when it cannot exceed five years; its seat; the functions and powers of the consortium organs; the rights, duties, quotas and conditions relevant to the admission, withdrawal or exclusion of members; and the sanctions for a breach of the consortium contract by members. The contract may only be modified with the consensus of all members (A.2607 cc). The Code does not require the establishment of an assembly, although in the silence of the contract on the matter, the rule appears to be one of collegiate decisions. Nor does the Code provide for an executive although as a matter of practice a common office appears to be a necessity for both management and control. The responsibility of the consortium managers is as set out in their mandate. The quota of an outgoing member accrues proportionally in favour of the other members of the consortium (A.2609 cc).

(iii) Consortiums with external relations. It may happen that a consortium needs to enter into legal relations with third persons in order to fulfill its objects. Although A.2615 *ter* cc admits the possibility of forming a company with consortium objects, the consortium may, without forming such a company, enter into legal relations with third persons through the establishment of a common office (A.2612 cc). In such cases the consortium contract must be registered in the registry of enterprises. However, such registration does not alter the nature of the

consortium nor does it convert the consortium contract into a contract of partnership. The consortium constitutes an imperfect patrimonial entity because, during the life of the consortium, the consortium fund, made up of contributions by members, is not subject to execution by the personal creditors of the members nor can the members seek its division or partition. Moreover, since the law of 10 May 1976 n.377, the representatives of a consortium are no longer personally liable for the contracts entered into on behalf of the consortium; their liability is limited to the extent of the consortium's funds.

B. PARTICIPATION ASSOCIATION (*l'associazione in partecipazione*)

An economic co-operation between two or more subjects may be achieved through forming, instead of a partnership or company, a participation association. The participation association is a contract which permits the associated person to participate in the profits or some other aspect of an enterprise upon payment of a defined contribution (A.2549 cc). The associated person does not become a partner but merely remains a creditor of the enterprise. The participation association differs to a partnership in the following ways: there is no common fund or partnership property; the enterprise remains, and the contribution of the associated person becomes part of, the personal property of the entrepreneur who alone acquires rights and obligations vis-à-vis third persons; the entrepreneur alone is liable to third parties (A.2551 cc); the management of the enterprise belongs to the entrepreneur alone and the associated person has only rights of account and inspection within the limits fixed by the contract (A.2552 cc); and the participation of the associated person in the profits and losses of the enterprise is regulated by the contract although his liability for losses cannot in any event exceed the value of his contribution (A.2553 cc).

C. THE TEMPORARY ASSOCIATION OF ENTERPRISES

This form of association, which is based on a Community model, was introduced by the law of 8 August 1977 n.584 and enables a joint tender for public works. It consists of several enterprises which, whilst maintaining their individual autonomy, associate through the grant of a collective, gratuitous and irrevocable mandate to one of the associates (the so-called 'head enterprise') who is thereby authorised to tender and later to contract on behalf of the group for the performance of all of the work associated with a given project (except for any part of the work excluded from the tender) by the members of the group.

D. TRUST CONSORTIUMS (*Consorzi-Fidi*)

The law of 12 August 1977 n.675 enables the formation of associations of small and medium-sized enterprises with the object of obtaining particular types of bank finance or additional credit at lower than market interest rates without having to provide real guarantees. The consortium forms a risk fund which is offered to credit institutions as a subsiduary guarantee which usually covers up to 50% of the risk in the case of the insolvency of a borrowing enterprise. This is sometimes supplemented with a personal guarantee from all of the member enterprises in the group equal to a sum which is a proportion of the maximum credit which can be made available to the consortium. The concession of finance to such consortiums is generally subject to a favourable report by a technical committee comprising representatives from both the consortium and the credit institutions.

Collective entrepreneurs or companies (le società)

A. INTRODUCTION

A company (*società*) is the collective exercise of an enterprise. From an organisational point of view, companies may be divided between companies of persons and share (or capital) companies. Companies of persons comprise the simple partnership (*società semplice*), the partnership (*società in nome collettivo*), and the limited partnership (*società in accomandita semplice*), all of which are characterised by the profit motive. Share companies, on the other hand, may have either a profit motive or an object of mutual benefit. Share companies with a profit motive are the public company (*società per azioni*), the stock company (*società in accomandita per azioni*), and the private company (*società a responsibilità limitata*). The share companies with an object of mutual benefit are the *società cooperativa a responsibilità limitata*, the *società cooperativa a responsibilità illimitata*, and the *società di mutua assicurazione*.

Although the legal nature of the formative act of a company has been controversial in the doctrine, the Civil Code specifically regards it as a contract. It can now, therefore, be regarded as settled in both the doctrine and the case law that it is a plurilateral contract in which all of the parties have a common object. Therefore the formative act of a company is subject to the general law of contract as to its necessary elements, interpretation and effects and, with certain exceptions, as to the capacity of the parties as well. The parties are free to select the type of company which is to be formed subject to one limitation only, namely, that a company with commercial objects cannot be a simple partnership.

The basic distinction between personal and share companies is that the latter have a perfect patrimonial autonomy, that is, the patrimony of the company is distinct from the patrimonies of its members as a result of which the members are only liable for the company's debts to the extent of their shareholding and, conversely, the company is not liable for the personal liabilities of its shareholders. In the case of personal companies, on the other hand, there is only an imperfect patrimonial autonomy because there may be the liquidation of a partner's share to meet his personal liabilities and, moreover, there is the unlimited liability of the partners for the obligations of the partnership. It is controversial whether a further distinction between personal and share companies is that only the latter have legal personality, although this appears to be the preferable view which has also been adopted by Cassation.

'National companies' only are totally subject to Italian law and these include both companies formed in Italy (A.2509 cc) and companies which, although formed abroad, have their administrative seat or principal activity in Italy. Foreign companies which have only a secondary seat with a permanent representation in Italy are only partially subject to Italian law, viz, they are only required to deposit and register their constitution in the registry of enterprises, publish their annual returns, and comply with the local law as to the conduct of the enterprise in question (A.2506 cc).

B. THE SIMPLE PARTNERSHIP (*la società semplice*)

This is the most elementary form of company and may be defined, by way of exclusion, as that type of company which cannot be constituted in any of the other forms permitted by law. Its fundamental characteristic is that it may only have a lucrative non-commercial economic activity. This form of company is, therefore, only available for the following purposes: first, and within certain limitations, agricultural activities; second, the management of immovables, provided, however, as also in the case of agricultural activities, that the activity of the company is not restricted to the mere enjoyment of its property or production, as the case may be, as this would eliminate the requisite of an 'economic activity' which is necessary for the company's existence; and finally, D.P.R. 31 March 1975 n.136 enables auditors to form this type of company. Part of the doctrine is of the view that this form of company has an unlimited use because it may be utilised for any activity defined as an economic activity by A.2247 cc provided that it is not also classified as a 'commercial' activity by A.2195 cc.

No particular form is required in respect of the contract setting up the company and it may, therefore, even be oral. However, because certain contracts are subject to registration, that is, where the contribution of a member consists of immovables or the company is to have a life exceeding nine years, the contract must in these cases be in writing. However, notwithstanding that in such cases the contract must be registered in the registry of deeds, it need not be registered in the registry of enterprises.

The company's capital consists of the contributions of members which may be in cash, kind, credit or services. The contributions or quotas are defined by the company contract or, in its absence, are deemed to be equal.

The general principle applicable to personal companies, and therefore to the simple partnership also, is that the right of management belongs severally to each partner who has an unlimited responsibility. However, the parties are free to vary the general rule and may provide for a joint management in which case the consensus of all management partners is required except where an urgent decision is necessary so as to avoid damage to the company. The Code does not provide for a decisional organ, such as a general meeting of members, and therefore it is sufficient to separately collect individual decisions without a formal meeting. Except for those decisions which are expressly required by the Code to be unanimous, the doctrine is in disagreement as to whether decisions must be unanimous or by majority.

The company name must contain the name of one or more partners but not the name of any partner who according to the partnership agreement is not personally liable for the company obligations.

Each partner, after approval of the accounts, has a right to receive his share of the profits. This is a major distinction between personal and share companies as in the case of the latter a member has only an expectation because the distribution of profits is subject to the deliberation of the general meeting. In the absence of definition by the company constitution, the division of profits and losses is presumed to be proportional to the contributions of the partners. If the contract defines the division of profits only, then any losses are presumed to be divisible in the same proportions. The partners are free to vary such criteria with the only limitation being that they cannot totally exclude any partner from participating in the profits and losses of the company as this would strike at the very basis of the existence of the company, that is, the profit motive which is connected with the element of risk.

A company, according to A.2266 cc, acquires rights and assumes obligations through those partners who are authorised to 'represent' it. Where, however, the company constitution does not provide otherwise, each management partner is entitled to represent the company. The liability for obligations assumed on behalf of a company are satisfied in the following manner and order. First, a company creditor may proceed against the company's patrimony (A.2267 cc). The creditor may be subrogated to the rights of the company against a partner who has partially or totally failed to make his contribution to the partnership. Second, a creditor may proceed against the partners who acted for and on behalf of the company. The liability of such partners is direct, unlimited, personal, and joint and several. When the creditor directly proceeds against such partners, the latter have the right to request that the company's patrimony be first executed upon (A.2268 cc). Third, the creditor may proceed against all other partners who are, subject to any agreement to the contrary, presumed to be personally and jointly and severally liable for the company's liabilities. Any limitation to the liability of a partner may only be raised against those creditors who had notice of any agreement to that effect. The possibility of restricting liability for company obligations to some members only of a simple partnership is a characteristic which distinguishes it from the ordinary partnership in which all of the members are unavoidably liable.

The patrimony of personal companies is said to be autonomous because, although it is available to company creditors, it is not directly available to the personal creditors of a partner: Artt. 2270 and 2271 cc. The rights of a personal creditor of a partner against the company patrimony may be summarised as follows. The creditor may always either execute against the profits due from the company to the partner or take any conservative proceedings to avoid the dissipation of the share due to the partner on liquidation. Moreover, if the other personal property of the debtor is insufficient, the creditor may seek the liquidation of the debtor's share in the company whereupon the company must carry out the liquidation within three months of the application. However, this latter remedy is not available in the case of either ordinary or limited partnerships: the personal creditor of a partner in such cases cannot, during the life of the company, seek the liquidation of the debtor partner's share.

A person may cease to be a partner by death, resignation or exclusion, none of which will, in general, determine a dissolution of the partnership. The death of a partner obliges the surviving partners to liquidate the share of the deceased for the benefit of the latter's heirs. In such an event, the surviving partners may also elect to dissolve the partnership or, if the deceased's heirs agree, to continue the company with them. As far as resignation is concerned a partner may resign from a partnership in the following circumstances: first, at any time, upon giving three months' notice, where the duration of the partnership is either indefinite or for the life of one of its members; second, for just cause only where the partnership is of a definite duration; and third, upon the occurrence of any event defined by the contract as entitling resignation. In every case, the resigning member is entitled to the liquidation of his share. A partner may, moreover, be excluded from the partnership either at the instance of the other partners upon the occurrence of certain causes defined by law, e g interdiction and the breach of certain provisions of the partnership agreement, or by operation of law where the continuation of the partnership is impeded through an occurrence referable to a partner, that is, the liquidation of a partner's share either at the instance of a personal creditor or pursuant to his bankruptcy.

A simple partnership is dissolved, according to A.2272 cc, in the following instances: lapse of time, where the partnership was for a limited duration and it has not been extended; fulfilment of the objects of the partnership or their supervening impossibility; agreement of all of the partners; a fall in the number of partners to one only unless the position is rectified within six months; and for any other cause provided for in the partnership contract.

c. PARTNERSHIP(*la società in nome collettivo: snc*)

The ordinary partnership is specifically regulated by Artt. 2291—2313 cc. However, the Code provides that any deficiency in its regulation is to be supplemented by reference to the provisions on the simple partnership (A.2293 cc). The two types of company are not in fact dissimilar, especially in relation to the internal relationships of the partners. Its fundamental and distinguishing characteristic is the unlimited joint and several personal liability of *all* of the partners for the partnership liabilities. The partnership agreement, which must contain certain details, must be in writing and registered in the registry of enterprises (that is, at the registry kept by each *Tribunale* pending the establishment of the registry of enterprises). Any modification to the partnership agreement must be unanimous and recorded in the registry prior to which it cannot be raised against any party not having notice of it. In the absence of agreement by the other partners, a partner cannot take part in any activity which is in competition with the company.

The patrimonial autonomy of an ordinary partnership is more rigid than that of a simple partnership. First, the liability of the partners for company obligations is both unlimited and joint and several, as a result of which the bankruptcy of the company necessarily results in the bankruptcy of the partners. However, the liability of the partners is a subsiduary liability only in that the company creditors *must* first execute upon the company assets and only in the case of their insufficiency may the creditors proceed against the personal estate of the partners. Second, the personal creditor of a partner cannot require the liquidation of the debtor's share in the company (A.2305 cc). He may, however, take conservative proceedings to prevent the dissipation of the debtor's share in the company, execute against the debtor's share of the profits, and provoke the debtor's bankruptcy (if he is a commercial entrepreneur) and consequently his exclusion from the company by operation of law. Third, every partner of the company becomes liable for obligations contracted before his membership of the company and outgoing partners remain liable for all obligations assumed by the company until its dissolution (A.2290 cc).

The company is required to prepare annual accounts comprising a balance sheet and a profit and loss account. The company may be dissolved upon the same grounds as for a simple partnership, as well as for bankruptcy or upon an order issued by the relevant government authority.

The following consequences arise where a partnership fails to register: the relationships between the company and third persons are generally regulated according to the norms applicable to a simple partnership; the company cannot enter into a bankruptcy agreement nor any agreement for its controlled administration (see p 421, below); the prescriptive period becomes ten instead of five years; and any partner may proceed to regularise the registration of the company or seek a mandatory order against the company managers to do so.

D. THE LIMITED PARTNERSHIP *(la società in accomandita semplice)*

The basic characteristic of this type of partnership is the existence of two classes of members: first, limited partners whose liability is limited to the extent of their contributions and who cannot participate in the management of the company; and second, unlimited partners who have an unlimited secondary liability for the obligations of the company and are entitled to its management. The existence of both types of partner is essential to the formation of the limited partnership and if either class subsequently becomes non-existent for more than six months the company must be dissolved.

All of the norms on ordinary partnership, as far as applicable, also regulate the limited partnership. However, the limited members cannot include their names in the company name which must be made up of the name of at least one unlimited partner and indicate the type of company. If this restriction, or the prohibition on management, is infringed by a limited partner, the partner loses the advantage of limited liability and, for the latter type of breach, may be excluded from the partnership. The rights of the limited members, according to law, comprise the performance of their duties although under the supervision of the managers, the right to receive and control the annual accounts, and the right to retain profits which were received in good faith and according to the regularly approved annual accounts although subsequently found to have been non-existent. The limited partners may be given, by agreement, the power to give authorisations and opinions, as well as powers of inspection and supervision. Given their limited influence upon the activities of the company, the shares of limited partners may be freely alienated both by will and, subject to contrary agreement, by *inter vivos* transaction provided that in the latter case the transfer is approved by a number of members representing the majority of the company capital. The transfer of the shares of unlimited members, on the other hand, depends upon the consensus of the partners, subject to any agreement to the contrary.

If the company remains unregistered, the relationship between unlimited partners and third parties is regulated in the same manner as for a simple partnership. However, the liability of limited partners remains a limited one unless they participate in the company's activities.

E. THE PUBLIC COMPANY (*La società per azioni: SpA*)

This is both the principal type of company and the most appropriate company structure for large enterprises which involve a considerable capital and the assumption of a notable risk. The peculiar characteristic of this type of company is that the relationship between the company and its shareholders is impersonal and anonymous; this explains why it was known as the '*società anonima*' under the previous legislation. The three distinguishing features of the SpA are: first, the liability of the shareholders is limited to their contributions; second, the participation of the shareholder in the company is represented by shares of equal nominal value; and finally, the company must have a minimum capital of no less than Lit.200 million so that companies with a lesser capital may only incorporate as a *società a responsibilità limitata* (see p 408, below).

The SpA is basically regulated by the Civil Code although there have been many recent changes introduced by special legislation. These changes comprise the increased publicity required of SpAs which are listed on the stock exchange by the introduction of a series of public controls administered by the newly established National Commission for Companies and the Stock Exchange ('CONSOB'); the introduction of a new type of privileged share, the investment share (*azioni di risparmio*); the better publicity and regulation of economic concentration; the better information of shareholders on matters of management; and a restriction upon the use of proxies at general meetings.

A public company comes into existence upon the fulfilment of three conditions. First, the stipulation of the company contract or Memorandum of Association (which is the constituent act) and the Articles of Association (which regulates the operation of the company). The Memorandum of Association must be, upon pain of nullity, in the form of a public deed prepared by a notary. Article 2328 cc lists those matters which must be specified by the company Constitution: the name, place and date of birth, address, and nationality of shareholders and the number of shares held; the company name which may even be fictional provided that it includes an indication of the type of company; the seat and any branches of the company; the objects of the company which are merely indicative of its activity as there is no doctrine of ultra vires; the subscribed and paid-up capital; the nominal value of shares; the total number of shares; the value of any credits and payments of kind, verified by a court-appointed expert; the criteria for the division of profits (subject to the restriction preventing the exclusion of any member from their enjoyment) in the absence of which there is a presumption in favour of their proportional distribution; the share of profits to be taken by foundation members; the number and powers of directors; the number of supervisory members; and the duration of the company. The stipulation of the company contract immediately gives rise to the three obligations contained in A.2329 cc which must be satisfied before the company can be incorporated, namely, the subscription of the whole of the share capital, the payment in cash of at least three-tenths of the nominal share value, and the procurement of all necessary governmental authorisations. Second, homologation by the *Tribunale* which effects a purely formal control to ensure compliance with all of the necessary conditions for incorporation whereupon the court may grant or reject the request for registration of the company. The *pubblico ministero*, the applicant, or any subscriber may, within 30 days, seek a review of the *Tribunale's* decree by the Court of Appeal. Finally, registration in the registry of enterprises and the publication of the Constitution and Articles of the company in the Official Gazette known as BUSA (The Official Gazette for Private and Public Companies). Upon compliance with both of these final conditions, the company comes into existence.

The major aspects concerning the pre-incorporation activities of a company (A.2331 cc) are: first, the prohibition on the issue and alienation of shares prior to the registration of the company and second, the joint and several unlimited liability of persons who have acted in the name of the company prior to its incorporation.

The valid formation of a company requires a plurality of subscribers, in whose absence the formative act is null. However, nullity does not occur where the absence of a plurality of members arises subsequent to the company's formation through the voidability of shareholdings as such a defect does not operate ab initio and does not therefore exclude the initial plurality of subscribers. Moreover, where the lack of plurality arises through a subsequent concentration of all of the shares in a single shareholder, this merely gives rise to the situation regulated by A.2362 cc which provides that where the company membership drops to one, the shareholder will have an unlimited liability for the company obligations arising during the period of his sole shareholding.

A shareholding in an SpA gives the right to vote at general meetings as well as certain patrimonial rights: the right to the dividend declared by the general meeting, the right to share in the residue of the company assets upon its dissolution, and the pre-emptive right to subscribe to new share issues. Shares must be nominative (and therefore transferable by entry in the company's register) except in the case of investment shares which may also be bearer. Shares are, like negotiable instruments, freely transferable although the company constitution may impose certain restrictions such as the requirement of certain subjective or objective conditions in the transferee, the subjection of the transfer to a discretion of a company organ which need not give reasons for its refusal, and pre-emption provisions in favour of existing shareholders. A company may have various classes of shares. First, ordinary shares (*azioni ordinarie*). Second, preference shares (*azioni privilegiate*) which confer a priority as to both the payment of dividends and the division of capital upon the dissolution of the company. They also generally confer voting rights although this may be limited by the company constitution to extraordinary general meetings. Third, stock (*azioni di godimento*) into which ordinary shares may be converted when, following a reduction in capital, the nominal value of shares is less than their market value because of the existence of capital reserves. These stocks therefore enable the stockholder to participate in the future economic fortunes of the company. Stockholders have a right to a dividend but only after other shareholders have obtained a dividend equivalent to at least the legal interest rate and, similarly, participate in the division of capital after the other shareholders have first obtained a sum equal to the nominal value of their shares. Stocks do not confer a voting right. Fourth, shares assigned to employees (*azioni assegnati ai prestatori di lavoro*) whose issue is subject to any special requisites stipulated by the company constitution relating to their form, method of transfer and inherent rights. Finally, investment shares (*azioni di risparmio*) which are directed to persons interested in small investments rather than participating in an economic activity. They do not confer a right to vote, but grant both a higher dividend rate and, at the dissolution of the company, a priority to the full extent of their nominal value. They also confer certain taxation concessions. They may be bearer and must not exeed half of the company's capital. The investment share is closer in nature to debentures than shares.

The Code contains a large number of provisions designed to protect the capital structure of the company. Briefly, these provisions: prohibit the issue of shares or convertible debentures at below their nominal value (Artt. 2346 and 2420 *bis* cc); subject to certain exceptions, prohibit a company acquiring its own shares or the shares of a company it controls (Artt. 2357 and 2359 *bis* cc); prohibit the reciprocal subscription of shares by companies (A.2360 cc); prohibit the distribution of profits not actually received (A.2453 cc); and oblige a reduction in capital in those cases in which the company assets have fallen by more than one-third as a result of losses (A.2446 cc). Moreover, A.2428 cc requires that at least 5% of a company's net annual profits be set aside in a reserve fund until an amount equal to one-fifth of the company's capital is accumulated. This statutory reserve cannot be distributed but may be diminished in exceptional circumstances after which it must be reintegrated when conditions permit. An additional reserve may be stipulated by the company constitution or the general meeting. The publication of a company's capital position is ensured through the detailed provisions in the Code which oblige companies to prepare clear and precise accounts at the end of each financial year.

A company, furthermore, may raise additional capital by the issue of debentures (*obligazioni*) which may be either nominative or bearer. The debentureholders are organised into a general meeting of debentureholders which decides matters of interest to them and elects a representative to act on their behalf. The representative executes the decisions of the general meeting of debentureholders, represents them in any bankruptcy or related proceedings, and protects their interests vis-à-vis the company. The existence of a representative satisfies the need to have a permanent spokesman negotiating with the company on behalf of the debentureholders.

The participation of a company in another company may give rise to either a control or association relationship. A company (whether an SpA or an SRL) is said to exercise a control on another company where the former first, has a number of shares or quotas sufficient to give it a majority of votes at the ordinary general meetings of the 'controlled company', second, is in a position to have a dominant influence on the life of the 'controlled company' as a result of particular contractual relations between them, or third, has a controlling shareholding in an intermediate company which in turn controls the 'controlled company' (A.2859(1) cc). The Civil Code prohibits a 'controlled company' from subscribing for or purchasing shares in the controlling company unless the subscription or purchase is made from the company's reserves other than from its statutory reserve (A.2359 *bis*(1) cc). A 'controlled company', moreover, cannot exercise the voting rights attached to its shares in the controlling company (A.2359 *bis*(2) cc). On the other hand, companies are said to be merely associated where one company participates in another company to a significant but insufficient degree to give rise to a control relationship; that is, where one company holds at least one-tenth of the share capital of another company, which proportion is reduced to one-twentieth where the relevant share capital is quoted on the stock exchange (A.2359(2) cc).

The regulation of the participation of companies in each others affairs has been made more rigid in the case of companies listed on the stock exchange as a result of the law of 7 June 1974 n.216. Article 5 of this law provides that every SpA or SRL which holds more than 2% of the share capital of a company listed on the stock exchange and every listed company which holds shares in an unlisted company or in an SRL in excess of 10%, are bound to disclose the position by written notice served on both the other company and CONSOB within 30 days of the above limits having been exceeded. If the disclosure is not made, there is a loss of the voting rights attached to the relevant shares. Where the participation is reciprocal, there is not only an obligation of disclosure but also of cesser to the extent that the participation exceeds the statutory limits mentioned above. In such cases, the company which first receives the disclosure is prohibited from exercising the voting rights attached to the shares held by it in the other company in excess of the statutory margin and, furthermore, it must dispose of the shares held by it in excess of that margin within 12 months.

The structure of an SpA consists of the general meeting (*l'assemblea*), the directors (*gli amministratori*), and the supervisory council (*il collegio sindacale*). The general meeting is the deliberative organ of the company although, in practice, the effective centre of power lies with the directors. Depending upon the matter for decision, the general meeting is either ordinary or extraordinary. The ordinary general meeting takes place at least annually and decides all matters of ordinary administration: it appoints the other company organs, approves the annual accounts, takes action in cases of maladministration and decides all other matters reserved to it by the company constitution or submitted to it by the directors. An extraordinary general meeting, on the other hand, decides particular matters such as changes in the constitution and articles of the company, debenture issues and the appointment and powers of liquidators.

The management of the company may be entrusted either to a sole director or to several of them in which case they constitute a board. Directors need not be shareholders and are appointed for three years with eligibility for re-election. Their appointment must be notified to the registry of enterprises which must also receive their specimen signatures within 15 days of their appointment. Moreover, directors must post a security in the form of nominative shares in the company or nominative government bonds. The directors have a tripartite responsibility. First, they are responsible to the company in damages for the inobservance of their duties. This is a responsibility which is based upon their contractual relationship with the company. Second, they are responsible to the company creditors for the inobservance of any obligation inherent in the preservation of the company capital.

Finally, they are responsible to the individual shareholders and non-creditor third parties who are directly damaged by their fault or fraud. Moreover, it must be remembered that as there is no doctrine of ultra vires, acts outside the scope of the company objects cannot be raised against a third party acting in good faith (A.2384 *bis* cc).

The supervisory council consists of either three or five permanent members and two alternate members elected by the ordinary general meeting from persons who need not be shareholders of the company. If the company has a capital of not less than Lit.500 million, at least one permanent member if the council consists of three members or two permanent members if the council consists of five members, and in either event one of the alternate members, must be selected from the role of auditors. The appointment of a council is, in any event, mandatory for all share companies of any type with a capital of not less than Lit.100 million. The members of the council remain in office for three years unless dismissed sooner for just cause. Its primary function is that of a supervisory organ: it reviews the activities of the directors, participates in the meetings of the Board, and may request any information of the directors. It also reviews the activities of the general meetings, participates in them, and may take proceedings to challenge any decision made by a general meeting that is contrary to law or the company constitution. It also has certain secondary functions of a supplementary nature: it may call obligatory general meetings where the directors have failed to do so, it may request a reduction in capital to cover losses where the general meeting has not done so, and it may perform acts of ordinary administration pending the appointment of new directors where the existing directors have ceased to hold office. The members of the council are personally responsible to the company for negligence and violation of secrecy in the performance of their duties and are jointly and severally responsible with the directors for acts or omissions resulting in damage which could have been avoided through a proper exercise of their vigilance.

The controls exercised by the supervisory council have been considered inadequate as the members of the council are, in practice, appointed by the same shareholders who control the general meeting and appoint the directors. To overcome this defect two external controls have been introduced. First, the establishment of CONSOB which has investigative and inspection functions over three types of bodies: share companies listed on the stock exchange; public corporations carrying on economic activities and whose shares are listed on the stock exchange; and unlisted companies which exclusively or primarily have interests in other companies or engage in certain defined activities and have a minimum capital and reserves totalling Lit.10,000 million. Second, in the case of companies listed on the stock exchange, the verification of accounts has been removed from the control of the supervisory council and given to so-called audit companies. These companies must be registered on a special roll kept by CONSOB and their objects restricted to the keeping and audit of business accounts. The appointment of an audit company, subject to the approval of CONSOB, is made by the general meeting of the relevant SpA. The appointment is for three financial years and may be renewed twice only. Moreover, it is always open to one-tenth of the shareholders or the *pubblico ministero* to request the judicial control of a company where there are well-founded suspicions of serious irregularities by the directors and supervisors in the exercise of their duties. The judicial authorities may thereupon order an inspection of the company and, if an irregularity is found, either convene a general meeting so that appropriate action may be taken or, in serious cases, dismiss the directors and supervisors and nominate a judicial director.

F. THE STOCK COMPANY (*La società in accomandita per azioni*)

This is an incorporated company in which the members possessing power (the director-members) have an unlimited personal liability for the company's obligations. It is the same as the SpA except that the power of management belongs to permanent directors who as a quid pro quo for their dominant position bear an unlimited, even if only a secondary, personal liability for the company's obligations. This form of company is today without a future and there are no more than 20 in existence. It has an affinity with both the limited partnership, because of the existence of two types of members (limited and unlimited members), and the SpA, because the members' participation in the company is represented by shares and the company must be registered in the registry of enterprises. The limited and unlimited members have the same shares, the only difference being that the unlimited members also exercise management functions which give rise to their unlimited liability. This type of company is regulated by special provisions supplemented, as far as applicable, by the norms relevant to the SpA. It must have a minimum capital of Lit.200 million and its name must include the name of at least one unlimited member and an indication of the type of company.

G. THE PRIVATE COMPANY (*La società a responsibilità limitata: SRL*)

This form of organisation enables smaller enterprises to adopt a non-personal company structure and therefore benefit from a limited liability. In other words, it is a form of organisation midway between an SpA and the personal companies or partnerships. It is regulated by specific Code provisions, some of which reproduce exactly the provisions applicable to the SpA and others of which merely apply, by reference, the norms applicable to the latter. In contrast to the SpA, it is characterised by a more flexible structure and greater participation of members in the company's management. The company must have a minimum capital of Lit.20 million which is *not* divided into shares but 'quotas' which, although may be of varying amounts, must be made up of multiples of Lit.1,000. Each member's liability is limited to the extent of his contribution or quota which is normally transferable and divisible. The company constitution must be in the form of a public or notarised deed and indicate the name and personal details of members, the company name which must indicate that it is a company with a limited liability, the company seat, the company objects, the amount of subscribed and paid-up capital, the quota of each member together with the value of any property and credits paid towards his contribution, the manner of division of profits, the number and powers of directors, the number of members on the supervisory council (if the company constitution provides for one) and the duration of the company. The company acquires legal personality upon its registration in the registry of enterprises. Membership of the company ceases by voluntary withdrawal, transfer of the relevant quota, execution upon the member's quota by his creditors, bankruptcy, forced sale of a member's quota to recoup arrears in contributions, and expulsion of the member. The SRL cannot, in contrast to the SpA, issue debentures. The company organs, like the SpA, comprise the general meeting, the directors, and the supervisory council. However, the management structure of an SRL differs to an SpA in the following ways: the company constitution may provide that the management of the company be entrusted to non-members; directors may be appointed for terms exceeding three years or indefinitely; and the directors are not required to post any security. The nomination of a supervisory council is only mandatory for companies with a capital of Lit.100 million or over. Where there is no council, the control over the company is exercised by the individual members through certain rights which are guaranteed by the criminal law, namely, the right to request information of the directors, the right to inspect company books, and the right of one-third of the members, at their own expense, to require an audit.

H. CO-OPERATIVE SOCIETIES (*Le Società mutualistiche*)

The common characteristic of these organisations, dealt with separately by both the Code and special legislation, is that of 'mutual advantage', that is, of providing goods and services directly to its members upon conditions which are more advantageous than those on the open market. The enterprise is collectively conducted by the persons who are to benefit from its goods or services so that its members and the recipients of its activities are identical. Provided that they comply with certain rules relating to the distribution of dividends and reserves, and the distribution of their assets upon liquidation, they enjoy certain taxation benefits. A co-operative society may be of a commercial or a non-commercial nature and may relate to consumption, production, services, credit or insurance (which is subject to particular regulation). It must be formed by a public or notarised deed and acquires its legal personality upon registration in the registry of enterprises. It must have at least nine members whose participation is represented by 'quotas', not shares. The liability of the members may be unlimited, in which case the members are personally and jointly and severally liable (which, however, is a secondary liability only) for the obligations of the company, limited, in which case the liability of members is limited to the extent of their quotas, or accessory but limited, in which case, apart from their quotas, the members are personally liable for a further multiple of their respective quota. The name of a co-operative must indicate whether the liability of members is limited or unlimited. All co-operatives are subject to strict governmental control and are required to publicise their affairs in the BUSC (The official gazette for co-operative societies).

The principal types of commercial contracts

The extent of commercial law is evident from the vast number of particular contracts denominated as 'commercial' by the doctrine and dealt with by the standard textbooks on the subject. They are categorised as 'commercial' because they are the types of contract which are necessarily or normally used by commercial entrepreneurs in the exercise of their economic activity. They range from the most important and common one, the sale, to such specific contracts as leasing, factoring, franchising, computer services, carriage, agency, banking, negotiable instruments, and insurance. Although the general principles of the law of contract are equally applicable to them, special rights and duties have grown around each particular type of commercial contract. However, it is not proposed to deal with all, or indeed, most of them. The sale has already been referred to in chapter 8 and this section will be restricted to bills of exchange and cheques.

Bills of exchange

This subject is dealt with by the special legislation of 14 December 1933 n.1669 which adopted the Geneva Convention of 1930 for the uniform law on bills of exchange and promissory notes. The doctrine defines a bill of exchange as a formal and abstract instrument payable to order that confers upon its legitimate possessor an unconditional right to the payment of a determinate sum at the stated date. The essential characteristics of a bill of exchange may be deduced from this definition. First, a bill cannot be a bearer bill but may only be transferred by order unless this too has been excluded by its indorsement with the phrase '*non all'ordine*'. Second, it is a formal instrument as its form is prescribed by law. Third, it must be complete in that it must contain all of the prescribed requisites on its face without reference to any other instrument. Fourth, it is abstract because it is not concerned with the legal relationship which gave rise to it. Fifth, it is self-executing provided that all stamp duty requisites have been observed, that is, no judgment is required against the debtor as a pre-condition for its enforcement. Finally, it enables the accumulation of several obligations having the same object, that is, the obligation of every successive indorser and guarantor is added to the original obligation. All such obligations, which are autonomous and therefore have a validity independent of each other, give rise to the joint and several liability of all persons who have indorsed or guaranteed the bill.

The Italian concept of a bill of exchange comprises two particular types. First, the bill of exchange in a strict sense (*la tratta or cambiale in senso stretto*) which is an order from one person (the drawer) to another person (the drawee) requiring the latter to pay a sum of money to a third party (the payee). Second, the promissory note (*vaglia cambiario o pagherò cambiario*) which is the principal type of negotiable instrument used in Italy and comprises a promise by one person (the maker) to pay a sum of money at a given date to another person (the payee).

A bill must be drawn on pre-stamped paper bearing the stamp duty corresponding to the amount of the bill. If a bill does not bear stamp duty *ab initio* it is not self-executing and has only the effect of an acknowledgment of debt or a promise to pay (A.1988 cc). A bill must contain the name 'bill of exchange', an unconditional order or promise to pay a defined sum which must be written in words and numbers with priority given to the former in the case of any difference between the two forms, the name of the drawee if it is a bill of exchange in the strict sense, the name of the first payee, the date of issue, and the subscription of the maker or drawer. If any of these requisites are missing, the instrument can only have the effect of an acknowledgment of debt. A bill need not contain the place of payment, in which case it is understood to be at the domicile of the drawee (or maker in the case of a promissory note), nor the date of payment, in which case it is understood as being payable on presentation.

The persons obliged on a bill of exchange may be divided into two categories: the principal obligors who are the maker of a promissory note and the acceptor of a bill of exchange; and secondary obligors whose liability arises upon a failure to honour a bill and are the drawer and indorsers of a bill. The guarantor (*l'avallante*) of a bill (see p 412, below) may be either a principal or a secondary obligor: he is a principal obligor if he guarantees the acceptor, otherwise he remains a secondary obligor. If the principal obligor refuses payment at the due date, the legitimate holder may proceed against any other obligor. The secondary obligor may then, in turn, seek reimbursement from preceding indorsers, the drawer or their guarantors. The obligations are autonomous because the invalidity (e g because of incapacity or forgery) of one such obligation does not affect the others, unless it is a nullity based upon the form or content of the bill caused by its drawer or maker in which event the nullity affects all of the other obligations arising on the bill.

The acceptance of a bill is the means with which the drawee obligates himself to pay the sum mentioned in the instrument. In the case of a bill of exchange in the strict sense, the drawer is obliged to pay in the event that the drawee fails to honour the bill as he is taken to have promised the act of a third party (A.1381 cc). Thus until acceptance, there is no principal debtor (unlike the promissory note in which case the maker is obligated from the start) and the drawer, indorsers and their guarantors are liable as secondary obligors. The institution of 'acceptance' was essentially meant to avoid the holder remaining in doubt as to the intent of the drawee. The holder is therefore able to exercise the action of regression (see p 413) against the drawer without awaiting the due date for payment where there has been a refusal to accept the bill. However, a bill need not be presented for acceptance until the due date unless it is expressly prescribed by the drawer or an indorser. Acceptance is expressed with the words '*accettato*', '*visto*' or equivalent expressions, or even by the simple subscription of the drawee on the face of the bill. Acceptance may be limited to part of the sum but no other conditions may be imposed.

As already noted, the transfer of a bill takes place through its indorsement which is a declaration written on the bill with which the indorser orders the debtor to make payment on the bill to another person (the indorsee). The indorsee acquires an original right free from any defects in the right of the indorser. The drawer or an indorser, however, may prevent the negotiation of a bill by making the bill not to order. Apart from the negotiation of the bill, indorsement also serves a guarantistic function because the indorser becomes obligated on the bill through its negotiation and is therefore jointly and severally liable for its acceptance and payment, although the indorser can avoid such liability by adding the words 'without guarantee' to his indorsement. The holder of a bill must present it to the debtor for payment either on or within two successive work days of the due date. In contrast to the general rule, the holder cannot refuse *part* payment because this partially releases the secondary obligors.

A bill of exchange may have one or more guarantors. A guarantee (*avallo*) is a declaration with which a subject (the guarantor) guarantees the payment of the bill for one of the obligors (drawer, maker, or indorser). Every successive holder of the bill acquires an autonomous right (that is, independent of the validity of any other obligation or of the relationship between the guarantor and the guaranteed party) against the guarantor for the obligations contained in the bill. Thus the right of a present holder is not prejudiced by any defences which the guarantor may have against any previous holder nor any defence which the guaranteed person may have against the present holder. Moreover, the holder is not required to firstly execute against the guaranteed person but may proceed immediately against the guarantor. A guarantor who effects payment thereby acquires an autonomous right on the bill, together with interest and costs, vis-à-vis the guaranteed person and those obliged to the latter on the bill. The guarantee must be written on the bill, the usual phrase being '*per avallo*' followed by the signature of the guarantor, although the signature alone on the face of the bill is sufficient. Although a guarantee may relate to part only of the sum in the bill, a guarantor may not impose any other conditions to his guarantee.

The holder of an unpaid bill may use the bill as an enforceable instrument and immediately initiate enforcement proceedings or he may initiate ordinary adjudicative or injunctive proceedings which allow a speedy recording of a hypothec against the defendant. In whichever form the action on the bill is taken, it is either a principal action, if it is taken against a principal obligor, or a regressive action, if it is taken against a secondary obligor. A principal action is not subject to any particular formalities but only to a three year prescriptive period. The regressive action, on the other hand, is subject to shorter prescriptive periods (one year in the case of actions by the holder against either an indorser or the drawer, and six months in the case of actions by an indorser against another indorser) and the onus of protesting the bill within the time strictly stipulated by law upon penalty of forfeiture of the right of action. A protest is a public act (usually drawn up by a notary or a judicial officer) with which a refusal either to accept or pay a bill is ascertained in a solemn form. The need for a protest may be expressly excluded by the use of the words 'without protest' or other equivalent forms. Apart from the protest, the holder must advise his indorser and any guarantors of the latter of the failure to accept or honour the bill, and each indorsee must, in turn, advise the preceding one, all within very short times and with particular formalities.

Apart from the proceedings on the bill (that is, the principal and regressive actions), the law allows as a final remedy the action of unjust enrichment so as to avoid that the holder remain prejudiced through the forfeiture or prescription of the actions on the bill. However, this action is of a strict residual nature in that it is dependent upon both the impossibility of bringing an action against *any* obligor on the bill and the absence of a right in the plaintiff to bring an action based on the fundamental relationship which gave rise to the bill. Therefore, if the latter right existed but was lost, unjust enrichment is not available. The action of unjust enrichment does not relate to the sum in the bill, but to the lesser amount by which the drawer, acceptor or indorser was unjustly enriched at the plaintiff's expense. The action must be brought within one year of the forfeiture or prescription of the action on the bill.

Cheques

The law on cheques is regulated by RD 21 December 1933 n.1736 which adopted the Geneva Convention of 1931 for the uniform law on cheques. The law on cheques is similar to that on bills of exchange, the differences between them being the result of the different functions served by the two instruments. A cheque, unlike a bill of exchange, is not an instrument of credit but a means of payment available to persons who have readily available funds in a bank.

Cheques are subject to a fixed stamp duty and are not subject to acceptance. A cheque must be presented for payment within eight days of its date if the cheque is drawn and payable in the same commune, or within 15 days if the communes are different. The drawer of a cheque is liable as a principal obligor and any indorsers as secondary obligors. The action of regression against secondary obligors is subject not only to the timely presentation of the cheque for payment but also to its protest. Cheques are necessarily payable on presentation. Part of the doctrine and case law consider undated cheques as null although this is a common practice given the very brief terms for presentation. Post-dated cheques are immediately payable notwithstanding any fiscal and criminal consequences. Proceedings on a cheque must be brought within a short prescriptive period and the action of unjust enrichment within one year of the forfeiture of an action on the cheque. In order to reduce the danger of payment in bad faith arising out of loss or fraud, various limitations may be placed on the negotiability and payment of cheques, e g by crossing.

A particular form of cheque is the bank cheque which obligates the bank itself on the cheque. It is more readily accepted because there is no danger that it is not backed by funds as there must be a special authorisation from the Treasury to issue bank cheques and the issuing banks must lodge as security with the Bank of Italy a sum equal to 40% of the total amounts in circulation in the form of bank cheques.

Bankruptcy

A. INTRODUCTION

Yet another important consequence of the qualification as a 'commercial entrepreneur' arises in relation to bankruptcy. The insolvency of a common debtor (that is, a person who is not a commercial entrepreneur) has only limited consequences as his sphere of activity is usually a restricted one. The law, therefore, restricts the individual creditor to recourse to ordinary enforcement proceedings against the individual assets of the debtor. There is no available system for the winding up of the affairs of a common debtor as a single unit, so that creditors who fail to intervene timely are merely left to the residue of the debtor's assets (see enforcement proceedings, ch 7, above). On the other hand, the insolvency of a commercial entrepreneur generally involves a vast group of creditors and has a broader repercussion on the general economy. The law does not allow individual enforcement proceedings but rather subjects the entire patrimony of the enterprise to judicially controlled proceedings to ensure an equal treatment of creditors. This form of collective enforcement, which has the object of liquidating all of the assets of the entrepreneur for the satisfaction of creditors, is known as the collective enforcement procedure or bankruptcy procedure (*procedura esecutiva concorsuale o fallimentare*), as distinct from the individual enforcement procedure which aims to satisfy the individual creditors of a common debtor. The essential characteristic of bankruptcy proceedings is that they are necessarily collective because they relate to all the property of the debtor in the interests of *all* his creditors. It is, moreover, based on the principle of equality according to which all creditors must be treated equally, subject only to cases of genuine priority.

B. THE ORDINARY BANKRUPTCY PROCESS

There are two prerequisites to bankruptcy proceedings. First, the subjective prerequisite, namely, the proposed bankrupt must be a commercial entrepreneur, whether a natural person or a company. However, small and agricultural entrepreneurs, public entities which are subject to the special proceedings analogous to a bankruptcy (forced administrative liquidation), and large businesses facing the economic difficulties defined in the special law of 3 April 1979 n.95, are not subject to bankruptcy. Article 1 of the Banruptcy Law (*lf*), however, expressly provides that a commercial company can never be regarded a small entrepreneur. Therefore, to satisfy the requisite of commercial entrepreneur for the purposes of the bankruptcy legislation, there must be an enterprise (as defined in A.2082 cc) which has a commercial nature (that is, not concerning handicrafts or agriculture) and which is not small (in the combined sense of A.2083 cc and A.1 *lf*). Second, the so-called objective prerequisite, namely, a state of insolvency which arises where the entrepreneur 'is no longer capable of regularly satisfying his obligations' (A.5 *lf*). Various situations constituting a state of insolvency are listed in A.7 *lf*. However, their common characteristic is that the state of insolvency must be permanent and not merely a temporary difficulty which can only give rise to controlled administration (see p 421, below) and not a bankruptcy.

Bankruptcy proceedings may be initiated at the instance of one or more creditors (even if the debt is not of a commercial nature), the debtor himself, the *pubblico ministero* who may act in the 'general interest' of all creditors, or the court ex officio where the insolvency of the debtor becomes evident during other proceedings. The competent court is the *Tribunale* that has jurisdiction in the place where the entrepreneur has his principal seat or, in the case of companies, where the company has its registered office irrespective of whether it coincides with the principal seat of the company. If the court refuses to declare the debtor bankrupt, the applicant may seek a review of the decision by the Court of Appeal. If the debtor is declared bankrupt, the debtor or any other interested person may bring an opposition within 15 days of the judgment. The necessary interest to bring an opposition may even be of a mere moral nature, e g the interest of the spouse of the bankrupt. The decision in the opposition proceedings is subject to appeal to the Court of Appeal and then to recourse to the Court of Cessation. In addition to declaring the debtor bankrupt, the judgment appoints the various organs necessary to the bankruptcy procedure (that is, the supervisory judge and the curator), orders the bankrupt to file accounts within 24 hours, fixes a term not exceeding 30 days within which all creditors must present their claims, fixes the date of the first audience for the verification of claims (which must be within 20 days), and, if necessary, issues a warrant for the arrest of the bankrupt and other responsible parties where there has been the commission of a bankruptcy crime, the most important of which is the crime of *bancarotta*. The bankruptcy judgment is publicised by affixture to the notice board of the court, publication in the legal notices for the province, service on the debtor, curator, creditors, *pubblico ministero* and the clerk of the *Tribunale* of the place where the bankrupt was born, and the registration in the bankruptcy register kept by the court.

Until a bankruptcy judgment is removed from the register for rehabilitation the registration gives rise to defined personal disabilities in the bankrupt such as the loss of the franchise, ineligibility to stand for public office, ineligibility to practise certain professions or to accept various positions of trust, and the inability to commence affiliation proceedings. On the other hand, however, the bankrupt is not excluded from conducting new commercial activities although their profits fall into the bankruptcy. The bankrupt is dispossessed of his property which is administered by a curator who takes possession of it. The bankrupt does not, however, lose title to his property but merely to the rights of its administration and alienation. The dispossession does not extend to the property listed in A.46 *lf* (that is, broadly, personal effects and those earnings necessary for the maintenance of the bankrupt and his family) and the family residence (but, again, only to the extent that it is necessary for the bankrupt and his family). From the creditors' point of view, the effect of the bankruptcy is that it commences the concurrent satisfaction of all creditors from the bankrupt's estate as a result of which, first, individual execution proceedings are inadmissible, save any rights of secured creditors, and second, all credits become non-interest bearing, except, again, in the case of secured debts as to which Artt. 2788 and 2855 cc apply.

The bankrupt estate may also comprise property which had been alienated prior to the bankruptcy declaration. The procedure through which such property is recouped for the benefit of creditors is known as bankruptcy revocation (*revocatoria faillimentare*) which may only be brought by the curator. The object of the action is to render ineffective any disposition which was made to defraud the creditors. Transactions subject to revocation may be grouped into three broad categories. First, transactions which are automatically ineffective vis-à-vis the creditors, that is, gratuitous transactions and the payment of debts falling due on or after the date of the bankruptcy, where the transaction or payment took place within a period of two years prior to the bankruptcy. Second, onerous transactions and the payment of statute-barred debts or guarantees where the transaction or payment was made within a period of two years (or in the case of certain transactions, within one year) prior to the bankruptcy and was surrounded by irregularities which arouse a suspicion of fraudulent intent. In such cases there is a presumption of fraud which may, however, be rebutted by the other party to the transaction by showing that he was ignorant, as at the date of the transaction or payment, of the debtor's state of insolvency. Third, onerous transactions and the payment of debts and guarantees where the transaction or payment does not appear to be irregular. Such transactions may only be revoked if the curator proves that the other party to the transaction knew, as at the date of the transaction or payment, of the debtor's state of insolvency. Finally, it should be noted that a bankruptcy does not per se rescind a contract.

The effect of a bankruptcy on the property acquired by the spouse of a bankrupt is dealt with by A.70 *lf* which provides that property acquired by the bankrupt's spouse within a period of five years prior to the bankruptcy forms part of the bankrupt estate. This principle is based upon the rebuttable presumption that the property of the spouse has been acquired with the funds of the bankrupt. If, in the meantime, the property acquired by the spouse has been alienated or mortgaged by the spouse, revocation is not available if the third party proves his good faith, that is, the absence of notice that the property had been acquired with the funds of the bankrupt. If, however, the third party is unable to show good faith, or the curator proves bad faith, the property does not automatically form part of the bankrupt estate but merely becomes subject to an ordinary or bankruptcy revocation. This presumption, known as the '*muciana*' presumption of the Roman law, however, is only of a limited significance nowadays because the usual communion of property regime, which is applicable to spouses, applies irrespective of whether the property was acquired by one or the other of the spouses (see p 326ff, above).

The bankruptcy process involves four different organs. First, the *Tribunale* which declares the bankruptcy and puts the process in motion. It has jurisdiction over every aspect or matter arising out of the bankruptcy. Second, the supervisory judge who directs the bankruptcy process and supervises the activities of the curator. All decisions of the supervisory judge are subject to appeal to the *Tribunale*. Third, the curator who carries out the bankruptcy process and whose principal duty is the administration of the property of the bankrupt. The bankrupt or any interested party may complain about any administrative act of the curator to the supervisory judge whose decision, as already noted, is then subject to appeal to the *Tribunale*. Finally, the committee of creditors which consists of between three and five creditors appointed by the supervisory judge. The committee has a purely consultative function whose opinions, even in those instances in which it must be sought, are not binding. Each member of the committee has powers of supervision and the right to be specifically informed on every aspect of the proceedings.

After a bankruptcy judgment is made, the bankruptcy process may be divided into five broad phases. First, the preservation and administration of the bankrupt's estate. The preservation of the estate involves the affixture of seals where the nature of the property permits it, the preparation by the curator of an inventory of the property, and the adoption of any measures necessary to prevent the deterioration and loss of the property. The administration of the estate is carried out by the curator who although may freely perform all acts of ordinary administration may only carry out acts of extraordinary administration after authorisation by the supervisory judge. Moreover, the bankrupt's enterprise may, in certain circumstances, be temporarily continued. Second, the determination of the claims and their priority. In this phase there is the individuation of the creditors who are to be admitted to the distribution of the bankrupt's estate. The creditors must submit their claims within the time fixed by the bankruptcy judgment after which the supervisory judge determines both the admission of the claims and their order of priority. The supervisory judge also decides if there are any transactions subject to revocation. Creditors who are not admitted to the bankruptcy or, if admitted, dispute their priority, may oppose the decision of the supervisory judge before the *Tribunale* whose decision may, in turn, be challenged before Cassation. Third, the determination of the assets. The assets comprise the actual estate of the bankrupt and those assets which, as a result of a revocation, are to be regarded as forming part of the bankrupt estate. Fourth, the liquidation of the assets. Movables are sold by either auction or private treaty, at the discretion of the supervisory judge. Immovables, on the other hand, are generally sold by auction although the supervisory judge may, at the request of the curator and upon hearing the committee of creditors, authorise a private sale. Finally, the distribution of the proceeds of sale. The proceeds are applied in the following order:

1 to the costs of the proceedings and any liabilities incurred by the curator,
2 to the payment of the secured creditors, and
3 to the payment of the unsecured creditors.

The distribution proposed by the curator is subject to approval by the supervisory judge after publication of the proposed order for a period of ten days.

The bankruptcy process may come to an end in either of two ways. First, by *closure* which may arise in the following cases: where the creditors do not submit any claims within the time fixed by the *Tribunale*; where all of the liabilities have been satisfied; where the bankrupt estate has been entirely distributed; or where a distribution is not possible because there are no assets. Upon any of these events, irrespective of the stage reached in the proceedings, various consequences follow: the bankruptcy process is terminated; all of the bankruptcy organs are dissolved; the debtor regains his patrimonial rights; and, moreover, if unsatisfied, the creditors re-acquire their right to receive payment. The personal effects of the bankruptcy, on the other hand, endure until the *Tribunale* declares the bankrupt rehabilitated. Where the bankruptcy was closed because there were no, or insufficient, assets, the bankruptcy may be re-opened within five years of the closure provided that it will be productive and it has been expressly requested by the debtor or a creditor. Second, by entering into a scheme of arrangement which realises an equal satisfaction of creditors without having recourse to the liquidation phase. A scheme of arrangement arises where the debtor proposes the complete payment of secured debts, the payment of a given percentage of unsecured debts, and the offer is approved by a majority of the creditors and the *Tribunale*. The bankruptcy process is terminated at the point at which the court's approval of the scheme becomes *res judicata*. The performance of the scheme is supervised by the supervisory judge, the curator and the committee of creditors. The scheme, however, may be either rescinded, if it is not performed, or annulled, if there was an intentional mistatement of the liabilities or a concealment or dissimulation of the assets. In either event the bankruptcy procedure is re-opened.

As already noted, the personal consequences of a bankruptcy do not cease upon the closure of the bankruptcy but rather upon the civil rehabilitation of the bankrupt. The conditions for civil rehabilitation are the complete payment of all creditors in the bankruptcy, the performance of all obligations assumed in any scheme of arrangement, and proven good conduct for at least five years after the closure of the bankruptcy. In any event, there cannot be a rehabilitation if the bankrupt has been convicted of the crime of fraudulent *bancarotta* (see p 422, below) or, unless also rehabilitated under the criminal law, of certain other crimes. The grant of civil rehabilitation will result in the removal of the name from the bankruptcy register, the re-acquisition of all personal capacities lost as a result of the bankruptcy, and the extinguishment of the crime of simple *bancarotta* (see p 422, below).

C. THE SUMMARY BANKRUPTCY PROCEDURE

The summary procedure, which is a simplification of the ordinary bankruptcy process described above, is available in bankruptcies where the liabilities of the bankrupt do not exceed Lit.1.5 million. However, if during the proceedings it is found that the liabilities exceed this sum then the ordinary procedure must be adopted. The features of this simplified process are: the *pretore* of the place where the indebted enterprise has its principal seat may be given the functions of supervisory judge; the appointment of a committee of creditors is optional; the verification of the assets and liabilities of the bankrupt is carried out by the supervisory judge without any intervention by the creditors; and the approval of any scheme of arrangement merely requires the consensus of the majority in number and value of the book creditors and approval by the supervisory judge whose decision is not subject to appeal. This procedure, however, is rarely utilised in practice.

D. THE APPLICATION OF THE ORDINARY BANKRUPTCY PROCESS TO COLLECTIVE ENTERPRISES

As noted at the outset, collective enterprises, or companies, are always subject to bankruptcy proceedings as they can never qualify as a small entrepreneur. The bankruptcy of a company necessarily means the bankruptcy of any member with an unlimited liability (A.147 *lf*), even if such member is not an entrepreneur, as well as limited members who, according to Artt. 2317 and 2320 cc, have clothed themselves with an unlimited liability vis-à-vis third parties. However, where a member becomes a unitary shareholder of a company, although he assumes an unlimited liability under A.2362 cc for the obligations arising during his unitary shareholding, he cannot be made bankrupt because the object of A.2362 is to protect third parties and not to clothe the shareholder with the quality of a commercial entrepreneur.

As incorporated companies have a legal personality separate from their shareholders who do not, therefore, become commercial entrepreneurs, the bankruptcy of the enterprise results in the liquidation of the company only and shareholders are merely liable to the extent of their shares or quotas. All of the provisions examined above relating to ordinary bankruptcies are also applicable to incorporated companies, subject to any necessary adaptations. In contrast to incorporated companies, the bankruptcy of a partnership of any type will also extend to individual partners with an unlimited liability whose bankruptcy is declared with the same judgment as that dealing with the partnership.

E. OTHER INSOLVENCY PROCEEDINGS

There are two special institutions which enable a debtor to avoid a bankruptcy judgment. The first is the so-called preventive agreement or composition with creditors (*concordato preventivo*). As its name suggests, it can only arise prior to a bankruptcy judgment and therefore avoids placing the enterprise into bankruptcy which could also be harmful to the creditors. The institution is only available to a commercial entrepreneur who is in a state of insolvency which has not yet been judicially declared. The debtor, through a judicial agreement with his creditors, either agrees to pay his secured creditors in full and his unsecured creditors in an amount of at least 40% of the debts owed or offers to his creditors all of his property which must be sufficient to cover at least the above amounts. Although a preventive agreement does not deny the debtor of the administration of his estate, nor the management of his enterprise, he nonetheless remains subject to the supervision of a judicial commissioner and the supervisory judge.

The second institution, known as controlled administration (*l'amministrazione controllata*), on the other hand, is available to a debtor who is in temporary difficulties (not a state of insolvency) to prevent his insolvency and therefore bankruptcy where there is a proven possibility of saving the enterprise. This, too, takes place through a judicial agreement conceded by a majority of the creditors the substance of which is to allow a delay of up to two years within which the debtor is to pay his debts fully. During that time the enterprise continues its activity under the management of the debtor who is supervised by a judicial commissioner and the supervisory judge. If, at the lapse of the relevant time, the debtor remains unable to meet all of his debts, then the procedure is converted into either a preventive agreement (upon request of the debtor) or a bankruptcy. In contrast to the preventive agreement, this institution aims at the payment of all debts in full within the time delay conceded to the debtor and it is based upon the assumption that the entrepreneur is in a temporary difficulty only and can therefore salvage the enterprise.

Finally, mention must be made of two further special procedures applicable to particular enterprises. First, compulsory administrative liquidation which is applicable to certain types of enterprises having regard to both the nature of their activities and the fact that they concern a vast range of persons, e g insurance companies, credit institutions and co-operative societies. This procedure, which is partly analogous to the bankruptcy process, comes within the jurisdiction of the governmental authority which has the supervision of the particular type of activity conducted by the enterprise. Compulsory administrative liquidation does not necessarily presuppose a state of insolvency because it may be put into motion for other reasons also, namely, irregularities in its operation and the violation of law or administrative norms. Generally, the availability of compulsory administrative liquidation excludes the possibility of bankruptcy proceedings. However, in those cases where both proceedings are available, the one requested first prevails.

Second, the extraordinary administration of large enterprises suffering economic difficulties which was introduced by special legislation in 1979 (DL 30 January 1979 n.26 which was ratified by the law of 3 April 1979 n.95). This procedure removes the enterprise from the ordinary bankruptcy procedure and subjects it to a procedure substantially similar to compulsory administrative liquidation. The procedure, which is directed and supervised by experts in the particular industry, the Minister of Industry, Commerce and Craft, and the Interministerial Committee for the Co-ordination of Industrial Politics, aims, through a total or partial reconstruction programme, to save and rehabilitate the enterprise in difficulty because of its technical, commercial, productive and employment value.

F. THE BANKRUPTCY CRIMES

It may happen that various acts committed by the bankrupt or certain other persons either before or during the bankruptcy proceedings constitute crimes. These are the so-called '*reati concorsuali*' or bankruptcy crimes which have as their prerequisite the existence of a bankruptcy or some other insolvency procedure. The typical bankruptcy crime is that of *bancarotta* which can be either fraudulent or simple depending upon whether it involves the fraudulent or negligent and imprudent diminution of the debtor's estate which would have otherwise been available for the benefit of creditors. The penalty for fraudulent *bancarotta* comprises imprisonment from one to ten years, the ineligibility for ten years of conducting a commercial enterprise, and the incapacity over the same period of accepting a management position in a commercial enterprise. The penalty for simple *bancarotta*, on the other hand, comprises imprisonment from six months to two years and the ineligibility of conducting an enterprise or of holding a management position for two years. There are also various other bankruptcy crimes which may be committed by either the bankrupt himself (e g abusive recourse to credit by concealing his insolvency) or other persons such as the curator, manager, or creditor of an entrepreneur.

Part IV
Hybrid categories of law

Chapter 10

Labour law

Introduction

Labour law, more than any other field of law, is constantly changing in response to social conditions. Since legislative action is almost entirely a mere adaptation to existing reality, labour law is an area in which the elaborations of the doctrine and the decisions and maxims of the case law assume an importance equal to legislation.

According to the prevalent doctrine the peculiar characteristic of 'labour', the object of labour law, is the subordination of its suppliers vis-à-vis the employer. The present trend is towards broadening the scope of labour law by including relationships traditionally excluded from the subject. In particular, there is a tendency to include those relationships which, although they lack a strict legal subordination, nonetheless manifest an economic subordination. This trend is evident in the 1973 reforms which extended the labour process to any person who supplies labour to another in a situation of economic and contractual subordination, thereby including many relationships foreign to the traditional concept of the labour relationship, e g agency and the independent contractor.

Although there is a formal or legal parity between the parties to a labour relationship, from an economic point of view the supplier of labour is in the position of the weaker contractual party. The State has sought to restore a position of substantive parity through two major avenues: the introduction of imperative norms, which cannot be eliminated by agreement, favouring the weaker economic party; and the recognition and protection of unionism. The doctrine was quick to point out that a strict contractual conception of the employment relationship imposes serious limits since often the relationship is a mere de facto one. Therefore, a major achievement in labour law has been the extension by case law of the protections available in a formal employment relationship to mere de facto relationships arising by implication.

As already noted (see ch 3, p 78, above), the scope and content of labour law is a matter of doctrinal controversy. This is mainly because the subject now extends beyond its traditional private law field to encompass aspects of constitutional, criminal, administrative, and international law. It is sometimes said that labour law is a hybrid category of law comprising elements of both private and public law. Be that as it may, from a methodological point of view the traditional tripartite division of labour law still remains valid, viz, labour law in a strict sense which concerns the study of the contract of employment and the de facto labour relationship; unionism which concerns labour associations, union relationships and collective agreements; and social welfare legislation which concerns worker welfare. In its entirety labour law is concerned with the protection of the liberty and person of the worker because of his position of dependence. In other words, it tends to attenuate the more harmful effects of subordination, especially those aspects which relate to human liberty, dignity and security.

The sources and basic principles of Italian labour law

The number and diversity of the sources of labour law give rise to problems of identification, classification, and priority. Generally, the sources of labour law may be divided into three broad categories. First, the formal domestic law sources which comprise, in decreasing order of importance, the Constitution, ordinary legislation including delegated legislation and legislative decrees, the delegated legislation made by the government pursuant to *l* 14 July 1959 n.741, as amended by *l* 1 October 1960 n.1027, which codified certain provisions of the then existing collective labour agreements, regulations, and finally, usages or customs which are not binding except in the cases contemplated by A.2078 cc, viz, in the absence of regulation by legislation or collective agreement, provided that a usage more favourable to an employee always prevails over a legislative provision but never over a particular contract of employment. Second, the international law sources which comprise international treaties, the conventions concluded by the International Labour Organisation, and the regulations and other norms of the European Community. Whilst the first two are indirect sources, as they must be ratified and received into the municipal system, the norms of the European Community are generally directly binding on member states. Third, union sources which include collective agreements (or collective contracts) either of national application (as is normally the case in which event they are referred to with the symbols CCNL) or merely provincial in scope (in which event they generally deal with wages only and not other aspects of the employment relationship), and company agreements (CCA) which are generally limited in scope to an individual enterprise and constitute a more detailed version of the collective agreement applicable to the industry in question.

A fundamental unwritten principle lying at the basis of Italian labour law is that of '*favor prestatoris*', where if several normative provisions are applicable to a given situation, the most favourable to the employee must be applied. This principle is a direct consequence of the necessity to counterbalance the differing contractual strengths of the parties to a contract of employment. The most important particular application of this principle is that an otherwise binding normative provision may be substituted with another more favourable to the employee.

Any basic principles are to be found in the Constitution, which not only contains certain general principles relevant to the subject but also a particular section entitled 'Economic Relations' which prescribes various specific norms. The Constitution places labour in a predominant position in the overall structure of the State. Article 1 C, by stating that Italy is a democratic republic based upon labour, affirms the importance of labour in a broad sense and imposes an obligation on the ordinary legislature to fulfil the constitutional provisions on the subject. Article 4 C declares that labour is both a right and a duty. However, this provision does not mean that the right to work is a true and proper subjective right but merely obliges the State to render the right effective by creating initiatives and removing obstacles. It is for this reason that in Italy the placement of labour is regarded as being a strict public function within the exclusive jurisdiction of the State with a corresponding exclusion, upon pain of criminal sanctions, of any private involvement in the labour market. The description of labour as a duty merely creates a moral duty without any sanction in the case of its non-observance.

Foremost amongst the specific constitutional norms relating to labour law is A.36 which contains three fundamental maxims. First, the right to remuneration which must be proportional to the quantity and quality of work and, in any event, sufficient to provide 'a free and dignified existence' for the employee and his family. This provision, also applicable to apprentices, ensures a right of action to require its observance and means that the court may utilise, apart from any legislative provisions, the relevant collective contract, even if not applicable to the particular employee, in determining a proper remuneration. Second, that the maximum duration of the working day must be exclusively defined by legislation so that collective or individual agreements may only reduce that maximum. Third, that weekly rest and annual holidays are irrevocable rights.

Other significant specific constitutional provisions include A.37 C which guarantees equal pay for equal work without discrimination on the basis of sex (although this provision was only fully implemented in 1977) or age, A.38 C which prescribes both the right to social welfare in cases of unfitness to work and the right to adequate support in cases of injury, pregnancy, post-birth leave, invalidity, age, and involuntary unemployment, and Artt. 39 and 40 which guarantee the right of unionism and the right to strike respectively.

The distinction between the master-servant relationship and the independent contractor

The labour relationship may be either a master-servant relationship (i e the subordinate labour relationship) or that of independent contractor (i e the autonomous labour relationship). Only the former, comprising the employer-employee relationship, forms the object of labour law. The latter, generally dealt with in commercial law, concerns an obligation to perform, in return for a quid pro quo, a task or service carried out predominantly with the contractor's own labour and without entering into a position of subordination vis-à-vis the purchaser (A.2222 cc). The obligation of the independent contractor is an obligation of producing a result, whether it be the delivery of goods or the performance of services, and the obligation of the purchaser is the payment of the contract price and, if agreed, the supply of the materials necessary to carry out the work. This relationship between the parties is characterised by the autonomy of the contractor who has a complete discretion, subject to the terms of the agreement, in relation to the time, place and mode of performance, and who generally bears the risk until delivery.

The master-servant relationship is regulated by both the Civil Code and special legislation. A subordinate is defined by A.2094 cc, in the context of an enterprise, as one who places his intellectual or manual labour at the disposal and control of an entrepreneur in return for remuneration. The distinguishing features of the relationship are the subordination of the servant to the organisational, managerial and disciplinary powers of the master, and the servant's collaboration in the enterprise. The principal obligations of the servant are to perform personally his duties in the manner, time and place specified by the master, to remain at the disposal of the master for the contract period, to submit to the master's disciplinary powers, and to collaborate diligently and faithfully with the master.

The rights of the servant are remuneration, weekly rest, annual holidays and the freedoms specified in the Labour Law of 1970, principally the freedoms of unionism and opinion. Other rights may arise either from the individual and collective contracts applicable to the particular case or by law as a consequence of the servant's particular status (e g working mother, minor or student), the servant's condition (e g pregnancy, sickness or conscription for military service) or the nature of the relationship (e g apprentice). The master-servant relationship is also characterised by the absence of economic risk as a result of which the servant is entitled to the agreed remuneration irrespective of the quantity and quality of work (subject only to disciplinary sanctions) and its continuity, i e the permance of the bond even during the normal interruptions in the prestation of labour.

Labour law, traditionally regarded as a strictly private law subject, does not include public employment which forms the object of substantive and procedural administrative law. As already noted, labour law has now assumed such peculiar characteristics that the doctrine generally doubts it can still be regarded exclusively as private law. These peculiar characteristics include an intensive limitation upon the freedom to contract in an attempt to avoid the substantive disparity between the parties to the contract of employment, a preponderence of imperative norms from which there derives a predominance of mandatory duties whose non-observance frequently attract criminal sanctions, and finally, the decline in importance of the individual contract of employment because most of its terms are now dictated by either collective agreements or binding statutory and constitutional provisions that cannot be varied by the parties.

Notwithstanding the basic distinction between subordinate and autonomous labour, there are various types of autonomous relationships characterised by the following: a continuing collaboration with the enterprise, an integration with the organisational structure of the enterprise, and a dependence upon the directives of the entrepreneur, e g piece work. In this regard there is a clear tendency to extend the law on subordinate labour to include these relationships.

The doctrine nowadays generally considers the definition of subordinate labour contained in A.2094 cc as being too narrow in that it excludes both subordinate labour not performed within the ambit of an enterprise in the technical sense (e g piece work) and labour performed without remuneration (e g the labour of students in school laboratories). Therefore, the doctrine has sought to elaborate a more comprehensive definition of subordinate labour as a result of which the dominant doctrine now takes the view that the key concept is *subordination* in the work relationship, irrespective of where the labour is performed. The case law does not regard any single element as being sufficient to distinguish between subordinate and autonomous labour and considers the former as being dependent upon the existence of all of the following elements: subordination, continuity, risk, collaboration and, although not a determining factor, mode of remuneration.

The content of the first three of these elements is as follows:

A. SUBORDINATION

Subordination consists of the subjection of the servant to the directives of the master or of his senior staff. It is the fundamental element of the subordinate labour relationship without which the relationship cannot exist, e g the sole director of a company cannot also be its dependant.

B. CONTINUITY

Continuity signifies, according to the doctrine, a relationship of 'permanent debt' manifest in the fact that the contractual power of the master over his servant continues uninterrupted throughout the normal intervals in the prestation of labour. This characteristic explains the existence of obligations other than the mere prestation of labour and its remuneration, e g the duty of faithfulness owed by the servant.

C. RISK

The master-servant relationship comprises several types of risk none of which directly burden the servant, even though the latter may suffer some of their indirect consequences. Thus the master must bear the following risks: an economic risk connected with the quantity and quality of work; a vicarious liability for those acts of his servant which damage third parties (although the servant remains jointly and severally liable with the master vis-à-vis the injured party where the injurious act was either intentional or arose through the gross negligence of the servant); a liability for work-related accidents or sicknesses (which, however, falls directly upon the relevant insurance fund and only indirectly upon the master who is responsible for the major part of the premiums); and a liability for the servant's inability to work for causes unrelated to the prestation of labour (which is also subject to obligatory insurance in relation to which the master must again pay the major share of the premiums). The employer is responsible for the payment of all insurance contributions, including any part which is to be contributed by the servant and which is to be provided through periodical deductions from remuneration. In any event, the insurer is automatically bound to the servant even if the entrepreneur has failed to pay the relevant contributions.

The contract of employment

A. GENERAL

The unique characteristics which distinguish the employment relationship from contracts in general, and in particular the way in which the mere prestation of labour without more can give rise to an implied relationship (the so-called de facto labour relationship) with all of the same rights and duties as in an express contract of employment, has led many writers to doubt the contractual nature of the labour relationship. Notwithstanding the significant legislative limitations upon the freedom to contract in this area of the law, the prevalent doctrine maintains that the relationship must be referrable to a contract (a union of wills) which in this case may even be constituted through a simple combination of an obligation to work in return for remuneration. The case law maintains that the employment relationship may arise out of an implied agreement stipulated through a conclusive course of conduct which reveals an intent on the part of the parties to constitute a valid contract. Accepting the contractual nature of the employment relationship, the question of its classification has also been controversial. Although the doctrine variously classifies the employment relationship into the different traditional categories, for instance, as a contract for sale, the approach which appears more in tune with the current social conscience and the legislation in the field is that which regards it as a contract *sui generis*.

The contract of employment, as already mentioned, contains various non-contractual elements. The presence of these elements is not intended to deny the contractual nature of the relationship but only to make certain correctives in favour of the weaker contractual party. These elements concern the following aspects of the employment relationship. First, the formation process of the contract, e g in the case of several classes of servant, employment is restricted to those persons who are introduced by the Provincial Employment Office in which cases the employer is restricted to the mere indication of the number of employees required. Second, the obligation to employ given categories of person (e g invalid persons and refugees) in a number proportional to the size of the total workforce in the particular enterprise. However, their employment is not totally automatic as it is dependent upon the consent of the worker who must successfully complete a probationary term. Therefore, a consensual element is to some extent preserved. Finally, the termination of the employment relationship which does not, in most cases, depend upon the discretion of the employer but must be supported by a just cause or a justifiable reason. Moreover, the relationship cannot be terminated for certain defined reasons, e g marriage or pregnancy.

B. THE SUBJECTIVE PREREQUISITES OF THE CONTRACT OF EMPLOYMENT

A contract of employment, like every contract, must be stipulated by subjects who possess both legal capacity and the capacity to contract. For the purpose of contracts of employment, an employee acquires legal capacity at the age of 15 (or 14 in the case of non-industrial activities which are compatible with health and educational requirements). It is a matter of controversy amongst the writers as to whether a minor then automatically acquires the capacity to transact or, as suggested by the prevalent doctrine, he nonetheless requires the assistance of his tutor or parent to conclude a contract of employment. It is only in rare cases that the law requires an express and autonomous authorisation from the parent or tutor of a minor. Since 1977, every form of discrimination, including in matters of capacity, based upon sex has been abolished in labour matters.

In certain instances, such as pregnant women and minors, the psycho-physical capacity of the servant becomes relevant, some writers regarding this as an autonomous requisite of the contract of employment. Technical suitability, which clearly appertains to legal capacity, is required upon penalty of the nullity of the contract, at least in those cases where technical ability must be evidenced by either registration with a given body or the possession of a diploma, licence or certificate. Some writers consider the so-called employment booklet, which sets out the personal details and employment history of its possessor, as a subjective requisite. The possession of an employment booklet is necessary for employment and enrolment on the placement lists maintained at the Employment Offices.

C. THE OBJECTIVE PREREQUISITES OF THE CONTRACT OF EMPLOYMENT

The requisites appertaining to the object of a contract of employment are the same as for contracts in general, namely, there must be a possible, lawful and determined or determinable object.

D. THE ELEMENTS OF THE CONTRACT OF EMPLOYMENT

The essential elements of a contract of employment are identical to those applicable to contracts generally, viz, the intention to enter into legal relations, form (although, as is the case with contracts generally, no particular form is usually required), cause (which, notwithstanding that the contract of employment is a nominate contract, the prevalent doctrine considers to be the exchange of labour and remuneration), and motives (mainly relevant to the illegality of the purpose of the transaction).

The incidental elements of a contract of employment (that is, those elements not necessary to its structure or constitution) include the following. First, suspensive or resolutive conditions, the former finding an important function in the case of probationary agreements. Second, the stipulation of a probationary term which, unless automatically applicable pursuant to law or the relevant collective contract, must be in writing. Its duration must be defined and it cannot, in any event, exceed any maximum stipulated by the relevant collective contract. During the probationary term, unless a minimum period of service is specified, either party may summarily withdraw from the agreement without either the payment of an indemnity or the specification of reasons, although the case law is not always consistent on the latter. At the conclusion of the probationary term, the relationship becomes indefinite and the probationary service is computed towards seniority. Third, the stipulation of a *term* which is of extreme importance and strictly regulated by law. Where a term may be specified at all, it must be in writing. The general rule is that all contracts of employment are deemed by law to be for an indefinite term, except in certain strictly defined cases in which a termination date may be stipulated, e g contracts for seasonal work and entertainment contracts. The onus of proving the legitimacy of a fixed term contract lies upon the entrepreneur. Managerial contracts may always contain a term but must not exceed five years and cannot be renewed more than once, whereupon, if the relationship continues, it automatically becomes a contract for an indefinite term. Employees on a fixed term contract enjoy the same rights as persons on a contract for an indefinite term. Although employment contracts are generally for an indefinite term, the inclusion of a permanancy provision is not without effect: although it does not affect the employees right of resignation, it limits the rights of the employer who during the term stipulated in the contract may only withdraw from the agreement for a *just cause* and not merely for a justifiable reason. In the event of an unlawful resolution of the contract, the employee is entitled to damages for, inter alia, loss of salary and interruption of career.

E. THE INTERRUPTION AND CONTENTS OF THE CONTRACT OF EMPLOYMENT

In these matters the ordinary civil law is applicable although certain aspects of the latter are accentuated in labour law. For example, usages which assume a greater importance than in the general law in the interpretation of employment contracts concerning merchants, artisans and agriculturalists, and A.1370 cc which, together with Artt. 1341 and 1342 cc, provides that ambiguous provisions in standard contracts are to be interpreted against their author. All matters not specifically dealt with by an individual employment contract are regulated by either an express or implied reference to the relevant collective contract or to the relevant legislation. Where an employer neither belongs to the organisation which stipulated the relevant collective contract nor intends voluntarily to receive it, he is bound to conclude more comprehensive employment contracts: the case law generally takes the view that in such cases the value of the collective contract is restricted to its use as a guide in determining a 'sufficient' remuneration.

F. THE INVALIDITY OF THE CONTRACT OF EMPLOYMENT

Labour law also follows the general civil law in relation to the invalidity of contracts although, again, with certain peculiar variations. In cases of total nullity, the conversion of contracts finds an extensive application and often results in a different intent being attributed to the parties, e g indefinite employment will be presumed if a probationary agreement is not in writing. In cases of partial nullity, there is extensive resort to both imperative norms and, where the parties are members of the stipulating organisations, the norms contained in the relevant collective contract: in the latter instance, all of the clauses in the individual contract less favourable to the employee than the corresponding provisions in the collective contract are null. Finally, in cases of voidability, which is of little practical relevance to labour contracts, the ordinary general law rules are applicable. In any case, the resolution of a contract for invalidity, in accordance with A.2126 cc, does not affect the period during which the relationship was operative (unless there was an illegal object) in respect of which the employee is entitled to remuneration and all the other emoluments provided for by law.

G. INTERMEDIATION IN THE EMPLOYMENT OF LABOUR

Contrary to the general law position, every form of intermediation in the employment of labour is prohibited. The prohibition aims at preventing both profit by third parties, which may result in a diminution in the remuneration of labour, and interference with the exclusive right of the State Employment Offices in the allocation of labour. For the same reasons, any form of employment for the performance of labour for the benefit of a third party is also prohibited. The only exception to the latter prohibition is contracts for the performance of team work in which case although the entrepreneur contracts with a team leader he directly employs the whole team, which is responsible for the result of its services as a single unit, the so-called collective piece work contracts.

The engagement of labour

As already noted, the formation of the contract of employment is unique because, inter alia, of the regime applicable to the employment (or conversely, the allocation) of labour. This results in a notable restriction upon the freedom to contract, especially as regards the selection of an employee.

In Italy the allocation of labour is a public function exercised directly by the State and reinforced with a corresponding prohibition against any private intermediation in the engagement of labour. It is the means through which the State controls and co-ordinates the conflicting interests of the opposite social groups which come together in the employment relationship. The allocation system has the following characteristics: it is gratuitous; it is necessary to the valid engagement of an employee; it is regulated by *imperative* norms; and it is directly administered by the State through decentralised Employment Offices of the Ministry of Labour. Its fundamental feature is that it is obligatory; that is, subject to express legislative exceptions, both an employer who desires to engage an employee and a person who seeks employment (either because he is unemployed or because he desires to change his employment) *must* follow the mandatory procedure stipulated for either a request or an offer of labour.

The employment process consists of various phases. First, a request by the person in search of work for registration on the employment lists kept by the Employment Offices. The requisites for registration are residence in the commune in which registration is sought, the possession of an employment booklet and physical suitability. Second, registration on the relevant lists. Registration is an administrative obligation and not a discretion as it is dependent, not upon any evaluative process, but the mere existence of the above legal requisites. Third, the classification, according to fitness, of registrants into various productive sectors. This classification is of central importance as it is binding upon an employer in the engagement of labour. Fourth, the determination of an order of priority according to which registrants are directed to requesting employers. The criteria for determining the order of priority includes the existence of dependants upon the registrant, the latter's economic condition, and any other pertinent factor. Where several persons have an equal priority, the period of registration and superior qualifications become decisive. Fifth, the request of labour by an employer. Subject to certain exceptions, an employer may only engage persons registered on the employment lists through forwarding his request for labour to the territorially competent Employment Office. This request may normally be numerical only, that is, merely indicate the number of employees required in each employment category. A nominative request is only permissible: first, in the employment of family members, managerial and clerical staff, certain categories of highly specialised staff defined in lists issued by the Minister of Labour, caretakers, and domestic staff; and second, in the case of enterprises which employ no more than three persons. Staff may be directly engaged in cases of emergency, subject to later ratification by the Employment Office. Sixth, allocation by the Employment Office which must satisfy an employer's requests. Although a registrant may refuse any given employment, even if at the cost of a loss of priority on the employment lists if such refusal is without reason, an employer is obliged to engage the person allocated, subject to probation, if the potential employee possesses the stipulated requisites since the registrant has a perfect subjective right to be employed. Should an employer not engage labour through an Employment Office, the contract of employment is voidable at the instance of the *pubblico ministero*. If such action is not brought within one year of a complaint from the Employment Office, the contract of employment becomes valid and binding as between the parties.

The above general allocation procedure is subject to various exceptions apart from the already mentioned cases in which nominative requests for labour are allowed. The first broad exception is that in specified cases employers are obliged to reserve a certain number of positions for defined categories of persons such as disabled servicemen, the widows and orphans of such employees, and civil invalids. In particular, all public and private employers having more than 35 employees must reserve a number of positions equivalent to 15% of their total workforce in favour of these categories of persons. Similar provisions are made for the benefit of deaf-mutes (in the case of firms with more than 100 employees) and refugees. The second broad exception is the existence of certain special allocation procedures created by recent legislation for particular categories of employees. First, the law of 12 August 1977 n.675 on industrial reconstruction and conversion contains important provisions relating to redundant employees of firms declared to be in a state of crisis. Such employees are given a priority of employment in firms having more than 35 employees and which have initiated reconstruction or conversion programmes, enjoy public financial assistance, or operate in the same industrial sector as the firm in crisis. Second, the law of 1 June 1977 n.285 concerning youth unemployment. This law facilitates the procurement of a first job for youth aged between 15 and 29 through the following provisions: the establishment of a special employment list; the absolute prohibition on nominative requests; the introduction of work experience contracts which provide for part time employment over a defined or fixed term; and the grant of financial concessions to employers participating in the employment of this class of person. Moreover the Regions and unions have sponsored various unpaid apprenticeship schemes.

The allocation system as a whole has been criticised in many respects. This is partly because the system is too rigid, formal and bureaucratic, partly because there has been a widespread introduction of special allocation systems, and partly because certain occupations fall entirely outside the system. This explains why recently there has been an increasing demand for a unified but more flexible allocation system.

Collective contracts

Article 39 C provides that registered unions shall have legal personality upon which they may stipulate collective contracts binding all persons belonging to the employment category covered by the contract in question. The registration of unions has not yet been introduced as a result of which they merely constitute unrecognised associations whose activities are regulated by the private law. It follows that the effect of any 'collective contract' stipulated by a union depends upon private law principles with the consequence that the collective contract will only bind the members of the stipulating organisations. A collective contract can only operate vis-à-vis a non-member of a stipulating organisation if it is expressly incorporated into the relevant individual contract of employment. Part of the case law maintains that even if an employee is not a member of the relevant stipulating organisation, the collective contract will nonetheless be applicable at his request provided that the employer is a member of one of the stipulating organisations.

Collective contracts may be either bi-union contracts stipulated by opposing organisations representing employers and employees respectively, such as the national collective contracts (CCNL), or contracts stipulated by an individual entrepreneur and the union representing the employees in the particular firm. The former type of agreement may in turn be divided between intersectional agreements relating to several sectors of an industry (e g commercial enterprises) or sectoral agreements relating to a specific sector of a given industry.

A collective contract is not normally restricted to the bilateral relationships between employer and employee, but also deals with other general matters of union interest, e g union representation within the firm, conciliation procedures for the resolution of union disputes and the like. The binding effect of a collective contract upon the members of the stipulating organisations results in the nullity of any provision contained in an individual contract less favourable to the employee than the corresponding provision which deals with the matter in the collective agreement.

Finally, it may be noted that there also exist 'interconfederation agreements' which deal with issues upon which there is no statutory regulation and as to which there is a conflict of interest amongst different unions. These agreements generally define, inter alia, the procedures for the settlement of differences between the stipulating unions on the subject matter covered by the agreement.

The content of the contract of employment

A. INTRODUCTION
Although the basic obligations inherent in a contract of employment are the performance of a service and remuneration, there are many other rights, powers and obligations which affect both parties to the contract and cannot be merely regarded as of secondary importance. On the contrary, they have important consequences: for instance, if the servant violates certain obligations, this constitutes just cause for dismissal under A.2119 cc and may give rise to damages. These additional rights, powers and obligations may be conveniently divided into the obligations of the servant, the rights of the servant, and the powers of the master.

B. THE OBLIGATIONS OF THE SERVANT
The servant has four basic obligations. First, the duty to provide the service for which he was employed. The service must be lawful, possible and determinate or determinable. It is strictly personal as it must be performed directly by the servant, unless provided otherwise by agreement or by operation of law. Second, the duty to perform the service with the diligence inherent in the nature of the service and the interests of the enterprise (A.2104(1) cc). This is the diligence required of a good paterfamilias, that is, the degree of diligence which is owed by every debtor in the performance of his obligation (A1176 cc). Third, the duty of obedience and collaboration (A.2104(2) cc) which requires that the servant observe the instructions of the master as to the performance and organisation of his labour. The managerial and disciplinary powers of the entrepreneur have their basis in this duty. Fourth, the duty of faithful service (A.2105 cc) which comprises two basic obligations: the obligation not to compete with the entrepreneur and the obligation not to reveal secret information concerning the enterprise. The duty of faithful service has its basis in the general principle contained in A.1375 cc according to which a contract must be performed in 'good faith'. It follows that a servant has a general obligation to abstain from any act which could injure the enterprise.

It also follows that an entrepreneur may have an interest in ensuring that at the end of the employment relationship the servant does not utilise information gained from his employment to his own advantage. The entrepreneur may, therefore, extend the servant's obligation not to compete with him beyond the duration of the master-servant relationship. Such agreements must not make it onerous for the servant to find new employment, especially as they sometimes limit the stipulation of certain types of contract (e g contracts of agency). Because such agreements could well become Draconian, particularly if the servant is required to enter into them as a condition of commencing his employment, the law imposes certain restrictions: they must be in writing; they must define the extent of the prohibition in terms of object and location; they must provide a quid pro quo for the servant;

and they cannot have a duration exceeding five years in the case of managerial staff or three years in any other case (A.2125 cc).

C. THE RIGHTS OF THE SERVANT

Apart from the rights to remuneration and certain work conditions, to be considered later, there are two further rights of the servant which must be examined. First, it is said that a servant has the right to perform his services. With certain exceptions, the doctrine is in disagreement as to whether such a right exists, especially in those instances where the servant is guaranteed his remuneration notwithstanding that the master is unable or unwilling to accept the services of his servant.

Second, and less controversial, it can certainly be said that A.13 of the Labour Law of 1970 (*ll*), which modified A.2103 cc, has established the right of the servant to perform only those duties for which he was employed, thereby placing a restriction upon the master's rights to vary his servant's duties. Article 13 *ll* provides that apart from the duties for which he was employed, a servant may only be given either equivalent duties at an equivalent remuneration or superior duties with an appropriate adjustment in remuneration. In the latter case, the superior duties become definitive after a period of three months (or any lesser period specified by the relevant collective contract) unless their performance was temporary as a result of a need to replace an absent servant who had the right to the preservation of his position. Apart from the above cases, a servant may refuse to perform any duty different from that for which he was employed and likewise any duty which, although not strictly 'inferior' to that for which he was employed, does not allow him to use his technical and professional skills. Moreover, the master's powers to vary his servant's duties are restricted by that part of A.2103 cc which provides that the servant cannot be transferred to a different production unit except for proven technological and productive reasons. Any agreement which varies the above restrictions is null.

These developments have modified the theoretical view that specific objects of the employment relationship (or duties) were dependent upon the servant's 'classification'. Since the introduction of the 1970 Labour Law, the tendency has been the converse, that is, that the duties effectively performed determine the servant's classification. This is clearly evidenced in the collective contracts which are all orientated towards systems of functional classification, job evaluation and classification according to the equivalence of duties. This does not mean that the division of servants into various classifications has lost all its significance, especially as the legal system still imposes an obligation on the master to assign the servant to duties corresponding to his classification. Rather, it means that if there is a difference between formal classification and the duties effectively performed, then the latter must prevail in the classification of the servant, both in relation to remuneration and career advancement.

The formal categories of servant defined by the present legislation on the subject are administrative or technical managers, employees, and labourers (A.2095 cc), a tripartite classification which is important in the area of collective contracts. Managers are the most senior category of subordinate workers and have powers comparable to those of the entrepreneur. Employees are professional and organisational staff who do not exclusively perform manual labour. Labourers are divided into three sub-categories, viz, specialist, qualified, and common, depending upon the degree of technical knowledge required in their duties.

D. THE POWERS OF THE MASTER

The master has a right corresponding to every obligation of the servant. There are two specific powers of the master which must be emphasised. First, the managerial power which is a necessary corollary of the subordinate labour relationship and may be defined as the power to adapt the useful activity of each worker to the needs of the enterprise. Second, the disciplinary power which arises out of the right of the master to control the material or actual execution of duties. The latter is an exceptional private law power whose rationale lies in the fact that the legislature considered the normal private law remedies for non-performance of contract as inadequate. The disciplinary power does not aim at restitution or damages but is rather a 'preventive' remedy, something like a criminal sanction, which favours the performance and preservation of the contractual relationship in contrast to the general private law approach of its dissolution. This is manifest in the fact that the proceeds of any pecuniary sanction arising out of a disciplinary remedy are passed on to charitable and welfare organisations. Therefore the disciplinary power tends to guarantee not the performance of the obligation, but the organisation of labour.

The disciplinary power is not unlimited. Article 2106 cc provides that the sanction must be proportional to the seriousness of the infraction and that the power may only be exercised in the cases and forms defined by law. The power is today particularised and regulated by the 1970 Labour Law which incorporates the general principles of judicial proceedings, that is, the laying of a charge and the right of defence. The disciplinary sanctions stipulated by the Labour Law are verbal and written admonishment, fine, and suspension from work and remuneration. The doctrine disputes whether dismissal is technically a disciplinary sanction, although most collective contracts regard it as such.

E. GENERAL LIMITS TO THE MASTER'S POWERS

The 1970 Labour Law has generally affected all the master's powers as a result of the provisions relating to the 'liberty and dignity of the worker'. Some of the most significant provisions are the right of the worker freely to manifest his political, industrial and religious opinions in the workplace, the prohibition on the master engaging watchmen to supervise the activities of labour unless for the specific protection of property, the obligation of the master to communicate the names and specific duties of personnel engaged to carry out any permissible supervision of labour, the prohibition against the use of audiovisual or other equipment for the control of labour unless with the agreement of the relevant union or Labour Inspectorate, the prohibition on the master engaging in any investigation concerning the discovery and establishment of an inability to work on the grounds of health or accident (which investigations are to be carried out by other organisations), the prohibition against body searches unless necessary for the protection of property belonging to the enterprise in which case it can only be conducted when personnel leave the workplace with all regard to the dignity and privacy of the worker, and the prohibition on the master enquiring into the political, religious or industrial opinions of the worker or any other matter irrelevant to the professional evaluation of the worker.

Special employment relationships

There are certain types of subordinate labour constituting special employment relationships which give rise to contractual relations different from the ordinary contract of employment. One of the most important is the apprenticeship, a complex contract with a mixed cause because the master has the obligation to give in exchange for service not only remuneration but also a certain level of technical instruction. The apprentice is bound to undertake courses of professional preparation outside the enterprise. Time spent on such courses is to form part of working hours for all purposes, including remuneration. At the expiration of the apprenticeship, in the absence of a notice by the master or a withdrawal by the servant, the relationship becomes a normal employment relationship and the period of apprenticeship is to be computed towards seniority. Other examples of special labour relationships are piece work (brought into the category of subordinate labour), domestic labour, and caretakers.

It is clear that the mere services of a partner in a company does not per se qualify him as a subordinate worker although the norms for the physical protection of subordinate labour in the workplace are applicable to partners. This does not prevent a partner assuming the position of a subordinate worker in the company. The problem becomes more difficult in relation to the status of a director of an incorporated company (whether an SpA or an SRL). The general rule is that the subordinate labour relationship is only excluded in the case where there is a *sole* director.

Problems as to the existence of the employment relationship also arise in the case of family labour because of the existence of a rebuttable presumption that the work of family members is performed for reasons of family collaboration and not because it is legally due. The presumption of gratuity excludes the relationship between family members not only from the category of subordinate labour but also from labour in general although in this case also the norms on safe and healthy work conditions are nonetheless applicable. It has already been noted that the reforms on family law have introduced the so-called family enterprise (see p 328, above) which, however, by express provision, is excluded from the ambit of labour law. Generally speaking, the participation of family members in the enterprise is as partners and thus labour law would have no application. Nonetheless, nothing prevents a family member from becoming a subordinate worker in which case the general labour law, with certain exceptions, becomes applicable.

It should be noted that the various peculiarities of nautical and aeronautical labour have justified a separate regulation contained in the Navigation Code.

The performance of the contract of employment by the servant

A. PLACE OF PERFORMANCE

The servant is required to perform the contract at the place specified in the contract or, in the absence thereof, in the place where the contract activity needs to be performed. As noted earlier, A.2103 cc prevents transfer from one production unit to another unless for proven technical, production or organisational reasons. For this purpose, a production unit signifies not only a plant, but also an autonomous department or division. However, temporary duties outside the contract seat and temporary transfers are always permissible as their temporary nature is such that it prevents any injury to the interests of the worker and does not affect the structure of the employment relationship. If the servant is a union official, the transfer requires the consensus of the particular union. Transfers for reason of the servant's industrial, religious or political attitudes are always prohibited.

B. WORKING HOURS

The servant is required to observe the working hours fixed in accordance with organisation of the enterprise, save always the limits prescribed by legislation and collective contract. The general rule is a maximum working week of 48 effective hours. The general maximum does not apply to certain categories of workers, such as travelling salesmen, whilst it applies with more rigour to certain other categories such as adolescents, working mothers, apprentices and student workers. Subject to the exceptions mentioned above, any agreement extending the working week beyond the general limit is prohibited by legislation.

As subordinate labour concerns an obligation for performance only, and not a result, working hours are strictly related to remuneration so that if the quantity of hours served is diminished for a cause not imputable to the master, the latter may, as a general principle, proportionately reduce remuneration. Because remuneration also serves a quasi-alimentary function, various correctives have been made to deal with situations in which a reduction of working hours is not imputable to the servant either: in some instances (such as licences and paid leave) the risk falls upon the entrepreneur who is required to meet the servant's remuneration, whilst in other instances (such as sickness, accident or pregnancy leave) the risk falls upon the compulsory insurer. There are cases in which the entrepreneur may, for economic reasons, be forced temporarily to suspend production or reduce working hours, in which event an Integrative Income Fund has been established to mitigate the alimentary needs of the servant.

The collective contracts may provide for overtime which is usually left to the discretion of the master provided that it does not exceed two hours per day and 12 hours per week (RDL 15 March 1923 n.692). It must be remunerated at an increased rate to compensate for the 'marginal sufferance' of the worker. The law of 30 October 1955 n.1079, in an attempt to alleviate unemployment, prohibits overtime in industrial enterprises unless it is merely casual, necessitated by exceptional technological-production requirements, or it is impossible to employ additional workers. Apprentices and mothers with a new-born child are in every event excluded from overtime whilst working students are not obliged to accept it.

After-hours work which is not part of regular shift work must be remunerated at a higher rate and is prohibited for certain classes of persons such as working mothers, apprentices, student workers, and adolescent labour.

C. LEAVE

Every worker is entitled to various forms of leave. Weekly leave is an irrevocable right and usually falls on a Sunday. Unless the right to weekly leave is moved to another day of the week, increased remuneration must be paid for Sunday work. Remunerated leave is given on all civil and religious public holidays proclaimed by law. Work on a public holiday always attracts increased remuneration. Annual leave is a remunerated and irrevocable right and should be granted as a continuous period of leave wherever possible. Other miscellaneous forms of leave enable a worker to attend to his civil and personal obligations. These include: licence which comprises unpaid leave granted to enable attendance to civic duties (e g to vote at elections and to appear as a witness in court proceedings) and the right to 24 hours' paid leave to make a blood donation; marriage leave which is paid leave whose duration varies depending upon the classification of the servant and the sector of his employment and must be granted upon request to every servant who contracts marriage; suspension of employment in the case of conscription together with the concomitant right to the preservation of the position; and the right of absence of either parent in the first year of a child's life for a period of up to six months at an indemnity equal to 30% of normal remuneration paid by a fund called INAM.

Remuneration

As a result of the combined effect of A.2099 cc and A.36 C, remuneration: must be sufficient for the vital needs of the worker and his family; proportional to the quantity and quality of work; and determined or determinable, usually with reference to the relevant national collective contract. It is an unrenounceable and obligatory right, rebuttably presumed to constitute the counter-prestation of the contract of employment, continuous in that in certain cases it is payable notwithstanding a suspension in either the employment relationship (e g sickness) or the mere prestation of labour (e g holidays), and, finally, is generally paid periodically.

Remuneration, known as 'salary' in the case of labourers and 'stipend' in the case of employees, comprises various elements: first, the basic wage; second, wage indexation which ensures the adjustment of wages so as to reflect its real value and generally takes place every three months in accordance with the cost of living index; third, indemnities which are paid in accordance with the various stages in the labour relationship (e g on transfer), the nature of the work (e g drill money), the nature of the employee, particular efficiency, and particular agreements (e g retirement allowances); and fourth, family allowances which are payments of a welfare nature made by INPS, through the employer, on the basis of contributions made by employers to a common fund managed by the Institute.

Article 2099 cc contemplates, in addition to the ordinary fixed and periodical salary or stipend, other forms of remuneration known generally as time remuneration such as remuneration on a piece work basis, participation in the profits or product of an enterprise, and remuneration on a commission basis. In order to guarantee the essential characteristics of remuneration, and in particular that of its sufficiency, the national collective contracts usually provide for a fixed minimum remuneration in addition to any time remuneration just described.

Functional defects in the contract of employment

A contract of employment may be affected by various functional defects: non-performance, supervening impossibility, or a supervening excessive burden. These defects are regulated in a manner different from that in the ordinary civil law and vary depending upon whether the defect is imputable to the master or the servant.

A. NON-PERFORMANCE

Where the employer fails to perform the contract, either through a total or partial failure to remunerate the servant or through a breach of some other subjective right of the servant, then notwithstanding that the servant may always withdraw from the contract, the servant has no means of self-protection other than recourse to the court. Where the servant fails to perform, the master may resort to self-protection which, in the case of minor failures to perform, is through the imposition of disciplinary sanctions or, in the case of serious breaches, by withdrawal from the contract for either just cause or justifiable reason. Whilst the master may always be ordered to perform the contract, the servant may not as this would constitute an obligation 'to do' which is not specifically enforceable.

B. SUPERVENING EXCESSIVE BURDEN

A contract of employment hardly ever becomes excessively onerous for the employee because of the various institutions providing for increased remuneration. On the other hand, although a contract cannot become excessively onerous for the master through the automatic increases in remuneration, as these are either provided for in the collective contract or merely constitute an equalising variation through indexation, it may become so for market or other reasons in which case the excessive burden may, depending upon the situation, give rise to any of the following solutions: dismissals so as to reduce personnel, resort to the Integrative Income Fund, the winding-up of the business, or bankruptcy.

C. SUPERVENING IMPOSSIBILITY

The obligation of the master, being a pecuniary obligation, can never become impossible.

On the other hand, insofar as the obligation of the servant is concerned, its performance may in certain cases become impossible for reasons referable to the master, viz, for subjective (such as lock-outs, and the restructure or closure of the business) or objective (such as closure on government order, economic difficulties and *forza maggiore*) reasons. Where such an impossibility is referable to the *will* of the entrepreneur it may be considered to be either equivalent to pure non-performance (e g in the case of a lock-out), in which case the master remains obliged to perform his part of the agreement (i e pay the servant's remuneration), or connected with the freedom of enterprise (e g in the case of a winding-up), in which case the termination of the employment relationship is considered to be justified. If the impossibility is independent of the will of the entrepreneur, then it may lead to either of the following consequences: the termination of the employment relationship for an objective justifiable reason (e g dismissals for the reduction of personnel); or the survival of the employment relationship with the concomitant risk falling either upon the appropriate assurance fund or directly upon the entrepreneur who therefore must continue to remunerate his servant even though the relationship may be regarded as having been suspended for other purposes.

Apart from the above cases of impossibility referable to the master and a large number of exceptions which result in either a suspension or a temporary modification of the employment relationship, the general rule is that the impossibility of the servant to perform will generally extinguish the relationship. A mere suspension arises where the employment relationship continues to exist notwithstanding that the two fundamental obligations (service and remuneration) are temporarily deferred. This may, for example, arise in the following cases: where the master fails fully to occupy the servant; the conscription of the servant; the exercise of the right of absence by a servant who has young children; the legitimate exercise of the right to strike; and as a result of the imposition of a disciplinary sanction. Modification of the employment relationship arises where the interruption of labour does not result in a loss of remuneration, even if the remuneration is only in the form of an indemnity. This arises, for example, in cases of re-call to army service, and maternity, sickness or accident leave.

Succession to employment relationships upon the transfer of a business

Article 2112 cc provides that where the alienor of a business has failed to give a timely notice of termination, a contract of employment shall not only bind the alienee but the servant shall continue to retain all existing seniority rights. This is substantially different from the case of other business contracts as to which A.2558 cc provides that the succession of contracts is always subject to any agreement to the contrary and that the other party to an inherited contract may withdraw from the contract for just cause within three months of notice of the transfer of the business. The succession of the alienee of a business to employment contracts arises in every case where there is a change in the person of the entrepreneur provided that the enterprise continues to exist. The notice to which A.2112 cc refers may only be given in the case of contracts of employment for an indefinite term.

Termination of the contract of employment

The employment relationship may come to an end by either the conclusion of its object (whether satisfactory or not) or the termination of the contract of employment. In the latter case, a distinction must be drawn depending upon whether the contract is terminated by the master or the servant.

A. WITHDRAWAL BY THE SERVANT

As to withdrawal from a contract by the servant, A.2118 cc remains unconditionally applicable. It provides that either party to an employment contract for an indefinite term may withdraw by giving a notice in the manner prescribed by the relevant collective contract, usage or according to equity, and that in the absence of such notice the withdrawing party must indemnify the other in an amount equivalent to the remuneration which would have been due over the period of the required notice. Where there exists a just cause, the servant may summarily withdraw from the contract of employment (A.2119 cc). If the employment relationship is for a defined period, a servant who withdraws prior to the end of the term is liable in damages unless there exists a just cause for the withdrawal.

B. WITHDRAWAL BY THE MASTER

In the majority of cases, there are severe limitations upon a withdrawal from a contract of employment by the master. In the case of employment contracts for a fixed term, the master may only withdraw for either non-performance by the servant (in which case the withdrawal is for a just cause or a subjective justifiable reason) or for supervening impossibility. In the case of a contract for an indefinite term the master may withdraw for the following reasons: dismissal of the servant by the service of a notice pursuant to A.2118 cc in the case of employment relationships as to which the laws of 15 July 1966 n.604

and 20 May 1970 n.300 (see infra) are inapplicable; for non-performance by the servant (for a just cauşe or a subjective justifiable reason); for an objective justifiable reason; and finally, for supervening impossibility.

C. THE EXTINCTION AND DISSOLUTION OF A CONTRACT OF EMPLOYMENT

A contract of employment may, apart from a withdrawal by one of the parties, be discharged because its object has been satisfactorily realised because of the lapse of the term, in the case of a contract for a defined period, or the performance of the work stipulated by the contract. A contract of employment may, furthermore, be automatically extinguished by reason of a natural dissolution of the employment relationship, that is, through either the death of the servant or the cessation of the enterprise which is regulated in the same manner as a withdrawal for an objective justifiable reason.

D. THE DISCHARGE OF CONTRACTS FOR A FIXED TERM

The grounds upon which a fixed-term contract may be discharged fall into two broad categories. First, for either performance of the work stipulated by the contract or the lapse of the contract term, in relation to both of which the ordinary civil law is applicable. Second, for certain reasons also applicable to contracts of employment for an indefinite term, namely, dismissal for a just cause or a subjective justifiable reason, the death of the servant, the permanent closure of the enterprise, and supervening impossibility. A withdrawal '*ad nutum*', through the pure service of a notice pursuant to A.2118 cc, is conceptually irreconcilable with an employment fixed term contract as, too, with a withdrawal for an objective justifiable reason except for supervening impossibility.

E. THE DISCHARGE OF CONTRACTS FOR AN INDEFINITE TERM

(*i*) *Dismissal*. Because contracts of employment for an indefinite term are widespread, the termination of such contracts has become an important area of labour law. The principal form of withdrawal from contracts of employment for an indefinite term is the voluntary withdrawal of the master by the dismissal of his servant. Although the original legislation on the subject and A.2118 cc placed no limits upon the master's power of dismissal, there are now large numbers of restrictions introduced by various industrial agreements and special legislation. In those cases in which no specific restrictions apply (industrial or commercial enterprises with less than 16 employees in the same commune, agricultural enterprises with less than six employees in the same commune, and all other employers with less than 36 employees), A.2118 cc remains totally effective with the consequence that a dismissal need not be in writing nor reasoned, that is, a so-called dismissal '*ad nutum*'. In any event, a dismissal is invalid if it is for an illegal reason, whether expressed or not.

Where restrictions are imposed upon dismissals, the restrictions may be either objective, if they concern the grounds which may constitute a basis for the withdrawal by the master from a contract of employment, or subjective, if they relate to the status or condition of the servant. Subjective restrictions are inapplicable to cases of withdrawal for either the closure of an enterprise or a just cause.

The subjective restrictions upon a withdrawal by the master from a contract of employment are as follows. First, the sickness or injury of a servant who in such cases has a right to the preservation of his position for a certain period (A.2110 cc). Second, the pregnancy of a servant during which, and until the first anniversary of the child's birth, any dismissal is ineffective. Third, the marriage of a female worker in which case a dismissal is null if notified between the request for the publication of the marriage and the first anniversary of its celebration. Fourth, the conscription or re-call to military service in which cases conscripted servants who were employed for at least three months are entitled to the preservation of their position until 30 days after their discharge and servants who are re-called to military service cannot be dismissed until the expiration of a period of three months after their return to work. Fifth, where a servant is a refugee, in which case he cannot be dismissed in the first two years of his employment. Finally, where the servant is an invalid or the widow or orphan of such a person (for which category of persons there must be reserved a certain proportion of positions in the total workforce of defined enterprises) in which case the servant cannot be dismissed except for just cause, closure of the enterprise, total incapacity, constituting a danger, or a reduction in personnel in the category to which the servant belongs because the number of employees in that category exceeds the obligatory quota.

Although the Civil Code was formerly limited to either dismissals '*ad nutum*' (with notice) or dismissals for just cause (summary dismissals), the law of 15 July 1966 n.604 has instead introduced various objective restrictions upon dismissals. Nowadays dismissals may only arise for a just cause (the dismissal may be summary) or a justifiable reason (there must be notice). Further, a justifiable reason may concern a notable non-performance of the contractual obligations of the servant (the so-called subjective justifiable reasons) or a matter inherent to the organis-ation and conduct of the business (the so-called objective justifiable reasons). Furthermore, a dismissal must always be in writing, reasoned either initially or within five days of a request by the servant provided that the request is made within eight days of the communication of the dismissal, and, in any event, is null if it is based upon political, religious or industrial beliefs. In every other case, a dismissal is invalid. However, the law of 1966 is inapplicable to a number of situations: where the master has less than 36 servants (with certain exceptions contained in the law of 20 May 1970 n.300); where the servant enjoys permanency either by operation of law or contract (in which case the servant cannot be dismissed for a justifiable reason); where the servant is a company executive; where the servant is employed under a contract of employment for a fixed term; during the first six months of a probationary period; where the servant possesses the requisites for an invalid or old age pension or, in any event, is over the age of 65; and in the case of collective dismissals for the purpose of reducing staff.

A just cause does not even permit a temporary continuation of the employment relationship (A.2119 cc). It concerns particularly serious matters committed by a servant which strike at the very basis of the mutual trust that previously existed between the parties.

A justifiable reason, as already noted, may be either subjective or objective. The former, like a just cause, also concerns matters imputable to the servant but, unlike a just cause, does not affect the temporary continuation of the employment relationship although it too definitively disturbs the trust of the master in the faithfulness, capacity or honesty of his servant. An objective justifiable reason concerns matters relevant to the conduct, organisation, and regular function of the enterprise.

(ii) Remedies against dismissal. Within 60 days of the communication of the reasons for a dismissal, the servant may challenge the dismissal by notice in writing served upon the employer. There is no prescribed form for the notice nor need it be a judicial notice, provided that its purpose is clear. If the servant fails to give written notice within that time, he forfeits any right to challenge the dismissal. If the dismissal has been challenged by the service of a notice, the servant may either proceed directly before the courts (i e the *Pretore*) or first attempt any available conciliation procedures. If such conciliation is successful, the servant cannot later proceed before the courts.

A declaration by the court that the cause for the dismissal did not exist or was illegitimate gives rise, depending upon the case in question, to the following effects. First, in the case of either a fixed term contract or permanent employment, damages in a sum equal to the remuneration not received as a consequence of the invalid termination of the employment relationship. Second, in the case where a dismissal '*ad nutum*' is permissible, the conversion of the dismissal into such type together with an obligation to pay an indemnity for the failure to give the necessary notice of dismissal. Third, in the cases where law n.604 of 1966 is applicable (that is, generally, enterprises with 36 or more employees), if the reason adduced as a just cause is insufficient as such but nonetheless constitutes a justifiable reason, the payment of an indemnity for the failure to give the necessary notice of dismissal; if the reason adduced does not even constitute a justifiable reason, the re-employment of the servant within three days or the payment of an indemnity equivalent to between five and 12 months pay. Fourth, in the cases where the Labour Law of 1970 is applicable (that is, generally, industrial and commercial enterprises with 16 or more employees, or agricultural enterprises with six or more employees, in the same commune), it provides as follows: that dismissals which are either not in writing or unreasoned are ineffective; that dismissals based upon political, religious or industrial beliefs are null; and that dismissals in which the master fails to prove a just cause or a justifiable reason are voidable. In all of these cases, the master *must* re-employ the servant and pay damages equivalent to not less than five months' pay. The master is also liable to pay the relevant salary or stipend from the date of judgment until the servant's re-employment. In the case of a nullity or an inefficacy of the dismissal, the employer is bound to pay any remuneration still owing for the period between the dismissal and the date of judgment.

As already mentioned, notice is necessary for a dismissal in the following cases: contracts of employment for an indefinite term, dismissals '*ad nutum*', and dismissals for a justifiable reason. The length of the necessary notice varies depending upon the relevant collective contract and the classification and seniority of the servant. The master may elect to pay an indemnity equivalent to the remuneration to which the servant would have been entitled during the relevant notice period in lieu of a notice of dismissal. Where it is the servant who withdraws from a contract of employment without giving the appropriate notice, he is liable to indemnify the master in a sum equal to his salary or stipend over the period of the necessary notice.

Where an indefinite contract of employment is terminated for any reason whatsoever, the servant is entitled to a seniority allowance proportional to his period of service. In the case of a contract of employment for a fixed term, the servant is entitled to a termination bonus proportional to the duration of the contract and equivalent to the comparative seniority allowance provided for in the relevant collective contract. In the event of the servant's death, his heirs are entitled to a sum equivalent to the relevant seniority allowance and the indemnity payable upon a failure to give the relevant notice of dismissal.

Guarantees for the protection of workers

The tendency of the law to favour the worker not only manifests itself in the formation of the contract of employment but also in relation to the protection of rights inherent in the employment relationship. The case law has, for instance, held that the acquiescence of a worker to a modification to the contract of employment cannot be evaluated according to the normal interpretative canons as the worker, being the weaker contractual party, may have been induced to postpone any protective action until the cessation of the employment relationship. Similarly, where the employment relationship is terminated at the will of the master, it has been held that the mere acceptance of the relevant allowances by the servant does not per se constitute an acquiescence in the dismissal nor an implied renunciation of any right of action.

The various means through which worker rights are guaranteed may be summarised as follows. First, by giving claims for remuneration and retirement allowances a certain priority vis-à-vis the creditors of the employer. Second, in accordance with the general system which regards remuneration as also serving the function of satisfying the vital needs of the servant and his family, there are various restrictions placed upon the disposability of remuneration, both by the worker himself and his creditors. Thus, family allowances cannot be alienated, sequestrated or attached; stipends, salaries and various other allowances may only be attached, subjected to conservative sequestration, or made available for damages up to one-fifth of their value; the special social welfare funds established by an employer are immune from the creditors of both the master and his servants; and finally, various social welfare benefits are totally immune from attachment. Third, the invalidity of any renunciation or transaction having as its object an irrevocable right (whether created by law or collective contract) of the servant. These renunciations and transactions, however, are not to be confused with the general releases that employers usually require workers to sign upon the receipt of various allowances at the conclusion of the employment relationship. Although considered separately by the doctrine and case law, such general releases have been held to be of no legal effect and therefore a worker remains free to bring any action within the ordinary prescription period for the recovery of all outstanding credits notwithstanding the execution of such a release. Fourth, the ordinary law on the prescription of rights takes on certain peculiar characteristics in relation to labour law. The relevant limitation periods contained in the Civil Code are the ordinary limitation period of ten years applicable to non-remunerative rights and the shorter limitation period of five years applicable to all periodical prestations, including remuneration. There are also certain relevant presumptive prescriptive periods (see p 334, above) which are one year for remuneration payable at intervals of no more than one month and three years for remuneration payable at intervals greater than one month, e g lump sum payments on termination of employment and annual allowances. However, the Constitutional

Court has held that the various prescriptive provisions were constitutionally illegitimate insofar as they permitted the limitation periods for remunerative rights to commence running during the currency of non-permanent employment relationships as they did not adequately protect those employees who, because they did not enjoy the stability of public employment, would 'impliedly' renounce their rights for fear of dismissal. The present position is as follows: first, if the employment relationship is a permanent one, then the limitation period for remunerative credits may commence to run during the course of the employment relationship; second, where there is no stability in the employment relationship, the limitation period for remunerative credits, which remains in suspense during the employment relationship, commences to run at the termination of the relationship; and finally, the limitation period for non-remunerative rights commences to run, in every case, in accordance with the general rules of the civil law.

Fifth, it may be noted that the rights of workers are protected through various public, private and union organisations. On the public plane there are the Provincial Employment Offices and Inspectorates to which a worker may refer any violation of labour rights.

Unionism

The organisation of Italian trade unions is of a complex dual structure. The vertical structure comprises basic territorial units for each industrial sector (provincial unions for each category) with always more extensive territorial units for the same category in an ascending order (regional and national federations for each category). The national federations for each category then form into various confederations. On the horizontal plane there are, at the provincial level, apart from the basic territorial units for each industrial category, the so-called 'territorial unions' which are provincial confederations comprising the various categories that belong to their respective national confederations. The provincial confederations are, represented in their respective national confederations. In the case of employers, the law of 22 December 1956 n. 1589 provides that public economic entities separate from and form associations distinct to the corresponding associations of private employers with the consequence that in the principal industrial sectors there are two collective contracts, one for the private sector and another for the public sector.

As there is no legislative definition of a union, the doctrine defines a union as an association of either workers or employers formed to protect collective professional interests against any other external organisation. The case law, moreover, holds that an association must assist and protect the interests of the whole category that it represents and not only the interests of its registered members before it can qualify as a union.

Article 39 C, which specifically enlarges upon the more general freedom of association contained in A.18 C, guarantees the freedom of unionism. Moreover, A.39 C provides that a union obtains legal personality upon registration (which is conditional upon it having an internally democratic organisation) in an apposite registry whereupon it can enter into universally binding collective contracts. However, the registration aspect of A.39 C, being only a policy provision, has remained a dead letter because the legislature desires to remain neutral in the area of industrial relations and because the unions resist any form of State regulation. As a consequence unions are technically 'un-recognised associations' and subject to the relevant provisions of the civil law. On the other hand, the first paragraph of A.39 C, which guarantees the freedom of unionism, is clearly regarded to be directly and immediately applicable. This aspect of A.39 C manifests itself in the right to form industrial associations, the right to membership and participation in such associations including the right to remain a non-unionist, the protection of union representatives, and the freedom of union activity. It also comprises an implied recognition of the 'plurality of unions' (that is, the right to organise several unions having similar objectives in the same sector) which characterises the Italian industrial scene. The State, through the Labour Law of 1970, has apparently abandoned its neutral stance by enacting many provisions directed of guaranteeing the freedom of unionism in the workplace and, in particular, by protecting that right from any interference or reprisal by employers.

The right to strike

Article 40 C recognises the right to strike within the limits defined by legislation. For obvious reasons, the legislature has not intervened as a result of which the case law has become important in this area. Notwithstanding the absence of legislation on the subject, the Constitutional Court has held that A.40 C, and therefore the right to strike, is directly and immediately operative.

Historically, the strike has been the instrument of economic struggle with the evident object of seeking, through self-help, to bring about a balance between the differing strengths of the parties to the employment relationship; it has been defined by the Constitutional Court as a total abstention from work by several subordinate workers with the object of defending their economic interests. It follows that although the strike constitutes an individual subjective right it always aims at the protection of the collective interest and therefore may only be exercised collectively. The case law and doctrine have had to face the problem of the 'political strike' which the Constitutional Court has held to be legitimate provided that it is not utilised to subvert the Constitutional system nor to impede or hinder the free exercise of the legitimate powers through which popular sovereignty is expressed.

As the strike is recognised as 'a right', it cannot give rise to criminal liability nor be regarded as constituting non-performance of the contract of employment. It follows that the fundamental effect of a strike is the suspension of the counter-prestations inherent in the contract of employment (i e labour and remuneration) as well as certain other directly connected rights (e g annual holidays and seniority). Even during a strike certain obligations remain effective, e g the employer is obliged to preserve the position of the worker and the worker continues to be bound by the duty of faithfulness. Certain rights of a social welfare nature also remain applicable during a strike, e g sickness benefits.

The various types of strike considered to be legitimate include the economic strike, the political strike, the general (or solidarity) strike and the sympathy strike. These types of strike may take anomalous forms which pose problems of validity. They include the following. First, the rolling strike which is an intermittent abstention from work. There are isolated case law decisions which regard such strikes as legitimate. However, if the work periods are too brief to be of utility to the employer, the latter may refuse to accept them and accordingly regard them as non-performance of the contract of employment with a consequent reduction in remuneration. Second, the selective strike which is a type of rolling strike but consists of a rotational stop-work by the various departments in an enterprise. Third, the work-to-rule strike which consists of a slavish application of work regulations thereby notably reducing the rhythm of work. It is generally considered to be illegitimate. Fourth, the go-slow strike which is certainly contractually illicit and, arguably, also falls outside the requisite of an abstention from work which is necessary for a legitimate strike. Finally, the go-fast strike which involves over-production and is considered to be illegitimate as it does not come within the concept of a strike in the proper sense.

No less complex is the problem of the validity of actions taken in support of a strike such as picketing, boycotts and blockades of merchandise entering or leaving the workplace. The general approach of the case law is that supportive action which is considered to be necessary to the successful outcome of a strike is legitimate provided that it does not injure some other primary interest protected by the criminal law. In particular, any activity directed towards the coercion of persons who are not participating in the strike is considered as falling outside the right to strike. Picketing is regarded by the dominant case law as constituting a crime where it is accompanied by violence or threats; otherwise it is a civil wrong based upon the violation of the constitutional right to work.

The lock-out

Whilst the Constitution pronounces itself on the strike, it is silent with respect to the lock-out which is regulated by the ordinary civil and criminal law (Artt. 502ff cp). It cannot be regarded as a right. The dominant doctrine inteprets the silence of the Constitution on the matter as 'codifying' the differences between the socio-economic power of the parties to the contract of employment so that only the worker has a right legitimately to suspend his prestation in the employment relationship. It follows that, according to the ordinary law, the lock-out would constitute a breach of contract by the employer thereby giving the worker a right in damages equivalent to the lost remuneration.

Relevant principles of Community law

The common economic policies relevant to labour law arising out of the European Treaties are: first, the free circulation of persons, and in particular, of workers; second, the improvement of employment opportunities and the general standard of living through the establishment of the European Social Fund; third, a common policy on matters of professional training; and finally, a unified social welfare system in relation to migrant-workers.

Of particular importance are the norms on the free circulation and equal treatment of workers in all member states as a consequence of which every form of discrimination, based on nationality, concerning employment, categorisation, remuneration or any other work condition has been abolished. Therefore, a citizen of any member state may be legitimately employed by an employer in another member state and, in particular, the Provincial Employment Office (UPLMO) in Italy cannot raise any objection based upon the availability of nationals with the same qualifications, unlike its obligation to do so in the case of the employment of persons from outside the EEC.

The other important aspect of Community law with relation to labour law is the power of the Council of Ministers to fix the general principles necessary to achieve a unitary policy in relation to professional training. This is a significant departure from A.35 C according to which professional training was an internal public function. The Community objectives in this regard are first, the realisation of conditions which will make effective the right to receive an adequate professional training, and second, to provide the various productive sectors with the necessary forms of labour. The policy generally aims at a high level of training, as well as versatility, so as to enable further specialisation and, if necessary, professional retraining.

The special procedure for the resolution of employment disputes

The law of 11 August 1973 n.533 introduced a special procedure for the resolution of employment disputes with the object of ensuring a more effective and immediate protection of the worker. In contrast to the ordinary civil process, the labour process is simpler and speedier. It is characterised by first, its orality, second, its immediacy which is ensured through rules such as the requirement that there be no more than 60 days between the filing of the summons and the hearing, and the prohibition against adjournments, and finally, the broadening of the instruction powers of the judge which, therefore, are only comparable to the powers of the criminal courts.

The competent court of first instance in all labour disputes is the *Pretura* from which there is a right of appeal to the *Tribunale*. All of the parties are obliged to appear in person, a requirement which also has the object of enabling the judge to attempt a conciliation. The judge may decide the cause upon the basis of the documentary evidence alone or he may initiate an instruction in which case, as already noted, he has wider powers than in an ordinary civil process. However, these broad instruction powers do not deny the proceedings of the fundamental characteristic of Italian civil procedure, viz, that a court cannot proceed *ex officio*. Union representatives may be called for the purpose of giving information, especially in relation to the relevant collective contracts. Judgments which order an employer to make the payment of a liquidated sum to an employee are, contrary to the general civil law rule, immediately enforceable.

Chapter 11

Environmental law

Recent developments in Italian environmental law

Since the 1960s there has been, after a long legislative pause dating from 1939, a renewed interest in the artistic, historical, and natural environment. The now popular concept of 'cultural property' has its origins in the work of the so-called Franceschini Commission of the mid-sixties which was given the task of inquiring into the protection of the nation's historical, archaeological, artistic and environmental heritage. The Commission devised a broad unitary approach to the issue through the concept of 'historical testimony' which comprises every aspect of the nation's history and civilisation, including its environment. The aspiration for a common regulation of this heterogeneous subject was manifested in the adoption of the unitary concept of 'cultural property' which included the natural environment. Cultural environmental property included, apart from the traditional naturalistic concept, everything which in a given territory was worthy of conservation and valued as a complete testimony of a certain civilisation. Cultural environmental property therefore consists of two broad classes of property: environmental and urban property. The former comprises both natural property (understood in a geographical or ecological sense) which forms part of natural history, and natural property transformed by man. Urbanism comprises structures of special merit that are living testimony of a civilisation through its urban history. In other words, cultural environmental property includes the natural geographical and biological environment and the artificial environment created by man through his technological and artistic achievements.

The work of this Commission was followed by the so-called Papaldo Commission which had the task of revising and co-ordinating the norms relevant to the protection of cultural property. In relation to environmental property, the distinction between natural and urban property was again drawn and the draft proposals envisaged that environmental property would be protected by giving it priority within the ambit of urban planning. The Commission's proposals were never acted upon.

The next development came about in 1974 when the need to entrust the administration of the nation's cultural and environmental heritage to a single ministry, with the object of ensuring its organic protection, led to the establishment of the Ministry of Cultural and Environmental Property and, within it, the National Council for Cultural and Environmental Property presided over by the Minister himself. The functions of the new Ministry were defined as the protection and realisation of the nation's cultural heritage and the dissemination of art and culture through the co-ordination and promotion of both internal and, subject to the functions of the Ministry of Foreign Affairs, external programmes. Five sectional committees were established for the following classes of property: environmental and architectural property, archaeological property, libraries and cultural institutes, historical and artistic property, and archives. The functions of these sectional committees are, within the general policies fixed by the National Council, to propose annual and longer-term programmes, to co-ordinate the means and criteria for action, to disseminate information, to express opinions on questions referred by the Minister, and to pronounce themselves on issues delegated by legislation or regulations.

The activities of the Ministry do not extend to every possible connotation inherent in the term 'environment'. Even on the legal or normative plane, there is no single approach to the problem of the environment and this has led, across the fragmentary and sectional interests in the subject, to the equivocal formulation of 'environment' as a legal notion. The doctrine uses the term 'environment' in at least three different senses: first, environment as public property, that is, as the natural framework of cultural property; second, environment as the object of pollution; and finally, environment as the object of the urban planning of the national territory, or of its territorial assets, which is to some extent inseparable from the environment as cultural and environmental property. Of the three meanings of environment only the first has become a concern of the new Ministry.

Existing Italian legislation on the subject is based upon an analytical division of cultural property: things of artistic, historical, archaeological and similar interest, that is, so-called 'things of art', regulated by the law of 1 June 1939 n.1089; the so-called natural landscape regulated by the law of 29 June 1939 n.1497; and archives regulated by the law of 22 December 1939 n.2006 as amended by DPR 30 September 1963 n.1409. All these laws are based upon the same fundamental concepts which have therefore enabled the formulation by the doctrine of the more abstract and unitary concept of 'cultural property' in its expanded sense, as described earlier. The same concept was officially adopted in the establishment of the Ministry of Cultural and Environmental Property by the DL 14 December 1974 n.657 ratified by the law of 22 January 1975 n.5.

Constitutional provisions

The Constitution does not contain any express reference to the environment as an object of protection. There are, however, two indirect references which imply a collective interest in the protection of the human habitat and the quality of life: A.9(2) C which declares that the Republic shall protect the landscape and historical and artistic patrimony of the nation; and A.32(1) C which provides that the Republic shall protect health both as a fundamental individual interest and in the interest of the collectivity.

The scope, source and content of environmental law

The variety of possible things deserving of protection by environmental law means that there is neither a single notion of 'environment' nor its organic protection by the public authorities; rather environmental law consists of a variety of interests worthy of protection. In other words, there is no unitary form of protection of the environment but rather a plurality of protections each of which is directly related to the interest worthy of protection. For instance, the environment in a natural sense finds its protection in the normative regulation of cultural property, the natural landscape, historical centres, forests and national parks; the environment in the sense of terrestrial, aquatic, and air spaces finds its protection in the norms on anti-pollution; and the environment in the urban sense finds its protection in the norms on territorial order, the location of installations and urban planning. If a still broader approach is taken, then the concept of environment extends even further to include the natural habitat within which man lives and acts and therefore environmental protection in this wider sense extends to a number of human activities such as agriculture, the exploration and exploitation of minerals, reclamation, forestation, hunting and fishing, the exploration and extraction of hydrocarbons, and nuclear energy. However, the novel and moral interest in the environmental phenomenon impedes a precise definition of the notion.

This chapter is mainly concerned with the pollution control of water, air and soil resources. Pollution control in Italy is characterised both by an increasing interest in any existing legal norm which may in some way constitute a means of protecting the environment and the passage of new Regional and State legislation which is directed to the integration and substitution of the now largely obsolete existing legislation. Notwithstanding considerable legislation on the subject, there remains the absence of a truly independent and organic legal regulation of pollution control which still depends upon very disparate sectors of the law.

The traditional legal categories and environmental control

A. THE PRIVATE LAW AND POLLUTION CONTROL

(*i*) *Article 844 cc.* This provision, the most important of the private law norms with respect to pollution control, allows an owner of land to seek a prohibition against the emission of smoke, heat, fumes, noises, vibrations or the like from his neighbour's hand beyond 'normal tolerability' which is determined by having regard to the nature of the neighbourhood. Article 844 cc allows a balancing of the relative interests of production and ownership as well as a consideration of the priority of a given land use.

The effectiveness of A.844 cc in relation to environmental protection is limited by several factors. First, because it is a private law norm, its application is dependent upon private initiative which may be lacking through either considerations of expediency or agreement. Second, it admits a wide discretion in the courts because of the absence of a legislative definition of 'normal tolerability'. The case law has generally adopted the approach that those emissions which are the result of the normal use of a property must be tolerated by a neighbour. In relation to noise, in particular, the recent case law has held that only that noise which exceeds the general noise level in the locality is to be regarded as intolerable. This wide discretion therefore contains the possibility of a progressive expansion of permissible emissions through a gradual change in the nature of the locality. Consequently, the only limit upon such an expansion is that it cannot exceed a level which would be intolerable in every locality or in every event. Third, it has a limited application with respect to commercial, industrial, agricultural or other 'productive' activities because even if the nuisance exceeds the normal tolerability levels, the relative interests of ownership and production must be balanced. This power to balance equitably conflicting interests is rare in Italian law and although the Code is silent as to the consequences of a finding that the defendant may nonetheless carry on his activities, the case law and the majority of the doctrine is of the view that the plaintiff in any event is entitled to an indemnity. However, the court must, if possible, order the adoption of technical precautions to eliminate the nuisance and only resort to indemnity if there is no alternative solution.

It is apparent therefore that the courts enjoy a wide discretion, also enhanced by their right to consider the priority of a given land use, in the application of A.844 cc. Cicala (*La tutela dell'ambiente nel diritto amministrativo, penale e civile*, Utet, 1976, pp 9ff) suggests that the court's overall discretion may become less elastic as a result of the so-called Antismog Law which defines certain tolerability levels that cannot be exceeded. The application of the court's discretion is limited to production activities and does not therefore extend to nuisances arising out of non-production activities such as recreational activities (e g a youth club).

(ii) Articles 2043 and 2050 cc. Article 844 cc is concerned with the elimination of a nuisance through prohibition. The same activity could be subject to an action for damages based upon A.2043 cc (that is, a civilly illicit fact) which has different requisites to A.844 cc; whilst it necessitates the proof of fault in the defendant by showing that he could have avoided the damage through normal diligence, it is broader than A.844 cc because it is available to non-owners (e g tenants). Where a peril or damage to health is adduced under A.2043, the criterion of 'normal tolerability' is inapplicable as a result of which any prejudice to the right to health is unconditionally illegal. The requirements of health and safety, as confirmed by A.890 cc, prevail over any considerations relating to 'production'.

Furthermore, in the area of tortious liability, A.2050 cc, applicable to damage caused by dangerous works, assumes a certain importance in pollution control as it is, unlike A.2043 cc, untrammelled by the requisite of a subjective element of fault in the defendant. There is a general tendency towards the objective responsibility of entrepreneurs for all damage, however caused, resulting from their firm or products; that is, a responsibility independent of any subjective element. This tendency has been fully realised in the case of damage caused by enterprises dealing with nuclear substances (see A.15 DPR 30 September 1975 n.519).

(iii) Article 890 cc. This norm, also of significance to pollution, provides that where the construction of ovens, chimneys, stables or the like, the deposit of humid, explosive or other substances, or the installation of machinery may lead to a danger of injury, all such activities must comply with restrictions relating to distances from boundaries or, in the absence of such formal restrictions, with the distances necessary to prevent injury to the integrity, health and safety of adjoining premises. It is clear that this norm consists of two basic elements: the possibility of a danger arising from the particular object; and an adequate distance between the dangerous object and the neighbouring property.

B. LABOUR LAW AND THE ENVIRONMENT

Many norms relevant to the protection of the environment are to be found within the context of labour law which is, inter alia, concerned with the maintenance of a healthy and safe work environment. The general constitutional provision which affirms that the Republic protects health as a fundamental individual right and in the collective interest is certainly applicable to entrepreneurial activities given that the Constitution provides first, that economic activities cannot be exercised in conflict with social utility or in a manner which injures human safety, freedom and dignity (A.41(2) C), and second, that the Republic recognises and guarantees the inviolable rights of man within the social formations with which he manifests his personality (A.2 C). These provisions constitute the key to the interpretation of A.2087 cc and all special legislation relating to worker health.

Article 2087 cc imposes a duty upon the entrepreneur to adopt those measures which, according to the nature of the work, experience, and technology, are necessary to protect the physical and moral well-being of his servants. It follows that it is not sufficient for an employer merely to adopt those measures prescribed by law but he must also adopt all those measures which science and technology have made available for the protection of worker health. The law therefore requires an employer to reduce, as far as technology permits, any danger to his servants arising from dust, noise and fumes. Where there is a conflict between worker health and production needs, the former must without doubt prevail. These considerations lead to the conclusion that there is a true and proper right in the worker to a healthy work environment; a right enforceable against the entrepreneur. A servant has a right to request the courts to order the entrepreneur to adopt any necessary health measures. It would seem that the worker could also refuse his prestation of labour where work conditions are harmful to health and this cannot constitute a justifiable reason for dismissal. Similarly, a violation by the employer of his obligation to ensure a healthy work environment may give rise to a justifiable reason for the resignation of the servant who would then be entitled to request compensation for damages. These are necessary corollaries of the fact that although the servant is bound to place his labour at the disposal of the employer, the latter is bound to utilise it without prejudice to the health of his servant.

Work conditions come within the scope of trade union concern. Article 9 of the Labour Law of 1970 specifically provides that workers have the right, through their representatives, to control the application of the relevant provisions for the prevention of accidents and industrial diseases and of promoting the research, formulation and fulfilment of measures suitable for the protection of their health and physical well-being. The existence of a situation dangerous to health may therefore constitute a ground for either an industrial dispute or a complaint under the criminal law. Moreover, A.9 of the Labour Law implies a right in trade union representatives to seek a declaration as to what health measures ought to be adopted by an employer and an order that the latter must execute such measures.

Apart from all of the above rights, which assist in an elimination of the pollution phenomenon, an important role also belongs to the Labour Inspectorate. The Inspectorate may both order the elimination of health risks that do not per se constitute crimes and impose sanctions against the illicit behaviour of an employer which affects the hygiene of the work environment. The most important forms of illicit behaviour are the criminal wrongs relating to the violation of the legislative norms on the following subjects: work hygiene, the prevention of accidents and hygiene in subterranean work, the policing of mines and caves, and the protection of workers and the public against radiation and nuclear energy utilised for peaceful purposes. In accordance with these provisions, unhealthy works, which also include noisy occupations, must as far as possible be segregated from the rest of the relevant enterprise so as to reduce the possibility of injury to persons who are not specifically assigned to the dangerous work. These norms also have a secondary role in that at the same time they protect persons other than the workers of the enterprise such as neighbours.

C. THE CRIMINAL LAW AND POLLUTION CONTROL

(*i*) *Introduction*. The criminal law contains many provisions useful in the struggle against certain forms of pollution and has been utilised for this purpose by the public authorities. Although the Criminal Code contains specific provisions on noise pollution only, and not in relation to air, water or soil pollution, it contains a complex set of provisions directed to the protection of persons and things, and since pollution results in injury to persons and things these provisions are useful in the struggle against pollution.

There are certain general difficulties in applying the criminal law to pollution control. The problem of identifying the responsible person or defendant, although this is a relatively simple task in the case of small firms in which the owner is also responsible for technical matters, is significant in the case of large industrial undertakings in which duties and responsibilities are divided amongst the various levels of the organisation. The necessity to identify the responsible party arises from two considerations: first, having regard to the case law in other areas of the criminal law, few writers would take the view that an entrepreneur is vicariously liable for every criminal irregularity in the conduct of a complex organisation; and second, in Italian law natural persons only may commit crimes. As an entrepreneur may delegate sectional functions to subordinates, who may therefore become criminally responsible in relation to the performance of their duties, the case law takes the approach that an entrepreneur may only escape liability where the relevant function has been delegated in the widest possible terms to a suitably qualified person in accordance with the company's constitution and pursuant to an effective, actual and constant requirement of the enterprise. Moreover, the responsible manager must have been furnished with all of the material means necessary to perform the duties delegated to him. As a general rule, an entrepreneur may escape liability if he can show that he has provided the enterprise with the necessary purifiers which have then malfunctioned through the negligence, lack of maintenance or other cause referable to his personnel. In a complex company, it is sufficient for him to show that the duty to provide for the purification process had been delegated to a competent person who had been given access to the appropriate financial means.

The identification of the pollution source is in most cases a collective phenomenon. Where the law merely punishes a person who discharges polluting substances, there is generally little problem. But where the existence of the crime depends upon proof that the defendant has produced a specific injury, or exposed certain persons or things to a danger of injury, the presence of a large number of possible concurrent causes gives rise to considerable evidentiary problems.

Whether any action may be taken where the polluting emission is the consequence of an activity which is specifically authorised by law is a difficult problem, as there is no general rule in Italian law according to which an authorisation per se frees its holder from every form of responsibility.

Finally, there is the interesting and unresolved problem, which shall only be mentioned, of the responsibility of public officials in relation to a deterioration of the environment. This responsibility may arise either through a material activity of the public administration which directly causes the damage complained of (e g the pollution of a river with sewerage) or through incomplete control over the activities of private individuals. The latter situation may, in turn, arise because the public official has either failed in his duties of investigation and supervision or authorised work beyond his competence.

(ii) The specific criminal norms of relevance to pollution control

(a) ARTICLES 437 AND 451 cp. Article 437 cp punishes persons who omit to install equipment or warnings directed to preventing work accidents or whomsoever removes or damages such equipment or warnings. This provision may catch an omission to adopt the necessary precautions for work hygiene. Similarly, A.451 cp punishes any person who, through his fault, omits to install or removes or renders unserviceable any instrument or means for the extinguishment of fires or for dealing with other work related emergencies. This provision may be applicable in cases where an establishment fails to provide the means of dealing with accidents.

(b) ARTICLE 635 cp This provision punishes whomsoever causes the destruction, dispersion, or total or partial inutility of a movable or immovable which belongs to someone else. It is apparent that this provision contains certain inherent limitations, an important one being that the damaged thing must belong to another person who, incidentally, may even be the State. Therefore, because air does not have an owner the provision is inapplicable to atmospheric pollution unless such emissions subsequently damage public or private property, although a mere defacing or soiling of property would not come within this provision but A.639 cp which only prescribes a mild pecuniary penalty.

Although not all of the doctrine is in agreement, it appea: ; that the crime in A.635 cp does not apply to water, soil or subsoil pollution as the special legislation of 10 May 1976 n.319 (see p 476, below) overrides all other norms which could be applicable to these forms of pollution. This does not mean that it cannot apply to pollution which is not strictly consequential to an illegal emission into water or soil, e g in the case of damage to other things which come into contact with the water or soil.

Notwithstanding that the territorial sea comes within the sovereignty of the State, it does not form part of the State's so-called maritime demesne which, in Italian law, is strictly defined by A.822 cc to include only ports, spits, lagoons, salt water basins and inland waters. Therefore, part of the doctrine is of the view that marine waters cannot come within the purview of A.635 cp as they lack the 'ownership' necessary for the application of the article.

Animals fall outside the scope of A.635 cp: if they are private property, then their injury is punished according to A.638 cp; if they are wild, in which case they belong to no one, then the special legislation on hunting and A.500 cp apply. Similarly with fish, although there is some dicta that a school of fish belongs to the State and therefore comes within A.638 cp. This is now of little importance as the law of 14 July 1965 n.963 provides for the specific crime of 'injury to the biological resources of marine waters'.

Article 635 cp is important in relation to water pollution because, apart from the fact that part of the doctrine does not regard the special law of 1976 as having ousted its application, it would nonetheless be applicable to pollution caused by emissions with which the law of 1976 is not concerned, even though such emissions would, indeed, be relatively small in number. It is clear that as far as water pollution is concerned, the offender would rarely cause the water's destruction or dispersion but rather its unsuitability for the purpose for which it was intended. Thus the use to which water is to be put becomes important as merely making it unsightly or smelly may not affect its use. In essence, the problem, which cannot always be easily resolved, is one of determining both the function or use of the water and whether the pollution in question hinders that use. For example, water pollution rarely hinders its use for navigation.

The uses of certain water resources are defined by the Water Legislation of 1933 which states that subterranean and surface waters in abstract suitable for consumption, agricultural or industrial purposes must be maintained in a condition such that they remain capable of being used for such purposes. This does not mean that they must be directly capable of being put to such uses but rather that they must not be put into condition so as to render their purification impossible or extremely costly.

The functions of public surface waters also include that of a natural habitat for water life, an object which may be deduced from the Laws on Fishing (1931) and Sea Fishing (1965). The case law has held that waters may be declared to be public because of their suitability as sources of fish. Therefore, an interference with such functions may lead to the crime in A.635 cp notwithstanding that most of the special legislation imposes its own particular criminal sanctions. All of these norms, in contrast to A.635 cp, prohibit the mere discharge of harmful substances into the water without the need to prove that the water has actually been rendered unsuitable for water life.

All of the above functions of public surface waters may be said to be general. More particular functions are to be found in A.226 of the Health Law which provides that industrial discharges need only be subject to a complete and effective purification where they flow into lakes, water courses or canals which in any manner service domestic use. Therefore it seems that only part of the public waters must be maintained in a condition suitable for domestic purposes which, apart from their use for consumption (which brings Artt. 439 and 440 cp into force), includes any use that brings the water into direct contact with man, e g washing. Therefore, the pollution of water so that it becomes unsuitable for domestic purposes would only attract the crime in A.635 cp where the water is actually being used for such purposes in accordance with municipal regulations or custom.

Finally, it appears that waters made unsuitable for swimming may also give rise to the crime in A.635 cp. However, a conclusion that water was intended for swimming is indirectly dependent upon the Decree of 1911 which delegated to the communes the duty of regulating swimming in public places. Because such legislation was not concerned with determining the destination of waters for bathing purposes it has been suggested that it may be more fruitful, in the case of waters made unsuitable for bathing, to rely upon A.674 cp (see p 468, below) in whose terms it may be argued that the polluting substances 'offend or soil or cause a nuisance' to persons who wish to 'pass' the water or make use of it to refresh themselves.

(c) DELICTS AGAINST THE PERSON: ARTT. 575ff cp. As pollution and health are connected, the criminal norms concerning the protection of the person may be useful in combating pollution. Articles 589 and 590 cp, which concern the delicts of unintentional homicide and personal injury, deal with the situation in which a person through his own fault, that is, for 'imprudence, negligence, lack of skill, or inobservance of legislation, regulations, orders or discipline', causes the death or a physical or mental injury of another person. This provision is applicable where the pollution of air, water or the work environment injures the health of citizens. Its application encounters serious practical difficulties such as the proof of a definite nexus between the pollution and the injury, although this is easier in the case of an injury in the work place. The escape of highly toxic vapours is dealt with by A.674 cp which more readily overcomes the problems of proof inherent in Artt. 589 and 590 cp.

(d) ARTICLE 650 cp. The contravention contained in A.650 cp provides that, unless the facts constitute a more serious crime, any person who fails to observe an administrative measure issued for reasons of justice, public safety, public order or hygiene is punished by either arrest of up to three months or amend of up to Lit.400,000. This criminal norm, therefore, provides a criminal sanction as a back-up to any administrative order which is issued to protect public hygiene. Such administrative measures are issued by the mayors and this therefore raises the question of the relationship between A.650 cp and A.106 of the Communal and Provincial Law (CPL) which punishes violations of mayoral orders with an administrative pecuniary penalty. However, as A.650 cp constitutes a more serious crime than the administrative penalty in A.106 CPL, where there is a violation of an order issued by a mayor on the subject of pollution, if the purpose of the order was hygiene then recourse must be had to A.650 cp whereas if the purpose of the order was to protect public or private property then A.106 CPL comes into play.

(e) ARTICLE 659 cp. Article 659 cp, which deals with a disturbance to either the work or rest of persons, sets out two distinct crimes relevant to pollution control. The first, which can be committed by any person, concerns any disturbance to either the work or rest of persons, including any disturbance to various types of gatherings, through rowdy or noisy behaviour, the abuse of sound instruments or acoustic signals (including signals pertinent to the circulation of motor vehicles), or by the provocation of, or failure to impede, noises caused by animals (A.659(1) cp). The second may only be committed by persons who conduct 'a noisy profession or trade' in breach of a law or regulation (A.659(2) cp). The two crimes are different for various reasons, the most important being that the former requires a precise event causing a noise which disturbs a certain number of persons thereby violating the public peace, whilst in the case of A. 659(2) cp it is enough if a given law or regulation is violated without the further need to prove that anyone has actually suffered a nuisance. All noise concerned with entrepreneurial or professional activities generally falls exclusively within A.659(2) cp (as A.659(1) cp is restricted to 'gratuitous' noises) and is only punishable if the noise is contrary to law or regulation, the relevant legislation being A.66 of the Consolidated Law on Public Safety (TUPS) and A.216 of the Health Law (HL) (see p 472ff, below). Therefore it is legitimate for an entrepreneur or professional to conduct a noisy activity, unless some particular or general norm prohibits or regulates it, as A.659(1) cp is inapplicable to them. Nevertheless, A.659(1) cp may find application in the case of unnecessary noises produced by entrepreneurial or professional activities, such as noises produced through carelessness or incivility, as well as noises which could be eliminated through recourse to appropriate technological developments. This means that industry has an obligation or duty to adopt the most recent silencing methods. Certainly, a similar obligation exists in relation to those measures which are necessary to protect workers from noises in the work place.

(f) ARTICLE 674 cp. Article 674 cp contains two contraventions: the first concerns the situation where a person throws or discharges upon a public place or private common property a thing which is apt to injure, soil or create a nuisance to persons, and the second concerns the same effects but this time arising from the emission of gas, vapours or smoke in circumstances not permitted by law. The case law has interpreted A.674 cp as extending its protection to every aspect of the person, for example, emissions which merely soil clothes and vapours which constitute a nuisance because of their characteristic odour.

As the emission of smoke is specifically referred to in the second part of A.674 cp, the term 'thing' in the first part of the article is regarded as not including minute particles which generally accompany smoke and therefore the first part of A.674 cp, in its application to atmospheric pollution, is limited to that pollution created by dusts which derive from the working of solid materials. Article 674 cp can also be utilised, as mentioned earlier, against water pollution, especially where the water is used for swimming or where the pollution causes a soiling of beaches. This would not appear to be affected by the special law of 1976 on water pollution, which repeals all other legislative provisions concerning the subject, as A.674 cp is not concerned with water pollution as such but rather with those conditions which constitute a nuisance to persons.

The second part of A.674 cp is of particular relevance to atmospheric pollution. The phrase 'in circumstances not permitted by law' in this part of the article has been interpreted by Cassation to mean not only that the owner of an enterprise must observe the specific requirements or precautions imposed by the relevant Authority but that he must adopt all the means which technology makes available to limit the dangers and nuisances generated by the enterprise. This is because the authorisation of an industrial activity must always be understood as referring only to its normal activity which includes the adoption of all measures which experience and technology make available for the protection of health. It follows that these measures must be continuously updated in order to keep abreast of that technological progress which protects the physical and psychological integrity of man. This approach by Cassation corresponds with the approach of A.20 in the 1966 Antismog Law which provides that industrial establishments must adopt all of the means which technological progress makes available for the minimisation of atmospheric pollution.

The existence of the Antismog Law has given rise to problems of its relationship with A.674 cp. Some writers take the view that the Antismog Law, as a specific piece of legislation, overrides the more general A.674 cp, although Cassation has several times rejected this approach. The best view appears to be that the Antismog Law and A.674 cp operate concurrently. Article 20 of the Antismog Law has a more expansive operation than A.674 cp as it catches certain types of pollution which per se are not prohibited by A.674. At the other extreme, it seems that the approach taken by certain courts of first instance, which have gone as far as to hold that the Antismog Law does not affect the application of A.674 cp, must be rejected as this approach would threaten the coherence of the system. Rather, it would appear that those emissions which fall below the prohibitions contained in the Antismog Law must be considered as being permitted by law and therefore as not coming within the crime contained in A.674 cp. In this way, the Antismog Law has integrated and rendered less elastic and less uncertain the application of A.674 cp. Those emissions which exceed the levels permitted by the Antismog Law must always be regarded as 'not permitted by law' but, in order to satisfy A.674 cp, they must also be capable of injuring, soiling or annoying persons.

The Antismog Law also serves as a useful point of reference with respect to those circumstances which fall outside its scope as it can be regarded as codifying the standards which the Authorities consider can be achieved with the present state of technology.

(g) ARTICLE 734 cp. The contravention in A.734 cp punishes anyone who, through construction, demolition or in any other way, destroys or alters the natural beauty of places which are subject to special protection by the Authorities. The norm, therefore, has broad application in that it comprises pollution which either causes the disfigurement of both immovable things of conspicuous natural beauty and villas, parks, gardens, lakes and rivers which have an uncommon beauty or otherwise disturbs the aesthetic aspect of these things and offends the pleasure of persons who would like and ought to enjoy them. The scope of this norm is limited as the words 'places which are subject to special protection by the Authorities' have been interpreted as referring to legislative provisions which protect particular things only and not to legislation which declares the whole of a given territory to be of public interest because of its natural beauty.

(h) ARTICLES 439 AND 440 cp. Water and other consumable substances enjoy specific protection under the 1976 law on water pollution (the so-called *Legge Merli*) which repeals all other crimes dealing with the same matters with which it is concerned, although A.26 of the *Legge Merli* (LM) saves those provisions in the Criminal Code concerning delicts against public safety. Consequently, the amend in A.249 HL, which concerns the pollution of consumable water, has been repealed in relation to pollution caused by emissions of a certain permanency but not as to pollution caused by an occasional act, e g by the dumping of a carcass into a water supply.

It follows that insofar as the Criminal Code is concerned the delicts in Artt. 439 and 440 remain in force. Article 439 cp punishes any person who poisons water or other consumable substances prior to their collection or distribution for consumption. Article 440 cp deals with the situation in which water or other consumable substances are not poisoned but merely 'contaminated or adulterated' to an extent which renders them 'dangerous to public health'. These provisions are applicable to private waters or substances provided that the use of the water or substance is not restricted to very few and defined persons as this would remove the element of a 'public danger'. It is apparent that the use of polluted water for irrigation may lead to the indirect pollution of 'consumable substances' such as vegetables or fruit. Theoretically there is no difficulty in applying Artt. 439 and 440 cp to such cases as long as there is a danger to public health which cannot be the case where the fruits of the soil have merely been fouled so that any danger to health may be overcome through normal washing operations. The latter situation is dealt with by the contravention in A.5(d) of the 1962 law on The Hygiene of Consumable Substances which concerns the commerce of 'filthy' consumables. The delicts in Artt. 439 and 440 cp find an easier application where the pollution causes an intrinsic alteration to a consumable substance, e g the presence of chromium in milk.

Procedure

There are two basic procedures for pollution control: criminal proceedings which, independent of any administrative action, are only available in the case of a few limited types of pollution of a rather macroscopic nature; and administrative controls. The latter may take the form of either an obligation upon the administration to establish suitable means and plants for the destruction of refuse thereby preventing pollution, or the control and regulation of the activities of private individuals with the object of preventing pollution. The administrative regulation of private individuals is through the issue of either detailed regulations which are authorised by State legislation or specific measures which are directed to certain individuals.

In addition, the Prefects and the communal authorities may emanate 'temporary and urgent' ordinances against citizens in the 'public interest', a non-compliance with which will lead to criminal penalties. The powers of the Prefect arise from A.20 of the 1934 Consolidated Law on the Communes and Provinces (TUCP) which authorises the issue of temporary and urgent ordinances on matters of building, local police and hygiene where these affect public health or safety over an entire province or several communes. If such ordinances are not complied with, the Prefect may take the necessary measures to have them executed. Where an exclusively local interest is involved, then the appropriate measures are to be issued by the Mayor or his delegate pursuant to A.153 of the CPL of 1915. These temporary and urgent measures are of greater relevance to the Prefects than to the communal authorities, which have broad powers under Artt. 216 and 217 HL to deal with industrial pollution, as recourse to temporary and urgent measures may only arise where the authority in question has no other specific legislative or regulatory right of intervention. The Mayor has had his authority to issue such temporary and urgent measures enlarged after the introduction of the Antismog Law which conferred upon the 'Regional Committees against Pollution' a priority over the communal authorities in those zones which are subject to the legislation. The communal authorities, having lost their power to deal definitively with the problem of atmospheric industrial pollution, have consequently seen their power to issue 'temporary and urgent' measures in this area broadened because they no longer have any specific legislative right of intervention. It is a useful power which can be utilised during the delay in implementing the complex procedures under the Antismog Law. The power to issue such measures is always limited to temporary and urgent measures. 'Urgent' has been restrictively interpreted to mean an unusual and unforeseen event and not one which has existed for some time. 'Temporary' relates to the elimination of an immediate danger pending the intervention of the organ competent to deal definitively with the dangerous situation; the temporary measure cannot embody a solution which has a definitive effect.

The regulation of unhealthy industries

The regulation of industries which are unhealthy, dangerous, noisy or a nuisance is surrounded by a vast range of complex problems which interfere with an efficient administration of pollution controls. The complexity basically concerns the co-ordination of the 1931 legislation on public safety, the 1934 legislation on public health and the 1966 Antismog Law which both specifically deals with industries which threaten atmospheric pollution and affects and varies the 1934 Health Law. Other legislation has modified the competence of the mayor, the communal junta, the Prefect and the Provincial Medical Officer, as a result of which there has arisen an uncertainty as to their respective functions. The general picture has been further complicated by the fact that the Health Law does not have its own regulations and therefore recourse must be had to the regulations passed under the earlier and now repealed Health Laws.

This complex and uncertain state of affairs certainly exists in relation to unhealthy or dangerous industries regulated by both the 1931 Public Safety Law (TUPS) (Artt. 64, 65 and 67) and the 1934 Health Law (HL) (Artt. 216 and 217). In general, the Health Law, which was later in time, takes priority but this does not solve all the problems, since A.216 HL is restricted to certain unhealthy industries which are contained in a list approved by Ministerial Decree. Thus, in accordance with A.216 HL, only those industries which come within that list are required to notify the local authorities and are subject to any systematic controls. In substance, therefore, unhealthy industries which do not come within the list have no obligation to give any notice of their intent to the communal administration which may only subsequently issue orders against them pursuant to A.217 HL where the need arises. The industries which are not on the list, moreover, do not appear to be under any obligation to make an application to the mayor for the specification of fit and proper precautions pursuant to A.64 TUPS which appears to have been repealed as a result of A.216 HL. In the end result, the law on public safety appears to be limited to oil wastes (A.63), certain other unhealthy or dangerous waste substances and certain aspects of noisy activities.

Article 216 HL provides that all industries which produce vapours, gases or other unhealthy emissions or which are in any other way dangerous to public health are to be divided into two classes. The first includes those industries which are to be restricted to non-urban areas, i e isolated from residential areas, whilst the second includes those industries which require special precautions for the safety of neighbours. An industry in the first class may be permitted into a residential area if the introduction of new methods or special precautions no longer makes it a danger to public health. Any person who desires to commence an industry contained in either list must give 15 days' notice in writing to the mayor who may, in the interests of public health, prohibit the activity or prescribe defined precautions. The basis of this bipartite classification is that the first class includes those industries which are presumed to be dangerous to public health and must therefore be excluded from residentail areas, subject to a communal authorisation to the contrary, whilst the second class comprises those industries which, although not dangerous, may be required by the communal authorities to adopt appropriate safety precautions. It is ironic, however, that this complex discipline is ultimately sanctioned by very modest criminal penalties, in the form of amends, for the failure either to give the requisite notice or comply with any prescribed precautions.

Article 216 HL is supplemented by A.217 HL which provides that where public health is or may be threatened by vapours, gases or other exhalations, water drains and solid or liquid wastes emanating from industry, the mayor may prescribe appropriate measures to prevent or impede any such risk or damage. This provision applies to all industries, whether or not they are in the lists contemplated by A.216 HL and irrespective of whether they received a prior authorisation to commence operations. The failure to comply with a mayoral order may lead to the execution of the order by the communal authorities at the cost of the defaulting industry and the prosecution of the latter under A.650 cp. Article 217 HL is, in fact, a useful and often utilised means of dealing with pollution.

Industries concerned with livestock, that is, the breeding of animals on an industrial scale utilising feed which is not produced or recovered from the same property, are dealt with by DM 12 February 1971 which classifies such industries as unhealthy industries under the first class in A.216 HL, that is, as industries which must be isolated from residentiaĺ areas. Thus, Artt. 216 and 217 HL also apply to the intensive breeding of animals. The breeding of animals on a non-industrial scale does not come within the Health Law except insofar as the activity can be defined as a 'stable' which may ŏnly be removed from a residential area pursuant to communal health regulations.

The regulation of noisy industries is confronted by several problems. First is the relationship between A.66 TUPS, which provides that the conduct of noisy or inconvenient professions or trades must be suspended during the hours defined by local regulation or mayoral ordinance, and A.659(2) cp, which, generally, punishes the conduct of noisy activities contrary to law or the requirements of administrative authorities. Cassation has recently held that the combined effect of the two provisions is that the local authorities are limited to regulating the hours of noisy industries although this restrictive interpretation has been criticised by the doctrine which points out that noisy industries are also subject to Artt. 216 and 217 HL on *unhealthy* industries and may therefore be the object of local health regulations pursuant to A.218 of the same law. This approach finds support in three factors: the express terms of A.216 HL itself; the fact that the Ministerial Decrees have included certain industries in the list of unhealthy industries merely because of the noise that they cause; and certain decisions of the Council of State. It follows that, at least in relation to those industries classified as unhealthy by the Minister, the local authorities may issue particular measures defining the precautions to be taken in order to contain the emission of noise and, moreover, where such measures are not complied with, A.659 cp, and perhaps A.650 cp, are applicable. It appears that A.66 TUPS has not been totally overcome through the operation of the Health Law as A.66 TUPS is applicable to every noisy profession or trade and not only industry. It follows that although communal regulations may deal with most aspects of 'industrial' activities they can only deal with operating hours in relation to trades which do not constitute an industry. Those activities which are not noisy or unhealthy, and which do not come within the Health Law or A.659 cp, but which are merely *inconvenient* through, for instance, vibrations, are dealt with by A.66 TUPS and may therefore be subject to local regulation or mayoral ordinance.

The Health Law confers various powers upon the mayor at the local level and delegates certain other powers to the Prefect at the Provincial level. However, the law of 1958 which created the Ministry of Health transferred competence in health matters from the decentralised organs of the Ministry of Internal Affairs to the local bodies of the new Ministry and, in particular, to the Provincial Medical Officers and, on the communal level, to the local health officials. This immediately gave rise to doubts as to whether the health functions which had hitherto been exercised by the mayor and the Prefect had been transferred to the local health officials and the Provincial Medical Officers. It is clearly settled that the powers in A.227 HL (which concern the determination of both the distance from residential areas that unhealthy waters may be discharged into water course without causing a risk to public health and the necessary purification processes before such discharge) now belong to the Provincial Medical Officer. The 1958 legislation, in fact, after expressly reserving to the Prefect the right to issue temporary and urgent measures, provides that all of the other functions of the Prefect in the subject of public health are to be exercised by the Provincial Medical and Veterinary Officers according to their respective functions. There is no provision in the 1958 legislation which operates an analogous transfer of the functions of the mayor to the local health officials, but rather it speaks in terms of the health officials assisting the communal administrative organs in the elaboration and execution of their health functions. This norm takes it for granted that the local health officials have not absorbed the functions of the mayor in the area of health; rather, the norm is based upon the assumption that the legislation has merely established the form and method of collaboration between the two organs. Therefore, the mayor only may properly issue ordinances under A.217 HL.

There is the question of whether any State health functions have been transferred to the Regions pursuant to the decentralisation of administrative powers in the 1970s (see ch 5, p 166, above). Although there has been a transfer of certain health matters to the Regions, competence in matters of soil hygiene, the hygiene of residential areas, atmospheric and water pollution, and unhealthy industries have been reserved to the State. The competence of the Ordinary Regions in matters of health, in contrast to the Special Regions, is a limited one of 'assistance' as a result of which the Ordinary Regions cannot interfere in the area of public hygiene. The decentralising legislation has delegated to the Ordinary Regions the Provincial Medical Officers and their functions within the directives set by the central government. Whether these functions have been further delegated to other Regional organs varies depending upon the particular Regional legislation.

Although Artt. 216 and 217 HL are of general application to unhealthy industries, there are many specific provisions concerning pollution control in particular cases, e g in relation to producers of toxic gases (A.58 TUPS) and mining industries (especially in the case of hydrocarbons). All industries which use nuclear substances are subject to the law of 31 December 1962 n.1862, as amended. All plants which present a danger of nuclear pollution must be authorised by the Minister of Industry, subject to the opinion of the National Commission on Nuclear Energy. The necessary investigations concerning the safety of nuclear plants and the protection of both the employees in such plants and the population at large from the risks of radiation consequent to the peaceful use of nuclear energy are regulated in detail by the DPR 13 February 1964 n.185. Special legislation regulates the siting of thermonuclear, thermoelectric and turbogas plants of the ENEL (National Electricity Commission): the laws of 18 December 1973 n.880 and 2 August 1975 n.393. This legislation incorporates the balance struck between the interests of having such plants and the protection of health and the environment. Thermonuclear plants must comply with the 1964 Presidential Decree referred to above.

The specific forms of pollution and its control

A. WATER AND SOIL POLLUTION

(*i*) *General.* The law of 10 May 1976 n.319 (the so-called '*legge Merli*' (LM)), as amended by the law of 8 October 1976 n.690, is concerned with water and soil pollution. The two fundamental characteristics of the legislation are: its total discipline of water and soil pollution, satisfying the desire to establish a unitary and comprehensive regulation of the subject; and the rationalisation of the administration and regulation of pollution control hitherto spread amongst a large number of State and local bodies. The legislation was to ensure an efficient protection of soil and water resources from pollution through the creation of an organic system of limits and controls upon the principal types of pollution and the provision of the necessary financial resources for the modernisation of the sewer network and its associated purification plants. Due to the poor balance of payments, the provision of financial resources was replaced with the conferral of various powers upon the Regions to raise the necessary finances. The transfer of this matter to the Regions combined with their limited availability of funds has meant that only certain of the Regions have been able to provide for the construction of purification plants. The elimination of State funding from the original '*Merli* draft' has therefore led to a weakening of the strict regulation of polluting discharges and the concomitant application of criminal sanctions against those responsible for the administration of public sewers in the event of discharges from them into surface waters or the soil. In the end, the reclamation of the sewer network has been left to the so-called 'Regional plans for the reclamation of waters'.

The most important object of the legislation is the regulation of every type of discharge, whatever its source (public or private, direct or indirect), into surface or subterranean waters (internal or marine, public or private), including into sewers, or onto or under the soil (A.1(a) LM). Although this provision appears to be very broad, it has certain limitations. It concerns only liquid effluents, not solid wastes whose collection and disposal is still regulated by the law of 20 March 1941 n.366. A further although implied limitation is that the discharges must be of a certain continuity and not merely occasional emissions such as the sporadic poisoning of a river. In other words, the legislation is restricted to those situations in which the waste originates from productive or residential units with a certain continuity and is not concerned with the isolated polluting act. The sporadic incident therefore continues to be regulated by the pre-existing system. Finally, the legislation is not concerned with the intrinsic quality of the substance being discharged but rather the object of the discharge: the legislation is only concerned with the dissipation of wastes which have no economic value and therefore does not catch the spraying of the soil with natural or chemical fertilisers which are dispersed into the soil not with the object of their disposal but to obtain an economic utility.

The legislation does seek to control soil and water pollution through the regulation of discharges but also pursues its general object through various other means which include the re-organisation of public services concerning aquaducts, sewers and purification works. The legislation itself does not regulate the subject in detail but to a large extent delegates regulation-making powers to an interministerial committee and to the Regions, communes, and intercommunal consortiums. Although the legislation contains an almost comprehensive regulation of discharges from productive units, it delegates extensively the detailed regulation of discharges from residential units and sewers. The difference in approach was largely necessitated by the financial and practical problems inherent in the various matters dealt with by the legislation, e g the practical problems inherent in the transformation of the sewerage system. The emanation of the detailed regulations contemplated by the legislation is to come about in a given chronological and logical order according to the various duties imposed by the legislation upon the State, Regions, Provinces and communes. In essence, the Regions are charged with the preparation of Regional plans for the reclamation of waters which are to be prepared having regard to both the guiding principles fixed by the State and the programmes and responsibilities of the communes

(ii) The control of water pollution prior to the 1976 Legge Merli. Prior to the *Legge Merli*, there was the absence of any direct and organic control over water pollution which was regulated through two basic instruments. First, certain provisions of the Criminal Code, some of which still remain relevant (see pp 463–470, above). Second, and more important, Artt. 226 and 227 HL. Article 226 HL prevents the discharge of dirty or unhealthy wastes originating from residential, industrial or medical establishments into lakes, water courses or canals whose waters are in any manner whatsoever used for consumption or domestic purposes unless such wastes are subject to a complete and effective purification process before their discharge. Article 227 HL, on the other hand, expressly prohibits the emission from sewers or canals of the wastes referred to in A.226 into water courses which cross inhabited areas unless such wastes are first subjected to appropriate purification processes. It was the Prefect, and now the Provincial Medical Officer, who defines both the distance from a city or populated area at which such sewers or wastes may be safely discharged into water courses without causing a risk to public health and the necessary purification process required prior to discharge. The combined effect of these two provisions was that discharges from industrial establishments

and communal sewers had to be purified before their emission into water courses thereby anticipating the obligations which were later to be stipulated by the *Legge Merli* of 1976. Such norms were never applied. Moreover, since neither provision contained a sanction their violation could be criminally pursued only if these provisions were incorporated into either the local health regulations or a general regulation under the particular law. The general regulations, which are still those under the pre-existing health law, did not incorporate the above specific provisions and the penalties under the local health regulations were almost illusory. However, some magistrates had dealt with this lacuna by charging the mayor or Provincial Medical Officers with the crime of failing to carry out their official duties where they had not enforced these provisions concerning discharges.

(iii) The regulation of discharges under the 1976 Legge Merli. The regulation of discharges is the primary object of the 1976 legislation. All discharges must be authorised and comply with the various 'standards of acceptability' defined by Tables A, B and C annexed to the legislation. These 'standards' fix the various tolerability limits for differing abstract situations. In the case of industrial establishments, the legislation distinguishes between new discharges and those in existence at the date of the legislation. New discharges must immediately comply with the tolerability limits defined by the legislation, and in particular: (a) if the discharge is into surface waters, it must comply with Table A, (b) if the discharge is into a public sewer, it must comply with either Table C where the sewerage system does not have a central purification plant (which is a common situation), or with the tolerability limits defined by the relevant communal authority which manages the sewerage system where a purification plant exists or is introduced, (c) if the discharge is directly into the soil, it must comply with the hygienic norms of the local health authorities pending specific regulation, and (d) if the discharge is directly into the sea, the tolerability levels in Table A are applicable. In the case of existing discharges, there are various time limits defined by the legislation within which the discharges must be made to conform with the tolerability levels for new installations.

Because A.9 LM requires the authorisation of 'all discharges', it follows that non-industrial or civil establishments must also be authorised. In the final legislative draft the sanctions for the failure to apply for an authorisation in the case of an existing urban discharge were abandoned and thus the obligation has remained a theoretical one. The regulation of non-industrial discharges is that discharges into a public sewer are always permissible, subject to the observation of the regulations issued by the local authorities, whilst discharges into other than public sewers must conform with the regulations to be defined by the Regional reclamation plans. This raises the distinction between an industrial and a civil establishment. Broadly, an industrial establishment is one which predominantly carries out the production of goods on a stable and permanent basis. Civil establishments include, broadly speaking, domestic habitations, hotels, and establishments connected with tourism, sport, recreation, education, health, the provision of services, and any other activity (including one concerned with the production of goods) which gives rise to discharges similar to those from domestic establishments. Moreover, civil establishments are defined to include agricultural enterprises. The distinction may, at first sight, appear to depend upon the quality of the discharge so that all activities which produce an industrial type discharge come within the category of industrial installations. However, such a broad rationalisation is imperfect because of the extensive scope of the concept of civil establishments, e g although industrial laundries produce wastes similar to those of an industrial establishment, they come within the category of 'services' and therefore qualify as a civil establishment. It follows that, in the end, the broad definition of a civil establishment imposes a severe restriction upon the direct control of pollution.

The same authority is generally responsible for both the administration of controls and the issue of authorisations: the provinces in the case of discharges into inland waters, the communes in the case of discharges into public sewers or the soil, the Head of the Maritime Department for discharges into the territorial sea, the Committee of Ministers for discharges into the open sea. The controls over discharges may be effected by the relevant authority at any time and in the forms specified by the legislation. Samples of wastes may be taken at the point of immediate emission and, in the case of defined substances, inspections may be effectuated within the industrial establishment itself in order to ascertain the conditions which give rise to the wastes. In such cases the authority may require, as a condition of an authorisation, that the wastes be treated before emission.

The only exception to the requirement for an authorisation to discharge wastes is in the case of existing civil establishments which do not discharge into the public sewers. In this case there is only an obligation to declare their position to the local authorities 'within the times and in the manner prescribed by them'. This is because their regulation will eventually be defined by the Regional reclamation plans. All other discharges must be authorised, that is, existing discharges from industrial establishments, existing discharges into public sewers from civil establishments, and new discharges from either industrial or civil establishments. The general rule is that an authorisation may only be released in a definitive form where it has been ascertained that the relevant discharge complies with the tolerability levels defined by law. However, prior to a definitive authorisation, there may be the release of provisional authorisations which provide for a progressive adaptation to the defined tolerability levels. Of significant importance in this context is that provision which states that a provisional authorisation is deemed to have been granted in those cases in which an application to the relevant authority is neither granted nor refused within six months of the application. This is the so-called 'licence to pollute' provision. In fact, provisional authorisations for the silence of the relevant authority is the rule. The reason for this is that the authorities are not usually in a position either to refuse the application or release an express authorisation. Apart from indecision and delay, which are characteristic of Italian bureaucracy, the position is rather due to the lack of sufficient qualified functionaries to carry out the necessary investigations. As a deemed provisional authorisation does not contain any conditions, the applicant is not bound to comply with any restrictions. It is only where there is an express provisional authorisation that the relevant discharge may be subjected to a progressive compliance with the pollution limits prescribed by law. To mitigate against this situation, the relevant authority is entitled to revoke its 'implied' provisional authorisation or to issue the provisional authorisation previously requested stipulating appropriate restrictions. Where the discharge fails to conform with the conditions contained in an express authorisation, the authorisation must be revoked. To attenuate further the serious consequences of 'implied' provisional authorisations, the legislation provides that those responsible for existing civil and industrial discharges must adopt appropriate measures so as to avoid even a temporary increase in pollution. This provision lacks an effective sanction and is ineffective because of the lack of sufficient personnel to survey the prior and subsequent condition of discharges in order to ascertain whether the relevant pollution is on the increase.

The restrictions on pollution defined by Tables A and C of the legislation are binding on industrial establishments only. Civil establishments or civil discharges will become subject to control after the preparation by the Regions, in conjunction with the relevant communes, of the so-called reclamation plans which will deal with aquaducts, sewers, purification plants, public works and programmes, and the times within which all types of discharges must conform with the prescribed tolerability limits. Until then, civil discharges will not be subject to any control. The failure of the legislation to prescribe an immediate regulation in the case of urban discharges, similar to that for industrial discharges, constitutes a serious gap in the struggle against pollution.

(iv) The criminal sanctions after the Legge Merli. The *Legge Merli* declares that it regulates exclusively all types of discharges referred to in A.1 (a) of the legislation and that all other norms which directly or indirectly concern discharges into water, the soil or subsoil and their consequent

pollution are repealed. This provision has been interpreted strictly to mean that only those norms which are incompatible with the new legislation are repealed. It is argued that this must be the correct approach otherwise the 1976 legislation would lead to the repeal of norms which have a broader object than the mere punishment of pollution. Therefore, the problem is to determine whether the criminal norms referred to earlier remain effective in relation to pollution control and, if so, the extent of their application. Apart from Artt. 439, 440 and 452 cp, which have been expressly saved by the new legislation, it appears that Artt. 635, 639 and 674 cp continue to remain effective insofar as their object extends beyond the scope of the 1976 legislation. A similar situation applies to RD 8 October 1931 n.1604 which concerns fishing. The 1976 legislation, moreover, by subsequent amendment, expressly saved the special legislation concerning the protection of Venice from water pollution. Finally, the 1976 legislation itself has created various criminal sanctions which are applicable to the following situations: the failure to apply for any necessary authorisation; the continued discharge of wastes after an authorisation has been denied or revoked; the commencement of discharges prior to the grant of an authorisation; the aggravation of the state of pollution prior to the date upon which compliance with the defined tolerability limits is required; the surpassing of the defined tolerability limits; and the failure to comply with any conditions stipulated by an authorisation.

(v) Conclusion. The 1976 legislation turned out to be weaker than orginally intended and contains several serious obstacles to an efficient protection of water resources. First, there is no sanction against unauthorised discharges from urban establishments which, moreover, are defined broadly to include establishments 'providing services' and agricultural enterprises both of which produce wastes similar in composition to industrial wastes. Second, there is the possibility of an uncontrolled discharge of wastes as a result of implied provisional authorisations. Third, there has been a failure by the Regions and the local authorities to issue transitional prescriptions which would have avoided the 'liberty to pollute' inherent in the implied provisional authorisations pending the total implementation of the new legislation. Finally, there has been a failure by the authorities which manage the public sewers to issue the relevant regulations and a failure by the Regions in producing the required Plans for the reclamation of waters. This inertia has left discharges by civil establishments free from prescription or control. The total implementation of the legislation has been hampered by the lack of adequate finances and personnel, the continued absence of which will lead to a mere partial fulfilment of the objects which inspired the legislation.

B. FURTHER SPECIAL LEGISLATION CONCERNING WATER AND SOIL
POLLUTION

Other legislative provisions of continuing relevance to soil and surface
and subterranean water pollution include:

(*i*) *Articles 226 and 227 of the Health Law* (see p 472ff, above).

(*ii*) *The law of 3 March 1971 n.125, as amended,* concerning the
biodegradibility of synthetic detergents. This legislation has the object
of protecting surface and subterranean waters and prohibits the
commerce, production or import of detergents which do not comply
with the prescribed levels of biodegradability.

(*iii*) *The Consolidated Law on Fishing (RD 8 October 1931 n.1604)* which
is still applicable to those emissions which do not come within the *Legge
Merli* of 1976.

(*iv*) *The Law of 20 March 1941 n.366* regarding the disposal of solid
urban wastes. The *Legge Merli*, as already noted, is also concerned with
the protection of the soil and subterranean waters from pollution
connected with the emission of liquid wastes: the object of such
protection is to avoid the pollution of the subterranean water-bearing
stratum and other forms of pollution harmful to agriculture. However,
as it appears that the *Legge Merli* deals with neither the discharge of
solid wastes nor sporadic or occasional discharges, the law of 20 March
1941 n.366 concerning the collection, transport and disposal of solid
wastes remains operative. This law, introduced during the war, is
preoccupied more with the recycling of useful wastes rather than the
rational and complete disposal of useless wastes. The communes are,
according to this law, obliged to recoup all that 'appears useful to the
national economy', a duty which is regulated in detail. In respect to
useless wastes, the law limits itself to asserting in a single provision that
they may be disposed of and destroyed. Article 17 of the law contains a
prohibition, incorporating a criminal sanction, against even the
temporary deposit of wastes on public or private property. Article 17
has been interpreted to apply to all forms of waste and not merely to
urban wastes.

(*v*) *The law of 30 April 1962 n.283* which has not been affected by the
Legge Merli of 1976. A further risk of soil and water pollution arises out
of the extensive use of chemical products, such as pesticides, in
agriculture. The most effective form of regulation in this area is
achieved through a control or prohibition upon the use of dangerous
substances. However, this is only partially achieved by the above-

mentioned law which is only concerned with the control of substances which may endanger plants and consumables and which may therefore give rise to contamination and pose a risk to human health; it merely prohibits the distribution of products for consumption that contain any residue of toxic substances used in agriculture for the protection of plants. The Ministry of Health defines for each authorised substance a tolerability level for this purpose and the minimum interval which must elapse between treatment and picking. Moreover, various regulations have been issued on the subject, the last being that concerning the use of DDT.

(vi) Various provisions of the Health Law which regulate seepage into the soil or water resources as a result of improperly waterproofed pavements, e g in the case of rural stables.

(vii) Miscellaneous provisions of a varying importance in certain pieces of legislation which have remained effective notwithstanding the 1976 *Legge Merli*, e g A.103 of DPR 9 April 1958 n.128 which regulates mining activities by requiring the adoption of necessary measures to prevent the dispersion of salt water, petroleum products, oils, residues or any emissions from storage tanks into or upon the soil, as well as, incidentally, the unnecessary discharge of gases into the atmosphere; and A.17 of DPR 19 March 1956 n.303 which concerns risks to health as a result of the storage and discharge of substances and in particular it prohibits an employer from keeping stores of rubbish, waste or other solid or liquid materials unless adequate measures are taken to avoid any harm or injury to his workers and neighbours.

C. POLLUTION OF MARINE WATERS

Article 11 of the 1976 *Legge Merli* makes all direct discharges into sea water subject to authorisation by the Maritime Authorities. A 'direct' discharge means all discharges other than through sewers (which must be authorised by the Maritime Authorities) and surface water courses, that is, it is concerned with the discharge of industrial and civil wastes into the sea through private drainage systems. A special regime applies to discharges into the high seas. Its regulation has apparently been excluded from the 1976 *Legge Merli* which, pending both the ratification of the 1972 Convention of London and the introduction of a comprehensive international regulation for the protection of the Mediterranean, reserves the control of discharges on the high seas to the directives of an Interministerial Committee which, in granting any authorisation (which must define the terms and conditions of the discharge), must take into account all the International agreements to which Italy is party including the Conventions on the prevention of the pollution of the sea by hydrocarbons through which the Italian State has bound itself to apply the same restrictions upon discharges into the high seas by its ships as are applicable to discharges into the territorial sea.

Prior to 1976, control over the pollution of the sea was almost exclusively through the law of 14 July 1965 n.963 on sea fishing and the regulations made under it. Except for the continuing partial relevance of certain of its provisions, the law of 1965 has been completely repealed in relation to discharges into maritime waters because of the effect of the 1976 *Legge Merli*. Therefore, A.15(e) of the 1965 law which prohibits the direct or indirect emission into the sea of polluting substances (substances that either cause a direct danger to aquatic fauna or cause changes which unfavourably affect aquatic organisms) remains applicable in respect to occasional and sporadic emissions only in which case it is, in any event, difficult to prove the necessary intent to found the subject crime. Of more importance is A.15(d) of the same law which prohibits injury to the biological resources of marine waters through the use of toxic substances which are capable of stupefying or killing fish and other aquatic animals. This provision probably survives the 1976 legislation in toto as the crime is consummated when aquatic life is injured and not through the mere emission of harmful substances. As a result of the express reservation in A.15, the absence of an authorisation for the subject discharge into the sea is a necessary prerequisite to found either crime.

Finally, it must be noted that because A.11(2) of the 1976 *Legge Merli* expressly preserves the powers of the Maritime Authorities in relation to the protection and availability of the maritime demesne and its safety for navigation, the provisions of the Navigation Code largely remain effective. The Code regulates matters such as the discharge of material of any specie into ports and other areas designated by the Maritime Authorities for the transit and mooring of ships and other traffic and fishing needs. It also prohibits the discharge into the terrestrial or aquatic zones of the port or in the open sea at a distance less than that fixed by the Port Commander of wastes emanating from ships. The Navigation Code contains provisions concerning industrial activities near waterways and the coastline: it provides that persons who conduct industrial activities or keep permanent deposits which cause the blockage of adjacent waters must both ensure the preservation of the proper depth of the waters in conformity with the prescriptions of the relevant department and avoid the pollution of the waters by plants and deposits. The Code requires the grant of a concession to locate and conduct establishments on or near the maritime demesne or anywhere connected with the sea or maritime courses and canals. These concessions may be subject to certain precautions which must be taken by the concessionary to avoid pollution and, logically, may only be conceded to establishments which have been granted an authorisation under A.11 of the *Legge Merli* to make discharges into marine waters.

D. ATMOSPHERIC POLLUTION: THE ANTISMOG LAW OF 1966

The law of 13 July 1966 n.615, commonly referred to as the Antismog Law, is the first attempt at achieving a complete solution to the problem of atmospheric pollution. Although the legislation has been subject to much criticism, it has sought to deal with the requirements of a modern industrial society by dealing with the following sources of atmospheric pollution: thermal plants, industrial establishments and automobiles. The legislation creates three new organs: the Central Commission Against Atmospheric Pollution which has primarily consultative functions and participates in classifying communal districts into zones A and B for the application of the legislation; second, the Regional Committees Against Atmospheric Pollution which have decision-making powers over industrial plants except for the central plants of the National Electricity Commission (ENEL) as to which the Central Commission may express opinions; and finally, the Provincial Commissions which have investigatory functions only.

In relation to thermal plants, there is a degree of uncertainty as to the applicability of the Law. Whilst the regulations made under the legislation go beyond what is strictly understood in common parlance as being thermal plants (i e plants whose primary object is the production of heat) as the regulations include baker's ovens and the plants of other artisans, on the other hand, the regulations are too restrictive as their application is limited to plants which have more than a defined capacity and which are located in zones A and B whereas the legislature had not only imposed an obligation to obtain a licence irrespective of location but prohibited the emission of smoke without any exception in favour of either low capacity plants or plants outside zones A and B.

Article 15 of the Antismog Law punishes by amend an operator of a thermal plant which emits smoke containing polluting substances in excess of the limits fixed by the regulations. The punishable conduct is the emission of the polluting smoke and there is therefore no need for further proof that the emission is either dangerous or creates a nuisance. In a case of repetition, the operator may also have his licence revoked. However, it should be noted that both the proprietor and administrator of a building may also be criminally liable if the cause of the pollution is imputable to them, e g for failure to install different equipment or for utilising a prohibited combustible substance. The law also punishes by fine any person who fails to adapt their thermal plant, upon request of the Provincial Fire Service, so as to comply with the regulations. Moreover, the installation of every thermal plant is subject to the approval of the Provincial Fire Service which must ensure that the plant complies with the regulations and, once installed, test the plant prior to its use. The legislation contains both a list of certain combustible materials which may be used without limit and a list of various 'solid or liquid mineral' substances whose use is subject to authorisation and testing. The legislation also contains a list of certain combustible substances which are subject to defined limitations and may only be used after a successful application to the communal authorities. Generally, the relevant penalties are imposed upon the user of the plant and, although this would seem to give rise to difficulties in the case of condominiums, it appears that the responsibility falls upon the administrator, as the person responsible for the 'ordinary maintenance' of the common services, unless the failure to comply with the regulations falls outside the scope of 'ordinary maintenance' in which event the various owners in the building are liable.

The second major matter dealt with by the Antismog Law is industrial plants. The basic obligation of the operators of industrial plants located within zones A and B of the national territory is, in accordance with the regulations made under the Antismog Law and apart from any obligations connected with their classification as unhealthy or dangerous industries under A.216 of the Health Law, to contain within the strictest limits made possible by technological progress those emissions which, apart from constituting a danger to public health, would contribute to atmospheric pollution. Although the regulations restrict this obligation to industrial plants located within zones A and B, the literal wording of the legislation is such that it can be said to extend to every industry wherever located in the national territory.

The Antismog Law, contrary to its application in the case of thermal plants, does not provide for a preventive procedure in the form of a power to require the provision of purification processes as a condition to the approval of *new* plants. The regulations have remedied the situation by requiring that the plans for new industrial plants be submitted to the Regional Committee Against Atmospheric Pollution. However, its only consequence is that upon a negative opinion of the Committee, the mayor may deny the issue of a building licence. Therefore, the effective control over the atmospheric pollution of industrial plants is concentrated in the local mayor. It is interesting to note that, according to the Council of State, Artt. 216 and 217 of the Health Law are no longer applicable in determining the compatibility of industrial plants with health considerations arising out of atmospheric pollution, and that the saving in the Antismog Law relating to the obligations of industrial plants arising from their classification as unhealthy or dangerous works under A.216 HL merely refers to those obligations connected to other than atmospheric pollution.

In relation to existing industrial plants recourse must be had to the complex and lengthy process of alleging their 'contribution to pollution'. Pending this slow process mayors may resort to their powers of making temporary and urgent ordinances to safeguard public health (see p 471, above). In order to facilitate the relevant investigations the owners of existing industrial plants are obliged to supply various data to the communal authorities but the regulations have not, and, indeed, could not, impose sanctions for non-compliance with this requirement although this lacuna may be dealt with by mayoral ordinances. It has been maintained that the mayor may even order the closure of a factory where the owners fail to provide the communal authorities with the information required under the regulations. In short, the owners of industrial plants have two basic obligations: obtaining municipal authorisation, although this duty is not clear, and ensuring a minimum contribution to atmospheric pollution by maintaining appropriate combustion systems.

The third major area of concern of the Antismog Law is that of pollution caused by motor vehicles. The legislation, inter alia, punishes the driver of a diesel-engined vehicle which emits gases of an opacity exceeding that fixed by the regulations. Whilst this provision was given immediate effect, there are still no regulations implementing the other parts of the legislation concerning the prevention of pollution by motor vehicles. The enforcement of the provisions concerning motor vehicles is not by the application of a criminal sanction but through the inspection, at any time, of a suspect vehicle consequent to which the registration of the vehicle may be suspended. These provisions complement the law of 3 June 1971 n.437 through which Italy implemented the EEC Directive concerning the approval of new motor vehicles with combustion engines thereby controlling pollution in this manner as well. Therefore, unapproved vehicles cannot obtain registration and thus cannot be used without incurring the penalty under A.58 of the Road Code. Analogous considerations apply to the effectiveness of DM of 5 August 1974 which gives effect to the law of 27 December 1973 n.942 in relation to the requisites for the approval of diesel-motored vehicles. It is worth noting that all the legislation is concerned with the control of pollution through the regulation of the vehicle itself as, for instance, by the application of purifiers. The Italian legislature has not approached the problem of motor vehicle pollution by acting upon the quality of fuels.

E. ATMOSPHERIC POLLUTION: SMOKING

The law of 11 November 1975 n.582 limits pollution in closed spaces by prohibiting smoking, upon pain of a pecuniary administrative penalty, in hospital wards and schoolrooms, on public transport (automobiles and metropolitan railways), in station waiting rooms, in non-smoking compartments on trains, and like places. Similarly, in the case of enclosed premises used for public meetings, enclosed cinemas or theatres, ballrooms and the like. However, the operators of the latter localities are not bound to impede smoking or evict offenders but are merely required, upon pain of pecuniary penalties and the suspension or revocation of their public safety licence, to exhibit signs indicating the penalty for offenders. An operator may obtain, from the mayor, an exemption from the observance of the prohibition on smoking upon showing that there is the existence of efficient means of air conditioning or ventilation.

F. NOISE POLLUTION ARISING FROM THE CIRCULATION OF VEHICLES

The basic legislative provisions in this context are the DPR 15 July 1959 n.393 (the Road Code) and the law of 27 December 1973 n.942 referred to above in connection with the approval of motor vehicles. The Road Code, makes the following provisions on the subject. First, that all auto vehicles, motor vehicles and motor cycles must have suitable devices to contain noises emanating from their motors within the limits stipulated by the regulations. The mere absence of such a device, as also any alteration to it or a failure to keep it in good working condition, constitutes an illegality. Second, that all noises causing a nuisance and arising from the manner in which the vehicle is driven must be avoided, e g the revving of motors or the screeching of brakes. Third, that all acoustic signalling devices must be used with moderation and their use is prohibited in urban centres except in cases of an immediate danger of an accident. The existence of any of these infractions does not exclude the crime in A.659 cp concerning the breach of the peace whilst, conversely, the legitimate use of either an acoustic signal or a vehicle prevents such crime. Although noisy vehicles, such as tractors, may only be used for work within the hours permitted by the communal regulations, they may otherwise freely circulate. The violation of any of the above norms is penalised by a modest pecuniary administrative sanction.

Town planning and the environment

Since a significant part of the pollution problem has its origins in construction activities, the protection of the environment may find its logical place within the ambit of town planning. The mayor controls the issue of two important licences: the building licence which is issued in his capacity as the head of the local administration; and the habitability licence which is released in his capacity as a government official.

In relation to the building licence, the case law has sometimes limited its function to the architectural aspects of town planning and not to the hygienic and environmental aspects of the proposed structure. The Council of State has taken the opposite approach and upheld the refusal of building licences where the proposed edifices would have had inadequate provision for the disposal of liquid wastes or would have disturbed the public peace through the emission of noises at such a level so as to constitute a nuisance. It has also upheld as legitimate the imposition of conditions for the elimination of noise. This approach is consistent with several provisions contained in various pieces of special legislation which enable a consideration of hygiene and pollution issues in building applications.

Article 221 HL provides that edifices cannot be occupied without the authorisation of the mayor which is conceded after the inspection of an edifice by the health official or engineer who confirms that it was erected in conformity with the approved plans and that the building is not otherwise unhealthy. This provision is related to the powers of the mayor in A.222 HL either to declare a building unhabitable or order its eviction under pain of the sanction contained in A.650 cp. It appears that the habitability licence can be included amongst those authorisations which are aimed at preventing the pollution of the environment. It, also serves, therefore, the function of ecological protection, apart from ensuring the hygiene of individual habitations. There is a tendency in the recent legislation to attribute to the habitability licence a function of verifying complex conditions unrelated to the internal health of the building in question.

A final useful development in town planning is a procedural one which enables 'any person' to challenge a building licence before the administrative courts. This legislative innovation of 1967 literally enables any person to challenge a building licence which is contrary to law. Notwithstanding that the Council of State has restricted its operation by limiting the action to persons who to some measure suffer a direct damage from an improper construction, it has provided a valuable means to persons seeking to protect the natural environment. For instance, the Council of State has allowed an appeal by *Italia Nostra*, an association concerned with the historical, artistic and natural wealth of the country, against an authorisation to open a road in an area of scenic and environmental beauty. The administrative case law has often recognised the fear of ecological damage as a sufficient interest to ground an opposition to improper building authorisations.

Regional legislation

Recently, regional legislation has been active in filling the gaps left by the inertia of State bodies in the subject of ecological protection, although much of the Regional legislation in this area has been superseded by the State legislation of 1976 on soil and water pollution. It is generally agreed that the Regions have a legislative competence in the ecological sector although there is a lack of agreement as to the subject heading in A.117 C (which gives the Regions their legislative competence) from which it originates. It is clear that the regions' competence in the ecological sphere may arise from any of several heads in A.117 C, eg 'local, urban and rural police', 'fishing in internal waters', 'town planning', and 'agriculture and forests'. It is apparent that pollution control cannot be restricted to any given legislative sector but is rather inherent in several of them, a large number of which are contained in A.117 C. However, the traditional sector utilised in pollution control which is missing from A.117 C is that of public health; A.117 C mentions only 'health assistance'. The Special Regions, on the other hand, have a specific and express competence under their Constitutions in matters of hygiene and public health, as well as fishing, town planning, industry and the use of public waters.

Part V

The research of Italian law

Chapter 12

Legal research and bibliographical notes

Researching Italian law

The principal sources of Italian law and their respective collections are as follows.

A. LEGISLATION

Although all legislative dispositions are published daily, upon their passage, in the *Official Gazette*, the latter is not a very convenient means of discovering the existing legislation in any given subject. In practice, extensive use is made of two collections, published quarterly, which also contain the more important extracts from relevant parliamentary and ministerial reports: *Lex* published by Utet, and *Le leggi*, published by the Società Editoriale del Foro Italiano. There are many other legislative collections such as *La legislazione italiana*, published by Giuffrè, and *Le leggi d'Italia*, published by PEM. On administrative law there is a particular and important legislative collection known as the *Codice delle leggi amministrative*, published by Giuffrè, as well as various collections on specific subjects such as taxation (*Codice tributario*) and environmental law (*Codice dell'ambiente*).

B. THE CODES

So far as the codes are concerned, there are various types of publications. Some deal with a single code, either with or without an appendix of other basic and related legislative texts, whilst others comprise all or some of the basic Codes, again either with or without an appendix of other basic and related legislation. Of the latter type, the two best known works are *Quattro Codici*, published by Cedam, and *I Cinque Codici*, published by Giuffrè. Every major legal publisher has publications of both types. Many editions are annotated to a varying degree article by article with legislative and case law references.

C. THE CASE LAW REPORTS

There are two general and, by now, classical case law collections. First, *La Giurisprudenza Italiana* which is published monthly by Utet. It is divided into four parts: the decisions of the International Courts, the Italian Constitutional Court, and the civil sections of Cassation as well as the civil decisions of the Courts of Appeal, the *Tribunali* and all other inferior courts; criminal law decisions; administrative and taxation law decisions; and a miscellaneous section. Second, *Il Foro Italiano*, published monthly by Società Editoriale del Foro Italiano. It comprises five parts: constitutional and civil law decisions; criminal law decisions; administrative law decisions; Community and foreign law decisions; and a miscellaneous section. Both publications contain selected decisions, and each report includes a headnote, a list of doctrinal and case law precedents, and, generally, critical notes by jurists. Both publishers also produce, on a monthly basis, the civil and criminal *Massimari*, which are chronological collections of all of the legal principles arising out of the civil and criminal decisions of the Court of Cassation. These works provide a speedy reference to the recent case law in Cassation. The same publishers, as well as the publishers of *Giustizia Civile* and *Giustizia Penale*, two important law reports on private and criminal law respectively, produce annual *Repertori* which contain in systematic order the maxims or legal principles arising out of all the decisions published in the various law reports, as well as any bibliographical and legislative developments.

There are a large number of other law reports, published on either a national or regional basis, such as *Il Foro padano*, *Diritto e Giurisprudenza*, *Giurisprudenza di Merito*, *Archivio penale*, *Rivista italiana di diritto e procedura penale*, *Rivista penale*, *Il Foro amministrativo*, *Giurisprudenza Costituzionale*, *Il Consiglio di Stato* and *Rivista amministrativa*.

D. JOURNALS

Whilst the works cited in the previous section are mainly concerned with the case law, the works referred to in this section are predominantly, although not exclusively, doctrinal in nature. These include *Rivista di diritto civile* (two-monthly), *Rivista trimestrale di diritto e procedura civile* (quarterly), *Rivista del diritto commerciale* (two-monthly, comprising both doctrine and case law), *Le nuove leggi civile commentate* (which is a commentary on new civil legislation), *L'Indice penale* (four-monthly), *La legislazione penale* (quarterly), *La questione criminale* (two-monthly), *Rassegna della giustizia militare* (two-monthly), *Rassegna penitenziaria e criminlogia* (two-monthly), *Il Tommaso Natale* (four-monthly), *Rivista trimestrale di diritto pubblico* (quarterly), and *Nuova rassegna* (fortnightly administrative law journal covering legislation, doctrine and case law).

There are also a large number of journals on more particular aspects of civil, criminal, and administrative law, e g *Rivista di diritto agrario; Il*

Diritto d'autore; Il diritto fallimentare delle società commerciali; Assicurazioni; Banca, Borsa e Titoli di credito; Rivista di diritto industriale; Rivista delle Società; Rivista di polizia; Rivista di diritto penitenziario; and *Rivista di medicina legale.*

E. SYSTEMATIC AND GENERAL COLLECTIONS OF LAW

Of this type of publication, the two most important works are: first, the *Novissimo Digesto Italiano*, which is being updated, published by Utet; and second, *L'Enciclopedia del diritto* published by Giuffrè. Both the Digest and the Encyclopaedia deal comprehensively with every legal topic.

F. MANUALS, COMMENTARIES AND TREATISES

The principal manuals (or institutional texts) and treatises are listed below in the bibliographical notes relevant to each chapter.

It should be noted that there are several important commentaries on the various codes, for example, A. Scialoja and G. Branca (eds) *Commentario del Codice civile* published by Società Editoriale del Foro Italiano, G. Cian and A. Trabucchi (eds) *Commentario breve al codice civile* published by Cedam, P. Perlingeri (ed) *Codice civile annotato* published by Utet, D'Amelio and Finzi (eds) *Codice civile; Commentario* published by Barbera, and Docenti and Magistrati (eds) *Commentario del Codice civile* published by Utet. The two best known commentaries in the criminal law field are G. Lattanzi (ed) *I Codici penali annotati* published by Giuffrè and A. Brancaccio and G. Lattanzi (eds) *Esposizione di giurisprudenza sul codice penale e di procedura penale* also published by Giuffrè. These works are an article by article commentary on the relevant codes.

Finally, Giuffrè periodically publishes a bibliography of all legal articles and books: Vincenzo Napoletano (ed), *Dizionario Bibliografico delle Riveste Giuridiche Italiane.*

Bibliography

In addition to the general works referred to above, the following principal works referred to in the preparation of the text may be used for further reading in the respective subject headings. Further and more detailed references are to be found within the works cited.

CHAPTER 1 THE HISTORICAL DEVELOPMENT OF THE ITALIAN LEGAL SYSTEM INCLUDING A HISTORY OF ITALIAN LEGAL THOUGHT

Barile, P. *Istituzioni di Diritto Pubblico* (4th ed, 1982) Cedam

Bobbio, N. *Teoria della Norma Giuridica* (1958) Giappichelli
Bobbio, N. *Teoria dell'Ordinamento Giuridico* (1960) Giappichelli
Cappelletti, M., Merryman, J.H. & Perillo, J.M. *The Italian Legal System* (1967) Stanford University Press
Fassò, G. *Storia della Filosofia del Diritto* (1970) Il Mulino, Vol III
Ghisalberti, C., *Storia Costituzionale d'Italia, 1848–1948* (1981) Laterza
Irti, N. *Scuole e Figure del Diritto Civile* (1982) Giuffrè
Lavagna, C. *Istituzioni di Diritto Pubblico* (4th ed, 1979) Utet
Merryman, J.H. & Clark, D.S. *Comparative Law: Western European and Latin American Legal Systems: Cases and Materials* (1978) The Bobbs-Merrill Company Inc
Messineo, F. & Cicu, A. *Trattato di Diritto Civile e Commerciale* (1952) Giuffrè
Mortati, C. *Istituzioni di Diritto Pubblico* (9th ed, 1976) Cedam
Romano, S. *L'Ordinamento Giuridico* (1967) Sansoni
Sandulli, A.M. *Manuale di Diritto Amministrativo* (13th ed, 1982) Jovene
Torrente, A. & Schlesinger, P. *Manuale di Diritto Privato* (11th ed, 1981) Giuffrè
Trabucchi, A. *Istituzioni di Diritto Civile* (25th ed, 1981) Cedam
Trimarchi, P. *Istituzioni di Diritto Privato* (5th ed, 1981) Giuffrè
Wieacker, F. *Storia del Diritto Privato Moderno* (1980) Giuffrè

CHAPTER 2 THE ITALIAN LEGAL PROFESSION

Carbone, C. & Carbone, B.G. 'Avvocatura dello Stato' in *Novissimo Digesto Italiano* App. Vol I, p 622
Coletta, U. 'Commercialista' in *Enciclopedia del Diritto* Vol VII, p 803
De Santis, E. 'Dottore Commercialista' in *Novissimo Digesto Italiano* Vol VI, p 295
Gallo-Orsi, G. & Girino, G. 'Notariato' in *Novissimo Digesto Italiano* Vol XI, p 356
Lega, M. 'Avvocati e Procuratori, Diritto Moderno' in *Novissimo Digesto Italiano* Vol I, Pt II, p 1666
Martra, M. 'Archivi notarili' in *Novissimo Digesto Italiano* Vol XI, p 389
Pizzorusso, A. *L'Organizzazione della Giustizia in Italia: La magistratura nel sistema politico e istituzionale* (1982) Einaudi
Scoca, S. 'Avvocatura dello Stato' in *Novissimo Digesto Italiano* Vol I, Pt II, p 1685

CHAPTER 3 THE DIVISIONS, SOURCES AND SPHERE OF APPLICATION OF ITALIAN LAW

Balladore Pallieri, G. *Diritto Internazionale Privato* (2nd ed, 1950) Giuffrè
Barile, G. *Lezioni di Diritto Internazionale Privato* (1980) Cedam
Calamandrei, P. 'La funzione della giurisprudenza del tempo presente'

in M. Cappelletti (ed) *Opere Giuridiche* (1965) Morano, Vol I
Fazzalari, E. 'Giudici, diritto, storia' in *Rivista trimestrale di diritto e procedura civile* (1982) p 757
Franceschelli, R. 'Consuetudine' in *Novissimo Digesto Italiano* App. Vol II, p 498
Gorla, G 'Giurisprudenza' in *Enciclopedia del Diritto* (1970) Vol XIX
Gorla, G. 'Civilian Judicial Decisions. An Historical Account of Italian Style' (1970) 44 Tulane LR 740
Grassetti, C. & Carnevali, U. 'Diritto Civile' in *Novissimo Digesto Italiano* App. Vol II, p 1160
Grasso, E. 'Equità (Giudizio di)' in *Novissimo Digesto Italiano* App. Vol III, p 443
Irti, N. *L'età della decodificazione* (1979) Giuffrè
Morelli, G. *Elementi di diritto internazionale privato italiano* (10th ed, 1971) Jovene reprinted in 1979
Rodotà, S. (ed) *Il diritto privato nella società moderna* (1971) Mulino, esp. pp 9–20
Torrente, A. and Schlesinger, P. *Manuale di Diritto Privato* (11th ed, 1981) Giuffrè
Trabucchi, A. *Istituzioni di Diritto Civile* (25th ed, 1981) Cedam

CHAPTER 4 THE ITALIAN STATE AND FOREIGN RELATIONS LAW

Barile, P. *Istituzioni di Diritto Pubblico* (4th ed, 1982) Cedam
Caron, P.G. 'Culti Acattolici' in *Novissimo Digesto Italiano* App. Vol II, p 953
Catalano, G. 'Concordato Ecclesiastico' in *Novissimo Digesto Italiano* App. Vol II, p 286
Clerici, R. 'Cittadinanza' in *Novissimo Digesto Italiano* App. Vol I, p 1265
Comba, A. 'Comunità Europee' in *Novissimo Digesto Italiano* App. Vol II, p 193
Conforti, B. *Lezioni di Diritto Internazionale* (2nd ed, 1982) Editoriale Scientifica
Durante, F. 'Diritto Comunitario' in *Novissimo Digesto Italiano* App. Vol II, p 1169
Maresca, A. 'Consolare (Ordinamento)' in *Novissimo Digesto Italiano* App. Vol II, p 473
Maresca, A. 'Consolari (Convenzioni)' in *Novissimo Digesto Italiano* App. Vol II, p 477
Maresca, A. 'Diplomazia Ed Agenti Diplomatici' in *Novissimo Digesto Italiano* App. Vol II, p 1091;
Monaco, R. 'CCE (Comunità Economica Europea)' in *Novissimo Digesto Italiano* App. Vol I, p 1116
Muratori, A. 'Esportazione e Importazione' in *Novissimo Digesto Italiano* App. Vol III, p 509

Olivero, G. 'Diritto Ecclesiastico' in *Novissimo Digesto Italiano* App. Vol II, p 1194

Politi, M. 'L'Immunità Giurisdizionale Dei Rappresentanti Degli Stati Presso La FAO' in *Rivista di Diritto Internazionale* (1970) Vol 53, p 526

Spinelli, L. 'Accordi Lateranensi' in *Novissimo Digesto Italiano* App. Vol I, p 33

Tedeschi, M. 'Chiesa e Stato' in *Novissimo Digesto Italiano* App. Vol I, p 1145

CHAPTER 5 THE CONSTITUTIONAL SYSTEM

Barile, P. *Istituzioni di Diritto Pubblico* (4th ed, 1982) Cedam

Branca, G. (ed) *Commentario della Costituzione* (1975) Zanichelli

Crisafulli, V. *Lezioni di Diritto Costituzionale* (2nd ed, 1970–1978) Cedam (3 Vols)

Giannini, M.S. *Istituzioni di Diritto Amministrativo* (1981) Giuffrè (2 Vols)

Lavagna, C. *Diritto Pubblico* (1979) Utet

Lavagna, C., Agro, A.S., Scoca, F.G. & Vittuci, P. *La Costituzione Italiana annotata con la Giurisprudenza della Corte Costituzionale* (2nd ed, 1979) Utet

Mortati, C. *Istituzioni di Diritto Pubblico* (9th ed, 1975–1976) Cedam (2 Vols)

Paladin, L. *Diritto Regionale* (3rd ed, 1979) Cedam

Sandulli, A.M. *Manuale di Diritto Amministrativo* (13th ed, 1982) Jovene

Virga, P. *Diritto Costituzionale* (9th ed, 1979) Giuffrè

Virga, P. *La Tutela Giurisdizionale nei Confronti della Pubblica Amministrazione* (3rd ed, 1982) Giuffrè

CHAPTER 6 THE RESOLUTION OF DISPUTES: CIVIL, CRIMINAL AND ADMINISTRATIVE PROCEDURE

(i) Civil procedure

Carnelutti, F. *Trattato Del Processo Civile* (1958) Morano

Chiovenda, G. *Principi di Diritto Processuale Civile: Le azioni; il processo di cognizione* (1980) Jovene

Costa, S. *Manuale di Diritto Processuale Civile* (5th ed, 1980) Utet

Fazzalari, E. *Istituzioni di Diritto Processuale* (2nd ed, 1979) Cedam

Fazzalari, E. 'Codice di Procedura Civile' in *Novissimo Digesto Italiano* App. Vol I, p 1291

Liebman, E.T. *Manuale di Diritto Processuale Civile: il processo ordinario di cognizione* (4th ed, 1981) Giuffrè

Lugo, A. *Manuale di Diritto Processuale Civile* (7th ed, 1981) Giuffrè

Redenti, E. *Diritto Processuale Civile* (3rd ed, 1980– by T. Carnacini & M. Vallani) Giuffrè (3 Vols)

Satta, S. *Diritto Processuale Civile* (9th ed, 1981 by C. Punzi) Cedam

Verde, G. *Profili Del Processo Civile. Parte Generale* (1978) Jovene

(ii) Criminal procedure

Bellavista, G. *Lezioni di Diritto Processuale Penale* (7th ed, 1982 by G. Tranchina) Giuffrè

Carnelutti, F. *Principi Del Processo Penale* (1960) Morano

Chiavario, M. 'Codice di Procedura Penale' in *Novissimo Digesto Italiano* App. Vol I, p 1299

Conso, G. *Codice di Procedura Penale e Norme Complementari* (2nd ed, 1979) Giuffrè

Cordero, F. *Procedura Penale* (6th ed, 1982) Giuffrè

Leone, G. *Manuale di Diritto Processuale Penale* (10th ed, 1981) Jovene

Malinverni, A. *Principi del Processo Penale* (1972) Giappichelli

Manzini, V. *Trattato di Diritto Processuale Penale Italiano* (6th ed 1967 by G. Conso & G.D. Pisapia) Utet (4 vols)

Pisapia, G.D. *Compendio di Procedura Penale* (3rd ed, 1982) Cedam

Vannini, O. & Cocciardi, G. *Manuale di Diritto Processuale Penale Italiano* (1979) Giuffrè

(iii) Administrative procedure

Alessi, R. *Principi di Diritto Amministrativo* (1978) Giuffrè (2 Vols)

Capaccioli, E. *Manuale di Diritto Amministrativo* (1980) Cedam

Giannini, M.S. *Istituzioni Di Diritto Amministrativo* (1981) Giuffrè (2 Vols)

Nigro, M. *Giustizia Amministrativa* (1981) Mulino

Sandulli, A.M. *Manuale di Diritto Amministrativo* (13th ed, 1982) Jovene

Satta, F. *Introduzione ad un Corso di Diritto Amministrativo* (1980) Cedam

Virga, P. *La Tutela Giurisdizionale nei Confronti Della Pubblica Amministrazione* (3rd ed, 1982) Giuffrè

Zanobini, G. *Corso di Diritto Amministrativo* (1958–1959) Giuffrè (6 Vols)

CHAPTER 7 CRIMINAL LAW

Antolisei, F. *Manuale di Diritto Penale* (8th ed, 1980–1982), Giuffrè

Bettiol, G. *Diritto Penale* (11th ed, 1982) Cedam

Mantovani, F. *Diritto Penale* (1979) Cedam

Manzini *Trattato di Diritto Penale* (1961– by P. Nuvolone & G.D. Pisapia) Utet (several volumes, some of which are in the course of re-writing)

Nuvolone, P. *Il Sistema del Diritto Penale* (2nd ed, 1982) Cedam

Pagliaro, A. *Principi di Diritto Penale* (2nd ed, 1980) Giuffrè

Pannain, R. *Manuale di Diritto Penale* (4th Ed, 1962–1967) Utet
Pisapia, G.D. *Istituzioni di Diritto Penale* (3rd ed, 1975) Cedam
Serianni, V. 'Codice Penale' in *Novissimo Digesto Italiano* App. Vol I, p 1286

CHAPTERS 8 AND 9 CIVIL AND COMMERCIAL LAW

(i) Treatises Three important treatises in this general area are:
Messineo, F. *Trattato di Diritto Civile e Commerciale* (1952– by F. Messineo and A. Cicu and continued by L. Mengoni) Giuffrè
Messineo, F. *Manuale di Diritto Civile e Commerciale* (9th ed, 1959–) Giuffrè
Vassalli, F. *Trattato di Diritto Civile* (1937–) Utet

(ii) Civil law
Alpa, G. 'Consumatore (Tutela Del)' in *Novissimo Digesto Italiano* App. Vol II, p 516
Barbaro, D. *Sistema del Diritto Privato Italiano* (6th ed, 1965) Utet
Galgano, F. *Diritto Privato* (1981) Cedam
Gentile, F.S. 'Trascrizione' in *Novissimo Digesto Italiano* Vol XIX, p 517
Rescigno, P. *Manuale di Diritto Privato Italiano* (4th ed, 1979) Jovene
Santoro Passarelli *Dottrine Generali del Diritto Civile* (reprinted 1980) Jovene
Scialoja, A. & Branca, G. *Commentario del Codice Civile* (1943–1978) Zanichelli
Torrente, A. & Schlesinger, P. *Manuale di Diritto Privato* (11th ed, 1981) Giuffrè
Trabucchi, A. *Istituzioni di Diritto Civile* (25th ed, 1981) Cedam
Trimarchi, P. *Istituzioni di Diritto Privato* (5th ed, 1981) Giuffrè

(iii) Commercial law
Ascarelli, T. *Corso di Diritto Commerciale; Introduzione e Teoria Dell' Impresa* (3rd ed, 1962) Giuffrè
Asquini, A. *Corso di Diritto Commerciale; Titoli di Credito* (1966) Cedam
Auletta, G. & Salanitro, N. *Diritto Commerciale* (2nd ed 1982) Giuffrè
Bracco, R. *L'Impresa nel Sistema del Diritto Commerciale* (1966) Cedam
Casanova, M. 'Concorrenza' in *Novissimo Digesto Italiano* App. Vol II, p 306
Cottino, G. *Diritto Commerciale* (1976) Cedam
Ferrara Jr, F. *Gli Imprenditori e Le Società* (1980 repr. of 6th ed. updated by F. Corsi) Giuffrè
Ferri, G. *Manuale di Diritto Commerciale* (1980) Utet
Ferri, G. *Delle Società* (3rd ed, 1981) Zanichelli
Galgano, F. *Manuale Elementare di Diritto Commerciale* (1980) Zanichelli

Galgano, F. *L'imprenditore* (3rd ed, 1980) Zanichelli
Galgano, F. *I Contratti di Impresa; I Titoli di Credito; Il Fallimento* (1980) Zanichelli
Galgano, F. *La Società per Azioni*, (3rd ed, 1980) Zanichelli
Graziani, A. *Diritto delle Società* (5th ed, 1962) Morano
Graziani, A. & Minervini, G. *Manuale di Diritto Commerciale* (2nd ed, 1974) Jovene
Rava, T. *Diritto Industriale* (1973) Utet Vol I
Rotondi, M. *Diritto Industriale* (5th ed, 1965) Cedam

CHAPTER 10 LABOUR LAW

Ardau, G. *Manuale di Diritto del Lavoro* (1972) Giuffrè (2 Vols)
D'Eufemia, C. *Diritto del Lavoro* (1969) Moreno
Garofolo, M., Giugni, G. & Liso, F. *Diritto Sindacale* (1980) Cacucci
Ghera, E. *Diritto del Lavoro* (1979) Cacucci
Ghezzi, G., Mancini, G.F., Montuschi, L. & Romagnoli, U. *Lo Statuto dei Diritti dei Lavoratori* (2nd ed, 1979) Zanichelli
Ghidini, M. *Diritto del Lavoro* (8th ed, 1981) Cedam
Mazzoni, G. *Manuale di Diritto del Lavoro* (5th ed, 1977) Giuffrè (2 Vols)
Pera, G. *Diritto del Lavoro* (1981) Cedam
Prosperetti, U. *Il Lavoro Subordinato* (2nd ed, 1971) Vallardi
Riva Sanseverino, L. *Diritto del Lavoro* (14th ed, 1982) Cedam
Riva Sanseverino, L. 'Diritto Sindacale' in *Novissimo Digesto Italiano* App. Vol II, p 1210
Riva Sanseverino, L. 'Diritto del Lavoro' in *Novissimo Digesto Italiano* App. Vol II, p 1240
Santoro Passarelli, F. *Nozioni di Diritto del Lavoro* (1980) Jovene
Scognamiglio, R. *Diritto del Lavoro* (1972) Cacucci
Scognamiglio, R. (ed) *Codice di Diritto del Lavoro annotato con la Giurisprudenza* (2nd ed, 1980) Zanichelli

CHAPTER 11 ENVIRONMENTAL LAW

Capaccioli, E. & Dal Piaz, F. 'Ambiente (Tutela Dell'). Parte Generale e Diritto Amministrativo' in *Novissimo Digesto Italiano* App. Vol I, p 257 (and the bibliography contained therein)
Cantucci, M. 'Bellezze Naturali' in *Novissimo Digesto Italiano* App. Vol I, p 710 (and the bibliography contained therein);
Cantucci, M. 'Beni Culturali e Ambientali' in *Novissimo Digesto Italiano* App. Vol I, p 722 (and the bibliography contained therein)
Cicala, M. *La Tutela Dell'Ambiente nel Diritto Amministrativo, Penale e Civile* (1976) Utet
Cicala, M. 'Ambiente (Tutela Dell'). Diritto Penale & Diritto Processuale Penale' in *Novissimo Digesto Italiano* App. Vol I, p 265 (and the bibiliography contained therein)

Nascimbene, B. 'Ambiente (Tutela Dell'). Diritto Comunitario' in *Novissimo Digesto Italiano* App. Vol I, p 274 (and the bibliography contained therein)

Ponticelli, P.G. 'Consiglio Nazionale per i Beni Culturali e Ambientali' in *Novissimo Digesto Italiano* App. Vol II, p 430 (and the bibliography contained therein)

Tamburini, M. 'Ambiente (Tutela Dell'). Diritto Internazionale' in *Novissimo Digesto Italiano* App. Vol I, p 283 (and the bibliography contained therein).

Index

Unionism
  labour law as to, 452, 453
  rights as to, 182, 183
Universities. *See also* EDUCATION
  Bologna, influence of, 5, 6
  historical influence of, 3, 4
  law degree of, 43, 57, 72
  law studies in, during middle ages, 4, 5–7

Warrant
  arrest without, 239, 240
  judicial—
    arrest, for, 240
    detention, for, 240
Water
  public. *See* PUBLIC WATERS
  soil and, pollution control of. *See under*
    ENVIRONMENTAL LAW
Will. *See also* SUCCESSION, LAW OF
  defect in, 375, 376

Will—*contd*
  definition of, 374
  holograph, 375
  mystic, 375
  notarial, 375
  prescribed forms for, 374, 375
  privileged, 374, 375
  public, 375
  revocation of, 376
  secret, 375
  special or privileged, 374, 375
  testamentary executor, appointment of,
    374
Witnessess. *See also* EVIDENCE
  evidentiary phase of civil proceedings,
    in, 198–200
  expert, 200
  instruction phase of criminal
    proceedings, in, 236, 237
Work. *See* LABOUR LAW